Just *Passing* Through

A GERMAN-AMERICAN FAMILY SAGA

Revised Edition

H. PETER ZELL

ARPress
ILLUMINATING IDEAS
EMPOWERING VOICES

ARPress
45 Dan Road Suite 5
Canton MA 02021

Hotline: 1(800) 220-7660
Fax: 1(855) 752-6001

Ordering Information:
Quantity sales. Special discounts are available on quantity purchases by corporations, associations, and others. For details, contact the publisher at the address above.

Printed in the United States of America.

ISBN-13:	Paperback	979-8-89389-376-2
	eBook	979-8-89389-375-5
	Hardcover	979-8-89389-377-9

Library of Congress Control Number: 2024916693

'Tis strange – but true;
for truth is always strange;
Stranger than fiction.

Lord Byron

In memory of Mutti
(1909 – 1998)

CONTENTS

PART II
Bothers and Sisters

APPENDIX

INTRODUCTION

From whence I came I shan't pretend
To know nor where it all will end.
About my journey this be true:
I'm in the world just passing through.

Seven years had passed since *Just Passing Through: A German-American Family Saga* first appeared in print and it seemed appropriate to bring out a revised edition to take into account the new information that had since become available and to correct some errors that inadvertently entered into the original. The reader may be pleased to know that this book is many things but that one thing it is not, namely, a family genealogy with an endless recital of statistics on who begat whom. Rather it is meant as a record of some tumultuous times in which members of my rather dysfunctional family were caught up in including the two world wars. In general, I have been less concerned with ancestry and lineage than with the lives of individual family members and how they coped with the sometimes momentous problems with which they were confronted.

I felt compelled to write this story because it is unique and different from anything to be found in the vast literature covering this important epoch in world history. Hopefully, it will help contribute in a small way to a better understanding of these difficult times. While I am a student of history, both ancient and modern, my education and professional experiences have been in the sciences and technology rather than literature and this makes me an unlikely candidate to undertake a task such as this. Nevertheless, I decided to embark on it anyway in the hope that Providence would be my trusty guide and make my efforts worthwhile.

My narrative begins with a prologue entitled *A German - American Childhood* in which I relate my near idyllic existence in the countryside in the southwestern part of Germany prior to World War II that came to an abrupt and near catastrophic end when I was brought to the city of Stuttgart when not yet eight years old. There I became an eyewitness to the fire-bombings of that city during an Allied air raid in which my mother, a sibling and I had a narrow escape when a bomb scored a direct hit on the public bomb shelter we were staying in. The immediate postwar period included the occupation of my new hometown by first French and then American forces, my family's emigration to America, our first experiences in our new homeland, and ending with my entry into high school in suburban Chicago. This part of the book was not written to draw undo attention to myself, arguably one of the least accomplished members of my family, but because I found it the best way to introduce the major characters and set the stage for the remainder of the book. Perhaps even more importantly, it is a grassroots, historical record of life during the Third Reich and a devastating war and its aftermaths from a child's perspective.

Children are known to see the world in ways different from that of adults and while they may not fully comprehend what is happening around them, their observations are usually closer to the facts and the truth because they are not yet weighted down by the prejudices and conventional attitudes of their elders. This particular history is therefore bound to raise some eyebrows because it is at odds with a number of myths, half-truths and, at times, complete falsehoods propagated since the war. These came about to bring Germany back into the family of nations after the disaster that was the Third Reich and to allow members of the new postwar German Establishment to adjust to the realities of the day in the most expedient and profitable manner and, at the same time, permit the victorious western Allies to assume and maintain the moral high ground they have become accustomed to and which they continue to highly cherish.

Like Caesar's Gaul, *Just Passing Through* consists of three parts. In *The Ancestors* I briefly tell the story of my mother's parents, who came from very different backgrounds, and their very interesting lives prior to World War II. In my narrative I do not go further back in time than my great-grandparents because little if anything is known about more distant relatives other than the information contained in a large cache of birth and death statistics. In the central part of the book entitled *Brothers and*

Sisters I write about the life experiences of my mother Annemarie, whom her children called Mutti (mom in English), and her two siblings, Ludwig (known as Lulu) and Emmi. Mutti's life was complicated by the fact that, while being born a Christian, she had been married to the son of a prosperous Jewish businessman from Höchst, a town near Frankfurt am Main, who had emigrated to America leaving their half-Jewish daughter Esther behind with Mutti.

The Third Reich was, needless to say, not a comfortable or safe place for Jews or people with Jewish ancestors and was, in fact, virulently anti-Semitic. Yet Mutti managed to have her daughter, my Half-sister Esther, outlive it by using a highly unusual and novel strategy suggested to her by her Brother Lulu. Remarkable was that Lulu was an early supporter of National Socialism and eventually became a devoted member of the Nazi Party himself. Mutti's Sister Emmi too was impacted by the Nazi regime but for a completely different reason. She made her way to Berlin during the "roaring 20s" where she became a celebrity of sorts and quite wealthy before moving on to Switzerland.

The title of the third part of my work, *All My Children*, was suggested to me by a letter Mutti wrote me in which she gave a brief account of her ordeal under the Nazis and declared her "faithful love for all my children." In this part, I describe the sometimes stormy relationships between Mutti and five of her six offspring, all of whom except two were half-brothers and half-sisters. All of her children eventually came to live in the United States where each pursued, with varying degrees of success, his or her own version of the American Dream. An *Appendix* to the book includes a family relationship diagram which should be helpful in keeping track of the principal characters. Also included is a large section entitled *People & Places* with a series of photographs selected from hundreds available to supplement the writing and give it another dimension.

Readers often wish to know something about the author of a book they are reading or have read and in the case of *Just Passing Through* I have included an *Epilogue* entitled *An Autobiographical Sketch* to address that question. My narrative includes some memorable life experiences and interesting people I met on my journey as well as my own weltanschauung. It concludes with some prophetic comments based on my unique interpretation of parts of the last book of the Bible, *The Revelation of*

St. John. Many readers will find my analysis and conclusions disturbing and even offensive because they are at odds with conventional American attitudes and expectations. In fact, they are so startling and frightening even to me that I have long hesitated to publish them. Nevertheless, I feel it is my duty to report these, as controversial and unpopular as they may be, knowing that I will be in good company for it is written, *A prophet is not without honor, save in his own country, and in his own house.* (Matthew 13:57). When people do not like the message they often turn on the messenger.

While *Just Passing Through* was originally meant to only peripherally touch on the Holocaust, my routine genealogical researches brought to light so many important items related to it that I felt compelled to expand these inquiries and make the Shoah an important part of the book. Indeed, all family members living during the times of the Third Reich, including myself, were in some way impacted by it in one way or another and foremost our late mother. Thus, I found that some family members either joined the Nazi Party or were enthusiastic supporters of the regime while others were strongly anti-Nazi or indifferent to it. Yet all were either victims or beneficiaries or both of the regime at one time or another. In fact, it came as somewhat of a surprise and shock to me when I first realized that had it not been for the Nazis I and three of my siblings would most likely not have come into the world. Hopefully, my researches and the insights gained will allow my work to become an important contribution to the ongoing study of the Holocaust.

My genealogical research was on one hand easy but very difficult on the other. The easy part was obtaining the church and state records on important life events such as birth, marriage, and death of the principal characters because these were available from my late Cousin Peter whose father, as part of his application to join the Nazi Party, had to submit theses in order to demonstrate his pure "Aryan" background. Unfortunately, Peter inherited these papers on his mother's passing and the two rarely discussed their contents during her lifetime. As to his father, he last saw him when he was just five years old which gave the two no opportunity to discuss family matters. I myself was a little more fortunate in that Mutti often related anecdotes about her upbringing and family members during her lifetime. Regrettably, I did not take any notes and only showed passing interest in her stories at the time. As a result, extensive outside research was necessary to obtain more information that at one time included enlisting the services of a German genealogy professional in the case of one key ancestor. Still, many unanswered questions remained and left to speculation as my readers will soon come to appreciate.

The surname Zell is not a common one even in Germany where it originated but it is quite ancient. The name is believed to be derived from the Latin *cella* meaning a tiny room such as a cell in a monastery. When Western European families began to adopt surnames during the Middle Ages, first the nobility and then commoners, these were usually derived from a person's place of origin or, in the case of commoners, their occupation. Someone living near a monastery or coming from there could well be named Zell. The best known places bearing the family name are Zell am See and Zell an der Mosel, two small towns in Austria and Germany, respectively.

Interestingly, there even exists a Zell coat of arms. It dates to the year 1282 and is recorded in Johannes Rietstap's monumental opus on European family surnames, the *Armorial Général*. The description of the shield, translated from the French is: "Blue; a silver dove flying diagonally, holding a green olive branch in its beak" while the crest (above the shield and helmet) is described as "A gold star between two silver wings." The family motto is given as *Gott Meyn Trost* [God My Consolation/Comfort]. It is very unlikely, of course, that the original owners of this coat of arms and motto were direct ancestors of my own family as there must have existed many unrelated families named Zell at the time. Nevertheless, I found the symbolism very intriguing because, as a childhood survivor of a terrible war, I too have a strong aversion to international conflict and war and, in accordance with the motto, find much comfort in my belief in the Almighty.

Many of the verbal and written exchanges among the family members in *Just Passing Through* were, of course, in German. In fact, after our arrival in America, we continued to speak German at home because Mutti insisted on doing so lest we forget our native tongue. Where I have used a German word not found in the English dictionary I have italicized it, at least for the first time, followed by its English translation in parentheses or brackets. Sometimes I have included an entire phrase or sentence of what was said or written in German or French. This was done for the sake of authenticity especially where an exact translation was difficult to find. Readings from Scripture are always italicized. Peculiar to German is that the first letter of every noun is capitalized and it is uncomfortable for someone familiar with that language and convention to write, for example, hausfrau instead of Hausfrau or kaiser in lieu of Kaiser. I have usually opted to use the original German spelling. Also, it should be noted, the umlaut "ö" can also be written "oe" (Höchst or Hoechst) while the letter "ß" stands for "ss" (Strasse or Straße). The letter "c" although part of the German alphabet, is considered somewhat foreign and often replaced by a "k" such as the town of Krefeld which earlier had been spelled Crefeld.

In order to guard the identities of and spare them unwanted publicity, I have refrained from using the surnames of family members and people they came in contact with except in circumstances where it did not either seem to matter or the names are well-known and already in the public domain. The main focus of my work is to tell the story of my family and relate the facts as they have become known to me and not to question the conduct, competency, or motives of various people. It must be assumed that most, if not all, behaved honorably and in good faith. Naturally, if someone were to be really interested to know more about one or the other, nothing would prevent him or her from piercing this veil of secrecy because the Internet and social media have nowadays turned most everyone's life, for better or worse, into an open book.

PROLOGUE

A GERMAN—AMERICAN CHILDHOOD

A Humble Beginning

My arrival in the world was accompanied by the peal of church bells and the sound of trumpet fanfares. Neither were, of course, meant for me as my beginnings were of the most humble kind. My birth took place in an ancient inn to an unwed mother who had come to a small village near the Rhine River to seek refuge with distant relatives during one of history's darkest hours, that brief period in time known as the Third Reich.[1] The church bells, rather, were the customary call to the Christian faithful to worship for it was a Sunday morning while the trumpets heralded the start of the Games of the XIst Olympiad of the modern era in faraway Berlin. Providence chose to endow me with the gift of life, the gift of faith, the gift of poetry, and many other worthwhile gifts. Truly, despite my humble start in life, I feel most blessed and could not have asked for more.

The village I was born in was Graben, a *Bauerndorf* [peasant village] located near the town of Bruchsal in southwestern Germany between the provincial capital of Karlsruhe and the university town of Heidelberg.[2] What had brought my mother to Graben was her Jewish connection. With the rise of National Socialism and what came to be known as the Nazis (in German "national" is pronounced "nazional") and the wave of intense anti-Semitism sweeping the country, Mutti suddenly found herself ostracized by friends and neighbors alike so as to make life in her native Schwanheim am Main, a village near Frankfurt am Main, increasingly precarious. Mother did not come to Graben alone but had brought along her retired and now ailing father Peter and her then nine-year-old daughter, my Half-sister Esther. Because a Jewish name like Esther was a strong liability at the time, Mutti called her Mädi.

On the 11th day after my arrival, I was taken to the local Evangelical (Lutheran) Church, simply known as the Grabener Evangelische Kirche, and christened Hans Peter Ludwig Zell. My first name is a variant of Johannes which is the German word for John. The names Peter and Ludwig were in honor of Mutti's father and favorite brother, respectively. My two sponsors were my Aunt Emmi, who had come over from Geneva, Switzerland, and Erika Kuchenbeisser of Graben, a distant relative. Since my mother was busy taking care of Mädi and her father, I was temporarily placed in the household of Julius and Erika Kuchenbeisser, a childless couple who wanted to adopt me. But that was not about to happen because I made such a fuss crying for my mother that she had to come and fetch me.

My next stop was the nearby town of Bruchsal where I was placed in foster care with an elderly couple surnamed Maier. In my earliest memory, I was playing in a sandbox in the front yard of my new Bruchsal home when I chanced to look up and see a monstrous object silently appear behind some houses. It was headed directly for me getting ever bigger as it approached and I remember being transfixed by fright. In my short life I had never seen anything like it and only much later realized what it probably was.[3] Before long my stay with the Maier family too came to an end when it was decided that I was not being cared for properly and needed to be placed with someone out in the country where the better nutrition and fresh air would be beneficial for my further development.

In the Country

My early travels came to a temporary halt with my arrival in a small village about 5 km northwest of Bruchsal called Forst. There, I spent my early childhood in the care of my new foster parents, Maria and Oskar Gartner. Mama and Papa were very good to me and I loved them dearly. Papa was a butcher by trade and worked in a hog slaughtering plant in Bruchsal. He was tall, slim, and dark-haired and wore black leather boots, tight breeches, and a dark pullover. I often proudly watched him from a distance as he confidently stood among other village men discussing the issues of the day. Some mornings when I was in bed between the two, I would rub my cheek against his to feel the sting of his beard. Papa, unfortunately, was not with us long because there was a war going on and he had been drafted into the *Wehrmacht* [German army]. At the beginning he was in France and from there he would send us packages with delicious chocolates, and, especially for Mama, fragrant soaps and perfumes. Sometimes he would return home from the front for a brief period of time and then be off again.

Mama was big and strong and her kindly face, even temper, and a warm and loving disposition made it easy for me to bond with her. I had been entrusted to her care and she took her job seriously guiding and instructing but never scolding me even when it might have been called for. She was an excellent cook making many local specialties including Spätzle, *Schupfnudeln* [potato dumplings also called *Bubenspitzle*], and *Dampfnudeln* [steamed flour dumplings], and I began to thrive and gain weight. When I was four, Mama asked me if I wanted to have a little brother or sister and I told her that I very much did and preferred a brother if that was workable so that I would have someone to play with. As I well knew, of course, babies were delivered by the stork and I duly placed a lump of sugar on the windowsill of my room. Every morning I would check if it was still there and if it was, I had to wait a little longer. Finally, the sugar was gone and shortly thereafter I heard a baby's cries in the next room. It was my little Brother Wolfgang.

Mama, Wolfgang and I lived at Burgweg 13. Like most other houses in the village, it was a one-story building with a sloping roof and dormers on both sides. Mama and Papa had rented the upstairs *Wohnung* [apartment] from a farming family named Leibold who owned the house and lived on the first floor. There were four children in the family, namely, twins Irmgard and Gerhard, Kurt, and the youngest, Herbert, who went to school with Wolfgang. Their property included a courtyard on one side of which stood a barn, which housed a few cows and pigs, topped by a hayloft. A lean-to served as a chicken coop. The other side was Mama's domain and included a shed with a slanted roof in which she kept a large rabbit cage. Rabbits were our chief source of meat because Mama did not own any of the livestock. Beyond the courtyard and behind a wire fence lay a large flower and vegetable garden half of which was reserved for Mama. Entrance to the Leibold property from the street was gained by a wide wooden gate that parted in the middle. The right part of the gate held an entry door.

Our *Wohnung* consisted of just four rooms the largest of which, the one facing the yard, was a spacious country kitchen which also served as our living room. There were two bedrooms plus an unfinished room which Mama used for a pantry. In the kitchen stood a large iron stove that was used for cooking and baking and for heating the place during the cold months. A heavy wooden table took up the center of the room. On it Mama would knead the dough for a large round loaf of sour-dough bread once a week which, along with other village women, she brought to the village baker for baking in his steam oven. A hand pump in a corner of the kitchen provided us with fresh water. In the yard near the fence stood a small privy for our use.

Forst, so named for the surrounding forest, was a small village that had just one of everything—a butcher shop, bakery, grocery store, apothecary, doctor's office, post office, church, schoolhouse, and Rathaus (town hall). There was one policeman who lived down the street from us. Nobody had a telephone but phone calls could be made at the post office. The local news was delivered by a man who traveled around the village on a bicycle and rang a bell to bring the people out. Later loudspeakers were attached to some buildings so the news could be delivered directly from the Rathaus with announcement being preceded by a lively song. For the national news, however, every home including ours had a *Volksempfänger* [people's receiver].

The villagers were for the most part *Bauern* [peasant-farmers] who owned their homes and a few acres of land outside the village which they worked with plows and wagons pulled by cows. These animals did double duty for they were also milked with a portion of the milk going to a local co-op for income. Only a few *Bauernhöfe* [farmsteads] also had draft horses, motor cars, or heavy farming machinery. The fields were planted with a variety of crops for animal feed and human consumption including wheat, clover, barley, beets, potatoes, and *Spargel* [white asparagus], a specialty of the region. Other fields were used as apple, pear, or cherry orchards while still others were reserved for more exotic plants such as poppies, sunflowers, and tobacco. On the edges of some fields there grew popular herbs such as chamomile which some villagers, including Mama, gathered to make medicinal teas.

Forst's fields, woods, and meadows were ideal for exploring and playing in. During the warm season, the many meadows were a riot of color and teeming with grasshoppers and bugs of every kind. We boys were especially fond of *Maikäfer*, large brown beetles with sticky legs that came out in May, which we collected in glass jars stuffed with leaves. Sometimes we would venture into the surrounding woods which were quiet, dark, and mysterious places. Between the trees bright shafts of sunlight would reveal small fields of forest flowers, mushrooms, and more exotic plants while the occasional rustle on the forest floor would tell us that we were not alone. The pride of our village was a pair of storks which returned every spring to the same nest on top of an abandoned chimney. These huge birds in their black and white plumage were fun to watch as they flew about foraging for twigs from the nearby forest and frogs and snails from the wetlands. In the fall, after raising their two young, the entire family would fly south to Africa again.

No less industrious than these big birds were the many barn swallows which made Forst their home. These little creatures were incredibly swift and agile flyers as they pursued their prey of *Schmeißmücken* [blow flies] that bred on the manure piles that were all about because of the farm animals. They were master builders whose round nests built of mud could be seen under the eaves of many houses.

As soon as I could walk and get about on my own, I started to explore the village and was gone for much of the day. On my rounds, one of my favorite stops was the village smithy where I loved to watch the horses being shoed. I would stand outside at the edge of the shop, which was completely open to the street, and stretch my neck to peek in. The old blacksmith was always completely absorbed in his work and if he ever noticed me, he never let me know. Afterwards, I would visit our church which was the largest building in the village and stood right in its center. St. Barbara's slender bell tower held the clock which was visible from all directions and struck every quarter of an hour to let villagers at home and those working in the fields know how far along the day was.

In the beginning, I was too small to reach the handles of the church door and I usually had to wait until someone came along to let me in. Inside the huge and magnificent sanctuary all would be quiet with not a sound to be heard. It was a holy place and I could sense the presence of the Almighty. After walking down the aisles, I would sit in a pew for some time to take in the beauty and serenity of the house and say a silent prayer.

One morning as I was coming out of church, a woman took me by the hand and led me to an ornate building which was across the square from the church. We walked up to an office on the second floor and there she introduced me to the village priest who, after a friendly greeting, opened the Bible and began reading to me. I marveled at the seeming profundity and majesty of the words although I did not understand much of what he was saying. Quite possibly, I heard the awesome opening verse from the Gospel of St. John: *Am Anfang war das Wort, und das Wort war mit Gott, und das Wort war Gott.* [In the beginning was the Word, and the Word was with God, and the Word was God]. Afterwards, the priest laid his hand on me for a blessing.

To my surprise, one day Mama told me that I was not really *katholisch* [Roman Catholic] like her and the other villagers but *evangelisch* [evangelical Lutheran] and that a woman of my faith who lived in Forst would come by next Sunday to take me to Bruchsal for worship services in her church.[4]

The lady arrived and we set off on the long trek to Bruchsal. Instead of the magnificent edifice and sanctuary I had pictured in my mind, this church seemed more like a meeting hall. The bare and unadorned walls and windows, the plain altar and the absence of statuary or other works of art immediately turned me off. Most disappointing to me was that in place of a priest in colorful vestments there was a *Pfarrer* [pastor] in a black robe with a white collar. The intricate ceremony that was part of mass in Forst including the attendance of acolytes, the burning of incense, and the sprinkling of holy water as the priest walked up and down the center aisle was completely absent. All we did was sit in the balcony and listen to the *Pfarrer's* sermon which I thought would never end.

On the way back to Forst the lady asked me if I wanted to return the following Sunday. I had anticipated her question and replied that I did but on one condition. First she would have to get me my own Bible. While I did want to own a Bible I was also secretly hoping that she would deny my request. To my surprise, she said she would try to get one for me. As it turned out, I never saw her again. Instead of spending Sunday mornings in Bruchsal, I continued to attend Sunday mass in St. Barbara's but usually all by myself. Mama was not much of a churchgoing person and came along only on major holy days such as Christmas and Easter.

Sometimes Mama took her bicycle to visit people in neighboring villages such as Kronau and took me along perched over the rear tire. In Kronau, Mama had a sister, a Fräulein Frieda Reichert, who lived on Seegasse 16. On arriving, my first stop was not Mama's sister, however, but a lady named Sophie Just who lived on the same street and on whom I could always count on to have a bag of candy ready for me. One time we bicycled to Bruchsal where unbeknownst to me my birth mother was living at the time although in dire circumstances. I had no recollection of her since we had parted when I was still only perhaps three years old. She was living in just one room surrounded by all her worldly possessions. My mother appeared cold and formal to me but I myself was not brimming with affection either and showed no particular interest in her. Mama told me on the way home that she had not been successful in getting the money for a new pair of shoes for me which had been the purpose of our visit.

Mama called me a *Lausbub* [a mischievous little boy] and for good reason because I got myself into all sorts of trouble. I was not yet in school when I struck my first blow for peace by inadvertently committing an act of sabotage against our country's military. Mama and I were at the home of a woman whose son had just come home from the Wehrmacht on furlough. While the adults were talking, I decided to go outside to get some fresh air. The way out took me past a bedroom whose door stood halfway open. There I spotted a gun standing in the corner against the wall. I immediately took hold of it, placed it on the bed, and began to disassemble it.

Stripping the gun proved surprisingly easy and I soon had most of its component parts neatly laid out in front of me. However, when I tried to put the weapon back together again, all of my efforts proved futile. Getting increasingly frustrated, I inadvertently dropped some parts on the floor which promptly disappeared in the cracks between the floor boards. Just then the soldier returned to his room. When he saw what I had done to his gun, he became furious and tried to grab me but I managed to slip away and run from the house.

One day found me on top of the henhouse observing the courtyard activities when I noticed the big rooster jump on top of a hen and peck her on the neck. It got me very upset and so I slipped off the roof, sneaked up behind the pair, and gave the rooster a swift kick in the butt that made the feathers fly. There followed a big commotion with the hens fleeing in all directions. Just then the rooster turned around and, with its wings flapping and claws extended, came at me forcing me to run for my life. From then on, every morning the irate rooster lay in wait for me as I came out of the house to carry Mama's chamber pot to the outhouse. Spilling much of the contents on the way, I usually barely made it before the rooster caught up with me. This went on for some time until one day Frau Leibold presented me with a bowl of soup. It seems the old cock had finally met its fate and been turned into chicken soup. I had finally won my battle with the rooster but I never lost the soft spot in my heart for the underdog.

I must have been between five years and six years old when Mama and I were at a neighbor's house and someone came in to tell us that Papa was seen walking on Burgweg on his way to Forst. I immediately took off and caught up with him just as he entered the village. My conquering hero, a soldier who had fought in many grueling battles all over Europe under the most famous generals, had finally returned home to us. He lifted me up and I fell on his neck with tears of joy running down my cheeks. Mama was not far behind me and she too was overjoyed at his safe return. Papa had much to tell us and I was all ears when he related his many adventures fighting for our country in one battle after another.

Papa's story of how he was nearly executed by an irate Wehrmacht officer affected me most. It seems that in the military Papa had been assigned to the transportation branch. This was not surprising since I had seen him driving trucks even when he was still in Forst. One day he was behind the wheel of a Wehrmacht truck when the attached trailer broke loose, veered off the road and turned over. Papa evidently did not notice what had happened and drove on until a command vehicle came up from behind and stopped him. The officer was furious and shouted to Papa, *"Stellen Sie sich in den Graben!"* [Go stand in the ditch!]. Papa did as he was ordered and the officer removed his pistol, took aim and was about to shoot Papa when another officer ran up and shouted to the would-be executioner to stop. For Papa it was a very close call.

Now, in the courtyard next to the house stood a water pump with a long handle. One day while Papa was still with us, I decided that the pump was not working properly and needed to be disassembled for an inspection. As I proceeded on my task, Papa spotted me and rushed over. He put me across his knee and with his right hand beat my butt very hard and long. When he finally let go of me I was absolutely furious. My body, my person, my dignity had been violated. I turned and pointing my finger at him screamed, *Faß mich nie wieder an!"* [Don't ever touch me again!]. Papa seemed shocked, drew back, and disappeared into the house. I immediately realized what I had done and was overcome with remorse. That day and the following days I made a strong effort to get back into Papa's good graces but to no avail. Papa persistently ignored all my overtures to please him. It seemed that to him I no longer existed.

One morning I did not see Papa and asked Mama where he was and she matter-of-factly told me that his furlough was over and he had returned to the front. I was in shock and could not believe what I was hearing. He had not said good-bye to me, I protested. At night I cried myself to sleep and for days I kept badgering Mama hoping that she would tell me something that would assuage my terrible pain. Had Papa perhaps looked in my room before he left and finding me asleep had told Mama to say good-bye for him? Had he at least mentioned my name during their last talk together? To all my queries Mama simply replied *nein* [no]. My pain was so much the greater because in my heart I knew that Papa was not coming back from the war and that I would never see him again.[5] This incident taught me a lesson I would never forget, namely, that the people you love the most can hurt you the most.

One of my happiest memories of these days was a vacation trip by train to the Schwarzwald (Black Forest) region where the youth authorities had sent me and other area children for a couple of weeks of *Erholung* [rest and recuperation]. We lived in a large *Kinderheim* [children's home] and almost daily the *Kinderfräulein* [governesses] would take us on long hikes during which we would walk hand-in-hand singing popular children's songs and Volkslieder they had taught us while they explained various sights on the way. Here I found a landscape that was completely different from that around Forst. The rolling green hills, dense woodlands, giant gorges, majestic waterfalls, and many exotic plants and flowers left an indelible impression on me. In the evenings the *Fräulein* would keep us entertained with various games and handicrafts.

My first day of *Volksschule* [elementary school] was an absolute disaster. I had just turned six and had been attending the village kindergarten, which was run by parish nuns, when I heard that I would be entering the Volksschule the following month. Now, the kindergarten building was located right next door to the schoolyard in the middle of which stood the 3-story red brick school building. One day after kindergarten, I went inside the school and finding it deserted checked out the large classroom on the first floor. There were four or five long rows of heavy wooden school benches for two students each facing a platform at the front of the room. On the window side of this raised area stood a lectern for the teacher. Sensing how important it was to be on the good side of a teacher, I decided that I would take the seat up front closest to him. This would allow for maximum eye contact and other friendly but discrete exchanges between the two of us.

Mama must have gotten me to school late because when we entered the classroom, most of the seats towards the front had been taken and, to my surprise and disgust, also the one I had selected for myself. I did not hesitate for a moment but immediately ran over to my chosen seat to claim it. When the boy in it refused to give it up, I pulled him out of it and soon the two of us were rolling on the classroom floor pummeling each other. The whole class was in an uproar when Mama and the teacher finally managed to pull us apart. The teacher now gave me a severe scolding and assigned me to a seat at the very back of the room.

A World at War

All of us kids knew that our country was at war because we had fathers or other relatives serving in the Wehrmacht and our *Volksempfänger* brought some news about it. But the war seemed far away and nobody talked to us kids about it. It finally came home to us unannounced like a thief in the night. One day I was out playing with my friends when a steady drone emanated from above that got ever louder. As we looked up we were amazed to see a huge formation of tiny silvery objects that glistened in the sun slowly but steadily make its way across the sky right above our village. We learned that these were enemy bombers that had come to drop their deadly loads on our country and people. One boy announced that the enemy were *Engländer* [Englishmen] who lived on an island in the Nordsee (North Sea). Another claimed that the bombardiers were little black men from America.

Now and then white puffs of smoke could be seen appearing amidst these aerial flotillas which some older boys said were made by our Flak antiaircraft guns that had been set up to bring them down. We intently watched for a hit but became increasingly disheartened when the bombers always seemed to get away unharmed. However, sometime later a group of older boys triumphantly marched into the village carrying part of the fuselage of an enemy bomber they had found in the woods. It was displayed in the village square where we kids took turns angrily kicking it.

I soon had my first direct wartime experience when Mama took Wolfgang and me to Bruchsal and from there by train to Karlsruhe, the largest town in the region, to see an eye doctor. We had developed eye infections that nearly closed up both of our eyes. I was sitting in the doctor's chair when I was startled by a high-pitched scream from a nearby siren. It was a *Fliegeralarm* [air raid warning] announcing the approach of enemy aircraft. Mama hastily led Wolfgang and me to the safety of a nearby *Luftschutzbunker* [air raid shelter] where we stayed for some time.

After the all-clear siren had been sounded, we all returned to the doctor's office where he applied a salve to our eyes which soon cleared them up. From the little I could discern with my bandaged eyes, extensive preparations had been made for fighting off the enemy aircraft. There were piles of sandbags on streets and squares, some streets had been cordoned off to traffic and on the ground and on the roofs of a number of tall buildings I could see Flak emplacements with gun barrels pointing skyward. Helmeted soldiers searched the sky with binoculars or scurried about. When I returned to Forst, my friends were much amazed by what I had to tell them.

Despite the war and the recurring appearance of the enemy armadas overhead, village life went on as usual. Our village's *Bauern* continued with their routine of plowing, sowing, reaping, and gathering. The Leibold family was up early every morning milking the cows and feeding their livestock. Afterwards some family members would ride to their fields on a four-wheeled wagon pulled by a couple of very lethargic cows. During the harvest season, Mama would occasionally supplement her small income from Papa's serving in the Wehrmacht by hiring herself out to one of the more affluent *Bauern*. A few times she yielded to my demands to take me along and we would find ourselves harvesting potatoes. This vegetable was a staple for us and people had learned to turn it into a large number of simple but tasty and nutritious dishes including fried and mashed potatoes, pancakes, and soup.

Mowing and gathering of the crops was an especially exciting activity to watch for us kids. The mowing was done with sickles and scythes and the cuttings loaded onto wagons with pitchforks. The straw was tied into bundles and left on the fields for later pickup. Somewhere in the village stood an immense threshing machine for separating the kernels of grain from the chaff. Its many levers, rotating gears, pulleys and belts, not to speak of all the noise and dust it generated, were a great source of wonderment for us all.

As the war continued and with most of the men gone off to fight in it, the farm and other chores were more and more left to the women and children and especially the older boys. The few men still around had been exempted from military service because of advanced age or a disability or because they were indispensable for the type of work they were doing. Needless to say, many of these people were not the most adapt at what they were called upon to do. One time I watched with great amusement from our kitchen window as one of the Leibold family's fattened pigs was about to be slaughtered. The animal had been brought to the courtyard but probably having sensed that its life was in grave danger decided to make a run for it. The porker began to race from one end of the yard to the other and whenever it was cornered and held down for the fatal shot from the *Böller* [a short, high-caliber handgun], it managed to break free again and the chase began anew. This went on for some time until the unfortunate victim became exhausted and collapsed and could then be dispatched.

The older boys were in charge of butchering the smaller farm animals like chicken and rabbits. In the case of Mama's rabbits, however, she needed no outside help and did the job herself. While I never saw her do it, I suppose it was a pretty bloody business. I noticed that our poor rabbits would retreat to the far ends of their cages whenever Mama showed up. After she had killed and skinned the animal, she would give me the pelt which I then carried to the village policeman and get a few pennies for it. According to Mama, the rabbit pelts would be worked into fur coats for our soldiers on the Russian front where it was extremely cold.

Once a year, in the spring, the public buildings and some of the private homes were adorned with long red banners bearing a black *Hakenkreuz* [swastika] within a white circle to celebrate the Führer's birthday. On these days, Mama and I, along with many other villagers, would assemble in the schoolyard to listen to a uniformed official who spoke to us from a window in the upper story of the schoolhouse. As usual when adults were giving speeches or sermons, I soon got bored because I could not follow what they were saying. What I did enjoy was watch and listen to a drum and fife corps of the Hitlerjugend (Hitler Youth) as it marched about playing martial music. The boys wore natty uniforms and down the side and affixed to a wide black leather belt each boy wore a small sheathed ceremonial dagger with an eagle insignia. At the conclusion of the speech there were excited shouts of *Sieg Heil* [Hail victory] followed by the singing of the national anthem *Deutschland über Alles* [Germany Over All].

Most villagers had heard the Führer speak on their *Volksempfänger* but none had actually seen him except for one girl who was a member of the Bund Deutscher Mädchen (Union of German Girls), or BDM for short. She had attended a rally at which the Führer appeared and spoke. On her return, she became a celebrity and was much envied by other villagers who asked many questions about what she had seen and heard.

One day Mama told me that a certain woman in the village had become the leader of the Forst BDM even though she was a *Jüdin* [Jewess]. Mama seemed very upset by it all. She did not explain to me what a *Jüdin* was and I did not ask but since Mama strongly disapproved of her, I surmised that being a *Jüdin* was not something praiseworthy. Furthermore, it was clearly not appropriate for such a person to be a leader in the BDM. This woman, Mama said, did not fool her. She could swear that she was *jüdisch* [Jewish]. I was so proud of Mama—no matter how people tried, nobody could fool my Mama.

While the girls played with their dolls or helped their mothers around the house, we boys loved to play soldier. Sometimes the radio brought us news from the front and the announcer would mention the name of one of our famous generals such as Guderian, Kesselring, Manstein, Paulus, Rimmed, or Rundstedt. Mama would then proudly tell me under which general Papa was serving at the time or had served in the past. This would usually get me into a soldierly mood. I would then bring out my toy helmet, which showed our country's symbol, an eagle, on one side and the *Hakenkreuz* on the other, plus my cap pistol and pretend that I was fighting the enemy alongside my Papa.

One time some of my friends and I were playing soldier in the vegetable garden beyond the fence of our house. We were lying in the grass banging away at imaginary enemies, when a real enemy plane appeared menacingly overhead. Our captain, an older boy, shouted for us to lie low and not to move but I became frightened and bolted for the barn. After the plane had left, our captain sharply reprimanded me for giving away our position and putting us all in mortal danger.

One of the most exciting things to happen in Forst at the time was the arrival from Bruchsal of several policemen on bicycles. News of their arrival quickly spread through the village and a crowd of mostly kids like myself gathered to watch the action. We heard that they had come to arrest a Wehrmacht deserter. It just so happened that this soldier's lady friend lived in a tall building next to our house and that is where the deserter had evidently found refuge. The policemen entered the house as we anxiously waited outside for a long time. Finally, they emerged with the deserter in tow and they all bicycled off for Bruchsal again where we knew there was a large prison. After their departure, we kids remained in front of the house for some time and, looking up to an upper story where the woman supposedly lived, we all chanted a nasty rhyme one of the older boys had invented.

One day my birth mother unexpectedly showed up in Forst. I was pleased to see that she had much changed from the time I had seen her in Bruchsal and for the better. Instead of the quiet and sullen demeanor I had come to know, she seemed energized and in high spirits. I also noticed that unlike the stocky and plain looking women of the village in their old-fashioned outfits, Mother was good-looking, slender, and well-dressed.

One could immediately tell that she was not the wife of a *Bauer*, a *Bäuerin*, but someone from the city. She obviously had class and I became smitten by her.

Mother told me to call her Mutti and while Mama had always referred to me as Hans-Peter as if it was one word, Mutti called me Peter and ever since I have been known by that name. Mutti also told me she wanted me to live with her and my Sister Mädi in their new *Wohnung* [apartment] in Stuttgart and would soon come to fetch me. Needless to say, this made me very apprehensive because I was very happy where I was with Mama and Wolfgang.

Nearby Bruchsal had been bombed several times during the course of the war but nothing had approached the blow delivered one night by an enemy air armada that completely obliterated the little town and left a great number of its inhabitants dead or injured. Many in our village including myself watched in horror from afar as Bruchsal stood ablaze and huge plumes of black smoke rose into the night sky. Many in the village had parents, children, or siblings working or living in Bruchsal. Early next morning a small procession of survivors in tattered clothing and in obvious shock followed by wagons bearing simple wooden coffins made its way along the Burgweg towards the village center as anxious villagers hurried to meet it. They scurried about the stragglers searching for loved ones and wept for joy when they had found them or sobbed in grief when told that they were among the dead.

The enemy may have had his way with the people of Bruchsal but not all of the bombardiers got away scot-free. A number of the enemy aircraft were shot down by either Flak or *Nachtjäger* [night fighter aircraft] and some of the bomber crews that had bailed out were captured outside of town. Irmgard from downstairs, who was then 14 years old, had shortly before started to work in Bruchsal after graduating from the Forst Volksschule. She was lucky not to have been caught up in the conflagration because she had come home during the day.

According to Irmgard, who had heard it when she returned to work, something quite gruesome happened following the enemy raid. It seems that a number of Bruchsal townsfolk were so enraged by the destruction of their town and the killing of their fellow townspeople that they brought the captured enemy flyers back into town and there, before the authorities could intervene, stood them among the smoldering ruins left by their handiwork and stoned them to death.

In Forst, a special evening requiem mass was said in St. Barbara's for the victims of the Bruchsal massacre in which most villagers including Mama and I took part. There was a blackout in force so as not to give away the village's location to enemy bombers and the worship service was held by candlelight. I stood next to Mama at the rear of the immense church, which was filled to capacity, as she and the faithful intently prayed the rosary.

After returning home from school one day, I was astonished to see barricades being built on Burgweg at the entrance to the village which was only a short distance away from our house. The workers dug large rectangular holes into which they drove thick tree trunks and these pilings were then filled in with gravel and dirt. Further out in the fields deep trenches were excavated and camouflaged. These were to serve as tank traps to slow the enemy's advance. The workers were prisoners of war, we were told, and indeed they looked like foreigners. A few Wehrmacht soldiers guarded them and marched them about. We kids got friendly with some of these men after we found out that they had shiny metallic rings that looked like gold which we could put on our fingers. The prisoners would part with a desired object in return for a sandwich. I nagged Mama a long time to make me one until she finally relented and I got my reward of a shiny little ring which I put on my finger.

That our country's situation was getting ever more desperate was brought home to me when Mama took me along for a meeting in another part of Forst. There, a roomful of villagers were discussing the so-called *Volkssturm* [people's charge] which was to be a last-ditch effort by our people to beat back the enemy invaders. One of the military weapons to be used against the enemy was the *Panzerfaust* [tank fist] which was a grenade that could be thrown at a tank from the side or behind to disable it. The enemy had much cause to fear the *Panzerfaust* because anybody, from kids to old folks, could use it and its effect on tanks and heavy vehicles was devastating. A number of these weapons were on display at the meeting and instructions given on how to use them. I told Mama that if she decided to join the *Volkssturm* to sign me up too because I was sure that I could handle a *Panzerfaust* as well as anyone.

I had forgotten that during her visit Mutti had told me that she would be back to take me with her to Stuttgart. She evidently meant what she had said because one evening in the middle of the summer she and Mädi arrived to do just that. I was taken by surprise because Mama, who most likely knew of their impending arrival, had said nothing to me. Mutti told me that we would be leaving before dawn on the day after tomorrow. The early morning departure was necessary, she said, for us to get to Bruchsal before the *Tiefflieger* [low flying fighter planes] arrived at daybreak.[6] This gave me just enough time to get my things in order and say good-bye to my friends.

Mutti made sure that my parting with Mama would be quick and low-key. We got up in the dead of night and after a short and tearful embrace with Mama at the courtyard door, Mutti pulled me away and, firmly anchored between her and Mädi who both held me by the hand, we marched off towards Bruchsal. A little ways out, I managed to steal a glance back in the direction of the sleeping village and noticed a red glow on the horizon and some distant rumblings as if made by thunder. When I mentioned to Mutti that I thought a storm might be headed our way Mutti replied that what I saw and heard was not an approaching thunderstorm but artillery fire. The enemy, she said, was approaching and would soon be on the Rhine River. The Rhine, I knew, was not far from Forst and this was very frightful news.

Mutti, Mädi and I continued walking towards Bruchsal and arrived there while it was still dark. The railway station there had been bombed out and we stopped instead at a small brick building alongside the tracks which was marked as belonging to the Reichsbahn (railway authority). Mutti called inside through an open window to ask if there were any trains running to Stuttgart and out of the dark a man growled, "*SA marschiert.*" [SA on the march].[7] That was the opening of a rousing marching song often played on the radio and Mutti said that the official's answer, which was unintelligible to me, meant that we had to keep walking. We were now again on the open road and making good progress but by now it was daylight and Mutti now and then anxiously scanned the sky for any signs of *Tiefflieger.*

Whenever Mutti spotted danger we would jump into one of the trenches that had been dug parallel to the road to protect travelers from enemy fighters. These trenches were narrow and just sufficiently deep so that one could hide by crouching down. However, they were not continuous but rather spaced some distance apart. Jumping in and out of these like jackrabbits was great fun but all of a sudden and out of nowhere a *Tiefflieger* swooped down on us and, unfortunately, at a section of the road where there was no trench. Mutti spotted him first and shouted for us to get down and lie flat on the ground. We dove for a row of hedges beside the road and almost immediately the fighter passed over us and so low that as he pulled back up, the wind of his propeller blew leaves and debris in our faces. If the enemy pilot meant to scare us, he succeeded because we were really shaken up.

Somewhere we must have managed to catch a train to Stuttgart after all because I remember a streetcar ride from the Hauptbahnhof (main railway station) to Heslach, the southwestern part of town where Mutti had her *Wohnung*. We arrived in the middle of the night and the city was pitch-dark with not one light to be seen anywhere. As the unlit one-car *Straßenbahn* [streetcar] groped its way through rubble-filled streets, I could see the silhouettes of collapsed and burned-out buildings. As we came to a large square we passed the façade of a 3-story burned-out edifice with a center section and two wings. It looked like the remains of a great palace. There was no traffic or people on the streets and the city was like an abandoned ghost town.

Mutti, Mädi, and I got off at Adlerstraße, turned left to cross the street and walked uphill on it until we came to its end where there was a broad stone stairway. Walking up the first flight of stairs, we almost immediately came to a handsome 3-story apartment building that stood on the left. A small sign next to the front entrance carried the number 8. To reach Mutti's *Wohnung*, which would be my new home for almost six years, we walked up two flights of stairs on a broad staircase of polished stone. Mutti unlocked the door to the left (there was a second *Wohnung* across from it) and I immediately liked what I saw because all looked new, modern, and spacious. In the first room to the right, which looked like an office, Mutti had set up a toy train as a welcoming gift. It included an oval track and a wind-up locomotive with three cars. Over the next few days, I played with it a few times and when I lost interest, the little train set disappeared again.

Dodging The Bombs

The three of us had hardly settled in when the nightmare began. There were air raids around the clock with the *Amerikaner* coming by day and the *Engländer* by night.[8] The enemy was relentless in his efforts to destroy the city and all that lived within it. I finally came to know where the huge air armadas that I had seen passing over Forst were going and what they were doing. Now I was right in the middle of it all. The bombs that rained down on us were of three types, I learned, namely, *Sprengbomben* [explosive bombs], *Brandbomben* [incendiaries], and *Zeitbomben* [time bombs]. These were used in combination for maximum effect and tore up the most well-constructed buildings and set everything ablaze. With every bombing raid the city was transformed and familiar landmarks disappeared one after the other until little was left.

The arrival of the enemy, which had been preceded by the shrill sound of an air raid siren that had been mounted on one of the taller buildings in the neighborhood, brought out the city's considerable defenses—a welcoming committee of sorts. As powerful searchlights scanned the nighttime sky to locate the enemy armada, our Flak antiaircraft cannon, which had been placed on the hills surrounding Stuttgart, opened up and relentlessly pounded away at the enemy. The combination of booming guns, the steady drone of hundreds of enemy aircraft overhead, the whistle and explosion of their bombs, and the resulting conflagration and rising columns of black smoke produced an unforgettable spectacle for eyes and ears.

The populace would not have survived had the authorities not set up fortified *Luftschutzbunker* in strategic locations throughout the city since cellars afforded little protection against the massive bombs, some weighing as much as 1,000 pounds, used by the enemy. The shelter we were assigned to, and which was the one closest to our house, had been dug out under a public square called Platz der SA. At one corner of the square stood a small terminal for the Zahnradbahn (cog railway) that led up a steep hill to Degerloch, a part of town overlooking Heslach.

Fortunately, the Platz der SA was easy to reach for us. Behind our building was a narrow, steep road called Schimmelhüttenweg which, going in one direction, led up to Degerloch and in the other joined Böheimstraße which passed below the other side of our apartment building. We just had to walk down this road and then along Böheimstraße for a short distance and we were there. The shelter was well constructed and, besides having a thick concrete cover, was subdivided into several small, heavily fortified compartments called *Zellen* [cells]. In this manner, if one cell was hit by a bomb, the people in other compartments still had a chance of surviving.

It was not long after our arrival in Stuttgart, that I had the most traumatic experience of my life. One night, on arriving at the Platz der SA bomb shelter, Mutti had a strange premonition and decided not to immediately head for the cell to which we had been assigned but to tarry instead in the large common room at the shelter's entrance. After staying there for a while, Mutti, Mädi and I started walking to our unit with me leading the way. We were only steps away from our cell when suddenly the lights went out and the whole bunker appeared to spin around. Just then a huge wall of rubble and dust came crashing down in front of me to my right blocking my way. Fortunately, the walkway behind us was still clear and we quickly retreated.

People who were in our assigned cell were either killed outright or buried alive.[9] From under the debris the distant and desperate cries of women could be heard begging for someone to save their children. A warden or two scurried about looking for shovels but none could be found so that nothing could be done for these unfortunate souls. The mothers' pleas for help persisted for some time and became ever fainter until they stopped altogether. There followed an eerie silence in the bunker. The survivors, including Mutti, Mädi and I, were overcome by shock and grief. We had miraculously escaped unhurt but I had breathed in and swallowed much dust which made me cough and vomit.

After the all-clear was sounded, we exited the bunker into the fresh night air and as we walked towards home, I stole a glance back towards the center of town and saw Stuttgart ablaze like the inside of a furnace. The shock of our ordeal was such that we said nothing to each other and never talked about it afterwards. We did not perish that awful night as we easily might have. The Almighty clearly had other plans for us.

With the bomb shelter at the Platz der SA out of commission, Mutti chose a new one that was more secure but, unfortunately, also further away from our house. It was located at the opposite end of our street, Adlerstraße, which ran north and south, and this required us to walk down

Adlerstraße to Böblingerstraße, where the streetcars ran, and then up the other side of the street about the same distance and finally up a long flight of stone steps that mirrored those on our side of the street. There a street tunnel known as the Schwabtunnel had been converted into a bomb shelter by closing it off to traffic and installing heavy steel doors on both ends to protect against bomb blasts.

Mutti, Mädi and I spent many nights sitting on hard wooden benches in the Schwabtunnel listening to the strange whistle of descending bombs and their subsequent impact. The shock waves made the huge steel doors rattle and we were fearful that they might not hold and come flying in. Now and then a runner would enter and announce which buildings had been hit or were on fire. This allowed people to choose between venturing out to salvage some of their belongings or just wait out the air raid. The fire brigades were no longer operating because either the fire houses and engines had been destroyed or they could no longer navigate the streets which were filling up with rubble from the collapsing buildings.

Once the all-clear air raid siren had sounded, getting back home was a dangerous undertaking in itself. We had to climb over all the rubble, old and new, that had piled up on our street and at the same time worry about unexploded bombs including time bombs that might go off at any moment. Another danger was posed by collapsing buildings. Mutti usually led the way with Mädi and I following close behind. When Mutti looked down on Adlerstraße from the top of the stone stairway and saw that there was much fire along the street, she would moisten handkerchiefs at the Schwabtunnel for us to hold against our faces to guard against the searing heat.

Some of the bombed buildings we passed offered remarkable sights. Usually the entire interior would be gutted right down to the cellar with only an outer wall or two and the chimney left standing. Then there would be a kitchen sink or a bathtub dangling high up in the air held to a wall by nothing more than a piece of pipe or other fixture. The ground would be strewn with pieces of china, silverware, toys and other items some of which were still in perfect and usable condition. It would have been inappropriate for us to pick anything up and we never did.

As time went on, our situation became increasingly more difficult. While in the past there had been sufficient time between the *Fliegeralarm* and the arrival of the enemy bomber fleets to get to a designated shelter, now this time became ever shorter so that we had little advance warning of an impending attack or none at all before the bombs began to fall. Often the very buildings on which the air raid sirens had been mounted were destroyed. Another happening was that the total blackout of the city to prevent the enemy from locating his target was no longer effective. To better zero in on the city center the enemy began sending out lead planes which dropped a large quantity of flares mounted on tiny parachutes. These lit up the entire city turning night into day. In fact, this occurrence was the best indicator for us that an attack was imminent.

Occasionally, I was to blame for us not getting to the Schwabtunnel on time. Because of the lack of sleep, I was always tired and became increasingly lethargic and dispirited. No sooner had Mutti gotten me ready to leave when I had disappeared and crawled back into bed. Despite the danger, I urged Mutti to leave without me because I was absolutely certain that I was safe and nothing would ever happen to me. She always insisted I come along. On a few occasions we sat through a bombing raid in the cellar of our building rather than venture outside and risk being killed on the way to the Schwabtunnel. These were anxious hours because we knew that we could never survive a direct hit.

Because the air raids came mostly during the night, I sometimes had the opportunity to wander the streets around our neighborhood during the early afternoon and survey the latest damages. One of the buildings bombed out was a large, 5-story red brick apartment building that stood at the northwest corner of Adlerstraße and Möhringerstraße, the next street down from Böheimstraße. A pungent, sweetish odor emanated from that place which I surmised came from one or more decaying corpses still left under the rubble. There was really no one around who could dig out people who for some reason did not make it to a shelter on time because first priority had to be given to save the injured and tend to the living. Here as elsewhere the fate of the building's inhabitants was scribbled on the still standing outer wall with white chalk. A last name followed by a cross meant the family had perished while survivors had their names followed by a street address where they had found refuge.

For the soldiers at the front the happenings at home were especially devastating. With neither big cities nor small towns now spared from devastating aerial attack and communication with home only sporadic toward the war's end, they were more worried about the safety of their loved ones than their own. One story to circulate was of a young Wehrmacht officer who was returning home on furlough and eagerly looking forward to be reunited with his wife and a baby son he had not yet seen. When he returned to his hometown and the house they lived in, he found the place destroyed. Neighbors told him that there had been an air raid just days before in which his wife and child had perished. The young officer thereupon went to the cemetery and at the grave of his loved ones took his service pistol and shot himself to death. Many such tragedies occurred and made the rounds.

The Flight to Austria

The enemy continued his relentless air attacks against our country's towns and cities including our hometown of Stuttgart as if driven by some primordial urge to kill and destroy.[10] In the meantime, Mutti had decided that the city had become too dangerous a place for Mädi and me and had made arrangements for us to take refuge in the Vorarlberg region of the Ostmark as Österreich (Austria) was known at the time. The Vorarlberg was a mountainous area, Mutti explained, with no big cities or industry and was therefore relatively safe from air raids. Mädi and I were soon on our way there by train.

Our destination was Bludenz, a small town near the westernmost tip of Austria and due south of Bregenz, the capital of the Vorarlberg. There we moved into a spacious corner room on the second floor of a hotel called Weisses Kreuz (White Cross). Mädi took a part-time job serving in the hotel dining room leaving me to my own devices. I occupied myself with exploring the town and the surrounding countryside which was resplendent with spectacular mountain peaks, deep forests, and pristine Alpine streams and lakes. But even in this remote part of Germany one could not escape the fact that the country was at war as enemy bomber fleets ominously crossed overhead with the drone of their engines filling the air.

It was not long before Mädi had an admirer who visited her regularly. He was a young and handsome Wehrmacht lieutenant by the name of Fred

Straka who hailed from the town of Graz in the Steiermark (Styria) region of Austria. There was a small Wehrmacht garrison in Bludenz and he was its commander. On some days very early in the morning, Lieutenant Straka and his men would march by our hotel. He would be on horseback followed by his unit on foot lustily singing popular German folksongs like *Schwarzbraun ist die Haselnuss...* [Ebony is the color of the hazelnut] and *Es steht eine Mühle im Schwarzwäldertal...* [There stands a mill in a Black Forest vale]. At their approach, Mädi would rush to open the window and I would bring up a footstool to stand on and as we looked down, Lieutenant Straka would look up and offer a smart salute. After reviewing the troops, Mädi and I would get dressed and go downstairs for breakfast.

The military had always interested me and as I was making my rounds through the town and its environs, one of my favorite stops was the *Kaserne* [army barracks] where Lieutenant Straka was stationed. There was a striped guardhouse at the entrance with an armed soldier standing in front of it. Maybe he knew that his commander and my sister were friends because he paid no attention to me as I just wandered in. Inside the *Kaserne* I would watch the soldiers go through their routines in the central courtyard. There were always drills to be conducted, horses to be groomed, and rifles and other weapons cleaned and maintained. Now and then, Lieutenant Straka, Mädi and I would have dinner together in one of the local restaurants or at the hotel. One day towards the end of our stay in Bludenz, Lieutenant Straka and his unit were ordered out to guard the Brenner Pass, which was a mountain pass between Austria and Italy, and they all marched off.

I suspected that something was up when one day Mutti came unexpectedly for a visit. Mother, I knew, never wasted time and whatever she did had a purpose. I loved to ride the train and so if she was going somewhere by train, I hoped she would take me along. *"Wo geht's hin, Mutti?"* [Where are we going, Mutti?] I asked her and was delighted when she told me that she was headed for Schruns and that I could come with her. "What's in Schruns?" I wanted to know. I wasn't quite prepared for her answer. "We are going to visit your Sister Ute," was her reply. I was flabbergasted because nobody had ever told me that I had another sister. I much enjoyed the train ride which led through several immensely long tunnels and after a few stops we arrived in the little village. I looked about and we were surrounded on all sides by huge snowcapped mountains. The house where Ute lived in foster care was typical of the area. It was mostly constructed of thick wooden planks and had a low and broad sloping roof with a balcony on the upper floor which encircled most of the house. Ute's foster mother, whom I later learned was a Frau Pfeifer, received us cordially.

Ute, who was about five years of age, seemed very withdrawn and shy. I thought I might have seen her before, possibly with Mama in Forst, although I did not realize at the time that she was my sister. Ute was a little on the pudgy side and her round face and big brown eyes never displayed any kind of emotion. She appeared sad and never smiled even though Mutti tried to cheer her up a little by stroking her cheeks. I wondered what might be wrong with her. On the train back to Bludenz and after a stop or two we passed another little village called Tschagguns and Mutti matter-of-factly mentioned that this is where my brother named Volker was living in foster care. This was another surprise Mutti sprang on me. I did not know I had a brother. Naturally, I would have liked to have met him too but, according to Mutti, there was no time for a visit on this trip. Shortly thereafter Mutti took the train back to Stuttgart.

It was now winter and getting cold out. One day Mädi told me that after the war the Ostmark would become a separate country and the people no longer be Germans like us and it would therefore be best for us to leave and return to Germany. Only this time there would be no train because they were no longer running, she said.

About the trip back, I remember only one incident. Mädi and I had joined a small group of our fellow countrymen and were walking along a road that cut through a forest when the group stopped at a house to ask for some water. The woman who came to the door was very friendly and accommodating. She took particular interest in me probably because I was the only child among the travelers and entreated me to have some milk or at least a little water. Despite being thirsty, I steadfastly refused to take anything offered. I felt that in these hard and terrible times I had to be tough like a soldier and not let myself be babied. Somehow we managed to get back to Stuttgart either by train or some other means. When Mädi and I got to our apartment, Mutti had left us a note saying that she was on her way by train to Bludenz to pick us up. It seems that not only transportation but all communications had begun to break down as well. Mutti eventually rejoined us back in Stuttgart.

Peace At Last

After the Schwabtunnel, our final bomb shelter was by far the best and took us to the end of the war. We were fortunate in that our apartment building adjoined the extensive complex of the Marienhospital (St. Mary's Hospital) whose administrators had decided to build their own bomb shelter with neighborhood participation. In these private initiatives, if an able-bodied family member helped with the digging, the entire family was entitled to a place in the shelter. In our case, Mädi helped dig out a network of horizontal shafts under a hill next to the hospital. Fortunately, the entrance of this new Marienhospital bunker was only a few minutes walk up the Schimmelhüttenweg from our house. Besides providing convenient access for us, this new shelter was also the safest. If there were any more bombs falling or fires raging in Heslach or in the city center, as I am certain there were, we never saw or heard any of it from here.

On the other hand, this bunker was not a very pleasant place to spend time in because, unlike the public shelters, it was very crudely and unprofessionally constructed. The walls of the narrow shaft we were sitting in were mostly bare dirt with just enough wood beams and boards to keep the ceiling from falling down. People sat on two rows of benches, one on each side of a dirt walkway, with their backs towards the walls. Electric lights strung along the ceiling dimly lit the place. Although I never saw more of the shelter than the section we had been assigned to, I heard that there were more spacious accommodations further inside that included patient wards and an operating room. Now and then someone announced that wounded soldiers were about to be carried in and all the occupants turned around to face the wall and thus be spared any unpleasant sights.

One day close to the end of the war, I found myself back at the Platz der SA running an errand for Mutti when a couple of municipal workers caught my attention. As I stepped closer to investigate what they were up to, I saw the man on the ladder take down the street sign that said Platz der SA and replace it by one that read Marienplatz (St. Mary's Square). In a flash I realized what was happening. Excitedly I ran home to tell Mutti the good news. I found her standing by the kitchen sink peeling potatoes. Breathless and full of joy I shouted, *"Mutti, Mutti, der Krieg ist vorbei!"* [Mutti, Mutti, the war is over!]. To my great surprise and disappointment,

Mutti said not a word and, seeming oblivious to me, just kept on doing her chores. How I came to associate the end of World War II with the change in street signs remains a mystery to me to this day especially since I knew nothing about politics or what the war was all about or why we were being bombed. Mutti rarely volunteered any information that would explain things to me and I rarely asked.

One morning we were again sitting in the Marienhospital bunker, which we had entered the night before because of another air raid, when Mutti gently shook me awake. I had sat next to her and, resting my head in her lap, fallen asleep. She told me that a French officer had just been here and told us that we could go home because the war was over. Exactly what had he said, I wanted to know, and Mutti replied that the officer had announced in perfect German, "*Fürchtet euch nicht, der Krieg ist vorbei.*" [Fear not, the war is over]. I was elated. Walking back to our *Wohnung*, I heard someone say that the French army was about to march in on Böblingerstraße in the area of the Matthäuskirche, our parish church, in the center of Heslach. That will be a spectacle, I thought, that I cannot miss.

I immediately ran off despite Mutti's frantic calls to come back. When I got to the designated place, a small crowd of mostly older kids and a few adults was already there waiting. In my mind's eye, I saw a triumphal parade with foreign soldiers marching five or even ten abreast pass in review with flags and banners flying. Riding on a *Schimmel* [white stallion] out in front would be the victorious French general surrounded by mounted officers of a lesser rank all in colorful uniforms. Behind them would be a big military band playing rousing marches followed by the rank and file of enemy soldiers.

As I waited and waited, I strained my ears to hear the military band or some other sound that would herald the arrival of a grand army. Finally, I made out the squeaky noise that sounded like tank tracks. Then came an incredible sight that left me almost speechless. A mud-covered, ungainly old tank came into view and then another and several more and sprawled across the deck of each were two or three unshaven and haggard looking soldiers staring into space. Where was the pomp and ceremony I had expected? Was it still to come or was this it? Were the French mocking us and our great city? Adding to my disappointment was that this motley little column of rumbling behemoths did not continue on Böblingerstraße towards the Marienplatz and the center of Heslach but instead proceeded north in the direction of the Schwabtunnel. The crowd waited to see more but nothing followed. This was it.

Throughout the drive-by there was no reaction from the onlookers. Nobody cheered and nobody jeered. Everybody including myself just stood there silently looking on not knowing what to make of it. When the crowd began to disperse, I too started walking back home anxiously expecting a tongue lashing when I got there. But I think Mutti was just happy to see me back safe and rather than scold me gave me something to eat.

Just before the arrival of the French military, a number of grocery stores, butcher shops, bakeries, and other establishments in the neighborhood had begun to give away their inventories to their old customers. They wanted to clear their shelves before a marauding foreign army could seize the merchandise, I heard. The proprietors announced that they would be closing their stores and not reopen for an indefinite period of time. Heinrich's grocery store on Möhringerstraße near the Matthäuskirche did just that. That is where Mutti shopped with our ration cards during the war and where I picked up our daily allotment of milk in the morning. Their good deed allowed Mutti to stock up with some food to tide us over uncertain and possibly desperate times.

A few days after the French had entered Stuttgart, Frau Rapp who lived in the dormer apartment above us, rang our doorbell and told Mutti to quickly follow her for an important radio announcement. Mutti rushed upstairs with me close behind and we sat down next to Frau Rapp's *Volksempfänger*. The set was tuned to Radio Hamburg and I heard what sounded like *Trauermusik* [a dirge]. Then the music stopped and the announcer came on speaking solemnly. As usual, I did not understand what he had said and so I asked Mutti for an explanation. "*Der Führer ist tot*" [the Führer is dead] is all she said or, at least, is all that I remember her saying. The Führer dead? I was in shock and could hardly believe what I had heard. That the Führer could die had never occurred to me. Our country, the Reich, without the Führer? What would happen to us now? While Mutti and Frau Rapp were quietly conversing with each other, I sat there dumbfounded trying to come to grips with what I had heard.

For the first time I realized what had happened—the war was not only over but our country had lost it! Not long ago, I remembered, our Wehrmacht had been fighting in France and in Russia and in many other places in Europe and Africa and had been victorious. Now our country had been defeated. It suddenly dawned on me that nothing in this world is permanent and enduring. Our enemies had destroyed and defeated our country and in time their countries too would be destroyed and defeated. It was all in the nature of things. The one thing one could always count on was God the Almighty. He and He alone was forever. I felt as if some irrefutable truth had been revealed to me and shared it with no one, not even Mutti. It was springtime now and I was eight years old. In another three months I would be nine.

The Conquerors

The French occupation troops came but they kept a low profile and were hardly noticeable in the lives of the average citizen especially us kids. They brought along some of their colonial troops which we heard were from Morocco. These were black soldiers and it was the first time we kids had seen *Neger* [Negroes]. We kept our distance and studied them in great wonderment. These soldiers caused some problems with the women, we heard, whom they pursued and threatened . They were soon pulled out and replaced with regular French troops. The *Wohnung* on the floor below and across from us, which I heard had once belonged to a podiatrist who was a Nazi, was now occupied by a French officer and his wife. It so happened that Mutti spoke some French and soon became very friendly with this couple. When Mutti apologized to the officer for her poor French, he told her that she spoke a better French than even his wife. Mutti was ever so proud and told the story to anyone who would listen.

The only people who really feared the French were their former countrymen whom our French occupiers labeled collaborators. These were Frenchmen who had befriended our German occupation army after their country's surrender. Many of these people had fled to Germany prior to the liberation of their country by the Allies. Some had settled in Stuttgart and taken German wives. One day a Frenchman of Mutti's acquaintance was picked up by the French authorities and shortly thereafter executed. Evidently he was one of these collaborators and his killing much upset Mutti. She told me that these people had collaborated with us because they hated the *Russischen Kommunisten* [Russian Communists] who burned down churches and committed other outrages against members of our Christian faith. According to Mutti, in the past war these godless people and the *Amerikaner* and *Engländer* were allied against us. Clearly, these collaborators were fellow Christians and our friends and I fully agreed with Mutti when she suggested that we help them out as much as we could. But how?

In talking with the collaborators, Mutti realized that they were starved for French-language books to read. They had trouble getting them because they were in hiding and dared not venture out as long as the French army was in town. It just so happened that right after their arrival, the French had set up a cultural center called the Institut Français that was not far from our house. Since the collaborators did not feel safe to go there themselves, Mutti decided that she and I would procure the books for them.

One time I was at the Institut Français again to return some books and present my list of new ones given to Mutti by some collaborators, when the librarian began to question me. She thought it remarkable how many books my mother was reading in such a short time. Mutti had anticipated the librarian's suspicion and coached me to respond by telling her that my mother loves anything French especially French literature and reads a book a day on average. The librarian seemed very pleased with my explanation and quickly packed up the books for me. My story was, of course, a complete fabrication. The truth of the matter was that I had never seen Mutti read a book in German, not even a cookbook, let alone one written in French.

The French occupation of Stuttgart did not last long, perhaps a couple of months or so.[11] One day they left as quietly as they had come only to be replaced by a new breed of occupiers. These were the *Amerikaner* whom the people called *Ami* for short. I first encountered them when Mutti, a couple she was acquainted with and I took a stroll through some woods above Stuttgart after the city's surrender. On our walk we came to a gun emplacement manned by heavily armed American soldiers in steel helmets. The gun was pointed skyward and the soldiers intently scanned the skies.

"*Was suchen die?*" [What are they looking for?] I wanted to know. "*Deutsche Flugzeuge*" [German planes], was the man's reply. That seemed incredulous to me. "Are we not in Germany? Are they allowed to do this?" Rather than answer my questions, Mutti and the couple looked at each other in bemusement. Evidently, I still had not yet fully comprehended what had happened—we were now a country under enemy occupation.

Nobody liked these arrogant and overbearing *Amis*. While he French had tried to blend in, these new occupiers made sure that everyone knew that they were around and in charge. Where the French moved into apartments among the people, the *Ami* appropriated entire communities for their use as, for example, when they took over Sonnenberg, a newer part of town next to Degerloch. The Hindenburgbau building across from the Stuttgart Hauptbahnhof, the Württemberg State Opera House, and other public buildings still left standing after the wartime bombings were converted to serve as social clubs, military department stores known as PXs (post exchanges), and the like. Young soldiers self-importantly raced around town in jeeps marked Military Police (in capital letters) under their windshields, stopping cars and trucks, of which there were very few left, to question perplexed drivers and passengers and often taking away their papers for no apparent reason.

It seems that every time I came to the center of town to run an errand for Mutti, the American military had again set up roadblocks and yet another reviewing stand for one of their many ceremonies. There would be military bands playing rousing marches and honor guards in polished boots and shiny helmets prancing about carrying a huge array of American flags and regimental banners of every description. There would be lots of saluting and shouting of orders. Photographers would scurry about to ensure that all was recorded for posterity from every possible angle. The masters of ceremony were kept busy because there was always a general who was visiting or taking command or being transferred or retiring. Other soldiers were being promoted or received medals and commendations. There would be just a few bystanders like myself around to watch the show. One could see older people look at each other and, shaking their heads, walk away in disgust.

With the end of the war and the arrival of the foreign armies of occupation, the Third Reich and Nazi rule were clearly over. A new order was now in place with a new government in the making. All that was previously good and in, it became clear to me, was now evil and out and what had been out and evil was now in and good. People all of a sudden began to speak of the Nazis and the evil they had done. I heard of Nazi leaders being tried and executed by the victorious powers. Many people had to undergo *Entnazifizierung* [denazification] which was supposed to purge them of their militaristic and nationalistic zeal. But I also remembered that while the bombs were falling not too long ago, these same occupiers were called terrorists and bloodthirsty murderers of women and children. I found the whole situation very perplexing and strained to make sense of it all. Perhaps I should have asked Mutti to explain things to me but that thought never occurred to me. As always, I needed to figure things out by myself.

One day Mutti was reading the *Stuttgarter Zeitung*, the major Stuttgart daily, when she asked me to guess who had been in town. I had no clue. Then she told me it was Mrs. Roosevelt, the wife of the late American president. According to Mutti, Mrs. Roosevelt had given a speech at the Württemberg State Opera House to a group of our countrymen who were part of the new government. The attendees, Mutti said, must have been carefully selected to ensure that Mrs. Roosevelt got a friendly reception. I knew what she meant because during the war no two people were more despised in Germany than the American president and his wife. That was because Roosevelt, we knew, hated our people and our country and both he and his wife lived very immoral lives. What a strange twist of events, I thought, to now see this woman being received in my hometown as an honored guest.[12]

A strict non-fraternization policy was imposed, I heard, by General Eisenhower, the American commander, whereby any social contact between American soldiers (called GIs) and Germans was forbidden. This policy did not hold up long, however. Below our house at the corner of Adlerstraße and Böheimstraße stood a *Gaststätte* [restaurant] appropriately named Goldener Adler (Golden Eagle). It was not long before the Goldener Adler became a popular meeting place between GIs and our people. This was probably because most of these soldiers were stationed in Böblingen, a small town southwest of Stuttgart where the U.S. Army had set up its headquarters, and Heslach was the closest part of Stuttgart to that town. These GIs undoubtedly enjoyed the taste of German beer but many also wanted to meet some local people since they were often themselves wholly or partly of German descent. A few even spoke some German.

Sometimes Mutti would let me come along in the evening. At those times the Goldener Adler would be packed with GIs and the singing and carousing would go on until late into the night. They would be singing their favorite hit songs including "You are my sunshine, my golden sunshine...," "Put another nickel in, in the nickelodeon...," and "Sonny boy, I love you so...."

The Goldener Adler was also where Mädi, now again called Esther, met her future husband Nick and his brother Joe. Nick was all right but Joe, I thought, was a little goofy looking. Both were serving with the U.S. Army at the time but had arrived after the fighting was over. The two had learned to speak German from their parents who were living in Chicago where Nick and Joe grew up. We learned that his parents were from the Ukraine and therefore *Volksdeutsche* meaning that they were ethnic Germans who were born and lived outside the borders of the Reich but retained their German nationality and cultural traditions. (People like Mutti and I, who were born within the borders of the Reich, were known as *Reichsdeutsche*).

One day, when I was not home, Mutti had a most unwelcome GI visitor. This soldier rang our doorbell and announced that he had been ordered to inspect our premises. Mutti, suspecting nothing since he was in uniform and presumably on official business, let the soldier in. The GI thereupon searched our entire *Wohnung* taking his time to go through everything. After he left, Mutti discovered to her great dismay that the jewelry collection she had inherited from her mother, and which she had kept in the drawer of her bedroom nightstand, was missing. Esther was immediately dispatched to report the theft to the local American military authorities. To her amazement, and even more so to mine after I heard the story, these people did not seem at least concerned. They shrugged it off saying that they could not possibly find out who the GI thief was since they had almost nothing to go on. They offered no help whatsoever in getting the jewelry back nor did they apologize. I figured that the reason was probably because this GI was just doing what occupation armies were expected to do which was to carry off as much loot as they could.

Some people made it safely through the war only to meet a sad fate after it was over. Adelheid was an example. She was the daughter and only child of Frau Bader, a friend of Mutti's who lived on the first floor of an apartment building at the end of the Schimmelhüttenweg just before it merged into Böheimstrasse. Adelheid was a tall and stately young lady with long blond tresses and an endearing smile. She was the most beautiful creature I had ever seen and I had a crush on her. Mutti used to visit Frau Bader now and then during the last part of the war and sometimes she took me along. One evening when we were there, Mutti and Frau Bader got down on the floor next to Frau Bader's *Volksempfänger*. They had the volume turned nearly all the way down so that what was being said was barely audible. That was because they were listening to an enemy broadcast which, according to Mutti, was verboten. When I asked Mutti what she found out, she told me that it was too complicated for me to understand.

Shortly after the arrival of the Americans, Adelheid became friends with a number of GIs. One night they went out partying and probably had too much to drink. She and three GIs were all riding around town in a jeep at a high speed when the driver missed a turn in the road and drove into the Neckar River. Adelheid apparently knew how to swim and, while trying to help one of her friends who could not swim, was dragged under so that both of them drowned. The other two GIs made it to shore. Such was the sad end of my beautiful Adelheid.

While the adults may have had their problems with their new overlords, we kids were fortunate in that GIs liked children and were eager to show their good side to us. I heard that they often visited *Kinderheime* [children's homes] and threw parties for the kids bringing candy and toys. One day they invited all the Stuttgart school children to the Stuttgart airport in Echterdingen to show them a good time and I came along. We were transported there in school buses and the GIs gave out bottles of Coca Cola, Hershey chocolate bars, Wrigley chewing gum, and other treats that were eagerly snatched up. There were many shows and activities. Among the contests were ones for the prettiest girl and the handsomest boy in each age category and the kid with the most freckles. Lots of group photographs were taken and these later exhibited at the Königsbau building across from the burned-out Neues Schloss (New Palace). I was a little disappointed not to find myself in any of the photographs to show to Mutti but it was all great fun anyway.

One day Esther announced that her GI suitor was about to be sent to an intelligence school in Oberammergau in Bavaria. This much amused Mutti and me because we had never heard of a school that teaches intelligence. Not being familiar with the English language at the time, we did not know that intelligence was an euphemism used by the American military for information gathering and spying.

As soon as Mutti heard the news, she decided that a little Alpine vacation was just what we needed after our wartime ordeal and booked us a room in one of the better hotels in town. As usual, we took the train. The surroundings in Oberammergau much reminded me of our stay in the Vorarlberg during the war but here everything seemed less rustic and more classy. This was probably because Oberammergau was a vacation spot where people came to relax and admire the beautiful scenery and the many houses adorned with colorful paintings of scenes from the Bible. The village was best known for its *Passionsspiele* [Passion Play] that brought visitors from all over to witness a reenactment by the villagers of the Passion of our Lord. These events were held only every ten years, however, and this was not a Passion year.

We stayed for only about a week but I had one memorable experience. On our second or third day there, Mutti, Esther and Nick wanted to go out in the evening to see a movie. When Mutti wondered whether she could leave me alone in our hotel room, I told her to go on and enjoy herself and not to worry about me because I could pretty well take care of myself. I was sound asleep when I was suddenly jolted awake by a tremendous clap of thunder. This was followed in quick succession by another and yet another and lightening so intense that it lit up the room as bright as daylight.

I became increasingly alarmed even though I was never the fearful type. Suddenly there came what sounded like a huge explosion and I was sure the house had been hit by lightening. Terrified, I fled our room and ran down the hallway. A man came out of another room and talked to me in what sounded like English. He took me to his room and motioned to me to get into bed. I hesitated a little when I noticed that there was a lady already in there but I got in next to her while the man stood by the window to watch the storm outside. I immediately fell asleep again and the next morning I woke up in my bed in our room down the hall. Mutti, who had never scolded me before, now gave me a severe tongue lashing. It seems that I had chickened out and abandoned our room for no good reason, left all our belongings unattended and, worst of all, had crawled into bed with complete strangers.

Home Sweet Home

Growing up in Stuttgart after the war was like living in my own magic kingdom. The town had all the attributes of such a place. In fact, many years before, Stuttgart had been the capital and royal residence of a real kingdom, the Kingdom of Württemberg, and home to illustrious dukes, kings and princes.[13] There was an imposing castle and a sumptuous palace from those days right in the center of town together with many ancient churches, stately public buildings, rich museums, and a handsome opera house. The many elegant squares, lovely parks and a profusion of fountains, monuments and statues added to the fairy tale atmosphere. Even the city's location had an enchanted quality about it. It lay serenely in a secluded valley surrounded by rolling hills. These were covered with leafy woods except in places where vineyards had been planted and these came down almost to the center of town. That is why Stuttgart was known as the *Stadt zwischen Wald und Reben* [Town midst woods and vineyards]. I would celebrate my hometown many years later with this verse:

> *Midst wooded hills and vineyards my dear city lies*
> *Of royal birth and fair, a feast to poet eyes.*
> *And though a cruel fate bade me the world to roam*
> *Shall I be true to her, my native land and home.*

During the years I lived in Stuttgart, I became ever more enamored of the place and often walked to the center of town for no other reason than to take in its beauty and to admire its imposing architecture. Stuttgart was considered a big and important city but it had a small-town quality about it. My route would take me first to the Marktplatz (Market Square) and the Markthalle where Stuttgarters bought fresh produce brought in from the countryside as well as meats, fish and gourmet foods.

A little beyond was the Schillerplatz (Schiller Square) which was named in honor of the famous poet and playwright who was born in the nearby village of Marbach and went to school in Stuttgart. In the center of this pretty little square stood a magnificent statue of the poet by the Danish sculptor Bertel Thorvaldsen. The weekly flower market was held around the base of the sculpture.

At one end of Schiller Square stood Stuttgart's oldest church, the Stiftskirche (Founder's Church) dating from the 13th century and on the opposite the Alte Kanzlei (the Old Chancellery) where the king's chancellor (prime minister) had his offices. Across from it stood the imposing Alte Schloss (Old Castle) which was completed in the mid-14th century and served the early counts of Württemberg as their Stuttgart residence.

Moving on I would come to the spacious Schlossplatz (Castle Square) which has been called one of the loveliest town squares in Germany. It was framed on one end by the Neues Schloss (New Palace), a magnificent U-shaped. 3-story building begun in 1746 by the Italian architect Leopold Retti. Facing it at the opposite end of the square stood an imposing pillared building known as the Königsbau (King's Building). In the center of the Schlossplatz stood the 30 meter tall granite Jubiläumssäule (Jubilee Column) erected in 1846 in honor of *König Wilhelm, Dem Vielgeliebten* [King Wilhelm, The Much Beloved]. Between the Königsbau and the Neues Schloss was the Königstraße at the end of which stood the imposing Hauptbahnhof, Stuttgart's main railway station. Past the Schlossplatz I would come to the palace gardens in which stood the former royal opera house and now the home of the Württemberg Staatsoper and the Stuttgart Ballet. In fact, all these great buildings I passed, with the exception of the opera house, lay in ruins now, destroyed during the recent bombing raids on the city, but I would simply give my imagination free reign and pretend that all was still there.

The southwestern part of Stuttgart, where we lived, was not one of the more sought-after residential areas because, instead of the nice private homes and villas to be found in some other parts of town and the surrounding hills, Heslach was mostly a working class neighborhood made up of 3- to 5-story apartment buildings, diverse retail shops, and restaurants. Interspersed were some small metal working, clothing, and other factories. Our building was located on a promontory above street level and separated from the expansive grounds of the Marienhospital by a long series of stone stairways called the Adlerstaffel that led from Böheimstraße up to Degerloch.

The Marienhospital, one of Stuttgart's largest, was owned and operated by a Catholic order of nuns and consisted of several 2- and 3-story buildings, a number of small pavilions, and walkways and manicured gardens all enclosed within a stone wall. The main entrance was on Böheimstraße but a back gate was on the Schimmelhüttenweg at a place we kids called the Totenplätzle (Little Square of the Dead). It got its name from the mortuary on the first floor of a modern 3-story hospital building that stood there just outside the hospital's back entrance. The building's upper floor with large windows all around was presumably a laboratory because people in white coats could be seen scurrying about. The little square was a way station during the hospital's annual Corpus Christi procession after Trinity Sunday. For us kids in the neighborhood, it was our main playground where we boys played *Fußball* [soccer] and the girls hopscotch or we all played tag or hide-and-seek together.

Our apartment building had been put up to serve the upscale housing needs of doctors employed at the Marienhospital. Each of the two main floors above the parterre contained two apartments of equal size. Our *Wohnung* was on the second floor on the side of the Schimmelhüttenweg. In addition, there were two smaller apartments, namely, one on the ground floor next to the building entrance which was meant to be the *Hausmeisterwohnung* [concierge apartment] and the other a dormer flat above ours. On the other side of the latter was the entrance to an area which contained four small rooms, a kitchenette, and a bathroom. These were to accommodate domestic help for each of the four main apartments. After the war, when housing was scarce, these rooms were converted into a seventh apartment. Also, each of the apartments came with a locked cellar stall for storage. Ours was on the side of the Schimmelhüttenweg. Here Mutti kept our supply of potatoes, which were our main food source during the war, and a pile of small egg-shaped coal briquettes for heating our place. It was also where we spent some nights during the war-time air raids.

Mutti must have been well-connected when she obtained our *Wohnung* through the Stuttgart housing authority. The rooms, located around a central hallway, were spacious and bright with tall double-pane windows that parted in the middle. Prior to our occupancy, our flat had been the home of a medical doctor named Liebendörfer and his family who had moved to Bad Liebenzell to escape the bombings.

The Liebendörfers must have left in a hurry or were simply unable to get movers under the wartime conditions because the first room to the right when one entered the apartment still contained the doctor's fully furnished *Herrenzimmer* [gentleman's room]. In it were an oversized desk with armchair and a bookcase with sliding glass doors that was nearly the length of one wall. The furniture was very solid and heavy but modern in style with a light and high-gloss finish. The bookcase had several shelves plus some drawers along the bottom and was chockfull of books many of which were in a large format and leather bound. It was my good fortune to have been assigned to this room in which a daybed had been installed. Next to the *Herrenzimmer* came a large corner room whose long side overlooked the Adlerstaffel while the shorter faced the Schimmelhüttenweg. It housed the ornate dining room furniture that had belonged to Mutti's parents. We used it as a combination living/dining room.

Three more rooms completed the layout. At the end of the hallway and facing the Schimmelhüttenweg was the one bedroom and which was used by Mutti and Esther. On its left was a tiled bathroom with a large built-in tub. To the left of the apartment entrance was the kitchen with a spacious pantry. Attached to the kitchen was a small balcony. Besides a gas range for cooking, the kitchen contained a special coal-fired stove for heating water for the kitchen sink and bathroom and also the hot water radiators in the three main rooms. The kitchen was just big enough to hold a small buffet and table and chairs for having breakfast.

Mutti did not use the stove because coal was hard to come by and heating the apartment via the radiators proved inefficient. Instead she had a small iron stove installed in the *Herrenzimmer* that was kept blazing hot and heated almost the entire apartment during the cold months. Like everybody else, we had no telephone although there was a connection for one in the hallway. It had been removed when the doctor moved out. For the occasional phone call, we would go to the Marienhospital next door which had a switchboard and some phone booths.

Mutti had a cantankerous side and did not get along with too many people especially with ones too much around her such as neighbors. Frau Rapp in the dormer apartment above us seemed to be an exception. She was a tall, refined, and friendly lady and she and Mutti had a genuine liking for each other. Herr and Frau Krüger and daughter Henni in the *Wohnung* below us was on Mutti's persona non grata list because she thought them pretentious which was strictly taboo with her. Herr Krüger was the only one in the building who owned a car, a sports car, which he parked on the Schimmelhüttenweg.

One day found Mutti and me standing near Mutti's bedroom window when Frau Krüger at the same place below shouted to Henni in a loud voice to hurry up lest they be late for the opera ball. Mutti immediately shouted back, "Peter did you hear that? The Krügers are going to the opera ball. Let's hope they get there on time and not miss part of the performance." Later, when Henni began to work for the American consulate in the Zeppelin building near the Hauptbahnhof, Mutti quickly changed course. She plied Henni with cakes and pastries from a nearby café at her office because she needed her for some paperwork related to our emigration.

Mutti especially disliked the elderly couple in the apartment across from us. Indeed, the two were very reclusive and mysterious. Herr Fischer was an air raid warden during the war and additionally walked the streets in our neighborhood to enforce the blackout rules in effect to prevent enemy bombers from finding their targets. He also helped out at the *Luftschutzbunker* on the Platz der SA to get people in and out in an orderly manner. Mutti was afraid of him for some reason despite the laudable services he provided and they did not talk to each other. As to Frau Fischer, I never saw her during the war although I knew she was around. Now and then I would hear them having breakfast on their little balcony and talk to each other very quietly. I could tell that she did not speak in our Swabian dialect but in the high German spoken in other parts of the country. Right after the war Mutti told me that Herr Fischer was a big Nazi and a real bad person. I consequently tried to avoid him whenever I could and rarely saw him.

One day Mutti happened to visit the offices of a Jewish organization called Hias which Mutti told me had been set up to assist the Jewish and so-called *Mischling* people such as Esther with their problems. To her great astonishment, while there she ran into Herr Fischer. Knowing that he had been a Nazi and that the Nazis had been responsible for putting Jews into concentration camps during the war and, furthermore, suspecting that he was after some favors by making false claims, Mutti confronted him and demanded to know what he was doing there.

What Mutti learned astounded her. According to Herr Fischer, his wife was a *Jüdin* [Jewess]. He had apparently joined the Nazi Party and did all these volunteer services for the sole purpose of protecting Frau Fischer and keeping her from being hauled away to a concentration camp (KZ). It seemed almost incredulous that Mutti had for years feared and despised Herr Fischer only to realize that they had shared the same predicament and succeeded in protecting family members but in completely different ways.

After the war, former Nazis were generally held in contempt and Herr Fischer consequently preferred to keep to himself. Frau Fischer, on the other hand, was now free to come out again. One day she met me in the hallway. She was a refined and genteel lady but already very old and frail. To my great surprise she presented me with the gift of a precious book. The Fischers had one child, she told me, a son who had served in the army and had fallen. The book she was giving me had been his. It was a copy of the 155th (1932) edition of the popular *Schmeil Leitfaden der Tierkunde*, a classic textbook on our planet's animal life that was extensively used in the German school system for many years. Schmeil's work described the habitats and manners of a large variety of land animals and fishes and was profusely illustrated with expert drawings and full color plates. Frau Fischer was obviously being very kind and generous. Regretfully, I do not recall having shown my appreciation commensurate with what that book must have meant to her. It became my favorite among all of my books and I much treasured it and still do.

Kid Stuff

There were hardly any cars on Stuttgart's streets after the war even after most of the rubble from the bombings had been carted away to a site that grew to a momentous height and was humorously called Monte Scherbelino (Mount of Shards). The few cars and trucks around were often a little bizarre looking. Very common were small pickup trucks that had only three wheels. The front wheel was located below a hood that had the shape of a triangle. Trucks and Mercedes-Benz passenger cars were equipped with cylindrical cast iron tanks about six feet or more tall that were mounted vertically behind the cab in the case of trucks or in the trunk area of the cars. A small circular opening on the side of the tank had a flap that continuously opened and closed and when open revealed that the tank was a fiery furnace that burned coal. Somehow the contraption produced the fuel for running the engine.

With the streets to ourselves, we kids soon put them to good use. A couple of the older boys constructed a vehicle that consisted of a heavy wooden board onto which they nailed cross bars in the front and back to serve as axles. Instead of wheels they attached four large ball bearings which they found somewhere. Sitting on the board with the feet resting on the front axle, which was movable for steering, we took turns rolling down Adlerstrasse. But one had to be careful not to run into a street car at the bottom, on Böblingerstrasse, because the cart had no brakes except for a piece of wood nailed to the board that could be turned to scrape the ground. Some boys also carried slingshots in their back pockets. These were easily made because there was an abundance of rubber of a pinkish color around after the war.

Naturally, we all loved *Fußball* and we played impromptu games whenever there were a bunch of us together. Since the streets were almost free of traffic, that is where we did much of our playing. We had no soccer balls in those days and so we played with anything that rolled. Sometimes a small rubber ball or even a tennis ball had to do. Two rocks set some distance apart served as goal posts. Since we all had different ideas regarding the rules of the game, there were quite a few heated arguments which would then be quickly resolved by a *Ringkampf* [wrestling match]. Whoever pinned the other kid down was in the right and the game resumed. My favorite position was goalie because winning or losing a game was much dependent on the expertise of the goalkeeper. We could never agree on how far apart the goal posts in our games should be and since it was my bad habit to secretly move the rocks closer together whenever my team was losing, I was rarely allowed to play my favorite position.

The biggest post-war event in Stuttgart, which brought people from all over Europe to the city, was a *Fußball* game between Italy and Germany. It was held in the giant Neckarstadion on the outskirts of town. The Italians had come up by train days before and the stadium was completely sold out. I decided to go there just to watch the excitement with no hope of being able to watch the game. People were walking around offering tickets at astronomical prices and all I had in my pocket was the streetcar fare back home Mutti had given me. Then, out of nowhere, a man came up to me and pressed a ticket into my hand saying he had one too many. By the time I had a chance to look up and thank my benefactor, he had disappeared. Inside the stadium and before the game got underway, a small plane flew into it and the pilot dropped the ball into a circle in the center of the field. That was fantastic and the crowd went absolutely wild with excitement. Since I do not recall who won, I suspect it was the Italian team. I was quite a hero with the neighborhood kids for a while since I was the only one who had actually watched the game and not just listened to it on the radio.

Mutti was not generous when it came to toys and I had none. The closest I got to them was the toy store Spielwarenhaus Hermann Kurtz that stood at one end of the Marktplatz near the Rathaus. The Marktplatz area had been heavily bombed during the war and there were no large buildings left but, like other merchants, this company had put up a one-story make-shift structure. On both sides of the main entrance, there were several large display windows with each one featuring toys of the same kind or by the same company. One window was devoted to Steiff bears and other makes of stuffed animals, a couple featured dolls and doll houses for girls, while others showed toys popular with boys like me.

At the time, every boy's heart would skip a beat at the mention of the name Märklin. That company, with its bright red logo, was one of the most famous toy manufacturer in Germany and the Spielwarenhaus Kurtz carried a large selection of their products especially their specialty which was model railroads. These were exact replicas to scale of those used by the German railway system. Other toys in their program were miniature and working *Dampfmaschinen* [steam engines] with copper boilers and *Metallbaukasten* [metal construction sets] of many types and sizes. As much as I longed to have a Märklin construction set, I never asked Mutti to get me one because I had my sights set on something I priced even more.

The object of my heart's desire was a small, rectangular, charcoal-colored box I saw in the window of a camera shop on Eberhardstraße. There were many makes of German cameras on display like the famed Leica by Leitz, and cameras by Zeiss-Ikon, Rolleiflex, and Voigtländer. But for me a simple box camera would do just fine. There were no lens openings or speeds to set or a focus to adjust much of which would have been too complex for me anyway. All one needed to do with the box camera was point in the direction of the subject, push down a lever on the side, and hope for the best. The camera held a roll of film for eight large black and white photographs.

Every time Mutti and I came near this shop, I asked her to take another look at it in the window. One day we passed the place and I again badgered Mutti to get the camera for me sometime soon. Quite unexpectedly she took me inside and, without further ado, bought the camera and handed it to me. I was ecstatic and taken completely by surprise because it was no special occasion. I had my precious box camera for many years and put it to good use taking many photographs of family and friends.

Hitting The Road

Toward the end of the war, travel by any means but especially by rail was a precarious undertaking because of the danger posed by enemy *Tiefflieger* which attacked anything that moved. Passenger and freight trains alike usually traveled by night when the chances of being strafed were considerably less. When daylight travel was necessary, trains raced for cover in railway tunnels whenever danger loomed. In general, passenger trains did not enter or depart from the main station of a major city, the Hauptbahnhof, but stopped in a smaller substation outside of town to take on and drop off passengers. This was done to avoid being caught in an air raid which usually targeted the heavily populated inner city where the Hauptbahnhof was invariably located. Needless to say, people did not travel much in those days so that once the war was over, there was much penned-up demand for rail service as everyone sought to visit relatives and friends they had not seen in a couple of years or more.

Mutti too joined the travel craze and took me along on several trips. She seemed to have relatives, friends, and acquaintances in many towns and our travels took us from Stuttgart to Frankfurt am Main, Heidelberg, Karlsruhe, Baden-Baden, and places on Lake Constance. Each trip was an adventure in itself. Because few trains were running these were overcrowded so that we rarely got a seat but were forced to stand in the aisles for an hour or two at a time. At every stop on our route, and there were many, workers from the Red Cross and other relief organizations would walk along the train and pass out water to the parched travelers. Mutti and I spent considerable time in the huge waiting hall at the Stuttgart Hauptbahnhof.

Mutti must have decided that I was too solemn and needed some cheering up and so she did her best to keep me entertained. One of her favorite tricks to get me to laugh was to try to reach her prominent nose with the tip of her tongue while rolling her eyes to see how close she was getting. She also loved to pick out an individual as he walked past and parody his behavior to the extreme. One time a corpulent man with a facial expression like an English bulldog walked by and Mutti softly muttered, "woof, woof." Still the man heard it and as he turned about facing us, I feared for Mutt's safety. Fortunately, the mastiff moved on after letting loose with some choice expletives. Perceived snobs were always on top of her list for being singled out for ridicule and for that she chose some imaginary Englishmen. While in the Hauptbahnhof restaurant, she once showed me how these people tried to eat peas with the fork turned upside down after which she went into an English tea drinking ceremony that had me laugh so hard that I nearly fell off my chair.

The end of the war had brought famine to the land. While the food supply during the war was adequate and well regulated through the use of ration cards, the system had now broken down as the well-oiled machinery of the state came to an abrupt halt. Stores that had survived the bombings and were open for business had little to offer. Meats and fish and such staples as butter, eggs, and flour were difficult if not impossible to get. If there was a rumor that a butcher or fishmonger had gotten in some product, there would be long lines forming outside his shop. Many people went hungry and became weak. Once I saw a woman pass out standing in line and, foaming at the mouth, fall to the ground as others also in line rushed to tend to her.

A shortage that did not directly concern me was that for tobacco. The only people who had cigarettes in any quantity were American GIs. Now and then I would see a GI smoke a cigarette half way down and discard it by casually flipping it in the air. Invariably some kids would run to retrieve it and the boy who got to it first would take it home to his father. The father would then combine the tobacco from a few cigarette butts and roll it in special paper to make a new one. I even saw grown men stoop to pick up just discarded cigarette butts. To me all of this was very disgusting and I was glad not having to get involved.

To remedy the food shortage, Mutti took part in what was called *hamstern*, a word derived from hamster and the practice of that rodent to tirelessly search for and store food in its over-sized cheek pouches.[14] Going *hamstern* with Mutti was always an adventure and I was delighted whenever she asked me if I wanted to come along. Mutti preferred to conduct business in the Remstal (Rems Valley) in a cluster of small villages north of Stuttgart whose *Bauern* were well stocked with edibles and which they were ready and willing to trade in for useful and essential products like clothing, shoes, and bed linen. Mutti came to the Remstal every two weeks or so.

Our trip would begin early in the morning with a streetcar ride to a road that led to the Remstal. There Mutti and I would stand, with Mutti holding on to a small suitcase full of merchandise with one hand and to me with the other and wait for a good Samaritan to take us along. Hitchhiking was an accepted practice during this postwar period and anybody who was traveling somewhere and had room in his vehicle felt obligated to carry someone without transportation along. We rarely had to wait long before we would be on our way.

Mutti was an excellent salesperson and had built up a loyal clientele in two or three villages she visited in turn. On arrival in a village, the first few stops were with customers for whom she had brought one or more items they had asked for. Mutti's customers were of many kinds and one could never tell what to expect. One time, when Mutti brought me along, we went to see a customer who had requested a pair of shoes. Before going inside, she took out the shoes to look them over. "Darn it," she said to me, "that *Schlemiel* gave me two left shoes." (Mutti often used Yiddish terms—*Schlemiel* is Yiddish for a bungler). Fearing an embarrassing encounter, I asked Mutti if I could wait outside. The transaction was evidently successful because she emerged from the house smiling with the food items she sought and minus the shoes.

Some visits were entertaining as well. One of the families we saw now and then had a young son about my age. No sooner had we stepped inside the house when he would come out of his room attired in priestly robes carrying a make-shift altar. After performing a lengthy ceremony in the manner of a Catholic mass, he would pick up his altar, march back to his room and remain there. The ceremony over, Mutti and the *Bäuerin* would start conducting their business. When I afterwards asked Mutti what she thought of it all, she replied that the kid was obviously meschugge.

After these initial deliveries, there was usually time left for some prospecting for new customers. In those days, the Remstal *Bauern* collected the manure from their farm animals in an open concrete enclosure that sat between the farmstead and the street. It was an unsightly arrangement but evidently the best way for the later removal of the manure to the fields for use as fertilizer. Mutti's technique for prospecting was very simple. Realizing that her chance of finding a customer interested in her barter services was directly related to the *Bauer's* affluence, she singled out the houses with the largest manure piles out front and skipped the others. The larger the manure pile, she figured, the more livestock the farmer had in his barn and the better off he must be.

Trying to be helpful, I once suggested to Mutti that since larger manure piles probably produced more *Schmeißmücken* [blowflies] instead of the manure pile we should be checking the flypaper that usually hung from the ceiling of a *Bauer's* living room. The more flies sticking to it, I figured, the larger must be the manure pile and the richer the *Bauer*. From the look Mutti gave me I could tell that I had said something really stupid.

The most enjoyable part of the trip for me was the train ride back to Stuttgart. In bygone days, the fabled Schwäbische Eisenbahn (Swabian Railway) was the butt of many jokes. Its national reputation for being antiquated, slow, and inefficient was popularized by a humorous song in the Swabian dialect entitled *Uf der schwäb'sche Eisebahne* [On the Swabian Railway] that was known throughout Germany. Things had not changed all that much since the old days. The train consisted of a small and ancient-looking steam locomotive and three or four equally antiquated passenger cars with hard wooden benches.

Once the station master had shouted *einsteigen* [all aboard] and blown his whistle, the train would begin to move and as it slowly wound its way between fields and farmsteads, the engineer would blow the train's whistle causing the startled cows, geese, and chicken near the track to flee in all directions. I usually stood by an open window and when the train went around a bend, I could see the little engine huffing and puffing all the while belching thick columns of black, sooty smoke. Eventually we would roll into the Stuttgart Hauptbahnhof after which we would take the streetcar back home to Heslach.

Mutti purchased the merchandise which she carried to the country from a Jewish couple surnamed Adler that lived in an apartment building on the western end of Reinsburgstraße, a street on the other side of the Schwabtunnel. According to Mutti, the entire complex of several modern 2-story buildings had once been occupied by Nazi officials and their families and now housed a colony of concentration camp survivors who were awaiting relocation to America and Palestine.

I distinctly remember coming along on two visits to this couple both of which could have turned out badly for us. On the first of these, Mutti, Esther, and I were on our way in a streetcar running along Reinsburgstraße to see this couple and while Esther and I got safely on board the second car, Mutti tried to get on too late while it was already moving. It quickly got up to speed and Mutti was still hanging on to the support rails on either side of the entrance. Other passengers frantically rang the streetcar's bell by pulling on an overhead rope to alert the driver in the lead car but he either did not hear it or was obstinate and did not stop. Finally, Mutti jumped up on the running board as some passengers pulled her inside. I still shudder to think what might have happened had she missed her step and fallen.

On the second visit I remember Mutti and I being caught up in a police raid in the couple's apartment with Mutti and Frau Adler barely escaping an arrest. Evidently *hamstern* was verboten for reasons unknown to me. To avoid being caught by the police, Mutti posted me at the open living room window of the second floor flat to serve as a lookout in case of any suspicious activity down below. As I was watching Mutti and Frau Adler examine the merchandise and haggle over prices, I heard some shouting in front of the building and looking down was shocked to see that some green, boxy vans of the sort used for transporting prisoners had pulled up.

When the car doors opened and policemen came running out headed for the building entrances, I began screaming at the top of my lungs, "*Razzia, Razzia*" which, I had learned, was the word for a police raid. Mutti and Frau Adler barely had time to gather up the goods when there was a hard knock on the door with a man shouting, "*Polizei, aufmachen! Polizei, sofort aufmachen!*" [Police, open up! Police, open up immediately!]. While Frau Adler hastily carried the goods to her bedroom, Mutti slowly walked toward the door and shouted in a loud voice, "*Ich komm ja schon.*" [I'm already on my way].

As soon as Mutti had unlocked the door, a burly policeman came charging in and, ignoring Mutti's friendly query as to what had brought him here, headed directly for Frau Adler's bedroom. When he opened the door, Frau Adler let out a bloodcurdling scream and he quickly slammed the door shut behind him. He then walked over to Mutti and brusquely said, "*Ausweis!*" [Identification papers!]. As he examined her papers, he asked her what she was doing here. "*Was ich hier tue!*" Mutti replied indignantly, "*Seit wann ist es verboten seine Freunde zu besuchen?*" [What I am doing here! Since when is it unlawful to visit one's friends?]. Angrily the policeman gave Mutti back her papers and stomped towards the door.

As he walked past me, he gave me a mean look as if I was to blame for the whole affair. That first scared and then angered me. Once he had passed by and was headed for the stairs, I did what we kids usually did when some adult tried to scare us—I stuck out my tongue after him, put my thumbs in my ears, and flapped my fingers up and down. When Mutti had determined that the coast was clear, she called out to Frau Adler who came out of her bedroom again carrying the merchandise and the two went on to finish their business.[15] Early the next morning Mutti and I were on our way to the Remstal.

Usually we got back home from the Remstal at a decent hour but one time, for some reason, we arrived at the Stuttgart Hauptbahnhof so late that the streetcars had stopped running and we were faced with the prospect of walking all the way home loaded down with supplies which would have taken us one to two hours. As we were on our way down Königstraße toward the Schlossplatz, a GI pulled up in a small U.S. Army pickup truck and motioned for us to get in. Since the GI did not understand any

German, let alone our Swabian dialect, and Mutti and I did not know any English, Mutti used hand signals to guide the soldier to our destination. He drove us past the Marienplatz, up the Schimmelhüttenweg and onto the Totenplätzle where he parked. When we got to our *Wohnung*, I was dead tired and immediately climbed into my daybed, which then stood in the large corner room, and fell asleep.

A short time later Mutti came in the room, pulled away the covers, and yanked me out of bed. I was in a daze when Mutti whispered to me that the *Ami* was still in the *Herrenzimmer* next door and that she wanted me to at once go in there and get rid of him. I protested that I was in my underwear and not dressed for the occasion but Mutti told me that the GI would not mind. Thus reassured, I walked to the *Herrenzimmer* as instructed, softly knocked on the door and, hearing no answer, walked in.

There on the sofa facing the door lay the soldier dressed in nothing but his khaki shirt and socks while his pants were draped over a chair. I was so startled that I promptly forgot what Mutti told me to say. Realizing that I was seeing something I was not supposed to be seeing and trying to spare the GI any embarrassment, I quickly averted my eyes and began to focus on the room's large window. Since I was in the presence of a soldier, I kept an erect military posture while the GI continued to lie on the sofa motionless and completely quiet so that I could barely hear him breathe.

It seemed like an eternity before the message Mutti had instructed me to deliver came back to me and, still focusing my eyes on the window, I told the GI in my best Swabian dialect that it was near midnight and that Mutti wanted him to go home. Having delivered my message, I made a military style about-face and marched out of the room. Mutti was anxiously waiting for me at the entrance to the corner room but before I could get there, the GI came running out of the *Herrenzimmer* completely disheveled. His shoe laces were not tied, his shirt not tucked in and, holding up his pants with one hand, he opened the front door with the other and stormed out of our *Wohnung*. I suddenly realized that I must have been the cause of this soldier's distress by what I had said. Overcome with remorse, I quickly ran into the hallway and, as the GI was bolting down the stairs, leaned over the railing and started shouting after him to please visit us some other time. But before I could finish the sentence, Mutti had come out and, after clamping her hand over my mouth, dragged me back inside and locked the door.

Besides doing a lot of traveling ourselves, we also had visitors. A little over two years after the end of the war, my Aunt Irma came over from the *Ostzone* (eastern zone of Germany) bringing along my Cousin Helmut who was three years younger than I. Aunt Irma was the wife of Ludwig, Mutti's favorite brother, who had fallen serving in the Wehrmacht on the eastern front. Their trip was not without peril and involved considerable hardship because, after the war, the Russian occupiers installed a Communist dictatorship in that part of Germany and that regime did its best to prevent people under their control from having contact with the West. This meant that my aunt and cousin had to cross the so-called Iron Curtain that separated the two parts of Germany to visit us. Helmut and I had much fun together. Since it was summer, we often took the streetcar to an outdoor swimming pool on the western part of Stuttgart. Mutti and Aunt Irma too found much to do together and spent much time away from our *Wohnung*. Our two visitors did not stay long before returning home. Mutti played it safe by never traveling to the *Ostzone* herself.

For my 11th birthday, Aunt Irma had brought me a peculiar gift of a slim, hardcover volume with a red border that carried no title. To my amazement the pages inside were completely blank except for some dedicatory remarks by my aunt, specifically, *Reif werden und rein bleiben*. [To mature and remain pure]. She told me the pages were blank so that I could fill them in. But with what? I asked myself because I knew of nothing important to write about. A year later, after a poem on the Christmas story had come to me and which I dedicated to Mutti, I converted the little book into a *Poesiebuch* [poetry book] in which I entered my poem followed by a number of proverbs and sayings which I thought useful as guidelines for my life.

Travels All Alone

With travel again possible, I much wanted to return to Forst for a visit with Mama, Wolfgang, and my friends as I missed them and the village. To my dismay, Mutti balked at taking me because she had other things to do but she said she would be happy to buy me a ticket if I wanted to go by myself. I was about nine years old at the time going on ten. The reason Mutti did not want to go was undoubtedly that she and Mama did not much like each other. Mutti always made snide remarks about Mama whenever I mentioned her and when I was with Mama she did not have anything nice to say about Mutti either. Still, I loved them both because each was very good to me in her own way. I finally decided to go on my own and took the train to Bruchsal, which was about one and a half hours away from Stuttgart, and there got on a bus for Forst. After a panic attack because I did not recognize the route being taken, I was happy to be back again.

To my happy surprise, Mama and Wolfgang were doing well and the village had survived the war unscathed. My arrival appeared to have been anticipated by the kids in the village as a sizeable number surrounded me and in a procession conveyed me to a certain house. Looking up to a second story window they began to chant, *"Maria, Maria / der Hans-Peter ist da."* [Maria, Maria / Hans-Peter is here]. This baffled me because I did not remember having had a girlfriend in Forst. I had no idea who she was or what she looked like and anxiously stared up at the window hoping for an appearance that would solve the mystery. Alas, my beloved never showed herself despite the vociferous chants and shouts of my companions. The romance had clearly not survived my brief absence.

My friends also gave me a rundown on all that had happened since I had been spirited away nearly two years earlier. I found out that some of the people who were in high places in the village during the time I lived in Forst were now decried as Nazis. I heard of one man who had even committed suicide. He did this on account of being ridiculed and disgraced by the other villagers. This made me reflect on the sudden shift in fortune of some people. Not long ago these men had proudly pranced about in their party uniforms and boots and made patriotic speeches from high balconies to enthusiastic villagers like Mama and me and our friends and neighbors. Now they were all of a sudden condemned and disgraced and some had even killed themselves. How about all the people including Mama and me who were there in the schoolyard and listened and wildly cheered because they, the adults at least, understood and liked what they heard? Nobody bothered Mama or me or the other villagers on account of this or called us names. It somehow did not seem right or fair.

The village kids had another bit of exciting news for me that they were sure would please me. There was a certain boy, Veith by name, who lived across the street from us. This boy was bigger and stronger than I and whenever he spotted me he would chase me down and then sit on my belly. After a while he would let me get back up without ever saying a word. I never knew if he liked or disliked me. The exciting news was that Veith was dead. It seems that one day right after the war and the French had occupied the village, he had gone into the surrounding fields and there found a metallic object which he began to examine. The object turned out to be a grenade which exploded tearing out his guts.

After the accident, I was told, Veith was taken to a French army field hospital in the area where he died. When I expressed the hope that Veith did not have to suffer long, one of the boys assured me that his end had come very quickly. The French have a custom, the boy explained, known as the *coup de grâce* in which they end the suffering of severely injured people by shooting them dead. According to his account, right after Veith was taken away, a loud bang was heard that sounded like a shot from a pistol. From this it was concluded that Veith had been given the *coup de grâce*. To know that Veith was quickly put out of his misery made me feel a lot better.

With my solo trip to Forst successfully completed, Mutti now felt that I was ready for an assignment involving a much longer one that would take me to the North Sea. It seems that Esther was laid up in the coastal town of Bremerhaven awaiting passage to America to join her father. Mutti wanted me to bring her a package of food to supplement her meager fare at the port. I accepted the assignment not that I was in a position to refuse. Mutti took me to the Stuttgart Hauptbahnhof in the morning and got me a seat on the train. I was told to keep the food package for Esther on my lap and warned not to lose it. To keep me entertained on my long journey, Mutti gave me an illustrated children's book that was chock-full of funny stories and cartoons. She then said goodbye and I was on my own. I was 10 years old at the time.

The train ride to Bremerhaven was longer than I had expected and as day turned into night we were still moving. All of a sudden in the middle of the night, the train stopped and everybody got off. I looked out to see the station but there were no station lights. In fact, there was absolutely nothing out there. Then why was everybody getting off? I finally too got off and walked with the others for some distance. But where was everybody going because I did not see any station lights ahead? Completely bewildered I sat down besides the rails and had a good cry. Soon after, a man walking with the crowd came up to me and took me by the hand for a very long walk that finally ended at the station. As I quickly realized, there was not much left of the Bahnhof, or for that matter, the entire town of Bremerhaven. Enemy bombers had razed it to the ground just like my hometown of Stuttgart.

After the stranger and I parted company, I somehow found my way through the mountains of rubble piled up beside the deserted streets to the barracks near the harbor where the emigrants were housed. My sister was in good spirits and I handed over the food package with a letter from Mutti. She then showed me to a communal bathing facility where I took my first shower and gave me a bite to eat. Esther then cajoled me to have a nap on her metal bedstead and I soon fell asleep. Some time after my return to Stuttgart, a postcard arrived from my good Samaritan. Mutti showed it to me and suggested that I write him back but playing obstinate, as I often did, I ignored her request. Much later I came to much regret my cold and ungrateful conduct when I recalled what had happened after we got to the Bremerhaven Bahnhof. I had to go to the bathroom and asked him to hold onto my food package while he stayed outside. When I came out, he was waiting for me with a kind smile on his face. It never occurred to me at the time that he could have easily absconded with my precious goods had he wanted to. It had been my good fortune to meet up with a truly good and decent man.

Back In School

During the height of the war and the bombings and even for some time after its end, the schools in the major cities including Stuttgart were closed. Most of the city children had been evacuated to the countryside in a program called *Kinderlandverschickung (KLV)* [Children Country Evacuation] and received their education in village schools. Some children whose parents decided to keep them at home in the city for the duration of the war and others, like myself, who were brought into the city from the country during the war, were essentially in limbo as far as formal schooling was concerned.

In my case, I had finished two years of schooling in Forst and was about to enter 3rd grade when Mutti brought me to Stuttgart. In Stuttgart, the schools did not reopen until September of the year following the end of the war. The two missed years of instruction, grades three and four, proved an almost insurmountable handicap for some years to come not only because I had not acquired reading, writing, and math skills on a par with my peers but I also lacked the motivation to give up my carefree lifestyle for the discipline required to do well in school.

While Mutti usually brought along a children's book or two for me to read in the air raid shelters, I rarely opened one up because I was always too tired for lack of sleep. Consequently, when I entered 5th grade in Stuttgart I could barely read and write and do almost no math. About this time, Ute and Volker returned from foster care in Austria and joined the family in our Stuttgart apartment. Of the two, only Ute was of school age. Esther was still living with us but only for a couple of months or so before her emigration.

Lerchenrainschule, the Volksschule (elementary school) Ute and I were sent to, was modern and attractive looking and located on a hill at the edge of a woods. It was a good walk from home along Böheimstraße past the Marienhospital and up a steep street that ran parallel to Adlerstraße and up to the end of the war had been named in honor of Manfred von Richthofen, the famous World War I flying ace. (At war's end, streets named for military heroes were all renamed). My home room teacher was Herr Mader whose favorite expression was *l-L-d-D* which stood for *lange Leitung, dünner Draht* [long line, thin wire]. He used it whenever one of his pupils was slow in catching on to something and for that he had my number too.

In fact, in Herr Mader's estimation I must have been one of the dumbest kids in class judging from the type of questions he asked me. One time he required me to come to the front of the class and transfer a fairly long piece he had written on the blackboard to the other side. Herr Mader asked me whether I thought it better to first make the transfer and then erase the original or erase the original first and then make the transfer. Naturally, the other kids in class snickered with delight. I then told Herr Mader that either way would work for me. To everyone's amazement, I first erased the piece and then wrote down an exact copy where Herr Mader wanted it. I may have been slow in catching on to things but I also had an exceptional memory.

My stay at Lerchenrainschule was short, just one school year, but it laid a good foundation and, thanks to Herr Mader, I began to read more than my favorite *Märchen* [fairy tales] by the brothers Grimm of which I owned a handsome volume illustrated with full-page color plates. I just loved to read stories that began with *Es war einmal* [Once upon a time] and read all of the many folktales the brothers had collected. A funny short story we had to read about a train ride so much delighted me that for the first time I took note of an author's name which happened to be Peter Rosegger, an Austrian poet and novelist. Herr Mader was also in the habit of visiting his pupils' homes to get to know their parents. When he came to our house, Mutti entertained him in the *Herrenzimmer*. I do not know what was said but I could not help but notice some overly solicitous behavior on Mutti's part afterwards. It caused me to cringe every time I heard a knock on the classroom door because I was afraid some kid would come in holding a carrot or an apple and ask if there was a boy named Peter in class.

Why did Mutti have to embarrass me by coming to school with these treats instead of giving them to me before I left in the morning?, I wondered. She had, after all, never been very affectionate or caring toward me otherwise. When she first brought me to Stuttgart I had now and then tried to give her a hug but she had always pushed me away saying she did not care for all that mush. After a while I just gave up. It really did not bother me because Mutti was otherwise taking good care of me and I could do without all that smooching. Admittedly, she showed her love in other ways as when she sat next to my bed for hours while I was down with the measles.

Sometime after the war Mutti also got involved in politics. She had made the acquaintance of an elderly couple who lived in a rundown and sparsely furnished apartment near the Matthäuskirche. These people had persuaded her to become active in the Heslach chapter of their organization which was named Vereinigung der Verfolgten des Naziregimes or VVN (Organization for Victims of the Nazi Regime). According to Mutti, this couple had spent time in a concentration camp and as victims of that regime were looking for restitution from the government. It was logical for Mutti to join since she and Esther too had been victimized by the Nazis. The local VVN chapter appeared to be very small because when Mutti took me along to a couple of their meetings, all the active members found room sitting around one regular sized table.

At one of these meetings in a room behind a restaurant's main dining room, it came to a little fracas. As we were all sitting at the table and Mutti and the others were having a discussion, one of the members got very angry and stood up to loudly and bitterly complain about the lack of progress the leadership was making. He asked the elderly couple whether this bottle of wine they had just handed out was the best they could do for him after years of membership. When he did not get a satisfactory answer, he told them that they could keep their wine and that he was through with them With that he stormed out of the room slamming the door shut behind him.

One day Mutti asked me if I would mind spending a little time after school now and then to collect membership dues for the VVN. I did not mind and she gave me a list of names and addresses. The members I visited appeared to be the poorest of the poor. They lived in rundown apartments in the poorest section of Heslach and did not seem to have a penny to their names. At one place, a haggard looking young woman came to the door holding a baby while other small children were screaming and scampering about inside. She then disappeared and after a long time came back to hand me the dues, which was just one Reichsmark, and hurriedly closed the door without saying a word to me.

I just could not handle all of that and after about a week asked Mutti to be excused from my assignment. I do not know whether Mutti stayed with this organization or left it because I never heard her talk about it again. Years later we learned that the VVN was a Communist front organization with many members also belonging to the Communist Party. Mutti had clearly been duped because she hated Communists.

A Swiss Vacation

Shortly after my year at Lerchenrainschule had ended and before the start of the new school year in September, Mutti told me that she was getting me a passport and a train ticket to visit my *Tante Emmi* [Aunt Emmi] in Geneva. I said, "*Wen?*" [Who?]. Mutti then explained to me that she had an older sister named Emmi who long ago had left the family home in Frankfurt am Main for Berlin and from there had emigrated to Switzerland. Well, by now nothing could surprise me anymore. Three years earlier I had found out that I had two siblings named Ute and Volker in Austria about whom I had known nothing before. More recently, I had heard about a third named Elke who was the youngest and lived somewhere else. Now I found out that I also had a Swiss aunt. It appears Mutti had not told me about her sister because the two had never liked each other from childhood and had not been on speaking terms for years. But it seems Aunt Emmi had persuaded Mutti to send me for a short vacation between school years. It sounded good to me. If nothing else, I would enjoy a look at the Swiss countryside and the train ride would certainly be a treat.

Subsequently, Mutti took me to the Stuttgart Hauptbahnhof and put me on the train for Basel where I would change for one going to Geneva. When I got to the Basel Hauptbahnhof, two nuns were waiting for me to take me into protective custody. They were tall and skinny and had pale, expressionless faces. At the station I looked into a kiosk and saw some very beautiful Swiss stamps showing ancient steam locomotives and hoped they would come over and buy me a couple. Instead, the two kept whispering to each other and paid no attention to me. Their stiff formality turned me off and I was glad to be rid of them once they had put me on the train to Geneva.

Aunt Emmi met me at the Geneva Hauptbahnhof accompanied by a man whom she introduced as my *Onkel Charles* [Uncle Charles]. At their home, I met two other members of the household which were the maid Nicole, who spoke only French, and Sambo, an energetic wire fox terrier. Aunt Emmi was a very lively and jovial person who spoke in rapid bursts of *hochdeutsch* so that I had difficulty following her. She was bigger than Mutti and her hair and complexion were somewhat lighter than hers. Uncle Charles was tall and slender and, while he was friendly and pleasant, seemed reserved and formal. Their house, called a villa, was located in the Champel area of Geneva at 23B, avenue de Miremont on a cul-de-sac off that street. There were three more large homes, all fenced in, on this narrow, semi-circular side street.

The 3-story Italianate structure had an asymmetrical look from the outside but the floor plan was very logical and uncomplicated. Past the front door, there was as an entrance hall which led to the various rooms which were, in a clockwise direction, a small salon, a large rectangular living room, a dining room of the same size, a half bath and an expansive kitchen with pantry from which tall French doors led to the yard. Beyond the dining room there was a glass enclosed and sun-filled *Wintergarten* [solarium] where breakfast was taken. A staircase between the entrance and kitchen led to the second floor which had a similar floor plan. Over the salon was a small bedroom, then came Aunt Emmi's bedroom, Uncle Charles' bedroom and study, a large tiled bathroom, and another small bedroom. On the third floor under the roof were two more rooms, namely, the maid's room and Aunt Emmi's sewing room, plus a half-bath.

Most rooms had a dark and gloomy look except for Aunt Emmi's bedroom which was bright and cheery not only because of the décor but it was on the sunny side of the house. The floors were covered by thick oriental carpets while the walls held many paintings including portraits of stern-looking ancestors of Uncle Charles. A door next to the kitchen led down to the cellar which held a wooden structure with a locked door for the storage of wine. There were two garages on the property, one at each end, as well as flower and vegetable gardens, some fruit trees and a stand of tall pine trees.

My visit got off to a shaky start. On the second or third day after my arrival, Aunt Emmi led me to the entrance hall where a group of people were seated awaiting our appearance. She introduced me in French and since I knew only my native Swabian, I could do no more than nod politely and pretend that I was pleased to make their acquaintance. Aunt Emmi's guests were the oldest people I had ever seen and looked like lifeless fossils from a bygone age. The icy stares with which they fixed me pierced me to the bone.

Perhaps they just did not like children, I thought, or maybe they disapproved of what I was wearing. I was dressed in the fashion of German boys my age at the time which meant Lederhosen, i.e., well-worn shorts of soft deerskin leather, leather suspenders with an inlaid imitation Edelweiss in the crosstie between the straps, a blue and white checkered shirt, blue woolen kneesocks and laced leather shoes. One wrinkled old lady raised her eyeglasses, which were fastened to a long ornate handle, and looked me over from top to bottom in the most condescending manner. I finally could take it no longer and fled into the kitchen and out the door to the yard. There I remained until they all had left despite Aunt Emmi's repeated entreaties to come back in again.

Nicole too took no liking to me and kept complaining to Aunt Emmi about that *enfant terrible* she had to put up with. She probably had good reason. One incident involved an electrical signaling device that hung in the hallway next to the kitchen and held a number of lights for letting the maid know if she was wanted and in which room. Rather than simply ask, I ran an experiment to find out which of the ten lights belonged to which room. The operation took much planning so as not to be caught and I had to hide in closets, behind curtains, and under beds until just the right moment to make my escape. Poor Nicole ran up and down the stairs for a couple of days as I kept repeating my experiment to make certain I had it right. On another occasion Nicole caught me going through Uncle Charles' large postage stamp collection after I had discovered the books at the bottom of a large wooden clothes closet in his room. Nicole almost went berserk because she suspected that I was about to make some changes in them.

After a while, things started to settle down. On some mornings Aunt Emmi and I would walk the short distance to the Plateau de Champel and take the streetcar to downtown Geneva for some grocery shopping. She had her favorite butcher, baker, and greengrocer, who all graciously addressed her as *Madame* which much impressed me. In Germany I had heard *gnädige Frau* [gracious lady] used as a salutation but *Madame* sounded even better. Aunt Emmi much enjoyed the personal attention given her and carefully inspected what was being offered before making her selections.

After these excursions, I soon felt enough at home in the new town to venture off on my own by walking down the Boulevard Helvétique to the Lac de Genève (Lake Geneva) to watch the tourist boats come and go. On the way, I would admire the stately public buildings and palatial private homes some of which were surrounded by tall and gilded wrought iron fences. The shop windows displayed a large variety of exquisite jewelry, clocks and watches, and other precious commodities. One could tell that Geneva was a town of great wealth which was not the impression I had of Stuttgart although my hometown had a beauty and charm all its own.

In the evening, after Uncle Charles had come home from the bank, we would all be together in the little salon where it was always nice and cozy. Several miniature Swiss clocks on stands fastened to the walls would be clicking and chiming away. There, at a small round table, we would have our evening meal brought in from the kitchen by Nicole. Uncle Charles was a wine connoisseur whose favorite brand was Châteauneuf-du-Pape and in the evening I would be given the key to the wine closet and asked to bring up a bottle of it. I too would be given Châteauneuf-du-Pape but much diluted with water since it was pretty strong stuff and once nearly put me out when I drank it straight.

After our meal and the dishes had been cleared off, the three of us would remain in the room and do our favorite things. Aunt Emmi would do *Handarbeit* while Uncle Charles would work on his large collection of rare and expensive postage stamps from many countries which he kept in leather-bound books. He would carefully examine his stamps under a magnifying glass and rearrange them in the books as necessary. Since I liked to draw, I would busy myself with doing the profiles of important men using as a guide drawings that appeared almost daily in a section of the *Journal de Genève* my aunt and uncle were subscribing to. Sambo, who was always tired in the evening after running around all day, would sleep peacefully in his wicker basket in the corner.

The daily routine was occasionally broken on weekends when Uncle Charles would take us to an old restaurant called the Auberge Communale de Carouge which Aunt Emmi liked because she claimed it had the best *gratin de pommes de terre* [potatoes au gratin].

Not everybody in Geneva shared in the good life as I soon discovered. Aunt Emmi's seamstress was an example. When this lady came to the house I could not help but notice her gaunt and haggard appearance and how focused she was on her sewing chores. She worked for Aunt Emmi but also made me a couple of outfits in the style worn by boys in Geneva after I was assured they would not make me look like a sissy. A couple of times she brought along her daughter, Madeleine, who was about my age. Uncle Charles had set up a net in the yard and there Madeleine and I would play a game of badminton while her mother worked in the upstairs sewing room. We would also have a little fun as Madeleine made an effort to teach me some French while I, in turn, tried to have her pronounce some words in my native Swabian.

One day Aunt Emmi went to see Madeleine's mother and took me along. Their second-floor apartment in old Carouge was reached by walking up an outside wooden staircase. When we entered I was shocked by the austerity of the place. There was one big, sparsely furnished room with bare walls and windows that were just tall narrow slits. Madeleine was not home since it was September and school was in session. Aunt Emmi sat down on one of the few chairs around and I stood next to her. During our entire visit, the seamstress remained behind her ironing board and never stopped working even for a minute. I now understood why this woman always seemed to be in such a cranky mood when she came to the villa. She worked hard and probably for little pay as Aunt Emmi, I learned, was not the generous type.

On another occasion Aunt Emmi announced that she and Uncle Charles would be going to Lausanne and I was welcome to come along. It was a balmy day in late September or early October and I much enjoyed the ride in Uncle Charles' big Mercedes-Benz. On the way there, Aunt Emmi gave me a choice of either going with her to a luncheon appointment with some ladies or with Uncle Charles who was planning to attend a postage stamp show. Neither excited me but I finally opted for the stamp show as the lesser of the two evils. For some reason, Uncle Charles tried to talk me out of going with him but I had made up my mind and would not budge.

When we got to Lausanne we parted company with Aunt Emmi going off in one direction and Uncle Charles and I in another. The two of us had already walked some distance when Uncle Charles had a change of heart. He had some other business to attend to first, he told me, and would return shortly to pick me up. With that he walked me back to the car, put me in the back seat, and walked off. I waited and waited and it must have been an hour or more and still Uncle Charles had not returned. That is when I decided to take a little walk and check out Lausanne until he came back. I walked down one street and then another all the while admiring the interesting architecture and landmarks and doing some window-shopping as I had done in Geneva.

I had been gone for a while when I decided it was time to return to the car to see if Uncle Charles was ready for the stamp show. Suddenly I realized that I had no clue where I had come from but remembered that when I got out of the car, I had seen a big statue of the Swiss folk hero Wilhelm Tell standing nearby. With the help of some people I ran into, I now found my way back. When I got there, both Uncle Charles and Aunt Emmi were standing by the car waiting for me. Aunt Emmi was overjoyed to see me and hugged and kissed me but I could tell that Uncle Charles was in a sour mood. Since it was already late in the afternoon and the stamp show had probably closed, Uncle Charles headed straight for Geneva.

All the way home Aunt Emmi was angry as a hornet and never stopped scolding him. How could he leave a 10-year old child all by himself in a car when the papers were full of stories about what was happening to children these days, she kept repeating. Actually, I was already 11 but decided to keep quiet. One of the things I remember her saying to him was, *"Charlie, hör zu! Das nächste mal wenn du auf eine Briefmarkenaussstellung in Lausanne gehst, da komm ich mit."* [Listen to me, Charlie! On your next visit to a stamp show in Lausanne, I'll be coming to the show with you].

At The Oberschule

It was now the beginning of September which was also the start of a new school year. After having finished 5th grade at the Lerchenrain Volksschule, I was now supposed to enter a Gymnasium or Oberschule (high school). The other option, namely, finishing 8th grade at the Volksschule followed by an apprenticeship, was not in Mutti's plans for me. If I did not show up for the start of classes at the Oberschule, it was because I was on vacation in Geneva and did not get back from there until sometime in early October. Blissfully unaware of the school opening date, and most other dates for that matter, and not at all eager to return to school anyway, I had never given the matter any thought while I was gone. I do not know the reason for my late departure for Switzerland but presumably either the required arrangements for my trip took longer than expected or Aunt Emmi and Uncle Charles did not get back from their second home in southern France in time. As a result, I had to take a special examination all by myself to be admitted to Schickhardt Oberschule, a prestigious boys preparatory school in Heslach.

The test, alas, laid bare my considerable educational deficiencies since I had only three years of formal schooling instead of the five of my peers. The written examination, which was loaded with math problems involving fractions and percentages, did not go well. It was all mostly Greek to me. I surmise that it was Mutti's good connections and superb persuasive skills that allowed me to be admitted anyway. After all, the lost two years of schooling were at no fault of my own and my forebears were educated people, she probably argued, making an apprenticeship inappropriate for me.

I was fortunate that she succeeded and the school took a chance on me because the two and one-half years or so I spent at Schickhardt Oberschule were life-changing learning experiences. The school was located at the opposite end of Adlerstraße across the street from the now reopened Schwabtunnel. It was housed in an imposing complex including two 3-story wings containing classrooms and administrative offices connected by a combination gym and assembly hall. Swimming lessons were provided in the indoor pool of the Heslach municipal baths located down the steps from the school.

That year, there were two entering classes of perhaps 60 plus boys in total and I was assigned to class 1b. The subjects taught were German, English, mathematics, geography, biology, art, music, religion, physical education, history (starting with the second year), and French (starting with the third year). Classes were held from Monday through Friday plus half a day on Saturday. We had only male teachers who were expected to not only teach the subject matter but also to help build character and self-esteem.

Our home room teacher, Herr Wahl, was a rugged outdoorsman who enjoyed to hike and hunt but was genteel and kind as well. Along three walls in his classroom he had put up signs in bold lettering proclaiming *Selbstzucht* meaning self-discipline. He admonished us that a man or boy must always be in complete control of himself so as not to succumb to the many sins and vices of the world. If we wanted to make something out of ourselves we must never waver from the straight and narrow, he told us. He taught mathematics and loved to put us through multiplication drills—we were required to know by heart the product of any two 2-digit numbers up to 20.

Herr Wahl took a special interest in me and became somewhat of a father figure although he was not overly pleased with my progress. At the end of my second year, he wrote on my report card, *"Peters Verhalten war geordnet. Fleiß und Aufmerksamkeit ließen zu wünschen übrig."* [Peter's conduct was orderly. Diligence and attentiveness left much to be desired].

That was an accurate assessment because instead of paying attention in class, I spent much time looking out the window and daydreaming. I could have sworn that school was only meant to keep people from thinking about things on their own.

The stories Herr Wahl told us showed a love of country and a strong Christian faith. In one, a severely injured man was found wandering the streets during the war and brought to a hospital where the nurses patiently tried to find out who he was and where he came from. But his mind seemed to be gone along with his ability to speak. They had already given up on him and were about to turn away, when the man folded his hands in prayer and laboriously and barely audible began to say, "*Unser Vater im Himmel....*" [Our Father in Heaven....]. Hearing the man recite the Lord's Prayer, his caregivers rejoiced and exclaimed, "*Er ist einer von uns—er ist ein Deutscher.*" [He is one of us—he is a German].

After Herr Wahl became severely ill and was much confined to his bed at his home in Degerloch, our new homeroom teacher was Herr Klein, a younger man who walked about with a cane after having lost a leg serving with the Wehrmacht. My grades immediately plummeted and, during my last full semester at the school, I received a grade of *ausreichend* [adequate] in all subjects except for religion where I continued to do very well. A grade of *ausreichend* was a 4 on a scale of 1 to 6, with 6 being a failing grade, and I could see the handwriting on the wall. If my grades did not improve, and there was no good prospect that would be the case, I would soon be out in the cold and at 14 entering into an apprenticeship with little chance of obtaining a university education.

I had three good friends at the Oberschule who were very different from each other. Jörg Reuschle was a curly haired blond kid who was always full of mischief especially when it came to playing pranks on the teachers but, unlike me, a very good student. Jörg lived alone with his mother near the Lerchenrainschule but because she was somewhat of a recluse, I never got to meet her. Gerhard Fehler was Jörg's friend before I met him and was a more quiet type. He was much burdened with the prospect of soon losing his mother who was dying of cancer. Because Gerhard lived far out near the western end of town and came in by the streetcar running on Böblingerstraße, I saw him only in school. However, one day I decided to go visit him and his parents. Before I left home, Mutti, whom I had told of Gerhard's mother, showed me a net full of a dozen or so exotic round fruit which she said were oranges. I had never seen an orange before let alone tasted one and I do not know where Mutti got them but she wanted me to take them along as a gift for Gerhard's mother.

When I got to the house, after a very long walk (for some reason, I did not take the streetcar), Gerhard and his father ushered me into a bedroom and introduced me to Frau Fehler who lay in bed looking very pale and emaciated. When I presented her with the oranges, she was so overjoyed that I feared she would leap right out of bed to give me a hug. Because I was not used to such emotional outbursts it startled and somewhat embarrassed me. What Mutti did for Frau Fehler was déjà vu for her. Her greatest pleasure came always from, in her words, "*Jemand eine Freude machen*" [To bring joy to someone].

My best friend at school was Hans-Eugen Wittmayr who lived on my way to school on the second floor of an apartment building on the southeast corner of Adlerstraße and Böblingerstraße. He was the smartest and most active of my friends. For some time Hans-Eugen walked around with his leg in a cast after falling off his bicycle which he used to ride at a fast pace down the hills of Stuttgart. Now and then he would give his head a quick upward jerk to clear away long strands of dark brown hair that kept falling down over his eyes. He was a friendly boy with an engaging smile. Hans-Eugen was very fond of his beautiful German shepherd dog and proudly showed her off whenever I visited him. The fact that his dog's ears pointed straight up and the end of the tail hung down without curling up at its end were proof that his was a purebred animal, he told me

One of our teachers, Herr Höger, was a strict disciplinarian and generated much angst among us kids. He was a former Wehrmacht officer who walked very erect and required us to sit up straight when he entered the classroom. Hardly inside he would complain about the foul air in the room and order the windows opened no matter what the temperature was outside. One day Herr Höger came in very angry. The source of his wrath turned out to be none other than my friend Hans-Eugen.

Now, across the street from where Hans-Eugen lived, on the other side of Adlerstraße, there was a streetcar stop and next to it stood a small wooden structure inside of which newspapers, magazines, and tobacco products were displayed and sold. On this particular morning, Herr Höger had gotten off the streetcar and entering this place to get the morning paper had apparently spotted Hans-Eugen in the back leafing through a magazine he did not approve of. Rather than confront my friend there, he decided to wait until he got to his classroom. When Herr Höger came in, he loudly complained that this very morning he was appalled to catch one of his pupils in that establishment leaving through a magazine full of naked women.

When Herr Höger had finished telling us of this student's disgusting conduct, he walked over to Hans-Eugen, who was sitting towards the front of the room and, without further ado, gave him a resounding *Ohrfeige* [slap in the face]. Hans Eugen was startled and manly tried to keep from crying when he lost control and the tears started pouring down both cheeks. His brown eyes glistened in anger and he reared back like a cobra ready to strike. Then he tilted his head forward in defiance as if to say, "Go ahead and strike me again, you big baboon," when Herr Höger quickly backed off and walked to the front of the room to begin with our geometry lesson for the day.

Starting with the third year at the Oberschule, we took up French and our teacher was Herr Dr. Traub who had a formal and aloof way about him. That was probably because he was the only one of our teachers with a doctor's degree. Dr. Traub's approach to teaching French involved an endless drill in proper grammar and the conjugation of verbs, regular and irregular. Unfortunately, his fixation on grammar and syntax came at the expense of a good vocabulary so that we made only slow progress speaking and writing that language.

Now and then Dr. Traub would bring in a young lady from the Institute Français to talk to us about French culture and customs. Indeed, after listening to her tour de force on French cultural achievements and the parade of famous composers, writers, painters, and scientists the country had produced, one was left with the distinct impression that French cultural achievements were almost on a par with our own German ones, if that were possible. The appearance of the French mademoiselle had a profound effect on Dr. Traub's behavior. Otherwise cool and distant, he now oozed utmost charm.

Upon her arrival and when she was not addressing the class, he literally danced around her as if they were performing in a ballet. He made all sorts of gracious and deferential gestures towards her including deep bows and fanciful arm and hand movements all accompanied by tidbits in French while she, obviously pleased by all the attention given her, profusely complemented Dr. Traub on his excellent command of the French language. At the end of class and after the mademoiselle's presentation, he would resume his flirtatious behavior and gracefully escort her upstairs to the teachers lounge while we would look after the two whispering *oh-la-la*.

Being *evangelisch*, I attended Pfarrer Gottlob Lang's religious classes at the Oberschule. The boys who were *katholisch* were taught by the local parish priest who also came to school. Pfarrer Lang was the senior pastor at the Evangelische Matthäuskirche which was the church of the Heslach Protestant congregation. I started attending it after the war once much of the rubble had been cleared away and it could be reopened for worship services. St. Matthew's was a very impressive church in the style of a Romanesque basilica with a floor plan in the shape of a cross. At the intersection of the nave and transept, the roof was topped by an octagonal cupola holding a cross. A massive bell tower in which was located the entrance portal stood on its west side.

The church had been severely damaged during the Anglo-American bombing raids on Stuttgart. The roof was mostly blown off and the sanctuary completely gutted including the stained glass windows and wall paintings, the pews, and the majestic pipe organ on the balcony over the main entrance. All that remained were the baptismal font and parts of the altar and pulpit. What was so strange about the destruction of St. Matthew's was that, unlike the inner city, Heslach was not particularly hard hit during the air attacks and most of the area around the church had escaped damage altogether. Rebuilding of the church started almost immediately and a second consecration was held five years after the war's end. I loved attending Sunday morning worship services at the Matthäuskirche even though I was almost always by myself as was the case in Forst. Like Mama, Mutti rarely went to church but encouraged me to go and say a prayer for her which I always did.

Pastor Lang, like some of my other teachers at Schickhardt Oberschule, became very influential in my life. He was a pious, kindly man whose father had been a church organist and composer. He gave us a good grounding in the four Gospels as well as the letters of St. Paul. He also taught us about the Reformation and the part played by Martin Luther and other church leaders in bringing about freedom of religion to Germany and Europe that came out of the Reformation movement. One day in class Pfarrer Lang told us a little secret. It seems that he had been imprisoned by the American occupation forces soon after the end of the war. But instead of being embarrassed by this assault on his pastoral dignity, he wore his imprisonment like a badge of honor.

One day, he said, the Americans had come to search the church and found a cache of Wehrmacht weapons hidden in the basement of St. Matthews. He knew about it and admitted he knew. Pfarrer Lang explained to us that he felt fully justified in allowing their storage towards the end of the war. The British and Americans had bombed and nearly destroyed his church and many other Stuttgart houses of worship, he said. These deeds were offenses against God and Christianity, he told us, and he had every right to help defend his church, his city, his country, and his faith against these godless foreign invaders. Pfarrer Lang was the only person I knew who dared to openly and defiantly speak out against our American occupiers.[16]

Our music teacher, Herr Bähr, was sill a young man who had received his degree at Heidelberg University. His finely chiseled face, double chin, dark locks, and expressive eyes left no doubt that he was an artist of some kind. He played the piano and the cello and was a sought-after choral director. Herr Bähr taught us about the development of German and European musical styles from ancient to baroque to classical to romantic to modern. For each period he would give us biographical information on the major German composers and, on the piano, play us short samples of their works.

Herr Bähr was also in charge of the school choir. He auditioned me like the others in class and found that I had an excellent treble voice and invited me to become a member of the school choir. This entitled me to sit in the front row of seats in his class. Many of our public performances were in war-damaged churches of both confessions where we sang in Bach's St. John and St. Mathew passions. At the non-church concerts, the emphasis was on old Volkslieder and lieder by 19th century German and Austrian composers. We became so well known that once we were bused to the studios of Radio Stuttgart where our program was recorded for later broadcast.

According to Herr Bähr, he had been drafted into the Wehrmacht close to the end of the war and early one morning he and a few other soldiers of his unit woke up to find themselves cut off from the main body of troops and deep in enemy territory. Wandering about and knowing the war was essentially over, they came to a farm house where they commandeered some civilian clothes. Soon after they ran into a French patrol. Herr Bähr, who spoke some French, addressed the officer as *mon général* and tried to explain to him that he and his companions were students at the Sorbonne in Paris and on an outing in the country. The officer, who just happened to have studied at the Sorbonne, did not buy his story and they all ended up in a French prisoner of war camp.

What we especially liked about Herr Bähr was that he also took us on many outings in and around Stuttgart. The dukes of Württemberg had built a number of palaces and hunting lodges in the area which were all worth exploring and Herr Bähr enjoyed serving as our guide. Among the places we checked out were Solitude, a small palace commissioned by Duke Carl Eugen and designed by the French architect Philippe de la Guêpière. The building was shuttered but we could peek inside and see the gorgeous interior. A perfectly straight road led from it to the great palace at Ludwigsburg, a town named for Louis XIV, the Sun King, which served as the summer residence for the Württemberg court. The story is told that this road, about 14 kilometers (9 miles) in length, was at least once covered with salt so that the duke and his party could take a mid-summer sleigh ride. Other royal residences we visited were Monrepos and Favorit.

One popular outing with Herr Bähr took place on a day in early September after the beginning of a new school year. Herr Bähr and his class would assemble at the Oberschule early in the morning and walk to the edge of a forest above Stuttgart. Here we would split up into two groups. One group would include Herr Bähr and a boy he had chosen while the rest of us comprised the second. Herr Bähr and this boy would be known as *Großer Bär und Kleiner Bär* [Big Bear and Little Bear]. In the game plan, the two bears would hike deep into the woods while we would leave about an hour later following a trail of broken twigs and other items left by the two. To keep us off track, the trail they left for us led to many dead ends. Once we had located the two ensconced on top of a hill, we would rush up and try to dislodge them. Afterwards we would sit in a circle and sing popular folksongs. I missed the first of the outings because I was on my Swiss vacation but did attend the second one and it was great fun.

The following year's outing, unfortunately, did not go as planned. To our amazement, when we came to the hill, the two bears were not on top but at its foot. Little Bear, a tall, blond boy from our sister class, lay there against the side of the hill in a crouching position. He was breathing heavily and seemed quite exhausted. Nobody knew what to make of it all and we were very disappointed that our fun had been cut short. Herr Bähr offered not much of an explanation. We then began the long trek back to the school with two of the older boys supporting Little Bear, who could barely walk, between them. One could see that both of his legs were discolored right up to near his buttocks.

Next day at school we learned what had happened. It seems that Herr Bähr had wanted to toughen up Little Bear before our arrival so that he would be in better shape to assist in defending the hill. But, alas, the exercises performed on him by Herr Bähr proved too strenuous so that instead of being strengthened by them the boy suffered a total collapse.

Parents who heard about the incident became very upset because they felt that this boy should not have been subject to such needless torment. Why would the school's music teacher get involved in physical fitness when the Oberschule had a professional and capable gym instructor? It was not long before some people complained to the school's *Rector* [principal], Herr Lehmann. The *Rector*, a stern and intimidating man, taught the upper classes and always carried a thick book with the title *Plato* on the cover around with him. He was *katholisch* and had been angry with his music teacher, who was *evangelisch*, ever since he had heard that Herr Bähr had been talking to our class about some early popes and their supposed shameless conduct such as fathering babies by nuns. Now with this latest incident, the *Rektor* had another reason to dislike our music teacher. All made us worry about what might happen to Herr Bähr and our yearly outings.

The subjects I found most interesting at the Oberschule were German and history. In German class we were introduced to the poetry of Goethe, Schiller, Fontane, Heine, Mörike, Uhland, and others and I developed a strong affinity for rhymed verse. In fact, I liked many of these poems enough to commit them to memory and recite them to myself whenever I was in the mood. With much of modern German history being very controversial, history at the Oberschule meant ancient and, specifically, Greek history. My reading in school texts were supplemented by books in the personal library of the previous occupant of our *Wohnung* on Adlerstraße, Dr. Liebendörfer.

To my great delight, the heart of the Liebendörfer library was a collection (in translation) of the Greek and Roman classics including the two epic poems attributed to Homer, *The Iliad* and *The Odyssey*, the histories of Herodotus and Thucydides, Plato's *Dialogues*, the works of Aristotle, and Plutarch's *Lives of the Noble Grecians and Romans*. The thoughts expressed in these works were, for the most part, beyond my comprehension at the time but I did peruse most of them gathering up as much as my mind could grasp. Other books in the library I much enjoyed were biographies of Alexander the Great and Cervantes' *Don Quixote de la Mancha*. With the addition of a daybed, the *Herrenzimmer* had been converted into my very own room giving me continuous access to the library. Sitting at Dr. Liebendörfer's big desk reading and taking copious notes often kept me up way into the night.

Emigration

In the meantime, Esther had been living in America for over three years and had moved from upstate New York, where she had been working in a resort town as a waitress, to Chicago. There she had joined up with her old boyfriend Nick and had gotten married. Mutti told us that Esther was now making arrangements to bring all four of us over too. I had mixed feelings about that. On the one hand, I would miss my friends and familiar surroundings especially my beloved Stuttgart while, on the other, I was not doing well at the Schickhardt Oberschule where my grades were slipping and I was fearful of not being able to continue after the present school year. It was near the end of the year and, according to Mutti, it might take three months for all the preliminaries to be completed including getting visas and booking passage. In addition, Esther and Nick had to first buy a house in the Chicago area so that we would have a place to live. At our end too there were many things to be taken care of including completing all that paperwork at the American consulate in Stuttgart.

Mutti was not at all enthusiastic about our impending move. I could tell that she had big reservations and perhaps even some dread although she did not talk to me about it. One thing that was sure to be on her mind was how we would fit into a culture that was likely to be completely different from our own. Mutti was now 40 years old and at that age taking on a new lifestyle and learning another language would not be the easiest thing in the world. In addition, she would most likely have to find a job and go back to work. And, of course, there was *Onkel Helmut*, Mutti's new gentleman friend. She would surely miss him.

The extended time frame before our move was sufficient for Mutti to make the other necessary preparations and get things in order. She had to decide what to do with our flat on which she held a permanent lease. Should she give it up or hold onto it and sublease it? Mutti had previously invited Aunt Irma to come to the West and take over our *Wohnung* but she had declined because she wanted to remain close to her parents and siblings. The next issue was what to do with the furniture and our other possessions, i.e., what to take with and what to leave behind and to whom. Mutti would have liked to have taken along her parent's dining room set but Esther, who would have to pay the transportation cost, said no to that idea. Also left behind was a grandfather clock that had been her father's retirement present from I.G. Farben.

There was, however, one item Mutti treasured above all others and that she did take. This was a foot-operated sewing machine by the well-known German sewing machine manufacturer Pfaff. The machine itself was housed in a solid oak case with an attractive door with inlaid marquetry. According to Mutti, it had been a last gift from her beloved father before his passing and she was not about to leave it behind.

Mutti also had them pack other useful or sentimental items. Among these were our goose down pillows and comforters and even our Christmas tree ornaments. Fortunately, over the years Mutti had also been very conscientious in holding onto and safeguarding important family documents and photographs despite her many moves and often haphazard living conditions. These she now had packed for their removal to America where they have survived to this day. As presents for Esther, Mutti had a solid oak coffee table with inlaid tiles made as well as an ornate wrought iron floor lamp. There was, alas, no room for my books including my collection of yearly editions of *Das Neue Universum* [The New Universe], a book series about nature, science, and adventure written for young readers. These I left in the care of two people we called *Onkel Josef* and *Tante Anny* with whom we often visited in another part of town.

I do not know how long Mutti had known Helmut Oswald but he had been coming to our apartment for a few weeks although my siblings and I rarely got to see him. Mutti must have purposely kept him away from us. He was a handsome man with a strong built and blond hair and we were told to call him *Onkel Helmut* [Uncle Helmut].

When I once asked him if he had fought in the war, he confided in me that he had indeed done so as a member of the Waffen SS. I could hardly contain my excitement because I knew that these men had been the best fighting unit, the elite, of our army. I did not know whether he was bluffing or telling me the truth and so I asked him for proof. Thereupon he took off his shirt, raised his left arm and told me to take a look. Sure enough, there above the armpit, was a small tattoo that looked like two parallel bolts of lightening. These, he said, were the insignia of their organization. Because I saw him very rarely, perhaps three times at most, I never had a chance to ask him any questions such as where he originally came from, what his rank was, or where he served.

At a going-away party Mutti gave at our *Wohnung* Uncle Helmut was there and a male friend of his. Also present were Robert Sokolov and Marcel Bosc, two French collaborators and their German wives, Liesel and Hilde, respectively. Frau Rapp from upstairs, and Elfriede Böhles, a lady friend of Mutti's, had also been invited. For the occasion, Mutti had ordered a large multi-layered torte, for which she had supplied the ingredients, from a local bakery. In addition, she served fruit cakes and assorted pastries plus wine, coffee and juice. Everyone was in a good mood and there was much chatter about the past and speculation on what the future might hold in store for us. On this occasion, Mutti also announced that due to the many uncertainties facing us she had decided not to give up the lease on our *Wohnung* but to sublease it to a couple of her acquaintance who needed a nice place to live. She would also hold on to the furniture and leave it in the apartment.

We knew little about America but many people listened to *Die Stimme Americas* a.k.a. *Voice of America* which painted a very rosy picture of the United States. It described the country as a veritable Garden of Eden where people from many different countries lived in harmony together and most owned their own houses and had a car. Frau Rapp was not convinced and gave me a book entitled *Das Land Ohne Herz* [The Country Without A Heart]. From the title I could tell that the country referred to was America because the prevalent opinion in post-war Germany was (most likely propagated during the war) that life there was a ruthless dog-eat-dog affair largely devoid of any compassion for fellow human beings. It turned me off and I do not recall ever looking into the book let alone reading it.

Our departure from Stuttgart on an afternoon train for Paris took place in early March. The train made a short stop in Bruchsal where Mama, who had bicycled down from Forst, was waiting to give me a sendoff. I got off the train and had just enough time for an affectionate hug and to take a picture of her with my box camera before the stationmaster blew his whistle. During a short layover in Paris, we had a chance to walk about and see parts of that magnificent city. Another train took us to the coastal town of Le Havre. When we arrived there it was too early for boarding the ship and so Mutti left Ute and Volker with some acquaintances at a large waiting hall at the docks while she and I went into town.

Le Havre, like Stuttgart, still showed the ugly scars of the last war for it too had been gutted. We stopped at a small family restaurant for a snack and were almost immediately joined by the proprietor. Mutti, who never missed an opportunity to practice her French, now had a field day as she and this rather corpulent Frenchman chatted about who knows what for at least an hour. Judging from her lively performance, I believe Mutti would have been equally at home in France as in Germany.

There were rumors all day that our ship's departure might be delayed or even cancelled because of an impending strike by French dock workers but when we got back to the docks, the immense ship called the SS *America* was ready for boarding and a great throng headed for the gangplank. It would be this ocean liner's 57th crossing of the Atlantic. Our accommodations left much to be desired as the four of us were given bunk beds in steerage deep inside the bowels of the ship. I was assigned to the upper berth of one bed and Volker to the lower while Mutti took the lower berth on an adjoining bed and Ute the upper.

When it was announced that the SS *America* would leave shortly, I rushed upstairs to one of the decks to watch the final preparations. It was night now and as the big ship slowly moved away from its moorings, one could make out the dock workers as they got on their bicycles and rode off. Shortly thereafter all the dock lights went out as the coast of France slowly receded behind us and we were on our way to the New World.

The crossing, which took nearly a week, was about as rough as could be imagined. We had been warned that crossing the Atlantic this time of year would be very tempestuous especially since we were headed west. This direction was opposite to the Gulf Stream, which flows east towards Europe, and also against the prevailing trade winds. The majestic SS *America* was a ship of the United States Line and one of the largest and fastest ocean liners afloat. It had been partly financed by the U.S. government and its design allowed it to be easily converted into a troop carrier in time of war.

So violent were the wind and waves at times that despite its huge size, the ship was tossed about like a flimsy paddleboat. The bow would rise way up into the air and a little while later come crashing down again while the stern went through similar contortions in reverse order. All the while the ship would precariously roll from right to left and back again. During high seas nobody was allowed on the open decks and ropes were tied throughout the hallways and public areas for passengers to hold onto.

Mutti and my two siblings were terribly seasick most of the time and stayed close to their beds. Poor Mutti, on one of her excursions on deck, was holding onto the railing when she had to vomit and inadvertently spit out her brand new dentures. I was spared from becoming seasick by strictly following instructions, i. e., by eating and drinking very little and spending most of my time walking back and forth in the fresh air on deck. Somewhere in the middle of the vast ocean between Europe and America Mutti turned 41 which meant that she could read the letter *Onkel Helmut* had given her to open on her birthday. She did not have a comment on its contents but I noticed no improvement in her dismal mood and it might even have changed for the worse.

One day I had been strolling on deck and was on the way to our room when a tall man came up to me, grabbed me by the arm and led me to an elevator despite my strong protestations and attempts to break free. The elevator took us all the way up to the first class section of the big ship. When we got off, it was like stepping into another world. The parquet floors, oriental carpets, chandeliers, and paintings and mirrors on the walls looked like they came from a royal palace. We passed wood paneled reading rooms, nicely furnished lounges, dining rooms of diverse sizes and decors, and a glass enclosed promenade deck. Unlike the ship's lower decks, which were teeming with people in all sorts of attire and babbling in many tongues, up here only a few people could be seen in the public areas and these were elegantly dressed and only spoke English.

My abductor led me to a mirrored barroom with a polished wood counter at which a few guests were seated enjoying divers beverages. There the man introduced me to his son who was sitting on a counter stool chatting with the bartender and without further ado left me with him. The son was a somewhat older boy and seemed a little bemused by my sudden arrival. He asked me to sit down on a stool next to him and told the bartender to get us a couple of Cokes "on the rocks." To see this kid sit on a bar counter with a bunch of adults and order drinks much amazed me. As this boy and I were sipping our sodas, he asked me to tell him something about myself and I began to do so in my halting school English.

I could tell that my new acquaintance was absolutely bored by my narrative and I, in turn, felt very uncomfortable with him and completely out of place. Fortunately, the boy knew how to break the impasse which was to excuse himself to go to the bathroom. When he had left, I made a run for the elevator and quickly descended into the belly of the ship to be once again among the multitude of immigrants where I belonged.

The much anticipated day of arrival in the New World was finally at hand. It was mid-March and nearly five years since the end of the war. In the distance appeared the unmistakable and impressive New York skyline. The SS *America* slowed down and tugboats came alongside to pull the great ship into the harbor. Before we got there, however, I went on deck holding my trusty little box camera and there patiently waited for the Statue of Liberty to come into view. I snapped the shutter at just the right moment to give me a fine, if slightly fuzzy, image of this world-renowned symbol of America.

I was 13 years old on that wintry morning when Mutti, my two siblings and I stepped on American soil. It was good to be back on terra firma and it seemed we had to learn to walk all over again. On the train that would take us to Chicago, I had a small inkling of what might be in store for us in our new homeland. We were all in our seats and excitedly chattering away when a man in a seat in front of me turned around for a chat. After a few perfunctory verbal exchanges, he asked me where we were from. When I replied that it was Germany, his previously friendly facial expression changed to a deep frown after which he abruptly turned back around again without saying another word. Sensing the man's hostility towards us, I turned to Ute and Volker and motioned to them to be quiet.

In The New World

The sky was gray and overcast when we arrived in Chicago. Sister Esther and husband Nick were at the station to greet us. I immediately made a faux pas by trying to give Nick an affectionate hug. After all, he was now my brother-in-law and I had not seen him in four years, and besides, we were all indebted to him for helping bring us over. Nick appeared repulsed by my friendly gesture and pushed me away. As I looked about, I could see just a handful of skyscrapers in the distance which was a far cry from the grand panorama I had seen in New York. There lay a pungent, sweetish odor in the air which I was told came from the Union Stockyards, a huge cattle and swine holding and slaughtering facility on the city's South Side.

From the station, we were driven to the home of Nick's parents, a first floor apartment in a 2-story building located in the northwestern part of town. This area near Lincoln Square was a neighborhood much favored by ethnic Germans. Nick's parents and siblings and diverse other relatives gave us a friendly welcome. We were happy to learn that most spoke at least some German. By the looks of the parents it was apparent that the family was of solid peasant stock. The mother was squat and broad shouldered and wore her hair in a bun while the father was tall and lanky and somewhat tongue-tied. Their weather-beaten faces suggested that their lives had seen much physical toil. We stayed there for a couple of weeks while Esther and Nick completed the purchase of a house.

Esther and Nick bought a small house on the south side of Oak Park, a village directly adjoining Chicago on the city's West Side. The village was one of those Chicago suburbs with a reputation for exclusivity and a certain snobbishness although many, if not most, of its inhabitants were not affluent or wealthy. The residents represented a good mix of working, middle, and upper middle class people which meant a diversity of housing from the modest homes south of the railway tracks to the grand apartment complexes near the center of town to the elegant homes and gated estates in the northern half of the village. An abundance of stately elms and oaks, which were home to countless squirrels and feathered creatures, and other greenery plus the nicely manicured front lawns of most homes gave the village a park-like appearance. This together with the upscale shops and department stores, excellent schools, churches of many denominations, and the many other amenities made Oak Park a very desirable place to live. It was easy to see why my sister and brother-in-law would choose this place for their home and Mutti, my siblings and I were fortunate that they did.

Esther's and Nick's house on 515 South Oak Park Avenue was located near the southwest corner of Oak Park Avenue, which ran north and south, and Madison Street which was at right angles to it and led to downtown Chicago going east and to other suburbs on the west. It was a so-called starter home, i.e., one that would fill the needs of the moment to be hopefully replaced by a more comfortable one as the owners prospered. As such, it was not much to look at being a 2-story stuccoed frame building with a couple of rooms and a kitchen on the first floor and three bedrooms with built-in closets and a bath on the second. It sat on a narrow but deep lot and had a small front yard and a larger, fenced-in one in the back. Part of the backyard was taken up by a garage that opened to an alley. The adjoining homes were of a similar design. Esther's place was sparsely furnished with the first floor living and dining rooms being almost devoid of furniture.

Shortly after our arrival in Oak Park, Ute, Volker and I were enrolled in the local elementary school closest to our house which was Emerson School on Washington Boulevard. The school building was a handsome 2-story brick structure of a lemon color with a number of very attractive classrooms plus a gym. Each classroom had huge windows and was furnished with several rows of individual student desks. As in Germany at the grade school level, boys and girls were taught together. All the teachers were women except for the boys gym teacher and a man who taught the woodworking class.

By age I should have been assigned to 8th grade but since it was getting to the end of the school year and it was thought that I would not be ready for high school in the fall because my English language skills still left much to be desired, I was put in 7th grade, or rather, in 1st grade of Junior High School since that was what the last two grades of elementary school were officially called. When I arrived at the school, Mr. Hebal, the principal, walked me to the second floor classroom where he introduced me to Miss Below, my home room teacher, and the class.

Among my classmates at Emerson, I got to know only a few and made no real friends. I was an immigrant and low on the class totem pole so that few wanted to bother with me and I myself was by nature not the outgoing type. Only one boy, Roger Nichols by name, reached out to me by offering me a used 3-hole binder for holding sheets of paper.

I had never noticed girls before but Gertrude (Trudy) Rathling was different. She was very pretty and spoke some German and I took a liking to her. It seems that her parents or grandparents had come over from the Old Country as people referred to any place in Europe their ancestors arrived from. To improve my English, Miss Below asked Trudy to give me English lessons in an adjoining classroom. I would read something and Trudy would tell me what it meant in German. Now and then Miss Below would poke her head inside to make sure that we were studying and presumably that there was no hanky-panky going on.

One day Trudy took me home to meet her mother. Mrs. Rathling took the occasion to deliver a lecture during which she made light of her German ancestry and let me know that her family was proudly American. She made me feel as if they had reached a superior status to which I could only aspire to. Presumably, I thought, this was the aftereffect of the war during which people of German ancestry were treated more or less like outcasts and to make life bearable they had to make a special show of their patriotism. I listened but made no comment. Nevertheless, I found the mother's remarks condescending and hostile and never returned there.

Trudy too managed to earn my ire by making a snide remark on a school bus that was to take us to our weekly Bible class at a church on Lake Street. I happened to be a few minutes late and when I arrived on the bus and apologized for my tardiness Trudy announced that they knew that somebody was missing but had they known it was me they would not have waited but left immediately. After this, I decided I did not need additional English lessons and our friendship came to an abrupt end.

Academically I did fairly well. Ms. Below taught us math and the angst I had of the subject began to disappear as I finally caught on to fractions and percentages. One time she brought me a copy of Mark Twain's *Adventures of Huckleberry Finn* from the school library. I did not know anything about the author or that the book was an American classic. When I briefly looked inside I decided that a story of a couple of characters floating down the Mississippi was not for me. After I had laid the book aside and not touched it again, Ms. Below took it back saying to Ms. Anderson, our English teacher, "Peter is not interested in literature." That remark much upset me. "What does Ms. Below know about me and literature," I said to myself, "I'm just 13 and have probably read more and better books than she has at 40 or 50."

My favorite teacher was Miss Bondurant who taught the science class. She liked my research on the involuntary nervous system and gave me a S+ (superior) for it . I was elated because I had finally received some credit for my work. Miss Bondurant also took us on walks around the village during which she taught us how to identify the different types of trees by the size and shape of their leaves.

A couple of my favorite classes did not engage my mind as much as my hands. In manual arts we could make things and I designed and put together a photo album into which I glued all the photos I had made with my box camera. The woodworking shop for boys had a good supply of boards, two-by-fours, dowels, and other stock as well as diverse hand tools for shaping and drilling. These we could use to build various practical items like book ends, bird houses, and foot stools. As my final project, I made a small table which I sanded down and varnished and triumphantly carried home.

Physical education classes were another favorite of mine especially the gym routines and competitive running. I much missed playing *Fußball* which was not played in American elementary schools where baseball was in. Unfortunately, I was completely inept at playing that game which required better hand and eye coordination than I could muster. Nevertheless I recognized that baseball and American football probably had more going for themselves than *Fußball* and I could see why the two games were so popular in the country.

Everybody in America had a job, I noticed, even kids. People worked hard and long hours. No job was guaranteed and people were continuously being hired and fired for cause or no cause. Kids worked for pocket money. When somebody wanted to do a boy a favor, he let him do a chore, like washing his car, and give him a dollar. Nick left for work in his car in the morning and took along Esther to drop her off at a different location in Chicago. In the evening, Esther came home on the Lake Street "L" (elevated train) which had a stop on Oak Park Avenue. Mutti too soon found work with a small company that made optical lenses and whose owner was of German descent.

I was in school hardly a week when Esther decided that I too needed a job. Without asking me, she volunteered my services to an Italian cobbler who had his shop in a building across the street from us near the southeast corner of Madison Street and Oak Park Avenue. The shop was small, cramped and dirty and my job was to sweep up and clean the sink and toilet. I was there only a couple of weeks when the shoemaker told Esther that he had found someone else. The sweeping part posed no problem for me but cleaning the sink and toilet did. The cobbler was in the habit of coughing up and spitting green and yellow masses into the sink and cleaning out the slimy mess was absolutely repugnant to me. It almost made me sick and I refused to continue doing it.

Having been unceremoniously fired from my first job, Esther decided that I needed a new one. Now, in Chicago the daily newspapers could be bought at a newsstand or subscribers could have their papers delivered to their homes early in the morning. For home delivery, there existed a number of newspaper distributorships which hired grade and high school boys to do the deliveries. Esther decided that delivering newspapers was the perfect job for me and so she took me to the Village Newspaper Agency, which was located on Oak Park Avenue just south and across the street from the Lake Street "L" station. The idea of delivering newspapers did not particularly excite me but I cannot say that anything really did at the time.

The interview with the agency's owner, Thomas Doherty, went rather well and I was immediately hired to work the route down Oak Park Avenue, from Madison to Harrison streets, and back north again on Euclid Avenue which ran parallel to Oak Park Avenue. Altogether my domain encompassed about 10 city blocks of private homes and apartment buildings.

The papers to be delivered were the two main Chicago dailies, the *Chicago Tribune* and the *Chicago Sun-Times*, plus a national financial paper, *The Wall Street Journal*. I had between 100 and 120 subscribers most of whom took the *Tribune*. This was, I was told, because Oak Parkers were mostly conservative Republicans and this paper represented their views. The paper route took me about one and one-half hours to walk and since school did not start until 9 a.m., I had plenty of time to get done. To carry the papers, we were each given a 3-wheeled wooden cart which we pushed in front of us down the sidewalk or, in the winter when heavy snowfalls and blizzards often blocked the sidewalks, down the middle of the street. The papers were delivered by a small van to the front porch of our house on South Oak Park Avenue very early in the morning so that I could just toss them into my cart, which I kept behind the house, and be on my way. The job did not allow for any days off during the year because a new edition of each paper appeared every day of the week including Sundays and holidays.

My job as a paperboy went exceptionally well and gave me much satisfaction. Neither Mutti nor Esther asked me for any of my earnings, which were $30 per month, but Esther did remind me that now that I had a job and an income she thought it proper for me to pay her back the cost of my sea passage. She mentioned a princely sum in relation to my earnings, over two hundred dollars, but I paid it out to her in weekly installments until all was paid off. Being the frugal type, I immediately opened up a savings account at Avenue Bank on Oak Park Avenue to help me manage my new-earned money.

Tom, as we all called him, was a very nice and friendly man of Irish ancestry. He had been a Chicago police officer before buying the newspaper franchise, he told me. Tom was tall and handsome and much reminded me of my Papa in Forst. Mrs. Doherty also worked in the office to do the billing and other paperwork. Fortunately for us paperboys, the bills were mailed out and paid by return mail so that we did not have to collect any money as was the case with boys who delivered the village weekly, *The*

Oak Leaves. The Doherty's son Tommy, who was about my age, had a paper route too while his younger sister, Susan, rarely came by. I did not get to see Tom or Tommy or any of the others people except perhaps on a Saturday morning when I sometimes stopped by the agency after working my paper route.

Fortunately, Tom and I got along well together and I became his favorite paperboy. Sometimes when I stopped by the office and read through parts of the *Chicago Tribune*, I felt like somebody was intently staring at me from the side. When I looked up it was Tom and we both had a good laugh. Tom had good reason to like me because he could depend on me which was not the case with most of the other boys. I was never late nor missed a day and was so punctual that my customers could have set their clocks by the time I came by every morning. I owed all that to Mutti who got me up in time every morning and, after fixing me breakfast, sent me on my way before going off to work herself. Now and then Tom would ask me to take along a new boy he had just hired to teach him my unique technique of delivering papers to the apartment buildings. Rather than running up and down the three flights of stairs at the rear, I would fold a paper into a tight bundle and by an underhand toss deliver it to the exact spot at the apartment's backdoor.

Probably to show his appreciation, Tom did some nice things for me that he did not do for the other boys. A couple of times he brought me to their apartment for breakfast with his family of pastries and hot chocolate. During my first summer in Oak Park, Tom even took me along for an outing with his family including Mrs. Doherty, Tommy and Susan, to Riverview Park which was a large Chicago amusement park located on Western Avenue in Chicago. There he treated us to rides, hot dogs, and sodas.

Tommy became my best friend even though I rarely saw him. He did not attend public school like me but went to a private Catholic elementary school. Tommy much reminded me of my best friend Hans-Eugen at the Schickhardt Oberschule in Stuttgart because the two had much in common in terms of looks and build and also personality traits. Now, Tommy liked to arm-wrestle and showed me how to do it. One interlocked hands and fingers and placed one's elbow on the table and then tried to push the other's hand down until the back of it touched the table. Whoever succeeded first was the stronger and won. One time Tommy and I were in the big room behind the office where the newspapers where temporarily stored and sorted before delivery. We had arm wrestled for a while and had gotten tired and stopped. For some reason we forgot to break and just stood there silently next to each other holding hands.

At that very moment Tom came out of the office and glanced over and saw us. I was so embarrassed that I wanted to crawl under the table and hide. Boys were not supposed to be holding hands, at least not real boys. Tom walked to the back of the room, checked that the door was locked and nonchalantly walked past us back to the office pretending he did not even notice we were there. He could have made a snide remark or otherwise made fun of us but he did not and for that I liked him even more.

One Saturday morning Tommy and I were wandering around the village when we came to a newsstand that stood on the northwest corner of Oak Park Avenue and North Boulevard. It was operated by a black man which was very unusual because in Oak Park these so-called colored people were looked on with distain so that none dared live in the village. Tommy was looking for a specific magazine and could not find it for some time. Finally he spotted it and pointing to it said, "It's way up there in nigger heaven." I was stunned that Tommy would say such a thing because by then I knew enough English to recognize the word "nigger" as a racial slur and presumably the ultimate insult to a black person. Instead of getting angry, the man remained perfectly calm, reached for the magazine and handed it to Tommy who bought it. I was much impressed by the man's dignity but sensed that he was hurt.

On the way back to the agency I urged Tommy to return to the newsstand and apologize but he said he did not have to. Back at the office, I could not get over what I had experienced and when Tommy continued to ignore my entreaties, I told his father about the incident. Naturally, I did not enjoy snitching on my best friend and I was much afraid that it might end our friendship but it was something I just had to do. Tom was furious and gave his son a severe tongue lashing that brought on tears. He told him to go back up there and apologize to the man and not to come back until he had done so. Tommy did as he was told and came back obviously relieved. Fortunately, the incident did not affect our friendship. I knew that sometimes being a good friend means not only to praise him for his accomplishments but to tell him when he has done something wrong.

Just about every boy in America owned or wanted to own a Schwinn bicycle and I was no exception. Like the automobiles for adults, for kids Schwinn bicycles were both transportation and status symbol. And like American cars, they were not built for speed but for comfort. Schwinn bicycles were marvelous creations of metal and chrome that sported fancy handlebars, saddle seats, wide tires and many accessories. From the day I first saw these attractive 2-wheelers, I pined to have one and since I now had a source of income, I was determined to have my dream come true. I had talked Mutti into letting me make a down payment on an especially attractive red and black model I saw in a bicycle shop on Madison Street and looked forward to the day when I had the rest of the money together and could take it home.

Just when that day had nearly come, there was an accident in which little Fritz Preiss, who lived in an apartment building across the street from us, was nearly run over by a car as he was riding his bike in front of his home. His family was German-American and we had befriended them. Other than for some minor cuts and bruises, Fritz fortunately escaped injury but Frau Preiss immediately took the bike away from him. This, in turn, made Mutti decide that she would not allow me to ride a bicycle either. I had to return to the bike shop and get my money back and was in tears. It seemed that I never got anything other kids had and took for granted.

Making Our Way

Americans had their own customs, traditions, and ways of doing things and these were mostly derived from England, I learned, which most people proudly claimed as their family's place of origin. Being immigrants, we were obliged to adopt most of these and did so, even if grudgingly at times, except where these conflicted with our own strongly held norms and traditions. The native language was English, of course, and we all learned to become more or less proficient in it but continued to use our native tongue even if it earned us condescending stares and snide remarks when we were out in public. We were pleasantly surprised that such Old World traditions as Christmas trees and Easter bunnies had made it to the New World although often in modified form. The tree was not put up and lit on Christmas Eve as in Germany but long before then and kids did not get their presents on Christmas Eve but on the morning of Christmas Day. One ancient German custom did not make it to America, namely, the ancient *Christkindlmarkt* [Christ child market] of which the one in Stuttgart was especially well-known.

Entirely new to us were the elaborate Christmas displays in the windows of major department stores with their beautifully costumed mechanical figures acting out scenes from Scripture and familiar fairy tales. Also, many home owners in the village decorated the outside of their houses with strings of miniature electric lights or featured lighted Christmas displays on their front lawns. Absolutely essential for Christmas was snow and Chicago, fortunately, had plenty of that.

There was no doubt that Americans ate much better than we had in Germany during and after the war. Truly impressive was the great abundance of food available to everybody. Americans ate a much greater variety of meats that, in addition to pork, included beef and chicken. Hamburgers and hot dogs (also called wieners or frankfurters) were a staple in the American diet to which we could easily relate because they were of German origin. Hamburgers were the German *Fleischküchle* [meat patties] and hot dogs were our *Würstle* [small sausages]. Many of the vegetables and fruits were entirely new to us. What we could not relate to was the American way of eating. For us it meant the knife in the right hand and the fork in the left during the entire meal with no switching. The American way may have been more practical but it was definitely not for us and Mutti had us continue to eat in our customary manner which she considered the only proper and civil way.

There were many new and unfamiliar things to cope with in America and it was inevitable that all three of us kids would have experiences we would most likely not have had in our native Germany. A most traumatic event for us all, and especially for Ute, was her accident at a playground on Lake Street. That street was the road that ran east-west through the center of Oak Park and at its western end was the main business district while at the other, that closest to Chicago, was more residential and home to a large playground. One Saturday found us at this place evaluating the various swings, slides, and other types of play equipment. Ute liked the slide, which was long and steep, and after coming down in a sitting position a few times, she decided to be a little more adventurous.

While I was testing out a swing to see how far up in the air I could propel myself, Ute lay down flat on the chute and came down head first at a good speed. Unable to brake at the bottom, poor Ute was tossed onto the hard cement base on which the slide stood. It shattered a number of her front teeth and when I got to her she was bleeding heavily. I managed to alert some adults and soon an ambulance arrived and took us all to the emergency room of a nearby hospital. Ute screamed in pain and I tried to calm her down while the doctor and nurses did their best to clean her up and repair at least some of the damage. Naturally, being the eldest, I should have been looking out for my younger siblings to keep them from harm but, as usual, I was off doing my own thing. Instead of scolding me, Mutti turned her wrath on the designers and builders who would cover a playground with asphalt instead of loose soil that would cushion the impact in case a child fell on it.

Brother Volker had an experience of a quite different sort. A little north of our house stood a large 2-story commercial building and in it, right across from the Italian cobbler and on the first floor, was a small grocery store. It was a favorite hangout for neighborhood kids because the grocer always kept it well stocked with many flavors of Popsicles and, furthermore, the place was air-conditioned which provided welcome relief from the sweltering heat outside. One day Mutti told me to check up on Volker who had been sent to the grocery some time earlier. When I walked inside the store it was empty but I could hear Volker giggling in a back room and immediately headed there.

To my amazement and shock, I saw my brother stand on a chair and the grocer in front of him with his hand up inside Volker's lederhosen. I got angry and, without saying a word, pulled Volker off the chair and dragged him outside. "Did I do anything wrong?" Volker wanted to know. "You should be ashamed of yourself," was my reply. "You stood there and let this nasty man play with your *Spitzle*. Just wait until Mutti hears about this." Volker pleaded that I not tell Mutti and I agreed if he promised not to do it again. This incident might have been avoided had not Mutti insisted that Volker keep wearing his lederhosen when American boys considered wearing short pants of any kind less than manly and wore blue jeans almost exclusively. In addition, his lederhosen earned Volker ridicule from classmates and teachers alike.

There are probably not many 13- or 14-year-olds who regularly read the newspaper but that is what I did because a perk of my paperboy job was a free copy of the *Chicago Tribune* every morning. By the time I was through with my paper route, Mutti, Esther and Nick had already left for work and I usually had some time to peruse the paper before I and my siblings left for school. Having access to the morning's paper allowed me to keep abreast of the war in Korea in which the United States was trying to prevent the North Koreans from overrunning the South and establishing a Communist dictatorship over the entire country. Keeping up with the war was important to me because we talked about it in class and having the latest information, supported by articles I had cut out from the *Tribune,* allowed me to score points with Miss Crabtree in social studies.

While my perusal of our local paper kept me up-to-date on world affairs it also opened up to me a world that was so gross, awful, and frightening that I could never have imagined it existed. Reading the *Chicago Tribune,* which carried the phrase "The World's Greatest Newspaper" in its masthead, made me realize just how strange and violent the world, and especially America, could be. It was so much different from what the daily broadcasts of the *Voice of America* had led us believe. The paper's fat headline broadcast the latest Chicagoland murders, rapes, robberies and other crimes on a daily basis and often with gruesome details. To stem the high crime rate, retribution was harsh and swift and the state's electric chair kept busy dispensing justice.

Besides the litany of ordinary crimes, there were numerous gangland slayings as members of the Mafia conducted their turf wars for control. This had been going on since the 1920s when Al Capone had ruled Chicago's underworld. His successor, Tony ("Big Tuna") Accardo, who likewise earned his living from the fruits of Chicago crime, lived like a country squire in a mansion in the neighboring village of River Forest while fellow mafiosi of lower rank too had homes there or in the less affluent Oak Park. Dead gangsters were forever showing up in the trunks of abandoned cars after having found themselves on some capo's hit list for one reason or another. It became apparent to me that, while Americans enjoyed great material prosperity and much individual freedom, they also paid a heavy price for it.

In these early days of the Cold War, there was a big hunt in progress for Communists who were said to have infiltrated the U.S. government and had ensconced themselves in many important positions. Americans now feared and hated the Russians even though they had only a few years ago been their trusted allies in the war against the Third Reich. Public scorn and hatred was not limited to the Communists but included the German people as well. These former enemies now turned into allies in the fight against Communism, became the target of a viscous hate and smear campaign in the *Chicago Tribune* and undoubtedly also in other American papers. The big American and British news services like Associated Press and Reuters and magazines of the day including *Look* and *Life* had a field day recounting all the atrocities allegedly committed by the German people during the war especially against the Jews. Being German was practically synonymous with being a war criminal. In fact, one hardly ever found the word German standing by itself—it was nearly always "German war criminal."

To see the country and people of my birth pilloried and exposed to hatred much embittered me and left its mark. That was because I still considered myself and my family very much part of this people and its culture. And what would qualify Americans to pass judgment on an entire people? Had the Americans and their British allies not long ago killed hundreds of thousands of my people in bombing raids on cities and towns to force Germany into unconditional surrender? Had the Americans not fire-bombed Tokyo and other Japanese cities and dropped atomic bombs on Hiroshima and Nagasaki to slaughter hundreds of thousands more? Had the victors not committed all these murders without the slightest feelings of guilt or remorse?

My Christian faith had taught me that all people are sinners without exception and, rather than being morally arrogant and self-righteous, Christians are called upon to ask for forgiveness for their own sins. What made Americans, who professed to be a Christian people, such unrepentant, self-righteous bigots and hypocrites? I did not dare ask such questions in school nor did I raise them at home but kept all these thoughts to myself.

Americans love war heroes and one was about to come to town. From what I read in the *Chicago Tribune*, in the Korean War fortune had now turned against the United States. China had entered the war to help the North Koreans push the Americans and South Koreans back south across the 38th parallel. At this point, General Douglas MacArthur, who had been America's top general in the war against Japan and now held the same position under the UN in the Korean War, wanted to drop atomic bombs on parts of China close to the North Korean border.

President Harry S. Truman, who had previously ordered the atomic bombing of Japan, was against expanding the war and ordered him not to publicly advocate it. When the general disobeyed the president's order, he was dismissed. This angered a bellicose part of the American public and General MacArthur was invited to address a joint session of Congress and given a tumultuous welcome in many American cities. One of the cities on his triumphal tour was Chicago. It would be a spectacle I did not want to miss. My friend Tommy was not interested and hence I went to the event by myself.

There was excitement in the air when I arrived in downtown Chicago by way of the Lake Street "L." Coming early, I got a choice spot on the parade route, which was down Michigan Avenue, Chicago's most fashionable street, and positioned myself on the curb on the other side and somewhat south of Chicago's famed Art Institute. Eventually thousands of people lined both sides of the street and when the general and his entourage came into view, a tremendous roar went up from the crowd. I had assumed that his motorcade would just whiz by on its way south to its destination which was the Hilton Hotel. To my great surprise, it moved at a snail's pace and when General MacArthur, accompanied by his wife and young son, came close he intently stared into the crowd. It seemed that he did not just see a faceless mass of people but a number of individuals whom he personally wanted to greet and thank one by one. I was much impressed because I had never thought that such an important celebrity could be so down-to-earth and personable.

It may have been just my imagination, but I believe that when the general's limousine came to the place where I stood, our eyes briefly met and after he had passed by he momentarily turned his head and looked back at me. Why would a great man like General MacArthur take notice of some scrawny little 14-year-old kid standing by the side of the road? If he did, it could have been because I must have stuck out among the wildly cheering and flag-waving crowd like a sore thumb. I carried no American flag and stood erect in a soldierly pose neither waving nor cheering like the others. That was not because I did not wish to honor the general (even though I did not care for his atomic bomb plans) but simply because I had never been the demonstrative type and would have found it completely foolish and out of character to behave as those around me.

After the motorcade had passed by, an avalanche of people came rolling down the street to follow it and I was swept along. Outside his hotel, the general's admirers kept cheering and waving their flags while inside, I learned, many dignitaries were awaiting him for a dinner in his honor. As for me, I walked over to the lakefront to admire Buckingham Fountain, the world's largest, and then left for home. It was a great day and I felt good having taken part in a genuine historical event.[17]

Tough Times

It was spring and Mutti, my siblings and I had now been in America for over a year. At home a storm was brewing and I sensed that the simmering feud between Mutti and Esther, which I had first noticed shortly after we had moved to Oak Park, would eventually come to a head. There was tension in the air and the slightest annoyance could set Esther off to deliver a verbal fusillade against our mother and the rest of us. We took our evening meals at the kitchen table but owing to the ugly atmosphere, I ate little for lack of appetite and consequently had gained little weight beyond the less than 100 pounds when I entered Emerson School. I also found it difficult to sleep and often forsook my metal cot and thin mattress, which was the only furniture in my room, for the small screened porch outside my upstairs bedroom to stare into the night. As it got warmer, the flashing lights of fire flies, which were unknown to us in Germany, provided a welcome diversion.

I was not quite sure about the precise cause or nature of the conflict between Mutti and Esther but I am certain that Mutti's pining for the lover she had left behind in Stuttgart was a big part of the problem. I had always been a blabbermouth of sorts and had told Nick's mother that Mutti had a friend by the name of Helmut Oswald in Stuttgart and, not realizing that it might not be the best recommendation for him, told her that he had been in the Waffen SS. I doubt though that I was giving away a big secret because Mutti would undoubtedly have had to explain to Esther why Uncle Helmut would not be allowed into the country. This is not to say, of course, that he ever wanted to come to America in the first place. His letter to Mutti which she opened on her 41st birthday aboard the SS *America* was probably a good-bye note and Mutti was simply not ready to accept that it was over.

The other issue was undoubtedly money of which there never seemed to be enough around even though all three, Nick, Esther, and Mutti, had good jobs. Esther was not happy with the two gifts Mutti had brought her from Germany. She called the massive end table and the wrought iron lamp chunk and said she would have preferred Mutti had brought her the money instead. Mortgage payments and other expenses seemed to consume most of the income leaving no money even for furniture. The small dining room remained empty and the only living room furniture was a few chairs and a small television set.

Undoubtedly, Mutti did not simply turn over her paycheck to Esther, as Esther might have expected, because if she ever contemplated returning to Germany she would need money to finance her trip. Consequently, Esther was constantly complaining that Mutti was not providing enough for the support of the four of us. Esther was probably right but it was no reason for her to take her anger out on her siblings. She and Nick worked hard and were undoubtedly eager to reach the American Dream already enjoyed by more affluent Americans and Esther became frustrated being held back by our mother and her three siblings by the half-blood who meant little to her.

Mutti had some moral support in our predicament from the Preiss family across the street. We visited them often and Ute and Volker and the Preiss kids, Heidi and Fritz, regularly played together after school. On a couple of occasions the family took all of us on outings in the country which is something Nick and Esther had never done. Thanks to Esther, however, this relationship soon came to an abrupt end.

According to Esther, Mr. and Mrs. Preiss had been members of an organization called the German American Bund that, prior to the war, had spoken out in support of the National Socialists. Esther somehow found out about it and started a campaign of harassment against the family. Mr. Preiss even fretted about losing his job after Esther had threatened to contact his employer if they did not keep to themselves instead of commiserating with us. Our new-found friends got so fearful of Esther that they asked us to please not to come see or call them anymore. This break was quite hard on us all because our friends were really nice and well-meaning people and we had much enjoyed their company, their assistance, and their moral support.

Late one Saturday evening, Mutti, my siblings and I came home on the Lake Street "L" from some German-American festivities in Chicago to find the front door locks changed and nobody home. Taken by complete surprise, we stood there for some time unsure of what to do. Mutti finally decided to seek the advise of Franz Gerstenberg, a Berliner who hosted the *Germania Broadcast*, the largest German language radio program in the Chicago area. Mutti had me call him at the end of his program at 9 p.m. from the drugstore in the building that also housed the cobbler and he suggested we contact the authorities. The police were located in the municipal building on Lake Street and so we walked up there to seek help. The policeman in charge seemed friendly and confided in us that his ancestors too were German.

After some time, two detectives brought in Esther and Nick who had evidently been at Nick's parents home in Chicago. The two were giving their side of the story and whenever Mutti tried to say something this previously friendly policeman shouted "*Halt's Maul*" [shut up]. That was extremely rude language and I had never heard it said in Germany to anyone let alone to Mutti. Despite his initial civility, the policeman turned out to be what we in Germany called a *Schweinehund* [son of a bitch]. It was our good fortune, however, that one of the two detectives sided with us and promised to help us find a place to live. He was a Mr. Bolstad, a big and friendly man of Swedish ancestry. But for the time being we were all brought back to Esther's house. Esther then filed charges against Mutti and one day found Mutti and me in court before a judge in the Oak Park municipal building.

I do not know what Mutti was charged with specifically but I would guess it was disturbance of the peace. Esther had brought her lawyer,

Anthony (Tony) Basile, who did most of the talking for her while Mutti relied on me to translate her arguments inasmuch as her English was not yet very good. It was an emotional and humiliating experience for both Mutti and me that brought me close to tears. The trial was short and Mutti was found guilty and given a hefty fine of over $200. A little later Mutti gave me the cash to bring to the courthouse while she was at work.

Detective Bolstad came through for us by putting us in touch with an elderly Oak Park couple which owned a 3-story apartment building in the Austin district of Chicago on the city's West Side immediately adjoining Oak Park. Fortunately, they had a so-called studio apartment for rent on the top floor and were willing to let us have it. Our new home was just a large furnished room with a kitchenette and bathroom. In the main room, there was a large bed that folded away into a closet in which Mutti and my two younger siblings slept while a large sofa became my bedstead. While quarters were extremely tight, we were happy to be on our own and away from Esther and Nick.

One irritation of living in this place was the loud prayers and chants emanating from the apartment below us that lasted way into the night and made it difficult for us to sleep. Often other neighbors would shout for them to stop because they were kept up too. The people were Orthodox Jews, we learned, and their two handicapped children were the reason for their father's nightly lamentations. They were a nice family otherwise and Ute, Volker, and I spent a number of evenings with them to watch Laurel and Hardy films from their collection.

Mutti continued working at the lens factory and since it was getting close to the end of the school year, my siblings and I were allowed to remain at Emerson School in Oak Park even though we now lived in a Chicago school district. We commuted there on the Lake Street "L" which fortunately had a station not far from our new apartment. I had to leave for Oak Park earlier than Ute and Volker because of my newspaper delivery job before school.

Mr. Bolstad came by now and then to check up on us and sometimes he would pick me up on a Saturday morning after I was done with my newspaper delivery job and put me to work painting the walls of his parent's new apartment. Now, there is an old America adage according to which there is no such thing as a free lunch. Officer Bolstad had procured new quarters for us and he now expected something in return. However, I had little talent or interest in painting apartment walls either for him or anyone else and when he realized it by the slow progress I was making on this chore, he discharged me from his services and hired a professional to do it.

An educational milestone for me was my graduation in mid-June from Emerson School. At age 14 going on 15, I was a full year older than my classmates. At least my English language skills had much improved and I had gotten rid of the accent I had acquired at the Oberschule that made me sound like a British schoolboy, to speak the American and, more specifically, the Midwestern version of English. My grades kept improving so that in my final semester, these were mostly "satisfactory" with a small sprinkling of "very good" in mathematics, gym, and personality and citizenship. Considering my unsettled life and the problems I had to cope with at home, I could be satisfied.

Graduation ceremonies were held in the Emerson School gym. Before that, we had our class photograph taken showing 49 graduates. I was probably the only kid at our graduation who was by himself. Mutti was too busy and could not come and Esther and Nick, at whose house I had stopped by before walking to Emerson, were not interested.

There was a dance and we graduates did the old two-step while parents and teachers watched from the balcony. At the end, when it was the girls' turn to choose a partner, all the boys had been picked except for me and two others. As probably the worst of the three disasters left on the bench, I did not expect to take part. Then up stepped Marie, the most popular girl in class, and to my great surprise offered me her hand. She could have picked any boy and he would have been proud to have the final dance with her but she had waited until all the other less popular girls had made their choices before making hers. It was a gracious gesture and brought grade school to a happy end for me.

Mutti had been talking about temporarily returning to Germany for some time. It was not just to see Uncle Helmut again but there were other matters she needed to tend to. One was our *Wohnung* on Adlerstraße which she had retained and subleased to a befriended couple and which still held most of our furniture. Mutti had promised me that she would wait at least until I had graduated from Emerson before leaving us. That day had now come. In the meantime, she had talked to Officer Bolstad about her planned trip and he had assured her that his parents, who owned a farm, would be happy to put us up for a month or two during her absence.

Unfortunately, just as Mutti was ready to leave, Mr. Bolstad informed her that his parents had changed their minds and would not take us in after all and that he could do nothing more for us. I suspect that my poor performance painting the walls of their new quarters had something to do with his parent's decision. Whatever the reason, it was very bad news for Mutti because an ocean trip took weeks of planning and preparation and with the ticket purchased, Mutti could not just cancel out without suffering a big financial loss. Besides that, she had quit her job at the lens factory and given up the Austin apartment as of the end of June. There was nothing to hold her back now and she was determined to be on the SS *Homeland* when it left New York for Bremerhaven. The realization that we were about to be abandoned worried me but I made no attempt to dissuade Mutti because I knew it would be useless. It was just something she had to do.

We took our leave in Chicago where Mutti boarded a train for New York. Her instructions to me were to return to Oak Park with Ute and Volker and present ourselves to officer Bolstad and his wife at their house. No sooner had she left than Volker disappeared but somehow, after a long search, we managed to find him again. With Ute and Volker in tow, I took the Lake Street "L" back to Oak Park to do what I was told. Getting off the train at Oak Park Avenue, we took the long walk to the Bolstad home which was located near the northeast corner of North Harlem Avenue and Augusta Street. The house was a modest 1-story stucco building with a slanting roof and dormers. I just dreaded the assignment Mutti had given me but finally mustered enough courage to ring the doorbell. Mrs. Bolstad was home and, needless to say, was surprised to see us but invited us in. We stayed at the Bolstad home for a couple of nights when we were turned over to Esther and Nick.[18]

A Homecoming

Once Ute, Volker and I were back at her place on Oak Park Avenue, Esther wasted no time making arrangements for our return to Germany. She immediately contacted the German consul in Chicago who issued us German passports which would allow us to reenter Germany. Mutti evidently thought the consul had persuaded us kids to return to Germany and wrote him an angry letter from Stuttgart to which the consul replied that Esther had informed him that our mother had left the country without arranging for our care during the duration of her absence and that she (Esther) could not accommodate us in her household.

Booking passage for us from New York to Bremerhaven was accomplished in record time so that towards the end of July, just one month after Mutti's departure, we were on our way back to Germany. We were in our train compartment at the Chicago station and Esther and Nick were standing on the platform outside our window when she motioned to me to write. I gave an affirmative nod but in my heart I had no intention to ever have anything to do with Esther again. She had no feelings or affection for any of us and I, for one, had none for her.

The ocean trip on a ship of the North German Lloyd was uneventful. The three of us made friends with kids near our own ages and took part in some of the many activities available on board. A day or two into the trip, the ship's chief steward took us out of steerage class and moved us to a comfortable cabin right across the one occupied by a boy I had befriended who was accompanying his father on a trip to England.

We arrived back in Bremerhaven on the last day of July just a couple of days short of my 15th birthday. To be back in my beloved hometown of Stuttgart and reunited with Mutti was the best birthday present I could have ever hoped for. Mutti was in high spirits and received us warmly. It was good to see that she was her old self again—full of joie de vivre and energy and ready for the next challenge. All the cares and problems of the past year seemed to have passed away. On her return, she had learned that Helmut Oswald was in a liaison with another woman and had confronted him at his workplace where, in front of his coworkers, she called him some choice names and ended their relationship, she told me, with a resounding *Ohrfeige*. "Bravo Mutti," I said to her in German, "I'm glad you got rid of that two-timing bum."

We were now all back in our old *Wohnung* on Adlerstraße 8 in Heslach. On her return, Mutti had arranged for the couple that had temporarily subleased the apartment in her absence to move out. We were not home too much during these lazy days of August because Mutti was never a homebody. She always needed to be among people and talking and interacting with others seemed to do wonders for her. There was no better place for meeting and talking with people than the many *Gaststätten* [inns] and Cafés in Stuttgart such as the Goldener Adler down the steps and across the street from us. While she would nurse a beer and I have a "Cola," Mutti would tell me something about her past including growing up in Schwanheim am Main and her plans for the near future.

Mutti never mentioned financial matters to me and money seemed to be no problem at the time. To take care of our Stuttgart expenses, she had gotten a temporary job as a retail clerk with a local Woolworth store on Königstraße near the Stuttgart Hauptbahnhof although that did not last long. She evidently made some unfavorable remarks about Woolworth stores to her German colleagues and the manager let her go. Perhaps more importantly, Mutti must have had child support payments accumulate in her account with the Stuttgart Landesgirokasse, her long-time Stuttgart bank, for the three of us during the time we were out of the country and even now for Ute and Volker.

Of immediate concern to Mutti was what to do with us before she could bring us back over to America. She had originally planned to return in August but with us kids being here now, she had decided to extend her stay for a few months more. Mutti told me that on her return she planned to find a job as a housekeeper in an affluent Chicago suburb and bring me over as soon as she had earned enough money to pay for my passage. My siblings, whom she might have to temporarily put into one of Stuttgart's children's homes, were to follow later.

Until my return to the States, Mutti had something special in mind for me, namely, a temporary stay in an *Internat* [boarding school]. There just happened to be a well-known one in a small village northwest of Stuttgart called Korntal. One day Mutti took me there to present her case. During the interview with its director, Mutti was animated as usual and talked up a storm on my behalf while I just sat there quietly contemplating the prospect of being cooped up for half a year or longer in this one-horse town in the boonies with a bunch of kids I did not know or care about. I wanted to live in Stuttgart and nowhere else. Mutti, however, was so taken in by the idea of me attending an exclusive boarding school that I decided to just play along hoping things would work out in my favor. Fortunately, they did.

A short while after our visit, Mutti informed me that she had received a letter from Korntal telling her that the school had decided not to accept me. I feigned surprise and disappointment but could scarcely contain my feelings of relief and delight. Mutti now rolled out Plan B which was to have her two friends, Robert and Liesel Sokolov, move into our *Wohnung* to look out for the three of us.

September 1, the traditional beginning of the school year, had now again arrived. While I had no particular desire to go back to school and would have been perfectly happy going to the Amerika-Haus, a cultural institution operated by the U.S. Government, to do some reading and playing table tennis until my return to the States, Mutti had other plans for me. Somehow she managed to persuade the school authorities to let me attend the Schickhardt Oberschule again although only to monitor classes and not as a regular student, i.e., I would do my class assignments but not be required to take any examinations and be graded. At the end of my stay, I would be given a certificate of attendance for presentation to the school authorities back in the States.

When I arrived at the Oberschule, I was happy to be assigned to my old class which was now class 5b and, at 30 students, about the same size as class 3b had been when I left a year and a half earlier. Some boys had left voluntarily or were not allowed to continue because of poor grades while others were new to me. Of my friends, Hans-Eugen was still there and so was Jörg but Gerhard had not made the grade and had dropped out. Walter Koch continued to get the best grades which made him class leader. He was a kid with a big head set on a smallish body. He wanted to be friends and I once shook his clammy hand but, since I did not care much for intellectuals, I avoided him. And there was Peter André, a new boy, who asked me what I thought he should choose for a career. When I told him that I could picture him as an airplane pilot, he was so elated with my answer that he almost fell on my neck. Of the teachers, Herr Bähr had been replaced by Herr Hildebrand as music teacher. I was told that Herr Bähr had been transferred to the Hölderlin-Gymnasium, a girls high school, where he was much adored by his female charges.

Immediately noticeable to me was that in the relatively short time I was gone, the atmosphere had changed considerably with the happy-go-lucky attitude of former days having given way to a strong competitive spirit. It was pretty much swim or sink at the Oberschule now. I also realized that I was now so far behind my classmates academically that the situation was hopeless. I did rather well in German and, not surprisingly, in English.

Mathematics was a complete disaster for me as the class was now deep into algebra of which I knew practically nothing. The problems were mostly about train schedules: If a train left A for B at a certain time and speed, when and where would it meet another train leaving B for A at a different time and speed. The closest I had come to algebra at Emerson School was what in American math classes was popularly known as the "rule of three" which was a simple technique for finding the fourth term of a proportion when three terms were known.

My long absence had put a chill into some of my former relationships especially that with Hans- Eugen but there were others to take their place. Undoubtedly, Hans-Eugen was a little envious of my overseas adventure but I too was at fault because I had made no effort to stay in touch. One time I overheard him tell a group of our classmates that other than knowing a few more words, I knew no more English than they did. Undoubtedly this was not true but, more importantly, I could not have a friend who would bad-mouth me behind my back.

Hans-Eugen's replacement was Paul Kage, a lanky boy who had come to West Germany from the *Ostzone* and shared my budding interest in science. After having been introduced to science and technology before my emigration by the books of *Das Neue Universum* [The New Universe], I now also came across a weekly newspaper with exciting stories about distant galaxies, UFOs, archeological digs, exotic sea creatures, and other strange things that I loved to read about. This was the type of stuff I could discuss with Paul because he was interested in the same topics.

The wealth of Paul's scientific knowledge much impressed me and I soon had occasion to put it to the test. Although Dr. Liebendörfer and his library were long gone, I remembered once finding some *Reagenzgläser* [test tubes] in one of the bottom drawers of the huge bookcase. These were the usual shapes used for chemical analyses—cylindrical, conical, and spherical. When I described them to Paul, he seemed familiar with all of them and immediately gave me both their German and Latin names. Asked by Paul to give me more shapes, I gave my imagination free reign and told him about test tubes shaped like helixes, cork screws, snail shells and other strange and exotic geometries. To my utter amazement, no matter how weird the shape I had dreamed up, Paul could immediately give me both its German and Latin name. Some of the names were really weird, I thought.

One day Paul told me he was taking me along to Kosmos, a Stuttgart society that published books and pamphlets on diverse scientific topics. It seems that Paul was a student member and he and others would now and then meet for scientific discussions and to socialize. At the society's headquarters, Paul led me to a room where a number of boys about our age were assembled and expecting us. Paul introduced me by informing the group that I had just returned from America where I had done some advanced research on a new *perpetuum mobile* and was on the brink of a major breakthrough. He was talking for me, said Paul, because my prolonged absence in America had diminished my fluency in German and we did not think it sensible for me to give my presentation in English since a few members had only a passing knowledge of that language. I then listened in stunned silence as Paul described my work and its scientific foundation and implications.

Paul touched on the whole gamut of laws and principles with any bearing on the case including Helmholtz's law on the conservation of energy, Newton's laws of motion, and the coefficients of friction and other properties of various materials. As I listened to my friend's discourse, my self-esteem, which had never been on the high side, began to rise considerably. To my dismay, however, when I looked about to savor the audience reaction, I could not help but notice some depreciating snickering among a few of the listeners that eventually brought Paul's lecture to a halt. It seemed to me that our audience did not think me capable of the research work so admirably described by my friend. To put an end to their patronizing attitude and restore some order to the proceedings, I stood up and with a frown on my face kicked one of the chairs. The snickerers got the message and made some apologetic gestures after which I sat down again and Paul continued with his presentation.

We left the meeting right after Paul had finished his presentation because, as he explained to our audience, we could regrettably not stay to answer questions because of another appointment. As we exited the building, I lashed out at Paul for having put me on the spot by not telling me about his planned presentation prior to the meeting. The one good thing, I told him, was that he got us out of there before I could be asked any questions. "And what is a *perpetuum mobile* anyway," I wanted to know. According to Paul, a *perpetuum mobile* is a mechanical devise that once set in motion continues in that motion indefinitely. That was in line with one of Newton's laws, he said.

However, according to Paul, his readings on the subject matter and his own experiments had convinced him that such a device could not exist in practice because it required the complete absence of friction which was unrealistic. There would always be some friction, however small, that would slow the mechanism down and eventually bring it to a halt. According to Paul, this was the reason that he had given up this project and started a new one which seemed more promising. He had been given a microscope for his last birthday, Paul informed me, and after a recent nocturnal occurrence while asleep and then having found a way to obtain more specimens, he had now turned his attention to studying the random motion of sperm.

Mutti returned to the States in mid-November on the SS *Homeland*. Just before her departure for the port of Hamburg, Robert and Liesel moved into our apartment. Since they were willing to look out for only us two older ones, Volker had to be placed in a Stuttgart children's home. Our two caregivers left Ute and me pretty much to our own devices and, even though Volker was not living with us, the three of us often got together on weekends. Since it was winter and snow was on the ground, we would sometimes take our sled to the hills around Stuttgart.

On one occasion, we decided to go down a hill that we knew was covered with ice rather than snow figuring that the ice would be more exciting because of the extra speed. With me sitting at the front and Ute and Volker behind me, the sled suddenly veered off the road and slammed into a tree at a high speed. The accident immediately brought a crowd of onlookers rushing to the scene. The impact had temporally knocked me out and when I came to some anguished looking faces were peering down at us. Miraculously, none of us was hurt but our sled was a total loss.

My relationship with our two caregivers, especially Liesel, was not particularly good. Ute and I had no contact with them before and Mutti told us almost nothing about them. They seemed to be somewhat on the coarse side. On weekends they enjoyed watching boxing matches and similar activities in steamy arenas and Robert would ride his motor bike around town with Liesel behind him. One time Liesel fell off it and suffered minor injuries. She was singularly unattractive with a thin face, high cheekbones, and bulging black eyes and had a personality to match. Robert was friendlier and spoke German with a strong French accent. The one thing I liked about him was the diligence he applied to important tasks I gave him such as doing my homework for French class. In fact, he did such an excellent job that Dr. Traub was astonished with what I could accomplish outside the pressures of the classroom.

In the evening Robert would entertain me with funny stories of his childhood which was partly spent in a boarding school. Once when he was 14 and home with his mother, she asked him to bring something to a lady friend who lived nearby. To his pleasant surprise, when he arrived this lady had baked a cake which she offered to share with him. Afterwards she led him to her bedroom where she induced him to join her in bed for a lesson in the art of love, he said. Robert asked me if I thought his mother was in on it. Since they were French, I suspected that she was but told him that from the little available information it was not possible to know for sure.

Confirmation in the Christian faith is an important rite for young Protestant believers and my unexpected return to Germany ensured that it would now take place in our old parish church, the Evangelische Matthäuskirche in Heslach. It had originally been planned for the St. John Evangelical Lutheran Church in Forest Park. That is where I had been attending a confirmation class conducted by Pastor Erwin Paul before leaving the country.

When I met up with Pfarrer Lang in Stuttgart again shortly after our arrival in August the year before and he found out that I had not yet been confirmed, he immediately enrolled me in his class. The festive confirmation service, conducted by Pfarrer Lang, took place on the 4th Sunday in March. Among the hymns the congregation sang that day was my all-time favorite—*Lobet den Herrn, den mächtigsten König der Erden*. [Praise to the Lord, the Almighty]. Very appropriately, considering my frequent travels and venue changes, the verse I was given to recite before the congregation was based on a passage from St. Paul's letter to the Hebrews

[13:14]: *Wir haben hier keine bleibende Stadt, sondern die zukünftige suchen wir.* [For here have we no continuing city, but we seek one to come].

Once Mutti was back in the States, she began to save up and when she had the money together, started to arrange for my return just as she had promised. She procured the required reentry permit, which Esther had neglected to do before she sent us back to Germany, and purchased a ticket for me in tourist class. A Stuttgart travel bureau made all the arrangements and managed to book me space on the TSS *Neptunia* of the Greek Line for a scheduled departure from Bremerhaven just three days after my confirmation at St. Matthew's.

As strange as it may seem, taking leave of Ute and Volker, of Robert and Liesel, of friends, classmates and teachers at the Schickhardt Oberschule, of neighbors and other people I had befriended or was acquainted with proved easier than saying good-bye to Stuttgart. Leaving the city that had been so much part of my life this time was an especially sad occasion because I suspected that I would not be back for a long time if ever. On the evening prior to my departure, I walked up to the nearby Karlshöhe, a hill above Stuttgart, to once more savor the panorama of glittering lights and illuminated landmarks of my beloved hometown below.

A New Beginning

If my first arrival on American soil two years earlier was more of an extended visit than an immigration, this time it was the real thing. Mutti and I had now come here to stay. As many immigrants before us had recognized, America was a land of opportunity where people could live up to their full potential free from the many restraints imposed by Old World governments, institutions, and customs. We were ready for the American Dream and its promise of material prosperity and personal freedom.

On my arrival in New York in early April, my first stop was not Chicago but the New York borough of the Bronx. Mutti had arranged for me to visit there with some people she wanted me to meet and, specifically, her former mother-in-law she called Oma Würzburger and my half-brother Friedrich. Since the Würzburgers had changed their family name to Wetmore after their arrival in America and Friedrich's first name was changed to Jerome,

Oma Würzburger was now Oma Wetmore while Friedrich Würzburger became Jerome (Jerry) Wetmore.

When I met up with them in the Bronx, Oma and Jerry were living in a small 1-bedroom apartment in a huge apartment complex. Oma was a very sweet lady and received me with a great show of affection and kindness as did her friends and neighbors who made a great fuss over me and plied me with gifts including several jigsaw puzzles. At nearly 24 years old, Jerry had no job as I could tell and slept on a sofa in his grandmother's living room while I did so on another one across from him. I do not remember much from this brief visit except that I do recall Jerry proudly introducing me to some of his friends on the street as his brother. For one much dependent for his emotional wellbeing on pleasant surroundings, the immense apartment blocks and treeless streets and squares of the Bronx had a depressing effect on me and I was happy to be shortly on my way again to meet up with Mutti in Chicago.

Mutti picked me up at the train station in Chicago and we took the "L" to Wilmette, an exclusive North Shore suburb, where she had found employment as a live-in housekeeper shortly after her second arrival in America the previous November. According to Mutti, she had found the job opening in Chicago's major German-language newspaper, *Sonntagpost und Milwaukee Deutsche Zeitung*. Mrs. Brown's parents were German and that would explain why she advertised in that paper.

The Browns were an affluent professional couple. Cameron Brown was a lawyer with the Chicago office of Lloyds of London. Mrs. Brown was a professor of painting at the University of Chicago and, according to Mutti, the youngest person ever to hold the position at this prestigious university. The family, I could tell, had class and they were courteous and friendly to boot. Mutti seemed genuinely happy working for them. She cleaned the house, cooked the meals, did the laundry, and took care of their young son Reed.

The Brown's home on 507 Lake Avenue was a prairie-style house by the famous Oak Park architect Frank Lloyd Wright. It was, unfortunately, defective in that whenever it rained, the roof, which was flat, leaked so that Mutti had to put out pots and pans in the living room to catch the water trickling from the ceiling. While Mr. Wright may have been a splendid architect and his buildings unique and attractive to the eye, their design and execution were evidently not always the most practical so that keeping his creations in good repair required special efforts by their owners.

During my short stay at the Brown home, I also got a lesson in modern art because Mrs. Brown had some samples of her artistic efforts hanging around the house. As Mutti explained it, these paintings belonged to the impressionistic school and were not to be confused with realistic painting in which the subject appeared as if it had been photographed. In impressionism, said Mutti, the artist tries to convey his or her underlying feelings about the subject rather than render it life-like. On viewing it, it was therefore often difficult to tell whom or what the picture represented. That undoubtedly explained why Mrs. Brown had lately begun to tell her guests something about a particular painting before she actually showed it to them. According to Mutti, there had been all too many occasions in the past when Mrs. Brown had led them to one of her portraits, such as one of little Reedy, and invariable a guest would ask, "Who is that supposed to be?"

Mutti had a nice suite all to herself where we both stayed and the Browns would have been happy to continue with this arrangement. They had even suggested that I be enrolled in Wilmette High School. Mutti, however, had other plans. She valued her freedom and independence and would never have been happy living in somebody else's home and be their servant for very long. Within a short time of my arrival, Mutti and I took our leave of the Browns and left for Oak Park. It was only logical for Mutti and me to be drawn back to this village where we knew our way around and still had friends and acquaintances. Mutti also undoubtedly wanted to remain close to Esther despite all that had happened before.

After apparently selling their home, Esther and Nick had moved further south to an apartment building in the 900 block of South Oak Park Avenue. Since the passenger list for the SS *Homeland*, the ship Mutti had returned on, gave that address as Mutti's destination on her arrival in the country, she must have temporarily moved in with them before leaving for Wilmette.

While still with the Brown family, Mutti had found a furnished room advertised in the *Oak Leaves* and arranged to rent it on a weekly basis. The house was a 1-story frame home on South Maple Avenue close to Madison Street. Our room which faced the street had probably been a family's living room. A young couple rented a room behind us and we shared the bathroom that separated the two rooms.

Our landlord was a Mr. Golden who was the proprietor of Golden's Pharmacy at the southwest corner of Madison Street and Harlem Avenue in Forest Park. He was well-to-do and owned, besides the drugstore, several rental properties and a mansion on Linden Avenue in Oak Park. He told us that he was about to sell out and move to Arizona to take advantage of an impending building boom there. He could foresee the day when Arizona would be covered with retirement communities owing to the sunny climate and the availability of huge tracts of desert land at cheap prices. He also wanted to get away from that nasty Chicago climate with its harsh winters that often brought snowstorms and blizzards with immense piles of snow. The summers were no better owing to the high humidity and stifling heat. According to Mr. Golden, it got very hot in Arizona too but it was a dry heat that people, especially the elderly, could more easily cope with. And besides, air conditioning was coming into use everywhere.

With the housing problem solved, some other matters needed attention. Mutti's first order of business now was finding a new job. Since her English was not yet good enough for an office position, her only option was one as a factory worker. Such jobs were plentiful at the time and she soon landed one in Chicago not far from where we lived and accessible by public transportation.

Needless to say, Mutti brought up the matter of my further schooling. Since it was now near the end of April and school would be out in June, I suggested to Mutti that we wait with my enrollment in high school until September. This would allow me to recover from all the stress I had suffered due the many recent venue changes. Some long-term damage to my psyche could not be ruled out, I told Mutti, if I did not get a break.

Mutti did not listen to me and dragged me over to Oak Park and River Forest High School, a big complex located in the northeastern part of the village near Chicago, to be enrolled. The school officials there wanted proof that I had attended school since graduating from Emerson School and I was glad that I had that certificate of attendance from the Schickhardt Oberschule to show them.

After being given a special examination, I was assigned to the freshman class which was shortly coming to an end. This was the class I would have been in had I not left for Germany. By age, of course, I should have been a sophomore. Since it was determined that my English vocabulary was still below par for high school, I was enrolled in both freshman English and sophomore German to help me improve my language skills. Other courses were algebra, freshman science, and physical education. By the end of my freshman year, I had nearly flunked them all, with the exceptions of German and gym, with grades of "D" which stood for "below average but passing." I clearly had much work ahead of me to catch up.

While I was in school, Mutti was busy finding us a more suitable place to live. Apartments were hard to come by during this first decade after the war. This was due to the returning soldiers from overseas who were setting up households plus all the European immigrants like us who were flooding into the country. After an extensive search, Mutti located a vacant apartment on the first floor of a townhouse located on Home Avenue just south of the Lake Street "L" which ran down one side of South Boulevard.

The building at 8 Home Avenue was a 2-story gray stone structure with a semicircular front that used to be the family home of a Mrs. Wright before she moved to California. After converting the place for multiple use, she rented out the first floor and basement apartments leaving the second floor, which used to be the family bedrooms, vacant. The caretakers of this and some other properties in the area were a black couple and probably the only people of color who lived in Oak Park at the time. They made their home on top of the garage of a neighboring apartment building. Mutti had to pay them a princely sum to get the place for us but she did not mind because the apartment was attractive, well located close to public transportation and, at $80 a month, very affordable.

Mutti and I were delighted to finally have a place to call home. We moved in on the 1st of May of the year and this was to be my home until I left for college and Mutti's for the next 13 years. At that time the building was sold after Mrs. Wright unfortunately died in an auto accident in California and the new owners wanted to move in. The downstairs of the townhouse was occupied by a Swedish-born single man by the name of Gustav Lindström who was the chef at Otto's Café, a well-known German restaurant in Forest Park. Gus told us that he was looking forward to his retirement in a few years when he planned to return to Sweden where his elderly mother was anxiously awaiting his return.

The flat Mutti rented was somewhat smaller in size than our Stuttgart *Wohnung* had been and less modern and airy but otherwise comfortable and adequate. The windows were in the smaller English style prevalent in America which were opened by raising the lower half in front of the stationary upper portion. This design was more economical and saved space but left less of an opening to the outside and made the windows much harder to clean than what in America were called French-style windows which parted in the middle and were standard in Germany.

Mutti assigned me to the largest and nicest room, which was the one facing Home Avenue, while she took a smaller one in the back as her bedroom. She made the center room with the apartment entrance into a combination living/dining room. Beyond this room was a small kitchen whose back entrance led to the back porch. Next to it was an old-fashioned bathroom that was accessible from Mutti's bedroom and the kitchen. Fortunately, we did not have to worry about heating the place in the winter because the apartment was connected to the village grid which supplied steam to the radiators.

The one thing we did not get used to was the presence of numerous cockroaches which were difficult to eradicate because they moved freely between the interconnected townhouses. I had never seen them in Germany but in America they were known as German cockroaches and so we had at least something in common with our visitors.

Mutti immediately went about furnishing our new home by using the American way of buying on credit. That was an innovation for her because in Germany it was the custom of saving up for things one needed and wanted and then paying cash. Mutti found everything at Wieboldt's department store which had a branch at the southwest corner of Lake Street and Harlem Avenue in River Forest and kitty-corner from the very exclusive Marshall Field's Oak Park store. For my room, Mutti selected a solid cherry bedroom with full size bed, a night stand, a tall chest of drawers plus a leather-topped desk. I was not along when she made the purchase and she did not ask me about my preferences. Perhaps she wanted to surprise me. Needless to say, I was very pleased when it arrived and saw it for the first time. The dining/living room furniture including a tall glass-fronted china cabinet and large table with six chairs was also of solid cherry wood. For her bedroom, Mutti selected a more economical fruitwood model also with a full size bed, a dresser with mirror, and a chest of drawers. The stove and refrigerator for the kitchen she bought in a German-American store on North Lincoln Avenue. It took her a while but she eventually had it all paid off.

The Boys Club

Being relatively new to the country and probably more naïve than most other 15-year-olds, I still had much to learn. Shortly after we were in our new apartment, Mutti and I happened to be at the main Oak Park post office, a handsome art nouveau building located on Lake Street near Oak Park Avenue, when a smallish, corpulent man with a ruddy complexion and a gun strapped to his belt walked up to us and introduced himself. His name was Red, he said, and he was the post office guard. Red, probably so named for the color of his hair, had overheard our conversation, he said, and guessed that we were probably from the Old Country.

According to Red, he was president of the Oak Park Boys Club and wondered if I might be interested in joining. I hesitated to say yes because the idea of membership in a boys club sounded much too exclusive to me. After all, we were just poor immigrants and I did not think that I would feel comfortable among Oak Park's upper crust. Mutti, however, immediately liked the idea and talked me into it because, she said, it could much benefit me to meet some American boys my age of some social standing. Red and I agreed that I would meet him at the post office the following Saturday around noon and he would take me to the club. We met as agreed and Red called his wife from a phone booth in the post office lobby. He told her that he was coming for lunch and asked her to set out another plate because he was bringing a friend.

When we got to Red's apartment, which was on the first floor of a red brick apartment building, his wife came to the door and when she saw me seemed surprised and befuddled. She did not even wait for Red to introduce me and rushed off to the kitchen. Lunch was standard fare consisting of a slice of meatloaf, some mashed potatoes with gravy, and peas and carrots. What much bothered me was that this lady kept her eyes focused on the plate in front of her and never once looked up at me or said one word to either one of us. In fact, the atmosphere was very chilly. Her obvious hostility robbed me of my appetite and I was happy when she had finished her meal and left to go back to work.

After lunch, Red escorted me to the basement and showed me the club room. It was nicely furnished with some lounge chairs, a billiard table and another one for table tennis. There was even one of those new television sets. On a wall I noticed several oversized photographs of the great ocean liners of the day. One was of the SS *America*, the very ship I had come over on, as well as one of her sister ship, the SS *United States*. He had no trouble getting the photographs, according to Red, because as president of a boys club, companies were happy to supply him with promotional materials for their products and services.

When I got back home, Mutti wanted to know if there was anybody I liked at the club. I had some difficulty explaining to her why there were no other boys and I was the first and only member. The club was still being formed, I told her, and Red was very selective and would not take just anybody. In fact, Red had confided in me that his was really an international boys club and that he intended to eventually turn it into world-wide organization. What qualified me for membership were my strong international credentials and there were few Oak Park boys who could match his very stringent requirements, I told Mutti. For some reason, Mutti seemed skeptical but eventually went along with my explanation.

At any rate, I never returned to the club or Red's home because I had had enough of his hostile wife. I asked him instead to teach me how to drive his car. This he did by several times taking me to a forest preserve in River Forest where I could safely practice my driving skills.

One Saturday morning, Red came by the house and announced that he owned several properties and would like to take me along to one of them so I could watch him collect the rent. This place was a large home in a style common in the village and called Victorian. Like others of its type, it was an asymmetrical wood frame house that sat on a stone foundation and included a large open porch, bay windows, a circular tower and small turrets for decoration. That style was popular with large families because the many bedrooms on the upper floor allowed each child to have his or her own room. Red led me up an inside stairway to the second floor and we started walking down a long, narrow hallway with several rooms on both sides.

Red's method of collecting the rent was very strange and unusual, I thought, and not like anything I had seen before. As we came to each room, Red would announce his presence by a hard knock on the door. The door would then open just slightly and a lady's hand come out holding the rental money. Without saying a word, Red would simply take it from her hand and move on to the next room. But at some rooms the lady tenants, unaware that Red was not alone, opened the door all the way. When they realized that Red had brought someone along and saw me, they invariably shrieked and quickly shut the door again. Apparently they had not enough time to put on some clothing after the knock and now stood there nearly naked. It was all very embarrassing and I wished I had not come along.

After taking care of business upstairs, Red led me down to the first-floor parlor. It was dark and musty in there with the heavy drapes covering the tall and narrow windows allowing only small shafts of sunlight to filter in. On the floor sat stacks of yellowed issues of the *Chicago Tribune* and a large pile of the *National Geographic*, a monthly picture magazine containing interesting articles on distant and exotic places as well as on plant and animal life. On the heavy wood table lay maps and atlases of all kinds and next to it stood a magnificent globe of the world. The people who had lived there were obviously much interested in the world at large. These folks were, in fact, Red's parents for this was their home and this is where he had grown up, he told me.

I was especially intrigued by the globe and as I was leaning over it, Red suddenly came up behind me, grabbed me around the waist and lifted me off the floor. I was surprised and shocked and froze whereupon he quickly set me down again. To assuage my obvious indignation and anger, he gave me a large atlas of the world and some of the magazines.

Late one rainy evening Red came by and invited me to an outing to Chicago's O'Hare International Airport. I readily agreed expecting to be taken to the observation tower to watch the planes take off and land. Instead I found myself standing next to a noisy runway in the dead of night with only an occasional car passing by and nobody else in sight. With Red standing behind me and knowing that he owned a gun, I was suddenly overcome by such angst that I began to sweat. He must have sensed my fear because after a while he suggested that he take me back home. On the way he talked of other future outings but I was not listening because I knew that I had to cut him loose. That was the last time I saw him. Later I heard that Esther had somehow tracked Red down and called him with the message to stay away or else.

Times of Contentment

Shortly after arriving back in Oak Park I had stopped by the Village Newspaper Agency to see if my friend Tom Doherty was still there. The agency had, in the meantime, moved to its own small building on South Boulevard near Oak Park Avenue and the Lake Street "L" station. Tom was happy to see me and we agreed that I would come back to work for him as soon as Mutti and I had found a more permanent home. As soon as that happened and I returned, Tom gave me the main route down Oak Park Avenue from South Boulevard to Madison Street and back up on Euclid Avenue. He also increased my pay to $50 a month which made me the highest paid newsboy at the agency.[19] The office was within walking distance of our new home on Home Avenue which meant that I could pick up my papers and delivery cart and start my route from there.

Working at our jobs and my going to school, still left some free time. The decade of the 1950s was known as the Golden Age of Television and Mutti had gotten us a small black and white television console so that we could watch all the popular shows of the day. Among the TV shows we enjoyed were *The Ed Sullivan Show*, a variety show featuring diverse artists, *The Jackie Gleason Show* with comedy skits called *The Honeymooners*, *Your Show of Shows*, another comedy show featuring Sid Caesar and Imogene Coca, *Arthur Godfrey's Talent Scouts*, a variety show, and *Your Hit Parade* which highlighted the most popular songs of the week.

For the entertainment of their male audiences the three major networks also offered a large selection of Westerns featuring such stars as Gene Audrey, the singing cowboy, Roy Rodgers, The King of Cowboys, Hopalong Cassidy, played by William Boyd, and the Lone Ranger, a masked former Texas Ranger and his American Indian friend Tonto. These were especially enjoyable for me because the heroes were tough hombres yet morally upright, the stories simple and easy to follow, and the endings satisfying with the bad guys either killed or hauled off to jail. Popular with us kids too were the Saturday matinees at Oak Park's Lake Theatre offering a double feature, usually including a Western, plus one or two Disney cartoons.

Much of our entertainment took place in Chicago. Usually on Sundays, Mutti and I would take the "L" to Lincoln Square, location of the Davis Theater, to see a double feature of German-language movies. The Davis Theater showed both American and German-language films but for the latter was called the Davis Mozart Theater. Operated by an Austrian couple, the movie house showed classic UFA (Universum Film AG) films from the past and newer *Heimatfilme* [homeland movies].[20] Part of our routine would be a visit to the Konditorei und Kaffee Kleinert on the corner of Lincoln and Leland Avenues for coffee and a slice or two of multilayered torte.

Late summer and early fall was an especially active time for Chicagoland's German-American community. First Mutti and I, and after she had also brought over Ute and Volker from Stuttgart, we all regularly attended the German-American Day festivities which usually took place on a weekend in August or September. The fest was held in a picnic grove in Riverview Park, a big amusement park on Western and Belmont Avenues on Chicago's West Side, and was always well attended.

This was an opportunity for new arrivals from Germany and Austria and those who had been here for some time to get together and pretend they were back in the Old Country for a while. The offering included parades by war veterans proudly marching behind American flags and brass bands playing John Philip Sousa marches, performances by various German-American children's and adult choirs, dances by regional *Trachtenvereine* [folk costume groups], stage plays, contests and, of course, all sorts of hearty German foods and beer.

Much of the credit for keeping me focused on my newspaper delivery job must go to Mutti. Because high school started earlier than elementary school, at 20 minutes past 8 in the morning, I had to be up very early to get through my route and to school on time. Mutti believed in a healthy lifestyle and the restorative power of sleep and she made sure that we got plenty of the latter. We went to bed early on most evenings after we had eaten and I finished my homework. In the morning she got me up, fixed breakfast, and sent me on my way before going off to work herself. Mutti let me keep all the money I earned while living at home and never asked for any of it nor did I volunteer to part with any. She knew that every penny I earned would go into my college fund so that I could realize my dream. Following in the footsteps of her father and my namesake, I had decided to become an engineer.

NOTES

1. The ancient and venerable word "Reich" and what it stands for needs some explaining because it has been associated primarily with the Third Reich and demonized especially in the Anglo-American world. When President Franklin D. Roosevelt met with Soviet leader Josef Stalin in Tehran in November 1943, he told him that "it was very important not to leave in the German mind the concept of 'the Reich'...The very word [Reich] should be stricken from the [German] language." (See Michael Beschloss, *The Conquerors*, 24). Nothing, of course, came of this ridiculous idea. The word Reich is derived from *reich* meaning rich or wealthy while *Reichtum* is the German word for wealth. Reich can stand for kingdom, commonwealth, or empire. The concept of a Reich has a very long history and goes all the way back to Charlemagne (742-814 AD), a Christian warrior of the Middle Ages who was king of the Franks, a Germanic *Volksstamm* [tribe] the Romans called *Franci*. The Franks became dominant in Western Europe after defeating another Germanic tribe, the *Alemanni*, in 496 AD.

    With his crowning in Rome on Christmas Day in 800 AD by Pope Leo III as *Imperator Romanorum* [Emperor of the Romans], Charlemagne (Karl der Große in German) became the founder of the Holy Roman Empire. The empire's head held the title Caesar (Kaiser in German) and its symbol was the Roman eagle. Charlemagne's capital was Aachen (Aix-la-Chapelle) now in the Federal Republic of Germany. Both Frenchmen and Germans claim him as their own but he was neither but always *ein Franke*. The Holy Roman Empire of the German Nation, usually referred to as the First Reich, existed for over 1,000 years until 1806 when it was dissolved by Napoleon after his conquests in Western Europe. The Holy Roman Empire was said to have been neither holy nor Roman nor an empire. The fact that it was not a military empire most likely accounted for its longevity.

German-speaking peoples have always and continue to pray the Lord's Prayer which includes the phrase, *Dein Reich komme* [Thy Kingdom come] in spite of all the "conquerors" past and present.

2. The village of Graben was first mentioned in historical records in the year 1306 AD. Translated into English, Graben literarily means ditch, trench, or moat In 1972, Graben joined a neighboring village, Neudorf, to form the village of Graben-Neudorf and the two villages are now known by that name. A history of Graben appears in Konrad Dussel's book *Graben: Vom Bauerndorf zur Modernen Industriegemeinde* [Graben: From Peasant Village to Modern Industrial Community]. A copy was given to me by the *Evangelische Kirchengemeinde* [Evangelical (Lutheran) congregation] of Graben on a visit there in early September 2006.

3. What I presumably saw as a small boy was a zeppelin, a rigid, gas-filled airships that was popular for long-distance travel for some years before large passenger airplanes were developed and commercial airlines could offer such service. The zeppelins flew out of Friedrichshafen on the Bodensee (Lake Constance) which lies about 110 miles southeast of Bruchsal by air. Transatlantic travel with zeppelins came to an abrupt end when on May 6, 1937, the dirigible *Hindenburg* caught fire at Lakehurst, New Jersey, after crossing the Atlantic, killing 35 passengers and crew out of the 97 people on board. The particular zeppelin I most likely saw was the *Graf Zeppelin II*, a Hindenburg class airship which had its last flight on August 20, 1939. If that is the flight I happened to witness, I would have just turned three years old.

4. Germans refer to themselves as being either *katholisch* or *evangelisch* depending on whether they belong to the Römisch-Katholische Kirche Deutschlands or RKD (Roman Catholic Church of Germany) or the Evangelische Kirche Deutschlands or EKD (Evangelical Church of Germany), the country's two major state-funded church bodies. Unlike in the United States where Christians belonging to one of the Lutheran synods refer to themselves as Lutherans, this is not the case in Germany where the term Lutheran standing by itself is not in common usage although the term Evangelisch-Lutherische Kirche is sometimes used.

One reason is that Lutheran was used as a term of disparagement after Pope Leo X had excommunicated Marin Luther (1483-1546), the church's founder. Another was that Luther himself was strongly opposed to have a church named after him. Luther, a former Catholic friar, taught that the sole authority on the Bible was not the Pope but the *Evangelium* [Holy Scripture] and his followers therefore referred to themselves as being *evangelisch*. A number of American Protestants are also known as evangelicals with their own belief system and doctrine which, however, much differs from that of original German evangelicals. To avoid confusion, in this book I will refer to them as "American evangelicals." In Germany, American evangelicals are known as *Evangeliker*.

5. My premonition turned out to be correct because Papa never returned from the war and must have been killed not long after I last saw him. As far as is known to me, Mama never heard anything about his fate. My recent online search in the files of the Volksbund Deutsche Kriegsgräberfürsorge e.V. (German War Graves Commission) in Kassel has Oskar Gartner listed as having been born on March 29, 1919 in Laas (since 1994 a part of Liebschützberg, Saxony) and gone missing on February 17, 1942. Further correspondence with the *Volksbund* revealed some surprising and disturbing information on him. Specially, Oskar Gartner was a private and served in an organization identified as "1./SS-Pol. Aufkl. A." It thus appears that he was a member of the feared political branch of the SS (Schutzstaffel) which was in charge of the Nazi extermination campaign against Eastern European Jews. Incidentally, the abbreviation *Aufkl.* stands for *Aufklärung* [reconnaissance, discovery].

According to the *Volksbund* report, Oskar Gartner fell on February 17, 1942 at Krasnogwardeisk near Leningrad and was first buried in the military cemetery in Gattschina. His remains were then transferred to the German military cemetery Sologubowka which lies 30 miles southeast of St Petersburg, the former Leningrad. This means that Oskar Gartner was not yet 23 years old at the time of his death and about 20 when he and Mama took me into their Forst home. Naturally, it pains me to know that my beloved Papa was a member of such a despicable organization. Because I knew him as a very kind and affectionate man, I am convinced that he did not volunteer for this terrible assignment.

6. *Tiefflieger* [low flyers] was the term used by Germans during World II for allied fighter planes whose mission was to strafe civilian targets and bring terror to the German heartland. *Tiefflieger* targets included towns and villages too small for the conventional bomber armadas which were reserved for larger towns and cities. Most *Tiefflieger* attacks were directed at almost any target that could be of value to the German war effort in the broadest sense—passenger trains, vehicles on the open road, *Bauern* working the fields, and even ordinary individuals riding their bicycles along a road. These fighters swooped down from great heights and then flew at tree-top level to surprise their victims with deadly effect. Despite some early moral qualms about wantonly targeting individual civilians, the attacks went on and killed thousands. (See Max Hastings, *Armageddon*, 323-325). American World War II historians have routinely denied their existences despite overwhelming evidence to the contrary. Numerous eyewitness reports of *Tiefflieger* encounters may be found in Wolfgang Samuel's *The War of Our Childhood*.

7. SA, an acronym for *Sturmabteilung* [Storm Unit], was a para-military, ultranationalist organization, also known as Brownshirts, which was instrumental in bringing the Nazis to power by acts of intimation and violence against all designated as undesirables including Jews, Bolsheviks (Communists), Socialists, Roma (Gypsies), and homosexuals. Their leader was Ernst Röhm, a close confidant of Hitler, whom the Führer had later executed for plotting against him and the Reich and immoral conduct. (Röhm was openly gay).

8. The Anglo-American air forces, i.e., the Royal Air Force's Bomber Command and the U.S. Army Air Force (USAAF), divided their task as follows: While the Americans conducted daylight precision raids on factories and rail and communication facilities, the British came at night to take out the inner cities and population centers. Stuttgart was the target of 53 mostly British air raids between August 25, 1940 and April 19, 1945, the dates of the first and last bombings. During these attacks over 8,000 mostly four-engine bombers dropped over 20,000 explosive and 1.3 million incendiary bombs on the city destroying two-thirds of the city center and killing 4,562 of its inhabitants with

another 8,908 injured. (See Heinz Bardua, *Stuttgart im Luftkrieg 1939-1945, 198-200*).

Admittedly, Stuttgart was an industrial center and home to large manufacturing firms, most notably automobile companies, and as such a legitimate military target since these firms contributed to Germany's war effort. However, as in most ancient European towns, Stuttgart's industrial plants and other legitimate military targets were not located in the city proper but outside of town. This was because industrialization came long after the cities were already in existence. As a result, the inner city of Stuttgart was mostly residential and the location of the town's major cultural and civic institutions.

So why was the center of Stuttgart as other city centers attacked so ferociously when they were almost entirely devoid of military targets? The reason was that the primary British objective was not destruction of Germany's military targets but the morale of the German people in the hope of speeding the Third Reich's collapse. In other words, the aim was the unrestrained killing of German civilians and destruction of their habitat until they surrendered. As one British historian noted, "From beginning to end, the Western allies encompassed the deaths of two or three German civilians for every German soldier they killed on the battlefield."(See Max Hastings, *Armageddon*, 299).

More than anything else could have done, the terroristic nature of the Anglo-American air campaign united the German people. Instead of breaking the home front, it strengthened it and instead of shortening the war it prolonged it. Incidentally, it was Churchill himself who used the word "terror" to describe Bomber Command's operations. In a post-Dresden minute to Charles Portal, the heard of the RAF, he stated: "It seems to me that the moment has come when the question of bombing of German cities simply for the sake of increasing the terror, though under other pretexts, should be reviewed." (See David Irving, *Apocalypse 1945: The Destruction of Dresden*, 267).

9. To verify the facts pertaining to my childhood recollection of the Platz der SA event, I contacted the Stadtarchiv Stuttgart (Stuttgart City Archives). Archivist Dr. Roland Müller replied that this particular bomb shelter was indeed hit towards the end of the war and, specifically, during one of four air raids between July 24 and July 29, 1944. In all

probability, Dr. Müller wrote, the Platz der SA event took place during the first and heaviest of these attacks, on the night of July 24/25. He referred me to a publication by the Stadtarchiv Stuttgart on the World War II Allied bombing campaign authored by Heinz Bardua and entitled *Stuttgart im Luftkrieg 1939-1945* [Stuttgart During the Air War 1939-1945]. An Appendix includes a lengthy report given by Stuttgart's mayor, Dr. Karl Strölin, to the city council on August 10, 1944 concerning the attacks of July 25, 26, 28, and 29, 1944 stating in part (in translation):

> *That the number of dead during these heavy attacks was kept within tolerable limits can be attributed to the fact that our population had so many bunkers, dugouts, and other safe places at their disposal. However, at the Platz der SA bunker an especially heavy direct hit came to explode within the ceiling ripping it open. Because the bomb unfortunately hit the partition wall between two cells, there were a total of 15 dead and 23 injured in the two cells. The remaining cells of the bunker remained intact. Efforts to repair the bunker are underway.*

From *Stuttgart im Luftkrieg 1939-1945*, 2nd edition, Stuttgart 1985. (Publications of the archives of the City of Stuttgart, Vol. 35), 254. Quoted by permission of the Stadtarchiv Stuttgart.

10. Stuttgart was just one of the many German cities and towns to suffer almost complete destruction. In fact, by the end of the war practically all of Germany's cities and major town had been reduced to rubble and on the order of one-half million civilians, including 70,000 children under the age of 14, killed. British civilian losses under what the British called The Blitz, were less than 10% of that number. In May 1942, Bomber Command sacked Cologne, an ancient town founded by the Romans, in a 1,000 bomber raid codenamed Operation Millennium. The bombings turned apocalyptical with the firebombing of Hamburg in July 1943, which the British codenamed *Operation Gomorrah*, and which took over a week to unfold with the objective of wiping the entire city from the face of the earth. Between 40,000 and 50,000 of the town's residents met a fiery death in the *Feuersturm* [firestorm]

the British managed to unleash. The bombings culminated in the immolation of Dresden, the capitol of Saxony, on February 13/14, 1945 by a combined British-American bomber fleet. That raid was initiated by British Prime Minister Winston Churchill to impress his Soviet allies with Anglo-American air power during his scheduled meeting with Roosevelt and Stalin at the Yalta (Crimea) Conference that month.

Bomber Command was led by British Air Marshal Arthur Harris who may be credited with destroying more towns and cities than any man in recorded history. He was to Winston Churchill what Adolf Eichmann was to Adolf Hitler and, like Eichmann, a psychopath. Both men were remorseless, unrepentant killers on a grand sale. When his superior, Charles Portal, suggested that he concentrate on military/industrial targets including oil plants, Harris replied in a letter dated November 1, 1944:

> In the past 18 months, Bomber Command has virtually destroyed 45 of the leading 60 German cities. In spite of invasion diversions, we have so far managed to keep up and even to exceed our average of 2 cities devastated a month.... There are not many industrial centres of population now left intact.....Are we now to abandon this vast task, which the Germans themselves have long admitted to be their worst headache, just as it nears completion?

(See Max Hastings, *Armageddon: The Battle For Germany, 1944-1945*, 304).

Harris concluded his letter by calling for the destruction of Magdeburg, Halle, Leipzig, Dresden, Chemnitz, Nuremberg, Munich, Coblenz, Karlsruhe and some undamaged areas of Berlin and Hanover. Portal, who was extremely deferential to his subordinate probably because Harris was in good standing with Churchill, gave the green light and the rampage continued with ever increasing intensity. At first, it was about breaking enemy morale and winning the war but eventually destroying and killing became an end in itself. For an overall history of the air war against Germany two books can be recommended: Randall Hansen's *Fire and Fury: The Allied Bombing of Germany, 1942-1945* and Jörg Friedrich's *The Fire: The Bombing of Germany 1940-1945*. Attacks on specific cities are chronicled in Keith Lowe's *Inferno: The Fiery Destruction of Hamburg 1943* and David Irving's *Apocalypse 1945: The Destruction of Dresden*. Incidentally, in order to discredit Irving's exposé of the Dresden massacre, first published in the U.S. in 1963, certain revisionist have managed to pin the label "Holocaust denier" on him. But as Shakespeare wrote, "Foul deeds will rise Though all the world o'erwhelm them, to men's eyes." (*Hamlet*, I.2). Also available is a DVD by PBS American Experience entitled *The Bombing of Germany*.

Arthur Harris is regarded as one of the heroes of the British Empire—after the war he was ennobled and in May 1992 had a statue erected in his honor in a London park. A monument honoring the over 55,000 Bomber Command aircrew who died in the campaign was unveiled more recently, in June 2012, by Queen Elizabeth II. In my personal opinion this memorial stands not only as a tribute to fallen bomber crews but also as a lasting reminder of the crimes, sins, and depravity of all military empires and their leaderships past and present. Beyond that, it also serves as a fitting tribute to the thousands of brave young German boys, some just barely into their teens, and old men who manned the antiaircraft guns and search lights and often paid the ultimate price in defense not of the regime in power but of their country.

11. The French occupation forces in Stuttgart turned the city over to the Americans in early July 1945 after just 10 weeks. The French under Charles de Gaulle, their provisional president, left very reluctantly because it was the only major German city under their control. President Harry S. Truman had to evict the general and his forces by threatening to cut off post-war financial aid to France if he did not comply. (See Michael Beschloss, *The Conquerors*, 276)

12. Some online research revealed that Eleanor Roosevelt did indeed visit Stuttgart after the war. The date was October 24, 1948. (I was twelve years old at the time). Mrs. Roosevelt's reception was not as friendly as Mutti had made it sound, based on the *Stuttgarter Zeitung* article she read, and Mrs. Roosevelt spoke not before politicians but to a group of German women doctors who were meeting there. According to her account, she was asked to come to Stuttgart by the governor of the

American zone, General Lucius Clay, and feared that she would receive a cool reception because of all the bad publicity she had received during the Hitler era.

Indeed, Mrs. Roosevelt found her audience was "cool and reserved if not bitter towards me" especially when she began denouncing the Nazi philosophy and actions and telling the doctors that the German people must bear their share of the blame. She then started to talk more approvingly, she wrote, saying that she hoped that the United Nations would bring an end to international wars and that Germany would flourish under a democratic form government. Her audience, she wrote, slowly warmed up to her and she could feel a change in attitude. Mrs. Roosevelt concluded her remarks with, "And now I extend to you the hand of friendship and cooperation." (See *The Autobiography of Eleanor Roosevelt*, 321).

13. The city of Stuttgart had its beginning around 950 AD when Duke Liudolf von Schwaben, a son of Holy Roman Emperor (Kaiser) Otto I the Great (912-973), started a *Stutengarten* [stud farm] to breed horses for the imperial army. This is the origin of the name Stuttgart and the city's seal fittingly contains a prancing stallion. The region around Stuttgart, like that of the city itself, went through a series of name changes but eventually became known as Württemberg. Württemberg was part of the Holy Roman Empire and ruled by counts of which the first was Ulrich I the Founder (1226-1265 AD). In 1495 the county became a duchy and in 1806, when the Holy Roman Empire was dissolved, Napoleon made Württemberg a kingdom. At that time, the adjoining territory of Baden became the Grand Duchy of Baden. After the Second World War, Württemberg (with Stuttgart as its capital) and Baden (with its capital in Karlsruhe) became *Länder* [states] in the newly created Federal Republic of Germany. A constitutional convention in March 1952 united Baden and Württemberg and the territory became the state of Baden-Württemberg (BW) with Stuttgart as its capital.

The region including Baden, Württemberg, and the western part of Bavaria is also known as Schwaben (Swabia) for the ancient Germanic tribe known to the Romans as the *Suebi*. The first known inhabitants of the region were the Celts. The Romans conquered the area in the first century AD only to be driven out by the Alemanni early in the third century. With their defeat by the Franks in 496 AD, the Alemanni were incorporated into the Frankish kingdom. During the early Middle Ages Schwaben was a duchy ruled by the Hohenstaufen family from which sprang several German kings and Holy Roman emperors (Kaiser) until 1268 AD when 16-year-old Conradin von Hohenstaufen was executed by Charles I of Anjou on treason charges in a dispute over the Kingdom of Sicily. With Conradin's death, the Hohenstaufen dynasty became extinct and the duchy was abolished. The native dialect of the region was *schwäbisch* [Swabian] which is now only spoken by old-timers. It has been replaced by *hochdeutsch* [high German], the language now taught in the schools throughout Germany, Austria, Lichtenstein, and parts of Switzerland.

14. What I did not know at the time was that what Mutti euphemistically called *hamstern* was actually part of a *Schwarzmarkt* [black market] operation. Black marketeering is defined as "illicit trade in goods or commodities in violation of official regulations." Black markets usually develop when there is a disruption in the distribution system so that the normal rules of supply and demand are no longer operative, i.e., one group of people may have goods that another wants and vice versa but they are unwilling to sell these on the open market for one reason or another. In Germany after World War II, some *Bauern* had foodstuffs and were in need of other essentials such as clothing or bed linen while some city dwellers had the merchandise but were short on foodstuffs.

The reason people did not sell their goods was because the currency, which was the Reichsmark at the time, was nearly worthless and each group was waiting for the so-called *Währungsreform* [currency revaluation] to come into effect. In the meantime a barter trade developed in which, although officially illegal, many people who had access to desired merchandise took part including ordinary citizens, concentration camp survivors, and American GIs.

The Jewish Holocaust survivors living in Germany after the war were supplied with merchandise by American relatives and Jewish relief organizations and were eager to sell their goods for U.S. dollars because they needed the money for their anticipated resettlement in the United States or Palestine. The long anticipated currency revaluation came on June 20, 1948 when 100 of the old Reichsmark (RM) were exchangeable for 6.5 of the new Deutsche Mark (DM). The previously horded merchandise now became available again in the stores and the black market came to an abrupt end.

Mutti participated in the *Schwarzmarkt* because, like many people at the time, she was looking for food to fill our pantry which would have been nearly empty had it not been for her efforts. While I never bothered to ask her how the scheme worked in our particular case, I suspect that it was as follows: Sister Esther, who was now employed in upstate New York, mailed Mutti a small sum of money every week or so—I heard it was just $10. Mutti took these dollars to Frau Adler on Reinsburgstraße and bought merchandise her customers in the Remstal were looking for. There she exchanged this merchandise for scarce food items. Most of this food she kept for our own use while the remainder she sold to friends and neighbors for needed cash in Reichsmark. These transactions were made illegal because they benefited only a minority of people, promoted hording of scarce commodities, and deprived the state of sales tax revenues. The police conducted sporadic raids on suspected black market operations in Stuttgart and elsewhere.

15. The police raid Mutti and I witnessed was most likely the one that took place a year after the end of World War II when the black market in Germany was in full swing. The raid in March 1946 (when I would have been 9 years old) is described by Oxford historian Nicholas Stargardt as follows:

> *But even in the US Zone, Jewish DPs [Displaced Persons] did not have an easy time. As Jews became a larger proportion of the remaining DPs, so the old image of the Jew as the archetypical swindler gained new currency. On 29 March 1946, 180 German police accompanied by dogs raided a Jewish camp in the Reinsburg Strasse in Stuttgart looking for black-market goods. Although they found only a few eggs, they provoked a full-scale fight with the Jewish DPs. One concentration camp survivor who had only recently been reunited with his wife and two children was killed. The American Military Government immediately responded by barring German police from entering Jewish camps.*

From *The German War: A Nation Under Arms* by Nicholas Stargardt, copyright © 2015. Reprinted by permission of Basic Books, an imprint of Hachette Book Group, Inc., 550 & From *The German War* by Nicholas Stargardt. Published by Vintage. Reprinted by permission of the Random House Group Limited © 2016.

16. Pastor Lang may be forgiven for being as embittered as he was and to loathe the American and British militaries for the destruction of Stuttgart's houses of worship. He was fully justified. Of the 36 churches in Stuttgart proper including Heslach, of which 26 were *evangelisch* [Evangelical Lutheran] and 10 *katholisch* [Roman Catholic], 23, i.e., close to two-thirds were either completely destroyed or severely damaged. Only four Stuttgart churches survived unscathed. (See Hans Bardua, *Stuttgart im Luftkrieg 1939-1945*, 309-310). One must surmise that the churches became prime bombing targets because when one attempts to demoralize a Christian population, as the British leadership did, one way to do so would be to raze the places where it would typically find hope and solace in times of trial and tribulation.

17. According to historical records, General Douglas MacArthur came to Chicago on April 26, 1951, 15 days after he was relieved of his NATO command in Korea. Chicago gave him a rousing welcome with three million people lining the official parade route along State Street and then down Michigan Avenue. In the evening, an enthusiastic crowd of 50,000 people heard him speak at Soldier Field, a stadium near Lake Michigan, followed by a fireworks display. In his speech, the general called for a realistic end to the Korean conflict with a minimum loss of American lives. America's goal, he said, should be "victory over the nation and men who, without provocation, have attacked us." The nation he was referring to was, of course, China. That country had, by its military intervention, forced him and his army to retreat to the 38th parallel dividing the two Koreas and thus to the starting point of the war. General MacArthur wanted retribution against China by use of the nation's nuclear arsenal which greatly alarmed many people at the time and especially President Truman.

18. None of the family saw Officer Bolstad again after Volker, Ute, and I stayed at his house. Sometime after my return to the States, I was

shocked to learn that our erstwhile benefactor had committed suicide. My more recent inquiry with the Oak Park police department revealed that the officer's full name was William H. Bolstad, that he joined the department on January 10, 1944, and died on September 18, 1951. His death, therefore, occurred just seven weeks after Esther had returned the three of us to Germany. It is very disquieting to think that this very good and compassionate man may have felt guilty enough to take his life after his parents had reneged on their promise to take us in during our mother's temporary absence. It was especially sad because for me and my two siblings our return to Germany was only a temporary setback and not a major calamity.

19. Tom Doherty and I stayed in touch after I left his employ following my high school graduation. He and his wife had moved to Florida after their retirement and bought a condominium in West Palm Beach. There Tom passed away after suffering a fall in his home in July 1999 at age 88. Susan, his daughter, wrote me of his death and let me know that her father had always fondly remembered me as his best and favorite newsboy.

20. *Heimatfilme* were very popular with Germans and Austrians during the 1950s and 1960s because, with the cities and towns lying in ruin after the recent war, people were drawn to the countryside. The venue of the simple love story was usually a picturesque little village in a scenically attractive part of the country such as Bavaria or the Black Forest. The story lines were diverse but in one popular one the protagonist would be a lowly but pretty country girl, such as the daughter of an innkeeper or a *Kinderfräulein* [governess], who would meet her prince charming in a high-status individual such as a member of the nobility, the scion of a wealthy family, or a medical doctor. After falling in love and successfully overcoming all kinds of obstacles, there would be a happy end with the two getting married in the village church followed by a procession of brass bands and villagers in folk costumes and a big wedding feast. Many of the most popular *Heimatfilme*, such as the 1958 comedy hit *13 Kleine Esel und der Sonnenhof* [13 Little Donkeys and the Sonnenhof] with Hans Albers and Marianne Hoppe, were later released as DVDs while some others have been uploaded to YouTube.

PART I

THE ANCESTORS

OPA

The Early Years

As some parents were wont to do, after the birth of Esther, her first child, Mutti referred to her father and mother as *Opa* [grandpa] and *Oma* [grandma], respectively. Opa Peter Zell was a native of Krefeld, a town on the Rhine River northwest of Köln (Cologne), where he was born an hour and a half past midnight on September 25, 1872 and baptized on May 11 of the following year in that town's Evangelical (Lutheran) Church. Peter was the son of Johann Peter Zell and his wife Louise Zell née Kirchhoff. My Great-grandfather Johann Peter came into the world on May 26, 1814 in Wuppertal-Elberfeld while my Great-grandmother Louise Kirchhoff was born on January 30, 1839 in Krefeld. Both were *evangelisch* and baptized shortly after their births.

The couple had married on January 5, 1872 in Krefeld. From these dates, it is apparent that at the time of his birth, Opa's father was already 58 years of age while his mother was just 33, an age difference of 25 years. But this was Johann Peter's second marriage and he had already sired six children, four girls and two boys, by his first wife, Anna Maria Zell née Backhaus.[1] Three more children came out of his marriage with Louise Kirchhoff, namely, Peter (Opa), Gustav Adolph, and Carl Wilhelm. Johann Peter passed away on October 29, 1895 at age 81 in Krefeld while his wife Louise followed less than a year later, on September 9, 1896, at age 57.

According to Mutti, her Grandfather Johann Peter was well enough off to retire early in life. The source of his supposed wealth is not clear, however. When he married Anna Maria Backhaus on May 21, 1842, at age 28, he gave his occupation as *Anstreicher* [house painter]. This does not suggest an affluent background unless he had his own business and did exceptionally well for himself. By the time of his marriage to Louise Kirchhoff 30 years later, his occupational status had changed to *Rentner* [retiree]. His new wife did, however, come from a well-to-do family. Her mother was Friederike Luise Kirchhoff née Wittig (1814-1870) and the Wittig family of Krefeld was in the *Samt und Seide* [silk and velvet] business.

Little is known of Opa's childhood or early youth. Presumably he attended the Volksschule in Krefeld and possibly a Gymnasium (secondary school). Since he carried the title *Ingenieur* [engineer] but not the more prestigious title of *Diplom-Ingenieur* [graduate engineer], it could be presumed that he studied at one of the many German engineering schools which had a more practical, job-related orientation rather than a Technische Hochschule (technical university). That presumption turned out to be correct because when Mutti's Brother Ludwig (Lulu) filled out his application for Nazi Party membership he stated that his father attended the Technikum Mittweida in Sachsen (Kingdom of Saxony) during 1892-1896. Inquiries at that school revealed that Opa was indeed a student at the Technikum Mittweida (since 1969 known as Hochschule Mittweida / University of Applied Science) but the dates were incorrect. According to the school's archives, Opa matriculated on March 3, 1890 to study *Maschinenbau* [mechanical engineering] but did not graduate. In fact, he was expelled on September 30, 1891 after just one full year of class attendance.

As the correspondence between the school and his father, then living in an apartment on Moerser Straße 91 in Krefeld, show, the reasons for Opa's expulsion were progressively worsening grades and several infractions including gross misconduct in two instances resulting in a fine of 10 Marks. He was also accused of an attempted deception of a teacher by submitting fraudulent drawings. Despite Johann Peter's desperate pleas to keep his errand son in school, a school official named Kirchhoff (also his wife's maiden name) wrote him on October 27, 1891 that the school regrets not being able to change its decision but could favorably consider an application for readmission after a year's gainful employment with good references. The correspondence also revealed that Opa was hard of hearing which was probably the reason he was later exempted from the military draft. According to Mutti, her father was an active member of a Rheno-Westphalian *Landsmannschaft* [fraternity] and this might partly explain Opa's disgraceful conduct because these student organizations were notorious for being rowdy. The records show that Opa never returned to the Technikum Mittweida to complete his engineering education.

An Engineering Career

After this shaky start, Opa was nevertheless able to build a solid career in engineering. According to Mutti, her father was employed as an engineer by a small company in Frankfurt am Main for several years and there learned all aspects of his profession. Around 1907, her father joined the Chemische Fabrik Griesheim-Elektron as an engineer. The company had its start in 1856 as a manufacturer of fertilizer and herbicides. Griesheim, where the factory was located, was a small town a few miles southwest of Frankfurt am Main and near the north side of the river. In 1925, the three largest German chemical companies of the day, namely, Farbwerke Hoechst, Badische Anilin und Soda Fabrik (BASF), and Bayer, combined with a number of smaller firms, including Chemische Fabrik Griesheim-Elektron (then also known as Autogen), to form I.G. Farbenindustrie Aktiengesellschaft (Syndicate of dyestuff companies), or I.G. Farben, for short. Henceforth, the Griesheim plant was called I.G. Farben, Werk Autogen.

What had attracted the attention of I.G. Farben was Autogen's expertise in electric arc and gas welding and cutting technology. Griesheim engineers were pioneers in that field and had perfected the technique in the years 1902-1904. It required the use and controlled release of certain gases, acetylene and oxygen, which, in turn, called for devices to control and measure gas pressure. This led Opa and the other Autogen engineers to develop pressure gauges and similar instrumentation. I.G. Farben eventually became Germany's largest private company but, unfortunately, also one of its most notorious because of its alleged collaboration with the National Socialists (Nazis) during World War II.[2]

By the time Opa started to work for Chemische Fabrik Griesheim, he and Oma had already lived in Schwanheim am Main, a village right across from Griesheim on the south side of the Main River, for a number of years.[3] Schwanheim was a small community of single family homes, some rental buildings, diverse retail shops, small manufacturing plants, and many *Gaststätten* [inns, pubs]. Schwanheimer were mostly *Bauern*, skilled craftsmen, shopkeepers, salaried employees, professionals, and *Beamte* [carrier civil service employees]. The population also included many blue collar workers who had found employment in Griesheim, Hoechst and other industrial communities in the Frankfurt area. Much of the social life took place in the Gaststätten where the many *Vereine* [clubs, social organizations] held their meetings. The community was tight-knit with many of the families being related to each other and of a long lineage.

One thing that set the Zell family apart from the other villagers was their religion in that it was *evangelisch* while most Schwanheimer were *katholisch*. In fact, three-quarters of Schwanheim's population, which by 1928 totaled about 5,800 souls, was Roman Catholic and worshipped in the imposing Mauritiuskirche, which, with its 235 foot bell tower, was visible from afar and popularly known as the Dom im Maingau (cathedral of the Main region). The *Evangelische Martinsgemeinde*, to which the Zell family belonged, did not get its own church building until November 1911 and before then worshipped in a chapel.

According to a *Heiratsurkunde* [marriage certificate] issued by the Standesamt (registrar's office) of the city of Frankfurt am Main, *Ingenieur* Peter Zell and Auguste Rosa Sareika, a native of Straßburg, were married on October 31, 1898. The union between Peter and Rosa was blessed by the arrival of four children—two boys and two girls: Carl Peter's birth in November 1899 was followed by Ludwig Friedrich's in February 1901, Louise Emma's in December 1903, and Anna Maria's in March 1909.

Since this was the period of the Kaiserreich (empire) and Kaiser Wilhelm II (reigned 1888-1918), it is not surprising that the nobility played a prominent role in the life of the family. In fact, two additional family members were of this select group even though it was just the dog nobility. These were the Irish setters Flora von Bärensprung and Asta von Warendorf. The "von" (from) in their names attested to their noble origins. In addition, there were two Angora cats whose names, alas, were not mentioned by Mutti and therefore cannot be recorded for posterity. Presumably, they were commoners and thus at the bottom of the family totem pole. This did not mean, however, that they were in any way treated with less deference.

When one of Mutti's friends came by the house once towards the evening, she was astonished to see the two hefty felines sitting on the dining room table enjoying supper with the rest of the family. To have four pets in a household at this time of food shortages was most unusual. When once one of the boys went to buy a bag of rice and, when questioned by the proprietor, told him it was for the family dogs, word quickly spread through the village and people became indignant. Perhaps it was just coincidence but not long after one of the two noble bitches died of food poisoning.

By all accounts, the head of the Zell household was an affable and cultured man whose one passion in life was his work. When World War I broke out in the summer of 1914 and Opa was employed by the Chemische Fabrik Griesheim, he began to energetically apply his engineering expertise to the war effort. At the time, the military airplane had been perfected and was being used by both sides to affect the outcome of the war by aerial combat between enemy fighters or bombing of military and even civilian targets.

The first enemy bombs had fallen on German soil and Opa was feverishly working on a technique to hide his factory as well as others from enemy attacks by engulfing them in clouds of dense smoke to make it difficult for enemy pilots to locate specific targets such as oil and gas storage tanks. These were much prevalent at the Griesheim factory which was one of the largest explosive suppliers to the German Army during the war.

Mutti remembered her father often working on his smoke generating experiments out of their home. For a long time, she recalled, every evening after supper and most Sundays her father would retreat to his laboratory to perfect his technique and thick clouds of white smoke could be seen billowing out of the upstairs window of a room on the garden side of the house.

Mutti's most vivid memory of the war years was when late one evening Lulu, who had just been paying a visit to the outhouse in the backyard, came running upstairs and started banging on his parent's bedroom door shouting, "*Papa, Papa, der Himmel über Autogen ist ganz rot.*" [Papa, papa, the sky over Autogen is completely red]. Opa jumped out of bed, saw the conflagration across the river, hastily dressed, and got on his bicycle to drive over the Main River bridge to the factory. He found the place engulfed in flames and cordoned off.

Recognizing him, the police let Opa pass and, with some fellow employees already lying dead or injured on the ground, he scampered up one storage tank after another to open the valves to prevent further explosions. Opa's heroic efforts, Mutti recalled, were reported in the papers and congratulatory telegrams received at home for several days thereafter.

A local paper, the *Höchster Kreisblatt,* carried the following report in their November 22, 1917 issue about the accident two days earlier (in translation):

Explosion in Griesheim

> It has been officially reported: Tuesday at 9:50 in the evening an explosion occurred in the factory "Griesheim-Elektron" which caused a fire that was visible from afar when it ignited a lumberyard. The well organized security measure worked superbly. Management and work force showed much circumspection and calmness. The factory fire department and those of Frankfurt and Höchst, which responded immediately, were soon able to localize the fire and put it out. Clearance work is already in progress; production will be maintained. Concerning human losses, no determination has as yet been made. Five people were reported missing and twelve injured.

The low-key reporting was in keeping with war-time practices not to reveal too much lest it alarm the home front and encourage the enemy. This is also why no names were reported of either victims or first responders like Opa. This explosion was actually the second to take place at the Griesheim plant. An earlier and much more severe one occurred on the afternoon of April 25, 1901 which took the lives of 26 employees and wounded 200 more.

While Opa much enjoyed his work as an engineer, he had other interests as well. According to Mutti, in his younger days her father was active in diverse sports clubs. He took part in rowing and biking competitions and owned a motorbike which he raced competitively. A photograph of him as a young man shows him with a sash down his chest covered with an array of sports medals he had won.

One of the civic projects Opa got involved in shortly after the family arrived in Schwanheim was the teaching of shorthand or stenography. He had evidently acquired that skill along the way. With the increasing industrialization of the country in the late 19th century and early 1900s there arose a demand for office workers. At the same time, there was an abundant supply of young people in the villages, including Schwanheim, eager to work in the relatively clean environment of an office while earning a decent wage. The key to success for these aspiring office employees was proficiency in shorthand and typing.

Among the papers left by Opa were the *Statuten* [by-laws] for an organization called *Stenographen-Verein Gabelsberger zu Schwanheim am Main* [Gabelsberger Stenographers Club of Schwanheim on Main] which he and two like-minded villagers founded on September 7, 1903 and registered with the village of Schwanheim seven days later. Purpose of the group was the promotion of stenography by the system known as Gabelsberger and specifically to i) offer instruction in shorthand, ii) train professional stenographers, and iii) build and maintain a library. There were to be regular, associate, corresponding and honorary members. Regular and corresponding members had to be proficient in shorthand. The board was to consist of a chairman, a secretary, and a treasurer. The 3-page document was signed by Opa, serving as chairman, and the two other officers.

As World War I came to an end in November 1918, Mutti recalled, her father dreaded the impending collapse of the old order and what might follow. All his life Opa had been *kaisertreu* [loyal to the emperor] and the slogan, *Gott, Kaiser und Vaterland* [God, emperor and fatherland] pretty much summed up his weltanschauung. He and his family were part of the establishment and he was very fearful of any change in the status quo. The post-war era would bring turmoil and street riots as Communists, Socialists, and ultranationalists would struggle for control of the state while anarchists would fight to do away with the state altogether, he predicted. The hoi polloi, which he had always disdained, would now be triumphant.

Opa never talked about democracy. Perhaps he did not think it would work in Germany where people always opted for strong leadership and considered democratic governments as inherently weak and dysfunctional. Opa's deliberations proved almost prophetic. The street battles did occur until one group on the extreme right would emerge victorious and, in restoring order out of chaos, turn the Reich into a Fascist dictatorship.

Shortly after the war, emissaries of the large American chemical and other companies started arriving in the country to recruit the cream of German physicists, chemists, and engineers for work in the United States. A delegation also arrived at the Zell home in Schwanheim am Main, Mutti remembered, and tried to persuade Opa to emigrate. Germany had been defeated and there was no future here, he was told, while in America new job opportunities and an affluent lifestyle awaited him and his family. According to Mutti, Opa listened for some time when he stood up and said, *"Meine Herren, geben sie sich keine weitere Mühe—ich bin Deutscher und bleib Deutscher."* [Gentlemen, do not trouble yourselves any longer—I am German and will remain German].

Opa had never particularly liked Americans whom he referred to as *diese Hottentoten* [those Hottentots]. Like the rest of his countrymen, he had read about the U.S. government-sponsored anti-German mass hysteria that had swept the country during the war and which had subjected Americans of German ancestry, a substantial part of the population, to severe harassment and every sort of indignity imaginable including the suppression of German-language newspapers, the public burning of German books and musical scores, and the boycotting of German-American businesses. With the entry of the United States in April 1917 on the side of England and France, a European war had became a world war and the large German-American community had quickly become America's pariah.

In the beginning, Autogen's acquisition by I.G. Farben in 1925 was very favorable to Opa's career and led to the expansion of his duties and responsibilities. The parent company's management recognized his unusual talents in solving technical and manufacturing problems and made him a trouble-shooter for the whole of I.G. Farben. His job was to ensure that its factories were kept running. Mutti remembered several occasions when at odd hours of the day or night the company car would come by to pick up her father and take him to the Frankfurt airport. There a plane would be waiting to fly him to some distant part of the country where he was urgently needed.

Mutti recalled a funny incident when her father was flown to a plant in eastern Germany because the technical staff had problems with a new piece of machinery. Management and technical personnel were standing by the equipment awaiting Opa's arrival anxious to see what *Oberingenieur* [senior engineer] Zell would do to get it started. It took him just a minute or two to find the source of the problem—one of the components had not been plugged into an electrical outlet. The red faced staff offered all sorts of explanations and apologies. "No wonder we lost the war," Opa supposedly quipped.

Despite the high esteem he was held by the company's management, Opa remained a very modest and self-effacing man. According to Mutti, her father was repeatedly offered a directorship on the company's board but always declined saying that he was happy with just being a good engineer and did not want to be bothered with management responsibilities.

Coping With National Socialism

Many changes came to Germany and I.G. Farben in the early 1930s with the arrival on the scene of the ultraright National Socialists or Nazis as they were derisively called by their opponents. At the beginning, Opa considered them and their Austrian leader just rabble-rousers that would eventually disappear again as had other upstart political organizations in the past. But this group proved to be entirely different—it became more than just another party but a movement with broad appeal to the masses. As a result of the prevailing chaotic political and economic conditions in the country following the Reich's defeat in World War I, their leader Adolf Hitler's oratory skills, and his promises to restore order and bring back jobs, the Nazis gained in strength and by January 1933 were in power.

Before long, most of the I.G. Farben management team had joined the Nazi Party, then simply known as *die Partei* [the Party], and the chief engineer at Autogen was among them. Opa's boss came by the house now and then, Mutti recalled, dressed in *Partei* uniform complete with boots and swastika armband and they would leave in the company car for Klingenberg am Main, a town about 40 miles southeast of Frankfurt, where I.G. Farben maintained a warehouse. Opa never became a member of the Party despite the pressures put on him to join. He had good reason to be anti-Nazi. The National Socialists were virulently anti-Semitic and his own daughter was married to a Jew while her in-laws, the Würzburgers, together with their friends and fellow businessmen from Höchst, the Schiffs, were all Jews.

It did not take long before the injustice created by anti-Semitism became intensely personal even for Opa and he could not simply remain a bystander. Jewish businesses were placed off limits by Nazi Brownshirts who posted themselves at the entrances to discourage shoppers from entering. Not surprisingly, sales at these establishments plunged and once thriving businesses began to flounder and fail as even loyal customers stayed away rather than confront these ruffians. Men of the *Sturmabteilung* [storm troopers] or SA also came to be stationed at the entrances of the Schiff and Würzburger stores with the inevitable results. After some time, the only shoppers to come by were family and good friends and a few courageous souls who dared show their defiance of the new regime and its policies.

Opa was one of the few to show considerable chutzpah in the face of gross injustice. He did not need anything in the way of new clothing or other items but he continued to shop at the Schiff department and Würzburger clothing stores anyway. As Mutti recalled, when her father showed up at the Würzburger haberdashery and was about to enter, he was confronted by a burly storm trooper standing at the entrance. The man gruffly confronted Opa saying, *"Wissen Sie daß Sie bei Juden kaufen?"* [Are you aware that you are buying from Jews?]. That was a loaded question because glued to the store windows were large notices warning potential shoppers that the store was Jewish-owned and was not to be entered. Now, Opa was a very mild-mannered and civil man and Mutti had never heard of him using profanity until this instance. *"Wo ich einkaufe geht Sie einen Scheißdreck an"* [Where I shop is none of your shitty business] was Opa's shocking reply.

At home, Opa was quiet and reserved. He loved the orderly life and did most everything by the numbers. While he exerted a strong influence on family affairs, he stayed mostly in the background and let Oma run the household. By nature he was somewhat aloof yet very approachable by his children. Mutti and her siblings were awed by their father's seeming encyclopedic mind because they could ask him a question on any topic and get a full and plausible answer.

Automobile ownership was not common at the time and the family did not own one. Fortunately, Autogen was within walking distance of the house. At Easter 1907, the first bridge in the area spanning the Main River had been opened connecting Schwanheim with Griesheim. Opa would leave early in the morning and walk across the bridge to work and return about noon for a long, 2-hour lunch break during which he would take a little nap or work the crossword puzzle. He would and then light his cigar and walk back to the factory.

On Saturday, Opa worked half a day and, after returning home, he would change and take off by himself for Frankfurt am Main on the Waldbahn. The Waldbahn (forest railway) was a privately owned, miniature steam railway that connected several communities with a terminal in the Sachsenhausen district of Frankfurt. This was Opa's time off from job and family. What he did in Frankfurt is anybody's guess but Oma suspected that he either had a lady friend there or frequented the red light district which was then (and is now) located near the Hauptbahnhof and, specifically, on some side streets off the Kaiserstraße, a broad boulevard that leads to the Hauptbahnhof.

One time her mother sent Annemarie to Frankfurt to check up on her father's extracurricular activities. After reconnoitering the Hauptbahnhof area, Mutti spotted him sitting at the Café Hauptwache in downtown Frankfurt having his coffee and reading the paper. When Mutti reported back to her mother, Oma interpreted this to mean that Opa was probably waiting to pick up some prostitute. Her husband's suspected philandering caused Oma much mental and emotional anguish. Her suspicions may not have been entirely unfounded as circumstantial evidence relating to his final illness would indicate.

Another one of his major faults, as Mutti saw it, was her father's lack of concern for his family's financial future. Thus, he never purchased a home for his family which his well paying position would have allowed him to do. In fact, it was quite unusual for a man in his position as a senior engineer with one of Germany's major companies not to own his own home. Instead, he preferred to live in rent like most of the non-salaried employees and hourly wage earners at Autogen. The reason, he explained, was that he did not want to be bothered with the responsibility that came with home ownership. According to Mutti, he had owned a house in Frankfurt am Main but sold it during the worst possible moment during the post-war financial crisis leaving him minus a house but a bundle of worthless cash.

Throughout most of his long career at I.G. Farben, the family lived at Feldbergstraße 8 in a nondescript working class house that was in the traditional two-story brick construction with a slanting roof.[4] These unadorned houses lined the treeless streets of old Schwanheim like soldiers in formation. This was the place Opa and Oma had moved into a few years after their marriage and the birth of their two children Carl and Ludwig in Frankfurt am Main. It was not until about 1930 when the family left the Feldbergstraße for more attractive, although smaller, quarters at Vogesenstraße 40. There they rented the second floor of a modern two-story building located in a leafy part of the village.

Opa's financial concept was that his family would enjoy a relatively affluent life style during his lifetime which he apparently assumed would be a long one since he was always in good health. Specifically, his two daughters would marry *standesgemäss* [in accordance with the family's social rank] and receive a generous *Aussteuer* [dowry] while the two sons would receive a good education and make their own way after that. Consequently, he left his children no real property. Mutti claimed that Opa's philandering and his refusal to buy a home were related. He spent so much money on his extramarital affairs, she claimed, that he could not also afford to buy a house even at his princely salary. What Mutti did not mention was that her mother was not herself a model of thriftiness and that a good portion of Opa's salary must have gone to support her costly lifestyle as she was fond of fashionable clothes.

The Final Years

The mid and late 1930s brought pivotal changes in Opa's life. In 1935 he had to accept early retirement presumably because of bad health. Whatever might have been its cause, it could only have been exasperated by the emotional turmoil he must have gone through at the time. Three years earlier Oma had unexpectedly passed away while recuperating from surgery. At work the atmosphere had become decidedly toxic for one not in tune with the new regime. On top of that, Opa's own son Lulu had announced his intention of joining *die Partei*.

The Nazis had by now fully ensconced themselves at I. G. Farben. In September 1934 a new factory code went into effect by which I.G. Farben employees, including those at the Griesheim factory, were urged to show "a joyful commitment to the National Socialist state and its Führer" as well as "unwavering loyalty to the plant community, the *Volksgemeinschaft* [national community] and the German fatherland." New words were coined to express the new leadership style. Thus, a factory became a *Betriebsgemeinschaft* [plant community], the company head was called a *Betriebsführer* [plant leader] and the employees the *Gefolgschaft* [followers].

Much pressure was exerted for managers and employees to join *die Partei* and most top managers did so. Early retirement was the fate of Jews and many who were eyed askance because of some Jewish connection. As to the nature of Opa's illness, Esther once told me he had contracted syphilis which, however, no other family member who would have known as, for example, Uncle Lulu's side of the family, could corroborate.

For whatever reason, by early 1937 Opa was in very bad physical shape. In a letter dated March 12, 1937, the head of the *Nervenklinik* [neurological clinic] of Frankfurt University, located in Frankfurt-Niederrad, wrote Lulu in Bitterfeld that his father was being treated for an *organische Gehirnerkrankung* [organic mental disease] the outcome of which could not yet be predicted but that his [Lulu's] presence was not required. In another letter from November of that year, Lulu wrote his Uncle Gustav that his father had suffered a severe stroke the previous April and that his sister [Annemarie] and their father had recently moved to Graben.

I.G. Farben's management, to its credit, did its best to smooth over Opa's transition into early retirement which would obviously be another severe emotional blow for him. He was given a monthly pension of 900 Reichsmark which was very generous for the time. The management also showed its gratitude for his many years of dedicated service by having a retirement ceremony for him and making him a gift of an attractive, modern-style grandfather clock. Now and then, Mutti recalled, the company car would stop by to take her father for a ride into the country. His desk at work was kept as he left it and he was allowed to keep a set of keys to the office and told that he was free to return at any time of day or night at his pleasure.

In the fall of 1937, Mutti and Opa permanently left Frankfurt-Schwanheim for Graben to be close to a relative, a *Tante Johanna*, for moral support and a helping hand. Despite his poor physical condition and mental impairment, Mutti recalled, her father retained his courtly and meticulous manner to the end. He insisted on being formally dressed every day and continuously checked to make sure that his tie was in place. The doctor in Graben, a typical country practitioner, could, understandably, not do much for Opa and after his condition kept worsening, Opa was brought to the university hospital at Heidelberg for treatment. The doctors' best efforts to save him proved in vain, however, and he passed away after a short stay.

Opa's death certificate issued in Heidelberg on May 17, 1938, states that *Oberingenieur im Ruhestand* [senior engineer in retirement] Peter Zell of Graben, district of Karlsruhe, age 65, born in Krefeld, widower of Auguste Rosa née Sareika, died on May 12, 1938 in Heidelberg. No cause of death is given. His body was cremated in Heidelberg and Mutti brought her father's ashes back to Frankfurt-Schwanheim for interment next to Oma in the old Schwanheim cemetery.

Opa had been employed by Chemische Fabrik Griesheim and I.G. Farben for 30 years yet practically no documentation about his employment there exists. After Farbwerke Hoechst was taken over by Sanofi-Aventis, a French chemical and pharmaceutical company, the personnel files of Hoechst and the associated I.G. Farben companies in the area were deposited with a new firm called Hoechst A.G. located in the Industriepark Hoechst (Hoechst Industrial Park). According to the Sanofi archivist there, no personnel files from the Griesheim plant, with a few exceptions, still exist. However, he did locate a brief notice announcing Peter Zell's passing in the July 1938 issue of *Von Werk zu Werk* [From Factory to Factory] for the Maingau region of I.G. Farben. It states that Peter Zell, a retiree, had worked at the Griesheim plant in the *Abteilung Gase* [Section Gases]. The other document attesting to his employment at I.G. Farben is an obituary that appeared in as yet unidentified publication:[5]

Am Donnerstag, den 12. Mai 1938, verschied nach längerer, schwerer Krankheit unser im Ruhestand lebender

Peter Zell

Ingenieur

Der Verstorbene war 30 Jahre bei uns tätig und hat uns infolge seiner vielseitigen Kenntnisse und Fähigkeiten besonders auch während des Krieges, wertvolle Dienste geleistet.

Durch seine persönlichen Eigenschaften und sein schlichtes Wesen, erwarb er sich die Wertschätzung seiner Vorgesetzten und Mitarbeiter.

Führer und Gefolgschaft
der I. G. Farbenindustrie Aktiengesellschaft
Werk Autogen, Ffm.-Griesheim.

Die Einäscherung im Krematorium Heidelberg ist bereits erfolgt.   [12907

The I.G. Farben obituary states that Opa passed away on May 12, 1938 after a long, severe illness. The diseased was with the company for 30 years, it states, during which he performed valuable services, especially also during the war, on account of his wide-ranging knowledge and abilities. The notice also lauds his character traits and unpretentious demeanor which earned him the esteem of fellow employees and the management

Opa's notice does contain one peculiarity. His death certificate, as well as other documents, list him as *Oberingenieur i. R..* [senior engineer in retirement]. The company obituary, however, refers to him simply as an engineer. Perhaps the ever modest Opa would have preferred it that way. But what would accounts for this post mortem demotion? Most likely it was another price Opa had to pay for his stubborn refusal to join *die Partei* and his obstinate and vociferous opposition to the new regime which had come to power five years earlier. At least Opa, by his early passing, was spared having to witness the start of yet another war and the horrors that would accompany it. That war, which came to be known as World War II, was just a little over a year away.

OMA

A Tough Beginning

When Peter Zell married Auguste Rosa Sareika it caused a rift between him and his family because his new wife was not *vom Stand* [of compatible social standing] meaning that she was socially unacceptable to the Zells and Kirchhoffs of Krefeld. In those days parity was expected of marriage partners in terms of social class and wealth. This was apparently not the case here and Oma suffered mentally and emotionally throughout her marriage from being snubbed by her husband's family. Augusta Rosa Sareika was born at nine o'clock in the morning of May 4, 1875 in Strassburg.[6] Oma's birth certificate gives her first name as Augusta but all subsequent documents refer to her as Auguste. She was the daughter of August Sareika and Maria Catharina Sareika née Wormer. Her birth took place at Langstraße 62 (Langstross 62 in Alsatian), which is now the Grand'rue and lies in the center of town. This confirms what Mutti told me, namely, that her mother was born *im Schatten des Münsters* [in the shadow of the cathedral].

Neither of Oma's parents was Alsatians by birth. Maria Catharina Wormer's birthplace was Landstuhl in the Pfalz (Rhenish-Palatinate) where she was born on July 20, 1848, the daughter of Thomas Wormer of Malsch (near Karlsruhe) and Rosina Wormer née Heigel of Landstuhl, while her husband August Sareika was a native of East Prussia. It is not known what brought Mutti's grandmother to Strassburg but that is not the case for her grandfather. August Sareika had taken part in Prussia's victorious campaign against France during the Franco-Prussian War of 1870-1871 and after coming to Strassburg with the army, had settled there.[7]

August Sareika led an adventurous life that, alas, ended in tragedy. According to his baptismal record, he was born August Schareika at seven o'clock in the morning of September 7, 1839 in Worplack in East Prussia and baptized in the Evangelical (Lutheran) Church in nearby Rößel eight days later. (Since the end of World War II, these places are part of Poland and called Worplawki and Reszel, respectively).

August was the son of Samuel Sareika, a master blacksmith, and Marie Elizabeth Sareika née Heldt. Interestingly, in August's baptismal certificate his parent's surname is spelled Schareika while in all subsequent documents, including his marriage certificate and military papers, his name and that of his parents is given as Sareika. Possibly the surname was misspelled by the clergyman making out the baptismal certificate or else August later changed it perhaps on joining the army. Inquiries concerning his parents with the Evangelical (Lutheran) church office in Reszel, Poland, proved fruitless. Even Uncle Lulu, when he was required to show proof of ancestry, could find no trace of his grandparents on his mother's side. The name is believed to be of Lithuanian or Polish origin.

When August was 18, he joined the Prussian army where he had a distinguished military career as a noncommissioned officer in the horse cavalry. An impressive document exists stating (in translation from the German): "By order of his majesty the *Kaiser und König* [Emperor (of Germany) and King (of Prussia)] Sergeant August Sareika of the 4th squadron of the royal East Prussian cuirassier regiment no. 3 Count Wrangel, is awarded this medal in recognition of his faithful participation in the victorious campaign of 1870-1871." The award was given at Königsberg, the capital of East Prussia, and dated August 1, 1871.[8] Shortly thereafter, on January 3, 1872, Sergeant Sareika, age 32, was awarded another certificate and medal for 15 years of faithful service in his majesty's standing army.

When August and Maria Catharina were married two years later, on May 28, 1874 in Strassburg, his occupation was listed as *Schaffner an der Eisenbahn* [train conductor] meaning that he had been discharged from active duty not long after receiving his service medal. Presumably, the war was over and its veterans no longer needed and sent home to try their luck in civilian life. August and Maria must have been somewhat of an odd couple and one wonders what attracted them to each other. He is said to have been a man large of stature and, having long served in the horse cavalry, presumably somewhat rough-hewn in manner while his wife was petite and a little fastidious. Also, he was nine years her senior although that was not that unusual at the time. A big oddity for the time, however, was that they were not of the same faith. While August was *evangelisch*, Maria Catharina was devoutly *katholisch*. That is undoubtedly why my great-grandmother had to forego a church wedding and settle for a ceremony in the Strassburg Bürgermeisteramt (office of the mayor).

The Sareika family including August, Maria and little Rosa subsequently left town for Karlsruhe, the capital of the Grand Duchy of Baden which was just an hour north by train but on the eastern side of the Rhine. The reason for their move is not known but there is a strong likelihood that August, as a former Prussian soldier, was not welcome in predominantly French Alsace-Lorraine and may have lost his civil service job as a train conductor. In Karlsruhe, according to Mutti, her grandfather became despondent and, tragically, committed suicide by hanging himself.

A search in the Karlsruhe city archives confirmed Mutti's story. Found was a notice prepared by the Karlsruhe state's attorney dated September 28, 1881 and appended to August Sareika's death certificate which states: "With respect to the *Selbstmord* [suicide] of the *Cementarbeiter* [cement worker] August Sareika....in accordance with §157 of the *Strafprozeßordnung* [Code of Criminal Procedure], permission is hereby granted for the burial of the above-named individual." Like the death certificate, the state's attorney's statement gives August Sareika's date and time of death as September 27, 1886 between 8:30 and 9:00 o'clock in the morning.

One can only speculate as to the reason for my great-grandfather's suicide at age 47. Perhaps he had problems finding suitable civilian employment in Karlsruhe ending up, as he did, as a common laborer. He could also have had martial problems. According to his death certificate, August was living at Kaiserstraße 51 at the time of his death yet an on-line search of the Adressbuch der Haupt-und Residenzstadt Karlsruhe (City of Karlsruhe address register) for the years 1884 through 1886 shows him residing at Brunnenstraße 3 where his widow continued to live after his death. Clearly, the couple lived apart.

Intriguing too was the venue of my great-grandfather's death. While he lived at Brunnenstraße 3 (officially at Kaiserstraße 51) at the time, according to the Karlsruhe state's attorney's report he took his life at Bismarckstraße 43. Another online search of the official Karlsruhe address register mentioned above revealed that the latter property was owned by *I.K.H. Prinzessin Wilhelm*. [H.R.H. Princess Wilhelm]. Princess Wilhelm was a granddaughter of Czar Nicholas I of Russia (1796-1855) and wife of Prince Ludwig Wilhelm August von Baden.[9]

Why would August end his life not at home but in the house of a royal stranger? Was he engaged in some manual labor for the princess at the time, such as doing repairs to the house or grooming her horses (he had been a cavalryman), and found this location for his self-destruction more opportune? Or could it be that he had been romantically involved with this lady and felt jilted? Many of the marriages among aristocrats were arranged for political and dynastic reasons and therefore often loveless. It was therefore not uncommon for people in their situation to have a paramour on the side. This may have been the case here although it is difficult to contemplate a royal princess getting romantically involved with a common laborer. Incidentally, the former royal residence is now part of a fashionable hotel.

It had been seven years since the untimely and tragic death of her husband when my widowed great-grandmother, then nearly 45 years of age, remarried. Her new husband was Clemens Schaub who was five years her junior and, like her, Roman Catholic.[10] According to the records of the Katholisches Pfarramt St. Michael Neuweier, Clemens was born on February 11, 1853, the son of Karl Schaub and Martina Schaub née Nesselhauf. He made his living as a *Händler* [dealer, merchant]. Clemens and Maria Catharina were married in Karlsruhe on June 13, 1893 and made their home there until his death on October 11, 1911 at age 58. Despite being 40 years of age when he married, the church records indicate that this was his first and only marriage and that he had no known children. He did have an older sister, born in December 1846, named Johanna. Apparently Clemens was a good and decent man and Uncle Lulu (Ludwig Friedrich Clemens Zell) was named after him.

According to Mutti, after Clemens' death her maternal grandmother lived with the family in Schwanheim for a short time but she and her mother did not get along and Maria moved back to Karlsruhe. There, she and a lady friend operated a store for *Südfrüchte* [tropical fruits] and Mutti used to come down on the train from Frankfurt am Main to visit her. Most notable about her grandmother, according to Mutti, was her extreme piety. Thus, while she was living with them, she never failed to attend early morning mass. In fact, when the bells of the Mauritiuskirche, which stood at the end of their street, started to ring for six o'clock mass and the rest of the family was still in bed, Maria was already on her way to church. Her grandmother died in Karlsruhe's municipal hospital on September 12, 1925 at age 77 when Mutti was just 16. Since Mother was only two years old when Clemens passed away and she never got to know her father's parents, Maria was the only grandparent Mutti had known.

A Beloved Mother

Oma did not talk much about her growing up in Strassburg and Karlsruhe and hence Mutti had nothing to relate on the subject. One reason undoubtedly was that she had been traumatized by the suicide of her father August which had happened when she was just 11 years old. Together with whatever may have been the situation within the home prior to his death, she seems to have had a rough start in life and preferred to keep these things to herself. While there is no indication that Oma ever attended a school beyond the Volksschule level, she was well enough educated to converse intelligently with people including Opa on many diverse topics. Not surprisingly, she was bilingual and spoke French and German or at least the Elsass (Alsace) versions of the two languages. She taught her children French and conversations at the dinner table were usually in one language or the other. This language proficiency would play a major role in the lives of all her children.

Oma, according to Mutti, was warm-hearted and generous and much touched by any kind of suffering. She was a doting mother and her children adored her. After the war, she was full of compassion for the returning soldiers who were flooding into Frankfurt am Main and the surrounding areas including Schwanheim on their way home in other parts of the country. Oma organized relief in the form of clothing and food drives and saw to it that individual soldiers had a place to stay and something to eat. This was at a time when food was scarce and the population as a whole was living at the bare subsistence level. No hungry person, it was said, ever got turned away at her door without having at least a bowl of hot soup offered him or her. She also endeared herself to the two village *Pfarrer* [clergymen] by having them over for the midday meal on a regular basis. One *Pfarrer* was *evangelisch*, the other *katholisch* but she played no favorites and treated each with equal courtesy and deference. She also had a great love for animals and was active in the local chapter of the anticruelty society. Now and then the family attended the horse races but when once a horse fell and had to be put down she was aghast and the family never attended another race.

As the wife of a well-paid *Angestellter* [salaried employee], Oma and the children had a somewhat privileged lifestyle not available to most other villagers. She had little to do in the way of housework as cooking, cleaning, and washing of clothes were performed by two sisters of the Raab family who lived across the street. One sister, Gretel, was the housekeeper and started early in the morning when she fed the family pets and fixed breakfast after which she did the usual housekeeping chores. Her sister Mina came over later to prepare the *Mittagessen* [lunch], which was the main meal of the day when Opa would come home from I.G. Farben in Griesheim and the children from school.

All meals had to be *standesgemäss* [in line with the family's social position] which meant that no foods were served which the less privileged folks were accustomed to eating such as beans and lentils. Meat was on the menu whenever available together with potatoes and other vegetables. Opa did not like popular dishes like goulash as he insisted that meats, potatoes, and other vegetables show up on the plate neatly separated. He rejected such staples as spaghetti and rice as being too foreign but found potatoes to pass muster as genuinely German. (Potatoes are actually of South American origin). The light evening supper consisted of rye bread and assorted cold cuts and cheeses served with wine and tea. This meal too was *standesgemäss* because it was too costly for most families who would usually end the day with leftovers from the noon meal or a soup with bread.

Other than what was required to tend to the needs of her children, Oma had plenty of spare time for other activities. She was a member of the Frankfurt café society and her daily afternoon routine was to take the Waldbahn to the Sachsenhausen section of Frankfurt am Main to visit one or the other of the many better Frankfurt cafés. There she would have her tea and torte and chat with friends and other patrons. Oma was also somewhat of a fashion plate who loved stylish clothes. She was said to have traveled to Strasbourg, her birthplace, and as far as Paris on occasion to find clothes and fashion items she could not get in Frankfurt am Main. She also wore lipstick and when permanents were introduced in the mid-1920s, she was one of the first in the village to have her hair done in this manner.

Needless to say, Oma stood out among the highly conservative and straight-laced women of the village who would discreetly watch behind their lace curtains as she took her stately walk, in her latest finery, down Alt-Schwanheim to the Waldbahn station which stood at its end. These pleasure trips aside, Oma was also a strong supporter and patron of the major Frankfurt civic institutions including the Zoologischer Garten (zoo), the Palmengarten (conservatory) and the opera to all of which the family had season passes.

In the fall of 1932, Oma entered a hospital in Frankfurt-Sachsenhausen to have a thyroid operation. The procedure was successful and she was making good progress recovering. Her doctors had warned her to remain in bed and nearly motionless because of the danger of a *Blutgerinsel* [blood clot]. Unfortunately, she got up for some reason which resulted in a thrombosis. Oma died on October 18, 1932 at only 57 years of age.

Oma's passing came as a great shock to the family and especially to Mutti who thought the world had come to an end. According to Mutti, family members were astonished when they recalled that about three years earlier Oma's father August had appeared to her in a dream saying, *"Rosa, Rosa, du hast eintausend Tage"* [Rosa, Rosa, you have one thousand days]. Her passing, not surprisingly, caused great sadness in her adoptive village as her fellow Schwanheimer remembered her many good deeds over the years and especially her efforts to alleviate the hardship in the village during and after the war. According to Mutti, her mother's funeral cortege three days later to the Schwanheim cemetery was one of the largest in village history.

Losing a Child

Losing a child is a nightmarish experience most parents do not wish to contemplate. For Oma this became reality and the most devastating event of her adult life from which she never fully recovered. According to Mutti, her mother was never quite the same after losing her beloved Karl.[11] Carl Peter, their first child and the apple of Oma's eye, had been born on

November 16, 1899 in Frankfurt am Main where his parents still lived prior to moving to Schwanheim and baptized there on September 2 of the following year. Unfortunately, no photos of him and few documents relating to his life have survived but, according to Mutti, her brother was a handsome, caring, and idealistic boy who aspired to become a doctor. He had turned 18, which was military age, in November 1917, and was attending the Gymnasium (secondary school) in preparation for the university. His *Jahrgang* [age group] graduated in June 1918 and Mutti remembers him and his classmates proudly wearing their colorful school caps and, exuberant and flushed with patriotic fervor, looking forward to joining the other young men from the village fighting for their country. As had been expected, they were immediately drafted into the army.

The family gathered in Hanau, a town southeast of Frankfurt am Main, to see their son and brother off. The train that would take him and his classmates to the front was already awaiting them. The war itself was called a *Stellungskrieg* [trench warfare] and there was a frightful slaughter of men on both sides with tens of thousands dying for territorial advances of just a few yards. By this time, the war was going very badly for the Reich and only a miracle could safe the country from defeat. The family, including Karl, was fully aware that they might not see each other again and at least not in this world. Young Karl made the situation even worse by telling his mother that he would not return a cripple. She vehemently protested that they loved him and would take care of him no matter what and to please come back. After final tearful embraces, Karl and his companions boarded the train and it rolled out the station headed for the killing fields of France.

According to Mutti, her mother could never accept the fact that Karl had been killed. She insisted to the end of her life that her beloved Karl would sooner or later show up in Schwanheim again. In fact, when plans were made in Schwanheim, as elsewhere in the country, to honor the fallen warriors with memorial plaques and monuments bearing their names, Oma vehemently objected to have Karl's name included.[12] Mutti too was led to believe that her brother had survived and been transported to England after being severely wounded. Her father supposedly wrote desperate letters to that country's Red Cross asking them about the whereabouts of his son but never received a reply.

Yet according to an entry in the family *Stammbuch* [ancestry book] prepared by Uncle Lulu in the mid-1930s, Karl died *auf dem Feld der Ehre* [on the field of honor] on August 23, 1918 near Arras in northern France. In fact, in my uncle's files was found a letter addressed to his father in Schwanheim from the Kriegsministerium (war ministry) in Berlin dated September 30, 1919 stating (in translation):

> The war ministry's central registry has the sad duty to inform you that the notice of the death of Musketeer Karl Zell of the 8th Company of Reserve Infantry Regiment 87, born on November 16, 1899 in Frankfurt am Main, is confirmed. He died on August 23, 1918 of his wounds. With sincere condolences......

One possible explanation is that Opa kept this letter from Oma to perhaps spare her further grief and leave her with the fond hope of a future reunion with her beloved Karl.

Just ten weeks after Karl's untimely death, on November 11, 1918, an armistice was signed ending what came to be known as the First World War. Oma never knew but Karl would not be the only one of her four children to die abroad. In fact, as fate would have it, not one would find his or her final resting place on German soil.

NOTES

1. Anna Maria Zell née Backhaus, my Great-grandfather Johann Peter Zell's first wife, was born on November 26, 1812 in Duisburg and died on May 24, 1867 in Krefeld at age 54. The couple was married on May 21, 1842 in Krefeld and had six children: Maria Friedrike (born in May 1845), Anna (November 1847), Friedrich (March 1850), Ludwig (March 1852), Auguste (September 1854), and Emma (February 1857). Opa Peter Zell's two full brothers, Gustav Adolph and Carl Wilhelm were born in October 1873 and February 1875, respectively. All nine of Johann Peter's children were born in Krefeld and baptized in the town's Evangelical (Lutheran) Church.

2. After World War II, the victorious western Allies seized control of I.G. Farben and dismantled it as a punitive measure for allegedly being involved in the crimes of the Nazi regime including supplying the armaments for a war of aggression, the use of slave labor including concentration camp inmates, and being a source of lethal gases used to kill Jews and other minorities during the Holocaust. An account of Farbwerke Hoechst's history during the war is given in Stephan Lindner's *Inside I.G. Farben: Hoechst During the Third Reich*. Farbwerke Hoechst was eventually taken over by the Paris-based firm Sanofi-Aventis (now Sanofi S.A.) while BASF and Bayer, two other major I.G. Farben components, continued operating as independent companies. The former is the world's largest chemical company by sales while the latter is one of the largest pharmaceutical companies in the world and best known for its invention of aspirin.

3. The village of *Sueinheim* is first mentioned in a deed signed in *Franconofurd* (Frankfurt) on November 17, 880 AD by Louis (Ludwig) the Younger who was a son of Louis II (Ludwig) the German, grandson of Louis the Pious (Ludwig der Fromme), and a great-grandson of

Charlemagne (Karl der Große). *Suein* in *Sueinheim* stood for swine, a highly prized commodity at the time. Sometime in the early 16th century, historical documents began referring to *Sueinheim* (home of swine) as *Schwanheim* (home of swans). Two very interesting books on the history of Schwanheim, both published by local historical societies, are *Suenheim, Sueinheim, Schwanheim* (1971), and *1100 Jahre Schwanheim* (1980).

The Main River, which passes through Frankfurt am Main, was known as the *Moenus* to the Romans. It is a tributary of the Rhine River and the longest river lying entirely within Germany. It originates in the Franconian Jura mountains and, passing through Würzburg (Bavaria) and Frankfurt am Main (Hesse), enters the Rhine at Mainz, the capital of Rhineland-Pfalz (Rhineland-Palatinate). Since 1992 the Main River has been connected to the Danube by the Main-Donau-Kanal a.k.a. Rhein-Main-Donau-Kanal or Europakanal, creating a 2,200 mile navigable waterway from the North Sea to the Black Sea. Incidentally, Main is pronounced "mine" in German.

4. After Schwanheim became part of Frankfurt am Main on April 1, 1928, certain Schwanheim streets were renamed to avoid confusion with existing ones in the city. The old Hauptstraße (Main Street) is now called Alt-Schwanheim and what used to be the Feldbergstraße, where the Zell family lived, became the Blankenheimerstraße.

5. Cousin Peter had sent me a copy of our Grandfather Peter Zell's death notice in November 2006. He had no further information about it and I have since not been successful identifying the newspaper it was published in. The obvious candidate was the *Höchster Kreisblatt* because it was the most important regional paper at the time and where one might expect the I.G. Farben management to place an obituary for one of its important salaried employees. This paper, which since 1965 is part of the *Frankfurter Neue Presse* of Frankfurt am Main, lost its archives during the war but most issues, I learned, were microfilmed with copies available in the municipal archives of the town of Eschborn and the Hessian state library in Wiesbaden. Both venues were contacted but the archivists at neither could locate the notice on microfilmed issues of the paper for May and June 1938. This means that either not all parts of the *Höchster Kreisblatt* were microfilmed or

else the notice appeared elsewhere—either in an internal I.G. Farben publication or another of the numerous smaller papers published in the area at the time and for which no copies have survived including the local *Schwanheimer Zeitung*.

6. At the time of Oma's birth, Alsace-Lorraine was part of Germany where the region was known as *Elsass-Lothringen* and its inhabitants as *Elsässer* who spoke their own German dialect. Strasbourg is the French name for Alsace's capital, which was originally known by its German name Strassburg [*Strasse* for street plus *Burg* for castle]. Alsace-Lorraine had been a bone of contention between France and Germany almost since the Treaty of Verdun of August 843 AD at which time the Carolingian Empire was divided up among the three sons of Louis I the Pious (778-840), the third son and heir of Charlemagne: Charles II the Bald (823-877) became king of the West Franks, and Louis (Ludwig) II the German (804-876) king of the East Franks while the middle kingdom, which extended from the Atlantic to Rome and included Alsace-Lorraine, went to Lothar I (795-855). The western and eastern parts of Charlemagne's former empire would eventually morph into modern France (*Frankreich* in German) and Germany (*Allemagne* in French), respectively.

Since the 10th century, Alsace had been part of the Holy Roman Empire of the German Nation. French rulers subsequently set out to expand their country's eastern borders claiming most of the lands west of the Rhine as part of France. The strategy succeeded because, until the rise of Prussia and the Franco-Prussian War of 1870/71, France was by far more powerful than the fragmented Holy Roman Empire of Germany. During the reign of Louis XIV (1638-1715), the region was annexed by France. For the ethnic Germans of Alsace-Lorraine this led to frequent expulsions and the suppression of their language and culture by the French authorities. After Germany's defeat in World War I, the teaching of German was prohibited and people who had moved into the region since 1871 were expelled. After France's defeat in World War II, the region became part of the Third Reich.

After World War II, the territory reverted to France and French was re-imposed—until 1984 newspapers were not allowed to have more than 25% of German content. In January 2016, the identities of

Alsace and Lorraine became further blurred when France, in a major reorganization, combined these former departments with Champagne-Ardenne to form a department called Grand Est with Strasbourg as its capitol. Since the 1990 Schengen Convention, which opened the borders within the European Union, citizens of signatory countries, including France and Germany, are free to move across borders to live and work where they please without governmental interference.

7. Under Frederick II the Great (1712-1786), the Kingdom of Prussia had become a formidable military power. In the early 19th century, Prussia helped Austria, Britain and Russia defeat Napoleon Bonaparte and his empire. Then, under Chancellor Otto von Bismarck (1815-1898), Prussia had united Germany to establish the Second Reich. (The First Reich was The Holy Roman Empire of the German Nation). After the defeat of the Third Reich in World War II, the victorious Allies decided to do away with Prussia which they identified with German militarism and nationalism and divided up its territory between the Soviet Union, Poland, and East Germany.

8. The military certificate issued to my great-grandfather, Sergeant August Sareika, was rich in symbolism. At the top there appears the slogan *Mit Gott für Kaiser, König und Vaterland* [With God for Emperor, King and Fatherland]. Two warrior maidens, one on each side, stand behind shields carrying the names of 14 towns including Amiens, Metz, Paris, Sedan and Strassburg (presumably important venues in the war) while at the bottom appear the fallen standards of the Napoleonic Empire (two banners carry the "N" insignia for Napoleon III, the French ruler at the time), the years 1870-1871, and the name of the long disputed territory—Elsass-Lothringen.

9. Princess Wilhelm was the name by which Maria Maximilianowna Leuchtenberg-Romanovskij (1841-1914), Duchess of Leuchtenberg, was known as after her marriage to Prince Ludwig Wilhelm August von Baden (1829-1897) in February 1863. Her mother was Princess Maria Nikolajewna Romanov, the eldest daughter of Czar Nicholas I of Russia. Prince Wilhelm was a general and politician who served in the Franco-Prussian War, in which he was severely wounded, and later in the Reichstag (parliament) in Berlin. Princess Wilhelm divided her time between Karlsruhe and Baden-Baden, a spa in the Black Forest.

At the time, Baden-Baden was a favorite with Russian royalty and literati who spent part of the year there to take the waters, play in the town's famous casino, attend the theater, or just enjoy the beautiful countryside and agreeable climate. Princess Wilhelm was best known for her charitable work and her successful efforts to give Baden-Baden a Russian-Orthodox church which was consecrated in 1882.

10. Clemens Schaub was born on February 11, 1853 in Neuweier (now part of Baden-Baden), the son of Karl Schaub, a *Landwirt* [farmer], and Martina Schaub née Nesselhauf. Karl Schaub and Martina were both Roman Catholics and residents of Neuweier. When Clemens Schaub married Maria Katharina Sareika née Wormer on June 13, 1893 in Karlsruhe, he was 40 years old and it was apparently his first and only marriage because a records search in Baden-Baden and Karlsruhe as well as the Roman Catholic diocese of Freiburg turned up no information on any other marriage nor the names of any children. Only an older sister, Johanna Schaub, born on December 20, 1846, was found in the records.

11. The letter "C" was not in common usage in the old German alphabet and there are few German words beginning with a C. The Latin C was always pronounced as a "K" (hard C) in German and so written. Presumably the spelling of Carl was changed to Karl when he was drafted into the army during World War I or even while still in school. The town of Krefeld was originally spelled Crefeld and both versions are found in old birth certificates and other documents. Similarly, Cologne is Köln in German and Caesar was pronounced *Kaesar* which morphed into Kaiser (emperor). Notable exceptions to the general rule are *Christus* [Christ], *Charakter* [character], *Chemie* [chemistry], *Chor* [choir], China, and Computer.

12. Oma was not successful in her effort to keep her son's name off the list of fallen soldiers because a small stone memorial plaque on an inner wall of Schwanheim's Evangelische Martinuskirche bears Karl Zell's name along with 24 of his fallen comrades. In the Roman Catholic Mauritiuskirche, a magnificent *Kriegergedächtnisaltar* [soldier memorial altar] was erected in 1927 which bears the names of 125 young men of the Catholic faith who gave their lives for their country in World War I. Considering that Schwanheim was just a small village,

the total of 150 fallen attests to the carnage inflicted on both sides during this 4-year conflict which was called the "the war to end all wars."

My more recent inquiry with the Volksbund Deutsche Kriegsgräberfürsorge (German War Graves Commission) found no record of Karl in their archives of fallen World War I soldiers. Presumably he found his final resting place in the German military cemetery St. Laurent-Blangy outside of Arras, France. Soldiers were buried in individual graves only if their identity could be firmly established while unidentified remains were buried in a so-called *Kameradengrab* [grave of comrades]. Presumably my uncle was buried in such a grave. The French authorities laid out the cemetery after the war without German participation and the Volksbund began taking care of it in February 1927. It holds the remains of nearly 32,000 German soldiers from World War I including 7,069 in individual graves.

PART II

BOTHERS AND SISTERS

LULU'S STORY

A Young Patriot

Ludwig Friedrich Clemens Zell, Peter and Rosa's second child, just missed being called up for military service in the Kaiser's army during the First World War but his turn came at the very beginning of the following one which was, more or less, a continuation of the first. My Uncle Lulu was born on February 6, 1901 in Frankfurt am Main and baptized in the Evangelical (Lutheran) Church of Griesheim on February 2 of the following year. It was Oma who gave him the *Kosename* [pet name] Lulu. After finishing his primary and secondary school education and coming of age, Lulu found his country in political and economic turmoil.

During the post-war economic crisis in Germany, caused by wartime depletion of resources and huge reparation payments demanded by France and Great Britain under the punitive Treaty of Versailles, in 1923 it came to hyperinflation. Prices were changing by the hour and by the autumn of that year a loaf of bread was selling for two hundred billion marks! People used to get paid and hasten to the grocery store so they could obtain the needed provisions before prices changed again. The national government in Weimar was unstable, millions were unemployed, and things looked extremely bleak. The country's experiment with democracy following imperial rule had failed.

Mutti had told me that her brother had served in the French Foreign Legion, known in Germany as the *Fremdenlegion*, in Morocco following the war and was discharged after contracting malaria. This account made me assume that my uncle, as had no doubt other young men, listened to the siren song from across the Rhine and had joined the *Fremdenlegion* becoming a mercenary for the French to escape the malaise prevailing in his home country. The assumption seemed logical because Lulu spoke

French and was somewhat acquainted with French culture through his mother. I was wrong as the actual circumstances were much different.

The true facts are recorded in Lulu's application for Nazi Party and SA memberships, a copy of which I received from his son Peter in July 2013. The SA, as previously mentioned, was a Nazi paramilitary organization that significantly helped Hitler's rise to power. The 20-question form Lulu was required to complete had the cumbersome title of *Heimatschein= (Staatsangehörigkeitsausweis=) Gesuch* [Application for Homeland and Citizenship Certificate]. Its purpose was to ascertain that the applicant was an "Aryan" (Nordic, Caucasian) individual and not a *Mischling*, i.e., a person of diverse, non-Aryan ancestry. With these facts and additional information much of Lulu's rather interesting life story can now be told.

According to local historians, soon after the signing of the Armistice on November 11, 1918, French colonial troops from Morocco arrived in Schwanheim after crossing the Main River bridge coming from Höchst. The purpose of the occupation was to form a border area outside neighboring Frankfurt am Main since that city was to remain unoccupied. To the villagers' great annoyance, barbed wire fences and other obstacles were erected to prevent anyone from traveling to or from Frankfurt. In addition, a nightly curfew was imposed and every Sunday morning all village men were required to appear at the restaurant Frankfurter Hof (popularly known as "Seppche") and present themselves to a French colonial officer, a Moroccan, to have their names checked off.

To the people of Schwanheim it was an affront and effort to humiliate them. When Frankfurt am Main too was occupied by Moroccans an incident there further inflamed the passions. On April 7, 1920 an angry mob of students were protesting the Frankfurt occupation at the Hauptwache (the old city militia building) in the town center, where the Moroccans had made their headquarters, when the Moroccans fired into the crowd killing 9 people.

In the meantime, several right-wing, para-military organizations had sprung up across Germany which were illegal by the post-war Treaty of Versailles. Lulu had, according to Cousin Peter, joined up with one of these known as the Freikorps (Free Corps). The Freikorps was initially very supportive of the post-war Weimar Republic and had helped the government put down several revolts by groups of left-wing agitators one of which, with the backing of the Kremlin, had proclaimed a Bavarian Soviet Republic. Based on the aforementioned application for SA membership, between the beginning of May 1919 and mid-January 1920 Lulu attended military training (with unspecified units) in three different locations in Germany. After these, for the brief period from January 20 to February 28, 1920, he lived with his parents in Schwanheim am Main.

While living with his parents, Lulu was arrested by the French occupation authorities on charges related to his Freikorps membership and military training and taken to Metz, France. Parenthetically, like Strassburg, the capital of Elsass (Alsace), Metz, the capital of Lothringen (Lorraine), was originally a German town. By the treaty of Verdun of 843 AD, both territories and towns had been assigned to East Francia, the largest component of the Holy Roman Empire (Germany).

According to Cousin Peter, in Metz his father was given the choice of either serving 5 years in a French prison or the same length of time in the French Foreign Legion. He chose the latter as the lesser of the two evils. Lulu never mentioned serving in the *Fremdenlegion* in his application but referred to the entire time period, including his imprisonment in Metz, as being in *französischer Haft* [French custody].

According to the application, Lulu was stationed in Morocco from March 18, 1920 until March 31, 1925 when he was discharged. A piece of correspondence to have survived from Lulu's service with the French Foreign Legion is a picture postcard from his mother, probably written in January 1924, with best wishes on his 23rd birthday.[1] After his discharge, Lulu returned to his parent's home in Schwanheim am Main.

Party Membership

According to Cousin Peter, when his father returned home from Morocco in early 1925 not much had changed for the better either politically or economically. After some minor jobs, he eventually got hired by Philipp Holzmann A.G., a large (now defunct) Frankfurt building contractor, as a *Bauleiter* [construction supervisor]. The company had a project in Bitterfeld, a small industrial and mining town near the cities of Halle an der Saale and Leipzig in eastern Germany, and sent him there. Lulu arrived in Bitterfeld in April 1928 and lived there until September 1939 when he was drafted into the Wehrmacht at the beginning of World War II. While with this company, Lulu also taught stenography and typing at the Höhere Handelsschule (business college) in Halle where he met and fell in love with Irma Schellberg. Lulu and Irma got married on February 7, 1931 in Bitterfeld and had three children—Marga born the same year followed by Peter and Helmut in 1937 and 1939, respectively. It just so happened that I.G. Farben, Opa's former employer, had a plant in Bitterfeld and Lulu left the construction firm to join I.G. Farben as a *Kaufmännischer Angestellter* [salaried clerk] in their commercial department.

It was while employed at I.G. Farben that Uncle Lulu applied to join *die Partei* and presumably also the SA although no separate documentation as to membership in the latter has been located. This required Lulu to submit documentation that he was racially pure, i.e., that there were no Jews in the family *Stammbaum* [family tree]. [2] As the captured records of the NSDAP showed, Lulu joined the National Socialists on May 1, 1937 as member no. 4046038.[2] According to Cousin Peter, his father served as a *Funker* [wireless operator] with this organization.

When Lulu joined the Nazis and the SA it was probably not one of his more fortuitous moves since by 1937 the SA was already on a steep decline as far as power and prestige within the Reich was concerned. In fact, after Hitler came to power in 1933 he had no further use for these ruffians and, rather than being an asset, they became an embarrassment and burden to the regime. Most importantly, their leader, Erich Röhm, was a radical Socialist who advocated a stronger voice of the proletariat (industrial workers) in the Nazi movement, nationalization of major industries, confiscation and redistribution of the country's private property, and more rewards, especially jobs, for SA members. He even called for a second revolution. To most Germans this sounded like Communism. Furthermore, the officer corps of the Reichswehr, the forerunner of the Wehrmacht, became alarmed by Röhm's ambitions and ever expanding power that would have subordinated the Reichswehr to the SA.

His closest advisors persuaded Hitler to act and act he did. On July 1, 1934 he had his old friend and comrade as well as other SA leaders executed on drummed-up charges of having plotted against the Reich and its Führer as well as moral turpitude. The final blow to the SA came on September

1, 1939, the first day of World War II, when Hitler had the entire SA membership, including Uncle Lulu, inducted into the Wehrmacht. At one fell swoop the Führer had solved the nation's continuing unemployment problem. Now they all had jobs!

About Lulu's military career little is known but he presumably first served on the western front and took part in the victorious campaign against France. It must have given him a measure of satisfaction to be able to exact retribution on the French after they had imprisoned him for over five years for his nationalist activities and opposition to French occupation. With the start of *Unternehmen Barbarossa* [Operation Barbarossa], the codename for the invasion of the Soviet Union on June 22, 1941, Lulu was transferred to the eastern front where he served with the 6th Army and took part in the famous battle of Stalingrad.

In Stalingrad the Red Army completely surrounded and destroyed the invaders forcing their leader, General Friedrich Paulus, to surrender the last remnants of his vast army on February 2, 1943. This catastrophic defeat marked the beginning of the end of the Third Reich and was a replay of sorts of the defeat inflicted on Napoleon's Grande Armée 130 years earlier. Both Napoleon and Hitler had underestimated the toughness and resilience of the Russian people, the resolve of their leaders, the immense size and resources of the country, and the harshness of the Russian winter.

For many years little was known about Lulu's ultimate fate. According to my Cousin Peter, the Deutsche Dienststelle (WASt) in Berlin, which is the German federal office in charge of maintaining the archival records of members of the World War II Wehrmacht, informed him that his father had taken part in the eastern campaigns having fought in Poland and Ukraine, that his rank was *Oberfeldwebel* [first sergeant], that he went missing on January 9, 1943 during the battle of Stalingrad, and that his ultimate fate was unknown. Ever hopeful that he would some day return, my Aunt Irma waited another 35 years before having him declared dead. An East German court established the official date of his demise as December 31, 1948.

Fortunately, within the last few years much of the uncertainty surrounding his fate has been cleared up to bring a measure of closure for the family.

From inquiries with the Volksbund Deutsche Kriegsgräberfürsorge we learned that Lulu served as a *Hauptfeldwebel* [master sergeant] with the second *Hundertschaft* [unit of 100] of Ukrainian Battalion 6 and went missing on January 9, 1943 in the vicinity of Stalingrad. He and 103,000 other missing Wehrmacht soldiers are memorialized in the German military cemetery of Rossoschka near Volgograd (formerly Stalingrad) where granite blocks have been erected holding the names of the missing in alphabetical order. The Volksbund mailed Cousin Peter photographs of block 126 with the inscription: LUDWIG ZELL * 6.2.1901 + JAN. 1943.

This begs the question why a very decent man from a good middle-class family would join the National Socialists. I suspect that for Uncle Lulu the party's attraction must have been more economic than ideological. The Nazis were racists but he was not. Lulu never showed by word or deed that he was ant-Semitic. In fact, it was through her brother's party membership and good advise that Mutti and Esther survived the Nazi regime. Like most others who joined *die Partei*, he most likely never anticipated that this new so-called *Bewegung* [movement] would lead to the "final solution" of the Jewish problem. His motive was most likely economic and, specifically, job-related. Hitler promised to create jobs and that he did by huge public works projects such as building a network of superhighways known as Autobahnen that crossed the country.

It is probably no coincidence that Lulu joined the Nazis on May 1 (May Day) which is celebrated as International Workers' Day or Labor Day in most countries with the exception of the United States and a few other countries. Incidentally, the U.S. had to choose another day for Labor Day because May 1 was chosen to commemorate Chicago's infamous Haymarket riot which began on May 4, 1886 as a public demonstration for an 8-hour workday, ended in a bomb blast, police shootings, and the prosecution and hanging of several prominent labor leaders some of whom were not even present at the rally. Lulu was working for I.G. Farben at the time and, as previously mentioned, employees of that industrial giant were under much pressure to join *die Partei* and Lulu would undoubtedly have complied to be sure he kept his job.

Although history has painted him a villain, Hitler was a populist and a hero to millions as contemporary newsreels unmistakably show. Many Christians saw the Führer as a savior providentially sent to save the

German people and the Reich from foreign oppression. He had put an end to Communism in Germany and helped thwart attempts to install a Russian-style Communist dictatorship in the country. The Pope and the Catholic hierarchy likewise greeted him as the savior of the West from the scourge of ungodly Communism. The *Reichskonkordat* between the Holy Sea and the German Reich signed in July 1933 in Rome was an agreement promising non-interference of the Reich in the affairs of the Catholic Church and vice versa and is still in force to this day. Parenthetically, Hitler almost immediately broke the pact but without earning the ire of most Catholics even after March 1937 when Pope Pius XI published the encyclical *Mit brennender Sorge* [With Burning Anxiety] warning the "venerable brethren" of the German Reich of the dangers posed by turning away from God.

The Führer spoke for the people when he renounced the infamous *Treaty of Versailles* by which the Western Allies, chiefly the French and British, made the Reich the scapegoat for World War I and following a policy of revenge and retribution stripped the Reich of all its overseas territories and possessions, forced the country to accept huge reparations payments it could not possibly make, and accept occupation of the western part of the Reich by France ostensibly to de-militarize the area. In March 1936, Hitler had defied the western Allies by sending troops into the occupied Rhineland and returning that part of the Reich to German control. The Führer promised to restore Österreich (Austria) to the Reich and make Germany a great nation again. Most importantly, he created jobs. All these measures must have resonated with Lulu, as with millions of his fellow countrymen, and encouraged him to support the regime in power.

When one time Lulu was home on furlough from the Wehrmacht, he told Mutti of the shocking atrocities he saw being committed against civilian populations on the eastern front. God forbid, he had said to her, if these outrages should ever be avenged on the German people. They were avenged and retribution was not long in coming. As the Red Army overpowered the Wehrmacht and rolled westward towards Berlin, millions of Germans fled in terror before it. Towns and villages were razed to the ground and inhabitants who had stayed behind were murdered. Countless German women were raped by Soviet soldiers in a systematic policy to avenge Nazi claims of German racial superiority over their Slavic neighbors. Around 12 million Germans were expelled from the eastern provinces of the Reich with their ancient homelands divided up among the victors.

The Anglo-Americans meted out their own form of justice in a relentless bombing campaign of sheer terror that pulverized the ancient towns and cities of Germany and killed over one-half million people. In the devastation wrought on Germany, historians have compared World War II to the Thirty Years' War (1618-1648), a war between Catholics and Protestants following the Protestant Reformation.

Yet despite the huge losses in lives and property, not all was in vain. The Thirty Year's War which had ended nearly 300 years earlier with the Peace of Westphalia had laid the foundation for religious freedom in Germany and the rest of the Continent. The latest war would lead to rapprochement between France and Germany, the Continent's ancient rivals, and the Treaty of Rome, an agreement signed in 1957 by Belgium, France, Italy, Luxembourg, the Netherlands, and West Germany to create a single European market for goods and services. The European Economic Community was successful and in 1992 led to the Treaty of Maastricht establishing the European Union (EU). Despite its many flaws, the EU has been a pillar of peace and prosperity on the Continent and is likely to remain so for many years to come.

The Post-War Era

After the war, the victorious Allies sliced up the old German Reich into four zones of occupation with the French and Anglo-Americans creating three zones in the West and the Russians one in the East. In May 1949 partial sovereignty was restored to West Germany with the creation of the Bundesrepublik Deutschland (BRD), in English known as the Federal Republic of Germany, while a few months later the leaders of the eastern zone announced the establishment of the Deutsche Demokratische Republik (DDR), i.e., the German Democratic Republic. Despite its name, the latter was anything but a democracy. Its leaders were German Communists who had fled to the Soviet Union when Hitler came to power and were brought back to Germany after the war to set up a Russian-style Communist dictatorship under the tutelage of the Soviet Union. Officially, the regime called itself Socialist and not Communist (Communist never rang well in German ears) but, if that was the case, it was an extreme left form of Socialism. The DDR existed for two generations and became extinct with the fall in November 1989 of the Berlin Wall, which had separated the two parts of the country, and the reunification of Germany on October 3, 1990.

The DDR was the ultimate welfare state with all the people's material needs, from cradle to grave, taken care of. There was near full employment as the state created jobs as needed while poverty was virtually eliminated by extensive social welfare programs. Because the free enterprise economic system prevalent in the West was economically more successful, the standard of living for East Germans was well below that of their countrymen in the BRD except for party functionaries and other privileged individuals who were able to enjoy the good life. Higher education was free but only available to those amenable to Communist ideology. For the citizens of the DDR life was relatively uncomplicated requiring little in the way of personal initiatives. With everyone reeducated and indoctrinated in Communist ideology and the values of the new regime, most East Germans made a remarkably smooth transition from Nazism to Communism, from the far right to the far left, in a very short period of time.

Not all East Germans were happy with the new regime. Many wanted to flee to the West to be reunited with relatives and/or for economic or political reasons. To prevent *Repulikflucht* [flight from the Republic], which was a crime punishable by years in prison, the DDR authorities began with the erection of a tall concrete barrier including guard towers manned by border police which the regime referred to as the *Antifaschistischer Schutzwall* [Anti-Fascist Protection Rampart]. This designation was in line with doctrine propagated by the regime that the West, including the BRD, was essentially Fascist with an agenda designed to thwart the will of the people to build a Socialist state. The Berlin Wall, begun in the summer of 1961, ran for nearly 100 miles through the middle of Berlin and much beyond. Border guards routinely shot people trying to cross it. Another innovation to keep its citizens in line was the creation of the Staatssicherheitsdienst (State Security Service) or Stasi for short, which employed nearly 100,000 agents supported by a large army of DDR citizens turned informants.

It should come as no surprise that the life experiences of the members of the eastern and western branches of the Zell family were much different. With her husband serving with the Wehrmacht from 1939 on, my Aunt Irma had to raise their three children, Marga, Peter, and Helmut, on her own. She seems to have done a solid job as all grew up to be decent and fairly well-adjusted adults. I had first met my aunt and Cousin Helmut as an 11-year-old when they came to visit us in the summer of 1947 in Stuttgart after a perilous journey across the border between East and West Germany. With the border essentially closed, visits to the West were now only possible with special permits and these were difficult to come by. Entry into the DDR was discouraged by a monetary measure whereby visitors were required to exchange their valuable Deutsche Marks or U.S. dollars for nearly worthless East German Marks on a one-to-one basis. This gave the regime the hard currency it needed for important purchases from the West but left the visitor with little buying power.

An exception to travel between the two German states was made for the elderly. At age 60 a person was allowed to visit relatives in the West once a year while at the age of 65, which was the official retirement age, retirees could leave the country with the proviso that they give up all claims to social security benefits, i.e., monthly retirement payments and health insurance. In a very generous gesture by the Federal Republic, upon arrival in West Germany these people were automatically enrolled in the social security system and extended full benefits as if they had paid into the system all their working lives.

One of the beneficiaries of this arrangement was Aunt Irma who had moved from Bitterfeld to Halle an der Saale where she was employed as a secretary. Irma Lina Zell née Schellberg was born on November 30, 1911 in Strelno (now Strzelno in Poland) in the province of Posen (Poznańska). While she was still living in East Germany, Aunt Irma and Mutti had corresponded only intermittently with years passing before they were in touch again. Much of that had to do with the fact that the DDR regime discouraged its citizens from having much contact with relatives or others in the West. Responding to a Christmas greeting from Mutti and with greetings on her sister-in-law's upcoming 63rd birthday, Aunt Irma wrote on February 29, 1972 (in translation):

> *My dear Annemie, how long has it been since we heard from each other. Years? .... Do you still remember how beautiful it was when I came to Schwanheim? I so often think of all the beautiful weeks I had there, then just with one child. Who would have believed that this terrible Hitler would bring us so much grief and misery. Even today one cannot fully fathom all the evil this person and his closest associates brought about!!! Neither I nor Marga, who is still searching for answers, have ever been able to discover anything about Lulu. We followed every lead, even the weakest. And now, after 29 years, there is little hope that Lulu is still alive. On the 6th, he would have been 71.*

She had just returned from her first trip to West Germany, Aunt Irma wrote, where she spent three wonderful weeks with Marga, her *Püppchen* [little doll], and relatives she had not seen in decades. She was very hopeful to see Mutti again sometime. "Won't you come back to Germany once more?" she wanted to know. Now that she could travel to the West, she wrote, they could meet even if Mutti could not or did not want to come to the DDR.

Aunt Irma's comment about Hitler was especially poignant because it reflected the experience of most Germans at the time. When *das Volk* [the people] so enthusiastically cheered the Führer because they saw in him the God-ordained savior of the nation, they could never have imagined what they were in for. Uncle Lulu had, of course, been one of Hitler's staunch supporters and had even joined the Nazi Party. That is probably why Aunt Irma wrote about Lulu immediately after denouncing Hitler and the Nazi regime. Understandably, she tried to disassociate Lulu from the regime's evil deeds by holding Hitler and his *engste Mitarbeiter* [closest associates] responsible for everything. In other words, the party rank and file was not to blame since they were duped as the rest of the people. It could be argued, of course, that had it not been for them, Hitler would not have come to power and been able to do the harm he did. On the other hand, Lulu did not join *die Partei* until 1937, when Hitler was already in power, and thus may best be described as what came to be called a *Mitläufer* [fellow traveler].

My aunt was eligible to leave the DDR for good in December 1976 but stayed a bit longer. According to a letter she wrote me from Halle in early January 1978 while I was living in Frankfurt am Main, she was just making preparations for her move to the West. It involved endless paperwork to comply with DDR regulations including a complete accounting of every item she was taking with her down to the last spoon. A check from Mutti for 30 Deutschmarks had just arrived, according to my aunt, and she was filling out the paperwork to get the money paid out to her. She was also looking forward to receiving a last package Mutti had mailed her. Her destination, she wrote, was Flörsbachtal, a town due east of Frankfurt am Main, where her older brother Otto Schellberg and his wife Margarete (Gretel) had settled after their retirement. She was also much looking forward to visiting Emmi in Geneva, who had cordially invited her, and Graben-Neudorf from where she had also received an invitation (presumably from Uncle Jule and Aunt Erika).

After arriving in Flörsbachtal, she and her sibling found an attractive little *Wohnung* for her in the Lohrhaupten part of the village. I had not seen my aunt in 30 years and much looked forward to meeting up with her again. That opportunity arrived in mid-March 1978 when I visited her and her brother and sister-in-law. It was just a week before my business trip to the Leipzig Trade Fair and a visit with my Cousin Helmut in Halle. Aunt Irma had just arrived and seemed very happy in her upstairs flat in a 2-story family home. We had many more opportunities for get-togethers that year in Flörsbachtal-Lohrhaupten and my flat in the Sachsenhausen district of Frankfurt am Main.

Sadly, the hoped-for reunion between my mother and aunt never took place. There had been a perfect opportunity in June 1982 when Mutti came to visit me just prior to my return to the States. While the main purpose for Mother's trip was to see her Sister Emmi in Geneva and we had less than two weeks, we still managed to visit just about everyone we wanted to see but neither Mutti nor I thought of dear Aunt Irma. The reason probably was that during my March and April 1978 visits, Aunt Irma appeared somewhat cool and detached. Our relationship was friendly but not particularly affectionate. When I mentioned it to Mutti, she thought that her sister-in-law had probably expected me to leave her some money to defray the cost of her recent move to West Germany. The thought had never entered my mind and, if it had, I doubt that I would have felt obligated to do so. She had, after all, her daughter Marga and brother Otto living in the West who both had good incomes. And why should I be financially supporting my aunt when I was not doing that well myself at the time? My American salary in dollars was not overly generous and Frankfurt am Main was an expensive town to live in.

Neither Emmi nor Mutti ever had many kind things to say about Irma. During her visit to her sister-in-law in Geneva, the two did not get along as they were of two entirely different temperaments. As for Mutti, she once insinuated that Irma had been unfaithful to Lulu. That was probably not true because I knew that Mutti was in the habit of accusing people of wrongdoing that had no basis in fact. Mutti also claimed to have once mailed Irma an expensive overcoat she had just worn a couple of times and Irma supposedly wrote back telling Mutti not to send her anything more if she could not afford something new.

While in Geneva, Aunt Irma apparently told Aunt Emmi that I was a cheap-skate who had given her son only 50 Deutschmarks after he had picked me up in Leipzig for the drive to Halle an der Saale and back. What my aunt did not know was that I had unexpectedly found myself strapped for Deutschmark on my trip because most places asked to be paid in Deutschmarks rather than the local currency, which I had bought at the official one-to-one exchange rate, and I had always obliged. Nevertheless, if Aunt Irma felt hurt by our neglect of her she was justified and I later much regretted not to have proposed to Mutti that we visit her in Lohrhaupten. Mutti herself never mentioned Irma during her visit. She apparently never forgave Irma for bad-mouthing her son in Geneva.

Aunt Irma, being a full-fledged participant in the German social security system with its generous allotments and health care benefits, lived in the West in comfortable circumstances for another quarter of a century. I had my last contact with my aunt in mid-December 1998, when I wrote her a long conciliatory letter in which I reminisced about Mutti who had passed away earlier that year and apologized for not having stayed in touch with her over the years or visiting her more often while I was employed in Germany. She never responded. She was, however, in continuous contact with Esther. Then one day I received a letter from Cousin Peter with the sad news that his mother had passed away on February 19, 2002 at age 90. According to Peter,

Aunt Irma was in relatively good health when she unexpectedly suffered a massive stroke, went into a coma, and died shortly thereafter. Her remains were brought to nearby Bad Soden - Salmünster, where he and his family had moved after leaving East Germany, and buried in the village cemetery.

Different Strokes For Different Folks

There is often something special about the first-born of a family and that, at least, was true about my Cousin Marga. She seemed to be the most adventurous of the three siblings because she was the first to leave East Germany for greener pastures in the West. Marga Annerosel Zell was born on August 3, 1931 in Bitterfeld. She made the painful decision to leave behind her family and friends knowing full well that she may not see them again for a very long time. She did so when told by the regime that she was not eligible for a university education or any career that seemed to be meaningful or of interest to her. The time was the early 1950s and, with a little gall, it was still possible to cross the border between East and West. Marga had saved some money and one day she got on a train for East Berlin and, taking advantage of the reduced security checks during rush hour, took a local train to slip into West Berlin. From there she found her way to Bonn, then the capital of the newly established Federal Republic of Germany. She subsequently attended school to become a medical technician and worked in hospital X-ray departments.

Marga also got married to one Anton (Toni) Isfort and henceforth took the name of Marga Isfort-Zell. Nothing is known about her husband's background. I was intrigued by his Anglo surname and when I asked Cousin Peter what he knew about Toni, I was told *nichts* [nothing]. He obviously did not approve of his brother-in-law. Only Aunt Emmi could provide some details about him and these were not flattering. She had invited Marga and Toni to Geneva a couple of times and described Toni as a "sometime architect and fulltime alcoholic" and a "*Säufer und Taugenichts*" [a drunkard and good-for-nothing] who just lay around the house all day slurping up her best wines.

Aunt Emmi felt quite differently about her niece whom she described as a very gentle and refined person for whom she felt sad because she always looked so tired and frail. Our cousin, we knew from Esther, was employed as a laboratory technician in the X-ray departments at a number of hospitals in succession and the hours and workloads were strenuous. According to Aunt Emmi, while she felt sorry for Marga, there was nothing she could do for her because she would never leave Toni even though Marga knew that he would never change. What Aunt Emmi most resented about him was that he counted on poor Marga and her modest income for nearly his entire support. He was living off her and that she could not tolerate. Aunt Emmi became so disgusted with Marga and Toni that, according to a letter she wrote Mutti in April 1980, she told the two that they were no longer welcome in her house.

Unfortunately, I never got to meet my cousin and her husband. In May 1977, I received a very friendly letter from Marga and Toni in Frankfurt am Main with an invitation to visit them in Rheinbach, a small town southwest of Bonn. They had just moved into a beautiful new apartment with a big balcony there, she wrote, and Toni even included a detailed sketch of it. Regrettably, my work kept me very busy and I never found the time to follow up on the invitation. Mutti and Esther knew Marga well, of course, and the three regularly corresponded.

According to Cousin Peter, his sister had the misfortune of contracting Hepatitis C at one of the hospitals she worked for, the last being the one attached to the University of Bonn. Hepatitis C is a blood-borne infectious disease caused by a virus that attacks the liver. The virus had not been discovered until very recently and no cure was yet available. Marga passed away on January 15, 1999 at age 67 while Toni had already predeceased her. It must have been a terrible blow for Aunt Irma who prematurely lost her beloved daughter who had devoted her life to help heal others.

The one family member for whom the new Communist regime held much promise was my Cousin Helmut whom I had first met in the summer of 1947 when he and his mother visited us in Stuttgart after the war. Helmut Ludwig Zell was born in September 1939 in Bitterfeld and just five years old when World War II ended. According to Peter, Helmut became a member of the Junge Pioniere (Young Pioneers) and other East German Youth organizations and volunteered to serve with the Nationale Volksarmee (National People's Army). These activities, according to Peter, gave his brother the credentials to obtain a university education and become a *Diplom-Ingenieur* [graduate engineer]. With Helmut's privileged status came a secure job as an engineer with one of the state-run companies, a nice apartment, and an automobile.

Our second and last meeting took place in mid-March 1978 while I was still on assignment in Germany. I had traveled to Leipzig to attend the Leipziger Messe (Leipzig Trade Fair) which had been Germany's biggest and most prestigious industrial trade fair prior to the war. (After World War II West Germany set up its own fair, the Hannover Messe in the town of Hannover in Lower Saxony). Helmut, like his mother, lived in Halle an der Saale, birthplace of the Baroque composer Georg Friedrich Händel a.k.a. George Frideric Handel. (A famous contemporary, Johann Sebastian Bach, was born in the same year, 1685, in nearby Eisenach). Unlike Marga and the rest of the family, Helmut seemed content with life in the DDR although he did not hesitate to criticize the regime for its many shortcomings.

While in Leipzig and Halle, I managed to get a glimpse of life under Communism or Socialism, the term preferred by the regime. In Leipzig, I sought out Auerbach's Keller, an old watering place made famous by Goethe's *Faust*. When I could not get timely service for some reason, I had to content myself with a fatty piece of pork belly with mashed potatoes at the Hauptbahnhof. I later learned that East Germans, especially waiters, tried to avoid any interaction with Westerners as such contacts were not encouraged by the regime. In my search to locate that restaurant, I noticed the complete absence of advertising or any form of sales promotion on the buildings or anywhere else as was common in the West. The reason, it occurred to me, was that the competition among suppliers of goods and services in the West that made advertising necessary was completely absent because the East German economy was completely under state control. When everything belongs to the same entity, there is no need for competition or sales promotion.

Helmut had offered to pick me up at my Leipzig lodgings and take me back there that evening. Hotel rooms in Leipzig were difficult to come by and the Fair management got me a room in a private home near the fairgrounds. My landlady made me a sumptuous breakfast that was unlike anything I had seen in East Germany and when she asked if she might have the room rent in Deutschmarks rather than the local East

German currency, I was happy to oblige. Helmut arrived in his Trabant, a 2-cylinder, gasoline and oil guzzling vehicle that was the standard make of automobile for those few privileged to own one. My cousin told me that he had already ordered its replacement because delivery normally took 7 years.

Christl, his wife, awaited us in their small but cozy apartment on Lutherstraße in one of those drab Stalinist style apartment complexes of that era. In his prior marriage with Heidi, Helmut told me, he had a son named Rüdiger who was now living with his mother and her new husband elsewhere in East Germany. Helmut apologized for the condition of their apartment which was in need of repair. Materials and repairmen were hard to come by, said Helmut, because there were no private contractors and to get anything done by the appropriate state agency one had to know and, on occasion, bribe the right party functionary. That was why so few people owned their own homes—it was simply too frustrating to keep property in good repair.

Before dinner, Helmut and I took a short walk around Halle. The air was putrid and a pungent odor engulfed the town. It came from the pollutants that were being daily spewed in the air by the surrounding chemical works. The state made no effort, probably due to the lack of funds, to remedy the situation. While doing some window shopping and looking into the windows of the closed shops, I noticed the absence of any brand-name products, such as Leica cameras, and assumed it was the night display since it was toward evening. Not so, according to Helmut, who informed me that any quality merchandise made in East Germany was exported for the hard currencies of the West, chiefly dollars and Deutschmarks, while the general public had to be content with other goods of lesser quality imported from neighboring Communist-bloc countries. For the lucky view with cash in hard currencies, however, special shops existed where quality merchandise could be purchased.

At the small food store we stopped at there was no need to decide what kind of meat we should buy—beef, pork, chicken, venison—because the choice had already been made for us. It was pork chops or pork bellies that day and nothing else. We brought home three pork chops, wrapped in newspaper, which Christl fried and served with a salad.

Over dinner, Helmut told me that he saw little hope that their economic system would survive much longer. The government, he said, worked out

5-year and yearly plans with production goals for various products. The plans also set the prices for theses goods. Unfortunately, production had no relationship with actual consumer needs or wants so that there was always an overabundance of some goods while others were in short supply or not available at all. Production goals were always met by the simple expedient of revising them downward whenever output fell short. Because the wages and salaries from the state-owned factories were automatically deposited into employee bank accounts, whether someone worked or not, there was little incentive to go to work. In fact, according to my cousin, they had employees at their plant who had to be periodically picked up by the authorities and brought in to do their jobs. All Communist economies, he said, worked this way. No wonder that a little over a decade later it all came to an abrupt end with the "fall of the Wall."

The Family Flees To The West

Cousin Peter, like his sister, was not happy with his life in the DDR and he and his family were among the many East Germans anxious to leave the country for the freer and more affluent West Germany especially after his mother had moved there in 1978. Peter Karl Rolf Zell, born on August 12, 1937 in Bitterfeld, was just two years old when his father left to serve with the Wehrmacht. Unlike his younger brother Helmut, Peter never became a friend of the regime. Not being allowed to pursue a university education, he was trained as a *Schlosser* [locksmith] and employed as a *Monteur* [construction worker] in the Halle/Bitterfeld area. His wife Karin, born on August 25, 1940, was the daughter of Günther Sommer, a salaried clerk, and Gertrude Sommer née Kunz. Peter and Karin were married on July 29, 1961 in Potsdam near Berlin. They had three children all born in Bitterfeld, namely, a son, Matthias, born in January 1962, and daughters Dörte-Christin (Dörte) and Beatrix (Trixi), born in June 1965 and November 1971, respectively. Since Peter and Karin were still well below retirement age, the East German regime was as eager to keep them in the country as the family was determined to get out.

Like all East Germans who wanted to leave, the family became suspect resulting in much harassment by the DDR authorities including special surveillance by the Stasi. Peter once told me that he and Karin kept up a lively correspondence with his mother and other relatives and friends in the West as a way of insuring that they would not some day be picked up by the Stasi and disappear without a trace. While contact with Westerners was not encouraged by the regime, Peter felt that staying in touch would diminish their chances of that happening because people would be alerted to their disappearance and make inquiries regarding their whereabouts. According to Peter, it took a concerted 3-year effort to obtain an exit permit before they finally succeeded.

In April 1984, he, Karin, and their three children arrived in the Federal Republic to join Peter's mother in Lohrhaupten. The following June Peter found employment in construction in a small spa town northeast of Frankfurt am Main called Bad Soden-Salmünster and relocated there with his family. I met Cousin Peter and his family for the first time on a Sunday in May 1993 while on a one-week vacation to visit Aunt Emmi in Geneva during her last illness and visits to Graben-Neudorf and Stuttgart. At that time, we also visited his mother in Lohrhaupten.

By the time I met up with Cousin Peter again, during a 3-week tour of Germany with a side trip to Rome in August and September of 2006, Peter's family had grown to include two of his children's spouses and four grandchildren. Matthias was divorced and had a son named Felix Peter (Felix), born in 1994, Dörte and husband Thomas had daughters Marie-Juliane (Julchen), born in 1984, and Neele-Frederike (Neele), born in 1996, while Trixi and husband Michael had a son, Tjard Berend (Tjard), born in 2001. At the time, Cousin Peter's oldest grandchild, Julchen, was a student at the Goethe Universität Frankfurt where she was studying history and German literature in preparation of becoming a teacher while her younger sister Neele had just begun attending the Gymnasium (secondary school). Felix had just turned 12 and the law now allowed him to choose the parent he wanted to live with and picked his father. (His mother lived with her new husband in Schwedt, a town in the state of Brandenburg near the Polish border). The youngest grandchild, Tjard, was a lively 5-year-old whom the family called *der Erfinder* [the inventor] because he continuously came up with new gadgets and ways of doing things.

By the time of my second visit in late summer of 2011, Julchen had graduated from the university and become a *Referendar* (teaching apprentice) in the town of Bingen on the Rhine. After passing a couple of more exams later in the year, she expected to obtain her teachers certificate and, after some years of teaching, attain the coveted title of *Beamtin* [female civil service employee with tenure]. She had a boyfriend named Kevin who worked as a traveling DJ and was making good money. Neele, her younger sister, was still attending the Gymnasium and considering an acting career. Felix planned to visit me next year after his Gymnasium graduation. He is a big fan of America, he told me, and loves everything American and someday wants to leave Germany for life in America. Tjard had just entered the Gymnasium and loved to write short stories and play the classical guitar.

Matthias, Thomas and Michael were all employed in technical services or sales support in and around Frankfurt am Main to where they commuted by train or car. Dörte and Trixi worked part-time in personnel management and accounting, respectively. The four families had managed to secure spacious and attractive flats within walking distance of each other which meant frequent family get-togethers. Peter and Karin's 5-room, balconied *Wohnung* was on the second floor of a 2-story home located on Frankfurter Straße right across the street from the village's Evangelische Kirche. The owner of the house, an elderly lady who lived on the first floor, was charging Peter a relatively low rent in exchange for taking care of the property including a large backyard with flower and vegetable gardens.

Life in the West was generally very good for the family even though Peter did encounter a major problem. When they arrived he was already in his upper 40s and with new job opportunities at that age limited, he returned to work in construction. In 1987, just three years after starting on his new job, he had the misfortune of losing his balance and falling off a roof. He suffered major injuries including a broken hip which laid him up for several months. The doctors inserted a nail in his hip joint which bothered him for the rest of his life.

While Peter and Karin never reached a level of affluence on a par with their fellow countrymen in the BRD, their generous social security income, which included regular plus disability benefits, allowed them to enjoy a very comfortable lifestyle. Since they had been cooped up in East Germany for most of their lives, they much enjoyed traveling about the country. For many years during the summer the two vacationed on Borkum, a German island in the North Sea. They regularly took day trips by train to Frankfurt am Main and other major towns throughout the country. Sometimes they returned to their roots in Bitterfeld where Birgit and Werner, Karin's sister and husband, still lived. On the occasion of their golden wedding anniversary in July 2011, their three children gave them a vacation trip with a week's stay in Berlin and Potsdam which they much enjoyed. During good weather, the two also took long bike rides to neighboring villages and through the scenically attractive countryside. When not on the road and weather permitting (the region is known for swiftly shifting winds and much rain), they enjoyed puttering around in their garden.

Like most former East Germans, Peter and Karin were not religious people. In fact, Peter told me that they do not believe in God even though both he and Karin were baptized and confirmed in the Evangelical (Lutheran) Church. The East German regime, whose prophet was Karl Marx and who declared religion to be "the opium of the people," was notoriously nontheistic and even replaced the Protestant rite of confirmation with a pagan state ritual called *Jugendweihe* [youth consecration]. Peter's children, although baptized in the Christian faith, also took part in this ceremony. As is common in today's secular Europe, two of his children pay the customary church taxes on income but attend worship services only on high Christian holidays if at all. Of Peter's and Karin's four grandchildren, three are baptized and confirmed Christians. The exception is Felix whose father was against it. Being non-believers, neither he nor Karin attended church except for the few occasions when one of their grandchildren was baptized or confirmed. According to Peter, when they came West and he found employment, he officially left the Evangelische Kirche to save the church taxes he would have been required to pay.[3]

Through my trips to Salmünster and our many letter and telephone exchanges, Cousin Peter and I got to know each other well and we became the best of friends. Despite having had only about eight years of formal schooling, Peter was surprisingly knowledgeable on many topics. He was an easy-going, unpretentious individual so that he reminded me much of how Mutti had described her father. Politically, he was aligned with the Christlich Demokratische Union Deutschlands or CDU (Christian Democrats), a center-right party and not, as one might have expected, the left-leaning Sozialdemokratische Partei Deutschlands or SPD (Social

Democrats). He told me that coming from East Germany he had enough of Socialism and Socialists to last him a lifetime. Like most of his countrymen, Peter was a die-hard *Fußball* [soccer] fan who spent much of his time in his easy chair watching the game.

For me Peter was a valuable source of information on our ancestors and contemporaries which much helped me write *Just Passing Through*. I was astounded by how thoroughly he had studied the ancestral records left by his father and the vital statistics he could recall about even distant relations. My cousin was very patient and forthcoming in answering the many questions I posed on the phone or in letters to him except in the case of Helmut. I had noticed that Peter never mentioned his brother and whenever I asked about him and how he was doing, he clammed up. He did, however, let me know once that they had kept Helmut in the dark about their planned emigration to West Germany because they could not trust him.

The whole operation was planned and executed, he said, in utmost secrecy with only their mother privy to the scheme. In fact, I heard that when their mother was still living in Halle before moving to the West, she and Helmut would take the same streetcar to work in the morning and not look at each other let alone say hello. Such was the distrust between mother and son. With the army of informants the Stasi had assembled to spy on relatives, friends, and neighbors who could blame Peter for being secretive with a family member who also happened to be part of the establishment? The resulting estrangement between Helmut and the rest of the family was so deep that when their mother passed away in February 2002 and Helmut came to town, he left for home immediately after the funeral service without even talking to his brother or anyone else in the family.

A Fatal Habit

Peter's one major problem was his severe addiction to that most deadly and wide-spread of all cravings, namely, tobacco. It would eventually cost him his life and, most likely, Karin hers. He was a chain smoker who went through two packs of cigarettes a day. Karin, who never smoked and was very health conscious, had even asked her husband to confine his habit to their half-bath (the flat also had a full bath) where he spent a few hours each day. My cousin's hacking cough every time we were on the phone much troubled me and, suspecting that it was on account of his heavy smoking, I continuously pestered him to see a doctor. He always countered saying he had his lungs checked every six months and they were always found to be clear.

It turned out that it was not Peter's lungs that suffered but his heart. In late February 2012, after not feeling well and visiting his physician, he was rushed to a local hospital where he received a defibrillator. The doctors found his heart scarred as a likely result of a silent heart attack which left this organ less than 30% functional. By late June, he was back in the hospital for follow-up surgery after his pulse again reached unacceptable levels. By the summer of the following year Peter reported that both he and Karin were suffering from circulation problems and so weak that they could no longer work in their garden and even had problems going up and down the stairs of their home. Fortunately, Trixi came by before work while Dörte, who lived across the street, tended to them after getting home from work.

It nevertheless came as a surprise and shock when I learned in early August 2013 that Karin had been admitted to a Fulda hospital and undergone surgery for breast cancer. It seems that she had noticed an abnormality and experienced severe back pains but, fearing the worst, had told no one about it, not even Peter. An examination revealed that her cancer was extremely aggressive and had already spread to her lymph nodes, spine, and liver, the latter of which was nearly gone. Karin subsequently had radiation treatment for her spine. The doctors debated the feasibility of chemotherapy for her liver and, after several weekly treatments, eventually stopped it and switched to drugs and hormones. Now and then she would be taken from home to a hospital, including the one at the Goethe University Frankfurt, for further treatments but, despite all the doctors' best efforts, she became progressively weaker.

Remarkably, Karin took everything in stride and insisted on dying at home. She rejected outside palliative care and even having a hospital bed installed in their apartment preferring to sleep on the family sofa. She was always heavily sedated and, according to Peter, in no pain and asleep most of the time. Karin passed away on the evening of Tuesday, January 28, 2014, at age 73, just six months after her cancer diagnosis. Peter called me the following day to give me the sad news saying he had sat next to her when she took her last breath. Needless to say, he was overcome by grief. They had been happily married for 52 years.

Things were not quite the same after Karin's passing. She had kept the family together and Peter seemed to become somewhat isolated from it. He wanted to show that he could manage on his own and rejected much of the help offered by his family. He cooked for himself although Dörte would have been happy to include him in the cooking for her family. Peter also went on another vacation by himself and in August 2016 took a train and ferry to Borkum where he rented a vacation apartment for three weeks. It was his 15th annual vacation there, he told me. As it turned out, it would be his last. By the end of the year, he complained of increasing weakness so that he hardly left the house anymore.

Peter began suffering from pain in the lower back and noticed blood in his urine. After doing tests on his bladder and kidneys in early February 2017, his doctors first concluded that the cause was the blood thinner medication he was taking but a CT scan done two months later revealed a tumorous left kidney. I talked to Peter for the last time on May 14 which was the day before his scheduled surgery. He feared that he might not survive because of his weak heart. I told him to hang in there because I had decided on a short trip to Germany during which I would stop by to help celebrate his 80th birthday in mid-August. In fact, I said, since our birthdays were only 10 days apart, we could celebrate both events together, mine at the beginning and his at the end of my trip.[4]

The following day I heard from Matthias that the operation was successful and that his father would be entering rehab. The bad news was that Peter had gotten out of bed and on the way to the bathroom had slipped and fallen braking his hip and hand. Peter had told him about my planned visit and they were looking forward to see me again, Matthias wrote. At the end of June Matthias e-mailed me *"Es gibt keine Hoffnung mehr"* [There is no hope left] and that his father would be entering palliative care in Bad Orb. It seems that after Peter had no appetite and was losing weight, the doctors had done another CT scan and found that his liver too was cancerous.

During his final days, according to Matthias, his father refused to take in any food or medication. On July 11, 2017 Matthias e-mailed me the sad news that his father had passed away on that day shortly after noon. The day was just a month short of his 80th birthday. With Peter's passing I had lost not only a cousin but my closest friend. According to Matthias, Peter would be buried in the local cemetery next to Karin. When I asked if a clergyman would be present at the funeral Matthias replied in the negative saying that his father was not a church member and would have preferred it that way. A week later Matthias e-mailed me a letter which, coming from a non-believer, was most remarkable. In translation, he wrote in part:

> *I take comfort in the thought that with death not everything has come to an end. I cannot conceive that with death we disappear without a trace and nothing remains. Maybe we will all meet again "above." Wouldn't that be something! As you know, we all were not raised as Christians but in a certain sense I believe in God. I cannot conceive that our lives and everything else on earth came about by chance... Anyway, I only wanted to say that I believe that after death something beautiful will await us—otherwise life would, in a certain sense, be quite meaningless.*

Could this be the beginning of a real conversion with tangible results, I thought, or just a passing notion to help him get over the emotional pain he was suffering?

A Family Feud

Germans are peculiar folks who are quick to take offense at any perceived slight. Even their neighbors, the French, have taken note and call a quarrel about nothing *une querelle d'Allemand*. Naturally, Elke and I contributed a wreath for his father's grave and Matthias sent me a photo of the gravesite showing it profusely adorned with several wreaths and bouquets of flowers. Another serious faux pass on my part would ensure that my friendship with at least one part of Cousin Peter's family would not last. I had taken special note of a photo of the gravesite Matthias had mailed me showing a temporary wooden cross (to be replaced with a more permanent marker later) with the inscription *Hier ruht in Gott Karin und Peter Zell* [Here rest in God Karin and Peter Zell]. I now had the nerve to question Matthias about it by mentioning that I was a little puzzled by these words since, as far as I knew, neither Karin nor Peter were believers. Even though I knew from Felix that his father had a short fuse, Matthias' response was unexpectedly angry. Evidently he mistook my comment as a direct attack on his father, which I had never intended, accusing me of being tactless and irreverent.

While his mother and father, Matthias wrote, were not Bible-thumping Christians and did not attend church on Sundays, they were more Christian than many churchgoers. All their lives they had endeavored never to harm others and had raised their children to follow their example. By the way, he wrote, they all said the Lord's Prayer at the grave. He praised his father as the most intelligent and well-read person he knew, a living encyclopedia, and yet one who was often belittled and ridiculed within his own family for being only a common laborer. Matthias concluded by putting me on notice that on the day of my planned visit, which would have been his father's birthday, he would not be available as he wanted to reserve that day in private contemplation. That I could well understand and wrote Felix proposing the following day, a Sunday, which would be the day before my return to the States.

Matthias' missive hinted at discord within the family and I only later learned that after Karin's death the once tight-knit family had split into two camps. It seems that one side accused the other of not coming to the house to visit their mother during her last illness when she asked them. Consequently, my visit became very problematic. On my arrival at Frankfurt's Rhein-Main airport on August 1, 2017 Felix was there to greet me. It was my custom to give each of my cousin's grandkids a substantial Euro gift when visiting and I gave Felix his. He must have been very disappointed because it surely was insufficient to get his car out of the garage where he had it for some time because he did not have the money for the needed repairs, he said. He nevertheless agreed to arrange a family get-together on the Sunday before my departure and try to contact his cousins.

When I arrived in Salmünster that Sunday Dörte's daughter Neele happened to be home and was surprised to see me. Neele informed me that she was making good progress at the Goethe University Frankfurt where she was following in the footsteps of her sister Julchen to become a teacher. Unlike Julchen, however, she had to take up English because there was no opening for her to study German literature. Her second major was history and she was just writing papers on the Holocaust and Caesar Augustus. She informed me that her mother and father were vacationing. They were on the island of Rügen, a German island in the Baltic Sea, where her father Thomas had an uncle.

At my request, Neele contacted Matthias and Trixi. Matthias replied that he was on the road and unavailable while Trixi said she was too busy to see me because she had to get Tjard ready for the beginning of school the following day. Consequently, I never got to see these members of Peter's family. At the village cemetery Neele and I visited Peter and Karin's grave and that of Aunt Irma which was nearby. After saying a prayer for their souls, Neele drove me to the Salmünster Bahnhof where I took a train to Schwanheim where I intended to spend my last night before my return home to Phoenix.

When I arrived in Frankfurt-Schwanheim late Sunday evening, a happy surprise awaited me. Kevin, Julchen's husband, showed up at my hotel to take me to their place on Altenhöferallee in Frankfurt am Main. Neele had just called her sister to let her know that I was in town and he had frantically searched to find me, he said, because nobody (meaning Matthias and Felix) had let them know I would be coming. At their flat in a leafy part of town I had a warm reunion with Julchen who showed off their beautiful new baby son Jasper. Jasper had been born prematurely, I learned, and was just two months old. His parents described him as the perfect baby who never cried but just peacefully slept in his crib or in their arms. Cousin Peter, I knew, had much looked forward to seeing his first great-grandchild but it was not to be. Kevin and Julchen had been married in a civil ceremony in nearby Wiesbaden in January 2016. According to Peter, who attended the wedding, of the family only Dörte with her family was there as well as Birgit and Werner from Bitterfeld while Matthias and Trixi with their families were conspicuously absent.

The happy couple was financially very well off. After spending some years in the Frankfurt am Main school system, in May 2015 Julchen had attained her goal of becoming a *Beamtin*. When Julchen met Kevin he was a DJ traveling throughout Germany for one-night performances. After years on the road, he decided on a career change and using his entrepreneurial talents and boundless energy started a German doughnut franchise business.

At the time few Germans knew what a doughnut was and none of the well-known American franchises specializing in these pastries had yet become established in the country. As it turned out, I was able to contribute in a small way to the financial success of this young family.[5]

Kevin started Tasty Donuts & Coffee, with a friend and fellow DJ as co-owner, in April 2012 with a tiny shop near the major Frankfurt shopping street, the Zeil. A local *Konditor* [confectioner] made the doughnuts for him while his coffee was a special blend he selected from a Hamburg importer. Using newspaper advertisements to attract franchisees, he rapidly grew his business and by August 2014, when he sold it to a Swiss investor, his chain of franchises had grown to 38, according to Kevin. After its sale he stayed on as general manger and had just started another franchise operation specializing in Italian foods. According to Cousin Peter, Kevin was paid 1.2 million Euros for his business, which after paying out his partner's one-third stake, still left him with a tidy sum. Yet despite his new-found wealth and enjoying a good income, home prices in the Frankfurt am Main area were so steep, said Kevin, that to buy their own home he and Julchen would still have had to take on a sizeable mortgage and restrict their comfortable lifestyle for years to come. This they were unwilling to do.

The family's 3-room flat in a newer building was bright and cheery and included a roof garden outside their spacious living room. The couple got around in three cars, one of which was used by Kevin for his business. According to Kevin, the only one of Peter's three children he and Julchen still have contact with is Dörte. When I asked him whether he would consider living in America someday he replied that he would do so in a heartbeat but it was not likely to ever happen because Julchen would never leave Germany since becoming a *Beamtin* in the German civil service system.

Of Cousin Peter's two grandsons, I only got to know Felix more than casually since he twice visited me in my retirement home in Arizona. During his first visit in October 2012, we had three weeks together during which we crisscrossed Arizona visiting most places of interest and, of course, Arizona's chief attraction, the Grand Canyon. We even made a side trip to Las Vegas. Felix was 18 at the time and had grown to nearly 6 feet tall and weighed 270 pounds. Hella, his father's new life partner, was a very good cook, he explained. (I had met Hella, a geriatric nurse, on my

2011 visit to the family). Felix was still much excited about America and things American. He especially liked Arizona, he said, because here he found himself free of the allergies that made life miserable for him back home. He came with a backpack stuffed with every type of electronic and optical gear imaginable which he carried with him wherever he went. His father had obviously spoiled him as a reward for choosing to live with him rather than his mother. Being a teen, he was infatuated with muscle cars especially if their engines made lots of noise.

When Felix came for a second visit, in April 2014, he brought along a friend also named Felix. This Felix had been to the States many times before because his parents, who owned a carton factory in Germany, owned a second home in Florida. The two young men rented a 2013 Mustang and drove to the Grand Canyon and from there to Las Vegas before returning to my place and home again.

Felix had matriculated at the Goethe University Frankfurt in the fall of 2013. Since he always liked mathematics, that was the curriculum he chose. Early in 2014, he wrote me that he had great difficulty with his courses and then, during his 2014 visit, revealed that he had failed two of his three courses and would likely have to repeat them. I then suggested that he take up business administration, like his friend, which could lead to many job opportunities. Instead, Felix struggled on with mathematics until the beginning of 2015 when he decided to drop out and learn a trade. One reason he chose math was because it required little reading. He absolutely loathed it, he told me, and had never read a book in his life.

After his return to Germany, Felix found an apprenticeship with a company that trains young people for employment with firms located in the Industriepark Hoechst (Hoechst Industrial Park), the same venue as I.G. Farben-Griesheim where Opa Peter had been employed. Incidentally, the German apprenticeship model that combines classroom instruction with on-the-job training during which time the apprentice is also paid ("earn while you learn") is a unique feature of the German educational system and now being copied in other countries including the States. Felix's apprenticeship, to begin on September 1, would lead to the title of electronics specialist for automation technology. Upon his graduation, his sponsor would become his employer. Neither Felix, his father nor I have been in contact since my 2017 visit but I have since learned that Felix has completed his apprenticeship and is gainfully employed.

Dörte's family and I, on the other hand, have stayed in touch. Julchen and Kevin informed me of the birth in June 2019 of their second child, a boy they named Jonte, and that they have since moved to another part of town. From Neele I learned that in October 2019 she passed her *Erste Staatsprüfung* [First State Examination] which completed her studies at the Goethe Universität Frankfurt. Beginning on November 1, 2020, she will be a *Referendarin* [female teaching associate] and in about three years or so will be eligible to take her second state exam. Assuming that she passes, she will be accredited as a teacher and *Beamtin* just like her sister.

Family members had, in the meantime, settled their differences, she told me, but that they were no longer as close as before when their Oma was still alive. According to Neele, she has been contemplating a sabbatical of a couple of months to perfect her English-language skills in London. She is also looking forward to take me up on my invitation to visit sometime soon and meet the American side of the family.

EMMI'S STORY

A Taste For Adventure

Mutti once derisively said of her older sister that she got her education on the *Abort* [privy]. That was because whenever someone was looking for Emmi during her early teens, she could be found in the family outhouse reading one of those trashy romance novels called *Schmöker* that were popular with German girls and young women at the time. They served as an escape from their humdrum lives in the very conservative towns and villages across most of the country including her native Schwanheim am Main. Oma evidently refused to let Emmi bring them into the house. Emmi must have taken much of what she read to heart because her life almost reads like a *Schmöker* even though it includes parts that not even the most imaginative writer of such literature could have ever dreamed up.

Louise Emma Zell, Peter and Rosa's third child and first daughter, was born in Schwanheim am Main on December 18, 1903 and, like all new members of the Evangelical (Lutheran) Church community, baptized in the chapel of the local Martinusgemeinde. In her case, this did not take place until May 29 of the following year. To the family she was simply known as Emmi but in later years she also liked to use Emmy or Emy when referring to herself.

From early on Emmi showed some peculiar behavior that did not endear her to the family and especially not to her Sister Annemarie of whom she was intensely jealous. Once, when Mutti was still a baby in her crib, her older sister was caught squeezing her nostrils shut or at least that was what it seemed she was doing. Thereafter, she was always watched and not allowed to be left alone with her baby sister. The family was also turned off by her singular selfishness as a child. Thus, during times of food shortage as during and after World War I, Emmi could be counted on to now and then sneak into the pantry to help herself to some scarce rations especially sugar which she craved.

That is not to say that Emmi had little going for herself. When she was in her mid-teens, Opa's family on his mother's side, the Kirchhoffs, invited her to spend a summer at their estate in East Prussia and when she returned from there, according to Mutti, she was a changed person. Instead of the easy-going Hessian dialect the family spoke, with the exception of Oma who's German had more of an Alsatian (Alemannic) flavor, Emmi now talked in the rapid fire high German spoken in Prussia, especially around Berlin and the eastern provinces. She also took on a sophisticated air and set herself apart from the family which she now considered hopelessly gauche.

Among Emmi's biggest assets were her stunning good looks combined with a quick intelligence and a bubbly, cheerful personality. In conversation she was charming and articulate and could talk knowledgeably on many topics. Presumably, she learned much from her father. These attributes made Emmi popular among her peers in the village. In fact, according to Mutti, Schwanheim's young male population was agog and she found herself the center of much attention. For Emmi, however, nothing homegrown seemed to hold much interest for her.

Emmi's first romantic encounter was with a Major Schneedecker, a French army officer who commanded the French occupation forces outside Frankfurt am Main after World War I. His headquarter was in Höchst am Main but a garrison of French troops was stationed in Schwanheim. Major Schneedecker soon heard of Emmi and her exceptional attributes and came calling. Judging from the major's name, it is likely that he came from Alsace-Lorraine, the region on the Rhine River that is now part of France but had been bouncing back and forth between France and Germany for the past few hundred years. He and Oma, who was born there, clearly had something in common, including the language, and he was at first a welcome guest. However, the major was apparently not a very tactful person and the family, according to Mutti, took offense with his overbearing attitude. On at least one occasion he made fun of a large photo in the family living room showing a proud Opa with his chest adorned with an array of medals he had won in competitive sports. Most importantly, the family discovered that Major Schneedecker was a married man and the relationship between the two came to a abrupt end when Emmi's parents told the officer that he was no longer welcome in their house.

Her independent streak and search for adventure led Emmi to Frankfurt am Main which was just a few miles down the road. She gradually drifted away from home and went there with increasing frequency on the Waldbahn steam railway. There she met up with a very unsavory character named Max Aeschbach. Max was a Swiss citizen from Zürich and nearly 9 years her senior. Nobody was ever able to figure out what Max's occupation was but Mutti probably came close when she once referred to him as *der alte Zuhälter* [the old pimp].

Max got Emmi pregnant which scandalized the family and, as Emmi would bitterly complain for the rest of her life, her parents simply tossed her out of the house and refused to have anything more to do with her. As cruel as her parent's conduct may have been, in a village where practically everyone was *fromm katholisch* [piously Catholic], Emmi's conduct was simply unacceptable and the family could not afford to see its reputation and social standing ruined because of one miscreant member who was out of control. Emmi had no choice but to cohabit with Max in Frankfurt am Main where, according to her sister, she had an abortion, which was illegal, so as not to lose her slender figure.

The Berlin Years

The end of World War I was followed by a decade of exuberance and high spirits that came to be known as the Roaring Twenties. In those days, Berlin, the capital of the post-war Weimar Republic, was the place to be not only for German but foreign highfliers as well. Most of the world's great scientists, including Albert Einstein, lived and worked there and so did the foremost artists, composers, painters, and writers of the day. It was an exciting, fun kind of place that attracted people from all over who came to sample Berlin's famous cabarets and other stage entertainments, and the diverse cultural offerings including world famous art galleries, museums, opera houses, and symphony orchestras. Great cities attract both the best and worst segments of society. Not surprisingly, this cultural Mecca also gained a reputation for unbridled vice and pleasures of the flesh.

Max Aeschbach too decided to partake of Berlin's delights and convinced Emmi that Frankfurt am Main was too small and provincial a place for them to be. They must head for Berlin where both the action and the money were and set up shop there.

In June 1931 Emmi invited Mutti to visit her and Max in their Berlin *Wohnung*. Mutti was just 22 years old at the time and her sister at 27 at the pinnacle of her Berlin career. Mutti came up by train from Frankfurt am Main and on arrival at the Berlin Hauptbahnhof was met by her sister who, driving a big limousine, brought her to her new home near the Bayerischer Platz in the Schöneberg district of town. There she found Emmi and Max ensconced in a luxurious flat in an attractive, 5-story apartment building located at Salzburgerstraße 11.

Mutti was taken aback by the opulence of their domicile. The period furniture was exquisite, the polished floors were covered by thick oriental rugs, chandeliers hung from the ceiling and the walls held oil paintings of the type one normally saw only in museums. There was even a maid, a young lady whom Emmi had brought up from Graben-Neudorf. Mutti's sister referred to her place as a salon where she entertained only the crème de la crème of Berlin's gentlemen population with a taste for beautiful and sophisticated women.

Emmi clearly was a success as she had beaten all odds by rising from an unsophisticated village girl with little formal education or means to become a celebrity and toast of a great metropolis. Mutti's account of her sister's Berlin years was later corroborated in court documents concerning the disposition of her estate after her death in Switzerland. An excerpt, in French, described her thus:

> *Louise Emma Zell est née 18 décembre 1903 en Allemagne. Elle résidait à Berlin où elle est devenue une personnalité très célèbre dans les années vingt, renommée pour sa beauté et son élégance notamment.*

In translation: "Louise Emma Zell was born on December 18, 1903 in Germany. She was a resident of Berlin where she became a celebrity during the 20s, especially renowned for her beauty and elegance."

Many of her clients, Emmi told her sister, were foreigners who all had one thing in common—they were very wealthy and sometimes even titled.

One of her clients was an oil baron from Texas who was very generous but always carried a gun on him which made her feel ill at ease. Another was a British lord who took her, along with her luxury sedan, on a world cruise which included India and New York City. That relationship soured, according to Mutti, after her sister continued to show interest in other men.

The apartment and its furnishings were not really hers, her sister confided in Mutti, but belonged to an elderly lady, a Frau Meier (or Maier) who had fallen on hard times but still maintained a room in the apartment. Frau Meier was the widow of a prominent Berlin banker who had lost his fortune during the economic upheaval and period of hyperinflation in Germany in the early 1920s. Since she was no longer able to maintain herself in her upscale home, this lady decided to enter into a novel but mutually beneficial arrangement with a person of means. How the two parties met is not known but Frau Meier agreed to let Max and Emmi use her flat as a salon and, in return, they would pay for the upkeep of the place and let her continue to live in her home as long as she desired. This arrangement seemed to equitably meet the needs of both parties and, on its face, should have worked out very well.

During her stay, Mutti had a chance to briefly talk with Frau Meier in private. What Mutti learned greatly disturbed her. According to this lady, Max and Emmi had come to severely restrict Frau Meier's movements and had confined her to a small room which she was allowed to leave only by permission. Furthermore, they had turned mean and abusive and had come to treat her not as the homeowner and lady of the house but as a housekeeper and servant at their beck and call. Mutti felt sorry for Frau Meier but, not wanting to cause problems with her sister, kept the troubling news to herself.

While Emmi was doing her thing, Max was engaged in another lucrative venture. Switzerland had always been known for its fine watches and there was a large and growing demand for this product in Berlin. The import tariff was, alas, very steep making Swiss watches very expensive in the city and anywhere else in the country. This is where Max stepped in to alleviate the situation and give average Berliners the opportunity to own this much valued commodity at an affordable price. He did this by cutting out the middleman or rather three of them—the state customs office, the importer, and the retailer. Max, according to Mutti, was on the Zürich-Berlin run of the watch import business and conveyed many Swiss watches from his hometown to his new domicile using his very cost-efficient technique.

On his many runs back and forth, Max would always manage to get the product past those pesky custom officials at the German-Swiss border by carrying an enormous, oversized handkerchief into which he had wrapped a large contingent of watches. On reaching the border, he would hold the stuffed hankie close to his face and coughing, sneezing and wheezing feign he had a bad case of the flu or something even more contagious like pneumonia. Invariably, one of the guards would recognize him and shout, "Oh, it's that sickly old Max again" and wave him through. It is difficult, of course, to believe that the customs officials at the border were naïve enough to consistently fall for this trick and were presumably in on the scheme.

The Berlin days of the happy twosome were numbered, however. National Socialism was on the rise in Germany and the Nazis were promising the people that once in power they would rid Germany of every vestige of that decadent western influence, mostly American and French, and all the vices that had taken hold in Berlin and elsewhere in the country after the war. They would do this by closing down the cabarets, the bawdy houses, the so-called salons and everything else they considered immoral and illicit and restore the country to the pure and pristine state that was supposedly the heritage of the German people.

Many people, especially foreigners living in Berlin, saw the handwriting on the wall and started to leave the city and the country. By the early 1930s, demand for Emmi's services had seen a steep decline and a once lucrative, although disreputable, business withered away. Max and Emmi decided it was time to leave town and fast and, since he was a Swiss citizen, to a haven awaiting them just across the border. They did so but not without first committing a most heinous act that would result in the death of Frau Meier.

It so happened that the lady of the house had to be out of town for a few days and Max and Emmi decided that this was the opportune time to pull off their diabolical scheme. They loaded all of Frau Meier's furniture, paintings, rugs, silver, china and everything else that was valuable and not nailed down into a truck and took off for Switzerland. When Frau Meier returned from her trip and saw the apartment emptied and stripped of all her possessions, she walked into the Havel (one of the two rivers that flow through Berlin) and drowned herself.

Back in Schwanheim Mutti learned about Frau Meier's suicide and the part played in it by Max and Emmi and was incredulous and shocked. She had, after all, known Frau Meier and commiserated with her but had, alas, done nothing to assist the poor soul to alleviate the terrible fix she found herself in. Of course, there probably was not much that Mutti could have done except go to the police. What was previously simply a case of sibling rivalry and mutual jealousies between the two sisters now blossomed into something that would result in long-term consequences for their relationship and beyond. Mutti began to loathe and despise her sister and could hardly ever talk of her again without bringing up the Frau Meier affair.

A Short Marriage

Instead of heading straight for Zürich, as might have been expected since that is where Max was from, the two made for Luzern (Lucerne) which lies some miles southwest of Zürich. There, according to the public record, Max Aeschbach and Louise Emma Zell were married on July 14, 1933. The couple then left for Genève (Geneva) in the French-speaking part of the country. This may have been at least partly Emmi's idea because she spoke a passable French and probably thought that life in little Paris, as Geneva was called, would be more to her liking than that staid and humdrum German-speaking Zürich. Max and Emmi got divorced in Geneva less than three years later, on June 17, 1936. At the same time, Emmi decided to forego the name Aeschbach and take back Zell, her maiden name. Their short marriage was interpreted, falsely as would later be revealed, to mean that Aunt Emmi married Max for just one reason—to obtain Swiss citizenship. In these turbulent times, this was a very prized commodity.

Despite their divorce, it had little impact on their relationship since Max and Emmi remained lifelong friends and companions. He spent his time commuting between Zurich, where he maintained a flat, and Emmi's home in Geneva. When he showed up at her villa in June 1975, Aunt

Emmi later recalled, he had come home to her to die. She cared for him for a short time but when the task proved too much for her, she reluctantly had him transferred to a nursing home in nearby Thônex, GE, on the French border. There he passed away less than a year after his latest arrival, on April 1, 1976 at age 81.[6]

A Wealthy New Partner

A few years after arriving in Geneva, Emmi's fortunes took a huge turn for the better when she met one of the most eligible bachelors in town—a wealthy investment banker by the name of Charles August Hirzel. According to Mutti, the two met in a Geneva night club. The year must have been 1940 or thereabouts because that was when Max left Geneva for Zürich and, according to his curriculum vitae, Charles Hirzel arrived in Geneva from Basel after the death of his mother. Charles was a 39-year-old bachelor who had never been married. This valuable catch at age 36 would attest to Emmi's continuing allure for men of means. Charles held dual American and Swiss citizenship having been born in Cornwall, New York, on August 27, 1901.

His father Karl Friedrich Hirzel, the scion of a wealthy Zürich merchant family whose *Bürgerrecht* [freedom of the city] dated to the first half of the 15th century, had founded and managed a successful export-import business in New York City at the time and also served as the agent for a major transatlantic steamship line. After the death of his first wife, an American named Maria Feltmann, in November 1895 Karl had married Adèle Valentine de Bondeli, the daughter of a noble family from Berne. The Hirzels had three children of which Charles was the youngest. Charles was only three months old when his father died. In January 1903, Adèle and her three children returned to Berne.

After attending schools in Berne, Charles left for Geneva in November 1920 to learn the banking business. He subsequently moved to London and from there to India where he made a small fortune in the cotton trade. He returned to Switzerland in 1928 and until 1940 worked for the Basler Handelsbank in Basel. Returning to Geneva in 1940, he became affiliated with Lombard Odier, a private investment bank founded in 1796. Charles subsequently opened up his own trade and investment bank, S.A. de Gérance et de Dépôts, in Lombard Odier's headquarters building at 11, rue de la Corraterie. Through his bank, Charles managed and invested the assets of his clients which were mostly wealthy Frenchmen.

As his fortune grew so did his valuable collection of vintage postage stamps from many countries which he had inherited from his father. His collection of early United States postage stamps is widely regarded as one of the finest in the world. It was last shown in the United States at the Sixths International Philatelic Exhibition (Sipex) held in Washington, D.C. during May 21-30, 1966 where it won the gold medal. Parenthetically, I had seen part of Uncle Charles' stamp collection as an 11-year-old during my visit to Aunt Emmi in September 1947 and again in May 1966 at Washington's Shoreham Hotel where the Sipex exhibition was held.

Sadly, Uncle Charles could not witness this highly anticipated event as he had passed away just three months earlier.

An announced agreement to bring the Charles A. Hirzel Philatelic Collection back to the United States for viewing at the Smithsonian's National Postal Museum in Washington, D.C. in 2008 and 2009 did not materialize when the Swiss decided it involved too much risk. Incidentally, today his collection is on permanent exhibit at the Museum für Kommunikation (Museum for Communications) in Berne.

Although Charles and Emmi lived together for a quarter of a century, they were never married. The reasons are not clear but it could have been that he or she simply did not want to enter into a formal marital relationship. It is also possible that he was discouraged from doing so by his family, i.e., his sisters Ester May Steinfels-Hirzel of Zürich, who was married to the owner of a well-known Zurich detergent manufacturer, and Evelyn Natalie de Pogranyi-Nagy of Berne, who had been married to a Hungarian nobleman. As to Evelyn, Charles generously supported her through the years since she had no substantial source of income of her own. Perhaps Aunt Emmi was not considered *vom Stand* [of compatible social position] or the sisters were concerned about the fate of their brother's and the family's considerable wealth in case of death or divorce. In any case, Charles and Emmi were in a relationship tantamount to marriage. (In some U.S. jurisdiction such an arrangement is called a common-law marriage).

A curriculum vitae, prepared for the exhibition of his postage stamps in Washington, D.C., tried to explain the relationship between Charles and Emmi this way (in translation from the German):[7]

> His [Charles Hirzel's] chronic Polyarthritis severely limits his activities throughout his life. He is dependent on constant care. A special relationship exists with his *Pflegefachfrau* [professional caregiver] who lives with him together with her husband in the same house. She completely isolates him from the outside. Even his family can visit him only in the offices of his firm. His philatelic life too plays out in his offices at 11 (or 13?), rue de la Corraterie. .... Charles August Hirzel dies in Geneva on February 11, 1966. His caregiver inherits his houses in Geneva and Grasse (France). As compensation for the *Wohnrecht* [occupancy rights] in the headquarters of Lombard & Odier, the management of Hirzel's accounts is turned over to this firm.

His biographer is to be commended for putting such a favorable spin on Uncle Charles' life in regard to his relationship with my Aunt Emmi. Of course, anybody who personally knew my aunt would also have known that she was not a professional caregiver and could not have acted in such a capacity by either training or inclination. On the contrary, she was independently wealthy when she arrived in Geneva and met Charles and was never his employee. The relationship between the two was from the start based on mutual attraction and friendship. The severity of Charles' arthritis also seems to have been overstated possibly to make Charles' need for a professional caregiver, and thus Aunt Emmi's existence in his life, more plausible. His arthritic condition did not prevent him from doing his job at the bank, work at his stamp collection, attend stamp shows, or engage in many other activities until the very last years of his life.

On the other hand, the claim that Emmi, Max and Charles lived together may well have been the case although when I visited Aunt Emmi in Geneva as a child, I never heard of or saw Uncle Max. Also, contrary to the biography, Emmi was not married at the time. If they indeed lived together as a threesome it would have been quite remarkable because Max and Charles would have had almost nothing in common except for their fixation on Emmi. For Aunt Emmi, this time would have been life at its most enjoyable because she once told me of a woman's dream existence in which she lived together with two or three men who each adored and treated her like a queen. "*Wäre das nicht schön?*" [Wouldn't that be beautiful?], she had asked me. I personally thought it a little weird but did not respond not realizing at the time that she may actually have lived that dream.

The mid-1930s through the early 1960s were undoubtedly very good years for Emmi. From the time of her arrival in Switzerland until 1945, the end of the war, she was living in relative safety in Switzerland away from the war and turmoil that would eventually engulf her homeland and the rest of Europe. And she had come not as a penniless refugee but, after her successful Berlin career (and act of thievery), as a woman of considerable means. Max Aeschbach was around whenever she needed him and, beginning in 1940, she also had a man at her side who not only loved and respected her but whose financial expertise made him and his clients extremely wealthy and was adding to her own fortune as well.

Their handsome residence at 23B, avenue de Miremont was located in one of the most fashionable parts of town and lavishly furnished. Nothing was lacking in the way of creature comforts. There was always one full-time maid living with them and sometimes two. At least once a year, the two would drive to Grasse, the flower capital of France and cradle of that country's perfume industry, to spend a few weeks in their second home on the French Riviera. There, in Chateauneuf de Grasse, a village a short distance north of Cannes, they would relax in Charles' villa La Rato Penado overlooking the Mediterranean Sea.

It seems sad and unfair at times, but all good things must eventually come to an end. Towards the mid-1960s, Charles' health began to fail. He had kidney problems plus suffered from constant pain in his fingers which were badly contorted from his rheumatoid arthritis. As mentioned by his biographer, he had problems of a different sort as well. It seems that as time went on, Emmi did her best to seal Charles off from all outside contacts, including his family, as she became increasingly apprehensive of her own unprotected status in case Charles should die or find someone else to consort with. Her vulnerable position and her constant suspicion that he was straying appears to have made her almost paranoid. Thus, it is known that for many years Emmi would incessantly call Charles' office to check up on him and his whereabouts. At times, she would even show up unannounced at the bank and, if felt provoked, create a scene much to his and the banking staff's great embarrassment.

Charles' condition eventually forced him to retire from the bank after which Emmi took care of him at home with the assistance of a nurse. When Uncle Charles passed away on February 11, 1966 at age 65 in their villa in Geneva, he left Aunt Emmi the house and their vacation retreat in Chateauneuf de Grasse. The bulk of his estate, which at one time was rumored to be on the order of two hundred million Swiss francs, including his valuable stamp collection, he bequeathed to his mother's hometown of Berne.

A Difficult Visit

Some four years later, in mid-April 1970, I myself arrived in Geneva after I had received my MBA degree and Aunt Emmi had invited me to stay with her while I was conducting my search for a corporate management position in Europe. To my surprise, Aunt Emmi was not alone but had Max for company. This is the first time I really got to know him although I had seen him once before as a young teenager. That was towards the end of 1951 when he had briefly stopped by our *Wohnung* in Stuttgart after Mutti had returned to the States and Ute and I were living there in the care of the French-German couple, Robert and Liesel. Uncle Max, who introduced himself as our aunt's former husband, seemed to have some other business in town to tend to because we got to see him only briefly before he was on his way again. Presumably Aunt Emmi had sent him to check up on us.

When we met this time in Geneva, Max had just turned 75. He was tall and gaunt and walked with a stoop. His lean, furrowed face reminded me of Andrew Jackson on the United States $20 bill. Living with Aunt Emmi, Max took it easy and daily slept almost until noon and, after having something to eat and lounging around the house for a while, he would take a walk to his favorite café on the other side of the Parc Alfred Bertrand. There he would spend most of the afternoon. On the way back, he would pick up a couple of girlie magazines und, after supper, study these until it was time for bed. I was not allowed to park my 1967 Mercury

Cougar which I had brought over, in either of the two garages on the property because both were supposedly occupied. They were indeed and when I once clandestinely walked into the larger of the two, I found two walls stacked high with uncle Max's extensive collection of his favorite magazines.

Being under the same roof with the two, was not a pleasant experience. I got much annoyed when I realized that Aunt Emmi was opening my mail and not passing it on to me. Some letters from Mutti which contained important information such as recommendations from former employers, which I needed in my job search, never got to me. When I wrote Mutti to complain about her sister's despicable conduct, she wrote back in June that both she and Esther had forewarned me, "*daß diese Person kein Gewissen hat*" [that this person has no conscience].

As for Uncle Max, we were two very different individuals and unable to bond. We never had an argument but nevertheless tried to stay out of each other's way. There was a certain coarseness about him that turned me off and his talk was liberally sprinkled with expletives. My opinion of Max was negatively impacted by what I had heard about him from Mutti so that I necessarily considered him somewhat of a lowlife who probably never held a real job and made his living by exploiting others including my aunt.

My bad impression of Uncle Max was confirmed when one day Aunt Emmi answered the phone and shouted (translated from the German), "Max, it's Düsseldorf, your wife wants to talk to you." I was stunned and asked Aunt Emmi for an explanation. It seems that during the war, Max had married a Jewish woman whose family owned a factory in Germany. Their marriage had put the business under the Swiss flag and thereby saved it from confiscation by the Nazis. This is presumably why Max and Emmi were married for only three years. Clearly, Max's second was a marriage of convenience and he had entered into it for whatever benefits it brought him.

My strong negative feelings for Max were matched by his for me. In a letter she wrote to Mother six years after my visit, Aunt Emmi spoke of Max's intense dislike of me and how he had agitated for her to show me the door almost from day one. My mother had evidently sung my praises to her sister, as mothers are wont to do, because Aunt Emmi wrote back that Mutti did not have to tell her how *anständig* [decent, trustworthy] her son was. *"Ich weiss das; ich habe ihn sehr gern"* [I know that; I like him very much], she wrote, and then explained that she could not involve me in her affairs (presumably financial) and keep me in Geneva because *"Max war furchtbar eifersüchtig* " [Max was terribly jealous] and continuously made the biggest scenes whenever I was temporarily out of the house.

Max's jealousy seemed well founded as we learned much later. In her will and testament Aunt Emmi had named Max as her sole heir. Her ex-husband was most likely fearful Aunt Emmi would change her mind and make a new will to include her favorite nephew and godchild. And so it came about that Aunt Emmi told me it was time for me to move on and after just five weeks with them, and before I had time to properly follow up on all of my job leads, I left Geneva for Cologne. There, working out of a hotel room, I found a sales job with an American computer company.

Mutti and her sister had not seen each other for many years and during my time in Germany an opportunity arose for the two to get together again. After a year with my new employer I had decided to return home to the States while Mutti had reached retirement age and was no longer working. This would be a good time for her to come over to visit our relatives and friends again. After much cajoling, I persuaded her to take one of the passenger ships then on the North Atlantic run and travel from New York City to Bremerhaven from where she could take a train to Frankfurt am Main and visit me in Frankfurt-Sachsenhausen where I lived in a rented studio apartment. We could return home together the same way and send my car ahead on a freighter. After her arrival in mid-June 1971, we used my Cougar to travel throughout the country for about seven weeks before returning home.

At the beginning of July, Mutti took a train to Geneva to visit her sister but was back five days later because she did not want to miss an outing to the scenic Odenwald region with her classmates from the Schwanheimer Volksschule the following day. She might have left for Geneva earlier and spend more time with her sister but because the two never got along, Mutti wisely decided that she did not want to overstay her welcome.

Time For Travel

My next opportunity to visit Aunt Emmi came in mid-May of 1977 after a Pittsburgh-based company sent me to Germany on an extended assignment. My aunt appeared in good health, although she had put on much weight, and was surprisingly upbeat. Long walks through the Parc Alfred Bertrand gave us the opportunity for some bonding. According to Aunt Emmi, after Max had died a year ago, she had indulged her love for foreign travel by taking the train to various places of interest. On a few occasions she had gone to Freiburg in the Black Forest to visit relatives of Max including his nephew Fritz and wife Erika, and to consult her eye doctor. On her travels, she said, she had gone as far away as Spain to enjoy its beaches and sunny climate. Since she made no mention of visiting the villa in Grasse which Uncle Charles had left her, she had presumably sold it by then.

One time Aunt Emmi showed up in Graben-Neudorf, where she had attended my baptism some 40 years earlier, to visit with Erika and Julius Kuchenbeißer. When Uncle Jule some years later talked of her visit, he said that when she arrived they were bewildered to see her looking more like a homeless person than the lady of means that she was.

Her most enjoyable trips, said Aunt Emmi, were to Rome where she had a good friend by the name of Theresa Rolli. They called each other regularly, she said, and she had visited her a number of times. According to my aunt, while she much enjoyed being with Theresa their get-togethers always left her a little embarrassed. It seems that whenever she arrived at Rome's Termini train station, Theresa would greet her in the Italian fashion with a profuse display of affection including bear hugs and ardent kisses on the lips. One day Aunt Emmi got a call from Theresa asking if it would be all right for her son Mario to stop by for a few days. He had planned a trip to London and wanted to check out Geneva on the way. She would be more than happy to accommodate her son, Aunt Emmi told her, especially since Theresa had always graciously put her up whenever she came to Rome.

When Mario arrived, Aunt Emmi was surprised to see him accompanied by a young boy whom he described as a relative. Aunt Emmi was charmed by the youngster and some maternal instincts apparently took hold of her. Without further ado, she dragged the startled kid upstairs, got the water running, put him in the tub, and proceeded to give him a bath. The boy, she said, was extremely shy but absolutely gorgeous with classic features, curly black hair, and soft white skin. After dinner, she assigned Mario to the bedroom next to the staircase and gave the boy the room next to hers, the one over the little salon. When Aunt Emmi had to get up during the night to answer nature's call, she noticed that the light was still on in the boy's room and when she walked across the hallway she found Mario's room empty. It was immediately obvious to her, she said, that Mario had joined the boy in his bedroom. This got her extremely upset. The next morning, according to my aunt, she wasted no time to vent her anger by telling Mario over breakfast that she wanted him and the boy out of her house as soon as they had finished eating.

Obviously, Aunt Emmi could have handled the situation more tactfully and, most importantly, should have called her friend in Rome before doing anything. What happened next was entirely predictable. The following day Theresa called absolutely furious by the way her son and his young companion had been treated. There followed a heated exchange that, alas, effectively ended their friendship.

According to Aunt Emmi, she was anxious to travel some more but as a woman now in her early 70s, she no longer felt comfortable doing so by herself. She was anxious to find a travel companion. This is where I came into the picture, she told me. How would I like to go on trips with her with all expenses paid? In addition, there would be a generous stipend for my services to boot. I would then no longer have to worry about having a job. She owned a great fortune, she told me (without offering any particulars), and was looking for an heir. She really liked me, she said. After once telling me that I reminded her of a little *Pfälzer Bauer* [peasant from the Palatinate], she now went on a charm offensive. *"Du hast grosse Augen"* [You have large eyes], she told me grinning impishly like a little school girl.

I told my aunt that her proposal was completely out of the question for me. I had made a considerable investment in my education and I was not about to throw it all away. I needed a regular job with a secure income and the proposed arrangement was not in line with my future plans and aspirations, I informed her. If she had no friend to travel with her, I suggested she advertise for a travel companion in the papers.

Her proposed arrangement, I knew, would have never worked out anyway. I was not the type who could live with somebody in a dependant relationship and subject himself to that person's whims and fancies. My aunt, I knew, was a very capricious person who had callously pushed me out of her house seven years earlier. I would not give her a second chance. Her volatile temper which showed whenever I inadvertently hit on one of her hot buttons filled me with angst. When I once reminded her how she used to shout at and berate Max for no good reason, she screamed at me saying how I could say such a thing. She had always treated that dear old man with utmost kindness and respect, she claimed.

Aunt Emmi's erratic mood swings and imperious and unpredictable behavior reminded me of the Roman emperor Nero as brilliantly played by Peter Ustinov in MGM's movie *Quo Vadis*. One lived with people like that at one's own peril. When I wrote Mutti about her sister's proposal, she was incensed and wrote Aunt Emmi to stop trying to turn me into a playboy and gigolo. She had nothing to worry about, Aunt Emmi promptly wrote back, since her son had neither the good looks nor the charming manner to be either.

During the following ten years or so of overseas corporate assignments, I made it a point to visit Aunt Emmi now and then just to say hello and spend a few days with her. Sadly, she was noticeably deteriorating physically and emotionally and no longer taking care of herself. For one, she was becoming terribly obese. In fact, food seemed to be the only thing left that interested her. Whenever I came down by car from Frankfurt am Main or Munich she had me bring along a pound or two of her favorite *Landleberwurst* [country style liver sausage], a couple of loaves of heavy German rye bread, and some bottles of *Appelwoi* [apple wine, a favorite Frankfurt beverage]. She did not share any of it with me and after two or three sittings, all would be gone. Her hair was never done and simply tightened into a bun in the back. Her front row of teeth showed unsightly gaps.

Much to my embarrassment, especially when we went out to eat or take a walk in the Parc Alfred Bertrand, Aunt Emmi dressed very shabbily in an outfit consisting of dark sweatpants and T-shirt over which she wore a beige cashmere coat. Instead of a necklace she wore a small chain around her neck with the house keys dangling from it. All this was in stark contrast to the other women in the park who staked their reputation on being worldly and chic on a par with their Parisian cousins. Aunt Emmi seemed not to notice their ostentatious display but to much enjoy walking among them looking like a homeless person with not a penny to her name. As to her assets and financial status, I never asked her about it as I did not think it proper and she, in turn, never volunteered any information on the topic.

Most embarrassing to me was her often bizarre behavior. For example, one time she took me to lunch at a fancy restaurant on the route des Acacias next door to a branch of the Banque Populaire Suisse. This is where she took her banker once a week, she told me. To my great surprise, the maître d' was reluctant to seat us making all sorts of excuses. Aunt Emmi finally prevailed, we got a nice table, and she ordered steak. The beef looked juicy and well-marbled but came with a thick border of fat. Aunt Emmi proceeded to cut out all the fat, move it to one side of her plate, and then, as if it was the most natural thing to do, toss the entire lot under her chair. Needless to say, I was shocked and glad to get out of the place before the waiter found the clumps of fat sitting on the beautiful oriental carpet in the place.

In another example of her eccentric conduct, it never mattered to her that there was no room if she wanted to sit down somewhere. She simply made room. On one occasion we came to a trolley bus stop in downtown Geneva on our way back to the Plateau de Champel. All the seats on the bench were occupied by a number of women probably headed home from a downtown shopping trip. Peering out from behind her thick eyeglasses, Aunt Emmi waddled up to the bench and, coming right up to the two women she intended to displace, moved in until she was practically eyeball to eyeball with them. She then planted her handbag right between them and proceeded to push the two apart. The two women, visibly in shock, got up and fled whereupon Aunt Emmi calmly sat down smiling contently. She was about to use the same technique on another occasion in a popular restaurant when I managed to pull her away and find another place for us to sit.

Things were changing in other ways too. Despite her supposed wealth, Aunt Emmi had become extremely miserly in her old age and so penny-pinching in fact that she walked to a post office near her house to make phone calls because, she claimed, it was cheaper than calling from home. She owned no television set or even a radio or any of the other amenities considered standard in even the most modest of homes. She preferred a quiet existence, she said, and did not want to put up with all that noise and commotion coming from the outside.

My aunt had given up employing a permanent housekeeper long ago, soon after Uncle Charles had died. Thereafter she had a string of part-time maids who were usually foreigners in the country on work permits and whom she paid as little as possible. The old adage that you get what you pay for was certainly true here because the only employees she could attract were women she could not depend on or trust. At least on two occasions I found her composing a note to the police to bail out a maid who had been caught using public transportation, which operated on the honor system, without having a machine-validated ticket in her possession. She suspected and continuously accused her temporary employees of stealing her silverware, rugs, and other valuables. This they undoubtedly did considering it just compensation for services not adequately compensated. It all added to the constant turmoil in the house and a high employee turnover.

Aunt Emmi was also not spending any money keeping up the place. The once gorgeous interior of the house was now in disrepair, the plumbing and heating units were no longer functioning properly, and parts of the once nicely manicured garden were overgrown with weeds. In a way, though, one could not blame her for neglecting her property because the neighborhood was rapidly changing although not in the usual sense, i.e., through the influx of low-income and economically stressed individuals. On the contrary, the new arrivals were well-off individuals and their families who were being employed by the many international companies and organizations, such as branches of the UN, that were setting up shop in Geneva.

With land for new construction being severely scarce, the single family homes and villas on the Plateau de Champel no longer represented a good and efficient use of land within the city. Consequently, the city and the developers were pressing the owners of these homes to sell out and free the land for condominium and rental apartment complexes. To attain their objectives, they were offering ever increasing incentives. Consequently, the small enclave of homes off the avenue de Miremont, where Aunt Emmi's house was located, was already surrounded on all sides by large multi-storied apartment buildings. As she well knew, it would only be a matter of time before the remaining homes were sold and came down as well. She herself was continuously being pestered by builders to sell her property. It simply made little sense to her to put more money into it.

Two Dubious Friends

While Uncle Charles was still around, he had set Aunt Emmi up with a financial advisor he knew and trusted to handle her investments. This man had unexpectedly died at a relatively young age leaving a wife and underage children. According to Aunt Emmi, she was approached by the widow with the request for some modest financial assistance for herself and her children since she was suddenly left without a source of income and her husband had unfortunately not sufficiently provided for the eventuality of his early passing. In making her case, this lady reminded my aunt of her husband's many years of faithful and competent service for which he had charged her only a nominal fee. Nevertheless, said Aunt Emmi, she did not feel at all obligated to help this woman out since her husband had been compensated for his services and, besides, the replacement she had found did an even better job for her than her husband had done.

This new man in charge of Aunt Emmi's finances, Eric Oppliger by name, worked for the Banque Populaire Suisse at their branch at 2, route des Acacias. She once took me to meet Eric over lunch at the restaurant next door to the branch but he professed to know neither English nor German and we were thus unable to have a meaningful conversation. By his appearance and attire, her "banker" as she always referred to him, appeared to me more like a low level employee or clerk. Despite being at least twice his age, Aunt Emmi obviously had a crush on Eric. She was much flattered by the attention he lavished on her whenever she met him at the bank and convinced herself that he had a genuine liking for her and even some romantic interest. When I asked her to stand next to him so I could take their picture together, she blushed, giggled, and squirmed like a school girl on her first date. Once she confided in me how deeply hurt she was when Eric had recently taken his wife and children on an extended vacation without bothering to inquire what she would be doing in the meantime.

Despite her infatuation, Aunt Emmi was nevertheless shrewd enough to eventually realize that her banker's interest was not so much in her person as in her assets. This became clear to her when Eric made her an offer by which he and his family would be moving into her villa and take care of her as long as she lived in return for her signing over the property to him and leaving his wife the priceless jewelry collection she kept in a safe-deposit box at his bank. Eric had already had the contract prepared and all she needed to do was sign it, she said. She had no intention of doing so, she told me, but kept the papers in her bank box to have proof of his intentions should she ever need it.

Another individual to take great interest in Aunt Emmi was Marie Kopf who was 22 years her junior. Marianne, as my aunt called her, came from the French-speaking part of Switzerland and, like many Swiss, was bilingual and able to speak both French and German. I met her a few times on my brief visits to Geneva and we got along very well. Marianne periodically checked up on Aunt Emmi, did some housework and other chores, and in her car took her on errands and even on drives in the country. She seemed like an excellent companion and just what my aunt needed. Marianne knew of Eric Oppliger and thought that Aunt Emmi was too much under his influence. The two were obviously rivals for my aunt's affection.

Marianne presented herself as a devout Christian although she never identified any religious affiliation she had. She told me that all her efforts on my aunt's behalf were motivated purely by Christian love and charity. While Aunt Emmi had been baptized and confirmed, her religion had obviously never played much of a role in her life. Marianne now reintroduced her to the Bible, she told me, and did her best to make a believer out of her. It was something that much appealed to me at the time.

Two Estranged Sisters

In the meantime, Mutti and her sister were continuously in touch by mail and occasional phone calls. Most of the communication was, however, in a westerly direction. Of the nearly one hundred letters from her we kept, two thirds were to Mutti while the remainder were to me. In her letters to her sister, Aunt Emmi kept pleading with her to come to Geneva to live with her. She needed Mutti and could offer her a comfortable lifestyle since she was very well off financially, she wrote. In a letter she wrote me in December 1980, Aunt Ernmi complained about Mutti's seeming ingratitude. Specifically, my aunt wrote verbatim (translated from the German): "My sister has forgotten much for example the 1,000 DM I gave her at the Basel Bahnhof, the money I continuously sent her to Stuttgart and the trip to New York I paid for; but that's how she is and has always been with me; for me too that was much money at the time, but it's of no consequence, only because you wrote me that nobody was helping you out" Mutti evidently had me write her sister begging for financial support after Ute, Volker and I were returned to her in Germany in 1951. This would explain why we could continue to live in our apartment on Adlerstraße without Mutti having a job to support us.

Mutti, in turn, did her best to make excuses why she could not come. She knew the two could never live together under one roof and would be continuously at loggerheads. Besides, she had her comfortable home in Oak Park surrounded by her family, friends, neighbors, and pets and saw no reason to exchange all of that for life in Switzerland and all the uncertainties involved in such a move especially at her advanced age. Sadly, Aunt Emmi could never understand why her considerable wealth were insufficient to entice her sister to come live with her.

The exchanges between the two sisters sometimes got unintentionally humorous. After Mother kept writing that she could not leave home because she had her beloved cats to take care of, her sister wrote back that her cats were as welcome as she was because she had always loved animals. Eventually, Mutti must have decided to take the bull by the horns. She wrote her sister that she had just ordered her passport and was getting herself and her four darlings ready for the trip. (This was two more cats than she actually had). Aunt Emmi immediately replied asking her not to come unless it was minus her cats. Her yard was full of birds she was feeding, she explained, and she simply could not have all these cats around the house. When Mother confided in her that she had a fear of flying, her sister wrote back she could hardly believe it since nowadays everybody flew. When Mutti pressed her to say whether she had ever flown herself she had to admit that she had not.

Mother also kept inviting her sister to come live with her knowing full well that Aunt Emmi had a peculiar aversion of coming to America even for a visit. Just as Mutti, Aunt Emmi offered all sorts of excuses for not changing her domicile. First of all, her doctor had advised against it, she wrote. Then there were Mother's cats. She just could not see herself living in a small house together with four cats. Also, there was the manner in which we heated our place. Gas heat was absolutely unacceptable to her because it was unhealthy, she claimed. (She had an oil furnace).

Aunt Emmi's letters were peculiar in at least two respects. First, they were never dated. Only the postmarks on the envelopes, if readable, would reveal when or where they were mailed. Most importantly, they were for the most part completely devoid of substance in that they never contained any information by which one could get more than just a passing glimpse of her life and activities. She would write about how well off she was but never give even a hint of what she owned or what she had coming in to support herself. She would write about just coming back from a trip to Freiburg or to Rome or to the south of France or to Spain but offer no further details such as whom she had seen or how she had spent her time. We never received any communication from her while she was away from Geneva—not one letter or postcard.

Much about Emmi's life remained a complete mystery to us leading to endless and useless speculation about her. Was she really as wealthy as she always claimed to be or was she just trying to make us envious or use her supposed wealth to entice Mutti to come to Geneva? Were the trips she claimed to be taking real or just pipe dreams? We supposed that since she had lived in Switzerland most of her life, she had succumbed to Swiss ways including a passion for privacy and secrecy. Nevertheless, her family was annoyed because she would confide the most intimate details of her life in her two Geneva friends, Marianne and Eric, while leaving her next of kin guessing and mostly in the dark.

The Presumptive Heiress

Wealthy people, especially childless ones, often find themselves the objects of undue and unwanted attention from potential heirs patiently waiting in the wings for their demise. Aunt Emmi was in that unhappy position especially with respect to Esther who kept our aunt in her crosshairs like a hunter stalking some priced elk. Of special interest to Esther was our aunt's jewelry collection, which she had been shown as a child, and which included some rare yellow diamonds. She also knew, possibly from Uncle Charles, that among our aunt's possessions was a large portfolio of corporate stocks including shares in Hoffmann La Roche, the Swiss pharmaceutical company. With our mother getting on in years it would only be a matter of time before Esther would come into the inheritance, or at least that part due our branch of the family, if she played her cards right.

Mutti was always fully supportive of Esther's pursuit and felt she deserved the inheritance not only on account of certain promises that had been made to her when Esther was still very young and used to visit our aunt in Geneva but also because Esther was, after all, her first-born and the legitimate offspring of her only marriage. This is a point Esther made sure Mother understood and never forgot. Although it is doubtful that Esther or our mother had ever heard the term primogeniture, their attitude was very much in tune with that concept which says that the exclusive right of inheritance belongs to the eldest son or, presumably, if there was no son, to the eldest daughter. All might have gone well had Esther not made some grievous misstep that would earn her the enduring wrath of Aunt Emmi.

Esther was fond of Uncle Charles, whom she called Charlie, with his great wealth most likely the major source of that attraction, and tried to keep in touch with him apart from our aunt. Since she knew that Aunt Emmi was not averse to opening mail addressed to him and that her letters would probably not get through, Esther began writing to him at the office. When our aunt discovered her niece's chicanery, she was furious. But worse was yet to come. When our uncle was in his last illness towards the end of 1965 and being cared for at home, Esther decided that she had to come to his aid and rescue him from our aunt's clutches. Her plan was to remove him from the villa and bring him back with her to Oak Park where she could arrange for him to get the medical and other care she thought he needed and did not get at home.

In a daring move, Esther traveled to Geneva but when she came to the house, Aunt Emmi, who had gotten wind of her niece's scheme, would not let her in. Supposedly, Esther then attempted to enlist the assistance of the police to intervene on her behalf but without success. Esther did not get to see our uncle and had to return home with her mission unaccomplished. To Aunt Emmi, her niece's conduct represented a scandalous breach of trust and a hostile intrusion into her private life that was inexcusable. For want of a better word, she excommunicated Esther. From then on our aunt never wrote her niece again or answered her letters. Whenever she called, Aunt Emmi would hang up as soon as she heard her voice.

Aunt Emmi never got over what Esther had done to her as her letters to Mother over the years revealed. In 1966, not long after the incident, she wrote her sister about that *armselige* [miserable] Esther who tried to alienate the man she loved above all else and with whom she had lived happily for decades. And when that did not work, she claimed, Esther had slandered her and thereby also him. Charles' testament proved everything, she wrote. If he had just a spark of affection for Esther, wrote our aunt, he would have left her at least a token amount of his vast wealth in his will. Evidently, he had left her nothing. Years later our aunt was still fuming when she wrote Mutti how her daughter had bombarded her beloved Charles with letters at the office and how he had handed them over to her unopened with instructions to return them to Esther and for her to write them both at home. That in no way dissuaded her niece, she wrote, from continuing the practice.

Subsequently, Esther made another big mistake when she enlisted a Geneva resident she knew to clandestinely keep an eye on Aunt Emmi and our aunt suddenly realized that she was under surveillance. To cover her tracks, Esther used Mutti as an intermediary. Annie Mühlhans was in upper management at Geneva's Hotel de Berne on the rue de Berne and Esther had met her on one of her overseas trips. Our mother was apparently introduced to Annie at her sister's house on her short trip to Geneva in July 1971 because in a letter to me back in Frankfurt am Main Annie congratulated me on the *Schmuckstück* [ornament] that was my mother. She found her very youthful, congenial, and straight-forward, she wrote, and asked me to again thank her for the delightful gift she had brought her. (Presumably that was a present Esther had asked Mutti to bring along).

I eventually had a chance to meet Annie at her hotel on one of my Geneva trips. Like many in the hospitality industry, Annie was a very attractive young lady with a charming personality. She told me how her position in a nice Swiss hotel was a dream come true after she had fled that oppressive East German regime for West Germany from where she had made her way to Switzerland. She also had a steady boyfriend by the name of Dominik Porisi, she informed me, who also worked at the hotel. Marriage, however, was not in the cards, she confided, because Dominik was not only too stingy for her taste but was always surrounded by a big flock of relatives besides his possessive mother and she could not see herself becoming part of a large Italian clan.

After we returned to the States in August 1971, Mother and Annie conducted a lively correspondence that lasted for five years. Most of Annie's letters appeared prompted by the latest gift Mutti had sent her. She congratulated Mother on her good taste and her success in finding clothing that was always a perfect fit. The jewelry too was always what she wanted but never got around to buying. Annie reminded Mutti that her friendship did not have to be repaid by presents and objected (but not too strenuously) to her sending them. Dominik especially should not be receiving any more since he was well off and already owned two condominium apartments, she wrote. Mutti, of course, always enjoyed remembering relatives and friends with gifts but in the case of Annie she also expected something in return. This was information on her sister, which, although of not much interest to her personally was to Esther who was its ultimate recipient.

In line with this mission and to keep the packages from America coming, Annie now and then called Aunt Emmi to see how she was doing. Being a secretive and suspicious person by nature, our aunt did not volunteer much information but at least Esther would know that our aunt was still around. Dominik too was employed in this enterprise. In her report to Mutti of January 1975, Annie wrote that during the Advent season of 1974, when he was reconnoitering around Aunt Emmi's house, Dominik happened to catch a glimpse of Max Aeschbach. He told his lady friend that Herr Aeschbach looked so run down and sick that he could barely recognize him. One time, Annie and Dominik decided to call Aunt Emmi and invite her over to the hotel for a visit. They really felt hurt when they were rudely rebuffed. She had so many friends, Aunt Emmi supposedly said, that she could not remember ever having met the two.

This mutually beneficial relationship came to an abrupt end with Annie's letter of early July 1976 to Mutti in which she described her last encounter with her sister. It seems that Mother, probably prodded by Esther, wrote Annie a postcard in which she mentioned Max's death three months earlier and asked her to stop by her sister's place to offer condolences. Annie did as she was asked and showed up unannounced. Aunt Emmi came to the gate and let her in but instead of taking her inside, set her down in front of her house. When Annie read from the postcard and came to Max's death, Aunt Emmi became furious. She told Annie that was nobody's business and accused her of having come to spy on her. Annie told her that she was there at the request of her sister and denied the spying charges. When Aunt Emmi did not calm down, she abruptly left after just ten minutes.

The next morning Aunt Emmi showed up at the Hotel de Berne and had Annie called to the lobby. There she began to scream and berate Annie demanding that she and Dominik leave her alone. Annie asked her to lower her voice since they were in a hotel and, when her visitor did not stop, just walked away from her. In her letter, Annie asked Mother not to write her anything more about her sister since it was really none of her business. While the tone of the message was very apologetic and cordial, Mother appears not to have replied to it. However, shortly thereafter Aunt Emmi wrote her sister, most likely in response to Mutti's query, that Annie's career had suffered a sudden and severe setback. She was now working in a *armseligen* [miserable] little hotel, crowed aunt Emmi. It appears that the altercation in the hotel lobby had cost poor Annie her job.

A Disastrous Visit

It had been 11 years since Mutti had last been back in her native country when she joined me in Germany in the second week of June 1982. At that time my latest corporate assignment there had ended and I was due to return to company headquarters in the States. It again seemed an opportune time for Mutti to come over and see her sister and other relatives and friends. It took some effort to persuade her to leave Oak Park because she did not want to be away from her two beloved pets for two weeks and, having never flown before, did not relish the idea of getting on an airplane and flying all by herself. After much cajoling, Mutti finally consented and Esther put her on the plane at O'Hare International.

On her arrival in Frankfurt am Main the next morning, her old school chum Mariechen from Schwanheim and I picked her up and brought her back to her birthplace. From there Mutti and I hit the road again. After stopping off in Graben-Neudorf to see Uncle Jule and in Karlsruhe to visit

Mama Gartner, we drove on to Geneva the following day arriving there in the evening. The two sisters greeted each other warmly and we stayed overnight with Mutti assigned to the small bedroom next to her sister's and me to the one next to the stairs.

By the next morning, the friendly atmosphere had decidedly changed and the old animosities between the two sisters began to resurface. Nevertheless, Aunt Emmi invited us out for lunch at her favorite restaurant in Annemasse, a small French town a short drive from Geneva. That lunch turned out to be a disaster as the two sisters began to verbally tear into each other. They spoke in French (or something close to it) since they evidently did not want me to understand what was being said but that only made the other diners perk up their ears and listen in as the argument got more heated and louder. I was fearful that the disturbance would result in us being evicted from the premises. Presumably, the two were regurgitating their old grievances with Aunt Emmi bringing up the ill treatment she had received as a teenager when the family kicked her out of the house while Mutti reminded her, among other acts of moral turpitude, of her illegal abortion and the Frau Meier affair in Berlin. There may have been considerably more.

Things did not improve in the afternoon back at the house. I was on the first floor when I heard a thumping sound as if someone had fallen and rushed upstairs. There on the floor of Mutti's temporary bedroom, I found the two sisters pummeling each other and calling each other names. Not wanting to get into the middle of a catfight by trying to separate the two, I grabbed Mutti's hand and yanked her up and away from her sister leaving Aunt Emmi sprawled on the floor. Mother and I quickly picked up our stuff and, without further ado, left the house.

The only place in town I knew well was the Auberge de Carouge on the rue Ancienne, and this is where we drove to have our dinner. The proprietor and I were acquainted from previous visits to his restaurant and he suggested we stay overnight in one of the upstairs rooms. The next morning after breakfast, I called Eric Oppliger to invite him to join us for lunch at the Auberge and meet his client's sister. He had since been transferred to Banque Populaire Suisse's branch in the Petit-Lancy section of town where we picked him up. The conversation between him and

Mutti was in French but, according to Mutti, neither of them said much of anything and they just exchanged some pleasantries.

In the afternoon, we went to visit Marianne Kopf at her pedicure salon on the second floor of a building at 25, quai des Bergues in downtown Geneva. While Marianne tended to Mutti's toe nails, we heard some groaning in the next room which Marianne explained came from a woman she and a lady friend were taking care of. It seems she and her friend were also qualified nurses and were taking in terminally ill people to take care of until their passing. Surprisingly, Marianne did not look in on their patient before we left while her friend seemed to be nowhere around. After coffee and pastries at a nearby café, the three of us went on a walk around the neighborhood and took some photographs. We soon met up with a slim, dark haired young woman whom Marianne introduced as Liselotte, a nurse who worked with her. At the time, Mutti and I did not realize what a central role Liselotte would eventually play in the life of Aunt Emmi and we paid little attention to her.

Late in the afternoon, Mutti and I left for Munich, where my company had its German headquarters, via the Bodensee (Lake Constance). On the way, Mutti finally volunteered to say something about what had caused the ruckus at her sister's place. It seems that Mother had found some cherry pits in her bed during the night and was convinced her sister had planted them there just to annoy her and make her uncomfortable. In the morning she had confronted her about it which led to their brawl.

Unfortunately, the short visit had produced the very opposite result of what had been intended which was for the two sisters to finally bury the hatchet and begin to respect and love each other. Aunt Emmi and her younger sister were now, after all, 78 and 73 years old, respectively, and there might not be too much time left for them to do so. It was hard to fathom but, clearly, the entire undertaking had been a complete and unmitigated disaster. The incident of the cherry pits would eventually lead to unforeseen and drastic consequences for the family.

An Ultimatum

This ill-fated visit should have ended communication between the two sisters but it caused only a temporary interruption. Remarkably, Aunt Emmi soon restarted her campaign to have her sister come and live with her. In June 1983 she wrote of falling on the steps leading to the upstairs of her house and injuring her knee. *"Wäre froh wenn ich Dich hier haben könnte. Vielleicht ist es Dir möglich zu kommen?"* [Would be glad to have you here. Maybe it will be possible for you to come?]. If she did, she even promised to return to America with her.

In an accompanying note to me, Aunt Emmi asked why my mother was not writing her. She wanted to know whether I was perhaps behind this. She really did not need anybody but since her sister and her had grown up together, she wanted to see her again or at least hear something from her. "Oppl." (presumably Eric Oppliger) was not well and planned on taking early retirement. She rarely saw him anymore but was now mostly with Marianne, she wrote. Marianne liked me and would be glad to see me again.

In November of that year, Aunt Emmi wrote her sister, *"Ich bitte Dich mich zu besuchen"* [I beg you to visit me]. She no longer wanted to live alone in that big house, she wrote. Mutti must have again proposed to her sister to come to the States instead because Aunt Emmi wanted to know whether Mother really thought she would exchange *die schöne Schweizerstadt Genf* [the beautiful Swiss town of Geneva] with Chicago? "Let me know soon whether you want to come or not because otherwise I'll give the house to friends and enter a *Damenstift* [convent] and then all will be over between the two of us; hopefully you won't let it go that far and you'll come to your sister," she wrote. "I'll make you a good life; I can do that if I want because I'm not a poor woman," she continued. She closed with *"Also komm meine Kleine."* [Come then my little one].

Aunt Emmi's letter also included a barb against me calling me *ein alter Kerl* [an old guy] too lazy to make even a bowl of soup for myself. She had heard from Esther, wrote our aunt, that I was the reason our mother was not coming to Geneva because I needed her in Oak Park to cook for me and do the household chores. She would not have to do any *Hausarbeit* [house cleaning etc.] as in Oak Park, aunt Emmi wrote, because she had a Portuguese man doing that for her for the past two years.

The following year, aunt Emmi sent her sister a cryptic and urgent message, written on two scraps of paper dated *Pfingstmontag* [Pentecost Monday], which would have been June 11, 1984, in which she instructed her to very quickly mail her the birthdates of Esther, Peter, Volker, Nick, and Elke—all or none. (Inexplicably, she left Ute off the list). She could also send her own birth date, she wrote. *"Mach schnell, mein Notar wartet"* [Hurry up, my notary is waiting], she demanded. If Mutti did not immediately mail her the birthdates, she would give everything to the City of Geneva for the poor, she warned. "Maybe it will be better if Esther writes the address and brings the document to the post office," she wrote, and "tell her to immediately come to you and take care of this." It was all in our own interest, she insisted, and added, *"Der arme Peter wird dadurch wie die anderen eine gesicherte Existenz haben—ich gebe ihm ein bischen mehr."* [Poor Peter will thereby have a secure livelihood like the others—I'll give him a little more].

When the letter arrived, it so happened that Mutti was pretty well stressed out as she must have felt abandoned by both my sister and me. I had recently accepted a position with the subsidiary of a German manufacturing company on Long Island and had left home assuming Esther would look out for our mother. Unfortunately, she did not but instead completely ignored her neither visiting nor wanting to talk to her on the phone. Presumably the reason was that Esther was faced with some severe mental health issues and felt that our mother was a major cause of these by continuously pestering her with a multitude of various little problems and complaints.

At the end of April, about six weeks before Aunt Emmi's letter arrived, I had received one from Mutti in which she bitterly complained about Esther's shoddy treatment of her. Since Mother did not drive, she had to do her grocery shopping by either taking the bus or going on foot. For groceries, Mutti preferred Jewel Foods on Lake Street in River Forest which was about a mile from our Oak Park townhouse. It was Saturday, she wrote, and she was on the way home carrying a load which was too heavy for her. When she stopped by Esther's place on Bonnie Brae and rang the doorbell, nobody answered even though she saw one of the family cars sitting in the driveway. Disappointed, she trudged home.

Repeatedly rebuffed by Esther in her attempts to be in contact with her, it is not surprising that Mutti never passed Aunt Emmi's letter on to her daughter. I found it in the top drawer of my desk when I was back home on a short vacation in early September. Thinking that Mutti had told Esther about the letter and the information request and the matter had been taken care of, I just left the letter where it was and forgot about it. That was a terrible mistake because it turned out that Esther knew nothing about our aunt's request so that our aunt never received the information she had asked for. This must have been a terrible disappointment because after this all correspondence between the two sisters came to an abrupt halt. By that time Aunt Emmi was 80 and her sister 75. The consequences for the family of this final breakdown in communication between the two sisters would prove far-reaching.

Living In The Mountains

Afterwards, whenever I called Aunt Emmi, I found it very difficult to reach her because she was now rarely at home. It seems Marianne had taken charge of our aunt and taken her to her new place in Sainte-Croix in the Jura mountains at irregular intervals and for extended periods of time. The few times I managed to talk to our aunt, the phone conversations were short because of her aversion to long distance calls which she kept insisting were too expensive. Sometimes, if she felt the conversation was getting too long, she would hang up on me in the middle of a sentence with some parting words about writing her instead. Now and then we would also hear from Marianne. A picture postcard she sent from Geneva right after New Year's of 1988, featured a cluster of houses on a hill named Résidences Les Petites Roches in Sainte-Croix in which she marked one as being hers. I did not quite know what to make of the message she wrote on the back. Translated from the German and signed Marianne Kopf, it read:

> *Your aunt is slowly becoming a believer. I pray for her every day*
> *and believe Jesus answers my prayers. She can barely free herself*
> *from the banker; he has enchained her for the inheritance; she*

cannot but wants to be free. I think that Jesus alone can do it; I thank him every day. I often go cleaning at her place and often without getting paid; as a Christian I do this for her conversion. I am fond of her. Thank you for your prayers for your aunt.... On this card you will see my house in the Jura mountains. God bless you.

Three months later Marianne called to warn me that Esther was bombarding our aunt with letters including disparaging remarks about me. According to Marianne, Esther continued to write that our mother was eager and willing to join our aunt in Geneva but that I was against the move for selfish reasons. Marianne called Esther a snake who could not be trusted. I need not worry though, she assured me, because our aunt had no love for Esther ever since she had tried to spirit her beloved Charles away from her when she (our aunt) was already in her 60s. She suggested I come soon and write often. This news about my sister's conduct did not surprise me because I had heard the same story from Uncle Jule in Graben-Neudorf whom she had called bad-mouthing me. He had gotten so angry at the time that he told Esther not to call him again.

It was three days past Easter Sunday in 1990, when I received a call from Marianne with alarming news. She had stopped by Aunt Emmi's house to check up on her friend and found her lying on the floor of the little salon unconscious. My aunt was rushed to a local Geneva hospital where she was diagnosed as having suffered a mild stroke. Marianne gave me the name and phone number of my aunt's notary, a Me Marc Pictet, and suggested I call him. This I did and Me Pictet confirmed what Marianne had already told me. Less than a week later, in late April, Marianne wrote with the happy news that my aunt was doing well and the hospital and her notary had arranged for her to return to her home. However, she wrote, my aunt could no longer live alone. She needed someone to stay with her and assist with meals, personal hygiene, laundry, and household chores.

If I could come Aunt Emmi and her would be delighted but to please let them know in advance because they may go to her (Marianne's) house in the mountains for some time. This is something the doctor had highly recommended, she wrote. In a postscript Marianne added that she was happy that God had given my aunt the opportunity to slowly turn to Him and that she could now be assured that my aunt would be allowed to spend eternity in heaven even though, she added, she was again full of *Lebensfreude* [joie de vivre] and savoring the spring, the trees, the flowers etc.. My subsequent phone calls to Aunt Emmi were not answered and neither were my letters and Marianne had never given me the address or phone number of her place in Sainte-Croix.

In line with my custom to call family and friends on New Year's Day, I gave Aunt Emmi a ring on the first day of 1991 and was surprised when she immediately answered the phone with her familiar "*voila*." She was very upbeat and talked a mile a minute so I could hardly get in a word edgewise. She had just been thinking about me, she said, and wanted to know when I was coming. She said she was living by herself again, although Marianne was still around, but wanted to shut the place down because it was too big for her. Unfortunately, she could not get any decent help and much of her silver and expensive rugs had been stolen, she claimed. She planned to move into a retirement home. Incidentally, this is something the family had hoped she would do for some time. Alternatively, I had suggested to her she get herself an experienced and trustworthy housekeeper from central Europe such as East Germany or Poland and pay her a competitive wage.

According to Aunt Emmi, she was doing real well except for the pain in her left knee which made it difficult for her to get about. Marianne, she said, had given up her pedicure business on the quai des Bergues and bought a house in the mountains near France. She suspected her of being after her house and money but, said Aunt Emmi, she would rather see the place burn down than give it to her. She praised her lawyer (probably her notary), her doctor, who was a friend of the lawyer, and Eric Oppliger who still did all her banking.

Aunt Emmi then asked about her sister and me and what we were doing even though I had pretty much kept her informed in my letters. I told her that I was studying for the Illinois bar exam coming up in February. To study law at my age was absolutely foolish, she thought, and again suggested I come and live with her instead. Mother was reluctant to come to the phone and after I cued Aunt Emmi in that her sister's short-term memory was not what it used to be, the two had a brief but friendly chat. Back on the phone with her, Aunt Emmi suggested I come over after my exams, around March, at which time she would show me all she had. I would be surprised, she said. Afterwards I called Esther who I knew was always eager to hear the latest news from our aunt. Esther suggested that our wily aunt was up to her old tricks which was to try to make people around her jealous of each other by one time favoring one person over another and then reversing the order. This would give her maximum leverage to have things go her way.

We were nearly two weeks into 1992 before I managed to get a hold of Aunt Emmi to wish her a Happy New Year. She was just closing the shutters to keep in the heat when she heard the phone ring, she said. She had been in the country with friends for two weeks and had just returned. (Presumably she was with Marianne and Liselotte in Sainte-Croix). She was doing fine, she said, but had developed arthritis in her right knee and with pain in both knees now she could no longer manage the stairs in her house. She had moved her bed to the little salon on the first floor where she was close to the kitchen, she said. Marianne was working locally and still looking out for her.

She had not received our Christmas card or my recent letter, she said. She can no longer get to the mail box (which was attached to the fence near the front entrance) because of her bad knees, she explained, and Marianne was taking in the mail. Marianne just could not be trusted, she said. According to Aunt Emmi, Eric Oppliger calls her daily. "*Er spekuliert aufs Haus* " [He is betting on getting the house], she said. She wanted me to know that Eric was no longer working at the bank but getting 3,200 Swiss francs a month in retirement pay but paying only 800 francs in rent.

When I told my aunt that I was now an unemployed lawyer looking for a job, she renewed her offer to come and live with her. She would pay me a generous monthly allowance. I was her only relative, she claimed. There were only three homes left in her area—the other two belonged to a dentist and a doctor, she said. Someone had offered her 3 million Swiss francs for the property, she told me, and all would go to me. I asked Mother to come to the phone and the two sisters had a brief chat. All I heard Mutti say was "*Es muss gehen*" [It has to go] which was probably her somber reply to her sister's query "*Wie geht es dir?* " [How is it going?].

Back on the phone, when I told Aunt Emmi about the passing of Sannche Heisack, a friend of both sisters, in May 1991 at age 82, Aunt Emmi replied that she had no further interest in those Schwanheim people. She has lived in Geneva a very long time and that was now her home, she said. When she mentioned she was nearly 90 years old now and I countered that she had just turned 88 only, she had a good laugh. She thanked me for calling and asked me to do so again soon but at night when phone calls were cheaper. As usual, she hung up while I was still talking. When I called Esther, I could tell she would liked to have talked with our aunt herself. Sadly, that was no longer possible as our aunt had written her off.

Alarming News

On Saturday, December 12, 1992 Mutti received a mailgram from a Pierre Toffel in Geneva asking her to call him during office hours; it was urgent and concerned her sister. I called him early on Monday morning and asked him if he minded talking with me since my mother had developed some memory problems and might have difficulty following what he had to say. He explained that he was an attorney and the court appointed guardian of my aunt's estate and had the sad news that she was severely ill. My aunt, Marianne Kopf and a nurse had returned Friday from Ste. Croix where they had lived in Mme. Kopf's house since July. She was now in her home being taken care of by Marianne Kopf and the nurse.

According to Maître (Me) Toffel, he had difficulty locating us because there were no papers in the house and he had found Mutti's address and phone number in a Bible only after a lengthy search. Mme. Kopf professed to be unaware of any family, he said, and claimed that, to her knowledge, my aunt had no contact with any family members. I explained that I had been writing to my aunt periodically during the last few months but had received no reply and that she did not answer her phone. We had just assumed she had taken off with her two friends for Ste. Croix now and then. Unfortunately, neither my aunt nor Marianne had ever given us an address or phone number where we could contact them there, I informed him, and since my aunt had always jealously guarded her privacy, we did not dare appear too intrusive by trying to track her down. If she wanted us to be in touch with her in Ste. Croix, we figured, she would have given us the information to do so.

According to Me Toffel, my aunt was very wealthy with millions in Swiss francs including large holdings in Hoffmann La Roche stock.

He was now trying to trace some 8 million francs which went missing. My aunt's safe-deposit box at her bank had been emptied and a jewelry collection she was known to have kept there was gone. Furthermore, the house appeared to have been stripped of most everything of value.

My aunt had made a will leaving her entire estate to Marianne Kopf and Liselotte Peter, Mr. Toffel informed me, and asked me what I knew about Mme. Kopf. I told him that my aunt and her were friends and that when my aunt began to need assistance with daily living, Marianne looked after her. Marianne professed to be a caring Christian, I said, but my aunt never trusted her and claimed she was only after her house and money. My own impression was, I told Me Toffel, that Marianne's game plan was to latch onto elderly widows of means and take care of them until they died while making sure, by one means or another, that she was richly rewarded for her efforts. That was possible, he said, because Mme. Kopf was already in court in another similar case.

Me Toffel suggested that I not contact Marianne and let her continue taking care of my aunt for the time being since she was doing a good job. We would simply have to fight the will in court after my aunt died, he suggested. Me Toffel had not heard of Aunt Emmi's notary, he said, and I gave him Marc Pictet's name and phone number. I told him that my older sister, Esther, would be best qualified to handle things on behalf of our mother and I would let her know about our phone conversation. In the meantime, to rebut Marianne's assertion that our aunt had no contacts with any next of kin and that she (Marianne) was unaware that my aunt had relatives, I would send him a detailed account of these contacts together with copies of photographs I had taken of Mutti, Marianne, and me during our visit to Geneva in mid-June 1982.

The news from Geneva energized Esther who immediately called the attorney. She also had her friend and personal psychiatrist Dr. Frank Murrin contact Aunt Emmi's doctor for an expert opinion on her condition. According to Frank, there was a strong possibility our aunt had colon cancer because of persistent rectal bleeding but that no firm diagnosis was possible because of her refusal to be examined. Her doctor, an American, said he and a psychiatrist had seen Aunt Emmi twice and she seemed alert and mentally competent but had "character problems." Esther was now contemplating a trip to Geneva. She and Frank had already obtained passports so they could leave on short notice. They did not want to take our mother along, Esther explained, because three people in a hotel room would be one too many and, besides, our aunt had never liked Mother anyway.

Still, Esther was somewhat in a quandary now because while Aunt Emmi may have disliked her sister (which was contrary to my own impression), she knew that our aunt not just disliked her niece but absolutely loathed her. What if she (Esther) showed up and Aunt Emmi refused to see her? Or, what if Aunt Emmi let her in but instead of repudiating the will leaving her estate to Marianne Kopf and Liselotte Peter, actually confirmed it? That would look very bad in front of the lawyers and caregivers who would be there. Perhaps it might be better to stay home and fight it all out in court after Aunt Emmi had passed on. Me Toffel, who was always on the side of the family, was said to have strongly advised against a visit.

From my point of view, it would be in both of our interests, Esther's and mine, to work together and in my subsequent dealings with her, I more or less proceeded according to this notion. What I did not realize was that my sister already looked beyond the present issue of whether or not Mutti would come into an inheritance from her sister. She assumed that to be a certainty and saw the matter as a contest between herself and me for who would inherit from our mother, then age 83, once she passed away. Esther managed to keep me in the dark about her true feelings and it was six years before a copy of a letter addressed to the recently appointed guardian of our aunt's estate came into my hands. The message, in German, was short and to the point and read in translation from the German:

Dear Mr. Toffel: January 7, 1993

Please direct all information concerning my sister, Mme. Emmy Zell, to my daughter, Esther Rose Holzman, as she is *meine einzige Erbin* [my sole heir].

(signed) *Anne Marie Zell*
970 Northcliffe
LAKE FOREST, IL 60045

The letter was notarized by Esther's Oak Park attorney whom she once introduced to me when she and Nick were still living in Oak Park. The note was ostensibly written by our mother but in reality, of course, by Esther while the address, which was Esther's, was to leave the impression that Mutti was living with her in Lake Forest when, in fact, our mother had never left our townhouse home in Oak Park. Interestingly, Esther's instructions to the attorney came just three weeks after Mutti had received the mailgram from Mr. Toffel. It was clearly a pre-emptive strike on Esther's part but probably not a smart one because it pointed to disunity and thereby weakness within our camp which could later be exploited.

The Visitors

The year 1993 proved to be crucial in the life of Aunt Emmi and her family. I had tried since New Year's Day to reach her when on the third Sunday in January someone finally answered the phone. It was Liselotte who, after it was established that the Peter on the line was the one from America and not the Peter (my Cousin Peter) from Germany, turned me over to Marianne. She had surprising news for me, Marianne told me. Esther had arrived in Geneva almost a week earlier and had come to see our aunt about four times since. According to Marianne, Esther had brought along an old man with whom "she sleeps with at the Richemond." (The Le Richemond was a 5-star Geneva hotel). She introduced him as a cousin of her husband Nick, said Marianne. On her second visit, Esther was in the company of our cousins Peter and Marga from Germany, she told me. It was the first time Aunt Emmi and Cousin Peter had met although Peter and his family had moved from East Germany to the West almost a decade earlier. She knew Marga, of course, from her visits to her with husband Toni.

Aunt Emmi must have wondered why Esther had brought along this stranger, Dr. Frank Murrin, and not her husband Nick whom she had met in Geneva and much liked for his easygoing manner. Some sort of suitable explanation was undoubtedly offered. The encounter with these relatives and strangers, some of whom she had never seen before and others whom she loathed, must have been a sobering experience for Aunt Emmi. She was on her deathbed and surrounded by a flock of vultures just waiting for her demise.

According to Marianne, Esther had no love for our aunt. *"Alles ist nur für das Geld—sie ist eine furchtbare Frau* [It's all about the money—she is a terrible woman], she said of my sister. Shortly after Esther arrived, said Marianne, she impudently asked to be shown her (Esther's) house to which our aunt angrily replied, *"Das ist mein Haus"* [This is my house]. According to Marianne, Esther, accompanied by Cousin Peter, tried to have our aunt sign something but she could not tell what it was. (Cousin Peter would later explain to me that they had asked our aunt to sign her name on a blank sheet of paper so they could verify she was still capable of signing a will leaving her estate to Marianne and Liselotte but that our aunt had refused to do so).

On one occasion, said Marianne, there was an argument between Esther and Dr. Murrin on one side and Dr. Simmons, the American doctor, on the other when a Swiss doctor was called in to mediate and supposedly labeled the goings-on "an American comedy." Esther used the occasion to bad-mouth me before our aunt, said Marianne, but with little success. When Esther told Aunt Emmi that I had several college degrees but was now working in retail sales, aunt Emmi countered with, *"Ist das eine Schande?"* [Is that a disgrace?].

Marianne confirmed what I had heard, i.e., that my aunt had made a will leaving everything to her. Aunt Emmi had prepared it *in den Bergen* [in the mountains] naming her, Liselotte and a religious organization as beneficiaries, she said. This was to compensate her for 20 years of work without pay. The will, Marianne claimed, was approved by my aunt's lawyer, Me Pictet, and that Me Toffel had been a witness. Changing topics, she was happy to assure me that my aunt was now *bekehrt* [converted] and was nightly saying very original prayers such as, *"Jesus, ich küsse Deine goldenen Füsse"* [Jesus, I kiss your golden feet]. My aunt had written me a New Year's card, said Marianne, which she will post shortly.

Marianne agreed to let me talk to Aunt Emmi but asked that I keep my conversation with her very brief so as not to put undue stress on her. In our short exchange, Aunt Emmi was mentally alert but I could tell from the sound of her voice that she was weak and tired. *"Wie geht es dir, Tante Emmi?* " [How are you doing, Aunt Emmi?], I asked. *"Ich bin gut versorgt—es geht mir gut"* [I am well taken care of—I'm doing fine] was her comforting reply.

I followed up with another call to her a week later. By that time, Esther and Frank had returned to the States. I found Aunt Emmi surprisingly upbeat and bubbly. *"Kennst Du mich "* [Do you know me?], I asked her. *"Natürlich, du bist der Peter. Komm doch mal rüber; es ist doch nicht weit; ich würde mich sehr freuen; es ist sehr schön hier"* [Of course, you are Peter. Come over sometime; it's really not far; it would make me very happy; it's very beautiful here], she replied in one breath. I promised I would come to see her as soon as I was able to do so.

A Sad Farewell

It was towards the end of May of 1993 before I could make good on my promise to visit our aunt. I had recently been informed at work that I had one week of vacation due me while American Airlines just happened to be offering a round-trip promotional flight between Chicago and Zürich. A rental car would get me to Geneva in three hours and a half and also allow me to make a whirlwind trip into southern Germany for brief visits with family. In Geneva, I would stay at the affordable Hotel de Berne which I knew, of course. Esther agreed to pick up Mutti in Oak Park in the evening and bring her back in the morning so she could spend her day at home with her two beloved pets, Tootsie and Struppi.

It would be the first time Aunt Emmi and I had met since that fateful visit I made with her sister in June 1982. *"Wer bin ich?"* [Who am I?], I said to aunt Emmi as I stepped into the room. *"Du bist der Peter"* [You are Peter] was her prompt reply. As we hugged I said to hear *"Ich hab dich sehr gern, Tante Emmi"* [I'm very fond of you, Aunt Emmi] to which she replied *"Ich dich auch"* [I am too of you]. I was shocked to see how the disease had ravaged her once sturdy body. The poor soul had been reduced to just skin and bones.

A special hospital bed had been set up for Aunt Emmi in the living room and that is where she spent most of her time. I noted the absence of the customary life-support hookups often found in hospitals next to terminally ill patients. Her bed and surroundings were clean, fresh and airy. Attending her were two attractive and courteous young people—Ann Marie, a nurse, and Andreas, a security guard. (In addition, I was told, there was another day nurse, Sarah, a night nurse, Jeanette, and another security guard, Bernard—five people in all). During good weather they would wheel her outside around noon to enjoy her flowering garden for an hour or two. I did not see Marianne or Liselotte—presumably Mr. Toffel had, in the meantime, banished them from the house because he had cause to suspect the two of stealing from and defrauding my aunt.

Before I left home, I had taken Mutti to Marshall Field's photo studio in their downtown Chicago store for some photographic work. In Geneva, I gave Aunt Emmi a 10"x 13" framed photo portrait of her sister along with a conciliatory and loving letter from her which I had helped compose. As I read it to Aunt Emmi, tears welled up in her eyes. This showed what I always knew, namely, that she had loving, sisterly feelings for her younger sibling even if these were not returned in kind.

There were some additional items I needed to take care of on my short trip. After two days with Aunt Emmi, I took the 7-hour drive up the Autobahn to Frankfurt am Main to stay at a small family-owned hotel I knew in the Sachsenhausen district of town. From there I made a brief Sunday visit to Cousin Peter and his family in Bad Soden - Salmünster. They were all in good health and doing well for themselves. Aunt Irma was living in neighboring Flörsbachtal and Peter and I went to see her bringing her my greetings from Mutti and Esther.

A brief visit with Uncle Jule in my birthplace Graben-Neudorf was next on the agenda. At 87, just two years younger than Aunt Emmi, he was in surprisingly good shape. He informed me that "*dein Vater*" [your father] Hans Schübelin, just passed away in Karlsruhe. I had never known the man and he had denied that he had fathered me and hence I had no feelings for him making this news of only passing interest to me. From Frankfurt am Main, I also made a couple of side trips briefly stopping off at the Kölner Dom (Cologne Cathedral) for a prayer for loved ones including Aunt Emmi followed by a stop-over in my hometown of Stuttgart for a quick tour of the old neighborhood.

Three days later, I was back in Geneva for more visits with Aunt Emmi. I was disappointed to find the photograph of Mutti I had brought over, which had stood on a highboy when I left, relegated to the chest's top drawer. My aunt, said her caregivers, had become upset whenever she saw it and they thought it best to just put it away. In fact, I was told, Aunt

Emmi had shown a similar reaction to letters she had lately received from her family and to avoid any distress they had no longer shown them to her. Presumably the disquieting letters were from Esther and the German side of the family, namely, Aunt Irma, and cousins Peter and Marga, because I had stopped writing after I realized Marianne was not passing my letters on to her.

While in Geneva, I had hoped to make courtesy calls on Attorney Pierre Toffel and Notary Marc Pictet. Me Toffel had expressed a strong interest in meeting me but when I arrived there, and despite having given him advance notice, I was told that he was out of town and not available. I did get to see Mr. Pictet, whom Aunt Emmi had always referred to as "*mein Notar*" [my notary] at his office at 4, rue de Rive in downtown Geneva. According to Mr. Pictet, he was holding my aunt's last will and testament in which she was leaving her entire estate, with the exception of two small bequests, to the City of Geneva. According to the notary, some time after making the will she had called back telling him she was not happy with it and planned to come in to change it but that she never did.

Me Pictet also gave me copies of relevant sections of the Swiss Civil Code, the *Code Civil Suisse* (CCS), dealing with probate and specifically articles 519 and 521. The former specified that a will is voidable if the testator had no testamentary capacity or was under undue influence. The latter stated that an action to void a will must be brought within one year or within 30 years against a beneficiary who had acted fraudulently.

Soon my all too short visit came to an end. Most of the time during the final three hours I sat with Aunt Emmi she was slumbering peacefully. According to the nurse, she was heavily sedated to numb the pain. Now and then she would open her eyes and a big smile would cross her face when she saw me. As I sat next to her holding her left hand and commented on her beautiful blue eyes, she beamed and playfully slapped it. I could only imagine what a lovely and elegant woman she must have been back in her glory days because she never showed me a photograph of her Berlin period, if she ever kept one, and Mutti had none either. (A small print showing her during her time in Berlin was later found among Aunt Irma's papers). It was already late in the evening when aunt Emmi was soundly asleep that I steeled myself to leave her side after saying a final *Vaterunser*

[The Lord's Prayer] for her. It was past midnight when I arrived at my hotel in Zürich next to the airport for the early morning flight back to Chicago.

Mutti, Esther, and Frank were there to greet me on my arrival at O'Hare International in the afternoon. I told them that I felt that our sister and aunt had only a short time to live. Esther and I discussed the prospect that the family would not share in our aunt's estate because we now knew of at least two wills in which either the City of Geneva or her former caregivers, Marianne and Liselotte, would be the beneficiaries. Since communicating by mail was no longer an option, we agreed that Esther should stay in touch with our aunt's caregivers by phone.

The sad but inevitable news came three months after my return from Geneva. At 3:20 in the morning (10:20 a.m. Geneva time) of Monday, August 23, my answering machine recorded this terse message:

> *Pierre Toffel speaking in Geneva. I have to tell you that your Aunt Emma Zell died last night. I would appreciate if you could call me back at my office and if you could give that news to your mother and your sister. Bye-bye.*

Even though Aunt Emmi's passing was imminent, the news still proved a shock to me and it took me a while to get over it. I called Mr. Toffel back an hour later and he confirmed his message. He wanted to know where my aunt should be buried. She had left no instructions, he said, but he thought it should be in Geneva. I suggested we leave the decision up to Esther since our mother had more or less designated her to take care of all important family matters. Besides Esther, he asked me to also contact my cousins in Germany to inform them of our aunt's passing. When I called Esther at about 4:30 a.m., she took the news very calmly. I had expected as much since Esther was a stoic and never one to show much emotion. She said she had told Mr. Toffel before that burial should be in Schwanheim with our grandparents and that she would call him back right away. I could not reach Cousin Peter but Aunt Irma was home. She too received the news matter-of-factly and told me she would inform Peter and Marga.

Mother came down for breakfast around 9 o'clock when I told her about her sister's passing. *"Sie hat keinen von uns leiden können; jetzt hat sie ihre Ruhe"* [She did not like anyone of us; now she has her peace], was her curt response. Esther called back to say that, according to the doctor, our aunt had died of colon cancer. She was heavily sedated and her heart had given out while she was peacefully asleep.

There was some initial confusion about the actual date of Aunt Emmi's passing. Since Me Toffel's message had said that our aunt had died "last night," we had assumed the date of her passing was August 22. That was a Sunday when Mutti and I happened to stop by Esther's place in Lake Forest on the way back from a buffet lunch at The Abbey, a resort in Fontana on Wisconsin's Lake Geneva. It just so happened that we had been talking about Aunt Emmi at the time. However, her official date of death is given as Monday, August 23, 1993, which means that she had passed away not the day before but on the morning Mr. Toffel had called.

It did not occur to me until much later but, by a remarkable and strange coincidence, Aunt Emmi had passed away on the very day that was also the 75th anniversary of the death of Uncle Karl. She had never talked about either of her two brothers, Karl or Lulu, and of her parents only disparagingly. While Uncle Karl had been just 18 years old when he succumbed to his wounds in northern France on August 23, 1918, his younger sister had made it to 89. One sibling was taken not long after he came into the world while the other had enjoyed a long and eventful life. One was an idealist and pure of heart while the other was a realist with a very tainted heart. Life can be so unfair! Sadly, no family member came to Aunt Emmi's funeral. I had expected that Esther and Frank or Nick or the German side of the family would attend but none were apparently able to make it.[8]

The Legacy

Aunt Emmi's passing focused attention on her legacy. Esther and I were already somewhat familiar with the Geneva laws of inheritance under the Swiss Civil Code (CCS). When aunt Emmi started to threaten her sister with leaving her out of her will if she did not immediately come to live with her in Geneva, Esther became concerned about what our mother's residual rights would be if either our aunt left Mutti out of her will or if she died leaving no will. Esther and I agreed that we should seek legal counsel and in early 1980, I wrote to the Geneva office of the Chicago law firm of Baker & McKenzie. An attorney there informed us that in the case of no will, under CCS Article 457, one-half of her sister's estate would go to our mother while her deceased Brother Lulu's three children, our German cousins, would inherit the other half.

In the case our aunt left a will, either of two sets of laws could apply—federal law or Geneva cantonal law. The latter was applicable if aunt Emmi's last domicile was in Geneva and she was a citizen of Geneva. Under federal law our mother would be entitled to a compulsory portion of the estate but not under Geneva cantonal law which suppresses compulsory entitlements by brothers and sisters. In other words, supposing that the two conditions for Geneva cantonal law were met in her case, our aunt could leave our mother out of her will and dispose of her estate as she saw fit.

The Geneva probate notification process was surprisingly prompt and efficient. A letter from the Geneva *Justice de Paix* (Justice of the Peace) dated September 1, 1993 gave official notification that (translated from the French) "Madame Louise Emma Zell, daughter of Peter and Augusta, née Sarcika (sic), born December 18, 1903, Genevese, divorced from Max Aeschbach, without occupation, resident of Geneva at 23B, avenue de Miremont, died in Geneva on August 23, 1993." The letter appointed Maître Pierre Toffel, a Geneva attorney, with offices at 29, Coulouvrenière, administrator of the estate. The distribution list included Me Pierre Toffel, avocat (attorney), Geneva; Me Pierre Mottu, notaire (notary), Geneva; Madame Anne-Marie Zell, Oak Park, Illinois, USA; Madame Marga Isfort, Alsdorf, Germany; Monsieur Helmut Zell, Halle, Germany; and Monsieur Peter Zell, Bad Soden - Salmünster, Germany.

A second letter from the *Justice de Paix*, this one dated October 19, 1993, and addressed to Monsieur Peter Zell, Oak Park, IL, USA made reference to articles 557 and 558 of the CCS and included six last wills that had been submitted for probate. In chronological order, these were:

#1) A holographic will made out in Geneva and dated June 3, 1966 which leaves her entire estate to ex-husband Max Aeschbach of Zürich. The will is signed but not witnessed and was presented by Maître Yves Aubert, a notary in Geneva, on September 20, 1993. The designated executor is Me Marcel Rehfous, a notary.

#2) A holographic will made out in Geneva and dated July 22, 1968 which leaves her Geneva residence to her ex-husband Max Aeschbach of Zürich; 100,000 Swiss francs to Leon Dufresne of Geneva; and the remainder of her estate to the societies for the protection of animals in Geneva and Zürich, in equal parts. The will is signed but not witnessed and was presented by Maître Pierre Mottu, a notary in Geneva, on October 12, 1993. The designated executor is Me Maurice Kervau, a notary.

#3) A holographic will made out in Geneva and dated August 14, 1982 disinherits her sister Anne-Mari Zell (sic) of Oak Park, Illinois, USA in accordance with Article 497 of the CCS because of an altercation she had with her in June 1982. Her bequests are 100,000 Swiss francs to Eric Oppliger of Geneva; 100,000 Swiss francs to the Berne Society for the Protection of Animals; and the remainder of her estate to the City of Geneva for social services and the care of the aged. The will is signed but not witnessed and was presented by Maître Marc Pictet, a Geneva notary, on September 15, 1993. The designated executor is Me Marc Pictet.

#4) A holographic will made out in Geneva and dated April 24, 1990 leaves her Geneva residence plus 50,000 Swiss francs to Marie Kopf of Ste. Croix; 100,000 Swiss francs to her nephew Peter Zell of Oak Park, Illinois, USA; her apartment in La Escala, Spain to Liselot Peter of Ste. Croix; 50,000 Swiss francs to Eric Oppliger of Geneva; 20,000 Swiss francs each to Victor and Nelson Ribeiro of Alcanede, Portugal; 50,000 Swiss francs to the Geneva Society for the Protection of Animals; 50,000 Swiss francs to the church of the Champel parish; and the remainder of her estate to a Christian foundation to be named "Fondation Chrétienne E. Zell" and to be administered by Marie Kopf and L. Peter. The will is signed but not witnessed and was presented by Maître Marc Pictet, a Geneva notary, on September 15, 1993. The designated executor is Me Marc Pictet.

#5) A typewritten will made out in Sainte-Croix and dated September 10, 1992 leaves her apartment in Maison Santana in La Escala, Spain to Liselot Peter and the remainder of her estate to Marie Kopf. The will is notarized as having been signed by the testatrix and two witnesses before Maître Pierre Guignard, a notary in Yverdon-les-Bains, and was presented by Me Pierre Guignard on December 15, 1993. There is no designated executor. A handwritten note by Aunt Emmi, which may have been appended to this will, reads (in a verbatim translation from the German):

Ste. Croix, September 11, 1992

Because of my family I have suffered much. I forgive because Jesus has become my help. But this leads to testamentary consequences for my family.

(signed) Emy Zell

#6) A typewritten will made out in Geneva and dated February 4, 1993 is a confirmation of the one notarized by Me Pierre Guignard. The will is signed by the testatrix, two witnesses and Maître Antoine Geroudet, a notary in Geneva, and was presented by Me Antoine Geroudet on August 31, 1993. The designated executor is Madame Tiziana Baud, a clerk in the office of Me Antoine Geroudet.

According to Geneva law and most other jurisdictions, the last two wills could be voided for two reasons. One was undue influence, i.e., the wills were not expressions of a "free will." Undue influence has been defined as mental, moral, or physical exertion which has destroyed the free agency of the testator. Since Aunt Emmi was living with and in the care of Marianne and Liselotte, it could be argued that she had been coerced or felt pressured to make a will naming them as beneficiaries. The other voidable cause would be the absence of testamentary capacity, i.e., it would have to be shown that at the time of the signing of the will Aunt Emmi was not "of sound mind." A finding of incapacity usually requires proof that, at the time of signing, the testator did not understand the general nature of the testamentary act or know the nature and the extent of his or her possessions. The presumption is that a testator was mentally capable to make a will at the time he or she did and cases where a will is voided for testamentary incapacity are therefore rare.

Regarding holographic wills, i.e., wills in the handwriting of the testator, are generally valid in all civil law countries (continental Europe including Switzerland), without attestation (witness signatures) provided the material provisions and signature are all in the handwriting of the testator. Aunt Emmi's four holographic wills (numbers one through four) were not witnessed but were presumably in her handwriting and signed by her and therefore valid. In case the last two wills were found invalid for either of mental incapacity or undue influence the prior will (#4) would normally be probated.

There was no doubt now that if Mutti was to become a beneficiary of her sister's estate, the family would have to go to court to void the last two wills by showing that Aunt Emmi was under undue influence or incompetent which would make the family, by default, the legal heir. What was not yet clear was whether the City of Geneva, named the primary beneficiary in will #3, would become a party to the lawsuit.

At a Thanksgiving dinner at Chicago's Como Inn that year, Esther told Mutti and me that she was about to hire a well-known Geneva attorney, Alexandre Davidoff, to represent our mother in the Geneva courts. (Me Davidoff was with the law firm Notter Blatter Davidoff & Associés with offices at 16, avenue Jules Crosnier). Maître Davidoff asked for $50,000 up front, she said, plus 15% of the inheritance should our mother's claim be successful. She planned to pay one-half of this amount on behalf of our mother and convince our German cousins to join the lawsuit and pick up the other half. Esther declined my offer to make a bank loan for a portion of the amount due saying she could handle it on her own. Cousin Peter and his two siblings subsequently agreed to join the lawsuit and pay half. On December 1, 1993, Esther mailed Me Davidoff a personal check for $25,000 with a copy to me.

Around Christmas, Me Davidoff informed Esther that the City of Geneva had informed him that they needed at least until mid-January 1994 for their decision because the case was so complicated. According to his fax, Mme. Kopf had made an offer to release the balance of the estate if she received the real estate plus two million Swiss francs.[9] At the end of January, the *Justice de Paix* wrote Esther that Marie Kopf had repudiated her interest in our aunt's estate in conformance with Article 572 of the Swiss Civil Code.

Me Davidoff's fax of mid-February 1994 to Esther brought both good and bad news. The good news was that, with Mme. Kopf now out of the picture, the family had officially become Aunt Emmi's legal heirs. As for the bad news, the City of Geneva had decided to start an inquiry to determine the feasibility of going to court to have the last two wills annulled because of suspected mental incompetence. The heirs, in turn, must now make the opposite argument, namely, that Aunt Emmi was fully competent when she saw the two notaries in September 1992 and February 1993, the attorney counseled. In line with this strategy, Me Davidoff wrote, he had started reviewing documents and interviewing witnesses to gather evidence in support of our position. In regard to our aunt's mental competency, we all felt we had a strong case because in all our personal contacts with her subsequent to the time the last two wills were made out, neither Esther nor I ever had the impression that our aunt was in any way mentally impaired but, on the contrary, smart and wily as ever.

In mid-April 1995, Me Davidoff faxed Esther that he had seen the lawyer for the City, a Mr. Zwallen (sic), to persuade him to settle out-of-court but was rebuffed. In the words of Me Davidoff: "A settlement before proceeding is not feasible because in the philosophy of the City, if something is due to them it is everything; on the contrary it is nothing! I tried as hard as I could to convince Mr. Zwallen (sic) that we have good witnesses and a strong position. I told him that your only concern was not to see the procedure last ten years and that you may be ready, to avoid proceeding, to pay to the city a symbolic amount of money." In mid-May Me Davidoff informed Esther that the City of Geneva had finally decided to go to court to have aunt Emmi's last three (not just two) wills voided. This would make the city of Geneva the legal heir under will #3 of August 1982.

With the lawsuit filed by the City of Geneva, relations between Esther and me progressively deteriorated. I had predicted the action because the City had nothing to lose and millions to gain. My sister did not share my opinion and, furthermore, encouraged by her lawyer, was convinced the case was winnable. Subsequently, Esther cut me off from any further information on the progress of the case. Aunt Irma and Cousin Peter in Germany were of little help having been instructed by my sister in November 1995 to keep mum. In mid-April 1997, I wrote Me Davidoff and when I received no reply, I asked John Roach, a lawyer I was acquainted with, to call him. Me Davidoff told John that he could provide no information on the case because he was working exclusively for Esther. Then, in June of that year, I wrote the clerk of the *Justice de Paix* who referred me to Maître Daniel Perren of the Geneva law firm Étude de Weck et Perren. Me Perren responded in July that he had been appointed administrator of the estate and would serve until a final judgment in the case had been rendered.

A Will Contest

The court battle between the City of Geneva and the Zell family over Aunt Emmi's estate was long and acrimonious. By the time I received Attorney Perren's letter of July 2, 1997, things were not going well for the family. Litigation was still in progress, the attorney wrote, but two judgments had so far been rendered in the case which were not favorable. Quoting Me Perren (writing in English):

– There has been a first judgment by the *Tribunal de première instance de Genève* deciding that the wills of April 24, 1990, September 10, 1992, [and] February 4, 1993 were null and void. As a consequence, the estate would be devolved to the City of Geneva in accordance with the will dated August 14, 1982.
– On May 23, 1997, the *Cour de Justice de Genève* gave a decision on appeal, confirming this first judgment.
– I can assume that the case will be brought to the *Tribunal fédéral Suisse*, which is the highest court and which will give a final decision on the case. (Unless the judges consider that other inquiries are necessary, the case would then come back to the Court in Geneva).
– So, at the present moment, it appears temporarily that your mother will not inherit from Emma-Louise Zell.

Mr. Perren continued, "Astonishingly, your mother's children are named in both judgments to which I referred, even if they are not involved in the proceedings. By receiving your letter, I could observe that your name is not mentioned in this list. It has no consequence but therein is something I cannot explain." He also informed me that there had been negotiations between Me Davidoff and Maria Kopf and she had been promised a substantial amount of money should his clients win.

I had asked Mr. Perren to advise me of the final outcome of this litigation and when I did not hear from him for nearly a year, I wrote back and in June 1998 received a fax message from him saying, "I can confirm that the Federal Court took two awards on March 10, 1998. As a result, Mrs. Zell's estate belongs to the City of Geneva. Mrs. Anne-Marie Zell and Mr. Helmut Zell were judged to pay 40,000 Swiss franks to the Court and 40,000 Swiss francs to the City of Geneva. Peter Zell and Marga Isfort withdrew from the proceedings." In other words, not only did the City of Geneva win their case but, adding insult to injury it seemed, Esther (in place of our mother) and Cousin Helmut, who had jointly appealed the case, were assessed 80,000 Swiss francs in court costs.

Being curious to know how much money the City of Geneva received from my late aunt's estate and how it was used, I contacted Me Perren a last time in early November 1999. In January 2000, the attorney faxed me: "I have no idea of the service of the City dealing with the money from Emma Louise Zell's estate. So, I regret not being able to be more helpful." I was not surprised because the Swiss are not known for their candidness.

The verdict of Switzerland's highest court in March 1998 brought litigation to an official end. Presumably because I was not directly involved in the law suit, although named a beneficiary in Aunt Emmi's fourth will, I had not received any documents regarding the litigation and its outcome from the Swiss courts. And, of course, Esther and her Swiss lawyer had not volunteered any information either.

It was nearly a decade before I again became interested in the case and asked Cousin Peter to send me copies of any court decisions he had in his file. He was happy to oblige. According to my cousin, the trial court made its decision in favor of the City of Geneva on November 14, 1996 but apparently did not issue a written opinion because he had nothing in his file. What he did find was a *Anklageschrift* (complaint) which, according to Me Davidoff, was a translation into German of his appeal of the verdict of the trial court. More importantly, cousin Peter's transmittal included the decision of the appellate court, the *Cour de Justice Chambre civile*, previously cited.

In his complaint, Mr. Davidoff accuses the trial court (the *Tribunal de première instance de Genève*) of having made errors in law and of gross misconduct in its function as fact finder in the case. Citing both statutory and case law, he accuses the (unnamed) trial judge of:

- showing bias in favor of the City of Geneva by making unfounded allegations, engaging in hostile interrogation of Me Davidoff's witnesses, systematically interrupting their testimony and putting words in their mouths resulting in a *Protokoll* [trial transcript] that distorts the testimony and intentions of his witnesses;
- arbitrarily ignoring the sworn testimony of several witnesses including notaries, psychiatrists, medical doctors, friends, and caregivers of the decedent who all had contact with the testatrix around the time the last wills were written and signed and all of whom testified that she would have been fully capable of freely expressing her wishes in a last will;
- arbitrarily and without proof accepting allegations made by Me Toffel that Mme. Kopf and Mme. Peter had stolen jewelry and cash from the decedent and coerced her to sign documents and making wills in their favor and then, after the trial court had decided the case, dropping all charges for lack of evidence;
- alleging that the decedent was mentally ill in contravention of the law which prohibits a judge from making such assertions without having first obtained the statement of a medical doctor;
- using the fact that the decedent had suffered a mild stroke to infer that she was mentally impaired and ignoring the law which holds that a testator may be mentally impaired but still, at the time of signing, be capable of making a will;
- contrary to law, shifting the burden of proof regarding testamentary capacity from the party challenging the will, here the City, to the party that seeks to uphold it;
- ignoring a rule of law (established in another case) which holds that the party that seeks to annul a will [here the City], must proof beyond the slightest doubt that the testator, at the moment he made the will, was so impaired mentally that he no longer knew what he was doing.

Mr. Davidoff also argued that the last two wills (those from 1992 and 1993) as well as the prior one (from 1990) were consistent with each other in that both Mme. Kopf and Mme. Peter are among the named beneficiaries while none of them named the City of Geneva. This should not be surprising, Mr. Davidoff stated, because Mme. Kopf was the decedent's confidant and best friend who prayed with her nightly and looked after her for 22 years without pay.

Mr. Davidoff asked the appeals court to overturn the verdict of the trial court, to order a new trial in which certain witnesses were allowed to testify a second time and in the case of one important witness for the first time, and to order the City to pay all litigation costs.

The 21-page opinion of the appeals court, the *Cour de Justice*, of May 23, 1997, in case no. ACJC/633/1997 begins with a list of the parties to the lawsuit including La Ville de Genève as represented by Me Alain Zwahlen of Geneva, and Madame Liselotte Peter of Bauma (ZH), who filed the appeal, Madame Anne-Marie Zell of Lake Forest, IL (USA), Monsieur Helmut Zell of Halle-an-der-Saale (Germany), Monsieur Peter Zell of Bad Soden - Salmünster (Germany), and Madame Marga Isfort née Zell of Irrel (Germany) as represented by Me Alexandre Davidoff of Geneva.

There follows a brief history of the case including the decision of *le Tribunal* [the trial court] rendered on November 14, 1996 in which the testament of April 24, 1990 is declared void, the public testaments of September 10, 1992 and February 4, 1993 are nullified and the testament of August 14, 1982 declared valid.. After the first couple of sentences regarding her Berlin days which have already been quoted above, her biography continues (translated from the French):

> In the 1930s she [Louise Emma Zell] made the acquaintance of Max Aeschbach, a Swiss citizen; in 1933 she left Germany to settle in Switzerland where she married Max Aeschbach whom she divorced in 1936. At that time she made the acquaintance of Charles Hirzel who became her life partner; they lived together until his death in 1968. As a citizen of Geneva and Burg/AG, Emma Louise Zell died on on August 23, 1993 in Geneva in her home at 23 B, avenue de Miremont. Her legal heirs are:
>
> – her sister, Anne-Marie Zell

 – the children of said sister: Jérôme Witmore (sic), Erwin
 Volker, Ute Niemeyer, Elke Peterson, and Esther Holzman
 – the children of her brother Ludwig, who fell in combat at
 Stalingrad: Marga Isfort, Helmut and Peter Zell

The decedent left a substantial estate estimated at between
20 and 25 million Swiss francs. She owned, in addition to her
Geneva residence, silverware, jewelry and a securities portfolio
worth on the order of eight million Swiss francs.[9]

In the spring of 1969, she makes the acquaintance of Marianne
Kopf, born in 1925, a retired pedicurist; they become friends.
In 1982, Marianne Kopf introduces her to another one of
her acquaintances, Liselotte Peter, a nurse born in 1936. The
three friends spend their vacations and weekends in a house
on chemin de Henriolettes in Ste- Croix (VD); the house
containing four apartments had been purchased in 1983 and
was co-owned by Marianne Kopf and Liselotte Peter. At Easter
1990, Emma Louise Zell suffers a *petite attaque cérébrale* [a
mild stroke] at her Geneva home; she is found lying motionless
by Marianne Kopf and hospitalized for three weeks. From then
on Marianne Kopf moves permanently into the home of Emma
Louise Zell to take care of her while Liselotte Peter offers
assistance during her times off. It should be noted that both
Marianne Kopf and Liselotte Peter were qualified caregivers
for the aged under the regulations of the Geneva Department
of Social Welfare and Public Health (as certified in October
1980 and September 1981, respectively).

The Court then lists the six testaments attributed to Emma Louise Zell
with the beneficiaries in chronological order, namely, those of June 3,
1966, July 22, 1968, August 14, 1982, April 24, 1990, September 10, 1992,
and February 4, 1993.

The decision in *Chambre Civile* case ACJC/633/1997, presumably
written by the president of the three-judge panel of the *Cour de Justice*,
a M. Pierre-Yves Demeule, rejects the appeal in its entirety and confirms
the ruling of the *12ème Chambre du Tribunal de première instance* of
November 14, 1996 in verdict no. 16904/1996 (case no. C/13891/1994-
12) and published on November 18, 1996 by which the will of April 24,

1990 is declared void, the *testaments publics* of September 10, 1992 and February 4, 1993 are also declared void and the will of August 14, 1982 made enforceable.

The last two wills are voided on account of testamentary incapacity and undue influence while the prior will, the one of April 24, 1990, is declared invalid because it does not comply with the provisions of the CCS. By Article 505 of that code, a holographic will must be handwritten, dated and signed entirely by the testator. This will, the court found, was not in the handwriting of the testatrix but was written for the most part by Liselotte Peter and partially by Marianne Kopf and then signed by the testatrix. The court also orders the appellants, i.e., Liselotte Peter, Anne-Marie Zell, Peter Zell, Helmut Zell and Marga Isfort, to pay court costs and attorney fees.

Esther, on behalf of our mother, and Cousin Helmut then appealed the case to Switzerland's supreme court, the *Tribunal fédéral Suisse*, which, as noted above, on March 10, 1998, confirmed the rulings of the Geneva courts.

A Conspiracy To Defraud?

After about four years of litigation in the Swiss courts, the outcome was a stunning defeat for the family and a financial windfall for the City of Geneva. Esther was the biggest loser because, having convinced herself that our mother was the legitimate heir of her sister's estate, and she, in turn, would inherit from our mother, she had made a large investment in terms of money, time, and work effort to secure Mutti's rights. After the final verdict, my sister was livid and used her business website to denounce the decision and the way the case was handled. Her customers and the general public would soon learn of all the chicanery that took place, she announced, in a publication to be called *The Swiss Conspiracy Book*. In the meantime, her website offered some interesting tidbits. According to Esther, she vainly tried to get her Geneva attorney, Alexandre Davidoff, to obtain a change of venue or at least try to get this apparently highly biased judge off the case when it became apparent that the trial was rigged.

Esther made some startling allegation to be further discussed in *The Swiss Conspiracy* book. She claimed that the attorney the City chose to represent it in the case, Alain Zwahlen, was chief justice of the appeals court for the canton of Geneva. Mr. Davidoff never objected to the ethical problems posed by this highly unusual situation, she wrote. She accused Marc Pictett (sic), her aunt's notary, of committing fraud by destroying a new will she had made out and filing one she had requested to be returned to her. She chided them all of being part of "an old boys club" that her Geneva sources told her run the Geneva courts and justice system. As to the "bank clerk Mr. Oblinger (sic)," Esther claimed he got the keys to her aunt's deposit box and helped himself to its contents. As with all of Esther's allegations, it is difficult to separate fact from fiction. Presumably some of these were true or close to the truth while others purely speculative.

Another big loser in the Geneva affair was Cousin Peter who lamented his misfortune in a lengthy letter of October 2002 to me which also included much information on his family. After his mother had received notice from an attorney in Geneva (probably Me Toffel) that our aunt was gravely ill, he had taken the train to Geneva where he met Esther in the offices of her Swiss attorney, he wrote. It was the first time the two cousins had met. Somewhat later in 1993, after our aunt's death, Esther persuaded him to join her in defense of the family's hereditary rights when the City of Geneva sued to have our aunt's last three wills voided. The attorney wanted $50,000 up front, he wrote, of which half was to be paid by the German side of the family, namely, Peter, Marga, and Helmut. At the exchange rate at the time, this came to about 15,000 DM for him and Karin but, because they did not have that kind of money, they had to make a bank loan at a very high rate of interest so that altogether the affair cost the two 23,000 DM, he wrote.

After the City won the lawsuit, Peter continued, Esther wanted them to join in an appeal but they refused. Parenthetically, cousin Peter seemed a little confused because the records show that both he and his two siblings took part in this appeal. It was only after this appellate court case was also lost and Esther wanted to bring the case to the Swiss supreme court that Peter and Marga refused to join. According to Peter, after the conclusion of these proceedings their attorney informed them that $10,000 was still left in their account and returned these funds to Esther. He and his siblings should have been entitled to half of this sum, he felt, but Esther claimed to have never received the money. After some bitter exchanges without a resolution, Peter wrote, he broke off all contact with Esther.

As for myself, I neither gained nor lost anything in Geneva and could be less troubled than my sister and cousins about the outcome. Admittedly, I fully expected to be remembered in Aunt Emmi's last testament if for no other reason than that I was her godchild and the only one of the family who was on friendly terms with her. She loathed Esther and had a strong dislike for the German side of the family as well including Aunt Irma and Cousin Peter because, I heard, they had pressed her for some financial support which she was not willing to give. That is why she would not take phone calls from Cousin Peter. My own expectations were met when I was the only family member to be included in any of her six last wills, namely, the one of April 24, 1990, in which she included my Oak Park mailing address and even telephone number. It is likely that she wanted to make certain that her American and not her German nephew would inherit from her.

Remarkable is therefore the fact that the *Court de Justice*, in its opinion, left off my name in the listing of our mother's children naming only my five siblings. Since this holographic will did not meet the requirements of the Swiss Civil Code and was declared void, this omission had no direct bearing on the case but it does point to a cavalier attitude on the part of the appellate court in its presentation of the facts some of which were incorrect such as, for example, when it is claimed that Aunt Emmi divorced Max Aeschbach when she met Charles Hirzel.

The outcome of this litigation should not have come as a surprise and it did not to me. When one has a city as a litigant (here the City of Geneva) and judgment is rendered by the courts of that litigant, the outcome is a forgone conclusion. According to the family's attorney, as described in his appeal of the trial court's ruling, that court went out of its way to claim testamentary incapacity and undue influence in order to be able to void the testatrix's last two wills. Yet there was no proof offered in court that she was unable to comprehend what she was doing when she signed the two wills nor that she signed these under duress. In fact, all who were around her could attest to the fact that she was lucid and articulate to the very end.

The winning will, so to speak, was the hand-written one dated August 14, 1982 and presented by her notary, Marc Pictet, which left the bulk of her estate to the City of Geneva. But to get to this will, her subsequent hand-written will of April 24, 1990 had to be voided. This was done by claiming that it was written by her two friends, Marie and Liselot, and merely signed by her and therefore did not comply with the law which requires that a holographic will must be written and signed by the testator. On its face, the court's ruling was probably correct. But this will, which did not pass muster, too was presented by Me Pictet.

This begs the question, Why did Mr. Pictet neglect to alert my aunt that her will did not conform to the Swiss Civil Code and would therefore not stand up in court? He dispensed legal advise to his clients and, in fact, had given me copies of pertinent provisions in that law on my visit to him in May 1993. It could not have been a simple oversight on the notary's part. Most likely his performance was calculated to deliver the estate to the City of Geneva of whose judicial system he was part. Could Esther have been correct when she claimed fraud? Could this case have indeed involved a conspiracy to defraud the estate of Louise Emma Zell? This is exactly, according to Esther, what one prominent Geneva legal scholar who had become aware of the case, later claimed.

Requiescat In Pace

Aunt Emmi's life story leaves many unanswered questions especially about her later years. With all her great wealth, why did she live like a pauper? After Uncle Charles' passing was her income perhaps insufficient to support the lifestyle she had been used to because her money was tied up in securities and real estate? If so, why did she not seek professional help to convert a portion of these assets into a steady income stream for her to live on? She might have, for example, sold her villa to one of the developers and from the proceeds bought a condominium in an assisted living community in the area. There she could have been taken care of for the remainder of her life Why was she so terribly secretive about her financial situation with all of her family some members of which were highly qualified to give her needed financial advice and assistance? Why did she let herself instead be used and victimized by some very disreputable characters who she knew were only after her money?

Aunt Emmi did not lead an unblemished life but few people do. She obviously made some very poor choices in her younger days. Her entire family treated her shabbily but foremost her parents, her sister, and her niece who showed little love, compassion, or understanding for her. Everyone self-righteously saw her moral shortcomings while blissfully ignoring the flaws in their own lives. They had all rejected her and at the end of her life she rejected them also. None came to share in her considerable legacy and none deserved to. For me personally it is of much comfort to know that Aunt Emmi could die in the familiar surroundings of her home attended by very caring people. Most importantly, she found her way back to her Christian faith leaving this world in peace with herself and with God. Nobody could have asked for more.

ANNEMARIE'S STORY

A Conventional Childhood

Anna Maria Zell was the last of the four children of *Ingenieur* Peter Zell and his wife Auguste Rosa Zell née Sareika. Annemarie or Annemie, as she came to be known to family and friends, came into the world at seven in the morning on Saturday, March 6, 1909 in her parent's home on Feldbergstrasse 8 in Schwanheim am Main. Her baptism did not take place until a year later, on March 20, 1910, in the chapel of the Evangelical (Lutheran) Martinusgemeinde of Schwanheim. Parenthetically, baptism and worship services were still being held in a chapel because Schwanheim's Protestant congregation did not get its own church building until November 1911 when the new Martinuskirche was consecrated. Presumably, her Christian names were chosen to commemorate the life of her paternal grandfather Johann Peter Zell's first wife Anna Maria Zell née Backhaus but never used except for formalities.

Annemarie's childhood was conventional and happy despite being overshadowed by a terrible war that came to be known as the First World War. Being the *Nesthäkchen* [youngest child], Annemarie was the darling of the family and adored by almost everyone including her parents and her two brothers Karl and Lulu. Only Emmi took a jaundiced view of the new arrival. Her brothers were fond of their little sister not just because she was cute. What most endeared her to them was her unusually caring and warm-hearted nature. The war, then described as the war to end all wars, had broken out when she was just five years old. As it dragged on and with mighty British naval forces blockading Germany's ports which prevented the import of foodstuffs, it was not long before these became a scarce commodity.

It was then that Annemarie insisted that much of her meager rations be divided among her teenage brothers who always seemed to be hungry.

They, in turn, showed their love and appreciation in many ways including building her a beautiful doll house. Her generous heart did have its price. While it was not otherwise noticeable or bothersome, an X-ray of her spine later in life showed that it had developed a curvature at its base that made her right hip slightly higher than the left. The condition was ascribed to childhood malnutrition and the onset of polio.

Annemarie arrived in the world during the *Kaiserzeit* [imperial age] when Wilhelm II was Kaiser in Germany. At the time, the citizens of all the major European powers were intensely nationalistic and did their utmost to differentiate themselves from their neighbors. When Mutti entered kindergarten at age five, the children were taught a verse that would establish their German identity:

> *Du bist ein deutsches Kind!*
> *Lass nie die Lüge deinem Mund entweih'n.*
> *Von Alters her im deutschen Volke war*
> *Der höchste Ruhm getreu und wahr zu sein.*

[You are a German child! / Let never a lie pass your lips / Among the German people from ancient days / The highest virtue was to be faithful and true]. Thus, while it might be customary for other people to lie, it was not allowable for Germans and definitely not for German children. Every morning, the kindergarteners would sing a lied that began:

> *Heil Dir im Siegerkranz*
> *Kaiser des Vaterlands.....*

[Hail thee in triumphal crown / Emperor of the fatherland...]. Ironically, the melody was the same as used by the *Engländer* [Englishmen], their sworn enemies, in their national anthem.

Annemarie was an outgoing child and made friends easily. In kindergarten, she became friends with three other little girls. One was Franziska Trops. In Schwanheim nobody went by his or her given name, and Franziska came to be known as Susie or "Sus" to family and friends. Another of her friends was Maria Siebenhaar, who went by the name "Mariechen." Social status meant much to people at the time and because

Mariechen came from an *Arbeiterfamilie* [worker's family], the friendship between the two girls was not encouraged by Annemarie's parents but that did not much affect their relationship. Her third school friend was Susanna Saffran, called "Sannche," whose parents owned and operated the Frankfurter Hof, Schwanheim's best-known *Gasthaus* [guesthouse, inn]. Here Sannche's father, Anton Saffran, gained a reputation as a chef par excellence for Hessian cuisine and people came to eat at the "Seppche," as the inn was popularly known, even from beyond the borders of Hesse.

When the three friends were six they entered the Schwanheimer Volksschule (Schwanheim elementary school) to begin their formal schooling. Two of the girls, Annemarie and Mariechen, were tomboyish types and took part in most of the activities of their male classmates. They climbed trees and played pranks on their elders. The two also loved to walk around on stilts until Annemarie had the misfortune of falling off injuring her right knee. It had to be stitched up, Mutti recalled, without the benefit of anesthetics which were unavailable at the time. As a reminder, she had a large scar on her right knee for the rest of her life.

One of Annemarie's most frightening childhood experiences was when their gym teacher took the class for a swim in the Main River. One of the girls started to go under and in panic clung to Annemarie dragging her down with her. It was only through the resolute intervention of their teacher who dived in and pulled both girls to shore that they survived. As a result of this ordeal, Mutti had a livelong fear of water so that she would stay away from lakes and rivers and not even step into a swimming pool for the rest of her life.

Two other Volksschule events are noteworthy. When one of the boys in school, who had the reputation of being a bully, started to harass the two girls, they decided to put an end to it. While Annemarie came up behind him and held his arms, Mariechen approached him from the front and delivered a ringing *Ohrfeige* [slap in the face] after which they both ran off. The two friends were never bothered again. A Volksschule experience of a more pleasant sort was being taught *Handarbeit* [needlework]. The girls were instructed in several types with an emphasis on knitting and crocheting. There was a practical reason for that because as soon as they were proficient, the children were asked to put their skills to use by knitting socks for the soldiers on the front. This they were apparently eager and happy to do. Knitting and crocheting remained Mutti's favorite pastime for the rest of her life.

Just how much formal education Mutti received is not known with certainty. Mother had told me that after attending the Volksschule in Schwanheim she finished her education at the Schillerschule, a girls Gymnasium (secondary school) in Frankfurt-Sachsenhausen using the Waldbahn to get there. This made sense since Schwanheim and the surrounding villages had no such schools and anybody wishing for an advanced education with the possibility of later matriculation in a university had to look elsewhere.

Children would normally spend the first four years in a Volksschule and after fourth grade, when they were 10 years old, transfer to a Gymnasium for eight more years of schooling. Students would now be ready to take the *Abitur*, a final oral and written examination, at which time they would normally be 18. Mutti had fond memories from that time because her mother would often pick her up after school, she said, and take her to one of her favorite cafes for some treats. The problem is that, despite extensive searches in the enrollment records of the Schillerschule, no evidence of an Anna Maria Zell attending there could be found nor that of a close friend at the school, a girl named Cornelia Textor.[10]

Nevertheless, there exists considerable circumstantial evidence that Mutti, who was never known for boasting, did indeed attend the Schillerschule although not as a regularly enrolled student on track for the *Abitur*. In early May 2009, when I was on the phone with Maria Schäfer, the daughter of Mutti's late friend Sus, I asked her if she had ever heard of a Schillerschule in Sachsenhausen and she promptly replied (in translation), "Yes, your mother went to school there, my mother told me about it." Mutti often fondly recalled her experiences at this school including the teaching staff and especially a couple of very straitlaced and frumpy schoolmarms who, with their old-fashioned ideas and habits, kept their young charges in stitches. Also speaking for her attendance at that school was her exceptional command of the German language, both in speech and writing, and her familiarity with Friedrich Schiller's plays and poems from which she was in the habit of quoting. Of these, his ballad *Die Kraniche des Ibykus* [The Cranes of Ibykus] was one of her favorites. This indicated an education beyond the Volksschule level.

From this and other pieces of evidence, not least of which was a get–together with her classmates from the Schwanheimer Volksschule during a visit to Germany in June 1982, one can conclude that Mutti most likely graduated from there at age 14 and was subsequently enrolled in a special program at the Schillerschule. She must have attended there for only a very short period of time, perhaps a couple of years, and then left because she had her first child when she was just 17.

Judging from photos of the time, Mutti matured into a very attractive young woman although she was no match for Emmi. Her dark brown hair and eyes put her more into her mother's side of the family while her prominent Roman nose was said to be a Zell family trademark. In fact, Mutti used to joke that if she ever had occasion to travel to her father's hometown of Krefeld and got off at that town's Hauptbahnhof, people would automatically point her in the direction of the Zell family home. But rather than being a distraction, her aquiline nose lent her face that appearance of character and dignity that was truly part of her nature. About her *Zinken* [prong], as she jokingly referred to her big nose, she would now and then declare, *"Ein schöner Giebel ziert das Dach."* [A beautiful gable is an ornament to the roof]. She was, however, happy that none of her children inherited it.

Both Mutti and her sister were slender and well endowed in a womanly way but while Emmi let herself go to become obese with age, Mutti retained her slim figure throughout her adult life. As to her temperament and personality, it seemed to combine the best features of two related and adjoining cultures. Thus, she had the warmth, the joie de vivre and the people skills often associated with Latin peoples but also the mental discipline, the stamina, and the sense of order so characteristic of Germanic types. Much like her father, she was highly intelligent and gutsy but, above all, unassuming and unpretentious.

A Fateful Marriage

Annemarie's parents must have taken a lesson from their disastrous experience with Emmi because they did their best to chaperon her and ensure she met only the right people. They were well aware that Annemarie and her friend Sus, both around 15 at the time, were occasionally seeing a couple of French officers with the garrison stationed in Höchst am Main and closely monitored that relationship. Annemarie had befriended one of the young men because she wanted to remain in touch with her beloved Brother Lulu who was serving with the French Foreign Legion at the time although not entirely of his own volition. It seems that the regimen in that organization for certain individuals like Lulu was very strict and one of the rules was that they were allowed only limited contact with their families. This particular officer volunteered to serve as an intermediary allowing a continuous flow of information between Lulu and Annemarie and their parents.

One Sunday afternoon, Annemarie and her parents were enjoying the amenities of a Frankfurt café when a young man came to the table and introduced himself as Friedrich Würzburger. Most people called him by his nickname "Fritz," he said. The name Würzburger immediately suggested to the family that Fritz was Jewish because Jews often took the names of towns where their ancestors had originally settled, such as Würzburg (Bavaria), or included some precious metal such a gold or silver in their family names. Fritz explained that he was from nearby Höchst am Main where his family owned a men's clothing store. Mutti instantly took a liking to the handsome and well-mannered young man. After a brief chat, Fritz asked whether they minded if his parents, who happened to be with him, joined them at the table. They did not.

Fritz's father and mother introduced themselves as *Kaufmann* [merchant] Julius and Mathilde Würzburger. After some initial exchanges it became apparent that the chemistry between the two sets of parents and their offspring was just right. There followed some delicate probing regarding Fritz's past and future plans and financial resources. The family's clothing store, where Fritz was employed, was evidently a financially sound and profitable business and would yield an income for a lifestyle at least on a par with what Annemarie was accustomed to. After getting this out of the way, the parents decided to stay in touch and see how their two children got along together.

Ingenieur Peter Zell must have decided that a marriage between *Kaufmann* Fritz Würzburger and his daughter met his criterion of being *standesgemäss* [socially compatible]. For both parties, such a union would make much sense. For the Würzburgers having a son marry into a solid middle-class Gentile family was a plus status-wise while Annemarie, vivacious and intelligent, would be an asset to their business. In turn, Annemarie's parents were assured that their daughter would be well taken care of and enjoy a comfortable lifestyle.

Annemarie was just 18 and Fritz 26 when they were married on February 14, 1928 in a civil ceremony in Höchst am Main which, incidentally, a few weeks later became part of Frankfurt am Main and henceforth known as Frankfurt-Höchst. Whether Mutti ever accepted the Jewish faith in the bargain or remained a Christian is not known for certain since the marriage certificate makes no mention of ethnicity or religious affiliation of either party while Mutti herself never talked about it. The strong presumption has always been that Mother never changed her faith when she married Fritz and remained a Christian and member of the Evangelical (Lutheran) Church throughout her life. What is known is that she at times accompanied Fritz to worship services at a local synagogue. Evidently, the Würzburgers were orthodox Jews because Mutti recalled that when they attended, the men and women worshipped separately. While she sat with the other women on an upper level of the synagogue, Fritz was with the men on the ground floor.

According to Mutti, her marriage with Fritz was a very happy one. Fritz's parents gave the couple a generous wedding present of a honeymoon tour of Italy in a new automobile, a Fiat, which had been ordered for them for pickup at the factory in Turin. From her parents, Mutti received a generous dowry of household goods and furnishings most of which was purchased at the well-known Kaufhaus Schiff, a large general merchandise emporium located down the street from the Würzburger clothing store.[11] The Schiffs, with whom the Würzburgers were befriended, were another prominent Jewish family in the area and highly regarded for their many civic and charitable activities.

It seems that Fritz did not waste any time getting acquainted with his new bride because their first child, Esther, was born in February 1927, a full year (oops) before they were married when Mutti was still just 17. A second child, named Friedrich like his father, and nicknamed Bodo, followed in June of 1928. Fritz let Mutti do her own thing at home because, as Mother happily noted, among Jews the wife is in charge of the household with little interference from her husband. Since Mutti did not know how to cook when she got married because her mother had someone else do that chore for her, her mother-in-law stepped in and gave Annemarie a short course in German-Jewish cuisine. Garlic cleanses the blood, Mathilde told her daughter-in-law, and Mutti liberally used that vegetable in all her cooking thereafter.

The Würzburgers circulated within a much larger social group than the Zell family and Mother got to meet many interesting people among the Jewish community including the Schiffs, the Leviens, and the Rothschilds. Fritz's and Annemarie's was a so-called *Mischehe* [mixed marriage] as a marriage between a Gentile and a Jew was known. As Mutti bemusedly recalled, people who knew only that theirs was a *Mischehe* but did not know them personally, naturally assumed that she was the Jewish partner and Fritz the Gentile. After all, she was dark-haired with a prominent *Zinken*, which was supposedly characteristic of Jews, while he had a very Nordic look with blue eyes and blond hair.

They both found this very amusing and played it up by Mutti liberally sprinkling her conversation with Yiddish words she had recently learned. Thus, to be *meschugge* meant to be nuts and a *Meschuggener* was a fruitcake. Mutti was a *Schickse* which was Yiddish for a female Gentile while the word *goy* stood for a male Gentile. *"Hoy, hoy, hoy – schigger ist der goy,"* was the jingle used by Jews to describe an intoxicated non-Jew. A *Schlemiel* was a bungling and incompetent individual. To Gentiles, on the other hand, a male Jew was an *Itzig* which implied a clever but deceiving and untrustworthy person. Mutti enjoyed using Yiddish words and phrases throughout her life.

Mother also learned from Fritz and her in-laws that there was a pronounced class distinction among Jews based on their place of origin. German Jews considered themselves the crème-de-la-crème among Jews while East European Jews such as those from Poland or Russia were regarded at being inferior culturally and socially. Incidentally, German Jews belonged to one of two major divisions of Jews—they were of the Ashkenazim branch, a name derived from *Ashkĕnāz*, the medieval rabbinical name for Germany. Their language was Yiddish, a German dialect. (The other branch was the Sephardim Jews of Spanish origin).

German Jews had good reason to be proud. Many of them had achieved international recognition for excellence in the sciences, the arts, and other fields and they could point with pride at the high esteem enjoyed by many of their compatriots. The list was topped by the physicist Albert Einstein, who had been born in Ulm near Stuttgart and by 1917 had reached the pinnacle of German science by being named the first managing director of Berlin's newly established Kaiser Wilhelm Institut für Physik. Einstein had received fame for his special and general theories of relativity. Other institute directors were the chemist Fritz Haber, a fellow Jew who earned renown for the direct synthesis of ammonia from nitrogen and hydrogen, and the physicist Max Planck for his work in quantum theory. Haber and Planck were the 1918 Nobel Prize laureates in their respective disciplines while Einstein was the 1921 recipient in physics. As every educated German at the time knew, the brightest university professors, researchers, medical doctors, and lawyers as well as the most creative painters and composers were Jewish.

Not surprisingly, with their business and financial acumen, Jews were especially well represented in the German business and financial communities.

Many financial institutions and retail establishments were owned by Jews while individual Jews materially contributed to the economy as consumers of goods and services. Jewish women, according to Mutti, were very competitive and always wanted the latest and best of everything and usually got it. The well-to-do ones dressed fashionably and their homes were filled with antiquities, paintings, and oriental rugs. And while some people took offense at all these Yiddish-babbling, self-indulgent, and often obese women populating the restaurants and cafés while forever complaining about the supposedly inferior service or something else, they were nevertheless highly valued by the proprietors. Retailers and shopkeepers as well as restaurateurs knew that Jews with money were more likely to spend it than the more frugal and penny-pinching Gentiles among their fellow citizens.

Jews were also among the foremost patrons and contributors to public institutions like libraries, museums, and zoos and many charitable organizations, according to Mutti. In Frankfurt am Main the major civic institutions heavily dependent on Jewish largesse were the Frankfurt Opera, the Palmengarten (conservatory), and the renowned Frankfurter Zoo.

Business was very good for the Würzburgers, the Schiffs, and other retail merchants when Mutti and Fritz got married. The Würzburger men's clothing store was strategically located in the center of Höchst am Main at Bolongarostraße 128 which was at the corner of Bolongarostraße and Königsteiner Straße. The handsome four-story red brick and sandstone building had been put up by Fritz's parents in 1899 and came to be known as the "Würzburger Eck" (*Eck* meaning corner).[12]

The store itself was located on the ground floor of the building while the Würzburger family lived in an apartment on the top floor with the two stories in-between containing rental units. The store was widely known for quality merchandise, reasonable prices, and excellent service. An advertising jingle summed up the Würzburger business philosophy:

> *Immer preiswert, stets modern*
> *Fertigkleidung für den Herrn.*

[Always value priced, ever modern / Ready-to-wear clothing for the gentleman].

When plans were underway for the *Eingemeindung* [incorporation] of the town of Höchst am Main into the city of Frankfurt am Main, the Schiff and Würzburger families supported the move because they realized that being part of Frankfurt am Main would draw more customers to their stores. In fact, when takeover by the city seemed imminent, the Schiffs decided the time was ripe for a major expansion. In 1928, the same year the community came to be known as Frankfurt-Höchst, the Schiffs put up a modern, 2-story department store on Königsteiner Straße that took up an entire city block. The Kaufhaus Schiff, just as the original store, offered value through quality merchandise at affordable prices and special sales events made it a favorite place for shoppers from Frankfurt am Main and the entire Taunus region. Because of its proximity to the larger store, the Würzburger haberdashery too enjoyed a surge in sales that warranted the opening of two branch stores in surrounding communities.

The entire Würzburger family was involved with the operation of the clothing stores including Fritz, his parents, and two younger brothers.

Soon after the birth of her two children, Mutti too went to work at the Höchst store as a saleslady while Oma tended to the children back in Schwanheim during the daytime. Mother, as predicted, turned out to be a major asset to the business. She was a quick study and got to know the merchandise and the various brands and, most importantly, learned how to turn prospects into customers. Her open and friendly manner made her a natural for the job.

Annemarie also had exceptionally good business sense. Thus, she soon realized that their customers were very price-sensitive. That gave her the idea that if the Würzburgers dropped prices a fraction below the competition and actively promoted these reductions by advertisements, they might be able to not only increase sales but improve profits as well. Her in-laws tested the idea and after the results turned out to be favorable, adopted it. Instead of going for high margins like their competitors, the Würzburgers now adopted more of a discounting strategy.

But it was not all work and no play, Mutti recalled. On days when business was slow, she and Fritz would take time off in their Fiat for an afternoon drive in the country to places as far away as Baden-Baden and Heidelberg. They especially enjoyed their sojourns to the nearby spa town of Wiesbaden for the five o'clock tea and dance at the Park Hotel. Mutti also learned to drive becoming one of the first women in Schwanheim and Höchst to obtain a driver's license.

Tumultuous Times

After her marriage, the good times for Mutti lasted only a few short years. In October 1932 she lost her beloved mother who was recovering from an otherwise successful thyroid operation. It came as a terrible blow to her because the two were more than mother and daughter, they were soul mates. Oma died at the relatively young age of 57 while Mutti was just 23. When she came out of the hospital in Frankfurt-Sachsenhausen after her mother's passing, Mutti recalled, she was completely dazed and bewildered. She could not understand why everything seemed to go on as if nothing had happened. The streetcars were running, automobiles were on the road, people were nonchalantly strolling by, and everybody was going about their business as usual. To her the world had come to an end. Did they not know that her mother had died? Did anybody care? Her grief was almost unbearable and long-lasting. Mutti often reminisced about her mother throughout her life and always spoke of her with great affection. More bad new, alas, was on the horizon. It was only three months after this unhappy event before she, the Würzburgers, the Schiffs, and millions of others found themselves caught up in the evil and self-destructive vortex of National Socialism.

When that virulent anti-Semite Adolf Hitler and his rough-hewn henchmen came to power in January 1933, the handwriting was on the wall for German Jews who were being increasingly harassed and their businesses placed off limits by Nazi Brownshirts. As previously noted, members of the SA also came to be stationed at the entrances of the Schiff and Würzburger stores to discourage shoppers from entering. The results were predictable. The few courageous souls who continued to shop there, such as Opa, were insufficient to save these businesses and one after the other failed. German Jews fortunate enough to foresee the greater evils lying ahead decided to leave the country for other European countries they considered more save, such as England, Portugal, and Scandinavia, or for more distant places as Palestine, the United States, and South America. Among these were the Schiff and Würzburgers families. They had no choice but to eventually sell their properties at distress prices and emigrate.

The rising anti-Semitism and failing business put a severe strain on Mutti's marriage. When as early as 1933 Fritz decided to leave Germany for America, he naturally expected Mutti and their two children to accompany him. That, however, was not about to happen. Opa was strongly opposed to the idea and immediately counseled his daughter not to leave the country. He had a strong dislike for Americans whose role during the last war led to the destruction of his beloved *Kaiserreich*. He also disliked them for their brash and overbearing attitude, as he saw it, and disrespect for most other countries and cultures. America was a jungle, a dog-eat-dog society, Opa told Mutti, where the rich and powerful exploit those less fortunate. It was also a lawless place where Mafia gangsters like Al Capone ran protection rackets, controlled the city governments and courts, and murdered their rivals with impunity. Only riffraff left their native land to emigrate to America, he maintained.

Opa further stoked Mutti's fears of life in America by telling her that the Würzburgers would be arriving in the United States virtually penniless and there would be no telling where she and the children would end up. In America she could look forward to a life of great hardship and an uncertain future, he told her, and out of necessity find herself scrubbing the floors of well-to-do Americans. Opa had another and more selfish reason for dissuading his daughter to follow her husband to the States. Since Oma had died the year before, Mutti had kept house for him in Schwanheim and now, with him getting older and physically impaired, he needed Mutti more than ever.

Mutti, much torn between love for her husband and abiding affection for her father, eventually decided to follow her father's advice and remain in Germany. With Mutti unwilling to leave her native land and family and Fritz and his family having no choice but to leave, the two agreed that the only viable solution to their dilemma was a divorce which would allow each to go his and her separate ways and allow Fritz to make a new start wherever he found himself. They parted amicably and the two parties agreed that Fritz and his people would take Bodo with them to America while Esther would remain with Mutti in Germany. The divorce between Friedrich and Anna Maria Würzburger née Zell, by order of the 7th Civil Chamber of the Landgericht (state court) in Frankfurt am Main, became effective on March 7, 1934, one day after Mutti's 25th birthday and in the 7th year of their marriage.

Because the Würzburger name had, in the meantime, become a strong liability in Germany, Mutti dropped it and effective October 12, 1934 officially reclaimed her maiden name, Anna Maria Zell.[13] While they were married, Fritz and Annemarie had made their home at Hauptstrasse 48 in Höchst am Main, where Fritz had lived when he got married, but after her divorce Mutti moved back to her parent's upstairs flat at Vogesenstrasse 40 in Frankfurt-Schwanheim. There she took care of the small household including Opa and Esther. Meanwhile, Bodo spent most of his time with his father and grandparents at the Würzburger Eck in Frankfurt-Höchst.

The Nazi racial doctrine was formally adopted in the *Nürnberger Gesetze* [Nuremberg Laws] of 1935 which attempted to define such terms as *Arier, Jude* and *Mischling*.[Aryan, Jew, and mixed breed].[14] These laws were complex and often confusing resulting in much uncertainty as to who could call himself or herself truly Aryan and who not.[15] At any rate, Mutti now found herself to be a Jewess and *Mischling*. As a consequence, she and Opa, who had once been respected and well thought of members of their community, began to be treated like outcasts, much like the proverbial lepers, by their fellow Schwanheimer who went out of their way not to have any more contact with them. Old friends and long-time neighbors quite literally turned their backs on them.

The final blow came when one day Mutti was walking down a Schwanheim street when on the other side and coming towards her was Mariechen, her best friend from kindergarten days, accompanied by her husband Wilhelm (Willi) Bub in Nazi Party uniform. As they got closer, Mutti overheard Mariechen say to her husband (in translation), "Willi, don't look across the street, it's that Zell Annemarie." (Schwanheimer had the curious custom of placing the given name after the family name). Needless to say, Mutti felt deeply hurt. It eventually occurred to her that while the Würzburgers were forced to escape to America, she and her father had to mount their own escape but closer to home. Incidentally, Willi was with the same company as Mutti's father (Opa) had been, namely, I.G. Farben-Griesheim, where he was employed as a welder on construction projects in Germany and beyond.

The year 1938 was a pivotal year for German Jews because it was the year of the infamous *Reichskristallnacht* or simply *Kristallnacht* [Night of Broken Glass] which came about less than six years after Hitler's *Machtergreifung* [Seizure of Power].[16] During this pogrom, conducted during the night of November 10/11, 1938, Jewish businesses throughout Germany and Austria were attacked and ransacked by Nazi storm troopers, synagogues set ablaze, and Jews beaten and hauled away to concentration camps. It was also the year many Jews, including members of the Würzburger and Schiff families, began fleeing the Third Reich.

The Würzburgers, and probably other Jewish families, did not leave as a family group but as individuals as each member found the most opportune time for this momentous move and after the necessary but difficult task of obtaining a U. S. entry visa and an American sponsor had been secured. Fritz was the first of the Würzburgers to emigrate and arrived in New York City on April 1, 1938 on board the SS *Washington*, according to the *New York Passenger Lists, 1820-1957*. Bodo, my half-brother, then 11 years old and probably traveling by himself or with a non-family member, joined him in New York two years later. He had earlier been sent to boarding school in England where he lived in the village of Waddesdon. On April 6, 1940 he boarded the SS *Scythia* in Liverpool, according to the ship's manifest. Fritz's Brother Herbert followed a couple of months later.[17]

The last to leave the country were Fritz's parents, Julius and Mathilde Würzburger. They came to America by way of Lisbon, Portugal, where they had boarded the SS *Mouzinho,* and arrived in New York on September 2, 1941. By this date, World War II was already in its second year. According to Mutti, her former parents-in-law were on the last ship to leave Portugal carrying Jews out of continental Europe. Not known is why the two waited such a dangerously long time to make their escape.[18] Perhaps it took that long for the required paperwork to be finalized or they just had difficulty tearing themselves away.

According to the *Mouzinho* manifest, the last permanent residence of Julius and Mathilde Würzburger was Stuttgart where a United States visa was issued to them on May 28, 1941. Because Mutti had lived in Stuttgart since at least November 1939 (when Ute was born there) and since her former in-laws were not known to have had relatives or friends in town, one must assume that they came to Stuttgart to be with Mutti.

Most likely Mutti, Esther, Julius and Mathilde lived together or in close proximity, which, considering that they were all on the regime's blacklist, would have been a very risky situation and shown continuing care and considerable courage on Mutti's part. After leaving Stuttgart by train, the couple still had a long and dangerous journey ahead of them in that, to get to their safe haven in Portugal, they first had to travel through German-occupied France followed by General Francisco Franco's Spain, which was allied with the Reich. Their American visas were evidently sufficient to grant them safe passage through these hostile territories and arrive at their port of embarkation in time for the ship's departure. After their arrival in New York, the elder Würzburgers initially settled in the Bronx where Fritz presumably had established himself. There the family patriarch died soon after at age 67. Since Julius Würzburger had been in relatively good health, his passing was attributed to heartbreak.

Perhaps to shed some Old World baggage and better fit in with their adopted country, sometime after their arrival in America the Würzburgers anglicized their name to Wetmore. Friedrich (Fritz) Würzburger officially assumed the name Fred Wetmore and his son Friedrich (Bodo) became Jerome (Jerry) Wetmore. There was no contact of any kind between Mutti and her former in-laws for the duration of the war. In fact, Mutti was unaware of the name change until after the war.

Mutti's former husband Fritz seemed to have suffered lasting emotional scars from his forced emigration to the United States at age 36. He went back to work in the retail trade but never achieved anywhere the success and prosperity his family, i.e., his father Julius, had achieved back in Frankfurt-Höchst. Fritz, now Fred, remarried and had a son but the marriage was apparently not a happy one. Mutti and her former husband met just once in the States and that was when the family gathered in Gary, Indiana, for the funeral of his mother, Mathilde. Neither Mutti nor Esther had kept up contact with him. It seems Esther and her father had a falling out soon after he had brought her to America while Mutti, in turn, did not want to interfere with Fritz's marriage.

I personally never got to meet Mother's former husband. There was an opportunity for such a meeting when I stopped off at the Bronx to see Oma Wetmore on my second arrival in the States in April 1952 but Fred Wetmore never showed up but, if he did, he never identified himself. Given the circumstances one cannot blame him for not wanting to have anything to do with me.

Then in the late 1970s, Mutti heard from her childhood friend Mariechen in Schwanheim that Fritz was trying to reconnect with some of his old customers and friends in Frankfurt-Höchst. He had placed an advertisement in a local newspaper asking people who knew him from his days at the Würzburger clothing store to write to him. The ad gave his new American name, Fred Wetmore, and American home address. It is not known whether he received any replies. Chances would have been slim because by then his friends and acquaintances were probably either dead or old and frail or had moved away. Still others may have been too discomfited to come forward and identify themselves.

This unsuccessful venture to reconnect with the past could only give momentum to Fritz's slide into a deep depression. One day in May 1979, his wife came home to find him hanging from a fixture in their bedroom. Fritz was 77 years old when he committed suicide. The Shoah had claimed yet another victim! Mutti was very distraught when she heard about his death. *"Er hätte es nicht tun sollen"* [He should not have done it] she lamented whenever she was reminded of her ex-husband's fate. When Esther heard about her father's demise, she was astonished to learn that he had left her out of his will.

Some Brotherly Advice

With National Socialism and its racial doctrines taking a firm hold in the newly minted Third Reich, it is perhaps not too surprising that Mutti would want to shed her Jewish past as quickly as possible. Life as a *Mischling* and an outcast was a dreadful thought and she was eager and determined to return to her roots as a German citizen and again blend in with the mainstream of German society. Esther, with her Jewish blood, would be in grave danger and, for the duration of the Nazi regime, Mutti had one overriding priority and that was to keep her daughter safe. The thought of Esther being sent to a concentration camp brought her to a near panic and she now turned to Lulu, with whom she had always been close, for advice. Lulu had not yet joined *die Partei* but he was well versed in its philosophy and racial doctrines and advised Mutti how she might use these to her advantage and thereby assure Esther's survival.

The Führer believed that the Aryan race was superior to all others and destined to rule the world, her brother told Mutti. The German people had to be cleansed of all foreign racial elements and a purely Aryan society established which would rule over inferior races such as the Slavs to the East. According to Lulu, the Führer had determined that the German people were in need of Lebensraum for their existence and survival. This could only be accomplished by an expansion towards the East. The Führer was laying the foundation for a new Reich that would rival the First Reich (the Holy Roman Empire of the German Nation) in longevity and last 1,000 years. Much of what Lulu told her was news to Mutti who, on Opa's advice, had avoided listening to Nazi propaganda because it was mostly anti-Semitic and likely to upset her. As a matter of fact, Mutti had little interest in politics at the time anyway and had not kept up with many of the prevalent political or economic issues of the day.

What her brother told her next was to change Mutti's life. According to Lulu, in order to reach this great goal for the new Reich, the Führer was encouraging German women to have large families. Boys especially would be highly prized because of the need for Aryan men to accomplish the eastern expansion of the Reich. Motherhood, Lulu explained, would be a an honored state in the Third Reich with many benefits including being virtually untouchable. Therefore, Lulu suggested to his sister, since she was now designated a Jewess and *Mischling* and remarriage was out of the question, she should consider again becoming a mother but this time of Aryan children.

The task could be accomplished by entering into a liaison with an Aryan type perhaps with a man of proven Aryan ancestry such as a member of the Party. Any children born of such a union would be considered fully Aryan since she was only married to a Jew and was herself free of Jewish blood. She could, of course, expect the state to cover the costs and arrange for adequate financial support for the child or children.

It took Mutti a while to digest what she had heard. The notion of having children for the state struck her as strange but she eventually decided that Lulu's was the only viable option. To keep Esther from harm, Mutti was ready to do almost anything and so it came to pass that Mutti had four more children, all of Aryan blood and by different fathers and all, of course, out of wedlock.

As fate would have it, the first manifestation of what might be called "Operation Save Esther" was my own birth. According to an original and detailed birth certificate a midwife, Mina Nagel by name, stated before the local *Standesbeamte* [registrar], that she was present at the birth of Hans Peter Ludwig Zell on August 2, 1936 at 10 o'clock in the morning at Rheinstraße 4 in Graben *bei Heil* [in the home of the Heil family]. The morning hour and the fact that it was a Sunday would give credence to Mutti's claim that she heard the peal of church bells when I was born. The birth certificate also states that the mother, Anna Maria Zell, was a divorced Würzburger with home address at Vogesenstrasse 40 in Schwanheim near Frankfurt am Main.

Conspicuously absent from the certificate is the name of my father. This could only mean that paternity had not yet been established and may have been in dispute which was not uncommon in the case of unwed mothers. According to an excerpt from the *Taufregister* [baptismal record], I was baptized on August 13, 1936 in the Evangelische Kirche of Graben. The mother is listed as Anna Maria Zell, divorced, *evangelisch* [evangelical (Lutheran)], daughter of the Engineer Peter Zell. Emma Louise Aeschbach of Geneva and Erika Kuchenbeisser née Heil are listed as *Paten* [sponsors].

My father's identity has never been firmly established remaining a mystery to this very day. Nobody ever took credit and I have serious doubts that Mutti's story as to my paternity is credible. She always insisted that my father was one Hans Schübelin, the son of the Graben postmaster and his schoolmistress wife.[19] Mother evidently became romantically involved with Herr Schübelin during a stay with a distant relative in Graben late in 1935 and appears to have been in love because whenever she spoke of him it was always with much affection. She even named me after him. According to Mutti, while she was with her lover, she had neglected to tell him that her former husband was Jewish and when he found out, he immediately dropped her. At any rate, a court established that Mutti and Hans Schübelin had been in a relationship and ordered him to pay child support for the next 14 years.

Strong circumstantial evidence regarding my paternity points in another direction. Despite the court ruling, Hans Schübelin always insisted that he was not my father. According to my foster mother, Maria Gartner, when I first arrived in Forst at about age three, he and a friend came to the house to check me out. I was asleep in my crib when he told her that he could not possibly have fathered me since I showed no resemblance to him or any family member. During one of my corporate assignments in Germany and while visiting Mama Gartner in Karlsruhe, I called Herr Schübelin to introduce myself. At the time he was living with his wife and daughter Ursula at Gluckstraße 14 and employed in the *Außendienst* [outside service] with Karlsruhe's tax office. During our brief chat he told me that he was not my father and declined my request to meet him somewhere in Karlsruhe. It was many years later and after I had learned more about certain family relationships that it dawned on me that my biological father in all likelihood was not Hans Schübelin but none other than Julius Kuchenbeisser, my dear *Onkel Jule*.

Mutti had often been in Graben to visit with her favorite aunt, *Tante Johanna*. The only thing I remember Mutti telling me about her aunt was that she was a distant relative and an excellent zither player. The designation "distant" was very appropriate and it took considerable time and effort to establish her identity and how Julius and Erika Kuchenbeisser came to be my first foster parents. Mutti's *Tante Johanna* was Johanna Heil, born on July 18, 1886 in Neuweier (now part of Baden-Baden) to Raimund Boy and his wife Theresia Boy née Schaub.[20] Clemens Schaub was my Great-grandmother Maria Catharina Wormer's second husband after the death of August Sareika.

On January 2, 1911, Johanna Boy married Friedrich Wilhelm Heil, a barber in Graben. On December 10 of that year, the Heils had a daughter named Erika who, in turn, married Julius Philipp Kuchenbeisser, a *Beamter* [civil servant] in Graben. Wilhelm Heil occupied the left half of a building known as Rheinstraße 2-4 and had his barbershop on the ground floor while he and wife Johanna occupied the apartment on the second. This is where I was born *bei Heil* [with the Heils]. The right half of the building, Rheinstraße 2, housed a *Gaststätte* [inn] called Zur Sonne (To the Sun).

Mutti always referred to Julius and Erika Kuchenbeisser as my *Onkel Jule* and *Tante Erika* and that is how I addressed them even though I had no inkling on how we were related, if at all. According to Mutti, one day the Kuchenbeissers gave a party for Jule's fellow Wehrmacht officers (he was a lieutenant) during which Erika had the misfortune of falling and breaking her hip. The surgery was botched and Erika, tragically, remained confined to her wheelchair for the rest of her life. The Kuchenbeisser marriage remained childless.

When Mutti came to visit me in Germany in June 1971 we also went to see Jule and Erika in Graben-Neudorf where I became reacquainted with the two although I no longer had any memory of them while I was briefly in their home after my birth. The Kuchenbeissers owned their own house at Spöcker Straße 9, a modern one story building with a sizeable vegetable and flower garden bounded by a small stream. I subsequently visited them whenever I was on a work assignment in Germany.

During my visits *Onkel Jule* always greeted me with such a display of affection including hugs and kisses that I felt embarrassed and thought he might be a little on the fruity side. The idea that he was my biological father had not occurred to me at the time. It is very likely that Mutti got involved with *Onkel Jule* while she was visiting with her *Tante Johanna*, his mother-in-law. That would explain why he and Erika were so eager to adopt me and Erika came to my Christening. Other clues exist not the least of which is that, on hand of an early photograph of *Onkel Jule*, the two of us showed a striking resemblance.

Remembering that Uncle Lulu had advised Mutti to look for a genuine Aryan individual for her liaison, I came to suspect that Uncle Jule was such a person and perhaps even a card carrying member of the National Socialists at the time. Sure enough, my inquiry at the National Archives and Records Administration in Washington, DC came back positive. While *Onkel Jule* was not yet a member of the Nazi Party when I was born, the records show that he did join that organization two years later. According to the membership files, Julius Kuchenbeisser, a *Beamter*, born on May 16, 1906 in Daudenzell (now part of Aglasterhausen, Baden-Württemberg), and resident of Rastatt, joined *die Partei* on November 1, 1938 as member no. 7031777.

The court's decision in a contested paternity case could have been predicted. Hans Schübelin was a single man while Julius Kuchenbeisser was a married civil servant. Had the court found Herr Kuchenbeisser to have been my ancestor, it would have scandalized the village and most likely ended his career. It therefore appears that the hapless Herr Schübelin was more or less framed with the unfortunate consequences that his and his parent's good names were tarnished and he ended up paying for the support of a child he had not fathered.[21]

If my conclusion about my paternity is correct, Herr Kuchenbeisser's conduct was reprehensible and inexcusable. He could be called a *Schlawiner* [rogue, fraud] which judgment must be tempered, however, by the fact that he was also a very loyal and loving husband who devoted much of his life to caring for his invalid wife. Both Mutti and I kept in touch with *Onkel Jule* by telephone and mail. When I called him on his 90th birthday on May 16, 1996 his house was filled with well-wishers including the village *Pfarrer* [pastor]. He much wished I could be there, he told me, so he could once more embrace me. We had last seen each other three years earlier when I went to visit him on my trip to Geneva during Aunt Emmi's last illness.

The year after our phone conversation *Onkel Jule* suddenly fell ill and was taken to Heidelberg University Hospital where he passed away on November 6, 1997 at age 91. Julius and Erika found an impressive resting place in the new Graben Friedhof (cemetery). The headstone on the expansive plot is a large rectangular granite block with the name Kuchenbeisser appearing in capital letters across the top and their respective birth and death dates beneath. Mutti once told me that *Onkel Jule* had relatives in the Pfalz (Palatinate) region of Germany and when he made out his last will and testament they most likely became his heirs. (Because of German privacy laws, the registrar's office in Bruchsal could not divulge any further information on my suspected ancestor's relatives since there was no hard evidence that we were related).

As to my birthplace on Rheinstraße 2-4, it has a long and fateful history that goes back over a quarter of a millennium. When on my way to church on the first Sunday of September 2006, I met a life-long Graben resident named Luise Metzger, aged 85, and asked her if she knew anything about the building, she told me that it was a *Judenhaus* [Jewish house]. According to Frau Metzger, the building's owners were two siblings named Khan who each occupied one half. The brother, who engaged in much Hebrew chanting, lived on the left side while his sister operated Zur Sonne on the right. Rheinstraße 2-4, which is located close to the village center, is a substantial two-story complex with an arched gateway and door in its center that leads to an inner courtyard. The gateway's keystone is inscribed with the year 1786 plus some letters in Hebrew indicating that it was built by a Jewish family.

A partial history of Zur Sonne, the inn that constituted the right half of the building (Rheinstraße 2), appears in a contribution by Guido Herzog, director of the local Heimatmuseum, entitled *Die Juden in Graben und Ihre Verfolgung* [The Jews in Graben and Their Persecution] in an illustrated hardcover history of Graben.[22] According to Herr Herzog's account, the property was in Jewish hands for 150 years, from 1786 until 1936. The last Jewish owners of Zur Sonne were David and Mina Prager. While Mina Prager née Rauh died in 1933, David Prager was caught up in the Holocaust. In October 1940, the Nazis transported him to the Gurs internment camp in southern France and in 1942 to the infamous Auschwitz (Oswiecim) concentration camp in occupied Poland where he perished.

As previously noted, Mutti and Opa arrived in Graben in the fall of 1937 after Opa had suffered a stroke in April of that year leaving him partially paralyzed. They had come to be close to *Tante Johanna*. Mutti rented a *Wohnung* where she took care of both her ailing father and me after I had been temporarily left with the Kuchenbeissers. In the meantime, Esther and Bodo remained back home in Schwanheim and Höchst where the two children went to the local Volksschule. On some weekends, Esther would come down by train for a brief visit and bring along Bodo before he was shipped off to boarding school in England.

According to Mutti, her father adored his three grandchildren and much missed Esther and Bodo when they were not around. One time, Mutti recalled, she was at a neighbor's house when she got the shock of her life. Through the open windows of the two adjoining buildings she could keep an eye on Opa and, when she chanced to look over, he had gotten out of his chair and reached into the crib to pick me up. Since Opa was very unsteady on his legs, Mutti feared for the worst and rushed over. On coming into the room she was deeply moved when she found him with his little grandson in his arms tenderly hugging and caressing him.

Surviving Two Curses

The next few years until the end of the war had many challenges in store for Mutti. When her father passed away in mid-May 1938 in nearby Heidelberg, she suddenly found herself without means of support because the minute he died, the pension checks from I.G. Farben abruptly stopped. Since she had no occupation or job training, which was not unusual for a woman at the time, getting work would be difficult. Fortunately, she had lived frugally and had some money in the bank to tide her over what were to be some rough times ahead financially. From Graben she moved to the nearby town of Bruchsal where she lived in a single room surrounded by all her worldly possessions including her parent's ornate dining room set she had brought down from Schwanheim when she gave up their apartment there. It is here where Mama Gartner and I met up with her on our short visit after I had been brought to Forst. The woman Mutti rented the room from was a dedicated Nazi and knowing of Mutti's Jewish connection, took full advantage of her vulnerability by appropriating several personal items including an expensive handbag, Mutti indignantly recalled later.

By August of that year Mutti had moved to Karlsruhe, the largest town in the area, where she found employment as a factory worker at a munitions plant known as Deutsche Waffen- und Munitionsfabrik Karlsruhe (German Weapons and Munitions Factory Karlsruhe). She was on the official payroll there until mid-December 1939 which was a little over three months after the outbreak of World War II. Presumably she left there for better and hopefully less dangerous employment in Stuttgart.

Mutti knew some people in Stuttgart and the city offered abundant job opportunities. Outside of town, in the suburbs, were the headquarters and main manufacturing plants of major automobile and aircraft companies and their supplier firms. The city was especially well known for the former because it was the headquarters of Daimler-Benz, the world's oldest continuous manufacturers of automobiles. Mutti was sure she could land a job in the city despite her poor preparation.

Her move to Stuttgart proved fortuitous in other respects as well. As a former royal residence, up to 1918 the capital of the Kingdom of Württemberg, the inner city with its handsome palaces, imposing public buildings, ancient churches, and manicured gardens was a work of art and Mutti felt animated by her pleasant surroundings. And while Stuttgart was a big city by German and European standards at the time with nearly one-half million inhabitants and with all the amenities that could be expected in such a place, the city had retained a small-town, laid-back atmosphere that much appealed to her. Mutti especially loved the people, the Schwaben (Swabians), whom she found down-to-earth and gemütlich and much in tune with her own personality. Mother made Stuttgart her home for over ten years until our emigration in March 1950. It is here where she brought me in the summer of 1944 when the city was under siege and where her last three children were born.

Mother's job search in Stuttgart proved successful and soon after her arrival in town she went to work for Daimler-Benz A.G. in the Stuttgart suburb of Untertürkheim where the company had its headquarters. She was employed by Daimler-Benz from the beginning of February 1940 until May 1942 first as a laboratory technician and then as a typist in their commercial department. The war was now in full swing and the Anglo-Americans were bringing the war to Stuttgart by pounding the city from the air. Daimler-Benz was bombed out and stopped production at that location in May 1942.

In early June of the year, Mother went to work for the aircraft maker Heinkel-Werke in the Stuttgart suburb of Zuffenhausen. There she was employed in their commercial department as a *Kaufmännische Angestellte* [salaried clerk] until May 1944 when that factory too was bombed out in an air raid. Her last employer was a small Stuttgart manufacturer of nuts and bolts named Purrmann Schrauben where she remained until near war's end when that place too was put out of commission.

Mutti had some interesting stories to tell about her wartime employment in Stuttgart. She told of one fellow employee who had a strong premonition of impending doom. The young woman broke out in a sweat and called her fiancée to come quickly to pick her up because she was absolutely certain she was about to die. He came on his motorcycle and as they were on their way home they were hit by a bomb and killed. There are some things, it seems, that simply cannot be explained. At Heinkel-Werke some of her co-workers, Mutti remembered, were from the Ukraine and other East European countries. Either they had volunteered or been forcibly brought to Germany to work in wartime production. As the war drew to a close and it was apparent Germany was about to be overrun by foreign armies, these women began to panic because they were afraid the Russians would take revenge and treat them as collaborators. Mutti and the other women in the factory did their best to reassure them that they were safe. It was not likely, they told these people, that the western Allies would allow the Red Army to come as far west and south as Stuttgart.

Meanwhile, "Operation Save Esther" continued to fully occupy Mutti. Her last three children were presumably her part of a bargain to have so-called Aryan children for the Reich although nothing in writing to that effect has ever been located. Her children arrived like clockwork, starting with my own birth in 1936, bringing a new arrival every three years until 1945 after the war had already ended. Neither this sacrifice nor the fact that her brother was with the *Partei* spared Mutti from harassment by the Geheime Staatspolizei (Gestapo) and unannounced visits from these people who had Mutti and Esther on their list of *Mischlinge* to be kept under surveillance.

As a reminder to the Gestapo of his Party affiliation, Lulu had given his sister a photograph of himself in Nazi Party uniform with instructions to frame and prominently display it at home. Mother took Lulu's advice and placed the portrait on Dr. Liebendörfer's desk in the *Herrenzimmer*. Whenever the Gestapo showed up, Mutti would proudly point to the picture and tell them of her brother's high position in the party hierarchy and the discreet circumstances that occasionally brought Lulu into close contact with the Führer himself. That was, of course, a complete fabrication because, as Mutti well knew, Lulu was just an insignificant foot soldier, a peon, in the party machinery. In fact, he was serving in the Wehrmacht into which he had been drafted along with his fellow *Partei* members at the very beginning of the war. She also suspected that the Gestapo was not fooled and fully aware of Lulu's lowly status but figured that her story would at least earn her some points in that, by showing pride in her brother's supposed association with the head of the Reich, she was demonstrating her high regard for its leader.

Mutti's situation became especially precarious during the last two years or so of the war as she faced two terrible scourges at the same time. Most Stuttgarters were confronted by only one and that was visits by the British and American air armadas that could come at any time during day or night with little or no advance warning. During the daytime at work, Mutti and her fellow employees were subjected to repeated American air attacks aimed at the factories and infrastructure of the Reich. At night, the British came to hit the inner cities and population centers and, with some luck, create a firestorm that would race through the streets immolating everything in its path. People used to hope and pray for bad weather because clear skies over Stuttgart were an open invitation to the bombers.

While Mutti and Esther, like the rest of their countrymen, bravely and stoically suffered through this horrible ordeal without complaint, sometime in 1944 even they had reached the breaking point. Mentally and physically exhausted after a series of heavy air raids, they made their way to Kloster Mariabuchen, a small Catholic convent near Lohr am Main, where they stayed for a week or two of rest and recuperation before returning to the beleaguered city.

The second curse Mutti and Esther had to contend with was, of course, the home-grown one. The Nazis' "final solution" which resulted in the slaughter of between five and six million Jews. After the war it came to be known as the Holocaust. When Mutti sent Esther and me off to Austria in the fall of 1944, it was ostensibly to escape the air raids. As I later learned though, the real reason was to get Esther out of reach of the Gestapo. The Nazi regime, rather than slow down in the face of its imminent doom, now became even more ruthless. Not only were the remaining European Jews being hastily rounded up and transported to concentration camps, but even *Mischlinge* like Mutti and Esther were now in grave danger of their lives.

It was hard to say which of the two scourges posed the greater danger or the greater evil. The masters of the British and American empires were happy to kill off as many German civilians as necessary to force the country into unconditional surrender while those of the Third Reich did their utmost to kill off as many of Europe's Jews as they could lest any of them be around to delight in schadenfreude at the fall of the Third Reich. Genocide and mass murder on both sides was the order of the day and Mutti and Esther, both German civilians and *Mischlinge* at once, had found themselves among the victims of demonic powers whose one thing in common was an utter contempt for human life. By the grace of God, they survived both evils.

The Post-War Years

The end of the war in Germany in early May 1945 brought new challenges. The Allied bombings and Nazi racial pogroms had stopped, all major German cities and most smaller towns lay in ruins, the well-oiled machinery of the state had ground to a halt, and foreign armies of occupation were once again ensconced on German soil. Not much had changed since the days of ancient Rome except that the Romans could claim they had brought civilization to their part of *Germania*. The Anglo-Americans were not received with open arms. The streets were not lined with wildly cheering crowds waving American flags as in France and Italy when they entered these countries. Frenchmen and even turn-coat Italians, who had a few years earlier given the world Benito Mussolini and Fascism, could claim to have been liberated but not Germans.

With unconditional surrender, the victors had the opportunity to transform Germany into a country more to their liking. A democratic form of government was installed or, rather, reinstalled, partial sovereignty restored and Germany turned into a loyal ally of the now global Anglo-American Empire. Long-term military occupation of Germany, paid for by the Germans, would ensure that America's sacrifices would be repaid in full and with interest. Ex-Nazis were required to go through a process of *Entnazifizierung* [denazification] that would rid them of their militarism, nationalism, and racism notwithstanding the fact that their occupiers were themselves long-time practitioners of these very evils.

The people of Stuttgart had the good fortune to have the first taste of foreign rule under the French whose occupation posed no extra hardships. For Mutti, especially, their arrival was a favorable turn of events because she could speak a passable French and claim, by stretching the truth a little, that her mother was born in France and that she was therefore partly French. In reality, of course, she had not one drop of French blood in her as far as is known. Her dark brown hair and eyes and vivacious personality made her story seem plausible and she could probably have gone anywhere in France and immediately fit in with the indigenous people and culture without missing a beat.

Mutti especially endeared herself to the so-called collaborators who had stood with Germany during the war against the Russians and Communism. Mutti was genuinely concerned about their lot and did her best to keep them out of reach of their vengeful countrymen. At the same time, she managed to be on good terms with the French occupation authorities. Stuttgarters in general, were sad to see the French leave after a stay of only ten weeks especially because of the uncertainties that awaited them with the Americans who would be a tougher and more hostile breed.

Many other notable events took place during this immediate post-war period. For most women the birth of a child is something extraordinary, but to Mutti the latest addition to the family in September 1945 seemed almost a nonevent. All was kept very hush-hush. In fact, I was not even aware that Mutti was expecting and did not realize I had a new sister until shortly before we emigrated nearly five years later without, however, little Elke coming with us. Evidently, my half-sister was immediately placed in a *Waisenhaus* [orphanage] where she stayed throughout her childhood.

The Stuttgart schools eventually reopened in early September 1946 but that was nearly a year and a half away from the end of hostilities. That would give me plenty of time to explore our beloved city of Stuttgart and

Mutti and I to go on visits around the country and do some *hamstern* [food gathering] in the Remstal north of the city.

Ute and Volker returned from Austria in September 1946 and nearly in time for the start of the school year although only Ute was of school age. The two had been sent off to Austria two or three years earlier as part of the Third Reich's huge *Kinderlandverschickung* [child relocation] program in which most of Germany's child population was evacuated from towns and cities to the countryside where it would be more safe from the Allied bombings. There the children lived with foster parents, as did my two siblings, or in *Kinderheime* [children's homes] or special camps for the duration of the war. There was probably no safer place within the Reich than an Alpine village in Austria and Ute and Volker were fortunate in being sent there where they were spared the horrors of the last year or two of the war. The program was voluntary and mothers who kept their children with them in the cities put them at great risk. But with husbands and fathers at the front or already fallen, many wanted their children with them and that is why so many became victims to enemy bombs.

Mutti never explained to me why she decided to bring me to Stuttgart in the summer of 1944 but presumably she realized the war was lost and wanted me with her because the regime had warned the people of the mass pillage, rapes, and killings that would follow an Allied victory. The regime had also informed the people of the so-called Morgenthau Plan (named for President Roosevelt's Jewish finance minister) which envisioned the de-industrialization of Germany and turning the country into pastureland. Most importantly, the plan envisioned splitting up the Reich into several independent states. This conjured up the possibility we might not be able to see each other again for years to come. While I myself have no recollection of the event, according to Ute, Mutti and I picked her and Volker up on the German side of the Bodensee (Lake Constance) where a Frau Pfeifer, Ute's foster mother, had dropped them off, and conveyed them by train to our *Wohnung* in Stuttgart.

About three months after Ute's and Volker's arrival, Esther left us for the United States after her father Fritz had sent for her. Because of the large age difference between Esther and her siblings by the half-blood plus the fact that she was often out with her new boyfriend Nick while we went to school, there was little interaction between her and us. Esther's departure was therefore hardly noticed. Her emigration left me the oldest of Mutti's children at home and Mother began to rely on me more and more for assistance with all sorts of chores and assignments. She might have asked me whether I felt comfortable doing them when I was still very young but she never did.

Mutti went *hamstern* probably until June 1948 when the *Währungsreform* [currency revaluation] went into effect and black marketeering was no longer necessary to keep people from starving. On June 24, according to a document left by Mother, she declared having 8,600 RM (Reichsmark) in her account at Stuttgart's Städtische Spar- und Girokasse (municipal savings and loan association) and receiving an advance payment of 250 DM (Deutsche Mark), the new currency, for herself and the three children living with her, namely, Peter, Ute, and Volker. After this change in currencies, the shops were again filling with goods and the *Bauern* resumed shipping their meats and produce to the cities.

Fortunately, Mutti escaped being caught in one of the many *Razzien* [police raids] conducted to catch black marketers like her after the war because with a police record she might have had trouble with her later emigration. In January 1949 the Stuttgart Office for Public Order issued her a certificate stating that her name was not found in their file of offenders.

Emigration

There was much work to be done in the way of preparation for our emigration but Mutti had lots of energy and great organizational skills so that all went without a hitch. One could tell though she was not overly excited by the idea of leaving Germany and all that was familiar to her for a strange new country of which her father had spoken with such disdain. On the other hand, Esther and Nick were already there and apparently doing well as far as Mutti knew. We would therefore not be alone when we arrived and in good company. Leaving Germany would also mean saying good-bye to Helmut Oswald, the gentleman friend Mother had been dating. She had hoped they would marry someday but as an ex-member of the Waffen SS there was little chance he would be allowed into the United States and that is presuming that he even wanted to leave the country. Would they see each other again? Mutti made sure the answer was in the affirmative by making plans to return to Stuttgart after a short overseas stay and not give up our *Wohnung* on Adlerstrasse 8 but to sublease it to a local couple so she would have a place to live after her return.

Mutti had just turned 41 when the four of us arrived on board the SS *America* of the United States Lines in New York City on Saturday, March 11, 1950. It turned out to be a relatively short stay for her. By June of the following year, she was already on her way back to Stuttgart. She had, of course, planned it that way even before we had left home and now, with her constant battle with Esther over money and other issues, she was happy to get away from it all. Mutti unceremoniously abandoned the three of us in downtown Chicago. With my two younger siblings in tow and with just enough money in my pocket to get us back to Oak Park, I followed Mother's instructions to report to Officer Bolstad's home in the northwest side of the village. His parents had earlier agreed to take us in but, in the meantime, had reneged on their promise. Not surprisingly, we ended back up in Esther's place on Oak Park Avenue. She, in turn, sent us packing after only a month or so.

In the meantime, Mutti's stay in Stuttgart had done wonders for her emotional well-being. She was very upbeat and took it all in stride when my two siblings and I arrived there at the beginning of August 1951, just in time for my 15th birthday. Mother was happy that the uncertainties with Helmut had been resolved and the affair was over. Mutti could now look forward to a new start in the States but this time free of Esther's control and minus the emotional baggage she had been carrying around with her. Incidentally, while Mutti was away, Herr Oswald had been dating the owner of a manufacturing company for whom he worked as an accountant and whom he later married, we heard.

Making A Living

Back in the States, Mutti wasted no time getting herself reestablished. She had returned in mid-November 1951 on the same ship, the SS *Homeland* of the Hamburg-America Line, she had taken to Germany in June. After bringing me back over in April of the following year and leaving her job as a domestic in Wilmette, she found us a place to live, a townhouse flat on

108 Home Avenue in Oak Park just south of the tracks of the Lake Street "L." (Years later, after a deadly accident involving the gatekeeper, the Lake street "L" was relocated upstairs next to the railway tracks). After a short-lived job in Chicago, in early 1953 Mother started work on an assembly line with a company in nearby Melrose Park that manufactured copper coils for the electrical industry. She was with Standard Kollsman Industry for nearly four years.

Realizing that life would become much easier if she could speak a better English and even get her into an office job and, furthermore, becoming an American citizen would improve her job prospects in general, Mother enrolled in a course in English and Citizenship offered at Oak Park and River Forest High School. The school awarded her a certificate of completion in May 1955, a month before my own graduation from Oak Park High. Her teacher, Farrand Baker, also happened to be my Latin teacher. In addition, she diligently studied my complementary copy of the *Chicago Tribune* which I brought home daily after finishing my paper route at the Village Newspaper Agency. A small English-German dictionary and a magnifying glass were her steady companions in this effort.

In the meantime, she had saved up what she could from her job earnings and by early November 1954 was able to bring over Ute and Volker who had remained behind in Germany—Ute with the French-German couple and Volker in a children's home near Stuttgart. With that, we were all together again except for Elke who continued to live in an orphanage.

Mutti made steady progress towards her goals of English language proficiency and becoming an American citizen. She eventually could speak the language fairly well but with a heavy German accent. Her habit of using the wrong words at times injected some humor into our conversations. Thus, when she complained about all those tenderloins on our lawn, I knew she meant dandelions. When she saw hitchhikers on the road she invariably labeled them hijackers despite my previous explanations about the difference. A hair salon was always a saloon. A rude or klutzy person was, as usual, a *Bauer* but instead of using the word peasant she would call him a pheasant. Unlike German, English spelling is difficult and not always logical and so she wrote little in the new language. Practically all of her correspondence with relatives and friends was confined to German. She might have made better progress had she not insisted on speaking German at home but that language was the mother tongue and she understandably did not want to let go of it. By the spring of 1957, she had reached her goal and landed her first office job, with a credit company.

On November 6, 1958, when she was 49, Mutti became a naturalized American citizen in a ceremony at the federal courthouse in Chicago. As was the case with many other immigrants, she took the occasion to officially change her name but not to anglicize it as was the usual reason. In her case it was to formalize what had already become her name back in Frankfurt-Schwanheim. The former Anna Maria Zell, or Annemarie Zell as she was known to her family and friends there, now became Anne Marie Zell. Her American friends and colleagues at work called her Annie.

Ideally, Mutti would have found a well-paying job with a good company and stayed there for the 20 or so years until she could comfortably retire from her labors. That was not to be, however. The past war still lingered in people's minds and speaking English with a heavy German accent was definitely not a plus. More importantly, American companies favored younger employees and people over a certain age were severely handicapped. She would have loved to go to work for the well known Mars Candy Company whose plant was on Oak Park Avenue just north of the village limits. But Mars, like many other companies at the time, had a cut-off age of 35 years for new hires. Mutti was way beyond that age, of course.

Mother also had no real job skills which made her very expendable. By law, the state of Illinois allowed companies to hire and fire employees "for cause or no cause" in a practice known as "employment at will." It allowed owners and managers to quickly adjust to changing business conditions by hiring and firing people with typically just two weeks notice.

Mutti, like many others, was often laid off or terminated. Sometimes she left on her own for greener pastures which usually meant better working conditions or more pay or both. According to her Social Security earnings record, Mutti had no fewer than 14 different employers in the 20 years between 1950, when we first arrived in the States, and 1970, when she officially retired. She variously worked as a domestic, factory worker, office employee, and retail sales clerk. Between regular jobs she would temporarily collect Illinois state unemployment insurance or support herself by doing housework. It seems that her father's dire prediction about her life in America had partially become true because she did end up scrubbing floors for more affluent Americans.

For reasons unknown, Mutti's office jobs did not work out for her and she switched to manufacturing. It could be that she did not like the low pay for office help. After a couple of these jobs, her next stop was a candy company which, although not Mars Candies, was just as well known. E. J. Brach & Sons had its headquarters and main plant on Chicago's West Side just east of Oak Park and near the Lake Street "L." Mutti was with Brach Candy from the fall of 1959 until the spring of 1962 when she was let go.

Mutti never gave a reason for her firing but one clue came from an incident she told me about there. In Brach Candy's product offering was a sugar coated confection that resembled a slice of an orange. One day when Mutti was on the production line for this particular item, a maintenance worker got up on his ladder and started dusting the light fixtures overhead. When Mutti saw the dust coming down and settle on the sticky sugar slices, she was appalled and, unable to contain herself, started to shout, "Stop the line, stop the line." It was not long before a manager came running over screaming at her, "I'm the production manager here and not you—it's up to me to start and stop the line." An entirely different version leading to her firing was provided to me by Elke who was living with our mother at the time. By this account, Mutti had Elke call her boss, a married individual on whom she evidently had a crush, and sing him "Happy Birthday" in a deep and suggestive tone. This was considered scandalous and Mutti found herself out of a job a week later.

After the candy maker, Mutti had a couple of short-term jobs as a retail sales clerk—one with a large department store in downtown Chicago called Wieboldt's. This was followed by Henry C. Lytton & Co., an upscale clothing store in Oak Park's business district on Lake Street. There she was terminated because she could not get along with a woman manager who just happened to be a fellow German-American and lived in a townhouse flat just two houses north of us.

In Mutti's longest lasting job, from the spring of 1963 through early 1970, she worked for Chicagoland's largest food retailer, Jewel Companies Inc., or Jewel Foods as it was generally known, in their Melrose Park grocery warehouse on North Avenue. She was hired after demonstrating her extraordinary skill with numbers. It was said that she could manually add a long column of figures faster than anyone there using a mechanical adding machine. At Jewel Foods she was assigned to the so-called cycling office where her job was to do the invoicing and other paperwork associated with loading the fleet of Jewel trucks that supplied the company's food stores. Because of time pressure, the work was very stressful. On an average 8-hour shift, she had 18 men manning the trucks to cycle out. Another hour was allocated to breaks and lunch but, in practice, she worked nine hours almost continuously. During her supposed lunch break, she helped out as a cashier in the company cafeteria.

The job was made more difficult by the fact that she was on the nightshift and had to take two different buses to get to work Because Chicago's public transportation system was not very reliable, especially during the blizzardly Chicago winters, Mother had to leave home at least an hour earlier than usual to be at work on time. If she then arrived before her shift began, she invariably found herself playing cashier again. Mutti received no extra pay but kept quiet since she was in her mid-50s already and happy to just have a job. According to Mother, all she did during these years was work, eat, and sleep with little time or energy left for anything else. Once a week, she went to the office of Dr. Fritz Herz, a German-Jewish physician, for a B-12 vitamin shot to steady her nerves.

The last couple of years or so of Mutti's nearly 7-year tenure with Jewel Foods were unusually difficult ones. In July 1967, at age 58, she needed a hysterectomy. According to Mutti, her medical problems were mostly due to the required lifting of heavy stacks of paperwork on the job. Esther wrote me about the surgery after it had already been done at Oak Park Hospital. It seems Mutti did not want to alarm me and had kept it a secret. When I heard about it, I immediately came up by train from Virginia, where I was employed at the time, to take her home from a nearby nursing facility. When she returned to work about three weeks later, Mutti refused to go back to the cycling office and insisted on being transferred to a less stressful office job. Her bosses reluctantly agreed.

Mother had two other reasons for wanting to get relocated. A couple of the warehouse managers in the cycling office, it appears, were sexist lowlifes. One time she overheard one of them say to the other, "We don't need old bags around here—we need sex." Applicants for clerical vacancies were judged not by their qualifications but their looks resulting in a constant employee turnover. The second reason was the pressure she had been put under to falsify the records by understating the actual shipments that left the warehouse. She realized that the extra produce on some of the trucks was being siphoned off possibly by members of the Chicago Mafia. Understandably, Mother was not happy having to sign off on something she knew was fraudulent and might make her an accomplice to crime. She made her objections known and her bosses were not too happy about her making an issue of it. Early one morning when it was still dark out and she was walking through the parking lot after having gotten off from work, someone threw a rock at her that barely missed her head.

After her refusal to return to work in the cycling office, Mutti knew that she was on the "shipping list" but still surprised when her boss handed her a paycheck and told her it was her last. She was given no reason or explanation for her dismissal and the law did not require one. The timing of Mutti's firing in early February 1970 was ideal from management's standpoint because it was one month short of her next birthday which would make her 60. At that age, she would be fully vested in the company's retirement trust fund which meant the company would have to match the payments she had made into it. But it so happened that, to get the job, Mutti had understated her age by one year—she had claimed to be 53 when she was, in fact, already 54. Hence, when the company terminated her she was already 60 going on 61 and vested.

The company's managers were taken by surprise and protested but, after some wrangling, the retirement fund trustees decided to give in and mail her a check for the full amount. The payout was somewhat over $4,000 and gave Mutti some money to invest. With her approval, I immediately put it in a safe, high-yield preferred stock of the local electric company, Commonwealth Edison, for her. After Mutti had left the cycling office, the warehouse managers went through a number of young female replacements for her former job before finally facing up to the fact that they needed two people to do the job Mother had done all by herself.

For Mutti, her firing was not the end of the matter. She was inconsolably about the shabby treatment she had received after so many years of hard work and loyal service. Jewel Foods had otherwise been very good to her and her fellow employees. The company had offered them many perks including profit sharing and, for its "jewels," sponsored an annual company picnic that was much enjoyed by everyone. Deeply bruised in her self-esteem, Mother needed to get even with her superiors. She did so by contacting the Chicago offices of the Federal Bureau of Investigation (FBI). The agents there were much interested in her story because Jewel Foods' shipments of groceries from Illinois to their stores in neighboring Wisconsin involved interstate commerce and that activity was regulated by federal law. The FBI brought in a mole who reported on the goings-on in the Jewel grocery warehouse. The culprits were soon caught in the act and fired.

I chanced to be home for a few days after Mother's dismissal and drove her to the Illinois state unemployment office in nearby Maywood. As we came inside, by coincidence some of her former bosses and other warehouse employees were standing in line to be interviewed for unemployment compensation. Mutti, never short on chutzpah, called out to them, "Hello boys, nice seeing you again." It was schadenfreude well deserved. According to Mutti, she also received a phone call from J. Edgar Hoover, the FBI director, who congratulated and thanked her for being such a good citizen and contacting the authorities about the thefts. He might bring her to Washington some day, he said, to testify before the Congress during possible hearings on criminal activities in interstate commerce. Nothing came of that, however, and the director died a couple of years later, in May 1972.

Mutti's last employer was Dominick's Finer Foods, a competitor of her former employer, where she essentially did the same work she had done in the Jewel Foods cycling office. She was on the night shift, as before, with a starting time of 9 p.m.. Incidentally, Mutti worked that shift at both employers partly by choice. At Jewel Foods they had a job opening for that generally undesirable time slot but eventually Mutti preferred to be at work during the night and at home during the day because, as a woman living by herself, she felt it was safer. Mother stayed with Dominick's only a few months until the end of October 1970. The work was as demanding and stressful as it had been at Jewel Foods and this company's warehouse in Northlake was even more difficult to get to by public transportation.

Mother was now worn out and nearly 62. At that age she could take early retirement but with reduced Social Security benefits. It was time to call it quits. For a short time, she collected state unemployment compensation until the first Social Security benefit check arrived. Shortly after she left Dominick's, she received a letter from one of that company's executives by the name of Erv Brinkman who knew Mutti from when they were both employed at Jewel Foods. In the letter dated November 5, 1970, Mr. Brinkman expressed his sadness in her leaving the company but understood since they were located "off the beaten path" and she did not drive. "As I know only too well, the volume of work which you handled so accurately is still somewhat amazing to us all," he wrote. Mutti much appreciated this token of appreciation. Knowing that she had done a good job probably meant almost as much to her as the money she had earned at both places.

Mutti's Place

While at Jewel Foods, Mutti also got a new home. She had lived at 108 Home Avenue for about 13 years when the building was sold and the new owner wanted it for his family. Esther owned an apartment building on South East Avenue in Oak Park at the time but for Mutti moving into one of her seven flats was not an option. She could not have afforded the high rent and Esther allowed no pets in her building. I happened to be home from my engineering job in Virginia at the time and decided to help out and buy some property so that our mother and her pets could have a permanent home.

Esther offered to conduct a search after my return to work and found an attractive row house, called a townhouse in local parlance, near the northeast corner of North Harlem Avenue and Augusta Street. The location was ideal in that it was in the preferred northwestern part of Oak Park across from exclusive River Forest plus there was a bus stop close by on Harlem Avenue so Mutti could get around. By coincidence, our new home was within a stone's throw of the late Mr. Bolstad's place on Augusta Street. Mr. Bolstad was the Oak Park police detective who had come to our rescue after Esther had locked us out of her house and where my siblings and I stayed for a couple of days after Mutti had left us to return to Germany almost 15 years earlier.

The townhouse I purchased was one of six units in a 2-story building that faced a second building to the north with another six townhouse units. The exceptionally large space between the two buildings was taken up by individual lawns and a common walkway. The complex had just recently been put up and the original owner of our unit had moved to a larger home in another Chicago suburb. The first floor of each townhouse included a large living room with separate dining area, a small kitchen and a half bath. Two bedrooms and a full bath were located on the second floor while the basement came with a large pine-paneled recreation room plus a separate utility room. The high ceilings, wall-to-wall carpeting, varnished hardwood floors (upstairs), and two-tone color scheme added to the attractiveness of the place. Mutti and her two pets moved into her new home in mid-August 1965 at age 56 and lived there happily until near the end of her life.

Mutti was appreciative of my efforts and told me that she did not want to live in the house for free since, after all, she was fully employed and making good money. In fact, looking me solemnly in the eyes, she said. *"Ich will dir alles zahlen solang ich nicht hungern muss"* [I want to pay you anything as long as I do not have to go hungry]. Naturally, I was touched by her offer but assured her that I was not looking to make money off her but would limit her monthly payments to a nominal sum which would be just enough to cover the yearly real estate taxes and insurance premium while I would take care of the monthly mortgage payments.

To this end we set up a joint savings account with her Oak Park bank into which she could deposit her monthly payments and I could withdraw an amount equal to the annual tax and insurance bills. We agreed on $100 which eventually rose to a maximum of $200 some 30 years later. This arrangement worked out very well for both of us. Eager to make her own contribution, Mutti had the back patio redone with sections of natural stone and awnings installed over the windows and rear door. (Her neighbors later followed suit). Other improvements included a door between the kitchen and the living-dining room and a stainless steel kitchen sink. The neighbors were congenial for the most part. Once a year, in the fall, all got together for a townhouse picnic between the two buildings. Mutti was very contend in her gemütlich new home which we came to call Mutti's Place.

Saving And Investing

Quite amazing was how well our mother managed her finances to keep herself above water considering her many changes in employment and fluctuating income. She had already demonstrated her financial skills back in Stuttgart. Mutti was neither a spendthrift nor was she overly frugal but always very conservative in money matters. Besides having a comfortable home, she did not need much in the way of material possessions to make her happy. For many years, she preferred paying her bills in cash or by a bank check. It was not until September 1, 1966, when she was already 57 and employed by Jewel Foods, when Esther was able to persuade our mother to open a checking account to make her money management and payment of bills more convenient. Once she had that account, she more or less became addicted to it and, as the 42 check registers she left behind attest to, kept meticulous track of all her income and expenses even the smallest ones writing out checks for as little as two dollars.

She was always very scrupulous in paying her bills on time. In fact, she fretted missing or being late on a payment and would call the utility company or other place if she thought she should have received a bill and it had not arrived. During the years we still had a mortgage on the house and I was employed away from Chicago, she hand-carried the monthly payment to the savings and loan on North Avenue in Chicago's Austin neighborhood to ensure that it arrived on or before the due date.

Mutti may not have been consciously working to achieve the American Dream of material prosperity but she nevertheless realized that for her financial security she had to save and invest. It was my own strategy and I urged Mutti to save by buying individual retirement accounts (IRAs) which she did.

Mutti may also have been the first in the family to own corporate stock. While employed at Brach Candy in the early 1960s, she bought shares in that firm presumably on an employee stock purchase plan. Unbeknownst to me and probably because I was mailing her a monthly check of $30 at the time to compensate her for keeping my room at our Home Avenue flat while I was away, she made me co-owner of that stock. Later I further built up her stock portfolio by investing her money in the preferred and common stock of major electric power and telephone companies. In addition, I now and then purchased stock with my own funds which I put in joint tenancy (with right of survivorship) with her so that in case of my untimely demise she would own it outright.

Since she would not be receiving a company pension, the interest and dividend income from these investments would serve to supplement her Social Security income which I feared would be too small for her to live on. She paid me a rare complement in a letter she wrote me in Munich at the end of February 1982. "*Ohne Dich hätte ich keinen roten Pfennig*" [Without you I wouldn't have a red penny], she wrote. It was a big exaggeration, of course.

Strangely, and again unbeknownst to me, according to her check registers during her years with Jewel she made some sizeable money transfers, often as much as $500 at a time, to her savings account at the Landesgirokasse (state savings and loan association) on Königstraße in Stuttgart. It is not clear to me why she did this because she never expressed any desire to return to Stuttgart to live there. She had maintained an account at this location since she had relocated to Stuttgart during the war. Even after we had come to America, she maintained the account presumably out of a sense of loyalty and for sentimental reasons. Her continuing connection with her beloved Stuttgart seemed very important to her. Naturally, my preference would have been that she had kept the extra money at home and bought more IRAs or certificates of deposit instead or let me invest it in more utility stock for her.

The financial good days ended with Mutti's retirement when her income took a dramatic plunge. Her first monthly Social Security benefits check paid in May 1971 was just $125 which was less than one-fourth of her previous monthly income. This was supplemented by interest and dividend payments from her IRAs, CD's, Commonwealth Edison preferred, and American Telephone & Telegraph (AT&T) and American Electric Power (AEP) common stock. Esther and I also made small monthly contributions which, however, never exceeded $150 in total. We could and should have given more but neither one of us was overly generous with our mother figuring she would get by somehow as she always had. Mutti recorded every payment from us in her check registers as either "check from Esther for myself" or "check from Peter for myself" as if to show her gratitude.

It would have been completely out of character for Mutti to ask for more financial support. Somehow she managed to pay all her bills on time. Things slowly improved financially with a rise in her Social Security benefits and the addition, starting in June 1981, of monthly *Altersrente* [old age benefits] from Germany for her wartime employment there. By March 1997, her Social Security benefits had climbed to $570 and her German benefits to nearly one half that amount and although her income was still small by most people's standards, her fixed expenses were equally small. As a result there was always a monthly surplus of a couple of hundred dollars which I could invest for her.

Faults And Virtues

Like all people, Mutti had her good and bad qualities but fortunately her positive traits far exceeded her failings. She was remarkably warm-hearted and compassionate and genuinely affected by the plight of others. She could not pass a beggar on a Chicago street without saying, *"ach je"* [how sad] and open her purse. She would be especially kind to anybody she felt was disenfranchised or had a tough time making a living. In department stores she bought almost exclusively from black Americans or other minority sales personnel because she wanted to ensure that they met their sales quotas and earned decent commissions. She generously supported Oak Park's Animal Care League and many charities around the country.

Mother was the model of what in German is called *Bescheidenheit* [unpretentiousness, modesty]. In stark contrast to Emmi and Esther, she was humble, self-effacing, and unassuming to a fault. In a restaurant, it was difficult to get her to decide on a menu item because she did not want to be a bother. "Just bring me what's easiest for you" would be her standard reply to the waitress' query as to what she wanted. After the meal, one had to restrain Mutti from gathering up the plates and wiping down the table with napkins to reduce the waitress' workload.

Mutti's children too were expected to be *anspruchslos* [undemanding] and to do with little. Birthdates were practically nonevents and one had to remind Mutti of one's big day which she would then reluctantly acknowledge but there would be no birthday cake or gifts. She herself took no notice of her own birthday. School or other achievements too were not recognized and one dared not say much about these for fear of being put down. Undoubtedly, she took satisfaction in our progress but she would never go so far as to acknowledge let alone praise it. She evidently did not want us to become haughty or proud. In this, she succeeded remarkable well except in the case of Esther. The lack of praise and recognition for hard-won achievements was tough on my younger siblings who saw in it as an absence of love and care.

That Mutti did, nevertheless, take pride in her children's accomplishments was evidenced by a set of photographs found among her papers. The packet in a plastic cover with a label on which she had written *Schulbilder von Peter, Volker, Elke* [School pictures of Peter, Volker, Elke] contained the large- format photographs from the grammar school graduation ceremonies for the three of us. All were signed by our classmates and teachers on the reverse side. (Ute's class picture was not among them but presumably our sister took it with her).

Mother had numerous good friends, neighbors, and acquaintances, mostly fellow German-Americans living in the village, neighboring communities, and Chicago, with whom she met regularly. She was unusually gregarious and eager to meet people. *"Ich will immer unter den Leuten sein"* [I always want to be among people], she used to say. When she heard someone speak with a German accent, that was a cue to become acquainted. Where were they from? When told the town or village, and if it was in southern Germany, she usually knew the place or at least had heard of it. Within a short time, she had a good part of the person's life history while the new acquaintance had hers.

Mutti loved to remember people with all sorts of presents and send untold gift packages to relatives and friends overseas although on no particular occasion. Her wish, *"Jemand eine Freude machen"* [To bring joy to someone] first expressed in Germany long ago, was something that always stayed with her. Despite that, Mutti was very reluctant to accept any presents herself because she always claimed to have all she needed. According to Esther, our mother's joy in giving but finding little pleasure in receiving was a sign of poor self-esteem.

One tradition my sister started was to take Mutti to lunch in a nice restaurant on her big day. After I had accepted a management position on

Chicago's West Side in the early 1970s, I too was able to partake of this ritual. My new employer had the very nice and unique custom of making the anniversary date of an employee's hiring a holiday. My anniversary date happened to be March 6, which coincided with Mutti's birthday, and hence I had that day off. Esther initially favored various French restaurants in the Chicago area but we eventually settled on the Como Inn as our restaurant of choice. Its location on North Milwaukee Avenue was not far from my place of employment and made it a favorite with my company's management for wining and dining our best customers. The restaurant was a cavernous place with a magnificent Italian interior and great food.

Mother's modesty and restraint were evident in all she did. She rarely used makeup and when she did only sparingly. She dressed simply but tastefully with a pleated dress, a skirt and blouse, or a two-piece *Kostüm* being her favorites. A good eye for color and what colors went together was one of her strengths in choosing her clothing. Mutti appeared to have a weakness for footwear and her large collection included shoes not even her size and which she could never put on. Presumably she found them on sale and could not resist taking them home. Mutti also had a weakness for fabric for dressmaking. She had a German-American friend named Mariele who worked for the local branch of Wieboldt's department store and whenever there was a fabric sale, she would buy an assortment from her and mail it to friends and relatives in Germany. She kept it all in a footlocker in her bedroom closet. Most likely her habit of collecting and storing footwear, fabric, and other goods became ingrained during her "hamstering" days in post-war Germany.

Conceit and vanity always struck a sour note with Mutti especially with people she thought had no good reason to be vain or smug. She especially much disliked haughty people or those who, in her opinion, thought too highly of themselves. While she regularly had her hair done at the beauty shop while she was working, she discontinued that practice after she retired and went instead to a unisex parlor. Her Dutch boy haircut was just what she needed, she said, because she liked the look and now could wash her hair as often as she wanted. She thought it ridiculous for some older working woman, like Helen in the building across from us, to leave the house in the morning made up, dolled up, and artfully coiffed as though she was on her way to an audience with Marie Antoinette.

While she did not want anybody to fuss over her or impose on somebody else, Mother had no qualms about putting somebody down who she thought was overreaching and imposing on her. While being unassuming, she was not meek. In fact she often displayed considerable chutzpah. One day we had gotten out of the car at an Oak Park savings and loan on Lake Street and Mutti was about to enter the place thinking I had gone ahead of her. Just then a burly police officer stepped right in front of her blocking her way so that she could neither move nor see ahead. The man was a veritable giant and Mutti, at just a couple of inches over five feet tall, did not reach much higher than this fellow's bellybutton or so it seemed. The officer looked down at her through his reflective sunglasses and in a commanding voice asked, "Looking for somebody?" Rather than being intimidated, Mutti slowly raised her head and scornfully looking at him snapped back, "Yes, but not for you." He got the message and quickly stepped aside. I happened to be right behind her.

Despite her fairly patriotic outlook, Mutti had no problem showing her independence when circumstances called for it. She was a Francophile and whenever the French were in the doghouse in America, such as occurred during the presidency of Charles de Gaulle, Mutti rallied to their defense. The Americans were outraged that the French president was keeping their British cousins out of the newly formed European Economic Community (the forerunner of the European Union). President de Gaulle had maintained that the British were not true Europeans but outsiders who did not share the traditions and values of the Continent. Their entry into Europe would be a Trojan horse meant to allow their American partners to increase their hegemony over Europe.[23]

The American public responded by no longer buying French goods and renaming French fries "freedom fries." Mutti had never bought French wine nor any other wine before but now she brought home bottles of it to give away as gifts. One time we were in Chicago's German neighborhood and Mutti spotted a car of French make with a man sitting at the wheel. She immediately bolted over to it and began circling the vehicle eying and admiring it and beguiling the driver with smiles of approval. It was her way of showing her contempt for some bad policy. When Charles de Gaulle died in November 1970, Mutti made it a point to show up at the French consulate in Chicago to sign a book of condolences. When I once asked her why she was so kindly disposed toward the French after all the grief these people had caused us Germans over the centuries, Mutti replied, "*Die Franzosen haben ein gutes Herz.*" [The French have a warm heart].

Although Mutti was people-orientated and made friends easily, eleven close townhouse neighbors to content with posed some problems for her. She had some neighbor problems even back in Stuttgart. Most townhouses belonged to singles or childless couples while just a few were owned by families with a child or two. Being sensitive and thin-skinned, Mutti was quick to note any slight by any of them. Her continuously shifting alliances made it necessary for me to keep up on who was "in" and who was "out" especially after an absence from home for some time. If she saw me talk with someone who had caused her some injury, real or imagined, she would not say anything to me but I knew she would feel deeply hurt because loyalty was all-important to her.

Her problems with neighbors were not always her fault. The widow Helen across from us had developed terminal pancreatic cancer and one day in the summer of 1986 she and Patricia (Patti), her daughter, took off on a trip to Rome to take part in a papal audience. Mutti, wanting to be nice and bring a little joy, as she was wont to do, asked Patti if she could get her something as a travel gift. Patti wanted some pieces of clothing which Mutti duly purchased and gave to her. On the day when the two were to be picked up for the drive to the airport, Mutti anxiously stood by the front window so that she would not miss the departure without saying goodbye and wishing her neighbors a nice trip. When she spotted the two leave by their front door, Mutti ran out her back door to see them off in the parking lot. She waved to them frantically but they apparently completely ignored her as they drove by. There was no chance they did not see her, Mutti claimed, because their car almost ran her over. Mutti felt terribly hurt and when I called her that weekend from Long Island, where I was employed at the time, she wept and could hardly be consoled.

With some people Mother could be very mean and vindictive if she thought she had been wronged. When she moved into our townhouse home, the unit to the east of us was owned by a nice, quiet couple who operated a draperies business in Chicago. When they relocated, the place came into ownership of a woman who liked to imbibe a little too much on occasion. Marge used to go out bowling "with the girls" and when she came home late at night she was stoned. One of her activities before turning in was to open and close her bedroom closet door. These doors were suspended on rollers so they could be moved back and forth. When closing the door, Marge would invariably slam it into the common wall that separated the two townhouse units and Mutti would be shaken from sleep and end up in a cold sweat.

Not to be outdone, Mutti would get up when she thought her neighbor was asleep and rap on the wall with her fist. When her neighbor Ann on the other side expressed sympathy with Marge, Mutti, thinking the two were in cahoots to keep her awake, gave her the same treatment. Once Ann told me that my mother was a sneak. While she never caught her in the act, Ann was certain it was she who occasionally raided some mulberry bushes next to the late Detective Bolstad's house on Augusta Street and threw the berries on her back steps to turn them purple. The feud, which lasted some three or four years, came to an end when Marge moved into an Oak Park retirement home and Mutti and Ann decided to make up.

A Feline Bond

Mutti's fondness for pets led to many opportunities for meeting people and socializing. The pet food section at the grocery store became a favorite venue for her. Anybody coming by and reaching for a can of cat food was like a fly that had fallen into a spider's web. She loved to swap stories about cat peculiarities and dispense all sorts of advise for their proper care. Anybody walking a dog would likewise be a target for Mutti to zero in on.

While she was still working at Jewel Foods on the night shift and coming home on the bus early in the morning, she used to see a lady walk her little poodle near the northwest corner of Harlem Avenue and Augusta Street, which was on the River Forest side of Harlem. It was not long before Mutti introduced herself and struck up a friendship. The lady turned out to be Mrs. Accardo, wife of Anthony ("Big Tuna") Accardo, the *capo dei capi* [boss of all bosses] of the Chicago crime syndicate. The Accardos had recently sold their River Forest estate and temporarily moved into a condominium building across the street from Mutti's Place before moving on to California. People like the Accardos usually preferred to stay incognito but Mutti somehow managed to get Clarice Accardo to identify herself. Mrs. Accardo was Polish-American and perhaps Mutti just happened to have a Polish ancestor to establish a relationship.

Mutti reserved her warmest feelings for her pet cats of which she always had from one to three in the house. Since she lived by herself for many years, her pets provided her with the companionship and affection she longed for. In her animals she saw the qualities she found lacking in people especially unconditional love and loyalty. For Mutti, cats, unlike dogs, were downtrodden creatures who lived in a hostile world. Few people really liked cats in her experience. Her attachment to cats much determined her relationship with people. People who liked cats were good, warm-hearted, and compassionate. When Mutti met someone new, she would invariably probe to see what the person's attitude was toward cats because she could only warm up to someone who was a cat lover.

Mother had a remarkable rapport with her pets. She essentially treated them like babies carrying them about in her arms and, looking them straight in the eyes, lovingly talk to them. She insisted that they fully understood what she was saying. In fact, Mother was convinced animals had intelligence and feelings just like people and all they lacked was the ability to speak. If they could talk, they could tell you things that would astound you, she claimed. "They are human beings too" she once said to me. Not true, of course, but I knew what she meant.

Unfortunately, Mutti also tended to overfeed her pets which did nothing for their health. One stray she brought inside developed a taste for fresh pork kidneys and would soon eat nothing else. Blackie, as she called him for the color of his coat, did not live very long. In fact, most of her pets tended to be obese because she would constantly ply them with food from the table as well as canned and dry foods. This too was most likely related to her childhood war-time experiences when hunger was a constant companion of people's lives. The fact that a domestic cat's life expectancy is just 13 to 17 years on average was unfortunate because every time Mutti lost a pet it was like losing a child and she was grief-stricken a long time thereafter.

Mutti had one pet cat that stood out among the others. It was a calico, a female as nearly all calicos are, she named Putzi from the German *putzen* [to clean] for her habit of constantly licking and cleaning her coat.

Mother acquired Putzi some years after we had moved into our townhouse apartment on Home Avenue and while I was away at school. One day she heard the desperate cries of a kitten and found it in a shoebox on the porch next door where a neighbor had left it when he moved away. Putzi was a gentle and affectionate creature which seemed almost human in her understanding and feelings. When Mutti had her in her lap, which was often, Putzi would show her affection by standing up on her hind legs and gently lick Mutti's cheeks. This is something seen in dogs, of course, but rarely in cats. The two were almost inseparable and when Mutti came home from work, Putzi would be sitting by the back door at Mutti's Place awaiting her.

Putzi must have been about 17 years old when she became weak and lethargic which the veterinarian ascribed to old age. One day, in early October 1977, Mutti noticed her missing and searched for her throughout the house when she found her lying on the floor inside the upstairs linen closet. She gently took her in her arms and talked to her. Putzi struggled to raise herself up, shakily stood on her hind legs, and intently looked Mutti in the eyes. It was as if she knew it would be the last time she would see her beloved friend and companion. Suddenly she collapsed and expired. Mutti was overcome with grief and called me in Frankfurt am Main, where I was working at the time, sobbing uncontrollably. She wanted Putzi's ashes brought to Germany and buried in Frankfurt-Schwanheim next to her parents but I managed to talk her out of it.

An Introspective Side

While not being an intellectual given to deep thought and analysis, there was a strong non-material, reflective, and spiritual side to Mutti. One could easily underestimate her until one got to know her better. She was a Christian believer who understood the basic tenets of her faith and tried to live by them as best as she could. She knew her Bible and in her letters often surprised me by quoting long passages which she had most likely learned by heart during confirmation classes back in Schwanheim. Her repugnance of arrogance, pride, and self-rightcousness was much in conformance with the Gospel writers who unequivocally denounced these traits and instead advocated humility and repentance for sin. Mutti prayed daily and her children were taught to do the same. We said grace before and after every meal and quietly and discreetly even when eating out.

But while our mother encouraged all of us to go to church, she herself was an indifferent churchgoer both before and after she came to the States. She would attend worship services only on high Christian holidays such as Christmas and Easter. On rare occasions when I was home, she would ask to come along. One could suppose that had Mutti believed that there was a direct relationship between church attendance and being on good terms with the Almighty, she would probably have attended more often and even every Sunday as her so pious maternal grandmother, Maria Catharina, had done back in Schwanheim.

Mutti's lack of enthusiasm for church attendance after we came to America must have come about from an unpleasant experience when we first settled in Oak Park. There we attended a church in neighboring Forest Park which was within walking distance of our townhouse flat on Home Avenue. That church, St. John's Evangelical Lutheran, still offered services in both German and English. The congregation made the Zell family church members and, in accordance with American custom, presented us with a set of envelopes for the weekly donations. We were unfamiliar with this practice because in Germany one simply put one's donation in the collection plate that was passed around and, consequently, we never used the envelopes. About a year after our enrollment, Mutti received a letter from the church office informing her that our family had been removed from the membership rolls because of non-attendance. Mutti took it all in stride but never joined another congregation. For her the whole church business was about money. When I was about to be late for church on Sunday mornings Mutti would tell me not to worry just as long as I got there in time for the arrival of the collection plate.

Not being a lover of books, it would have been inconceivable to see Mutti read one, least of all a novel, or anything else besides a newspaper or magazine regardless of whether it was in German or English. When Esther got her a copy of *Das Kochbuch Fürs Leben* [The Cookbook for Life] by Rotraud Degner for Christmas 1971, it was likely the first and only book Mother had looked into since leaving school. This work was richly illustrated and contained over 1,000 recipes including traditional German ones and dishes adopted from the French and Italian cuisines. Mutti did not hesitate to add her own comments to some recipes—in red ink no less.

Mother did like to buy books as presents and endowed me with at least three. For Christmas 1967 she gave me a copy of *Deutschland im Farbbild* [Germany in Color] "*zur bleibenden Erinnerung an seine alte Heimat*" [for a lasting remembrance of his old homeland] while for my 32nd birthday I received *Opfergang Eines Volkes: Der Totale Krieg* [Martyrdom of a People: The Total War] by Erich Kern on the fate of the German people during World War II. Now and then she even stepped into the Oak Park branch of Chicago's famous Kroch's & Brentano's bookstore on Lake Street to browse through their shelves. There, in 1974 she bought me a copy of Fawn Brodie's just published *Thomas Jefferson: An Intimate History* as a Christmas present.

Mutti was also fond of rhymed verse in our native tongue and I sometimes wondered whether my own modest poetic gift came from her. As previously noted, she liked to quote verses from Friedrich Schiller, a contemporary of Wolfgang von Goethe in 18th century Weimar. On the back of an envelope containing a letter from Mama Gartner in Karlsruhe she had written, *Lampenschimmer / ganz allein im Zimmer / ich und Du / beim ersten Rendezvous.* [The glow of a lamp / all alone in the room / I and you / on our first rendezvous]. Most likely though it did not come from her but she found the little verse in one of her German-language ladies magazines such as *Die Hausfrau* and liked it enough to jot it down.

Rather than read, be it for knowledge or pleasure, Mutti preferred to write. She had a great need to express herself in letters and postcards. Throughout most of her life, she kept up a lively correspondence with relatives, friends, and acquaintances on two continents. When, during leisure times, she was not doing *Handarbeit* she was invariably writing somebody and they usually wrote back requiring yet another response. Letters she received and found interesting, she kept and consequently she wound up with quite a collection spanning many years. Whenever we were on a trip together, she spent considerable time writing picture postcards to family and friends Stateside and in Germany. Sometimes I found this exasperating because she preferred to do so while we were out having lunch and I wanted to move on and do and see other things. When I was away from home, we exchanged a letter a week on average in addition to the occasional phone call. Not receiving an expected letter from me because it took longer than usual or even got lost, would get her into a panic mode.

Unlike the letters of her sister, Mother's were not without substance. While often short on facts, they were chock-full of impressions, opinions, and advice, and liberally sprinkled with exclamation marks, often a number in a row, while important passages were underlined, sometimes two or three times, for emphasis. Her handwriting was almost childlike in appearance with the individual letters of the alphabet large, well formed and voluptuous. A graphologist studying her penmanship would undoubtedly have seen in it a reflection of her basic sincerity and warm personality. As might be expected, she had good advice for me on almost any topic. She was especially fearful that I might succumb to the many temptation life had to offer and that I might be out late at night carousing and not getting the sleep all Zell family members supposedly needed. Her letters usually ended with, "*Tausend Küsse und sei Gottbefohlen*" [A thousand kisses and God be with you].

As is the case with most people who have been blessed with a long life and have gone through many and varied life experiences, Mutti developed her own weltanschauung. Not surprisingly, she often saw the dark side in people. Having seen or heard just about everything before, she was always suspicious of people's true motives. People always looked out for their own interests, she assumed, and what they did was invariably self-serving. She did not trust anybody before they had proven their trustworthiness and could be very cynical about people in general. From the daily dose of stories on crime and gangland killings, corruption, frauds, and scams she read about in the *Chicago Tribune*, she was quick to generalize. "*Zustände wie im alten Rom*" [Goings-on like in ancient Rome] was one of her favorite expressions, one that had been handed down through the ages in the Old Country. Rome was, of course, the nemesis of the *Germanen* [ancient Germans] and the destruction of their empire by these forebears had always been justified by Rome's many evils and excesses.

Mother was a fount of wisdom and insight and her counsel was always good and to the point and to be taken seriously. If I did not take her advice, which was more often than not, I would come to regret it. One of these times was when she thought leaving my job with the federal government for corporate America was very foolish and pleaded with me not to do it.

She was right and I came to regret the move. Later she advised me to stay in touch with as many people as possible within and outside my company including competitors. That, of course, is the basis for networking and considered the most effective way of finding a new job if the old one did not pan out. She also told me to be especially attentive to lower level employees who could help further my career. It is the secretaries who are among the first to know about job openings or impending changes within the company, she claimed.

When I once lamented my slow progress with a particular employer, she consoled me with, *"Was für dich bestimmt ist, wird auf dich zukommen."* [What is meant for you, will come to you]. That notion of predestination flew in the face of the prevalent American attitudes, of course, since from childhood Americans are taught that they are masters of their own destinies and encouraged to be all they can be. What Mutti was saying, in effect, was that nothing people could do by their own efforts would alter the ultimate fate they had been assigned to. What of free will and the notion that we are all responsible for our own acts? Are evildoers, for example, to be left unpunished because their deeds were written in the stars? Mutti clearly hit on a riddle that has never been solved.

In keeping with her introspective and self-effacing nature, Mutti was always keenly aware of her own mortality. Sometimes, if I showed myself skeptical about one of her more cynical interpretations of some event, she would warn me with, *"Wenn ich die Augen zumache, gehen deine auf."* [When I close my eyes, yours will be opened]. She always considered me much too gullible and naive for this world. This was her way of telling me we lived in a tough world that left little room for idealism or naivety. But it was also meant as a grim reminder that her stay in this world, and that of all of us, was of very limited duration. When people contemplate their own demise, they often make out a last will and testament. This is what Mutti did at the end of April 1966, while I was away in Virginia, when she went to see a lawyer. The date of the will was not insignificant because Mutti was 57 years old at the time and that was the age her beloved mother had passed away nearly 35 years before.

Following A Family Heritage

After coming to America, Mutti participated in many German-American social activities. She and the rest of us, except for Esther who no longer identified with her German heritage, always looked forward to German-American Day which took place on a weekend in late summer or early fall in Chicago's famed Riverview Park.[24] After its closing in 1967, the festivities were moved to other venues and attendance dropped markedly. One reason was that the event attracted many new arrivals from Germany and Austria and by that time their number had been diminishing steadily as economic conditions in the Old Country were steadily improving. Another yearly event was the Schwaben-Picnic, sponsored by the Schwaben Verein. It was a smaller version of German-American Day and was usually held on the grounds of the Altenheim (Old People's Home) in neighboring Forest Park. We were especially drawn to that event because there we could meet fellow Swabians from Stuttgart and the surrounding area.

At all of these events there were always plenty of speeches by politicians who did their best to establish some sort of connection with the Old Country preferably through ancestry. The large German-American vote could always be helpful in an upcoming election. One perennial visitor was Everett M. Dirksen who, with his white mane, looked every bit the distinguished senator he was and who always patiently sat at a table, a stein of beer at his side, trying to accommodate as best he could a horde of enthusiastic autograph seekers. He was a popular and influential Republican and, after his death, the federal building in downtown Chicago was named after him. Another politician to invariably make an appearance was the Cook County State's Attorney John Gutknecht who kept reminding his audience that his name, *gut(er) Knecht*, meant good servant and that is exactly what he intended to be.

Always conspicuous by his absence was Richard J. Daley, the long-time (21 years) and popular mayor of Chicago. This descendant of Irish Catholics was indisputably the most powerful man in Chicago and was generally referred to as "the Boss." He ran the "Daley machine" and if one wanted a job with the police, fire, or water and sewer departments, or required some other favor, such as a zoning change, he or she would see the alderman for that ward, give an appropriate donation to the Democratic

Party, and the alderman would see what he could do. Many reasons were given for the mayor's slight (some German-Americans rated it an affront) but the most likely one was that Mayor Daley was a staunch Democrat and most German-Americans, including Mutti, consistently voted Republican.

Like most German-Americans, Mother was drawn to the conservative, law-and-order agenda of the Republican Party which she joined in the mid or late 1950s. German immigrants were somewhat unique in their choice of political party because most other newcomers to the United States, such as the Irish, Italians, and Poles, supported the Democratic Party which was more working-class and immigrant orientated. Germans coming to this country had usually learned a trade before leaving and were better off allowing them to assimilate more quickly than other ethnic groups. The Republicans contacted Mutti at least once a month soliciting money to continue the fight against those "liberal Democrats" in the Congress and Mutti responded generously even after retirement when she should have slowed down somewhat with her giving. Her reward was an occasional certificate of recognition from the National Republican Congressional Committee "in grateful appreciation for your valuable support in electing Republicans to the United States Congress." Not all German-Americans were die-hard Republicans, however, and found the Democrats more to their liking or, like myself, called themselves independents with no party affiliation.

Another organization that attracted Mutti's interest was the Deutsch Amerikanischer National Kongress or DANK (German American National Congress). Its objective was to publicize the cultural contributions of German-Americans to their new country and to represent their interests on relevant issues with American governmental and civic bodies. Since the organization was founded in 1959 in Chicago, a certificate of recognition from this organization dated May 1980 "for 20 years of faithful membership" would indicate that Mutti was with DANK from its very beginning. Their bimonthly, bilingual paper *The German-American Journal* (formerly *Der Deutsch-Amerikaner*) helped her stay in touch with important issues of concern to German-Americans.

There were two other German-American publications she enjoyed reading. She subscribed to the monthly *Die Hausfrau*, a ladies magazine featuring short stories, poetry, informational articles, and recipes that was published in Chicago until the early 1990s. Afterwards she temporarily received *Das Fenster* (The Window), a magazine of similar content, but she did not subscribe to it. On weekends, she would read the *Sonntagpost und Milwaukee Deutsche Zeitung*, a weekly newspaper in German and published in Chicago. She took the bus to pick it up at a newsstand on the corner of Harlem and Grand avenues in Chicago. That paper and its daily edition called *Abendpost und Milwaukee Deutsche Zeitung* ceased publication in September 1991.

Mutti loved Chicago and spent much of her free time there especially North Lincoln Avenue, a three-block stretch of German shops, restaurants, cafés and a movie theater just south of Lincoln Square on Chicago's Northwest Side. It was all that was left of a once thriving ethnic neighborhood where many Germans had settled during the 19th century. Mutti often went there on Sundays, alone or with one of her lady friends, to get the things that had been part of her lifestyle in Germany and which she could not get elsewhere like *Bauernbrot* [peasant rye bread] and different kinds of wurst from Delicatessen Meyer; German chamomile and senna teas, ointments and Uralt Lavendel (a brand of cologne) from the Merz Apotheke, a traditional German apothecary shop founded in 1875; and her favorite German ladies magazines from Schmidt's Imports.

Usually her excursion to Chicago and North Lincoln Avenue included the Deutsches Kino in the Davis Mozart Theater followed by coffee and torte at the Konditorei und Kaffee Kleinert. At other times she would take the Lake Street "L" to downtown Chicago to have lunch at The Berghoff, a well-known restaurant featuring German cuisine, or go shopping in one of the big department stores on State Street. She also enjoyed going to Oak Brook Shopping Center, a beautifully landscaped outdoor shopping area with many upscale stores, which was easily reached from Oak Park by bus.

Reminiscences

Mutti rarely talked about her experiences during the Third Reich. People who have had traumatic events happen to them rarely do. Most soldiers who come home from a horrific war, such as one of the two world wars or more recent ones like Vietnam or Iraq, invariability clam up unwilling to share their adventures with family and friends. What they saw and did would remain secrets they would take to their graves.

Life for a designated *Mischling* and Jew must have been hellish for Mutti since she had to constantly fear for her daughter's life especially towards the end of the war when things really turned ugly. Anytime during day or night there could be a knock on the door with the Gestapo outside ready to take Esther away. This despite Mutti's presumed strange and degrading arrangement with the Nazi regime to have children out of wedlock for the benefit of the Third Reich. Had she been asked about those days, Mutti would undoubtedly have answered any questions as completely and honestly as she could have. Neither I nor my siblings, alas, asked many questions. We were too busy finding our own way in a land where we had no roots and not much of a support system. Each one of us was essentially on his or her own to pursue what people called the American Dream and that kept us fully occupied.

Only once did Mother reveal her feelings on the subject to me and that was in a letter dated April 28, 1984 when she was already 75 years old. Her letter brought out the predicament she found herself in nearly four decades earlier. After complaining about the shabby treatment she was receiving at the time at the hands of her daughter and son-in-law, she wrote (translated from the German):

> The reason I had you [my siblings and me] after her [Esther] was only and solely in the hope that by making a new home for her she would not be taken away from me and sent to a *K-Z*!!! A Nazi had defended me just before the end of the war telling the Gestapo that she gave the "Führer" 4 children and nobody dared say one more word against me and the "Judenehe" [marriage to a Jew]. In her lifetime Esther can never make amends for what I had to go through with her during the Third Reich alone! She is sick and has become inhumanly cold and brutal. When my blessedly good mother had died, her first words were, "What do I inherit from her?" 5 years old!!! Even then I nearly had a stroke. My dear Peter, let us nevertheless thank our dear Lord God and be glad that she did not inherit her father's affliction. Like her, he too always cried and hanged himself 3 years ago as a 79-year-old in New York! Let it be and remain with you as an *eternal secret*. In faithful love, *for all my children*, especially *for you*, your Mutti.

The Nazi Mutti presumably referred to was Elke's father who would have been the last one she knew because Elke was born just four months after the end of the Third Reich.

Being curious, I once did ask Mutti what life was like during the Third Reich since my own childhood experiences must have been much different from hers and other adults. Specifically, I wanted to know why the Jews were so hated in Germany and whether people knew they were being exterminated in the gas chambers of the concentration camps. The people were well aware of the existence of concentration camps, she said, and these were known to be terrible places but not as death camps per se. Rather, the *Konzentrationslager* [concentration camp], KZ for short, was regarded as a work camp where inmates were required to perform hard labor for long periods of time. State propaganda had emphasized this point by using the slogan *Arbeit macht frei* [Work makes free]. According to Mutti, many people accepted the Nazi argument that Jews were lazy and greedy by nature who never did any real work but made their living by engaging in shady business wheeling and dealings. They thought it a good idea to send them off to a KZ for a while where they would finally have to work like the rest of the people.

The KZ was a terrible place, according to Mutti, but the idea that Jews were being gassed by the millions entered nobody's mind since it would have been completely outlandish and unbelievable. Nothing like that had ever happened in Germany or, in fact, the world before. The radio and newspapers were under government control and no contrary information was made public so that the majority of Germans were kept in the dark about the real fate of the Jews. The few people who knew the truth and had spoken out against the regime were considered traitors and often ended up in a KZ themselves. Consequently, according to Mutti, people learned not to ask too may disturbing questions and to keep their mouths shut.[25]

Religious affiliation did not make much difference in who supported National Socialism, Mother said, and it did not matter whether one was *katholisch* or *evangelisch*. Most people focused on patriotism and loyalty to the Reich or, more precisely, the lack thereof. Jews were considered warmongers who had led Germany into World War I and had collaborated with the western Allies to bring about the defeat of the Reich. They were alien, disloyal, and cowardly with young Jews having gone to great lengths to avoid military service during the war. While they did not themselves want to fight wars, they were nevertheless the instigators of wars and always found conflict between non-Jews to their liking, according to Mother who, rubbing her hands together with a gleeful expression on her face, tried to emphasize the point.

Mother's comments reflected the prevailing attitudes during the Third Reich. They were the result of a deliberate defamation campaign instigated by the Nazi regime because historical data has shown that more Jews, in proportion, served in the Kaiser's army, fell in battle, and received commendations for bravery, than their non-Jewish comrades.[26] While as patriotically German and as committed to German culture and values as non-Jews, it was the Jewish population's great misfortune to have never been able to fully assimilate and to remain outsiders in a society not known for much tolerance especially not in times of national crises.

Mother was a victim of Nazism as it destroyed her happy marriage and forced her to debase herself to keep herself and Esther alive. Yet, while she never had anything good to say about the Nazis, she also never expressed any bitterness toward them after their downfall. Perhaps the fact that the Gestapo never came for Esther and she was able to safely bring her through the war mellowed her opinion of them. Also, her beloved brother was with the Nazis and many other people she knew as well. Mutti felt that the depiction of Nazis by the Anglo-American Establishment and mass media as Jew-baiting Neanderthals was simplistic that had no basis in fact. Most Nazis, she said, were decent, law-abiding citizens who loved their country and their families just like everybody else.

According to Mutti, most of the Nazi party membership was made up of so-called *Mitläufer* [fellow travelers] who were not Nazi ideologues but joined, mostly after *die Partei* was already well established, to gain some kind of advantage from this association. Some hoped to protect a non-Aryan spouse or family member as was the case with our Stuttgart neighbor, Herr Fischer. For others, like uncles Lulu and Jule, membership was required or advantageous to get or hold a job or advance their careers. Still others yearned for the social status associated with membership in the ruling elite. Many recruits saw the good the Nazis had already done for the country, such as bringing about political and economic stability, destroying Communism and similar leftist ideologies, and drastically reducing unemployment. Most recruits believed that the Nazis would bring peace and prosperity to the country. This, unfortunately, proved to have been illusionary. The hard-core Nazis, the racist ideologues who brought Hitler and his National Socialists to power and instigated the Shoah, were very few in number, Mutti maintained.

By most accounts, for ordinary Germans, the ones who did not belong to one of the groups of outcasts or agitated against the state, life during the 12 years of the Third Reich was not bad and much better than in the years before. They lived in a dictatorship but one headed by a charismatic leader who was wildly popular as newsreels of the 1930s and early 1940s attest to. As their official name *Nationalsozialistische Deutsche Arbeiterpartei* [National Socialist German Worker's Party] indicated, Nazis were above all committed socialists who espoused the cause of the working man. Their aim was an egalitarian state with no class distinctions. Joblessness was eliminated by massive public works projects like the building of the autobahns while the tax burden was shifted from working-class families to the more affluent members of society.

Expansive social welfare programs encompassed universal health care, free higher education, subsidies to low-income families, supplementary child support payments, and free annual vacation stays for working-class mothers and children. The arts were fostered and heavily subsidized but woe to the painter or sculptor who produced works the regime deemed "degenerate." They were ostracized and their works banned. To ensure the good will and loyalty of the people, the Nazis made it a top priority to keep them well nourished and adequately supplied with consumer goods and subject to a minimum of war-related privations. Nobody at the time asked where these goods came from. As conquerors had done from times immemorial, the Nazis simply stripped the occupied lands of their natural resources including foodstuffs and shipped it all home leaving the subject populations starving.

Getting To Know The Country

Thanks to a son who was mostly away at school or pursuing a business career, Mutti got to see more of her adoptive country than many native-born

Americans. Her travels began with two or three train rides to Champaign-Urbana in southern Illinois after my transfer there in early 1958 to continue my studies at the main campus of the University of Illinois. The size of the campus impressed her as it had me but, alas, it was stripped bare of its beautiful trees due to an outbreak of Dutch elm disease. Mother's visits were short, two or three hours at the most, because I could not make more time for her. The school's engineering curriculum was tough for us all, and especially for me, and I needed to devote as much time to my studies as I possibly could.

Her next trips by train took her to Virginia where I had found employment as an engineer after my Army service. On her first visit, in June 1964, she saw historic Jamestown, where in 1607 the first permanent English settlement in the New World took place, and Colonial Williamsburg, the restored capitol of the British colony of Virginia where in the late 18th century George Washington, Thomas Jefferson, and other patriots had plotted the American Revolution.

A highpoint for Mutti was a trip to Washington's Arlington National Cemetery for a stop at the grave of President John F. Kennedy who had been assassinated the previous November by a man who, coincidentally, shared the same last name with *Onkel Helmut* in Stuttgart. The Kennedy gravesite was then just a mount of dirt topped by an eternal flame and surrounded by a white picket fence. A photograph shows Mother at the site dressed in a black silk *Kostüm* [skirt and jacket] and wide-brimmed hat striking a somber pose with hands folded in prayer. That really made her stand out among the crowd of tourists in colorful summer attire engaged in lively chatter. Mutti always had a love for the dramatic and playing the part.

On Mutti's second visit, in August 1968, we saw more of Colonial Williamsburg, enjoyed the beaches of nearby Virginia Beach, and drove to Charlottesville where we visited Thomas Jefferson's home of Monticello and the University of Virginia from whose engineering school I had graduated a year earlier. Shortly after her visit, I left for New York City to study business.

Our home state of Illinois and neighboring Wisconsin too offered many interesting and historic places to explore. Mutti and I drove down to Springfield, the state capital, and saw Abraham Lincoln's home before he became president and his impressive tomb erected after his assassination. At the outbreak of the Civil War, U.S. Grant, the last commander of the Union army and future president, lived in Galena on the Mississippi River and there Mutti and I toured the general's house which the town's grateful citizens had gifted him after his victory over Robert E. Lee and his Army of Northern Virginia. Americans hailed the two Illinoisans, Lincoln and Grant, as saviors of the Union.

Each big American city, it seems, has its own playground. Thus, New Yorkers have Long Island and Bostonians Cape Cod and Martha's Vineyard. On weekends, Chicagoans generally head north for Wisconsin and especially for Lake Geneva. Mutti and I spent many Sundays in this little town enjoying rides on paddle wheel steamers cruising the lake and sampling the excellent American and German-style dishes at a large and popular restaurant called Popeye's on Lake Geneva. Their specialty was pit-roasted pork and when the piglet was done, a couple of stout men would parade the spit-borne victim through the restaurant. Popeye's also put on a month-long Oktoberfest. The Abbey Resort in nearby Fontana featured an excellent Sunday brunch and we would go there as well. Mader's Restaurant, a famous German-American restaurant in Milwaukee, was reserved for special occasions. Sometimes we would drive up to Racine, Wisconsin, where I was once employed, to visit their zoo and boat harbor.

Florida was another state Mutti got to see. On our first trip there, in September 1976, we made the mistake of taking the train. Mutti insisted that was the safest and least stressful way to take a long trip especially since she was much afraid of flying. The ride to and from St. Petersburg turned out to be an adventure in itself as our train was repeatedly shunted to side rails and left standing there for an hour or more at a time as heavily loaded coal trains rumbled by on the main rail. Each way took several hours longer than scheduled and, in fact, the entire railway operation did not appear to follow a time schedule at all. Once in St. Petersburg and ensconced in a nice hotel there, we made side trips to places of interest including Disney World in Orlando. Mutti was not much impressed by people walking around in Mickey Mouse and other Disney character costumes and complained about too much kitsch.

Our second visit to the sunshine state together, in early October 1985, went much better. Since Mutti had, in the meantime, had her first flights (to Germany and back), she did not object when I told her we would be taking the plane this time. We flew into Miami for a tour that was both a pleasure and business trip. After vacationing for a few days along the Atlantic Coast visiting West Palm Beach, Pompano Beach, Fort Lauderdale, and Miami Beach, we crossed Florida via the Everglades Parkway (Alligator Alley) to the steamy Gulf Coast. After again visiting St. Petersburg and enjoying the beaches of Clearwater, we returned to Chicago flying out of Tampa.

While in the area, I showed Mutti the one-half of a newly built duplex I had bought a couple of months earlier in a community for seniors called Highland Lakes in Palm Harbor, a small town just north of Clearwater. It was meant to be a retirement home for both of us although, at less than 50 at the time, that event was still some years off for me. The property was also meant to be an income tax shelter as I was making a good salary at the time. Rather than let it stand idle, I rented the place out to help pay off the mortgage. Mutti liked our second home especially since all the rooms, unlike in our Oak Park townhouse, were on the same level which meant no more climbing of stairs.[27]

Not all German and Austrian post-war émigrés to North America settled in the United States. A good percentage chose Canada instead. They looked on that country as having the more traditional European-style socioeconomic system which they were accustomed to. While this would provide less opportunity than the free-wheeling capitalism practiced in the United States, it would still be better than what the Old Country had to offer right after the war. Canada could be expected to present less of a culture shock and a better blend with their former lifestyles and conservative values.

One of these families was Manfred and Nelda Straka who chose the Toronto suburb of Willowdale as their new home. Fred had served in the Wehrmacht during the Third Reich and been Esther's first beau when the two of us briefly lived in Bludenz. Nelda was from Fred's home town of Graz, Austria, and after the war they had married and emigrated to Canada. Fred had earned a doctorate in mathematics and become a university professor in Toronto. Mutti was fond of Fred and had stayed in touch with him and his wife. Their letters and picture postcards were always addressed to "Mutti Annemarie." It was great to see Fred again after some 30 years when we visited them and their family in July 1974. They took us to their Austrian club for dinner and there was a lively conversation about our different experiences in the New World.

From Toronto, we drove to Montreal where Mutti felt very much at home. The French language was music to her ears and the interesting sights and excellent French-style food made for an enjoyable stay. There was one memorable incident involving Mutti. As we were walking from our hotel to dinner at a nearby restaurant, we were approached from behind by a car chock-full of young people who were probably students at the local university. As the car slowly passed us, one of the students cautiously directed some words at us in French. Presumably he wanted to check whether we were English- or French-speaking types and preferably the latter. There had always been some friction between the two cultures with the French minority feeling dominated by the British who had wrested Canada from their ancestors in the mid-18th century. Mutti could not make out the students' words but her face spontaneously lit up and, bringing both hands to her lips, threw them a kiss. The response was immediate and noisy as the entire party exploded with car honking and shouts of joyful approval. It made Mutti's day and probably the students' as well.

On our second auto tour of Canada, at the end of August 1978, we again saw the Straka family in their suburban townhouse. By then, Fred and Nelda were already looking forward to retirement in southern Spain where they spent a few weeks every summer. Even Canada, it seems, was a poor substitute for Europe especially for the warm, southern part like the Costa del Sol where several communities had sprung up favored by German and Austrian expatriates and where houses could still be had at reasonable prices. The Strakas had purchased an older home in Oliva in the province of Valencia which they were remodeling and improving during each trip over. In Toronto, where Mutti and I rented a small studio in an apartment hotel, we took in the major tourist attractions making side trips to Stratford, home of the Stratford Shakespeare Festival, and the Canadian side of Niagara Falls.

Visits To The Old Country

Mutti returned to Germany only three times after our emigration in March 1950. This included her trip back in June of the following year to settle her affairs in Stuttgart. At the same time, no relative or friends from Germany ever came to visit us even though they were invited often enough to do so. Ocean travel between the two continents was, despite modern technology, still an often stressful and time-consuming enterprise especially when people got to a certain age. With a steamship crossing typically taking a week or more, it meant over two weeks on the high seas plus travel times to and from the sea ports and that was too much for many people.

When the travel mode began to change from steamship to airplane and travel time was reduced to hours, many of the older generation, like Mutti and her friends from Schwanheim—Mariechen, Sannche, and Sus—could not contemplate traveling by air. Aunt Emmi and our other relatives showed no interest either. Not even Mariechen's daughter Elke, who was living near Denver with her husband Robert and two sons, could entice her parents to make the trip. They all said that nobody would ever get them into an airplane. For Mutti that promise did not pan out because she would eventually fly four times on trips to and from Germany and later Florida.

In the summer of 1971, Mother had recently retired and I was about to leave my Frankfurt sales job, when I invited her over so we could visit relatives and old friends together and do some sightseeing. Mutti left New York on the TS *Bremen* of the North German Lloyd line on Sunday, June 13, and arrived in Bremerhaven on the following Sunday. From there she took a train for Frankfurt am Main. When I picked her up at the Hauptbahnhof late that evening one of her first comments was, *"Hier wollt ich nicht mehr leben."* [I would not want to live here again]. These were my own sentiments exactly. America had become our new home and we had gotten used to the much freer lifestyle and all the amenities that country had to offer. That chapter of our lives had ended 20 years ago and there would be no going back. A rented studio apartment in a high-rise at Grosser Hasenpfad 1-11 in the Sachsenhausen district of Frankfurt served as our home base and the 1967 Mercury Cougar I had brought over a year earlier as our means of transportation. We were together for over seven weeks before returning to the States.

Our first stops after Mutti's arrival took us to Frankfurt-Schwanheim and Stuttgart. In Schwanheim we met up with Mariechen Bub, her husband Willi and brother Fritz. We also visited Elli Lauer who had been Esther's one and only friend in Schwanheim during these difficult years when they were growing up together and Esther was being taunted by other children for being Jewish and a *Mischling*. Later in the week we spent a couple of days in our old home town of Stuttgart. There we went to see Hilde Bosc, the widow of a war-time French collaborator with Germany and Mutti's best friend in town. Hilde lived in modest circumstances on a widow's pension from the French government. On the following day we spent an afternoon at our old home on Adlerstraße 8 where we visited our erstwhile neighbor, Frau Rapp. It had been over two decades since our emigration but she still lived in her comfortable flat above our former *Wohnung*. Frau Rapp poured her heart out lamenting the sad fate of her beloved Ursula.

As a boy, I had known Ursula but even though Frau Rapp and Mutti were together fairly often, I saw her not more than a couple of times. Unlike beautiful Adelheid, Ursula was not at all pretty in my eyes. Like Adelheid, she had met an American GI who I heard was *ein Schwarzer* [a black man]. Neither Frau Rapp nor Ursula could have imagined at the time what this would entail especially after Ursula and her suitor got married and he took his bride home which was somewhere in the Deep South. Unbeknownst to anyone in Germany at the time, that part of America was extremely racist with blacks consigned to the bottom of the totem pole. According to Frau Rapp, her daughter now found herself in an unfamiliar and strange setting which she could not handle emotionally and from which there seemed no escape. As time went on, Ursula's letters to her mother revealed increasing despair until they stopped coming altogether. One day Frau Rapp received a note from her son-in-law's family with the terrible news that Ursula had died. The cause of death was given as an auto accident but Frau Rapp was convinced that Ursula, her only child, had taken her own life.

July was a very busy month for us. After Aunt Emmi had insisted that her sister come to see her as soon as possible after her arrival in Germany, Mother took a train leaving the Frankfurt Hauptbahnhof in the early afternoon of July 2 and arriving in Geneva late that evening. The two had never been close and Mutti decided on a short visit. Her return was timed so that she could be with her classmates at the Schwanheimer Volksschule for their annual *Jahrgang 1909* [birth year 1909] outing planned for the afternoon of July 8. The bus excursion took us to the Odenwald region, a nature preserve south of Frankfurt am Main. About 20 took part including her best friends at the school, i.e., Mariechen, Sus, and Sannche. We much enjoyed the beautiful countryside followed by dinner at a restaurant and brewery and ending with an evening stop at the Seppche restaurant in Frankfurt-Schwanheim for a round of *Äppelwoi* [apple wine in the Hessian dialect].

Shortly after, Mutti and I stopped by Graben-Neudorf to see *Onkel Jule* and *Tante Erika*. There the three reminisced about the days past as they leafed through a couple of thick photo albums containing a treasure trove of pictures that included ones of Oma and Opa, and their children. Parenthetically, when I many years later became interested in my family's history and would have liked to look at these albums again, I was unable to locate them. After Uncle Jule died, these books presumably went to his heirs. As previously mentioned, because no direct relationship between the Kuchenbeisser and Zell families could be proved, Germany's strict and sometimes very absurd privacy laws prevented me from obtaining their names or whereabouts.

While we sometimes stayed in Frankfurt am Main for some shopping, sightseeing, or visiting an outdoor pool in Neu-Isenburg to cool off, we spent most of our time on the road visiting people and taking a number of sightseeing tours through southwestern Germany. One trip took us to the Romantische Straße (Romantic Road) and its many picturesque towns and villages including the medieval, walled towns of Rothenburg ob der Tauber, Dinkelsbühl, and Nördlingen. Mutti had a lady friend, Elfriede Böhles, living in nearby Blaufelden and we stayed with her a few days. Other tours took us to the Black Forest (Freiburg im Breisgau, Baden-Baden.), the university town of Heidelberg, and towns and villages along the Main River including Lohr. Lohr am Main was the venue of Mariabuchen where Mutti and Esther spent some time recuperating during the 1944 bombing of Stuttgart. In addition, I took a few days around my 35th birthday to visit Paris and the Sun King's palace at Versailles while Mutti was with Sus and her daughter Maria Schäfer, then living in Frankfurt-Zeilsheim, and her family.

Naturally, Mutti and I also went to see Mama Gartner who was then living in Karlsruhe. After the war, she and Wolfgang had moved there from Forst to be close to Robert, her brother-in-law. When Robert retired he had moved in with her to share expenses.[28] Whenever I was in Germany on temporary work assignments, I visited them several times in their spacious third-floor apartment on Winterstraße 26B, near the city's zoological garden. Wolfgang lived nearby with his wife Elvira and their two children, Andreas and Manuela, and was employed as a salesman with Karlsruhe's biggest Mercedes-Benz dealer.

Both Mama Gartner and I had fond memories of Forst and whenever I stayed with them we would drive to Forst which was just one-half hour up the road from Karlsruhe. In Forst, Mama Gartner had a good friend, a widower named Artur Böser, who made his living as a *Bauer* cultivating, among other crops, *Spargel*, the white asparagus the area is known for. By the time Mutti and Mama Gartner met again on the fourth weekend of July, they had warmed up to each other and become good friends. One thing that helped was that Mother had been very generously mailing my former foster mother many packages of clothing and fabric for her and her grandkids.

After our visit in Forst and dropping Mama Gartner off in Karlsruhe we returned to Graben-Neudorf for an overnight stay with the Kuchenbeissers. From there, we returned to Stuttgart where Mutti wanted to visit with Jörg Reuschle, one of my friends at the Schickhardt Oberschule. She had always liked Jörg and stayed in touch with him and his wife Carmen over the years and, as was Mutti's habit with good friends, had mailed them packages of clothing for their two children. Jörg had moved up through the ranks and become a judge with the Landesgericht (state court) of Baden-Württemberg. He and his family owned their own house in a Stuttgart suburb where we met up with them. The dinner at home did not go too well, unfortunately, as Carmen made a couple of disparaging remarks about her husband that we thought unbecoming of a wife let alone one whose husband was a judge. Mother was especially offended and, considering Carmen ill-mannered and uncouth, broke off all further contact with the two.

In early August, after a last trip to Karlsruhe, Graben-Neudorf, and Forst and just before our planned return to the States, my Cougar broke down. Fortunately, there was a Ford garage in town where some emergency repairs were made. The following day, I drove the car to Bremerhaven in a little over five hours (a near record) and got there just in time for the August 6 departure of the New York bound freighter it was to be on. The next three days gave us time to say goodbye to all our friends in the area and make a last visit to the Schwanheim Waldfriedhof (forest cemetery) where Oma and Opa had been laid to rest. We then took an overnight train to Bremerhaven for a return trip on the TS *Bremen*.

The ship departed, as scheduled, around 1 p.m. of Tuesday, August 10 and, with the sea calm, the crossing was pleasant and uneventful. When we arrived in New York seven days later the freighter was still out at sea but did arrive in Port Newark, NJ, the following day where we picked up our car for the drive to Chicago. The freighter's delayed arrival allowed me to show Mutti some New York City landmarks and take her up to Columbia University where I had gotten my business degree three years earlier.

There was also a financial component to our trip. Since Mutti was now retired and her Social Security benefits were rather meager, the question came up whether she might have some benefits due from Germany since she had paid into the insurance fund for *Angestellte* [salaried employees] during her war-time employment there. The German consulate in Chicago furnished the necessary information regarding eligibility for retirement benefits, known in German as *Altersruhegeld* or *Altersrente*, on reaching age 65. Near the end of July we visited Daimler-Benz in Stuttgart-Untertürkheim for an enjoyable visit with the management which presented her with a necklace with a three-pointed star pendant and, most importantly, an *Arbeitsbescheinigung* [work certificate].

The application for German social security was subsequently approved even though her war-time employment was of relatively short duration and probably less than the minimum requirement of five years. When a law was passed in July 1987 whereby mothers born before 1921 could collect additional benefits for *Kindererziehung* [child rearing] expenses, Mutti applied for that also. This application, with attached birth certificates for all of her six children, too was approved which had the effect of doubling her basic monthly retirement benefit payments from Germany. Nobody can ever claim that the Federal Republic was less than generous in its social or other commitments.

Mutti joined me for her third and final visit to our native land during the second week of June 1982. It was at the end of another overseas work assignment—this one with a Wisconsin company at their German offices in Munich. Since she refused to be separated from her beloved pets for any longer, Mutti could be persuaded to stay for only two weeks. Needless to say, this was a major undertaking for her especially since she would be stepping into an airplane for the first time and, on top of that, she would be flying alone. When Esther put her on the plane at Chicago's O'Hare International Airport, she had a talk with the head stewardess telling her that her mother was 73 years old and had never flown before and to please look out for her.

This she evidently did because when Mutti arrived in Frankfurt am Main, she was relaxed and upbeat. Mariechen and I picked her up at the airport and drove the short distance to Schwanheim where Mariechen's husband Willi, her brother Fritz, and daughter Elke and her two sons, Steven and Mark, were awaiting us. Elke and her boys were on vacation from Albuquerque, New Mexico, where her husband Robert was stationed with the U.S. Air Force at the time. For transportation on our travels, I had secured permission to use my company car.

After paying a visit to the grave of Opa and Oma in the Schwanheim Waldfriedhof, Mutti and I drove south—a peace mission to Aunt Emmi in Geneva was the main item on the agenda for this trip. On the way, we stopped off in Graben-Neudorf to visit with *Onkel Jule* and stayed at his house overnight. (*Tante Erika* had passed away just four months earlier). Next morning we visited Mama Gartner, Wolfgang, and Robert in Karlsruhe. Wolfgang had, in the meantime, divorced Elvira and married Bärbel whom he had met on a skiing trip. He had also left his employer to try his luck at running a used car lot. From Karlsruhe we drove to Geneva where we arrived that evening.

The peace mission, as previously reported, turned out to be a disaster and after only three days, we left for Munich where I had rented an apartment while working in town. We traveled by way of the Bodensee (Lake Constance) and Bavaria's beautiful Allgäu region on a leisurely trip that included an overnight stay in Konstanz and visit to Mainau, known as Germany's *Blumeninsel* [flower island]. After showing Mutti around Munich, we made a day trip to Salzburg to tour the castle and other venues.

Since Mutti again wanted to see her lady friends, we more or less retraced our itinerary of eleven years earlier adding some venues and leaving off others. Thus, we were back in Frankfurt am Main, Stuttgart, and Blaufelden visiting with Mariechen, Sus, Hilde, and Elfriede while also doing more sightseeing.

Near the end of our trip, we were back in Graben-Neudorf for a second overnight stay with Uncle Jule and then, on the way back to Munich, stopped by in Karlsruhe to say goodbye to Mama Gartner, Robert, and Wolfgang. In Munich, Mutti and I took our leave of the office staff and closed down the apartment. From there we left for Schwanheim where we said auf Wiedersehen to our friends and stayed overnight for our return flight. Esther and her friend Dr. Frank Murrin met us at O'Hare airport anxious to learn what we had or had not accomplished in Geneva.

A Gradual Decline

Mutti enjoyed robust health throughout most of her life which was an exceptionally long one despite the fact that neither of her parents lived to an old age. She suffered from no major illnesses and had no surgeries except for the hysterectomy in the summer of 1967 at age 58. One factor contributing to her good health and longevity was a very healthy lifestyle. She ate in moderation and was well aware about *Diät* [proper diet] which meant avoidance of organ and fatty meats in favor of leaner cuts and the consumption of plenty of vegetables. Mutti never smoked and would not tolerate anybody smoking in the house. Her drink of choice was hot black tea with lemon and honey as a sweetener. Occasionally she would treat herself to a cup of Sanka, a brand of instant decaffeinated coffee, or chamomile medicinal tea from Germany.

Mutti avoided alcohol except the occasional glass of beer and constantly warned me against the consumption of hard liquor. One time on coming home from an overseas trip, I brought her a small bottle of Grand Marnier. Mother would not touch the liqueur until I told her that I had heard that it had some medicinal qualities. When I opened the bottle to pour some into a glass, she waved me off and insisted that the only way she would take it was from a teaspoon. She took one spoonful and then another and another until she had taken about five. I was much amused when I found the bottle a few days later hidden away and nearly empty.

Exercise is good for the circulation and Mutti got plenty of it. Because she did not drive and using the bus was often too much of a bother, Mutti routinely walked to do her chores in the village. She was also aware that she needed her sleep to stay fit and so, during her working days, she left all non-essential activities for the weekend and made getting plenty of rest her priority.

Old age usually brings its own challenges in the way of medical and other problems and Mutti was not spared any of these. I noticed a marked change in her in late July 1986 when I returned home for a two-week vacation on the occasion of my own 50th birthday. She was 77 then and despite her pets about her for company, she seemed downbeat and dispirited when I arrived. One cause was undoubtedly the death of her childhood friend Mariechen on June 5th of breast cancer and diabetes. (She had kept the latter a secret from even her family). Sus, her other childhood friend, had already passed away the year before. Only Sannche of her *Jahrgang*, who lived to age 82, was now still around of her old Schwanheim pals. Mutti was also distraught because Esther and Nick had sold their house on Bonnie Brae in River Forest and together with their good friend, Dr. Frank Murrin, had moved to temporary rental quarters in another Chicago suburb. They were planning to relocate to the exclusive North Shore suburb of Lake Forest, about 40 miles up the interstate from Mutti's Place, once they found something suitable.

Her daughter's strange animosity towards her, which always surfaced at unexpected times, also weighed heavily on Mutti and added to her misery. She had often expressed her gratitude to Esther for paying for the yearly upkeep of her parent's grave in the old Schwanheim cemetery. Esther had done so for several years, according to Mutti. But her daughter got absolutely furious with our mother when the bill for a wreath Mutti and I had contributed to Mariechen's funeral inadvertently showed up on her cemetery bill. Instead of letting us reimburse her, Esther sent the bill back unpaid and we had to make other arrangements.

Besides her emotional turmoil, Mutti had developed a number of medical problems which took their toll. Despite being on medication, she only got four or five hours of sleep a night which she blamed on her noisy neighbor Marge. Fortunately, she was able to get some rest during the daytime when Marge was at work. Her lower extremities and feet had begun to hurt. In addition, her bladder felt as if it had descended and was hanging out. She thought it was the result of the hysterectomy she had two decades earlier. Her doctor counseled against corrective surgery because of her advanced age. Both conditions made walking very difficult for her and she rarely ventured out anymore. I left for work on Long Island with a heavy heart knowing she was by herself with nobody looking out for her and now regretted having accepted that position so far away nearly three years earlier.

From my subsequent Sunday phone conversations with her, I sensed that Mutti had difficulties coping even though she never said so outright and pretended that all was well. Mother obviously needed help and I realized that the time had come for me to give up my management job and find employment closer to home. When I informed my superiors on Long Island and Germany of my impending departure because I was required back home, they preempted my formal resignation by terminating my contract.

On my return to Mutti's Place on the day before Thanksgiving of 1986, I was shocked to find her looking terribly run down. She had developed severe sciatica with excruciating pains along her lower back and down both legs that made it difficult for her to walk and perform even simple household chores. She continued to get only four or five hours of restless sleep at night despite sleep medication. In addition, Mutti had no appetite so that her weight had dropped from her usual 125 to just 109 pounds. She had also developed high blood pressure and was on medication for hypertension. All her pills made her woozy, according to Mutti, making it difficult for her to keep her balance. Needless to say, Mutti was happy to see me back and it seemed that I had just returned in time. I moved into our large basement family room where I could work, sleep, and move about at any time of day or night without disturbing her sleep in her second-floor bedroom.

Esther, Nick, and Frank moved into their new Lake Forest home on Thanksgiving 1986, the day after my permanent return to Oak Park. Since they needed to unpack and get settled in, we were not invited for a visit until a Sunday in mid-December. The property they had purchased at 970 Northcliffe Way was strategically located close to the intersection of two major roads—Waukegan Road, which led up from Chicago, and West Deerpath Road while their street led directly into the center of town.

Their new home was an attractive 2-story brick and frame building with a sloping roof and dormers. Attached to one side was a 2-car garage while on the other was a small fenced-in backyard holding some conifer trees. While the house was not typical of the type of homes in this exclusive and affluent suburb, it was certainly more than adequate for a comfortable lifestyle for the threesome. Across the street on an expansive and well-manicured lawn stood a huge stone mansion which, according to Esther, belonged to a member of the Chicago Mercantile Exchange. Clearly, Esther and Nick and their friend Frank were in the company of the rich and beautiful people although by far not in the same league with them.

The inside of the house was bright and airy. As one entered, immediately to the right was a half-bath and beyond that a cozy, wood-paneled den. On the left upon entering, a staircase led up to the second floor. Straight ahead and opposite the entrance was the large rectangular parlor which held Esther's nicest furniture including a couple of hand-painted pieces and an expensive sofa with matching chairs which she kept under plastic covers. A thick oriental rug covered the floor while the walls held a number of paintings which, according to my sister, were by famous contemporary artists. To the left of this room was the house's formal dining room but which served as an all-purpose room and office where Esther did most of her paperwork. To the left of the entryway and behind the staircase one entered a large country-style kitchen with a breakfast area and past this room lay an expansive family room with a fireplace and a floor-to-ceiling window looking out on the backyard. Esther had always been on the secretive side and Mutti and I were not shown the upstairs with the bedrooms and the sleeping arrangements during this, our first visit, nor any subsequent ones.

During our visit, Esther and I discussed Mutti's situation and decided that our mother needed medical assistance beyond what her regular physician was providing and that I would go about finding it. Getting relief from her sciatica seemed the most pressing problem but it took some time as initial attempts to find a cure proved unsuccessful. All her regular physician, Dr. Fritz Herz, himself elderly and close to retirement, could prescribe was pain medication and sleeping pills. A geriatric specialist at the Loyola University Medical Center in nearby Maywood, who had been recommended to us, was of not much help. He suggested Mutti use a cane to get about. This was unacceptable to her as it would make her look like an invalid and, furthermore, do nothing for her sciatic pains.

Our next stop was an Oak Park chiropractor who took an X-ray of her spine. It showed a small curvature at the base which he suggested might be the cause. We already knew of this condition, of course. He prescribed a series of heat treatments which, alas, did not bring more than passing relief. After a while, we stopped seeing him.

Mutti had another problem that became apparent soon after my return. She had become unusually forgetful. When in late March of 1987, I noticed Mutti becoming frustrated balancing her checking account, I took a look at her check register and was shocked at what I saw. It was a mess with several duplicate entries, many of them crossed out and blotches of ink throughout (she still preferred an ink pen for writing). That was not like the mother I knew who had always been precise, very neat in her bookkeeping, and proud of her numbers skills.

Notwithstanding her physical condition, it made me think she was getting lazy and sloppy and I scolded her. She said nothing in her defense but looked at me with very sad and pleading eyes. I felt terrible and regretted my outburst. There was obviously something else going on. Could Mutti have Alzheimer's? The thought scared me and I quickly put it out of my mind. We agreed that I would henceforth do her check register entries and balance her account while she continued to write out her checks as usual.

Since her friend, Frank Murrin, was a medical doctor, I kept pressing Esther to come to our mother's aid. If Frank did not know how to deal with her sciatic pains, he might know of somebody who could. Esther and Frank finally came by the house in mid-August 1987 to take Mutti to the offices of Dr. John Hanni in nearby Hinsdale. This doctor was, like Frank, a psychiatrist and, besides being his best friend, Esther's psychiatrist as well. The good doctor had Mutti's blood tested and found an imbalance in her serotonin level. His diagnosis was clinical depression for which he prescribed a daily dose of the anti-depressant Elavil (Amitriptyline). Within about a month of her first visit to this doctor's office, Mutti was free of most of her sciatic pains, slept through the night without sleeping pills, and regained her appetite. In fact, she soon put on so much weight, she had to be placed on a diet.

Mother's improvement was truly astounding. The thought that sciatica was associated with depression and that a psychiatrist could cure somebody of sciatic pains had never occurred to me and I wondered why Esther had not suggested taking our mother to Dr. Hanni before especially since she was on the same medication as Mutti. But the new treatment did not resolve all the problems in that her wooziness and floating sensation persisted. Mutti said it felt as if she was going up and down in an elevator. *"Ich flieg wieder"* [I'm flying again], Mutti would say. She always kept her sense of humor though and now and then would move her arms about simulating an airplane flight. The sciatica was gone, thank God, but her excellent mind and memory and her energetic stride and surefootedness were things of the past also. It was clear that she could no longer cope by herself and needed continuing care.

During the following months, I became increasingly concerned with both Mutti's short-term memory loss and her floating sensation and so at the end of April 1988, when she was 79, I took her to Gottlieb Memorial Hospital in neighboring Melrose Park for a brain scan. The MRI showed some brain shrinkage and minor damage which, I was told, was not unusual in people her age and that I should not worry about it.

Thinking her floating sensation might perhaps be caused by some defect in her inner ear, which helps keep the body in balance, I next brought Mutti to an ear, nose and throat specialist who examined her and found no abnormality. The doctor did suggest, however, that I talk to her psychiatrist about changing her anti-depressant medication. Dr. Hanni would have none of that. The Elavil he had prescribed was doing its job and he did not think it had anything to do with her floating sensation. He was probably correct since Mutti had complained of wooziness even before she was put on the anti-depressant. At that time she was only on medication for hypertension and sleeplessness. It appeared that Mutti just had to get used to this problem because nobody had an answer to it.

Despite Mutti's memory problems, she was still able to pick up on some unpleasant things which I tried to keep from her like my frustrations in my search for a new marketing management job in the Chicago area, a project I had begun soon after I had returned home. Mother wanted to know what the problem was and when I explained to her that the job market for marketing managers in their 50s was tough especially in these bad economic times, tears welled up in her eyes and she said, "*Wenn man mal fünfzig ist und nochmal von vorne anfangen muss.*" [When one is 50 and has to start over again]. I told her not to worry—it was just something that had to happen and things would turn out just fine as they always had in the past.

Keeping Active

With Mutti's most serious health problem resolved, we got back into our usual but somewhat modified routine. To prevent her from turning into a vegetable for lack of exercise and mental stimulation, I decided to take her on all my errands including grocery shopping which was a chore she had always enjoyed. One time we were at Jewel Foods on Lake Street in River Forest and, as usual, I held Mutti by the hand so she would not fall when a woman came up to me and asked, "Is this your mother?" When I answered in the affirmative, this person gushed, "I just wanted to tell you—she is as cute as a button." Indeed, with her radiant smile for everyone, Mutti was the picture of contentment and happiness with not a care in the world. Her walk was much slower now and she did not want to go too far since some pain and stiffness in her lower extremities persisted, especially on the left side, but now only when she was on her feet.

We were both sun worshippers and loved to spend time at the outdoor swimming pool and hence when the pools opened in the spring that was our destination on most weekends and holidays. We both held season passes for many years. Oak Park had two outdoor swimming pools—one on Lake Street, the other on the south side of the village. The latter, the one we preferred, was located in the middle of an expansive open area named Rehm Park and consisted of three different pools including diving, Olympic-size swimming, and wading pools, a large deck with umbrellas for sunbathing and a separate section with a snack bar and tables. Mutti spent most of her time lying in a deck chair getting a tan while I tried to get in as much lap swimming as I could. She was happy when she was, in her words, "*braun wie ein Bär*" [brown as a bear]. While she never stepped into the pool because of her water phobia, she did enjoy the water. Sometime when she did not come out of the ladies room and I had to send somebody in to look for her, they usually found her under the shower. They would lead her out soaking wet and impishly grinning from ear to ear.

With the swim season being relatively short—from Memorial Day at the end of May to Labor Day at the beginning of September—and with neither Mutti nor I being homebodies, we spent many fall weekends on North Lincoln Avenue, downtown Chicago, the Oak Brook Mall, or Wisconsin. Lake Geneva with its many fine restaurants, gift shops and lakeside activities was less than two hours up the road and we went there often. I had worked in Racine on Lake Michigan, which was even closer, and there we especially enjoyed visiting the zoo and the boat harbor. Sometimes all these activities got to be even too much for Mother. "*Du willst immer nur Vergnügen*" [All you ever want is have a good time], she once told me. That was unfair because I did these excursions to make sure she was adequately stimulated and had a good time herself.

On the way back to Oak Park we made it a habit to stop by Esther's place in Lake Forest. The visits were not always opportune because Esther's mail order business took much of her time and she often appeared stressed out. She could be very gracious and friendly and serve coffee and *Schwarzwälder Kirschtorte* or *Sachertorte* [Black Forest cherry or Viennese torten] from Chicago's Café Lutz or be short and rude. When we had evidently overstayed our welcome and Esther handed Mutti her handbag we knew that the audience was over.

During much of the week, Mutti enjoyed sitting in her easy chair by the front window of our little townhouse to do her *Handarbeit* while keeping an eye on the neighbors as they came and went. On her lap would usually be our tomcat—a black and white American shorthair which had shown up at Mutti's back door, where she fed several strays, and taken him inside and named Tootsie.

Like her sister Emmi, she had no use for television and rarely turned on our big Sony Trinitron TV console during the day. Even our Grundig-Majestic (2320) FM radio with its rich sound usually stood silent. She always disliked noise of any kind preferring quiet surroundings. *Handarbeit* once meant knitting elaborate pieces like sweaters and winter headwear but now she preferred crocheting, which required only one needle, and her creations were pillow or chair seat covers. Afraid she might hurt herself or start a fire (we had a gas stove), I kept her out of the kitchen and cooked all our meals.

When I suggested to her she do a little more around the house, besides spraying the coffee and end tables with furniture polish, and take the Electrolux for a little spin now and then she shot back "I'm not your housekeeper." She never had been much of a Hausfrau in the traditional sense and the housecleaning was left to me. Other than that, Mutti insisted on maintaining her independence and taking care of herself. Because she had difficulty getting up from the tub after a bath, I got her a special chair for inside the bathtub and in lieu of a bath she now took a shower in a comfortable sitting position.

One of the routines she had adopted every morning before getting up, was to do some sit-up exercises in bed to loosen up and strengthen her lower extremities. Then one morning she turned on the small Sony television set in her room and discovered a program featuring a group of young ladies in their early 20s doing some rather strenuous gymnastic exercises. When I heard some unusual noises coming from her room and rushed upstairs, I found Mutti a full participant. Her exercises included intricate dance steps, kicking her legs up in the air, and whirling about like a dervish. She was already in her early 80s and very unsteady on her legs and, naturally, I was afraid she might slip and fall especially since the upstairs bedrooms had varnished floors, and at her insistence, these were covered only by small area rugs. She was not happy when I removed the TV set from her room and requiring her to resume her sit-up exercises..

While her memory loss was not yet too serious, she occasionally did have some lapses but I decided early on not to correct her but to be wherever she found herself. If she was back in Schwanheim with her family, that is where I would be also. This sometimes let to some funny incidents. One time, when I was in the basement family room reading law, she excitedly came running in the house by the back door (after having quietly sneaked out) shouting, "*Papa, papa, draußen steht ein Alfa Romero*" [Papa, papa, there is an Alfa Romero outside]. I went upstairs and, taking her by the hand, we walked to the parking lot behind our townhouses. Sure enough, there stood a car with that company's logo on its grill. "*Ja, mein Kind,*" I said, "*das ist ein Alfa Romero.*" [Yes, my child, that's an Alfa Romero]. "*Kind,*" she shot back, "*du nennst mich Kind? Ich bin nicht dein Kind, ich bin deine Mutter!*" [You call me child? I'm not your child, I'm your mother!].

Germany is known for a rich musical tradition with some of the world's foremost composers and classical works having originated there. These compositions, however, represent only the tip of the musical mountain. Below lies a treasure trove of wonderful Volkslieder, many of them hundreds of years old. Both Mutti and I had always enjoyed these songs and now that Mutti was in her dotage, I kept her entertained and further stimulated with a daily dose of *Volksmusik* [folk music]. With the closing of the Deutsches Kino on Chicago's North Lincoln Avenue we found ourselves without our customary entertainment and I decided to purchase a 32" Sony Trinitron television console (which was the largest screen size at the time) with an attached VCR for viewing German-language videotapes. The system was delivered just before Christmas 1992.

Our routine before turning on the TV usually began with Mutti making sure that we both looked presentable. This included checking that her dress was over her knees and my shirt properly tucked in. The reason was that, for some reason, Mother had come to believe that whoever appeared on the television screen could look out and see us. When an entertainer's image appeared on the screen, Mother would beam approvingly and with a slight bow of the head acknowledge his or her presence.

Some of the most popular *Volkssänger* [folk music singers] of the day included René Kollo and Rudolf Schock, both of whom also appeared in operas and operettas, and Heino who specialized in this genre.[29] In his *Sing Mit Heino* [Sing With Heino] video recordings, Heino used the actual locale where the songs played for his performances. Thus, if he did the old student song, *Ich hab' mein Herz in Heidelberg verloren* [I lost my heart in Heidelberg], he would be walking around Heidelberg castle or along the Neckar River.

One song's lyrics came from a famous Goethe poem about a rose and its fate and so the venue for Heino's performance was a rose garden. In one scene, as Heino was singing, a couple came by with a dog on a leash. After we had watched this particular tape a number of times, Mutti turned to me and said, "I really like these people." I asked her why and she replied, "because they love animals." How could she tell, I wanted to know. "Well, haven't you noticed," she said, "every time they come by they have their dog with them." Clearly, Mother had gotten a little meshugge.

Mother and I got along very well together despite our very different personalities. That was probably because we respected and rarely criticized each other nor did I ask any embarrassing questions about the past. This did not, however, mean that we did not have some spats now and then. These invariably involved either our pets or Esther. Our cats had their feeding station in the kitchen and Mutti always kept their bowls filled to the brim. When it seemed to her that they were not eating properly, she carried the bowls into the living room and set them under their noses. Since our cats were usually obese anyway this practice irked me.

Once I pointedly asked her if she ever cared about anything else besides her cats. When she repeated the old refrain that animals were innocent, I reminded her that so were children. Well, she always cared about Esther, she said. That I knew, I told her. When I reminded her of all I had done for her over the years, she laughed almost hysterically. "What have you ever done for me?" she exclaimed.

Had I not bought her a house so she and her pets would have a permanent home, taken her on all my vacations while Esther never took her anywhere, supported her financially and bought her stock so she would have something to fall back on, and just recently given up my job on Long Island so that I could take care of her? She laughed telling me that I had never been able to hold on to a job and had been let go and that was why I was home.

When I asked her if that was what Esther had told her, she did not say another word. That evening when I came home from work, she tearfully apologized for what she had said. She wanted me to know how much she appreciated all I had done for her. She had always worried about getting old and feeble and left to fend for herself, she explained. I replied that her being nasty to me was an odd way of preventing that from happening.

Who Should Get What

It seemed strange to me that instead of being thankful for my efforts on our mother's behalf, Esther was becoming increasingly hostile and resentful towards me. She had been calling Mutti fairly often lately. I was not privy to their conversations but once overheard Mutti say to Esther, *"Nein, der Peter tut so was nicht."* [No, Peter doesn't do something like that]. I always wondered what Esther had insinuated I was supposedly doing. I knew Esther had been bad-mouthing me because I had heard it from different sources including Uncle Jule in Germany and Aunt Emmi and Marianne Kopf in Geneva. It was obvious she was now also working on our mother.

Since with Esther there was always one common denominator, which was money, I surmised she was fearful of losing out on the expected inheritance from our Aunt Emmi. Esther knew that our aunt had an intense dislike for her and would probably not leave her anything and that the most likely candidates would be either our mother or I or both. She therefore found it to her advantage to discredit me with our mother, our aunts Emmi and Irma, and anybody else in our circle.

In mid-December 1992, we had heard from Geneva Attorney Pierre Toffel that our Aunt Emmi was terminally ill with colon cancer and Esther immediately suggested we take Mutti to Esther's attorney to have her prepare a last will and testament. I was not enthused about the idea because Mutti's short-term memory was impaired and she no longer knew or cared about the details of her holdings having left the management of her financial affairs to me. More importantly, I thought the wills she had already made out earlier should do. These were prepared by Attorney Anthony (Tony) R. Basile of Oak Park, who was Esther's lawyer at the time.

On April 30, 1966, when she was 57, Mutti prepared a Last Will and Testament in which she stipulated that her estate be divided equally between her daughter, Esther Rose Holzman, and son, Hans Peter Zell, with Esther serving as executor and Peter as successor executor. Mother gave just one dollar each to Uta (sic), Elke, Volker, and Gerry (sic). Mr. Basile had recommended that she name all her children including the four she was excluding from her will.

On February 28, 1978, at age 68, Mutti had Tony Basile prepare a revised will with more specific bequests. She left her preferred and common stock in American Home Products Co. (the former Brach Candy) and all her common stock in American Telephone and Telegraph Co. (AT&T) to her son, Hans Peter Zell, her preferred stock in Commonwealth Edison Co., her bank Certificates of Deposit at Great American Federal Savings & Loan, and the remainder of her estate equally to Hans Peter Zell and Esther R. Holzman. She again left just one dollar each to Jerome, Ute, Elke, and Volker. In this will, signed by three witnesses, our mother named Esther and Peter as Co-Executors.

In-between these two wills, in June 1971, at age 62, Mutti wrote out a last will in longhand. The occasion was her impending ocean trip to Germany. Her written English was bad but her intentions were clear when she wrote:

Last Will. Oak Park, Ill. 6-10-1971

Before I am making a trip to Germany I like to make sure, in case of an Accident (?) or so, my two children: Esther Holzman geb. [geborene, i.e., née] Würzburger and Hans Peter Zell are sharing ½ + ½ everything I leave behind.

My children: Jerry Wetmore, Ute Niemeyer geb. [née] Zell, Volker Erwin Zell and Elke Zell now Ev. Peterson should become each one $1.00 (one Dollar) paid by my oldest daughter Esther Holzman, 122 So. East Ave. Oak Park, Ill. 60302

(signed) Anne Marie Zell bor. [née] Zell
1009-A No. Harlem - Oak Park, Ill. 60302

Incidentally, I was working out of town when these three wills were prepared and knew nothing about their existence until my permanent return home in late 1986.

Rather than take Mutti to Esther's new attorney (Mr. Basile had passed away), we agreed the lawyer should be neutral and a day before Christmas Eve 1992 we met at the Oak Park offices of an attorney who had been recommended to me by our neighbor Patti. When Mutti and

I got to First Chicago Bank, in which Attorney Michael Susman's office was located, Esther and Frank were already awaiting us. The attorney suggested that rather than having Mutti make out a traditional will, we should opt for a package deal that included a living (inter vivos) trust and three other documents. That would save the cost and time of probate and we readily agreed. The lawyer then took Mutti into a back room for a private conference and the two almost immediately came back out. To my astonishment, the attorney announced that Mutti was leaving everything to Esther Holzman. Esther immediately spoke up telling me not to worry because she intended to share half with me anyway.

Not wanting to rely on Esther's generosity, I asked Mutti in German who should inherit her estate and she replied "Esther und Peter." After a second private conference with our mother, the attorney announced that Mutti wanted Esther and Peter to share equally. Mutti would be trustee and beneficiary of the trust during her lifetime, according to the attorney. Esther then insisted being named sole successor trustee after our mother passed away. This was necessary, she claimed, to strengthen her hand when she went to Geneva to settle our aunt's affairs after Aunt Emmi had passed on. This was not acceptable to me and I told Esther that I could not agree to have her in sole control of Mutti's estate and that we should both serve as successor trustees. To this Esther was adamantly opposed.

Three days after our meeting, Mutti asked me if we had been in court recently and, Had I noticed how the judge had always agreed with her? We were not in court, I informed Mutti, but in a lawyer's office. When I reminded her that on the first occasion the lawyer had announced that she wanted to leave everything to Esther, Mutti emotionally denied ever having said that. According to Mutti, when asked about her wishes she had said, "Esther is the oldest" and when the attorney asked her if that meant that Esther should therefore get her estate, she had replied "yes." But she did not think that meant everything, she explained. I called Mr. Susman back and told him that I did not think the matter was handled properly and that I was not bringing our mother in for the signing of the documents. I told him that to have Esther named sole successor trustee would leave me out in the cold in case our mother came into an inheritance from her sister, and would be contrary to the provisions in our mother's three previous last wills.

When the attorney offered to call Esther and ask her and her husband to come back in to resolve the issue, I asked him, "Have you met Esther's husband"? to which he replied, "Well, who was the man she was with?" I explained to him that Frank was not her husband but a close friend and a psychiatrist. Mr. Susman next wanted to know about Mutti's mental state. I told him that while she could remember much from her childhood and later years, she had trouble remembering more recent events. No, I told him, she had not been diagnosed with Alzheimer's but that an MRI done about five years earlier at Gottlieb Memorial Hospital had shown some brain shrinkage.

"Mental dementia" was the attorney's immediate response. He then suggested I have Mutti's physician write out a note on her mental state and, based on that, he would write Esther that he could not proceed on the matter. Mutti's next appointment with her physician was at the beginning of January 1993 at which time Dr. Khan gave me the requested statement according to which our mother was suffering from dementia. This I forwarded to the attorney with payment of his entire fee. That I thought was the end of the matter. It was not—years later I learned that Esther had found another way to achieve her goal by taking our mother to her attorneys in Lake Forest who did her bidding.

A Brewing Storm

Esther and I never talked about the Nazi era since it did not exactly conjure up pleasant memories and especially not for her. It was therefore quite out of the ordinary when we found ourselves talking about this very topic on Mutti's 85th birthday in March 1994. It happened to be a Sunday and after Mutti and I had attended worship services in River Forest, we met Esther, Nick, and Frank for lunch at the Como Inn in Chicago where I had invited them. To our great disappointment Mutti had no appetite and ate almost nothing. Esther started talking about the Nazis claiming, among other things, that Hitler was gay and that Dr. Goebbels was the smartest of the bunch. As usual, Esther did almost all of the talking. I had not much to contribute while Mutti stayed mum.

When Frank asked me, "Who was Dr. Goebbels?" I told him that he was the Nazi propaganda minister and if he wanted to see him, he could do so on a DVD I had at home. Esther immediately piped up with, "I don't think the doctor is interested in your Nazi films." The film I had referred to was *Triumph des Willens* [Triumph of the Will] about the 1936 Berlin Olympics by the prominent filmmaker Leni Riefenstahl. The Riefenstahl film was the only "Nazi film" I owned and had bought it because I happened to be born at the start of these games and the film was considered a sports classic.

After dinner, I confided in Esther something that I had only recently come to realize, namely, that had it not been for the Nazis, I would not even be around. Her response, "That would be good" shocked me coming from a sister. Incidentally, it only later dawned on me that Frank had set me up because he would have known all about Dr. Goebbels as did most adult Americans who were around during World War II. He was clearly testing me regarding my attitude toward the Nazis and the Third Reich and I fell into his trap. I should have said, You have not heard of Dr. Goebbels?

Mutti had invited the three to join us after dinner for coffee and cake at Mutti's Place. For the occasion I had bought a large multi-layered Black Forest Cherry torte at the Café Lutz. Mutti had helped set the table with her best china. We anxiously awaited their arrival but they never showed up and Esther never called. *"Bei der Esther weiß man nie wo man dran ist"* [With Esther you never know where you stand], was Mother's sad lament. Esther had once again managed to ruin what would otherwise have been a perfect day.

It was most likely all part of Esther's overall strategy, although I did not realize it at the time, when she began to question the quality of care I was providing for our mother. Specifically, she expressed concern about the prescription drugs and the dosage I was administering. Dr. Hanni had prescribed 50 milligrams (mg) of Elavil for Mutti but Esther kept pressing me to give her more which I refused to do. In late September 1995, she left a message on my answering machine demanding I give Mother another 25 mg of Elavil beyond her normal dosage. "I talked with Dr. Hanni—if she doesn't get her medication, I have to take drastic steps and you know me, I'll do it," she said. I was not in favor of a higher dosage because when I had tried it once before, after Esther pressed me to do so, Mutti had walked around the house like a zombie as if she was in a trance.

To resolve the issue, in early October I took our mother to Dr. Hanni who informed me that he had not recommended a higher dosage in his phone conversation with Esther as she had claimed. Since Mutti was due to see her regular physician in a few days, Dr. Hanni suggested I ask Dr. Khan to arrange for a blood test and report back to him. Dr. Hanni called back a few days later to tell me that Mutti's serum level was quite appropriate and her thyroid function was normal (low thyroid activity can lead to memory loss, he explained) and that I should continue to give her just 50 mg at bedtime as before. I had been vindicated but I knew that this would not be the end of the matter because Esther, once she had fixed on something, would not let go. She was absolutely convinced that Mother was not getting enough anti-depressant.

The year 1996 started out poorly for Esther and this had its effect on all of us. Just before Christmas 1995, she had been informed by her Geneva attorney, Alexandre Davidoff, that the judge in the case had scolded him for challenging the court's findings and told him that a ruling in favor of the City of Geneva was forthcoming. This meant that the city would take our aunt's entire estate leaving the family with nothing. Esther now had to look forward to a lengthy legal battle to get the court's verdict overturned and, as she knew, the chances of success would be slim. She was clearly stressed out and became increasingly unglued.

When in mid-February, I took Mutti to Dr. Khan for another scheduled physical examination, he had excused himself and asked a lady colleague, Dr. Susan Thomas, to examine Mutti. This physician showed me a letter Dr. Khan had received from Esther accusing me of not giving Mutti her medications including Elavil and Dyazide (for hypertension) and, furthermore, that no record of purchases on these prescriptions could be found at our local pharmacy.

Dr. Thomas assured me that neither she nor Dr. Khan believed any of these allegations especially since our mother's condition was always found normal. I told the doctor that Esther had been leaving hateful phone messages on my answering machine and mailing me open postcards with these same unfounded allegations. On one particular disturbing one she wrote, "Not only does mother not get her pills on time but your behavior towards her is not acceptable—if you do not change your ways I will make drastic changes—don't push me." I had no clue as to what she meant about my "behavior" towards our mother.

When I brought Mutti to Dr. Khan three months later for another scheduled checkup, her blood pressure and other readings were again normal. The doctor told me Esther had called and screamed at him for supposedly not doing more for our mother especially regarding her dementia. She thought he should have prescribed some medications for that disease notwithstanding the fact there was none available for it at the time. Dr. Khan said Esther had a habit of becoming very intense for a while and then, all of a sudden, withdrawing again. He speculated that she might be manic-depressive and in need of help. His impression that Esther was mentally ill is something I had long suspected. Yet she was under the care of two experienced psychiatrists, Dr. John Hanni and Dr. Frank Murrin, I thought to myself. If these two could not stabilize her mentally, who could?

Neither Esther nor I wanted to face the fact that Mutti may have Alzheimer's and we had avoided ever mentioning the word or obtaining a diagnosis regarding her memory lapses. Even without an official diagnosis of her mental condition, it was obvious that things were not quite normal with her. In the evening, she could not remember what she had for lunch or if she even had lunch while events from the distant past seemed like yesterday to her. She often repeated the same thing over and over in a relatively short time span. Esther finally got up the courage to confront the issue. She and Dr. Murrin took Mutti to Rush Presbyterian St. Luke's Hospital in Chicago for an evaluation.

On their second visit to Rush Presbyterian in mid-June 1996, they were told that our dear mother did indeed have Alzheimer's. It was devastating news for all of us even though we had suspected as much all along. There was no cure or treatment available, Esther and Frank were told, and all we could hope for was that the disease would progress very slowly. According to the doctors, this was, in fact, a realistic prospect for people who were already up in years when diagnosed and Mutti was now 87 years old. Hopefully, something might even become available, in the meantime, to at least hold the disease in check. I was to give Mutti big daily doses of vitamins C (250 mg) and E (400 mg) and keep her stimulated, according to the doctors.

The summer of 1996 was the last time things were normal around the house. As most Chicago summers it was hot and humid and Mutti and I again spent time at the Rehm Park pool. We celebrated my own 60th birthday at the beginning of August with a Sunday trip to Lake Geneva for a pleasant day out. Esther, who had the habit of blowing hot and cold, surprised us the day after by inviting Mutti and me to a birthday luncheon at the Como Inn. Frank drove us there and, as usual, Nick stayed at home in Lake Forest. Poor Mutti had again no appetite and did not touch the chicken cacciatore Esther had ordered for her.

Towards the end of the month, we had our 8th annul townhouse picnic and our neighbors who, in the meantime, had learned about Mutti's Alzheimer's were especially nice to her. Then, on a Sunday in mid-September, Mutti and I attended a *Deutscher Tag* [German Day] event, sponsored by a local German-American society, near Lincoln Square which turned out to be our last such event together. Meanwhile, Esther and Frank continued to come by on Fridays to take Mutti to the Como Inn for lunch, which they had started doing about three years earlier, even though Mother no longer had much of an appetite and probably ate little or nothing at these outings.

The Nightmare Begins

Our near-idyllic existence came to a shattering end and a 18-month nightmare began in mid-October 1996. In the past 10 years, I had done my very best taking care of our mother. Making certain that she got her prescribed medications and in the correct dosages was especially important to me. Thus, when Esther left another hateful phone message on my answering machine accusing me of not giving Mutti her Elavil, I was outraged. In her tirade Esther claimed that our mother had been sounding depressed lately and she knew for a fact that she was not getting her Elavil and that I had repeatedly lied to her. She concluded with:

> *If you don't follow her Elavil procedure, I'll take Mother home and there isn't a damn thing you are going to do about it because I have enough money to fight you off from here to Virginia. Now you just remember that. I'm not fooling around. I have the backing*

*and I can do it and I have the lawyers. Now you better get busy
and give her the Elavil.*

Esther had never before mentioned wanting to take our mother to
Virginia but I knew that the three contemplated buying some property
in Charlottesville and moving there. (I had gone to school in that town
and had told Esther about its great location in the mountains and many
amenities). I was especially annoyed by Esther claiming, in effect, that
Mutti's Place, where our mother had lived for the past 30 years, was not
her real home and implying that her house in Lake Forest was.

Esther's latest allegations were the last straw and, on October 17, I fired
back with an angry 5-page letter that I later came to regret writing because
it was essentially a declaration of war and there would be no turning back.
In my missive I laid out the story of her life as I knew it. I told her how her
spiteful and vindictive conduct had torn our family apart but, despite all
of that, how my siblings and I had always treated her with kid gloves never
criticizing her or doing anything that would offend her because our mother
had told us that, being the oldest, she was entitled to deferential treatment.

I reminded Esther how she had always taken the high road leaving it
to others to make the sacrifices and then stepping in only when she saw a
benefit for herself. After years of neglect, she was now masquerading as our
mother's benefactor and guardian of her health. I told her that I was not
afraid of her money or her lawyers and while she could buy the lawyers,
she could not buy the law. Then I offered this broadside:

> *Only someone with a heart and mind of a reptile like you could
> keep accusing a brother of willfully withholding medication from a
> mother he dearly loves and has lived with and taken care of the past
> 10 years. How dare you miserable viper call me a liar. What would
> motivate me to not let Mother have her medication or lie to you?
> If there is one liar in the family it's you. You lie so much you can
> no longer tell the lie from the truth. Your whole life is one big lie.*

In the same letter I let Esther know that I was not opposed to have
our mother live with her in Lake Forest but only on condition that Mutti
expressed her wish to do so in the presence of both of us or, alternatively, in
case she could no longer make this decision on her own, if both Esther and

I agreed it was in Mutti's best interest. If our mother moved in with her, I wanted written assurances that i) she was given her medications (Dyazide and Elavil) only in dosages prescribed by her personal physicians, ii) she could have her beloved pet cat Tootsie live with her, iii) she would not be taken out of state without my prior written consent, and iv) I was allowed to see her at least once a week at dates and times mutually agreed on. It seemed like a very reasonable proposal to me if Esther really had Mutti's best interests in mind. I concluded by urging Esther to obtain outside professional help before she did more damage to others and herself since it was obvious that she was mentally ill.

Esther's response was not long in coming. On November 6, Katherine Levy, a lawyer in the Lake Forest offices of Jenner & Block, a prestigious Chicago law firm, sent me a letter stating, "Mrs. Holzman has asked me to determine whether charges should be filed against you for the dangerous neglect of a senior citizen." Ms. Levy wrote that Esther had taken our mother to Dr. Robert Bonow, a professor and chief of the division of cardiology at the Northwestern University Medical School in Chicago. (Dr. Bonow was a personal friend of Dr. Murrin). "I have been advised," Ms. Levy wrote, that "Dr. Bonow determined that Mrs. Zell suffered a silent heart attack which could have been brought on by the failure of Mrs. Zell to receive her regular dosage of Dyazide." Furthermore, the letter claimed that there had been an uneven purchase of Dyazide and Elavil at Walgreens, the pharmacy that held Mutti's prescriptions. The lawyer wanted me to forward any purchase records of the two drugs in my possession.

Needless to say, I was stunned and immediately called Dr. Khan who confirmed that Dr. Bonow had found an irregularity in Mutti's electrocardiogram and had called it a silent heart attack. According to Dr. Khan, such irregularities are common in someone of Mutti's age and that no amount of Dyazide could ensure against it. He called Esther crazy and paranoid. I also made an appointment for Mutti with Dr. Hanni. After examining her in private, he found her doing "amazingly well" and out of her depression. He said Mutti could be taken off Elavil altogether but it might be better to reduce her dosage to 25 mg. To placate Esther, who kept insisting that our mother was "down" because she was not getting enough Elavil, I persuaded Dr. Hanni to keep Mutti on the original dosage of 50 mg.

In my response to Ms. Levy, I appended the requested information on drug purchases. From my own records and with the assistance of the Walgreens pharmacist, it was possible to trace two years worth of Elavil and Dyazide purchases. These showed that more than an adequate supply of both medications had been purchased. There was an interesting twist, however, that laid bare one of Esther's little wicked schemes. The Oak Park purchases of Elavil were, in fact, insufficient which left me perplexed because I always had enough of the drug on hand to give Mutti her daily dosage. On further computer research, the pharmacist found that additional Elavil purchases on Mutti's prescription had been made at one of their Lake Forest locations.

This explained why, during a few of Esther's visits, when I wandered into the kitchen, where I kept Mutti's prescriptions, I found Esther with an open bottle of Mutti's Elavil in her hands. I had thought nothing of it at the time. What she was apparently doing was to add a small quantity of pills on every visit and since I did not reorder until the bottle was nearly empty, I always had an adequate supply and did not get a refill. What Esther did not realize was that the Walgreens pharmacist could trace purchases to other stores. When the purchases at the two stores were added up we had more than an adequate supply of both medications.

I concluded my letter to Ms. Levy with a restatement of my previous offer, namely, that I would be happy to turn our mother over to her client's care provided she could persuade our mother to live with her and I received written assurances that I could visit at least once a week. In a curt reply the lawyer informed me that her client was not willing to negotiate with me or enter into any written agreement. To me that meant Esther most likely planned to take Mutti to Lake Forest regardless of our mother's wishes and without my having any assurances regarding visitation rights.

In the meantime, Esther kept calling Mutti telling her to "come home" and live with her and "the family" in Lake Forest. After one such call, poor Mutti was quietly sobbing when she got off the phone. "*Ich muß heim gehen aber wo ist heim?*" [I have to go home but where is home?], she said to me. Mother was obviously under terrible pressure. While she did not want to offend Esther, she also did not want to leave her Oak Park home.

Mutti was not in the habit of passing out complements or showing much appreciation for things people did for her. I was therefore moved when, on the Sunday before Christmas, I came to her room to wake her and her first words were, "*Ich bin glücklich daß ich bei dir bin*" [I'm happy that I'm with you]. It had been many years since she had paid me a similar compliment although indirectly. One day I had walked into the village on some errand when our neighbor Marge found Mutti in the parking lot washing down my Mercury Cougar. "Why are you doing all these things for your son?" Marge wanted to know. "Because he takes good care of me" was Mutti's prompt reply, according to Marge.

When I realized that Esther would persist in her false and malicious allegations, I decided to seek legal counsel and in early January 1997 hired Susan Kennedy, a Chicago attorney with some expertise in elder law. She was on a list of lawyers recommended to me by the Alzheimer's Association which I had contacted. Susan told me that she had just recently started practicing law after a career in nursing. She immediately wrote Ms. Levy a conciliatory letter in which she stated that removing Mutti to Lake Forest appeared like a reasonable solution in light of the fact that her client was again employed and could therefore not be with our mother full time while the household of Ms. Levy's client contained three people who were usually at home. Another alternative would be to hire a caretaker for our mother during the day with expenses to be shared by Esther and me.

Susan also admonished Ms. Levy to have her client cease her unfounded allegations that I had failed to administer our mother her medications as prescribed. She called it a gross exaggeration to conclude that a "silent heart attack" is attributable to missed dosages of Dyazide or that Mrs. Zell is depressed as a result of not being given her Elavil. Susan concluded by suggesting that, in light of the controversy between their clients, Mutti might need guardianship of person and estate and proposed filing a "Petition for Adjudication of Disability." She would be happy to discuss the matter in a telephone call from Ms. Levy and expressed her hope the issue would be resolved in a mutually satisfactory manner.

Early in January, I also took Mutti to Dr. Khan for her regular 3-month checkup. Her blood pressure was normal at 120/70, her pulse regular and her weight at 127 pounds somewhat high but acceptable. During our visit, Dr. Khan performed his own electrocardiogram but did not find the condition Dr. Bonow had described. Even if it had shown up, said Dr. Khan, he would not be alarmed because 35% of people Mutti's age have such an irregularity. A blood test showed normal readings except for a high cholesterol level and a small kidney problem but neither were anything to be concerned about. Dr. Khan instructed me to make Sunday a Dyazide-free day and recommended more vegetables and fruit in her diet.

Subsequently, Esther and Frank took Mother to Dr. Bonow for a re-evaluation. During another visit to Dr. Khan's office, he gave me a copy of a letter he had received from Dr. Bonow dated January 21, 1997 in which the cardiologist stated, "An electrocardiogram performed today reveals normal sinus rhythm with right bundle branch block and probably prior inferior wall myocardial infarction." Furthermore, wrote Dr. Bonow, "Mrs. Zell remains stable from a cardiovascular standpoint. Her blood pressure continues to be well controlled on the Dyazide. At this time we have recommended no changes in her medical therapy."

Meanwhile, Mutti continued to show the effects of Alzheimer's. A few days after our visit with Dr. Khan, as Mutti was preparing for bed, she suddenly asked me, "*Wo ist meine Mutter?*" [Where is my mother?] and when I explained to her that her parents were in heaven with the angels now she asked, "*Seit wann?*" [Since when?]. She then asked about her sister and I repeated what I had said before. "*Nein, nein*" [no, no] she cried out and began to sob as I held her in my arms trying to console her.

The Abduction

Esther carried out her plan to carry off our mother without agreeing to my demand of guaranteed visitation rights with speed and determination. On the last day of January 1997, she faxed a typewritten message to Firstar Bank of Oak Park supposedly from our mother with instructions to "Transfer all incoming checks be it my S.S. $566.00, my German S.S. $269.80 or dividend checks in my account to my new account in Lake Forest, Il." The letter was signed by our mother while the letterhead contained Esther's Lake Forest address implying that Mutti was already living there. Incredibly, three days later the bank made a wire transfer that included the American and German social security benefit checks payable on February 1 to the Lake Forest account specified by Esther without making any prior inquiries. Shortly after, Mother's personal checks were being returned for insufficient funds. About the same time, Mutti received a notice from the Oak Park post office that they had received a change of address order.

The real shocker came on the evening of February 3, a Monday. After I got home from work, we had eaten and watched our *Volksmusik* VCR tapes, it was bedtime for Mutti. When we got to her room, I found that it had been ransacked. Everything including the bedding, all of Mother's clothes, and all photographs and other personal items had been stripped from the room and carried off in the footlocker Mutti kept in her closet whose contents, mostly fabric and shoes, had unceremoniously been dumped on the floor.

Since all of Mutti's underwear and nightgowns were also taken, I surmised that Esther and Nick had come to take Mutti herself as well who must have struggled and refused to leave with them. Mutti could offer no coherent explanation of what had happened during Esther's visit. The next morning, when I took Mutti to our other bank, First Chicago Bank on Lake Street, and informed them of the situation, they immediately put a "fraud alert" on her savings account to prevent Esther from having those funds transferred to Lake Forest also. We also went to the main Oak Park post office, where our postmaster, Ron, put a stop order on the change of address they had received.

Returning from work in the evenings, I never knew whether Mutti would still be there or had been taken away although I did come home during my lunch breaks to check up on her. The telephone was of no use as Mutti had stopped answering it after Esther kept calling to put more pressure on her. During early February, Esther came by the house repeatedly trying to remove Mutti but with no success. One evening I noticed that Esther had been to the house and when I asked Mutti if Esther had tried to take her with her, she replied, *"Immer aber ich hab ja dich"* [Always but I have you, after all].

When I asked Mutti why she thought Esther was so desperate to have her live with her, she just rubbed her fingers together in the universal sign for money. I had, of course, long concluded that Esther's true motivation was money but I found it interesting that Mutti too was fully aware. If anybody knew Esther, it was our mother, of course.

February 11 was Esther's 70th birthday and I suspected she would celebrate it by finally carrying out her plan to carry off our mother without a visitation agreement in place. I therefore switched my regular hours at work to be home and, unbeknownst to Mutti, stayed in the basement family room. Sure enough, towards evening Esther came to the back door trying to get in but Mutti had engaged a latch blocking her entry. (Esther had a key to Mutti's Place to allow her to check up on our mother whenever she wanted to). Upstairs I heard Mutti shout, "*Tootsie, geh nicht an die Tür*" [Tootsie, don't go to the door]. There was much banging on the door and a commotion outside until it was quiet again. Our neighbor Patti later told me that Esther and a man she did not know had stopped by her place and asked if she knew where her mother was. The unknown man must have been Dr. Murrin because Patti knew Nick.

Despite Mutti's long and valiant fight to remain in her home, Esther finally succeeded in seizing her. She came for her on the afternoon of February 17, another Monday, while I was at work. By some ruse, most likely by telling Mother she was taking her to a doctor, Esther managed to get Mutti to open the back door. As I left for work, I had spotted Nick in his station wagon cruising around the neighborhood and alerted the Oak Park police. When I returned home and found Mutti gone and called the police again, an officer came out and showed me a paper Esther had handed them. It was a "Designation of Guardian" Mutti had signed on March 11, 1993 naming Esther Holzman as the guardian of Mother's person and estate "in the event I am adjudged to be a disabled person." Serving as witnesses were the head of Esther's Lake Forest law firm, Addis Hull, John Hanni, M.D., and Frank Murrin, M.D. who all signed "believing Anne Marie Zell to be of sound mind and memory at the time of signing."

The date of the signing was significant because some weeks prior, in late December 1992, we had taken Mutti to Michael Susman, the Oak Park attorney, who had decided that Mutti's mental state precluded him from proceeding on the testamentary documents. Clearly, Esther had now surreptitiously taken our mother to her own lawyers who did her bidding. The Oak Park police considered the paper they were handed sufficient to allow Mutti's removal from her home. That was an obvious mistake because they asked for no proof that our mother had been adjudged to be disabled. Esther, Nick, and Frank had come in two cars to take Mother to their place in Lake Forest and besides removing Mutti they also carried off Tootsie, a lounge chair, and some other items. As fate would have it, Mutti remained her daughter's quasi-prisoner for the remainder of her life. The immediate problem for me was that I might not get to see our mother again if Esther had her way.

A Custody Battle

The drawn-out legal battle began when two days after Mother's abduction, on February 19, 1997, my attorney filed a "Petition for Appointment of Guardian for Disabled Person" in the Circuit Court of Cook County - Probate Division.[30] Susan followed up with a "Petition for Temporary Guardianship." Even though I was not interested in becoming Mutti's guardian of either her person or estate but only in obtaining firm, scheduled visitation rights, counsel advised that my objective was only possible through a guardianship proceeding. Esther's lawyers responded with a cross-petition to be appointed guardian of our mother's person and estate and a "Petition for Change of Venue" to which was appended the "Designation of Guardian" our mother had signed in March 1993. A hearing on the petitions was scheduled for the morning of February 26 in the chambers of Judge Richard E. Dowdle on the 18th floor of the Richard J. Daley Center in downtown Chicago. On the way to the courthouse Susan said that we were lucky because we had a judge who was both fair and experienced.

Esther had left Nick at home with our mother and, as usual, brought along her friend and counselor, Dr. Frank Murrin. It was a tactical error because poor Frank, who was in his upper 70s then and ailing, looked disheveled and haggard. When he spoke up and out of order, the judge addressed him with, "And who are you?" to which Frank replied, "I'm the in-house doctor." "Are you Mrs. Zell's doctor then?" the judge wanted to know to which Frank replied "No." At this point Susan piped up saying, "He is no doctor—he is a psychiatrist and he hasn't been practicing for years." Frank spoke up a couple of more times saying some really dumb and irrelevant things that did not further Esther's cause. In an aside to me, Susan said, "He is a wacko." I could not fail to note the irony in that comment since Frank was in a profession that supposedly tries to cure people of their mental problems.

The outcome of the hearing was that both of our petitions, Esther's and mine, were denied. Horace Jordan, the energetic young lawyer who represented Esther, got off to a bad start when he began praising the affluence and amenities of Lake Forest and the good life that awaited our mother there plus the benefits of having the hearings scheduled in Lake County. When the judge cut him short, Mr. Jordan apologized saying he really did not mean it the way it sounded. To the judge's query, "How long has Mrs. Zell lived in Lake Forest now?" Mr. Jordan replied "two weeks" to which Susan quickly retorted, "not true—10 days, your honor." "Last week it was Cook County, this week it's Lake County—I suppose next week it will be Dupage County." Susan also pointed out that most of Mutti's assets were still in Cook County as were her doctors and the witnesses. Then came the Judge Dowdle's fateful words, "Change of venue denied." This was an important victory for us in terms of convenience and litigation costs. The judge also ruled that the guardianship issue could only be determined in a plenary (full) hearing which was subsequently scheduled for March 20.

When Esther refused to let me see our mother, even on Mutti's 88th birthday on March 6, Susan filed an "Emergency Petition for Visitation of Alleged Disabled Person." In it, she asked the court to impose a visitation schedule. Esther filed a cross-petition opposing the emergency petition in which she asked the court to deny the petition or, in the alternative, rule "that Petitioner be limited to visitations with Mrs. Zell (a) on Tuesday and Sunday afternoons following 24-hour advance notice of the visit; (b) for one hour only on each of these days; and (c) with Mrs. Holzman in attendance if requested by Mrs. Zell." This visitation schedule and the conditions imposed were not acceptable to me. I wanted more visits and more time during each visit. Additionally, I did not care to have Esther sit in and monitor my conversation with our mother now that she and I were in court.

Since Tuesday was my day off from work, I would have preferred to see Mutti in the morning and stay with her at least a couple of hours. That was not possible, according to Esther, because Mutti slept late and often did not get up until noon. Since our mother had always been an early riser when she was with me, this news alarmed me because it suggested the strong possibility that Mutti was being given heavy doses of sedatives and other drugs. Dr. Murrin was, after a all, a medical doctor who had retained his medical license, even though he had long ago stopped seeing patients, and could therefore prescribe anything Esther wanted him to although not ethically, of course.

Before the scheduled plenary hearing, the court appointed a guardian ad litem (GAL) whose function is to represent the interests of an alleged disabled person before the court. Mary interviewed Mutti in her new home on March 9. On recommendation of Esther's counsel, Mary brought along a professor of German at Lake Forest College to assist with the translation. According to the GAL's report to the court, Mutti was incoherent and showed no interest in the petitions or the court proceedings. During the conversation, Mother thought they were all in Frankfurt and that even the man in the big house across the street was from there. When asked about guardians, Mutti stated that her parents were her guardians. She said she had never visited America but that everybody else had gone there and left her behind in Germany. Mutti was unsure if she was ever married. She claimed she had no children and could not identify Esther or Peter. She did not recognize the names of her other children when they were read to her. Mutti had no idea what the year was or her age but thought she was born on March 6, 1914.

Mutti became agitated and walked to the window refusing to say anything when queried about the petitioner and cross-petitioner (Peter and Esther). According to Mary's report, she would not express a preference as to who should serve as her guardian. The report concluded with a recommendation that a guardian for Anne Marie Zell's person and estate be appointed and her appearance at the hearing be waived. It was obvious to me from the report that Mutti had decided that the safest option for her was to be evasive and not to cooperate with the GAL.

The hearing on the emergency petition on visitation took place on the morning of Tuesday, March 11. After their trouncing in the first hearing, Esther and Frank wisely decided to stay away and leave it to their lawyer to represent them. In the meantime, Susan had taken Esther's measure. On the way to the courthouse, she said to me, "Esther is evil—she is so evil it's frightening." I could not agree more. After the guardian ad litem had presented her report, Mr. Jordan read out the visitation schedule and conditions set forth in their cross-petition.

This was precisely why we were in court, Susan told the judge. When the lawyer again claimed that morning visitation was not possible because Mutti slept late, the judge announced that the Petitioner must be able "to see his mom and if she is asleep while he is there he will sit next to her bed and watch her sleep." "Her loving daughter," he said, will undoubtedly have nothing against that. I was much touched by Judge Dowdle's kind and insightful remark.

Without further ado, the judge then granted our petition for emergency visitation and told the two counsels to work out a visitation schedule. Susan, Horace (or "Hob" as Esther referred to him) and I agreed that I should be allowed to see Mutti on Mondays and Fridays from 10 to 11 in the morning, on Tuesdays anytime between 10 a.m. and 6 p.m., and on alternate Sundays between noon and 5 p.m.. Furthermore, "The visits will be private between son and mother without interference by Mrs. Holzman." Susan wrote out a so-called "Agreed Order" in longhand, brought it up to the bench where the court clerk stamped it as filed and the judge, who was hearing another case, initialed it.

My reunion with Mutti three days later was an emotional affair for both of us. I got my first inkling that I was not welcome at the house when I drove up and found the driveway entrance blocked by Nick's and Frank's cars which were aligned in parallel facing the street. Nick unlocked the front door and Mutti fell in my arms. Where had I come from she wanted to know. She had been waiting for me a very long time, she said. Aside from a brief encounter in Dr. Hanni's office at which Mutti broke down on seeing me and was quickly hustled away, this was the first time we had met since she was taken away over a month earlier. Mutti looked good and was upbeat. She had obviously been well taken care of. She liked her new place, she said, and proudly showed me the little den next to the front entrance where she spent most of her day. There stood the easy chair that had been removed from our townhouse and her knitting basket filled with bundles of wool.

What did she do all day, I asked. "*Häkeln*" [crocheting] was her prompt reply. The only thing I found missing was Tootsie but decided not to say anything to Mutti. Because it was just a week past her birthday, I pretended it was that day and brought her flowers, a big box of cream chocolates, some more wool and a couple of her favorite *Volksmusik* videotapes. Nick allowed me to take her to their family room where the television set had an attached VCR. We watched one *Volksmusik* program when it was time to leave again. Mutti wanted me to stay but I promised to be back the following Tuesday. On the way out, I asked Nick about Tootsie and he assured me that our beloved pet was safe. Because Esther had her own small dog in the house (who barked a lot but never showed up), Tootsie had his home in the basement and was brought up occasionally to spend time with Mutti, according to Nick.

It had been expected that at the March 20 plenary hearing, at which Esther was present with Frank, Mutti would be adjudicated a disabled person. That did not happen because the two lawyers had not stipulated which of three reports on Mutti's condition filed with the court should be used—the GAL's, Dr. Khan's, or Dr. Hanni's. The two physicians agreed that Mutti had an extremely poor memory, was confused and disoriented as to place and time, and was totally incapable of making personal or financial decisions. Dr. Khan diagnosed her condition as "severe dementia of Alzheimer's type."

A new Agreed Order was entered providing for a two-day hearing, on July 22 and 23, on the matter of "who would serve the best interest of the respondent as guardian of the person and estate." The visitation schedule of March 11, 1997 remained in place except that on the Tuesday visits I was now allowed to take Mother outside the house for four hours. Allocating two hours total on the road, this would be enough time to take our mother back to her old and familiar surroundings in Oak Park and spend a couple of hours there visiting friends and neighbors and for us to enjoy a meal together.

In return, I agreed to Esther's demand to immediately hand over all of Mutti's jewelry. It had been kept in a bank safe deposit box and included a heavy jewel-encrusted gold ring in Mutti's possession for many years plus a braided gold necklace and bracelet, which Esther had once purchased for Mother, a strand of pearls, and some lesser items. I was happy to oblige and brought everything up on my next visit to Lake Forest. Mutti was there and when she saw her jewelry she exclaimed, *"Das gehört mir"* [That's mine] but Esther immediately handed the box over to Nick who left with it presumably to take it to their bank for safekeeping.

On the following Tuesday, March 25, Mutti saw her old home for the first time again. It had been five weeks since she had been spirited away and she was obviously delighted to be back. We replaced her clunky shoes with her comfortable house slippers and she settled down in her easy chair by the front window just like in the good old days. All that was missing from the happy scene was her beloved Tootsie on her lap. While I prepared a small lunch, she delightedly watched a *Volksmusik* tape. Some neighbors stopped by to say hello. Mutti's happy mood quickly changed when it was time to leave. She became very angry and grabbed some legal papers she saw lying on top of the Grundig radio and stuffed them in her handbag. Mother had evidently thought she had come back to stay and now felt betrayed.

On leaving, she clung to the back door so that I had to pry her lose and forcefully coax her toward the car. In the car she struggled to keep me from putting on her seat belt. As we turned the corner to drive north on Harlem Avenue and passed the townhouse complex, she anxiously looked back and began to sob. Naturally, I felt terrible and wondered if it was such a good idea to bring her back again. I had done it to reassure her that her former home was still there and she really had two places now she could call home. By the time we were back in Lake Forest, Mutti had calmed down but, on seeing the house, protested that this was not her home.

The following Tuesday, I decided not to take her back to Oak Park but to Racine, Wisconsin, which was also familiar territory for her. While I was employed there during the early 1980s, Mother had come up by train or bus for a weekend visit a number of times. I thought lunch there at her favorite restaurant followed by visits to the Racine zoo and boat harbor would cheer her up. It did not turn out that way. Poor Mutti was dispirited throughout our little outing. *"Es ist nicht mehr wie vorher"* [It's not like it used to be], she lamented. When I told her that I loved her, she responded with, *Das ist was sie alle sagen* [That's what they all say]. Could she be blamed for feeling the way she did? Undoubtedly, she heard the same line from Esther. Everybody professed to love her but why then was she no longer in her home in Oak Park and instead in a place she did not want to be?

A provision in the latest Agreed Order stated: "All Respondent's assets will remain with Petitioner Zell, who will reimburse Cross Petitioner upon receipt of any reasonable invoice in providing for the care of Respondent." It seemed forthright enough but led to an immediate squabble. Esther now decided to go on a buying spree on Mutti's behalf including a new wardrobe. None of this would have appealed to Mutti had she any say in the matter and Esther had never before mentioned anything about Mother's need for more clothes.

My fax machine was kept busy spewing out invoices and receipts with demands from Esther for immediate payment including $1,000 a month for room and board. In the meantime, she had contracted with an agency for daycare services for Mutti and told them to fax me the invoices for payment. I found that outrageous because Esther had taken Mutti to Lake Forest claiming there would be three people to look after her. We could have hired someone in Oak Park as well and then Mutti could have stayed in her beloved home.

I paid as many of the bills as I could from Mutti's checking account but refused to liquidate her assets to pay for the remainder. The matter got more complicated after I complained to the Social Security office that Esther was now collecting our mother's monthly benefits in contravention of the Agreed Order which put me in charge of our mother's assets, and they stopped making further payments.

Since Mutti was happiest when in her old Oak Park home, I brought her back as often as I could which turned out to be only four times in total because of intervening events. Her second visit on a Tuesday in mid-April turned out much better than the first. By then she had come to realize that it was not one place or the other but that she could freely move between her old and new homes. When I picked her up in the morning, she was in a jovial mood but had much difficulty walking to the car. When we got to Mutti's Place and she settled down in her easy chair by the front window, I realized why. Her clunky new shoes had been put on backwards, i.e., the right shoe was on the left foot and the left on the right. That explained the weird smile I noticed on Esther's face in place of her usual frown when I picked up our mother. Whenever Esther smiled I had cause to worry because inside she was all anger and spite. While Mother was clapping her hands with the music of another *Volksmusik* tape, I prepared one of her favorite dishes—smoked butt cooked in sauerkraut with potato pancakes. I babied her a little by spoon feeding her and she had a surprisingly good appetite which was not normally the case.

A Terrible Diagnosis

Towards the end of April 1997, which was 10 weeks after she had been taken to Lake Forest, Mutti was found to be suffering from severe anemia. Esther had become concerned because of our mother's shortness of breath and elevated heart rate and taken her back to Dr. Bonow. The doctor found a dangerously low hemoglobin level (5.6) and recommended an immediate blood transfusion which was performed the following day. When I called Mutti's primary care physician, Dr. Khan, he told me that he had received Dr. Bonow's report and expressed surprise by this sudden turn of events because all previous blood tests had come out normal. He did not think that it was a dietary problem but most likely the result of internal bleeding such as from an ulcer.

When I saw Mutti a few days later during a scheduled visit, she looked well but appeared tired. She pointed to the staircase and said, "*Danauf will ich nicht*" [I don't want to go up there]." When we got to the end of my stay, she started to become restless. "*Komm wir gehen jetzt*" [Come let's go now], she said and when I asked, "*wohin*" [where to], she replied "*heim*" [home]. After I told her we would do that but first she needed to get well again, she was satisfied.

On Dr. Bonow's recommendation, Mutti was taken to Dr. Kenneth Breger, an internist in Highland Park. When I called this doctor he told me that Mother's hemoglobin level had improved after the blood transfusion (to 11.5) but that another specialist would have to examine her because of a possible intestinal tract problem. Two days later, on April 25, I received a letter on my fax machine from Esther's lawyers, informing me that her internist had found blood in Mutti's rectum and, suspecting she may have colon cancer, had ordered a colonoscopy at Highland Park Hospital. I hoped and fervently prayed it would not be true.

When I picked up Mother on the last Tuesday of the month for another Oak Park excursion, I anxiously asked Esther whether Mutti was able to eat solid foods again. "Yes, she can eat solid foods," was her reply. Since Mother had her colonoscopy the previous day, I was elated because it meant that Mutti was probably alright and no evidence of the dreaded disease had been found. After our usual routine of having our *Mittagessen* [lunch] followed by another viewing of some favorite VCR tapes on our TV, I let Mother know that it was time to go back home again. "*Heim?* she said, "*hier bin ich doch daheim!*" [Home? I am at home!]. Although she was disappointed to have to leave again, she fortunately made no scene again. As it turned out, my elation regarding Mother's condition was premature because the laboratory results had not yet been in when I had picked her up.

Friday, May 2, 1997, turned out to be one of the darkest days in my life. When I came home from work, Susan had left me a message to call her immediately. She read me a fax from Esther's lawyers that said in part, "I regret to inform you that a malignant growth was found in Mrs. Zell's colon. Apparently, the doctors have indicated that this condition may have gone undiagnosed for five years. At the doctors' suggestion, Mrs. Zell has not been informed of her cancer. We would appreciate it if Mr. Zell would maintain the confidential nature of this condition. ....Due to the need for additional medical treatments, it may not be possible to strictly adhere to the visitation schedule outlined in the court's orders."

I was stunned by this horrible turn of events and asked myself how this could have happened. Both of us were patients of Dr. Khan and I had taken Mother to see him every three months, as he had instructed me, and she had been given blood tests, X-rays, and EKGs whenever he thought it necessary. We first came to Dr. Amjad Z. Khan in mid-February 1991 after our previous physician, Dr. Vinay Keesara, had closed down his Oak Park practice to continue his education in the field of cardiology. Dr. Keesara turned us over to Dr. Khan who owned his own clinic on North Harlem Avenue just a few blocks south of Mutti's Place. Later, after selling it, we saw him in the Oak Park Hospital professional building.

Dr. Khan had a sterling reputation as a board certified internist who was also president of the Oak Park Hospital medical staff and Mutti and I felt fortunate to be in such capable hands. In light of the fact that Mutti's sister had died of that very disease nearly four years earlier, Esther and I should have taken note that family members were susceptible to colorectal cancer and alert Mutti's doctors. Unfortunately, we did not make that connection at the time and the topic never came up between us and our physicians including Dr. Khan.

The first Tuesday in May (May 6) turned out to be the last time Mutti would see her Oak Park home. Since the following Sunday was Mother's Day, we did the customary thing for us which was to stop by a florist near North and Harlem avenues and pick out our supply of geraniums, pansies, and other flowers for the front of the townhouse and the planter on the rear patio. To my happy surprise, Mutti had a good appetite and ate a nice portion of the light lunch I made for her of tuna salad, pasta, and spinach. While I planted the flowers, Mutti stayed in the house enjoying more of her favorite *Volksmusik* tapes. All that was again missing from this picture of happy contentment was our beloved Tootsie on Mutti's lap.

More Visitation Issues

It was my sincere hope that with this great calamity that had befallen us, Esther and I could finally come to terms and stand together in support of our mother as she was battling colon cancer. If a trial to gain custody of Mutti's person and estate made little sense to me before, it made absolutely no sense to me now. Despite my lawyer's strong objection, she agreed to contact Esther's lawyers with my proposal to drop my petition for custody in return for generous visitation rights. Hoping the spirit of the day might pave the way for a resolution of our differences, I suggested a family reunion on Mother's Day (May 11). Esther was not interested, she told her counsel. Nevertheless, I was able to see Mutti for my scheduled two hours on that Sunday and brought her a pot of Azaleas and a large strand of one quarter inch cultured pearls from Marshall Field's which I placed around her neck. While Mutti never cared much for expensive jewelry, I knew Esther would most likely appreciate having it.

Unfortunately, my peace offering was for naught and my visit on the following day brought about an especially ugly scene. As I sat with Mutti in the open, doorless parlor, where Esther could observe us, Mutti suddenly got up and shouting, *"Komm wir gehen"* [Come let's go] ran to the front door to unlock it. Esther held her back and screamed at me to get out of her house and not to come back until I had paid all her bills. She also claimed that I was responsible for the shape Mutti was in. A few days later, Susan received a fax from Esther's attorneys formally rejecting my proposal to drop my petition for guardianship in return for visitation rights. To resolve the matter without court intervention, the letter stated, I must be willing to immediately turn over to Esther all of our mother's assets and withdraw my guardianship petition unconditionally. With no guaranteed visitation rights, this left me with only one option, namely, to prepare for the July guardianship hearing.

Most guardianship cases involve a financial element and this one was no exception. As part of the pre-trial discovery phase, Susan received a 7-page document entitled "Cross-Petitioner's First Document Request" in which opposing counsel asked for all of my and our mother's financial records dating back to January 1, 1986—a period of over 12 years. To be included were income tax returns, bank and brokerage account statements and records, cancelled checks, and complete data on all incomes and disbursements. In addition, I was to submit all documents pertaining to each and every job, position or other form of employment, and "all journals, diaries or other documents which contain daily or other periodic notations or descriptions of any events, including but not limited to financial transactions on behalf of Mrs. Zell." For Mutti all documents relating to her health care including medical and hospital records, lab tests and results, and prescription drugs were to be submitted.

The document request was a tall order but, fortunately, I had always kept Mutti's financial accounts separate from my own and maintained detailed records of all my and Mutti's financial transactions. In addition, I had for years kept journals for recording important life events. Nevertheless, getting all the data together was a momentous, time-consuming undertaking. After I was done, I put all the papers in a briefcase and hand-carried them to Susan's Chicago office in mid-May. Susan arranged to have them copied and shipped to Lake Forest together with the invoice, all in accordance with instructions from opposing counsel. According to Susan, the cost came to several hundred dollars which Jenner & Block duly paid.

Later we learned that after the lawyers had examined all the submitted documents and found no evidence of any wrongdoing on my part, Esther refused to reimburse her lawyers for the cost of the copying claiming that she had never authorized it. I had no sympathy for her lawyers because, in my view, they had overreached and improperly used the statutes to harass and intimidate me. It was sometime later when I made a similar request for information from Esther and I was strongly rebuffed by opposing counsel who gave me absolutely nothing when I realized that Susan should have thwarted their effort but did not perhaps because of inexperience or other reasons.

The last half of May and most of June was a tumultuous period. When on a scheduled visit on Monday, May 19, nobody came to the door to let me in, I went to see Jenner & Block in their Lake Forest offices to complain. The attorneys assigned to her case, Horace Jordan and Art Gollwitzer, and I had a long, friendly chat which gave me the opportunity to present my side of the case. Surprisingly, I found both lawyers very empathetic. One of the two called Esther and had her agree to let me see our mother for an hour on the following evening. Evidently they were not home during my scheduled visit because they had taken Mutti for blood and other tests.

Mother was very happy to see me and said a few words to Esther in an attempt to get her to talk to me when Esther shouted, "I don't want to see him, I don't want to talk to him, he won't be coming here much longer." After hugging Mother and saying good-bye I walked toward my car when Esther shouted after me, "How dare you come here, you murderer." Her outburst baffled me and I asked myself, Why is she calling me a murderer? Whom did I supposedly murder? Despite her lawyers' strenuous attempts to have Esther comply with the court visitation order, I continued to have a very difficult time seeing Mutti.

Coincidentally, in May both Esther and I made changes in our legal representation. The July court date on the guardianship issue had, in my opinion, been set too far out but according to Susan it was the earliest the court calendar would allow. In the meantime my legal fees were becoming substantial—on the order of two to three thousand dollars a month. Because of other financial commitments and only a modest income at the time, I needed to keep these expenses down.

To accomplish this, I asked Susan to accept the position of co-counsel and let me become lead counsel in the case. I was, after all, a registered attorney in Illinois although I had not practiced law and lacked experience.

Susan reluctantly agreed and I consequently entered my appearance with the court on May 21. Hopefully, this would put an end to Susan's costly work effort including unsolicited and lengthy strategy proposals and her many heated exchanges with the two Jenner & Block attorneys that added much to the cost of litigation but did little to resolve the conflict.

About the same time, Esther and her attorneys decided to part company. Jenner & Block filed a motion with the court to withdraw from the case and did so at the end of May. Her attorneys offered no explanation but when one has a client who is out of control by refusing to comply with court orders and may also be erratic in paying her bills it was easy to see why.

Most of my visits with Mother were difficult and emotionally wrenching. They always took place in the parlor opposite the front entrance with Mutti seated on the plastic covered sofa and I on an equally protected arm chair in front of it. Esther would usually walk by at irregular intervals to keep an eye on us. I never understood why that was so important to her except that it must have satisfied her need to be in complete control. One of her house rules was that I was not to bring any food or drink inside and when one time she caught me breaking her rule, she nearly went berserk. I had brought up a small plastic container of chilled grapes as a little treat for Mother. When Esther discovered me now and then put a grape in Mutti's mouth, she warned me to never let her catch me doing anything like that again. "The whole place is beginning to smell like a urinal," she shouted.

The parting with Mutti at the end of my visits was usually very problematic because she invariably wanted to come with me. I kept devising new ways to make the break as quick and easy as possible without creating a scene. Sometimes I would pretend to go to the bathroom or the kitchen and then quickly exit the front door before Mutti realized I was gone. Mutti invariably sensed that I was about to leave and that was her cue to run to the front door, which was kept locked, and try opening it. Sometimes Nick came to restrain her so that I could get out the door. One time Mutti struggled with him and cried out, "*Laß mich los, das ist der Peter—das ist mein Bub*" [Let me go, this is Peter—he is my boy]. As I hurried towards the car, she looked after me through the small window in the front door and tearfully waved me goodbye.

Something that appeared to terrify Mutti in Esther's place was being taken upstairs where her bedroom was presumably located. I was never shown Mutti's room and, as a matter of fact, neither Mother nor I were ever taken upstairs during our visits after they bought their Lake Forest house. The layout and occupancy of the second floor rooms as well as the basement, where Esther conducted her mail order business, remained a mystery to me. I could only surmise, based on what I saw on Bonnie Brae in River Forest, that Dr. Murrin occupied the master bedroom suite and Esther and Nick had a smaller bedroom or each had a separate one.

When we passed the staircase, Mutti would invariably point to it and say "*furchtbar*" [terrible]. One time after exiting, I heard a commotion inside the house which made me look back in. What I saw much upset me but I could no nothing about it without putting my all-important visitation privileges at risk. Poor Mother was desperately clinging to the bottom post of the banister as Nick and Esther were dragging her upstairs. I suspect that they kept her locked up in her room for much of the day and night so that they did not have to continuously watch her especially since she was always ready to make a run for it. Being cooped up like that would have been a frightening experience for her especially at night.

On June 1, a Sunday and the day after her lawyers' withdrawal from the case, Esther faxed me a typewritten note advising me that because of our mother's frail health visitation needed to be reduced to one hour a week, to Tuesday from 12 noon to 1 p.m., and in the house or patio only. Needless to say, I did not think one hour a week to spend with a terminally ill parent was sufficient time. Esther had never liked the visitation schedule worked out by the two opposing attorneys and made part of the two Agreed Orders of March 11 and March 20. She claimed that because she was not present and had never given her approval, she was not bound by these rules.

Notwithstanding Esther's new visitation schedule, I kept returning to the house according to the schedule in the court order but was locked out except for the one hour on Tuesdays. I therefore suggested to Susan that we renegotiate the visitation schedule with Esther but my co-counsel insisted that, since Esther was not the negotiating type, going to court would yield more concrete results. I finally agreed and prepared a "Petition for Rule to Show Cause" why the Cross-Petitioner (Esther) should not be held in contempt by violating the court's order on all points including visitation rights, privacy requirements, and health care notification.

After about a month, Esther hired a new law firm headed by Janna Dutton, Esq. who was considered an expert in the field of elder law and guardianship matters. Susan and I met one of her associates, an attorney named Mike Wood, who was "of counsel" to the firm, at the June 25 hearing on my petition for a contempt of court citation. That hearing was rescheduled to July 10 to give Mike more time to prepare a response. Meanwhile, on June 20, I had filed the customary pre-trial "Request to Admit Facts and Genuineness of Documents," a document designed to allow the parties to stipulate which facts each could agree on and which were in dispute.

This lawyer, in his response of July 18, admitted only a few of the 30 statements of fact objecting to most as being vague, argumentative, not relevant to the proceeding, or outside his client's knowledge. Remarkably, Mr. Wood even denied the statement that on February 17, 1997, his client had entered our Oak Park residence in my absence and removed our mother to his client's place in Lake Forest. It was now clear to me that the upcoming trial would be a highly contentious one.

On July 3, Janna herself entered the fray by faxing the judge a "Cross-Petitioner's Rule to Show Cause" for non-payment of expenses. The total amount payable, according to this attorney, was $8,794 including $4,250 for room and board (at $1,000 per month), $1,408 for home nursing care, $982 for clothing, and $372 for hair care. In my response, filed with the court on July 10, I informed the judge that I had fully complied with the court order of March 20 by which I was to hold our mother's assets and reimburse Esther for any reasonable expenses in providing for her care.

Furthermore, I took the latter part of the Agreed Order to mean that expenses were to be paid from Mutti's monthly income. The problem was that there was nothing coming in. Soon after Esther had taken our mother to her place, she had contacted Social Security to have Mutti's benefit checks deposited in an account in Lake Forest. When the court put me in charge of our mother's assets, I asked Social Security to redirect these payments into an Oak Park account instead which would allow me access to the funds. Social Security demurred because this was not authorized by the beneficiary. Because there was now a dispute regarding who should receive our mother's benefit payments, Social Security stopped making payments altogether. For me this made payment of major invoices impossible without liquidation of our mother's assets. My argument was that such liquidation must await the outcome of the two-day hearing later in the month.

A Plenary Guardian

Thanks to Esther's new lawyers the remainder of July 1997 saw much progress in resolving our dispute over visitation rights. On July 9, the day before the scheduled hearing, I received a call from a Dr. Steven Fox of Wellspring Services in Chicago who told me that he was working with Janna as an independent and neutral consultant on health care issues involving the elderly. He had seen Mutti earlier and she looked good and well taken care of, he said. She did have difficulty walking and her deformed spine did not help any in that regard. Regarding her Alzheimer's, his theory was, he said, that the disease has seven stages the last one (7) being the most severe where a patient no longer recognizes himself/ herself in a mirror. He estimated Mutti to be in stage 5½ since she still knew her children besides being able to recognize herself. Hospice, the nursing care service for the terminally ill, had also been in, he said, but Esther was not interested because, she claimed, they would take charge of Mother and her care and that was not acceptable to her. I confirmed what he had been told, namely, that my major interest in the lawsuit was visitation rights and not guardianship.

Dr. Fox assured me that my visits were good for our mother and that I should have continuing visitation rights with quality time in private. As for excursions outside the house, he recommended a time not to exceed two hours. Longer trips, such as taking our mother back to Oak Park, were not recommended because of the health situation, the physical and emotional stress, and the possible after-effects the following day such as weakness and fatigue. He wanted to know who Dr. Murrin was and why Esther had taken our mother out of her home and I gave him a full account. In a parting word, he told me not to leave it to the courts to find solutions as they are only good at signing off on solutions already found. It seemed like good advice.

At the hearing on July 10, both parties were present including Esther, again accompanied by Dr. Murrin, and her Attorney Janna. Susan and I also got to meet Dr. Fox and we had a nice chat. After some negotiating, a new Agreed Order was entered with a revised visitation schedule and the inclusion of Dr. Fox as a neutral monitor of Mutti's health care needs. The new schedule gave me visitation rights of two hours each (11 a.m.-1 p.m.) on Tuesdays and alternate Sundays and one hour (10-11 a.m.) on Fridays for an average of four hours per week. At my discretion, I could take Mutti outside her new home on any visit as long as the sojourn was within the local area. Visits inside the house were to be held in the family room rather than in the parlor and were to be private and undisturbed.

In the new Agreed Order, Dr. Fox was given authority to review all of Mutti's medical records, contact any treating physician, and inform both parties of any change in her health care status. The new visitation schedule was a compromise between Esther, who still thought it was too much time (her ideal was no time at all), and me who would be satisfied with fewer hours than I had been allotted previously but now under more favorable conditions. At least now Esther could no longer claim that the visitation hours were worked out between the lawyers without her input or approval. As a further concession to Esther, I let her know through her attorneys that I would exercise my right to take our mother away from her new home only on Tuesdays. In this way she would have to get our mother ready only once a week. The two hours on Tuesdays would allow me just sufficient time to take Mutti out to lunch in a local restaurant.

It had been over two months since I had last taken Mother outside her new home when I picked her up on the following Tuesday, July 15. She was all dolled up and happy to see me. We drove south on Waukegan Road and found an Applebee's Restaurant at Deerbrook Mall where we had lunch. To my dismay, Mutti had little appetite and ate almost nothing even though I tried to spoon-feed her. She did, however, show a lively interest in her surroundings studying the other patrons, as she was wont to do, and offering her sometimes humorous comments.

On the road back to the house I told her I would be back Friday for another visit to which she replied, *"Du kannst jeden Tag kommen"* [You can come every day]. When I repeated the same remark back at the house, she emphatically said, *"Ich hab dir doch schon gesagt, du kannst jeden Tag kommen*" [I already told you, you can come every day]. That exchange was encouraging because it meant that, despite her advanced Alzheimer's, Mutti's memory was still fairly good. In fact, I began to question Dr. Fox's estimate of her place on his Alzheimer's scale. I felt that had he been able to communicate with Mother in German, he might have placed her more in the 4 to 5 range or better rather than between 5 and 6.

With the guardianship hearing just around the corner, it was time for Susan and me to finally decide on what we really wanted and then negotiate with opposing counsel and their client to see if we could reach an agreement. Neither side looked forward to a trial in open court since we knew it would be acrimonious and gut-wrenching for all concerned. Furthermore, the outcome would be very uncertain. If there was a trial, I felt fairly confident I would prevail because I had the law and the facts on my side. I could also count on the testimony of neighbors half a dozen of whom offered to come to court to testify on my behalf. On the other hand, Esther had that "Designation of Guardian" document which would serve as prima facie evidence that Mutti wanted Esther to be her guardian.

Among the guardianship options Susan and I discussed was having a public guardian appointed for Mutti. The big fear on my part was that this individual would simply put Mutti in a nursing home. That thought was abhorrent to me based on a personal experience. When I came to Virginia on my first job back in 1962, I had taken a room with a couple named Dickinson who had the woman's elderly mother living with them. This sweet little lady was still in good health and, in order to be of as little bother as possible to her daughter and son-in-law, stayed in her room day and night only to occasionally come out to go to the kitchen or bathroom. She much dreaded, I heard, being put in a nursing home. One day the couple did just that and when I visited the lady she wept bitterly saying that she wanted very much to die at home. Sadly, there was nothing I could do about it. Not long thereafter I heard that this poor soul did die in the nursing home and felt that her removal from her home most likely hastened her demise. That is when I vowed to myself that our mother would never end up in a nursing home as long as I had a say in the matter.

Susan and I explored other options that led to my final decision. Because she could take better care of our mother, especially now that she was terminally ill, Susan felt that it would be best if Esther became guardian of Mutti's person with me becoming guardian of her estate only. On further thought, however, being guardian of Mutti's estate made little sense now since the expectancy of a windfall from the estate of Mutti's sister was virtually nil. The case before the Geneva courts was lost, I knew, even though the final decision had not yet been rendered. Furthermore, holding on to Mutti's assets and receiving her income while Mutti lived with Esther would result in the sickening prospect of a continuing battle with Esther over receipts and disbursements.

My conclusion was that it was best for all concerned to let Esther become the plenary (full) guardian in return for visitation rights in accordance with the schedule already in place. When Janna called, I told her of my decision but had one caveat. How could I be assured that Esther would not simply cashier Mutti's assets and make them her own? Janna explained that she would have Esther agree to a monthly budget. Any changes would have to be approved by the court and if she did not adhere to it, she would be personally liable. That was satisfactory to me.

A preliminary hearing was scheduled for Tuesday, July 22, at 10 a.m. with the guardianship hearing to start at 2 o'clock that afternoon if no agreement had been reached. Susan and I appeared in court while Janna had sent Mike who, as usual, had not brought all the necessary papers. All we could do is tell the court that we had an agreement and the afternoon session was no longer necessary. Judge Dowdle smiled and was obviously pleased. The formal signing of the Agreed Order by the court was postponed to the afternoon. Since it was my visitation day, I drove to Lake Forest to see Mutti and when I returned home I got a call from Susan that Mike had shown up in court late and once more unprepared. When Susan grumbled about a third appearance, the judge agreed it would be unfair to our side and said he would sign the final Agreed Order the following day.

On that day, Wednesday, July 23, 1997, Judge Dowdle signed the final Agreed Order and also a statement informing Mutti (via her counsel) that she had been adjudged a disabled person and that a guardian had been appointed for her. Under this new Agreed Order Esther became the plenary guardian of our mother's person and estate. The earlier Agreed Order entered on July 10 regarding visitation rights was to remain in full force and effect. I, in turn, agreed to turn over to Esther all of our mother's financial assets including all bank accounts, stock certificates, and other personal property. Mutti's furniture and furnishings and other tangible property in our townhouse, of which I was to make an inventory, was to remain in my possession. Esther now crowed that she always knew the judge would rule in her favor while I began to fret whether I had abandoned Mutti to a lunatic.

The asset transfer and other provisions in the court order were accomplished without a hitch. All financial assets held by Mutti in her name, including bank accounts and stock certificates, were delivered to Janna's office on Tuesday, July 29. Mike, who signed for them, was obviously pleased and paid me a rare compliment. "Despite what Esther says," he told me, "I think you took very good care of your mother." These assets became part of an "Inventory" of the real and personal property Esther filed with the court and which the court formally approved on September 16.

The total value of Mutti's estate including the joint tenancy stock was given as just short of $60,000—a small amount on its face but large considering that Mutti's entire earned income from jobs she held between 1950 and 1970 was only $70,000 according to her Social Security records. Among her holdings were 700 shares of corporate, telephone and electric utility stock, 300 shares of which were in joint tenancy with me, a $12,000 certificate of deposit and her savings account with the Landesgirokasse in Stuttgart with a balance of 18,500 DM ($10,000).

Mutti's yearly income, exclusive of stock dividends and CD interest, was listed as $9,200 which included $532 in monthly Social Security benefits plus $234 from German social security (*Altersrente*) for a monthly total of $766. (The exact dollar amount of Mutti's *Altersrente* depended on the exchange rate when payment was due because the benefits were calculated in Euros and then converted to dollars prior to payment by check). In addition, $3,200 in unpaid benefits from Social Security were expected to come into the estate.

While the 300 shares in joint tenancy were listed in the Inventory of Mother's estate, I did not turn them over to Esther's attorneys in July, despite their protests. A major portion of this stock had been purchased with my own funds and I was not about to hand it over to opposing counsel without something in return. This stock, I told Mike, would be forthcoming as soon as the assets I had already turned over to him were spent and he could give me an accounting. When Susan and I terminated our retainer agreement as of July 31, she had warned me that in all likelihood more litigation lay ahead because Esther would continue her efforts to prevent me from seeing our mother despite any court orders. If that was the case, I wanted to retain some leverage which, in Esther's case, could only be money. Holding back on the joint tenancy stock turned out to be a fortuitous move.

A Continuing Battle

Now that Esther was plenary guardian of our mother, things calmed down somewhat but, as Susan had predicted, the battle was far from over. My Friday and alternate Sunday visits to Mutti now took place in the family room in the back of the house where I could be assured of more privacy. The room was the largest on the first floor and had a fireplace on the further end while one side held a floor to ceiling glass window that looked out on a small patio and enclosed backyard.

The room was sparsely furnished with old, dilapidated pieces of furniture that looked as if they had been picked up at a flea market. For exclusive Lake Forest, it was a sight to behold. The sofa along the wall opposite the window had arm rests in which parts of the upholstery were gone exposing the wood underneath. Another piece was an ancient club chair with foot stool which belonged to Frank while a smaller easy chair was used by Nick when he read his spy novels. A beat-up coffee table, a large-screen television set and a cheap floor rug completed the furnishings. When I came in the room, Mutti was usually lying on the sofa with her head supported by a thin pillow on the arm rest and her eyes closed. As I passed my finger playfully along the ridge of her nose, she would open her eyes and exclaim, "*Mein Peter.*"

The effects of Mother's Alzheimer's were mostly negative, of course, but there were even some consequences one could call beneficial. While Schwanheim and Stuttgart still meant something to her, when I mentioned Oak Park she had no reaction and I thought it best not to remind her of Mutti's Place. Hopefully, she had forgotten about her former home and thus be spared the grief of no longer being there.

Something else I did not dare mention to our mother was my suspicion that when Esther and her two companions took her away, they immediately delivered Tootsie to a veterinarian to have him put down. Despite Nick's repeated assurances that our pet was safe, I never saw him again. Mutti, who was always so close to her animals must have missed him terribly at first. Perhaps her Alzheimer's had mercifully let her forget about him. Tootsie had been in perfect health and a beloved member of our little family. This beautiful animal too, I felt, had a right to enjoy the brief life it had been given in this world.

Undoubtedly, the greatest benefit from Mother's Alzheimer's disease was that she was never aware of the other one—her deadly colorectal cancer. Neither Esther and her family nor I ever brought up the subject and most likely Mutti never suspected that she was terminally ill.

In the beginning, these post-arbitration visits with Mutti were mostly very enjoyable. She was no longer aware of the days and times of day and so when I showed up on a scheduled visit it was invariable a surprise and she would happily greet me with her familiar "*Mein Peter!*" My visits usually started with a series of opening questions about me such as where I now lived and how I got there to visit. She then got me involved in her crocheting which continued to keep her busy. The bundles of wool I brought her had to be unwound and rewound into a ball allowing her to easily feed the yarn to her crocheting needle. Hence, much of our time together was spent doing just that with Mutti holding the bundle between her two forearms and me winding the yarn into a ball.

I was surprised by how good she still was with her *Handarbeit* chores. Her creations, although no longer the useful items of former days such as sweaters or sofa pillow covers, showed much artistic talent. Among the pieces she proudly showed me was a large circular one with concentric bands of five different colors with openings spaced at regular intervals for holding ribbons.

Sometimes we just sat there on that miserable sofa holding hands, praying, talking, or looking through a photo album or picture book I had brought up. At times Esther and Nick would busy themselves in the backyard. I knew, of course, that her yard work allowed Esther to keep an eye on us despite the fact that my visits were to be private. Yet I still managed to put a piece of butterscotch candy, her favorite, in Mutti's mouth now and then even though that was strictly verboten by Esther's house rules.

Before leaving, I would say a prayer followed by the *Vaterunser* [Lord's Prayer] and was happy to find that Mutti still remembered the conclusion, "*Denn dein ist das Reich und die Kraft und die Herrlichkeit in Ewigkeit, Amen*" [For thine is the Kingdom, and the power, and the glory, for eternity, Amen] in which she usually joined in.

Naturally, I much looked forward to the Tuesday outside visits with Mutti but to get to see her I had to be very punctual. Once, after I was late arriving at the house because of an accident on Interstate 94, Esther faxed me that if I was not there within 15 minutes of the scheduled visitation time, the visit was automatically cancelled. It took me about an hour to get up there and to arrive precisely on time I would leave home early and park for about a quarter of an hour nearby before proceeding to the house. Mutti usually awaited me sitting patiently on a chair in the hallway.

Sometimes Esther had her very nicely dressed wearing an overcoat and scarf and clutching a handbag while at other times her attire was absolutely minimalist. Her good-looking and comfortable shoes of fine leather had been replaced with a rough-hewn, clumsy pair that looked a size too big for her. She usually wore no jewelry except for a huge faux diamond ring Esther had put on her finger. Sometimes she was with and sometimes without her dentures but it did not matter much because Mutti usually took them off and gummed her food.

The two of us stopped for lunch at different restaurants in the area including Applebee's and Bakers Square which had some dishes on their menus which were tasty and easy for her to chew. To my great alarm, however, she usually ate little and sometimes hardly touched her meal at all. I did not know whether she perhaps had a good breakfast or her disease was progressing and robbing her of her appetite. Her face became thin and she lost weight. Despite this, she continued to take a lively interest in her surroundings and especially in the other patrons. She even tried to impress me by demonstrating her continuing prowess with numbers by counting things like the light fixtures overhead or the number of tables in the place. She still could count up to at least 20.

The last two Tuesdays in September of 1997 turned out to be especially stressful in that Esther's old animosities resurfaced. On the first of the two,

Janna had faxed me that today's visit was off because Mutti had to be taken to her doctor's office to treat an upper respiratory infection. I asked Janna to keep me posted and when I did not hear from her all day, I drove up to see Mother anyway arriving at about four in the afternoon. Nick ushered me in telling me in a hushed voice that Mutti had pneumonia and was resting on the sofa. When Mutti heard me enter, she opened her eyes and said softly, "*Mein Bub* [my boy]."

As I knelt next to our mother and held her hand, Esther suddenly burst into the room shouting, "I don't want anybody in the house when I'm not here—there are important papers here which nobody should see and I mean nobody." She then began to berate me. "Mutti was well until you came Friday and brought up the germs," she shouted, and "this is not a hospital or a nursing home" and "you can go to court anytime you want to and I'll meet you there until you are broke." My visits were only upsetting to Mother, Esther claimed. She then mumbled, "You don't belong up here." In the meantime, Mutti had sat up on the sofa and began to sob. Frank made a cameo appearance to say that he and Esther were on their way to a talk on Alzheimer's. The two soon left.

As I tried to calm Mutti down, she pulled me towards her, went through my hair and kissed me tenderly saying, "*Ich liebe dich.*" [I love you]. It was an outpouring of affection I was not used to. She looked drawn and fatigued and I had her again lie down on the sofa to rest. "*Laß mich doch mitgehen*" [Let me come along] she pleaded and then wistfully added "*dann wär ich doch frei*" [then I would be free]. With Esther occupied with her business venture and the Geneva litigation, Nick was mostly in charge of Mutti's care and on leaving, I entreated him to look out for her. He promised he would and I think he did. Mutti had gotten a shot of penicillin, he told me, and showed me a vial of antibiotics which he was giving her as prescribed by her doctor.

On the following day, I decided to get an independent professional opinion concerning my visits and called Dr. Fox. I told him about Esther's latest tirade and asked him if he thought that my visits were emotionally damaging to our mother as Esther had claimed. Should I, and could I, just stay away and leave Mutti to her fate? Dr. Fox described my sister as a very sick person and advised me to continue seeing our mother regardless of what Esther wanted. He believed that my regular visits were a great source of comfort to our mother that contributed to her well-being and happiness. His advice was reassuring and I decided to continue my visits no matter what obstacles were thrown in my way. Presumably Esther based her allegation on what Dr. Murrin had told her but I did not think that his opinion was a reliable guide in this matter because of his personal involvement. It could be expected that he would tell Esther anything she wanted to hear and do whatever she wanted him to do.

A Heated Exchange

The last day of September of 1997, a Tuesday, was a day to remember because on that day Esther must have decided to have it out with me. On the previous Friday Mutti had made a nearly complete recovery. In fact, she was in rare form—bubbly, talkative, funny, and obviously very happy to see me. So when I came up to take our mother to lunch, I was surprised when Esther claimed that Mutti still had a fever and needed to stay in. That was alright with me and I headed for the family room for an inside visit. Mutti and I sat on the sofa next to each other holding hands and talking when Esther suddenly burst into the room and claimed I was sitting too close to our mother and to move. I reminded her that my visits were to be private by court order and refused to move. She told me I could go to court anytime I wanted to since, as Mutti's guardian, she could now have all her legal expenses paid out of Mother's estate.

When I suggested that could be changed requiring her to foot the bill, she started a long tirade only interrupted now and then by some retorts of my own. For the first time, Esther revealed what was bothering her and I got an insight into the workings of her mind which I concluded was a very sick one despite being under the care of two psychiatrists. Throughout our nearly 2-hour exchange she kept repeating, "This discussion never happened—there are no witnesses." Mutti listened stoically and spoke up only once saying, "*Laß mich doch ein bischen an die frische Luft gehen*" [Let me go out into the fresh air a little] but when I reminded her that she was still not well and needed more rest, she relaxed and stayed put.

Esther began her harangue by telling me that I had never amounted to anything. I had four degrees and was now working in a furniture store.

I had been let go by my company in New York because I was paranoid and could never hold on to a job. I told her that at least I had an education while she lied about hers claiming to have a chemistry degree when, in fact, she had never gone beyond 8th grade.

Most stunning was her allegation that I had lived off our mother for the past 10 years. That was, of course, a blatant lie because I had always had more than a sufficient income to support myself. Furthermore, she claimed that I had once called her a bastard (which I never did). It was I who was the bastard, she said. Her father and mother were properly married when she was born, she claimed. She threatened me with a new lawsuit and that she would be after me until all I had was spent on lawyers and I was broke.

In my reply, I told Esther that I intended to sue her for elder abuse by forcibly removing our mother from her long-time home and transported her to her lair in Lake Forest causing our Alzheimer's afflicted mother irreparable trauma. Her sole purpose for doing so, I told her, was to get her hands on the money Mutti was expected to inherit from our Aunt Emmi. Inexplicably, Esther did not respond. She knew it was true.

Among Esther's other allegations were that I had lied to my lawyer when I told her that I needed to keep my legal expenses down because of my limited financial resources when, in fact, they were very substantial. Surprisingly, she quoted me my net worth that was not far off. According to Esther, she had received a call from Susan in June wanting to know about my financial situation and that the two had exchanged much useful information. She had passed it on to her lawyers, she said.

I replied that at least I paid my attorney, while hers, I had heard, were not so lucky. She owed her lawyers nothing, she claimed, except $800 for copying my financial records. She refused to pay them, she said, because she had not authorized the information request and the lawyers told her the documents proved to be of no use in the case. Her lawyers had asked her to come by their office to pick them up which she refused to do. "I'm not stupid," she said. "No, stupid you are not but evil," was my reply. "Are you evil, Esther?" I asked her and she replied with an emphatic "yes." Two more times I said to her, "Are you evil, Esther?" and each time she answered with a resounding "yes." Remarkably, she did not try to explain herself.

The heated exchange also revealed why Esther had called me a murderer nearly four months earlier after we first learned that our mother had been diagnosed with colon cancer. According to Esther, Dr. Khan was incompetent and she would sue him for malpractice and ruin his reputation and career at Oak Park Hospital. "To save his skin," she said, he would testify that he had told me on several occasions to take Mother to a specialist to have her colon examined but that I had neglected to do so. This allegation was, of course, a malicious lie because Dr. Khan had never mentioned colon cancer during any of our visits let alone ordered a colonoscopy for either one of us.

Of special interest to me during this confrontation were Esther's future plans for me especially when I heard they called for my quick demise by murder. She told me in graphic detail how she would eliminate me using "hired killers who worked quickly and efficiently and left no trace." She could easily afford the $½ million fee for the hit men plus overseas travel expenses. "My parting word to you is—watch your back," she said.

"You have a killer instinct, Esther," I said to her to which she replied that one had to kill to survive and by killing me there would be "one less to share the wealth with." When I again reminded Esther that the only reason she had brought our mother to Lake Forest was for the money, she did not deny it but said money was needed for many things including hired killers. Her response to my suggestion that she consider her own mortality, was, "Ha-ha, I'm in perfect health—I [will] live forever."

Esther promised to make life even more miserable for me. The best advice she could give me is to get out of town—and fast. "Are you going to call your lawyer now?" she asked knowing full well that I had released Susan two months earlier. "No," I replied " I'm going to call your lawyer." "Oh, to get information," she said. "On the contrary," I replied, "to give information."

When she again bragged of having been appointed guardian by the court, I reminded her once more that she had become guardian when I agreed to it and not because the judge was on her side. She was not worried about being charged with elder abuse because she and the doctor had credibility while I had none, she claimed. I told her that, in my opinion, neither she nor Frank could count on much credibility in a court of law.

When my two hours were up, I headed for the front door with Esther and Mutti following me. As we were passing through the adjoining kitchen, Frank was sitting in the breakfast area having his usual steak lunch. I was shocked to see him look so haggard and rundown and wondered if he might be gravely ill. Esther immediately let him know what I had said about his credibility. "Did you say that?" Frank wanted to know. Much embarrassed, I replied, "Doctor, I don't want to argue with you." "You are so ignorant," was his response. I decided to hold my tongue. If that was his opinion, so be it. While I saw him only two or three more times, we never spoke to each other again. Presumably, he stayed in his upstairs room during most of my subsequent visits.

When we got to the front door Esther, still mad as a hornet, screamed at me, "Get out, get out" but the door was locked and she had trouble finding the keys. When she finally located them and I managed to affect my escape, Mutti nearly slipped away too but Esther got a hold of her just in time. With Esther standing beside her fuming, ever spunky Mutti rapped on the door's window and waved me good-bye. I really wished Mutti did not make such an overt display of her feelings since it was an obvious embarrassment to Esther who might take it out on her after I had left.

A Calming Of Emotions

My visits during the remaining months of 1997 went fairly smoothly. Two things happened after my last visit that temporarily put Esther in a more benign mood. One was that the financial matters were finally settled. At the beginning of October, Esther received a lump sum payment from Social Security for six months of benefits which that agency had been holding back because of the custody dispute. She also received Mutti's monthly income of nearly $800 in American and German social security benefits besides her interest and dividend income. Secondly, I had written Janna giving her a complete rundown of my Tuesday visit including Esther's death threats. I am sure that either she or Mike had a serious talk with Esther about possible consequences and told her to desist or else risk being dropped as a client.

Soon after that heated exchange, I purchased a microcassette recorder which I carried clandestinely on my person during subsequent indoor visits just in case there would be more confrontations. As an added benefit, it allowed me to memorialize my subsequent visits. Fortunately, Esther now stayed away letting Nick usher me in. Still, her terrible anger was not completely assuaged and she found yet another way to torment me. Since I was not allowed to park in their driveway, I was obliged to do so on Northcliffe Way. It took a flat tire after one visit and two more nails in my right rear tire after another before I realized that my sister and brother-in-law were strewing nails where I normally parked possibly even while I was visiting. I consequently left my little Toyota in random places some distance from the house which solved the problem.

It was just too bad that Mutti never came to feel at home in Esther's place. On the Sunday before Thanksgiving, as I was about to leave, Mutti again tearfully pleaded with me to let her come along. As we were walking towards the front door through the kitchen and she saw Esther standing by the sink, she suddenly stopped and calling out to her, "Elle, Elle" (she must have temporarily forgotten her daughter's name) tried to pull me over towards her when Esther shouted back, "I will only talk to him in court." As on other occasions Mutti was hoping to get us to make up as she must have realized that it was the only way for her to get out of the terrible fix she found herself in. Her prospects of being free once more shattered, poor Mutti was again in tears.

Why had Mother not better adjusted after all these months? I asked myself and concluded that it was the chilly atmosphere and lack of warmth in her new home. Mutti, now more than ever in need of love, compassion, and companionship, received nothing of the kind. By nature, Esther was cold and completely lacking in natural affection and was simply unable to respond. Also, it was no secret that Esther was given to sudden angry outburst (I had heard of some that had occurred in places outside the house) and I am sure poor Mutti found herself the target of a screaming diatribe whenever she did or said something that angered or frustrated her daughter. Last but not least, in the evening Mutti continued to be hustled upstairs and locked up in her little bedroom for the night which was something that must have terrified her.

In conformance with my court-approved visitation schedule, I continued seeing Mutti on Fridays and alternate Sundays in the family room and taking her to lunch on Tuesdays. I always addressed her not with Mutti but the more gentle *Mütterchen* [little mother] or *mein Kind* [my child]. On my arrival, I would say something like, "*Du bist mein Mütterchen, ich bin dein Peter, und ich hab dich lieb, gell?*" [You are my mom, I am your Peter, and I love you, isn't it so?] to which she would reply "ja" or "*Das weiß ich doch*" [I already know that]. My introduction was usually followed by many questions: "*Wo wohnst du jetzt?*" [Where do you live now?], "*Wo ist das denn?*" [Where is that?], "*Kann ich da mal vorbeigehen?*" [Can I come by there once?], "*Mit wehm wohnst du jetzt?*" [With whom do you live now?], "*Bist du jetzt verheiratet?*" [Are you married now?], "*Wie bist du hierher gekommen?*" [How did you get here?], "*Was ist heute?*" [What day is this?], "*Wo warst du so lange?* [Where were you so long?].

By this time it had been nearly a year since she had been taken to Lake Forest and she probably no longer had a clear memory of Mutti's Place. Wenn I tried to explain to her that I still lived in Oak Park where we used to live together, her usual reply was "*Das kann ich nicht verstehen*" [I can't understand that]. She did, however, mention Schwanheim now and then. When I told her that her longtime friend and neighbor Dolly McNamara had passed away she had no reaction. Similarly, she no longer seemed to remember Jule Kuchenbeisser in Graben when I told her of his passing. She did, however, mention Tootsie once and when I asked her if she thought that I looked like a cat she could not stop laughing.

We kept up our normal Sunday routine during which I watched Mutti crochet her latest creations. and keep her entertained. In developing our visitation schedule, Susan and I forgot to make arrangement for holidays and hence this year I could spend neither Thanksgiving (Thursday), nor Christmas Eve (Wednesday), nor Christmas Day (Thursday), with Mother and had to contend with the two following Fridays. Still, my visits on both days turned out to be very pleasant. For Christmas I had gotten Mutti a cashmere sweater from Marshall Field's and a whimsical Mickey Mouse wristwatch with a red armband. Mutti was absolutely delighted with the latter and continuously raised her arm to admire it. The ever stern Esther, however, seemed to see nothing amusing in my gift and I never saw the watch on Mutti again.

For a change of pace, from mid-November on I brought Mutti to Denny's in Highland Park for our Tuesday lunch outing where I tried to coax her into eating her meal but with varying degrees of success. I would choose a dish that was easy to chew and digest and spoon-feed her constantly saying "*Mündchen auf*" [open up] and admonishing her to eat or she would fall ill. Sometimes she would finish almost her entire meal while at other times barely touch it or even spit out what she had eaten. In retrospect, it was absolutely foolish of me to virtually force-feed her when I knew she had colon cancer. Nevertheless, she was always happy to see me and on my last visit of the year said to me, *Es ist schön wenn wir zusammen sind* [It's nice when we are together]. I could hardly agree more.

A Final Year

When Mother was diagnosed with terminal colon cancer on May 2, 1997 she was given just six months to live and so it was apparent to everyone that the following year would be a pivotal one in her life. On my visit the day after New Year's 1998, a Friday, she was still in good spirits. When I awakened her on the family room sofa, her face lit up and sitting up she started to chatter and giggle. She asked the usual questions about where I was living now and how I had come. When I left, Steffi let me out. She had flown in from Washington, DC for Christmas and was ready to return to her government job there.

Just two days later, during my Sunday visit, Mutti showed the first sign of having abdominal pains. She rubbed her tummy and said "*Ich hab's am Magen*" [It's my stomach] when I asked her what was wrong. On the following Tuesday, she seemed better again and I took her to lunch at Denny's. To my great disappointment, however, I could get her to eat only a bowl of her favorite cream of potato soup with bacon but not her pot roast with mashed potatoes.

Mutti was cheerful again when I saw her the following Friday in the family room but Esther and Frank, sitting in the breakfast area, seemed in a somber mood as they whispered to each other. A big article in the *Chicago Tribune* that morning eulogized the death the previous Monday (January 5) of Dr. John Hanni at age 75 following heart surgery. With his passing, Esther lost her psychiatrist of many years and Frank his best friend.

The new year, as usual, brought the flu to Chicagoland and we were all infected including, unfortunately, Mutti. When I took her to lunch on the following Tuesday, it turned out to be the last take-out visit with her. As before, all she would take in was her favorite cream of potato soup. On my visit in the family room on the following Friday, I found her on the sofa breathing heavily and coughing. She seemed unusually fragile and weak but that did not deter her from doing her *Handarbeit*. Much of what she said was pure gibberish and she knew it. In fact, we both had a good laugh about it.

The next day, I received a fax from Esther that Mutti could not be taken out on Tuesday because of an "upper respiratory infection." I became quite alarmed when on each succeeding visit her cough had become more severe. She was always happy to see me and usually wanted to get up but I persuaded her to remain on the sofa. As much as it irked me to see her lie on that dilapidated piece of chunk with her head resting on a thin pillow that covered the nearly bare arm of the sofa, I dared not say anything for fear of enraging Esther and giving her cause to unilaterally cancel future visits.

When by the last Tuesday in January, Mutti's condition had not improved, I called Dr. Fox to tell him of my concern. He wanted to know how long she had been coughing and when I told him at least 10 days, he said that was unusually long. He was going to check if she was being treated and get back to me. Next day he gave me the disturbing news that Mutti had been diagnosed with pneumonia. According to Dr. Fox, he had been able to talk only to Nick who had been given the job of caring for Mother. Neither Esther nor Frank were available.

Mutti's illness was obviously of grave concern and on the following Thursday, I contacted Mike who confirmed the diagnosis and told me she had been taken to Dr. Breger in Highland Park twice and given antibiotics. I wanted to know if Esther and Frank had taken off for Virginia, as she had planned for years, and left Mutti in the care of Nick. Evidently not. In fact, Mike confided in me that Frank was seriously ill and had entered Lake Forest Hospital. He would not tell me the nature of his illness and asked me not to mention anything to Esther.

The next day, after seeing Mutti, I had a long phone conversation with Dr. Fox about what we should do next. Esther had finally called him that morning, he said, and told him that with both her mother and Dr. Murrin being sick and Mutti having become incontinent, she is close to burnout. According to Dr. Fox, Mutti's physician was doing a good job regarding her pneumonia—he had seen her twice and put her on a powerful new antibiotic. The test had apparently been done at Highland Park Hospital and Dr. Breger wanted Mutti to be admitted but that Esther had strongly objected.

Dr. Fox told me that Esther planned to place our mother in a nursing home. I replied that I did not think that was a good idea and Dr. Fox heartily agreed. He said Mutti's removal to Lake Forest had caused her immense trauma and contributed to her mental and physical deterioration. Another such move could be fatal, he said. The doctor expressed concern that, in her condition, Mutti had to be taken to her upstairs bedroom via a long flight of stairs. I suggested a hospital bed on the first floor to which Dr. Fox replied that he had already proposed that to Esther plus some in-house nursing help. Despite the fact that Medicare would pay for both, Esther had not acted on the idea, he said. He planned to again discuss the matter with Attorney Mike.

The first day of February was a Sunday and a scheduled visitation day. Nick let me in and told me to follow him upstairs. It was the first time I was allowed to see where Mutti spent the night and now apparently also the day. She was in bed and still coughing heavily but happy to see me. The bedroom was in a corner of the house overlooking the driveway. It was bright and cheery but tiny with just enough space for a twin-size bed, a couple of small chests and an upholstered chair. According to Nick, this was Steffi's room when she came home for visits. A portable toilet next to the bed confirmed my suspicion that Mutti was locked in her room during the night and not let out to use the bathroom. Understandably, this was done for safety reasons. If she would have been allowed to leave her room at will, Mother could have become disoriented and fallen injuring herself. She might even have tried to go downstairs to make her escape and fallen down the stairs.

I now came to realize why Mutti was so terrified when she was hustled upstairs in the evening. The nightly routine of being locked up must have been a continuing source of trauma for her. Just being confined in a close space would have been frightening enough but she must also have realized that in case of a fire she could easily be trapped. In fact, that was a fear she harbored even in Mutti's Place. I sat with her the full two hours while now and then feeding her some orange juice that had been left in the room.

Meanwhile, Nick busied himself downstairs while Esther was presumably at the hospital staying with Frank.

The following day, Monday, February 2, Mutti was admitted to Lake Forest Hospital. A fax from Mike gave me the news with instructions to contact either the hospital or Dr. Breger for more information. When I called the hospital after work, the nurse on duty told me that Mutti was alright and getting antibiotics but that she was uncooperative, would not eat, and seemed disoriented. On my scheduled visit next morning, Mutti was sitting in a wheelchair outside her room near the nurses station holding court. Several nurses and fellow patients stood and sat around her as she entertained them with her happy chatter and comic antics. She had evidently been brought into the hallway because she was afraid to stay in her room by herself.

A nurse now wheeled her inside her room for my visit. Mutti seemed content but ate almost nothing of her lunch. When I left in the afternoon so she could rest and sleep a little, she became agitated and wanted to leave with me. On my return in the evening, she was in the same place outside her room with Esther in attendance who immediately left when Mutti saw me and called out my name.

We had a nice visit when Mutti said she was "*müde*" [tired] and wanted to go to bed. A nurse wheeled her from her old room to another one nearby in outpatient oncology where she and an aid got Mutti in bed and connected IV tubes to her hands to keep her hydrated. All was well until I got ready to leave when Mutti almost went berserk. She started tearing away the adhesives holding the tubes in place and tried to rip away the strap across her chest holding her down to keep her from falling out of bed while shouting at me to help her get up. A nurse finally arrived to calm her down with some sedatives and replace her IV tubes as I hurriedly left for home.

Although I had no visitation rights on the following two days, I went to the hospital after work anyway hoping to avoid Esther who might possibly create a scene. My Wednesday visit was especially fortuitous. In order to prevent a repeat performance of the day before, the nurses had tied both of Mutti's wrists to the side of the bed while using a heavy belt across her abdomen to hold her in place. When I came in the room, she was struggling and unable to move. More alarmingly, her fight was for air which I only realized when she gasped, "*Ich krieg keine Luft*" [I can't breathe]. I then noticed that while her back was lying flat, her head was propped up by pillows and bent forward which compressed her chest and cut off the air supply. When I pulled her up and repositioned her pillows, it brought instant relief making her exclaim, *"Du kriegst alles"* [You get everything]. Strangely she added, *"Wenn ich nicht mehr leben will, dann sterbe ich."* [If I don't want to live anymore, I will die].

Rather than confront any of the nurses and create a scene, I decided to fax Esther and let that battle-axe do a number on, what seemed to me, a harebrained nursing staff. Esther's frivolous and uncaring reply shocked me. I was to direct all faxes and phone calls to Attorney Mike. During my visit on the following evening, a nurse was feeding her a liquid dinner and, to my delight, Mother ate it all. I just missed Nick, who had been sitting with her, the nurse told me. The good news was that Mutti's lungs were clear again. The nursing staff continued to wheel her into the hallway during the day and giving her a sedative in the evening before bedtime. By Sunday, Mutti was her old self again—she took in some food, was jovial and even watched some television. Her IV tubes had been removed the day before and she was due for release the following day—exactly one week after entering the hospital.

While Mother's cure from pneumonia had lifted my spirits, the remaining three weeks or so of February brought much tension and anxiety. Mutti had been returned home and put in bed for further recuperation. When on each of my scheduled visits I found Mutti in the same place and position, I became increasingly alarmed. She was flat on her back lethargically staring at the ceiling and hardly took note of me. Her bed smelled of urine and indeed, when I reached in, her sheets were wet. There was no indication that she was given anything to eat or drink. On one occasion I noticed a car entering the driveway and three nurses, one male and two female, get out and bolt up the stairway. To my dismay, they did not come to Mutti's room but had evidently been called to tend to Dr. Murrin who was back home.

After ten days of this, I sounded the alarm by phoning and faxing everybody I thought could possibly help. Dr. Breger told me that he had not seen Mutti since she left the hospital and had asked Esther to bring her to his office but that she had evidently decided to take her to a doctor in Lake Forest. He was not in favor of such fragmented care, he said, and considered himself out of the picture. He would, however, be happy to continue treating Mutti if Esther so desired. To keep things in perspective, said Dr. Breger, he did not expect Mother to live much longer and certainly not to 1999.

Mother's physician at the hospital, I was told, was a Dr. David Slivnick of North Shore Oncology of Libertyville. When I called him, he informed me that he had been seeing Mother at the hospital as had his associate Dr. Robert Mandal. He had told Esther at the hospital that he wanted to see Mutti in two weeks but that she had not made an appointment. According to Dr. Slivnick, Mutti's pneumonia/bronchitis was of a mild form and they had kept her at the hospital a little longer than was needed. He agreed with me that it was not a good idea for Mutti to be kept in bed this long.

My main contact was Dr. Fox who went to bat for me towards the end of the month after my fax to him describing Mutti's condition. He had, in the meantime, talked with Dr. Slivnick who told him that he really knew little about Mother and had only become involved because he was treating Dr. Murrin. (Since Dr. Slivnick was an oncologist, this told me that Frank's illness was probably cancer also). Dr. Slivnick had proposed a house call, according to Dr. Fox, but Esther had not given her approval.

Dr. Fox then informed me of Esther's plans to place Mutti in the Westmoreland Nursing Home next to Lake Forest Hospital although he did not think that was the ideal place. I informed him that I was no longer opposed to a nursing home for Mutti because I did not think she was getting the care she needed at home and was just wasting away. A good nursing facility, we agreed, would lead to an improved quality of life during her remaining days. Dr. Fox subsequently talked with Dr. Breger who agreed that Mutti should not be laid up in bed this long and suggested a nursing home even though she would have to get a new doctor because he did not make house calls. Dr. Fox also warned me that Esther would again attempt to limit my visitation with Mutti even in a nursing home.

On her lawyers' advise, said Dr. Fox, he had no direct contact with Esther. He said he would now write Janna and Mike to put the ball in their court. In his letter of February 26, with copies to Esther and me, Dr. Fox wrote:

I concur with Drs. Slivnick and Breger that Mrs. Zell's physical condition and functional abilities have deteriorated. As a result, the type and extent of personal and medical care needs have changed. I would recommend an immediate placement of Mrs. Zell into a certified (Medicaid) long term care nursing facility. I believe her condition will continue to deteriorate unnecessarily if she does not immediately receive 24-hour nursing care.

Attorney Mike called me the following day to discuss Dr. Fox's letter and other matters. He did not understand parts of it and would call Dr. Fox back, he said. He confirmed that Esther planned to place Mutti in Westmoreland Nursing Center and said that Dr. Fox now agreed with Esther that it was a good choice. Esther had been having problems with Mutti lately, he said, like getting her to eat and out of bed. A nurse had been to the house to see Mutti, Esther told him.

Mike also volunteered some confidential information. He said that after Esther took Mutti to Lake Forest, she never wanted me to be able to see our mother again. She had recently asked him to petition the court to further curtail my visitation rights. He prepared the petition, he said, but told Esther that she must bring him a sworn affidavit from a treating physician in support of the petition before he would take it to court because as a son I had an absolute right to see my mother. Esther never produced the affidavit, he said. He suggested that having Mutti in a nursing home would also make it easier for me to have more time with her. That was one reason I was now eager to have that happen, I told him.

On the financial side, Mike said that Mutti's present assets would suffice for just two months in the nursing home and if she lived longer they would have to petition the court for the remaining assets, i.e., the stock certificates held in joint tenancy with me. The news that all of Mutti's life savings, which I had turned over to Esther at the end of July of the previous year, plus the lump sum payment from Social Security, and her monthly income from various sources, including American and German social security benefit payments, were already close to being spent caught me somewhat by surprise. I told Mike that I would be happy to release the remaining funds provided the guardian gave me some sort of accounting. That would pose no problem, said Mike, and would be forthcoming along with the request.

In A Nursing Home

Mother was admitted to Westmoreland Nursing Center on the last day of February 1998. For years I had vowed that she would never end her days in a nursing home but on this day I signed an Agreed Order by fax giving my consent because I knew it was the right thing to do. Mutti would now get the around-the-clock professional care she needed and deserved and not die prematurely from neglect. In addition, I would presumably be able to see our mother as often and as long as I wanted. Westmoreland was conveniently located only a 3-minute drive down the road from Esther's house and on the grounds of Lake Forest Hospital.

Shortly after Mutti entered Westmoreland, Esther faxed Dr. Fox that she no longer wanted him to be involved. When he sent her his bill via her attorneys, she wrote at the bottom that it was the last one she was paying and whoever wanted to continue using his services should pay for them. Dr. Fox's unilateral dismissal was, of course, in direct violation of the Agreed Order signed by Judge Dowdle back in July 1997.

March 1 happened to be a Sunday and a scheduled visitation day and hence I came up for my fist visit at the home. The 2-story dark red brick building appeared gloomy and forbidding on the outside but the inside was bright and cheery. I was delighted to see Mother sitting in a wheelchair fully dressed, the first time in six weeks, in the second-floor hallway near the nurses station. I had brought her a large bouquet of pink mini-carnations with baby breath and she was delighted to see me. Esther had also brought over Mutti's small (13") Sony TV set with a VCR belonging to Esther which allowed the two of us to enjoy a *Three Tenors* and other videotapes.

Mother's large private room, number 222, was airy and nicely furnished with a hospital bed, a tall armoire, a chest of drawers, an easy chair, a round coffee table surrounded by four club chairs, and a long, narrow desk with chair facing one wall. A multi-section picture window, two sections of which could be opened to the outside, looked out on the well-kept grounds. Adjoining this room was an extra-large tiled bathroom. The place reminded me of a comfortable studio apartment minus the usual kitchenette. Patients were under the care of a large staff of full-time and part-time nurses and nurses assistants. Some more affluent people hired private caregivers who stayed with their loved ones in their rooms and took them out only for group activities.

I was hoping that Sunday's visit would be the model for subsequent ones and I could visit with Mutti undisturbed for as long as I wished. My second visit on the following Tuesday showed that my expectation was a fantasy. I had come up in the morning and found Mutti in bed watching television. A couple of nurses assistants took her to the bathroom where they washed and dressed her and put her in her wheelchair. It was about 2 p.m. as Mutti and I were watching some travelogues, when Esther suddenly stormed into the room shouting, "Out! Out!" According to her attorneys, she proclaimed, my Tuesday visitation hours remained as always from 11 a.m. to 1 p.m..

When I ignored her, she desperately tried to get Mike on the phone but he was unavailable. (I always pictured poor Mike trying to hide in a closet whenever Esther called). "I saw the letter you wrote to Dr. Fox," she shouted, and "I'll haul you into court and sue you for defamation of character until you're financially ruined and have lost everything including your house." I told Esther to do whatever she pleased but that I would be staying with Mutti another hour just the same. She kept up her tirade but finally left. Mutti had remained calm and paid no attention to the ruckus.

To me the Agreed Order of July 10, 1997 was to ensure my visits were on a firm schedule and not arbitrary as to date and time. This would allow Esther to plan for my visits and cause the least disruption in their daily routine. With Mutti now in a nursing home and that home open to legitimate visitors at any time during day and night, my contention was that my visitation rights were no longer restricted to those agreed on. In fact, in a phone conversation I had with Dr. Fox after he informed me of his dismissal he told me that, in his opinion, I should not be limited to the visitation schedule agreed on prior to Mutti's entry into Westmoreland and that he would be happy to testify in support of my position in court.

Besides, Esther's lawyer had assured me that I would get more time with Mother once she was in a nursing home and which was one reason I had agreed to the move. If Esther had a problem with that, she could go to court and tell it to the judge. While I did not limit myself to the visitation times in the Agreed Order, I did adhere to the days, namely, Tuesdays and Fridays and alternate Sundays.

March 6, a Friday, was a very special day for Mutti because it was her 89th birthday and, sadly, I knew it would be her last. When I arrived at Westmoreland in the morning, Mutti was nicely dressed in her blue silk dress sitting in her wheel chair in the hallway watching the big-screen TV. I was taken aback by the cool and indifferent way she greeted me. I wheeled her into her room and when I gave her my birthday card, she flung it across the room. She ignored the big bouquet of roses and my gifts—a robe, a bed jacket, and some nighties from Marshall Field's.

Esther had seen Mutti earlier, according to Judy, a nurse's aid, and I suspected that she had bad-mouthed me as she was wont to do. Perhaps she had told our mother that I was responsible for her being put in a nursing home making our mother feel that I had abandoned her. To my disgust, Esther had taken home her VCR so that we could no longer watch music and other tapes together. Judy had some confidential news for me. Dr. Murrin, she said, too was staying at Westmoreland and in a room on the first floor directly below Mutti's.

To my big relief, my Sunday visit went much better. This time, Mutti was delighted to see me. I was upset when I found the bouquet of flowers I had brought Mutti on her birthday in the trash can where Esther had apparently dumped them. Also my birthday gifts were gone. Monica, another nurse's aid, told me that earlier that day Esther had taken our mother to the first floor and there Mutti, wanting to stand up in her wheelchair, had fallen backwards bumping her head on the floor. Fortunately, she was not seriously hurt but they had put her in bed where I found her.

Monica also informed me that Esther planned to move Mutti to the first floor into Dr. Murrin's room and bring him back home. Per Monica, all the nurses and caregivers on the second floor love Mutti. She has a great sense of humor, she said, and is very sweet and loving. The staff all call her "grandma," she said.

Friday the 13th sounds ominous but that was the day Esther and the nursing staff chose to move Mutti into the room vacated by Dr. Murrin after he had been taken home. This new room was a replica of the one she had been in and its location on the first floor was preferable because it was in proximity to the Solarium where most group activities took place. Mutti was in a delightful mood and very talkative although much of what she said was pure gibberish. She was obviously happy to see me. As before, I stayed longer than the one hour allotted me by the Agreed Order hoping Esther would leave us in peace.

On my previous visit on Tuesday I had met with the Westmoreland Nursing Center staff, namely, Karen Forchette, the general manager, and Ginger Seff, the director of long-term care to give them some pertinent information about myself, Mutti, and Dr. Fox. Most importantly, I asked them to notify me or Dr. Fox in case of any emergency. They both assured me that they would do so. According to Ginger, the cost for a stay at Westmoreland was $190 a day or $5,700 per month. I also learned that Westmoreland was not a Medicare approved facility. Esther had instructed them, I was told, to move Mutti into Dr. Murrin's room and get him ready to be taken home.

Nurse Lori later confided in me that Dr. Murrin had a brain aneurysm and had to be carried out on a stretcher. The staff was quite shocked by the whole thing but Esther told them that Westmoreland was not good enough for the doctor and he would get better care at home. According to Bonnie, another caregiver, Dr. Murrin had been operated on for a brain tumor at the hospital next door. Esther vainly attempted to make him walk and just could not understand why he was unable to do so, she said. Esther had told them the doctor was her uncle.

Esther used her position as Mutti's plenary guardian to exercise complete control over her. The staff at Westmoreland was intimidated by her and all but stood at attention when she entered the premises. One of the first things she did was to post a long set of instructions on the armoire door for the guidance of Mutti's caregivers. The posting was signed "Esther Rose Holzman, Daughter and Guardian." One of the instructions was that Mutti was not to wear makeup or have any other cosmetic treatment done to her. Esther also went to great lengths to let the staff know of the special relationship between her and our mother and especially that I had no standing. When during one of my visits a caregiver tried to put in a good word for me, Esther said to her, "He is not my brother—I don't know where my mother picked him up."

At Esther's behest, room 122 had a completely Spartan look being completely devoid of any ornamentation or amenities. Thus, for example, she wanted no flowers or plants in Mutti's room. This was in sharp contrast to the homey rooms of other patients which were filled with photographs of loved ones, favorite pictures and artifacts, plants and flowers, and stuffed animals. The only item of a personal nature Esther allowed in the room was a Xerox copy of a photograph showing her as a small girl standing next to our ailing Oma, seated in a chair, shortly before she passed away. Esther put the image in a Plexiglas stand and set it on the room's desk.

Susan, another caregiver, asked me who the two people were. The photo was so sad, she said, it reminded her of a concentration camp. How remarkable for Susan to mention that word, I thought. Indeed, it seemed to me that Esther had turned Mutti's last domicile into something like a concentration camp and was herself playing the camp guard. This, ironically, after our mother's self-sacrificing efforts to keep her out of just such a place.

Mutti was probably the only patient at Westmoreland who refused to stay in her room by herself. She had always said, "*Ich will immer unter den Leuten sein* " [I always want to be among people] and that was now more true than ever. Being in the company of others raised her spirits and she obviously felt uncomfortable being shut up in a room alone. Not surprisingly, Mother was never in her room when I got to Westmoreland. Most of the time I found her sitting in her wheelchair near the nurses station and at other times before the big-screen TV in the hallway or in the Solarium.

The Solarium was the venue for diverse social activities including bingo games, fun and fitness exercises, movies, painting classes, sing-alongs, and, on Sunday mornings, interdenominational worship services. The staff would routinely wheel Mutti there to participate. After the activity, I would wheel her to her room for some quality time together and then, after my visit was over, take her back out again and park her near the nurses' station. When the caregivers put her to bed in the evening or for an afternoon nap, they always kept her room door partially open.

While Mutti's physical needs were obviously well taken care of at Westmoreland, I was not so sure about her mental and emotional ones. Naturally, I was delighted that Mother had found such a wonderful new home. The facilities and amenities were outstanding and the nursing staff just superb in its professionalism, compassion, and friendliness. So I kept asking Mutti, "*Gefällt's dir hier?*" [Do you like it here?] to which her standard reply was "*ja*." Notwithstanding her high approval rating for the nursing home, her constant pleas were to be taken home: "*Ich will heim*" [I want to go home] or "*Komm wir gehen*" [Come let's go] or "*Laß mich heimgehen*" [Let me go home]. Sometimes she even uttered, "*furchtbar*" [terrible]. I am not sure where home was to her at this stage. It could have been with me back in Oak Park or with Esther on Northcliffe Way. This despite the fact that Esther or Nick came by continuously to check up and sit with her and I would be visiting two or three times a week for several hours.

Clearly, an institution no matter how admirable cannot ever replace home especially for a mentally impaired person who has lost control over his or her affairs. All I could do was reassure our mother that we all continued to love her very much and that she was here to get the best possible care until she had regained her strength so that we could take her back home.

One of the most memorable days at Westmoreland was St. Patrick's Day which is celebrated on March 17 and this year fell on a Tuesday, my major visitation day when I could be there for her noon meal. My visit had started out on a sour note when a couple of caregivers excitedly greeted me with the shocking news that the big diamond in a ring Esther had put on Mutti's finger was missing. Knowing that Esther would never have been foolish enough to have Mutti wear an expensive piece of jewelry in a nursing home, especially since she was mentally impaired, I suggested to them that the stone was mostly likely faux rather than the real thing. When Esther heard about the missing diamond and made no fuss, it confirmed my suspicion.

On that day, Westmoreland's management invited visitors to the home's library for a traditional St. Patrick's Day dinner of corned beef, cabbage, and boiled potatoes followed by desert. To my astonishment and delight, for the first time in a long time Mutti ate a complete meal. It was marvelous to see her swallow everything I put in her mouth without the slightest complaint until her plate was empty. I came to call it the miracle of St. Patrick's Day and fervently hoped that this change in her eating habits would be permanent.

My wish did materialize because for the remaining Tuesdays of March, throughout April, and until the first Tuesday in May when lunch was wheeled to her room around 1 p.m. Mutti ate most of her meal as I spoon-fed her whatever was on her plate. A typical Tuesday meal would consist of either orange roughy or turkey casserole, mashed potatoes, spinach or another vegetable, ice cream, and diverse liquids including Ensure and hot tea. This was usually followed by a small cup of liquid iron for her anemia although Mother eventually refused to drink it because of its bad taste. The diet was clearly a low-carb one as I noticed the complete absence of pasta, rice, or bread. After her meal, her caregivers normally put her in a walker for a short indoor walk and then in bed for her afternoon nap.

Many people with Alzheimer's are known to undergo significant personality changes as the disease progresses. Previously gentle and kind individuals may turn cantankerous and mean-spirited while others may experience a reverse transformation. Fortunately, as her disease progressed, Mother became ever more affectionate, kind, and loving. She regressed to the days she grew up in Schwanheim when she was somewhat of a love sponge. That really showed itself at Westmoreland. During my Easter Sunday visit, in mid-April, several of her caregivers came up to me to let me know how fond they were of Mother. They loved her cheerful, sweet, and affectionate nature, they said, and she never complained. Her need for love and affection was so great, I was told, that Mutti wanted to constantly embrace and kiss everybody who took care of her. Supposedly, in one such encounter, a caregiver even lost an earring.

Not that she was an angel. On the third Sunday after her arrival at the home, she had an especially bad day. She was having her hair done in the hallway and greeted me warmly. After I had taken her to her room, she suddenly turned moody and irritable. "*Geh, geh*" [Go, go] she shouted at me. Caregiver Lori told me that on the previous day she had flung an empty can of Ensure, the high-protein drink, right across the Solarium for no apparent reason. On another occasion, when I came to Mutti's room, the door was closed and there was a commotion inside. I first heard her caregiver shout "no, no" and, after a brief pause, Mutti laughing heartily. When Mary, a nurse's aid, wheeled her out, she told me that while she was getting her dressed, she had to hold on to Mutti's hands because she tried to slap her. Those were the rare exceptions and showed her at her worst.

When, two days after Easter Sunday, I found the pot of Easter lilies I had brought up and Mutti's television set gone from the room and told that Esther had taken them away at night, I wrote Janna to complain about Esther's oppressive conduct. Esther replied almost immediately accusing me of having violated the judge's visitation rules for the past six weeks and of interfering with the rules of Westmoreland. Furthermore, she claimed, the staff resented the fact that I only spoke in German with Mother. "I will be at Westmoreland every Tuesday at 1 p.m. sharp," she wrote, "to see that my mother is bedded for her nap and alone in her room to rest with the door open for nursing staff to look in on her. The same routine will be followed on Sundays. You, Mr. Zell, are a visitor only not a guardian—you make no rules." Westmoreland had no fixed visitation hours and no staff member had ever complained to me about violating any of their rules. Consequently, I had no intention of following any of the rules and procedures unilaterally imposed by Esther.

A Fateful Month

May was to be a critical month for our dear mother. Despite her deteriorating health and general weakness, Mutti did relatively well until the middle of the month which was about 10 weeks after she entered Westmoreland. Mother's Day (May 10) was a Sunday not on the visitation schedule as I was allowed visits only on alternate Sundays, but since this was most likely the last Mother's Day for the two of us together, I decided to see Mutti anyway and drove up early before Esther would show up. Mutti was already up and in her wheelchair watching television in the hallway when I came in. She greeted me joyfully with her usual, *"Ach, mein Peter"* and many hugs and kisses.

Mother was in great form—I had rarely seen her so bubbly, energized, and talkative. A nurse's aid pinned the corsage I had brought up to Mutti's dress and promised to keep an eye on my bouquet of roses just in case Esther decided it was not appropriate for Mutti's room. We spent most of my short visit before the hallway TV watching an episode from the fantasy television series *Xena: Warrior Princess* playing on one of the channels. Mutti enjoyed Xena's antics and laughed heartily throughout the program.

The following Tuesday's was a watershed day for Mutti. The early part of my visit went rather well. To my happy surprise, my Mother's Day bouquet and greeting card were still in the room. Mutti much enjoyed a *Volksmusik* videotape entitled *Einmal am Rhein* [Once on the Rhine] featuring the popular tenor Rudolf Schock with songs and scenes from the Rhine River region. We played it on the hallway console and Mutti, as usual, happily clapped her hands with the *Sonntagskonzert* [Sunday concert] theme song.

It was not long after this happy episode when things quickly went downhill. Lunch was served and when I tried to put something in Mother's mouth she shrieked, "*nein, nein*" [no, no]. All she would take in was some Ensure. Afterwards Esther, a nurse's aid, and I took her for a little walk and since Mutti seemed very tired, Esther put her to bed. Mutti did not go to sleep, however, but remained half awake. As I sat next to her, she kept opening her eyes to check that I was still there. When I held her hand she firmly grasped it and would not let go. Whenever I assured her that I would be back in three days, she anxiously asked, "*Was ist es heut?*" [What day is this?] and plead "*Bleib doch hier*" [Do stay here] or "*Bleib bei mir*" [Stay with me].

Mother clearly sensed that something was not normal. She also wanted to tell me something but was unable to finish her sentences saying, "*Ich wollt einmal.....*" [I once wanted to....] and "*Wenn du mal...*" [If you sometime....] When, after about five hours, she finally dozed off I left her bedside to return to Oak Park not knowing what to make of it all.

I had been warned that conditions with the terminally ill like Mutti can change quickly and unexpectedly and just a few days later they did. On my Friday visit Mutti looked pale and tired. She had not eaten her breakfast and refused lunch. After Mary got her dressed, I wheeled her out on the patio for a short stay in the fresh air and warm sun but she remained lethargic and was obviously not feeling well. She kept falling asleep with her head tilting to one side. When she said, "*furchtbar*" and I asked her what was so terrible, she replied, "*Das weiß ich auch nicht*" [I don't know either].

When I came up for my next scheduled visit, which was the Sunday after Mother's Day, Kathy, who was on duty at the nurse's station, told me that on Saturday Mutti had suddenly become sweaty and ashen-faced. They called in Dr. Slivnick who determined that it was nothing too serious but ordered bed rest and a liquid-only diet for the day. I found Mutti in bed and surprisingly lively and alert and happy to see me. It was a great comfort to see her take in some of her liquid lunch including a vanilla shake, Jell-O, cranberry juice, and Ensure. Because there was no television in the room, after Esther had taken Mutti's little Sony TV home, and Mutti had to stay in bed, we just kept company for the next four hours or so alternately chatting and praying together until she began to feel tired and dozed off.

As to Dr. David Slivnick, I unfortunately never had a chance to meet him. He was, however, the one and only physician treating Mutti. On one of my visits a nurse lamented the fact that Mutti had no regular doctor saying that Dr. Slivnick was an oncologist and not an internist which is what she needed. That was somewhat ironic since, when Mother was in my care, Esther had continuously complained that our mother was not getting proper medical attention despite our regular visits to the offices of Dr. Khan.

My visit on Tuesday, May 19, started out on a high note but ended in tragedy. When I arrived at Westmoreland at close to 10 o'clock, I found Mutti in her wheelchair giggling and laughing at the dining room table. She was full of beans and greeted me affectionately. A caregiver had just finished serving her breakfast and she ate well, I was told. As a special treat, I had brought up one of her favorite *Volksmusik* videotapes, a *Sonntagskonzert* featuring Volksmusik groups from each of Germany's 16 Länder (states) followed by a program appropriately called *Der Mai ist gekommen* [May has arrived]. The latter featured traditional songs of spring by popular folksingers and choirs performing out-of-doors as they strolled through the verdant German countryside.

We watched the show as usual on the big-screen TV set in the hallway. Mutti was laughing and giggling in delight clapping her hands along with the music and even doing some mock conducting. The program was fairly long and towards its end I noticed Mutti doze off now and then. Afterwards, I wheeled her to the patio where, under a shady tree, we could enjoy the pleasant outdoors and fresh air.

Back inside at the dining room table, Mutti had no appetite and took nothing of her all-liquid lunch despite my repeated pleas *"Mäulchen auf"* [open up]. When I asked her why she was constantly rubbing her forehead and *"Fühlst du nicht gut, mein Kind?"* [Are you not feeling well, my child?] she simply said *"ja."* Sharon, her caregiver for the day, and I decided to have her take a short indoor walk and then put her to bed. The walk went very well and I praised her effort.

As we put her to bed, we noticed that Mutti's left leg was turning blue. Alarmed, I asked Sharon to please call the hospital for a doctor but her caregiver said she will call Dr. Slivnick instead. In the meantime, a nurse, Kathy, was alerted and arrived. When I asked her if Mother's bluish leg was a sign of a blood clot she affirmed. A gurney was brought in and Mutti rushed to the emergency ward in Lake Forest Hospital by way of an underground passageway.

At the hospital, Mutti was examined by a Dr. King, the emergency room physician, and a blood pressure monitoring devise put on her arm. The doctor was not sure if the blood clot was in a vein or an artery and called in a specialist who arrived shortly. The type of clot was important because a veinal clot could be dissolved by drugs but not an arterial one, Dr. King explained. In the meantime, Esther too had been alerted and arrived. Her remark to Dr. King, "We have to stop meeting like this, doctor, before people start talking about us" went over like the proverbial lead balloon. She then called Nick, who had returned home after dropping her off at the hospital, to have him ask Dr. Murrin which type of clot he thought it might be but Frank apparently refused to offer an opinion.

After examining Mutti's leg, the specialist concluded it was a clot in a vein. By now, the leg discoloration had largely disappeared. Mutti was then wheeled into a small, dark room for a so-called Doppler ultrasound test. The lengthy procedure, which produced colored images of blood flow, found no clot in the leg. After about three hours in the hospital, Mutti was wheeled back to her room at Westmoreland. The leg now turned bluish again and the nurse reported that a blood clot had shown up in the Doppler photos after all but not in the leg but further up in the groin area. Mutti was subsequently injected with Lovenox, a blood thinner, and put on a ventilator to help her breathe. She was absolutely quiet but kept rubbing her forehead. The attending nurse believing Mutti had a headache gave her Tylenol in water.

Saying Good-Bye

As Esther and I were sitting by the bed, Esther on the window side and I on the other, each holding Mother by the hand, Mutti slowly raised herself up and, without uttering a word, first turned to her left looking Esther long and intently in the eyes. She then turned to her right to long and intently look at me and finally back to Esther for another look at her. After this, Mutti slumped back on her pillow and closed her eyes. Both Esther and I stayed with our mother until late in the evening. Esther busied herself crocheting as she sat next to Mutti while I stayed outside the room but looked in on her every 15 minutes or so to find out how she was doing. When Mutti appeared restless and unable to fall asleep, she was given a tranquilizer to calm her down.

At about nine in the evening, just before Esther left, a man she called Fred came to the room. Esther had evidently hired him as a private caregiver to sit with Mutti through the night. I later learned that Fred Lehman had previously been employed in a similar capacity for Dr. Murrin. I stayed until after Esther had left and then hugged and kissed Mother and, although she gave no indication that she heard me, assured her that she would be alright and I would be back tomorrow.

As I left, Mutti had her hands folded in front of her and looked perfectly serene. Dr. Slivnick was scheduled to see Mutti later in the evening or early next morning. The nurse thought that Mother would be all right again by tomorrow and I returned home with a heavy heart. What neither Esther nor I realized at the time, was that when Mutti raised herself up to look both of us in the eyes she knew her end had come—she was essentially saying good-bye to us! Our mother was henceforth in a comatose sleep and never regained consciousness.

The following day was not a visitation day but I took off from work and drove north at midday to see if Mutti had improved any. She had not. She lay in her bed with her eyes partially open—eyes that no longer saw or recognized me or anyone else. All I could do was sit next to her, hold her hand and pray. A little after 2 o'clock, I temporarily left the room to get something to drink. When I returned shortly after, Esther was in the room. When she saw me, she began to shout that it was Wednesday, that I had no visitation rights that day, and to stay out.

Esther tried to close the door on me and when I pushed myself in, she grabbed the cup of cranberry juice in my hand and tossed the contents in my face. "Get the hell out of here unless you want to get killed," she shouted. The commotion brought Karen, the manager, and Lori, the caregiver, to the room. As I stood there with juice running down my shirt and tie and explaining to Karen what had happened, Esther calmly said, "I never touched him, I never threw anything." I told her that she was a lying bitch who had been lying so long that she no longer knew the truth from the lie.

Claudette, a nurse, told me that Dr. Slivnick had come by to see Mutti around midnight. His heartbreaking diagnosis was that the blood clot was secondary to Mutti's colon cancer and that nothing more could now be done for her. When I called back in the evening, Mary told me that Esther was in the room with Mutti. According to Mary, in addition to the oxygen, IV tubes had been connected to keep Mutti hydrated. When Mother became restless and agitated again, Mary said, she was given more sedatives.

At this point, Esther's lawyers made themselves heard again. On Wednesday afternoon, after I had returned from Westmoreland, I received a call from Mike telling me that Mutti's assets would soon be exhausted and it was necessary to liquidate the joint tenancy stock. I asked him whether he had obtained the accounting which he had promised would be forthcoming prior to the transfer. He had asked Esther for it, he said, but she had not yet responded. Regardless, he said, if stock is held jointly by a parent and child, it legally belongs to the parent. When I asked him if he could cite me the relevant statutory or case law, he replied he would look for it. When I informed him about the incident earlier in the day, he asked me if I had exceeded my visitation hours. Of course, I had, I told him. No wonder, he said, I had not petitioned the court for a schedule change and Esther was justifiable angry.

To check up on Mutti without, hopefully, running into Esther, I left for Lake Forest very early on Thursday morning but, because of an obstruction on the interstate, did not get to Mutti's room until 8 o'clock. Fred was there and Esther had arrived to relieve him. Mutti was lying on her right side sleeping peacefully. The ventilator was running and the IV tubes connected while a heating pad had been placed under her left leg.

As I began to stroke Mutti's face and hair and talk to her quietly, Esther shouted, "My mother is sleeping—leave her alone."

After a while, I went outside and found Claudette. We had a long chat on the patio about Mutti's condition. It was not, as I had assumed, the heavy sedation Mutti was under that was keeping her from recognizing her surroundings—she was at a different level of consciousness now, i.e., semi-conscious, Claudette explained. She could no longer be fed because she was unable to swallow and might even choke if something was put in her mouth. The IV tubes were only keeping Mutti hydrated, she said, and did not supply nutrients. The leg problem was evidently the tumor blocking circulation.

Claudette and I also talked about the nature of colorectal cancer, a treacherous killer disease that appears practically without warning. By the time it makes itself known by abdominal pains or rectal bleeding, it is often too late. Had the disease been detected early enough in Mutti, the cancerous part of her colon could have been surgically removed and she could have made a complete recovery. But then, of course, she would undoubtedly have succumbed to her Alzheimer's.

As we were talking, another caregiver came by to reminisce about how affectionate Mutti had been with the staff during her nearly three months there and how she always wanted to hug them and be hugged. They missed her very much, she said.

On Thursday evening, I faxed Mike my conditions for acceding to their demand. One was a statement listing the major sources and uses of funds and the amount still remaining in Mutti's account. The other was a new Agreed Order signed by both parties and Judge Dowdle extending my visitation hours. In my letter I told him that it was unconscionable to restrict my visits at the nursing home to the same hours as before since our mother was now on her deathbed.

Specifically, I demanded four hours on Tuesdays and alternate Sundays (up from two each) and two hours on Fridays (up from one) for a total of 8 hours on average per week plus up to 15 minutes on all other days. Obviously, I wrote, I would prefer unrestricted access, but I could live with the proposed schedule. In a subsequent phone call, Mike demanded that I immediately sign the necessary papers and I told him there would be no further transfer of funds without a new Agreed Order. In that case, he said, he planned to go to court the following week. I wished him good luck.

Praying For A Miracle

Even with Mutti in comatose sleep and Dr. Slivnick's dire prognosis, I never gave up on Mutti. *Dum spiro spero est* [While there is breath there is hope] was how I viewed the crisis. That is why, in retrospect, my letter to Esther's lawyers seems a little ludicrous. Claudette had let me know that Mutti was no longer receiving any nutrients which should have told me that she was, in fact, consigned to die. While Mutti's demise might come within days, I was making long-term plans for more hours on certain future visitation days. The message Claudette had given me had obviously not fully sunk in. Mutti was a fighter, I knew, and would not give up easily.

There was even some exciting medical news that gave me hope. On experiments with mice, a Harvard researcher had discovered that certain statins made tumors shrink and disappear. The technique worked by cutting off the blood supply to cancer cells. There was an outside chance that an experimental drug would become available in time to save Mutti. I also believed in the power of prayer and never felt having been let down in the past after earnest entreaties for something that seemed reasonable.

Even though she was semi-conscious now, I was certain Mutti would pull through this crisis and be around for at least another few weeks or even months. She had, after all, twice fought off pneumonia since being brought to Lake Forest over a year ago. I expected to come to Westmoreland some morning when she would suddenly open her big brown eyes and greet me with that radiant smile and those familiar words, *"Mein Peter."* As things turned out, Mutti had a little more than a week to live.

Fred, Esther's nighttime caregiver for our mother, had some comforting news for me when I called him on Saturday evening. According to Fred, Mutti's eyes were open staring at the ceiling but that she was not responding to anything. In fact, one could turn her on her side and she would not react in any way, he said. Despite all this, Fred explained, it was very likely for Mutti, as other people in a semi-conscious state, to be cognizant of a loved one's presence even though they were no longer able to respond.

That comforting thought was the reason for my practice of continuously talking to Mother and assuring her of my love and the love of our Lord Jesus who was watching over her. Soon she would be reunited, I told her, with her dear Mama and Papa, Karl, Lulu, and Emmi, and I too would follow soon. Never before had I prayed so much or so intently as during these final days. They were prayers of thanks and gratitude for Mutti's long and meaningful life, prayers of repentance for her and my own grave sins, and prayers for eternal life together in His heavenly Kingdom.

During Mutti's remaining days, Esther continued her attempt to enforce the visitation schedule in the old Agreed Order. The following Sunday and Monday were not scheduled visitation days but I managed to see Mutti for short periods of time anyway. Fred had told me that he would not report me to Esther but, at the same time, he would not lie to her if she asked him about my being with Mother.

When I arrived at Westmoreland early on Sunday morning, Fred informed me that there was no change in Mutti's condition. According to Fred, a morphine patch was keeping Mother from experiencing any pain. The morphine, he said, was keeping her on a middle ground where she would not experience any pain yet, at the same time, not be completely unconscious. He did not rule out the possibility that Mother had suffered a mild stroke. That it was a stroke was later confirmed by Bonnie who heard it from Dr. Slivnick. According to Fred, despite our differences, my sister and I had one thing in common—we both loved our mother very much.

I told Fred that I wanted very much to be by Mutti's side when she passed away and gave him an index card with my home and work phone numbers with a request to call me in case of an emergency. He promised to do so. When by a phone call to Fred at 9 a.m. Esther announced her arrival, I hastily prayed another *Vaterunser* and took my leave.

Taped to the door of Mutti's room that Sunday morning (May 24) was a note by Esther in red capital letters stating, "Nothing to eat or drink by doctor's orders. May 21, 9 p.m.." I was appalled by this insensitive and public posting of Mutti's imminent demise. While I held Mutti's hand and caressed her cheeks, she now and then slightly raised her head and opened her eyes. As she fixed the ceiling with a distant, absent stare, she gave no indication that she saw or recognized me. To brighten up her otherwise cheerless room, I had brought up a bouquet of her favorite pink mini-carnations hoping that Esther would not throw them out again.

Monday, May 25, was Memorial Day (Observed) and I went to see Mutti very early in the morning. Fred was just changing Mother and when he was done I returned to the room. When I reached for her hand, Mutti opened her eyes and moved her lips as if she wanted to say something. Now and then, however, her eyes opened very wide as if she was in shock while she seemed to be gasping for air. This much unnerved me but Fred assured me that she was not in pain or lacked oxygen but that it was a mere reflex action.

Fred told me that on Sunday afternoon a clergyman had come by to perform some religious ceremony at Mutti's side. He did not elaborate. Presumably, it was the sacrament of last rites of the Roman Catholic Church and most likely arranged by Nick, a devout Catholic. Although this rite is not observed by Protestants, it gave me much comfort to know it had been done for her. When, after about an hour mostly spent in prayer, Esther unexpectedly walked in I hurriedly left. During a late evening visit, Bonnie, the nurse in charge, had just changed Mother's IV setup by attaching a new fluid bag and moving the IV tubes from the left to the right hand. She told me that all of Mother's vital signs were normal. Unlike in the morning, her breathing was no longer strained and she slept peacefully.

The following day, Tuesday, was a scheduled visitation day for me and I extended my allotted two hours to five, three in the morning and two in the evening, hoping that Esther would leave us in peace. Mutti had now been in a comatose sleep for a full week. During my morning visit, I met Bonnie in the hallway. She told me that in all her many years as a nurse, she had never experienced a situation where one sibling had tried to keep another from their mother's deathbed. She thought it absolutely shocking.

Denise, a day nurse hired by Esther, was sitting with Mother as I entered the room. To my surprise, yesterday's flowers were still in the room. In fact, Esther had brought in a pot of pink azaleas. As I sat next to her, Mutti again experienced a number of spasms when her eyes opened wide, her lips were pressed together, and she seemed to be gasping for air. These episodes were followed by periods of peaceful slumber during which her eyes were half open and she was breathing normally.

When I arrived at 7 p.m. for my evening visit, Nick also drove up and we both sat with Mother with Nick reading a book while I held Mutti's hand and gently talked to her. Thankfully, she had no spasms and breathed normally. Shortly after we were joined by Fred and about two hours later Claudette entered the room and made a comment to the effect that only the IV tubes were keeping Mutti alive and a decision had to be made—it all dependent on what one wanted. That angered me because it suggested that they were about to prematurely end Mutti's life and I came down hard on the three telling them to not dare disconnect Mutti's life support system. Esther was in the hallway and when she heard the commotion she called for Nick who came back in the room to exclaim, "No decision, no decision."

When I called Fred early on Wednesday morning I was happy to hear that Mother had made it through the night and was resting peacefully. It was not a visitation day but I drove up in the evening after work anyway. I was greeted by Maria, a caregiver who happened to be from Austria and spoke German, who warned me that Esther was in Mutti's room. When I entered I expected her to immediately order me out. She did not and it soon became apparent to me why—it was because she wanted me to witness something. I sat down next to Mutti's bed across from Esther and holding Mutti's hand began to silently pray for her.

When after some time I happened to look up, I saw something that seemed surreal. There sat Esther grinning broadly as she perused what I perceived to be legal documents. She examined each one in turn nodding approvingly. Presumably, they were the papers she had Mutti sign when she had taken our mother to her Lake Forest lawyers. How quintessentially Esther, I thought to myself. Mutti is fighting for her life, I am praying for a miracle, and my sister is calmly savoring the spoils that were due her as soon as our dear mother had passed away. When Fred reported in at 9 p.m., Esther called Nick to inquire how Frank and Steffi were doing and to come pick her up. Before leaving, she told Fred to come in the room as she did not want me to be alone with her mother.

When I returned early the next morning Fred was there and told me that Esther was due between 7:45 and 8:00 a.m.. This gave me just one-half hour. It pained me to see Mother breathing heavily and rapidly again with her mouth open and her eyes partially closed. According to Fred her reflex action was constantly changing from serene sleep to heavy breathing. He assured me that her morphine patch, which was changed every three days, was keeping her from experiencing any pain and that her oxygen level was normal. When I called the nurse's station in the evening, Monica told me that Mutti was still much the same and that Nick was with her and had been there for much of the day.

Friday morning, May 29, was destined to be the last time I would see Mother alive. I had called Fred very early to obtain a status report on Mother and let him know that I was on my way. When I got to the room shortly after 8 o'clock, I found Esther sitting in a club chair and using the desk chair as a footstool. She had been perusing and reshuffling her legal file again and was now placing the papers in a big accordion folder. Breakfast was wheeled in and Esther helped herself to a tray and leisurely ate her meal. When Denise reported in at 9 o'clock, Esther called Nick to pick her up and, without further ado, marched out.

Mutti was lying on her back with her head turned facing the window. She was sleeping serenely and made no sound. Her breathing was normal and relaxed. Her mouth was half open and her eyes nearly closed. A nurse named Paula, whom I had not met before, came in to check on Mutti's vital signs—body temperature, pulse rate, blood pressure, oxygen level— and found them all normal. Concerning her blood pressure (116/56), I thought the second number (diastolic pressure) seemed unusually low but Paula assured me that it was nothing to be worried about. She informed me that Mutti's morphine patch had been replaced earlier that morning and gave Mutti another injection of blood thinner.

As usual, I sat with Mutti gently stroking her face and hair and alternately talking to and praying for her. I marveled at her pink cheeks and how youthful and healthy she still looked. When it got close to 11 o'clock, the end of my visitation time by the old Agreed Order, Denise came in the room to let me know that my time was up. She busied herself going through the chest of drawers and when she opened the armoire doors I noticed that it was almost empty except for the bed jacket I had once given Mutti. It was another ominous sign that Mutti was not expected to live much longer.

On the coffee table Esther had left a copy of the *Diplomatic List* with the names and addresses of the Washington diplomatic corps. She was obviously trying to impress the Westmoreland nursing staff with the fact that her daughter was employed by the State Department. Holding Mutti's hand in mine, I said a final *Vaterunser*, kissed her on the cheek, and said good-bye to Denise telling her I would be back in the morning. Nothing led me to suspect that I would not see Mutti alive again and that within a few hours she would be gone.

The Finale

The sad news came early next morning, May 30, and traditionally Memorial Day, when I called the nurses station and asked to speak with the nurse in charge for a status report on Mother. After a long while I was connected to someone who identified herself as Barb. She was a substitute nurse, she told me, and was sorry she had to tell me that "your mother died last night." I was stunned. How could this be? Mutti had done so well the day before and looked like she would be around for a few more days at least. On top of that, nobody at Westmoreland had called me. I had, after all, prepared index cards for the two Westmoreland managers and major caregivers including Fred with complete contact information and each had solemnly promised that they would call me in an emergency. Needless to say, I had gone almost nowhere for over a week to make sure I was around when a call came in.

When I arrived at Westmoreland an hour later, the place looked deserted. There was nobody at the nurses station. Mutti's room looked abandoned and eerie. The hospital bed, now less bedding, had been raised high and all three lamps in the room were lit with their shades removed. There seemed to be nobody around but I finally ran into a caregiver I had not seen before and said something like, "My mother died here last night, her name was Annemarie, and I don't know where they have taken her." She had no clue.

After some time Ginger showed up at the nurses station. She explained that on Friday (May 29) at around 4:30 p.m., both of Mutti's legs turned bluish, an indication that her heart was giving out, and they immediately called Esther. According to Ginger, she, Claudette, Esther, and Fred were with Mutti when she stopped breathing at around 8:45 p.m. with no overt signs of pain or discomfort. She and Fred had wanted to contact me, she said, but Esther had told them in no uncertain terms not to call me. Mutti's body had been moved to the Lake Forest Hospital morgue, she said, and recommended I take the tunnel to the hospital and there contact the hospital supervisor.

My efforts to find out what happened to Mutti's body was like a tale from Arthur Conan Doyle's *Sherlock Holmes*. At the hospital, a supervisory nurse told me that the body had been taken to the Wenban Funeral Home in Lake Forest. When I called there I got the director, Jim Iacubino, on the line who told me that Esther was there with him but that he could not provide any information. Suddenly the phone went dead. I immediately drove to the funeral home. According to Mr. Iacubino, Esther, who had just left, had disconnected the phone while we were talking. He again informed me that because Esther was our mother's guardian she had all the rights including funeral arrangement and he could therefore tell me nothing without her explicit permission including where Mother's body was or if any funeral arrangements had been made. I had hit a brick wall and returned home dejected.

On the following day, Sunday, I steeled myself and called Esther's house hoping that Nick would answer. He did and I asked him if he knew where Mother's body was and what funeral arrangements, if any, had been made. According to Nick, he had no knowledge of a funeral but, in a hushed voice, confided in me that Mutti's body had not yet been released and was still at the hospital morgue. In the background, I heard the family dog bark and footsteps. Nick immediately hung up. A few minutes later, Esther left a short message on my answering machine. "Don't you dare to ever call my house again—don't you dare," she growled. I now suspected that there would be no funeral and Esther would simply have Mutti's body cremated and the ashes disposed of as she saw fit.

Desperate to see Mutti one last time, the next morning I called the Lake County coroner's office and was fortunate to find in the coroner, Barbara Richardson, a real human being. It was absolutely essential that I view my mother's body to have closure, she told me. She would delay pickup of the body at the hospital morgue until 12 noon to give me time to get up there. I was to proceed to the Wenban Funeral Home and there call her back for further instructions.

The coroner's plan for me almost went awry because Esther had apparently anticipated my intentions. As I was getting myself ready, a pounding on my front door was followed by an anxious phone call from a neighbor, Charles Feldt, who told me that he and another neighbor, the Reverend James Yuan, had just been to the parking lot and noticed that my car had been vandalized during the night. I rushed outside to find my Ford Escort sitting flat on the ground with all four tires slashed. I had no enemies or quarrels with anyone and immediately knew that only Esther could be behind this outrage. She had obviously arranged for someone to stop by the house to do this hateful deed and possibly one of Nick's brothers who was a laborer for the village's Parks & Recreation Department and had stopped by Mutti's Place a few times.

When I told Charles of my predicament, he immediately volunteered to drive me to Lake Forest. When we got to the funeral home, Mr. Iacubino told me he had been contacted by Ms. Richardson and I immediately called her. She instructed me to tell the funeral director that I was returning home to Oak Park but instead I was to proceed to the emergency entrance of Lake Forest Hospital where a deputy coroner would meet me.

At the hospital, the deputy and a hospital employee escorted me past the emergency ward, down a long corridor and into a large, empty room. From an adjoining vault, the employee wheeled out a gurney carrying a body wrapped in a plastic bag. He slowly unzipped the bag to reveal the lifeless body of my dear mother. To my dismay, she lay there completely naked except for a diaper around her midsection. After some prodding, the employee found a sheet in a table drawer which he draped over the body up to the shoulders. I asked the two men to please step outside for a few minutes so that I could be with my beloved mother alone for one last time.

Once the spirit has left a person, what remains is rarely a pleasant sight. The awful disease and the absence of nutrients had taken their toll and Mutti's once well-proportioned and attractive form had been reduced to mere skin and bones. She lay flat on her back with the head tilted all the way to the left. Her mouth was partially open and her tongue, which appeared rough and blistery, pushed all the way into the opening. Her prominent nose appeared slightly bent out of shape. Shocked at what I saw, I came to wonder if Mutti's departure from this world was really as serene and peaceful as it had been described to me. Her left eye was half open and her right one fully closed. In the corner of the nose below the right eye I noticed a large drop of water. Was it a tear? I gently wiped it away and, loosing my composure, wept uncontrollably. Holding on to Mutti's hand, I fervently prayed for her soul.

After taking one long final look at Mutti's mortal remains, I left the room. It was just minutes before noon which was the time the body was scheduled to be picked up for cremation. On the way back to Oak Park, Charles tried to keep me entertained with some amusing stories but I was not listening. I felt very much like Mother had when her own mother had passed away some 66 years earlier—she thought the world should stop turning but, to her dismay, nobody took notice of this monumental event in her life. Like Mutti at Oma's passing, I felt a dreadful emptiness enter into my own life. I had lost my soul mate and the only human being I had ever truly loved and cared for.

After my car was repaired, I returned to Lake Forest to pick up a copy of Mutti's death certificate in the registrar's office. According to this document, Mutti died on May 29, 1998 at 8:50 p.m. in Westmoreland Nursing Care in Lake Forest. It was signed on June 1, 1998 by Dr. David Slivnick of Libertyville who stated that he last saw his patient alive on May 21, 1998. He gave the cause of death as CVA (cerebrovascular accident) due to left leg arterial embolism. Listed as contributing factors were colon cancer and dementia. According to this certificate, cremation had taken place on June 1, 1998 at Mount Olivet Cemetery in Zion, Illinois. Incidentally, a certificate issued by Mt. Olivet Memorial Park gives the date of cremation as June 2, 1998. When I called Mount Olivet, I learned that Mutti's ashes were picked up by Wenban Funeral Home presumably for delivery to Esther.

Fortunately, neighbors, friends and colleagues at work were wonderfully supportive and helped me cope. My Christian faith was, as ever, invaluable in getting through this ordeal. Mother was in the world for 89 years plus 84 days and I could be nothing but immensely grateful to the Almighty for the long life he gave her. I knew that this was not the end for Mutti but the beginning because our Christian faith teaches us that we live to die to live again.

Mutti's ashes were with Esther for the following 12 years when, perhaps sensing her own imminent demise, she mailed them to me by FedEx where they arrived at my Arizona home on April 10, 2010. The container was a substantial and impressive piece of copper/bronze with an engraved front plate bearing our mother's name and birth and death dates plus a replica of Albrecht Dürer's praying hands. I replied with a thank-you card expressing my joy in receiving this precious gift, wishing her well, and expressing the hope that Ute, who had in the meantime gotten in touch with her again, would continue to be at her side if and when she needed assistance.

Finding Closure

Most people find closure after the passing of a loved with the various rites and ceremonies designed for that purpose. In my case such a comforting sense of finality was not possible. There had been no funeral service or graveside ceremony and there was no stone or plaque to indicate Mutti's final resting place where I could come to visit. Not even the customary death notice in the *Chicago Tribune* announced her passing. To inform friends and neighbors, I called or visited them. As a way of finding closure, on the second and third anniversaries of Mutti's passing, I placed "In Memoriam" notices in the *Chicago Tribune* with a passage from Scripture or one of my own little poems.

I still often think about Mutti and what her life meant to me. In fact, I pray for her soul every day. When I once asked her if she was afraid of death she replied, *"Nein, dann hab' ich meine Ruh"* [No, then I will have my peace]. It was a reflection of the obvious fact that life had not always been easy for her and often treated her very harshly. Yet she took everything in stride and met every challenge like the trouper she was.

Mutti was strong in her Christian faith and tried to live by its tenets. She was good of heart and had compassion for the poor and disenfranchised and tried to alleviate their misery wherever possible. Mutti treated all people with respect and courtesy without giving any thought to their ethnicity, religion, or social status. Her outgoing personality, warmth, and sense of humor made her popular with all who got to know her. She was good and generous with all who treated her with a measure of respect and forbearance, as every human being is entitled to, and to many, both in America and her native Germany, she was and remained a devoted and loyal friend. She was honest to a fault and always tried to do the right thing. Mother was modest and unassuming and disliked all those who thought too highly of themselves and was not averse to putting them down when she thought they deserved it.

Mother was no angel but a human being with all the faults and flaws this entails. The major blot on her life was her inability to fully accept and bond with her three youngest children and at times treat them very harshly. Ute, Volker, and Elke deserved better despite the unusual circumstances by which they came into the world. The three must have been a constant reminder of her degradation during the Nazi era. At the same time, Mother was slavishly devoted to her first-born, Esther, while I too much benefited from her love and care.

While I was not fully aware of her great shortcomings as a parent until Mutti had passed away and I heard it from my siblings, it did not much change my esteem for our mother because I knew that she lived through some very trying times. I also came to suspect that some of my siblings' abuse allegations were embellished and strongly shaped by the oldest of the three and must therefore be taken with a grain of salt. It was my siblings' own character flaws and deep resentments that contributed to the animosity between her and them and they must therefore share in at least part of the blame. If Mutti did not show much love and compassion towards them neither did they for her. All three never appreciated what our mother did for them while the childhood neglect suffered by Elke was, of course, inexcusable.

To me personally, Mutti was a caring parent, a loyal friend, and a wise counselor. We were as one says in German, *Ein Herz und eine Seele* [One heart and one soul]. I greatly admired her and, I suppose, the feeling was mutual. I believe we brought out the best in each other. Fortunately, I was able to bond with her from the day I was born. Had it been otherwise, my life would have been completely different. My last name would most likely be Kuchenbeisser and I would have grown up in the German countryside with limited opportunities.

Even before her passing, I felt guilty not having done more for Mother while she was having a tough time making a living on her own in a man's world when women were often exploited in many ways. I was too wrapped up in myself and my own career goals to pay much attention to anybody else even to Mother and she was too modest to ask for help. That is why I was so willing and happy to come to her aid when she needed me. Those ten or so years when I was able to take care of her were the most satisfying ones in my life. Her parents passed away at relatively young ages and most of her school friends died in their 70s but Mutti made it to 89 and I like to think that I had something to do with that.

Mother longed to be home during her last days in the world and I feel guilty for having been involved in denying her that big wish. The first time she was taken away neither our mother nor I had a say in the matter. The second time I acquiesced to the move because I thought it was the right thing to do. Was I being selfish in wanting to keep Mutti alive when all hope for a recovery was long gone? Should I have kept quiet and let her die at home with my sister but perhaps a few weeks earlier than she did at Westmoreland? Had Esther only agreed to Hospice care in her home so that I could be assured that our mother received the care she needed while allowing me reasonable visitation rights. That would have been the ideal solution but it was not to be.

Ten days after Mother had been removed from her Oak Park home back in February 1997, I had a chance to talk with her on the telephone. It was only the second time since her abduction that I was able to do so. It was a Thursday and when I told her that I would be picking her up on the following Tuesday she was elated and exclaimed, "*Da bin ich aber glücklich—ich will sein wo du bist*" [That will make me happy—I want to be where you are]. I took her words to heart. It is, of course, a fundamental tenet of our Christian faith that we and our loved ones will some day be reunited in His heavenly Kingdom for life everlasting and it is of immense comfort for me to know that at the end of my earthly journey there will be someone very special awaiting my arrival for a joyous reunion in a place far removed from this vale of tears.

NOTES

1. Since the postcard to Lulu from his mother bears no address it was most likely mailed in an envelope or hand delivered by a French intermediary to his military unit in Morocco. It reads (in German): *Mein lieber Bub, Gottes reichsten Segen zu Deinem 23ten Geburtstag. Gebe Gott daß Du ihn im nächsten Jahr in unserer Mitte erlebst. Sonst noch alles wohl. Papa und die Mädchen gratulieren ebenfalls. Tausend Grüße und Küsse, Deine Mama.* [My dear boy, God's richest blessing on your 23rd birthday. God willing your next one will be in our midst. Otherwise all is well. Papa and the girls also congratulate you. A thousand greetings and kisses, your Mama]. On the side, presumably written by his father, appear the words, *Gott schütze Dich.* [God protect you].

2. After World War II, the U.S. Army assembled the captured membership and other records of the NSDAP (Nazi Party) in the Berlin Document Center in preparation for the Nuremberg war crimes trials. These records where subsequently microfilmed and sent to the National Archives and Records Administration in Washington, DC. When I contacted the Simon Wiesenthal Center in Los Angeles, I was referred to that agency. These records are now located in the Textual Archives Services Division of the National Archives and Records Administration in College Park, MD. In August 2004, that agency mailed me photocopies of Ludwig Zell's *Zentralkartei* and *Ortsgruppenkartei* [central and regional party membership registers] listing his name, birth date and place, occupation (*kfm. Ang.*), Bitterfeld address (Hermann Göringstraße 8), membership number, and enrollment date.

3. In Germany, as in most European countries, the churches are financed by the state which, in turn, raises the funds by placing a tax on income.

The *Krchensteuer* [church tax] varies by the Bundesland (federal state) and was 9 % in the state of Hesse where the Zell family resided. For a small fee, one can leave the church, known as a *Kirchenaustriitt* [church exit], and thereby save the church taxes. Presently only a little over half of the population still pays church taxes and holds official church membership. Leaving the church does have consequences, however, especially for Roman Catholics who may be excommunicated or refused certain sacraments of the church. Refusal to allow burial in a Christian cemetery or the attendance of a clergyman is another possible consequence for former members of either church.

Parenthetically, this arrangement between church and state was the result of the secularization of church property during the latter half of the 19th century during which both the Roman Catholic and Evangelical (Lutheran) churches were stripped of much of their vast wealth in land and real estate holdings while the state, in turn, agreed to compensate the two churches for their losses by payments from the state budgets. The arrangement has worked out well as there have been no significant complaints of state interference in the affairs of the churches or vice versa with the exception of the Nazi era when individual clerics were often seized if they spoke out against the regime and its policies. The most notorious case was that of the Evangelical (Lutheran) Theologian and Pastor Dietrich Bonhoeffer who was a founding member of the Confessing Church. His public condemnation of the pogrom against the Jews led to his arrest, trial on treason charges, and hanging in April 1945 just prior to the end of the war.

4. Purpose of my August 2017 trip to Germany was not only to celebrate our birthdays, Cousin Peter's and mine, and to visit some venues important in my life such as Stuttgart, Graben-Neudorf, and Frankfurt-Schwanheim, but to take part in the festivities surrounding the 500th anniversary of the Protestant Reformation. The year 2017 was much celebrated throughout Germany because on October 31, 1517 Martin Luther had nailed his 95 theses on the door of the castle church in Wittenberg (Electorate of Saxony) in eastern Germany which was the beginning of the Protestant Reformation.

5. Kevin, Julchen's fiancé, and I met for the first time when the two came by my flat in Sachsenhausen on the last day before my return to the States at the end of September 2011. Kevin, who was then in his late 20s, told me that he was tired of traveling the country as a DJ and wanted to buy into an American franchise like McDonald's or Starbucks. The problem was that most of these firms either preferred to own their own restaurants rather than take on more franchisees or required more money than he could put up.

   I then told Kevin about my Berlin experiences earlier that month that included a visit to a Dunkin' Donuts restaurant on Unter den Linden close to the Brandenburg Gate offering donuts and bagels along with their famous coffee. The shop was doing a land-office business with people standing in line to get in, I told him. If he managed to open a donut shop in Frankfurt am Main, I suggested, he could gain a foothold in the coffee and donuts business before his more powerful competitor arrived and kept him out. Remarkably, it took Kevin just half a year to follow through on my proposal. According to Kevin, when Dunkin' Donuts finally opened up their first restaurant on the Zeil in Frankfurt am Main in May 2013, it had no impact on his business enabling him to expand to other cities in Germany and Austria. His donuts, he said, were more to the local taste, i.e., less sweet and included a great variety of covered and filled confections not available from his big American competitor.

6. According to the Bevölkerungsamt Stadt Zürich (Population Office of the City of Zurich) Max Aeschbach was born on March 22, 1895 in Burg, AG (Canton of Aargau) and first arrived in Zurich on August 30, 1901 at age six. He left town for places unknown on June 30, 1914. He then apparently lived in Geneva from where he returned to Zurich on July 22, 1940. Max left for Geneva for the last time on June 2, 1975 at age 80. The information on Max's marriage to Louise Emma Zell, his divorce, and subsequent death are by courtesy of the Regionales Zivilstandsamt Menziken (regional registrar's office) in the canton of Aargau.

7. Information on Charles August Hirzel is taken from a curriculum vitae prepared by Jean-Claude Lavanchy, curator of philately at the

Museum für Kommunikation (Museum for Communications) of Berne, Switzerland.

8. Unanswered is the questions of the whereabouts of Aunt Emmi's remains. In anticipation of my 2011 tour of Germany and a possible visit to her gravesite, I had asked Trixi, Cousin Peter's daughter who is familiar with French, to assist me in this search. She contacted the City of Geneva and tracked down the funeral home where Emmi's body was taken, namely, the Pompes Funèbres Générales Genève in Carouge. An employee there replied that she was cremated on August 26, 1993 and the ashes taken away. Further inquiries by both of us regarding their final disposition were not answered. In response to my inquiry, Attorney Daniel Perren informed me by e-mail in May 2011 that the recipient of the ashes was most likely Eric Oppliger who, he wrote, finally inherited the 100,000 Swiss francs left him in her will of August 1982. Esther injected some drama into the search by claiming on her website announcing *The Swiss Conspiracy Book* that she relentlessly searched for her aunt's remains for seven years and finally found them "in an unmarked grave minus a head stone overgrown with weeds" in a small (unnamed) cemetery outside of Geneva.

9. In a fax of January 1994 to Esther, Me Davidoff quoted assets on the same order as given by the *Cour de Justice* less about 5 million Swiss francs to be set aside for taxes. That would leave a net estate value of between 15 and 20 million Swiss francs. At the end of 1993, the year Aunt Emmi died, the exchange rate was approximately 1.5 Swiss francs to the dollar. Thus, the estate's net asset value (after deduction of anticipated taxes) was between $10.0 million and $13.3 million.

10. My effort to obtain particulars on Mother's schooling extended over several years beginning in late 2007 when I contacted the Schillerschule with a request to search their *Aufnahmebücher* [registration books] for 1919 and 1920, the years Mother would have been expected to transfer from the Schwanheimer Volksschule to the Schillerschule had she been a regular student. The school secretary informed me that, regrettably, no entry for my mother or her friend Cornelia Textor could be found. In late September 2011, during my trip to Germany, I stopped by the Schillerschule and was given the opportunity to check out their books myself but found no relevant entry for these two years.

My last day of my 2017 trip to Germany, August 14, also happened to be the first day of school in the state of Hesse. Despite it being very hectic at the Schwanheimer Volksschule (now called the August-Gräser-Schule), Saskia Ghribi and Margret Michel, the school principal and secretary, respectively, gave me a cordial welcome. Frau Ghribi allowed me to inspect and photograph the inside of the building, a handsome 3-story brick structure located at Geroldsteiner Strasse 2, while the children were in church for the traditional worship service on this first day of school.

According to the school principal, the school has no records prior to 1928 when Schwanheim became part of Frankfurt am Main but recommended that I contact the Institut für Stadtgeschichte Frankfurt (Frankfurt Historical Institute). An employee there informed me that due to *Kriegsverluste* [war losses] no records from the Schwanheim school system prior to 1928 have survived and that, furthermore, nothing pertaining to my mother could be found in the entrance or graduation records of the Schillerschule.

In early October 2019, I contacted the Schillerschule a final time to ask them to extent their search to the year 1923, when Mutti would have been 14 and may have been enrolled as a special student after her graduation from the Schwanheimer Volksschule. The results of their search was again negative, I was informed, as no enrollment records were found for either Anna Maria Zell or Cornelia Textor.

11. That at least part of Mutti's dowry was purchased at the Schiff department store was confirmed when, after she had passed away, I found one section of an attractive lace curtain among her belongings with *Kaufhaus Schiff Höchst am Main Abt. Innen Dekoration* [Department Store Schiff Höchst on Main Dept. Interior Decoration] stenciled on the top border. There were also bed sheets and pillow cases bearing her monogram in red which most likely also came from the Schiff store. Mutti had obviously kept these items for sentimental reasons.

12. In early September 2006, during an extended stay in Germany, I drove into Höchst and found the Würzburger Eck at the corner of Bolongarostraße and Königsteiner Straße just as Mutti had described it. Nearby I had a chance encounter with three elderly ladies, one 85

years old, out on a Sunday stroll. When I lamented the fate of the Würzburger family and their store during the Nazi era one of the women sighed, *"Das waren schlimme Zeiten"* [Those were terrible times] and volunteered to lead me to another building that also had once been owned by Jews. As we walked down Königsteiner Straße we came to a huge 2-story building that took up an entire city block. To my astonishment it turned out to be the former Schiff department store Mutti had so much talked about. It seems that after having gone through several post-war owners, it now stood empty and abandoned. Shoppers, I was told, now preferred to travel to Frankfurt am Main with its many retail establishments or frequent some new shopping malls in the area. The women described the Schiff family as very kind and generous. They did much for the community, they said, and spoke fondly of the annual Christmas party they gave for the children of Höchst and surrounding areas.

At the former Schiff store entrance and encased in the sidewalk I found a large circular commemorative tablet which, I was told, had recently been placed there by a Schiff family member on a visit to Frankfurt-Höchst. The inscription read:

DAS BELIEBTE HÖCHSTER GESCHÄFT, 1901 VON NIKOLAUS SCHIFF GEGRÜNDET, WURDE 1928 VON DEN BEIDEN SÖHNEN ZU EINEM MODERNEN KAUFHAUS ERWEITERT. DAS BOYCOTT DURCH DIE NATIONALSOZIALISTEN FÜHRTE NACH 1933 ZU EINEM DRASTISCHEN GESCHÄFTSRÜCKGANG UND 1938 ZU ZWANGSWEISEM VERKAUF. BERAUBT UND MITTELLOS GELANG DEN BRÜDERN UND IHREN FAMILIEN ENDE 1938 DIE FLUCHT IN DIE USA.

[The popular Höchst store, founded by Nikolaus Schiff in 1901, was expanded in 1928 into a modern department store. After 1933, the National Socialist boycott led to a drastic business decline and in 1938 to a forced sale. Robbed and destitute the brothers and their families succeeded in their escape to the USA.]. Incidentally, the Schiff building has since been restored and turned into an indoor shopping mall. A brass memorial tablet entitled "Kaufhaus Schiff" affixed to the building near its entrance provides more details about the Schiff family and the building's history.

13. Documentation of the Würzburger-Zell marriage, Friedrich's (Fritz's) and Anna Maria's subsequent divorce, and Anna Maria Würzburger's resumption of her maiden name Zell, is all part of a one-page *Heiratsurkunde* [marriage certificate]. (By courtesy of the Standesamt Mitte (Höchst) in Frankfurt am Main).

14. The racial laws known as the *Nürnberger Gesetze* [Nuremberg Laws] were promulgated at a Nazi Party congress called *Reichsparteitag der Freiheit* [Party Congress of Liberty] held in Nürnberg (Nuremberg) on September 15, 1935. By these laws, a *Volljude* [full Jew] was a person who had three Jewish grandparents while a *Jude* [Jew] or so-called *Mischling* [mixed breed] was someone who had two Jewish grandparents or was married to a *Volljude*. These laws stripped *Volljuden* of their German citizenship and right to vote. In addition, they could not hold public office, be employed by government, or teach. Marriages between Jews or *Mischlinge* and persons of "German blood" were strictly verboten. (See Wilhelm Wagner, *Neuer Bildatlas Zur Deutschen Geschichte*, 311).

15. What may have been one of the best-kept secrets during the Third Reich was the strong likelihood that Adolf Hitler himself was partly Jewish through his paternal grandfather. In his authoritative biography, John Toland offers a Hitler family tree which lists a Frankenberger as one of three possible paternal grandfathers. The author does not elaborate on the issue. (See John Toland, *Adolf Hitler*, 10). George Bailey, an American journalist with first-hand knowledge of the era, provides more details. (See George Bailey, *Germans*, 259). According to his scenario, a Maria Anna Schicklgruber, who in 1837 was a cook in the household of wealthy Jews named Frankenberger in Graz, Austria, had an affair with the family's underage son who got her pregnant. Maria named her child Alois and, there being no one to claim paternity, he was given his mother's surname, i. e., Schicklgruber. Since it was pretty much established who Alois' father was, the elder Frankenberger reputedly paid child support for Alois for the legally required 14 years.

Five years after Alois' birth, Maria married a miller's apprentice named Johann Georg Hiedler. When he was already 40 years old, Alois Schicklgruber changed his surname to Hitler, a slight variation of his stepfather's name. On January 7, 1885 Alois Hitler married Klara Pölzl in Braunau am Inn, which was just across the border from Germany, where Alois served as an Austro-Hungarian customs official. Alois' and Klara's fourth child was born on April 20, 1889 and named Adolf. (See John Toland, *Adolf Hitler*, 7, 10-11). If Bailey's account is correct Adolf Hitler was one quarter Jewish and therefore a *Mischling* by Nazi racial doctrine.

16. The infamous *Kristallnacht* of November 10/11, 1938 was occasioned by the murder of an official in Germany's Paris embassy, Ernst vom Rath, by a disgruntled teenage Polish Jew named Herschel Grynszpan on the day before. It just so happened that when the news from Paris came in, the top Nazi leadership, including Adolf Hitler, was meeting in Munich. After briefly conferring with Dr. Joseph Goebbels, his minister of propaganda, Hitler abruptly cancelled his highly anticipated speech and left. Goebbels thereupon began a virulent ant-Semitic tirade calling for retribution after which telephone orders went out to the various SA units throughout the country to begin the pogrom. (See Wilhelm Wagner, *Neuer Bildatlas Zur Deutschen Geschichte*, 306).

17. Towards the end of August 2011, during another extended stay in Germany, I stopped by the Jüdisches Museum Frankfurt to present them with a copy of my recently published *Just Passing Through: A German-American Family Saga* for their collection. As I was talking with Christine Wern, the head librarian, and mentioned the Würzburger family of Höchst, Frau Wern pulled a booklet entitled *Die Vergessenen Nachbarn: Juden in Höchst* [The Forgotten Neighbors: Jews in Höchst] from the shelves. To my astonishment, in it I found photographs of the Würzburger and Schiff stores and another one of the three Würzburger boys, namely, Friedrich (Fritz), Herbert, and Erwin. Frau Wern graciously arranged to obtain a copy for me from one of the library's patrons. In the photo acknowledgment section of the booklet I found the notation "Herbert Wetmore, USA."

18. The elder Würzburgers were more fortunate than other German Jews and especially Jews in Nazi occupied territories because only a few months after their escape, on January 20, 1942, the infamous Wannsee Conference in Berlin was held during which members of the Nazi leadership, led by the director of the Reich security office, Reinhard Heydrich, established procedures for the *Endlösung der Europäischen Judenfrage* [Final Solution to the European Jewish Question]. What

had previously been a random program to transport Jews and other undesirable, including Communists, Socialists, homosexuals, Roma (Gypsies), and people who spoke out against the Nazi regime, to concentration camps now became a systematic and focused national effort. The world would come to know the program as the Holocaust or, in Hebrew, the Shoah.

According to the latest researches, on the order of five million Jews, mostly from Eastern Europe, died in concentration camps between 1939 and 1945. In the early 1930s there were roughly 570,000 Jews living within the borders of Germany which was less than 1% of the population. It has been estimated that of these two-thirds emigrated and the remaining 190,000 perished in the death camps and ghettos. Between 1939 and 1940, the Nazi regime actively promoted the emigration of Jews from the Third Reich and 160,000 left the country. (See Wilhelm Wagner, *Neuer Bildatlas Zur Deutschen Geschichte*, 295, 311).

19. According to a newspaper obituary notice given to me by my *Onkel Jule*, Hans Schübelin, born on November 20, 1911 in Karlsruhe, the son of Albert Friedrich August Schübelin and Lina Auguste Schübelin née Schulz, died in Karlsruhe on May 12, 1993. His occupation was listed as *Steuerrat a. D.* [tax councilor, retired]. The notice lists a daughter named Ursula Schübelin as survivor. According to an earlier death notice for his wife, Hans Schübelin had been married to Anna Maria Schübelin née Elfner who was born on October 31, 1907 and died on November 16, 1982 in Karlsruhe.

20. According to her death certificate, Johanna Heil née Boy, widow of Wilhelm Friedrich Heil, passed away on March 29, 1968 in the home of *Regierungsamtmann* [government official] Julius Kuchenbeißer. My *Onkel Jule's* address is given as Talstraße 66 in Stuttgart, an upscale apartment building in the eastern part of town. Presumably, he was employed in Stuttgart by the state of Baden-Württemberg at the time before he and Erika returned to Graben-Neudorf upon his retirement.

21. DNA test procedures are nowadays routinely used to determine paternity and had these been available in the 1930s my own would not be a mystery. Out of curiosity, I had my own DNA tested and found that my ancestry is 100% European and composed of four

ethnicities: North & West European (78.9%); East European (16.7%); Irish, Scottish & Welsh (2.3%); and Spanish (2.1%). Interestingly, none of my DNA was found to match any close family member but over 1,500 distant relatives were located in the U.S. and Europe.

22. When I visited my baptismal church in Graben, the Evangelische Kirche, on the day I met Frau Metzger, co-pastors Andreas and Silke Obenauer presented me with a copy of *Graben: Vom Bauerndorf zur modernen Industriegemeinde* [Graben: From Peasant Village to Modern Industrial Community] in which the article by Guido Herzog on the Jews of Graben appears. On my last visit to Graben-Neudorf, in early August 2017, I found my birthplace in a very dilapidated state even though the property was still occupied by a number of families. Neighbors told me that the village wanted to tear it down because it was an eyesore but that Graben's small Jewish community had objected because of its historic significance. Unfortunately, neither party was able or willing to put up the funds to rehabilitate and maintain the property. A local friend recently informed me that the village of Graben-Neudorf, as part of a project to restore the historic center of Graben, has completely renovated the building's interior and exterior including the installation of a new roof.

23. When the European Economic Community (EEC) was created by the Treaty of Rome in 1957, its six founding member were France, Italy, West Germany, and the Benelux countries, namely, Belgium, Netherlands, and Luxembourg. Around that time, during the presidency of Dwight D. Eisenhower (1953-1961), the government of the United Kingdom unsuccessfully sought American assistance in scuttling European plans for economic integration and subsequently got together with Denmark and others to form a rival economic block. When, in 1961, four countries including the U.K. and Denmark applied for membership, French President Charles de Gaulle caused the application to be rejected. Only in January 1973 were Denmark, Ireland, and the UK admitted to the EEC. By the 1992 Treaty of Maastricht the EEC became the European Union (EU) which now comprises 27 member states. In a referendum in June 2016, the British electorate voted to leave the EU (Brexit) and as of January 31, 2020 the UK is no longer part of it.

24. October 6, 1983 marked the 300th anniversary of the arrival of the first group of German settlers in Colonial America. The 13 families came from Krefeld in the Rhineland and were Quakers and Mennonites led by Pastor Francis Daniel Pastorius. Traveling on the *Concord*, they landed in Philadelphia on October 6, 1683 where they founded Germantown, the first recorded German settlement in the English colonies. The new arrivals came at the invitation of William Penn, a Quaker and founder of the Province of Pennsylvania. In 1983 President Ronald Reagan proclaimed October 6 an official holiday to be known as German-American Day to honor German contributions to America. When, on August 18, 1987, he signed S. J. Resolution 108 into law, October 6 became a permanent American holiday. Few Americans know about it and, like most other official holidays, it is not celebrated by the general public. It is, however, marked by local German-American groups in towns and cities across America and often celebrated in conjunction with Oktoberfest.

25. An important factor relating to the Holocaust Mutti did not articulate is the following. If ordinary citizens did not show more concern about the fate of their Jewish neighbors, it is most likely because they had more pressing problems to contend with. Most importantly, during this period of time Germany was at war. It was a savage war in which huge battles were fought with staggering losses on all sides. Germany's cities and towns were being pulverized by the western Allies and hundreds of thousands of their inhabitants slaughtered. People worried about the fate of their loved ones on the front and surviving the bombings at home. In most cities and towns across the country staying alive was a full-time occupation that left little time or inclination to worry about others and especially not about minorities including Jews. These historical facts are often ignored by people who grew up after Word War II resulting in a distorted view of German history.

26. According to historical records for World War I, of the 550,000 Jews living within the Reich who held German citizenship, 100,000 served in the Kaiser's Army with 80% being front line soldiers. Altogether 12,000 German Jewish soldiers fell in battle (12%) while 35,000 (35%) earned citations for bravery. (See Wilhelm Wagner, *Neuer Bildatlas Zur Deutschen Geschichte*, 294).

27. As it turned out, neither Mutti nor I ever returned to Florida to either visit or live there. It was unrealistic of me to expect Mother to move and live there by herself when she was already in her mid-70s while Esther and the rest of the family were back in Oak Park. Renting out the property brought its own problems typical of those of an absentee landlord. After my permanent return home, the continuing repair costs especially on a continuously leaking roof and the property tax bills that arrived punctually every three months put a severe strain on my finances and I decided it was time to sell. It came as great relief when I was able to unload the white elephant in late October 1993 although at a considerable financial loss.

28. Mama Gartner was born Maria Reichert on July 22, 1912 in Minseln (since 1972 part of Rheinfelden, Baden-Württemberg), a village nine miles east of Basel on the Swiss-German border. Sometime after Robert had died and she had trouble getting around, Mama Gartner moved across the street to the St. Josephshaus, a church-affiliated assisted living home. There she fell from her wheelchair breaking a hip. When the St. Josephshaus was now no longer able to care for her, Wolfgang and Bärbel brought her to a nursing home. There she felt abandoned and became increasingly despondent. His mother, Wolfgang wrote me, was much looking forward to a possible visit by me on her 80th birthday. Being temporarily between jobs at the time and in no mood for foreign travel, I decided to stay home. It was a decision I later much regretted because Mama Gartner passed away shortly thereafter, on August 19, 1992. According to her son, she was in fairly good health but on the day of her passing took lunch, laid down for a nap, and never woke up.

I was able to visit Mama Gartner's grave in the Karlsruhe Hauptfriedhof (central cemetery) during visits to Germany in the summers of 2006 and 2011, the first time with her grandson. At the time, Andreas worked as a cartographer for the state of Baden-Württemberg in Stuttgart, where he commuted by train, while wife Brigitte was with the tax office of the City of Karlsruhe. When I visited them, the couple owned their own home, a 3-story townhouse in Karlsruhe, and had two young children, Tobias and Rebecca. As to Wolfgang, he returned to his old employer after his venture with the used car lot failed. After his retirement, he and Bärbel moved to Efringen-Kirchen (Baden-Württemberg), the most southwestern corner of Germany, where she owned some property.

29. The *Volksmusik* productions issued as videocassettes by diverse artists were much enjoyed by music lovers in Europe's German-speaking countries. One series produced by ZDF, one of two German public television channels, was called *Sonntagskonzert* [Sunday concert] and featured out-of-door concerts by local choirs, brass bands, and other musical ensembles in villages and towns across Germany, Austria, and Switzerland. The event was usually held in the town square and started punctually Sundays at noon with a choir singing their popular theme song. Having sung in a school boys choir in Stuttgart and being an amateur poet, one *Volksmusik* offering much to my liking was a videocassette that came out in 1982. It was a co-production by ZDF of Germany and ORF of Austria featured the most renowned five boys choirs in these two countries accompanied by such well-known vocalists as Anneliese Rothenberger, Peter Schreier, and Hermann Prey.

The filming was done on location and featured the Regensburger Domspatzen, the Thomanerchor of Leipzig, the Tölzer Knabenchor, the Vienna Boys Choir, and the Dresdner Kreuzchor. Between the musical selections the actor Will Quadflieg recited poems by Goethe and others. The production entitled *Leise Flehen Meine Lieder - Eine Poesievolle Reise Durch die Jahreszeiten* [Gently Implore My Songs - A Poetical Journey Through The Seasons] was also available in the States through a *Volksvideo* label but, like many other outstanding Volksmusik offerings, this videotape was, unfortunately, not reissued as a DVD. Incidentally, the Regensburger Domspatzen (Regensburg Cathedral Sparrows), which serves St. Peter's Cathedral in the Bavarian town of Regensburg, was founded in 975 AD and is the world's oldest choral ensemble. Its director at the time of the recording was Georg Ratzinger whose older brother Joseph would later become Pope Benedict XVI.

30. After filing of the "Petition For Appointment Of Guardian For Disabled Person" in The Circuit Court of Cook County, Illinois, County Department, Probate Division, the case became known as "Estate of Anne Marie Zell, An Alleged Disabled Person, Case No. 97 P 001648, Docket 263, Page 256."

PART III

ALL MY CHILDREN

ESTHER'S STORY

A Promising Start

The Old Testament book of *Esther* tells the story of a Jewish girl who becomes the wife of Xerxes I the Great (519-465 BC), the ruler of the mighty Persian Empire. She saves her people from certain destruction by their enemies led by the king's grand vizier Haman. The heroine risks her life to frustrate Haman's evil plan and it is Haman and his followers who are executed on the very date assigned to the massacre of the Jews. Unique about *Esther* is that it is the only book in the Bible that never mentions God. On the Jewish calendar the event is celebrated as Purim, a two-day festival in the spring. When Fritz and Annemarie Würzburger named their first child for this ancient Jewish heroine they could not have foreseen that their daughter would be caught up in yet another pogrom designed to destroy the Jewish people, this time in the Nazis' "final solution" that came to be known as the Holocaust or Shoah.

Our story begins on February 11, 1927 when Esther Emma Rosa Würzburger is born to Friedrich (Fritz) Würzburger and his wife to be, Anna Maria Zell, in her maternal grandparents' home in Schwanheim am Main. Her father and mother were not yet married most likely because Annemarie was short of the legal age of 18. The couple's marriage took place one year later on February 14, 1928 in Höchst am Main by which time Esther was a one-year-old and her mother was already four months pregnant with their second child Friedrich. Esther had always taken special pride in her legitimacy vis-à-vis her younger siblings who, with the exception of her full brother, Friedrich (Bodo), could not make such a claim. Her birth certificate and the more recently obtained copy of her parents' marriage certificate prove otherwise.

Esther had an auspicious start in life. Her parents were solidly middle class people in the very status-conscious German society of the time, well off financially, and conventional in their attitudes and lifestyles. She was the apple of her grandmother's eye who spoiled her as grandparents are wont to do. Oma was charmed by the cute little girl who had inherited her parents' good looks and their outgoing and pleasant personalities. Esther was dark-haired like her mother but had the clear blue eyes of her father. Oma was already much looking forward to seeing her grandchild enter the Schwanheimer Volksschule at the beginning of September 1933 when she would be six years old. But that was not to be as she passed away nearly a year before.

The affection she and her grandmother had for each other makes the earliest recorded event from Esther's childhood all the more remarkable. According to Mutti, when she returned home from the hospital to tell Esther that her Oma had passed away, Esther had calmly asked, *"Was erbe ich von ihr?"* [What do I inherit from her?]. Mutti, beside herself with grief over her beloved mother's early passing and shocked by the callous question of her young daughter, had for the first and only time slapped Esther's face. In fact, Mutti never forgot Esther's remark and when she once reminded her about it many years later, Esther suggested that her Oma Würzburger may have put her up to it. Nevertheless, some character traits manifest themselves very early in life and, in Esther's case, her question turned out to be a true indicator of her character and future conduct.

The Nazi Years

With the rise of virulent ultranationalism in Germany, which came to be known as Nazism, Esther's hitherto happy childhood came to a premature and abrupt end. The Jews were made scapegoats for Germany's defeat in the world war, later to be called World War I, and Esther had a Jewish father which made her a *Mischling* [mixed breed]. School children, who in the process of socialization appear to require a pecking order, are quick to note one or the other in their midst who does not fit the norm especially if they have been alerted to which group is in and which is out in the social hierarchy. Esther was certainly different and when she got to the Volksschule she found out just what that entailed. According to Mutti, some of her classmates began taunting Esther with vulgar rhymes like

"Jud, Jud—scheiß in die Tud" [Jew, Jew—shit in the bag]. Most kids would not play or associate with her. In fact, only one Schwanheim girl, Elli Lauer by name, would not join the others and instead become a good and lifelong friend.

After attending the Schwanheimer Volksschule, Esther came into what during the Nazi regime was called *Pflichtjahr* [compulsory year in domestic service] or *Stellung*. All girls after leaving the Volksschule went into *Stellung* for a year or two during which they lived with a family to learn the skills of a Hausfrau and help out with household chores. This was the female version of the apprenticeship served by boys who were required to learn a trade unless they were attending the Gymnasium or Oberschule in preparation for the university. According to Mutti, Esther's experience in *Stellung* was not a pleasant one. The people she worked for were exploitive expecting much work from her while giving her little to eat so that she often suffered hunger pangs. Parenthetically, it may be assumed that the major beneficiaries of this cheap domestic help were well-connected Nazis.

There was at least one bright spot during Esther's early years. That was when Aunt Emmi and Uncle Charles invited her to spend time with them in their homes in Geneva and Grasse. The visits were an eye-opening experience for Esther and set the stage for many of her future plans and activities. She was fascinated by her aunt's and uncle's wealth and opulent lifestyle and especially by their beautiful vacation home in the south of France. Their villa La Rato Penado in Chateauneuf de Grasse was located amidst a sea of fragrant flowers, herbs and shrubs including roses, violets, jasmine, lavender, lilac, and mignonette that stretched down the hills to Cannes and the Côte d'Azur. The oils derived from these plants formed the basis for a flourishing perfume industry that made Grasse the perfume capital of the world. While there, Esther reputedly formed a strong bond with Uncle Charles, or Uncle Charlie as she later liked to call him.

According to Mutti, her sister did not bring Esther to Geneva and the French Riviera to see the sights and smell the roses but to put her to work cleaning house and doing chores. Esther happily obliged especially after Aunt Emmi promised her, so Esther and Mutti would forever claim thereafter, that someday she would inherit all of her aunt's wealth including her fabulous collection of rare yellow diamonds. Back in Schwanheim, Mutti wasted no time telling relatives and friends that Esther was her wealthy sister's designated heiress. For Esther, Aunt Emmi's reputed promise was like money in the bank and she made sure throughout her life that nobody got in the way of what she saw as her rightful inheritance.

It appears that despite the dangers posed for a *Mischling* during the Third Reich, Mutti's collaboration with the Nazi regime kept Esther insulated enough from its persecution of Jews including *Mischlinge* to allow her to lead a relatively normal life. In Stuttgart, where Mutti had relocated by 1939 when her daughter was 12, Esther received some excellent occupational training and found employment. She did not attend a Gymnasium (girls were much less likely than boys to receive a higher education in those days) but, after graduating from the Volksschule and doing her *Pflichtjahr*, was admitted to the private classes of a Dr. Binder, a well-known Stuttgart chemist and educator. This being the early 1940s and the war in full swing, his school served the needs of industry for more technical help than the public educational system could provide. Under Dr. Binder's tutelage, Esther learned the rudiments of organic chemistry and was apparently a very bright and gifted student.

On successfully completing the course work, Esther was immediately hired by the firm of Robert Bosch GmbH, an electrical company that supplied spark plugs and other electrical equipment to Daimler-Benz AG and other manufacturers in Germany and abroad. According to Mutti, the Robert Bosch company was one of the few employers to hire *Mischlinge* and other minorities during the Third Reich. At Bosch, Esther was assigned as an assistant to a Dr. Hausemann who was in charge of a company laboratory located in the Stuttgart suburb of Feuerbach. Its main function was the analysis of engine oils. Esther was very *tüchtig* [capable, energetic] according to Mutti, and the two had a profitable relationship. Eventually, towards the end of the war, Robert Bosch and the laboratory were bombed out, like many other German manufacturers, and Esther became unemployed.

Just about this time, the Nazi persecution of the Jews took on an increased intensity as did the Anglo-American bombing of Stuttgart and Mutti thought it prudent to send Esther to Bludenz in the Tyrol region of Ostmark (Austria). As previously mentioned, Mutti sent me along and we stayed in a small hotel called Weisses Kreuz (White Cross) where Esther helped out in the restaurant. She was nearing 18 at the time and beginning to attract the attention of the opposite sex. Her first suitor was the young and dashing Wehrmacht lieutenant Manfred Straka, an Austrian by birth but a German citizen after the so-called *Anschluss* [annexation] by Adolf Hitler of his native Austria to the Third Reich. The romance did not last long as his unit was deployed to the Brenner Pass (the Alpine boundary between Italy and Austria) and Esther and I returned to Stuttgart.

Back home, Esther did a valuable service for us all by helping with a neighborhood initiative encouraged by the regime which was to construct bomb shelters to supplement the public ones already in existence or being built. This particular private initiative was sponsored by the Marienhospital (St. Mary's Hospital) next door to our apartment building on Adlerstraße 8. The project was to dig a bomb shelter into the side of a hill at a location on the Schimmelhüttenweg that was a short distance from our home. It kept us and our neighbors and the patients, nurses, and doctors of the Marienhospital save from enemy bombs for the duration of the war.

Emigration

After the war, Esther met Nicholas (Nick) Holzman at the Goldener Adler restaurant across the street from our apartment building. Nick, a 25 year-old GI from Chicago who spoke some German, was not as dashing and debonair as Lieutenant Straka had been but more of a good-natured, nice kind of guy. Nick and Esther became good friends and subsequently spent as much time with each other as his Army duties would allow. With the help of the Stuttgart offices of the Hebrew Immigrant Aid Society (Hias), Mutti and Esther were able to locate Esther's father Friedrich, her grandmother Mathilde, and brother Bodo in the United States. The task was complicated by the fact that, unbeknownst to the family, the Würzburgers had changed their names to Wetmore sometime after their arrival in America.

The Wetmores were found living at 2170 Walton Avenue in the Bronx, a borough of New York City. There being no postal service between Germany and the United States during and immediately after the war, Nick was enlisted to use his Army mailing privileges so that the two sides could correspond. Eventually Fritz (now Fred) agreed to become his daughter's sponsor for her emigration to America and provide a place for her to live. In late November 1946, just a year and a half after the war's end, Esther said good-bye to her family and Nick and left Stuttgart for the port town of Bremerhaven and life in the New World.

Little is known about Esther's first few years after her arrival in New York City in mid-December 1946 at age 19 because she never talked much about it. In line with other members of her father's family, she adopted Wetmore as her surname and called herself Esther Rose Wetmore. According to Mutti, she first lived with her family in the Bronx and then found employment as a waitress in the Adirondack Mountains in upstate New York which was a well-known vacation destination for well-to-do Jews from New York City. From her earnings, which were said to have been meager, Esther mailed Mutti a small sum each week, reputedly $10, which Mutti skillfully used to become a successful entrepreneur in the flourishing post-war activity known as the *Schwarzmarkt* [black market]. As a consequence of Mutti's efforts, our little family was much better off than our friends and neighbors as far as foodstuffs were concerned. For reasons unknown, Esther and her father and her brother, now called Jerry, did not hit it off well together because she subsequently had little contact with the two. She did, however, renew her bond with her grandmother and the two stayed in close touch for the remainder of the latter's life.

Esther was not happy with her situation in New York and when Nick contacted her after his discharge from the U. S. Army and suggested she come to Chicago to become his bride, she was all too happy to oblige. First she had to become a Catholic and after accepting that faith, Esther Wetmore and Nicholas Holzman were married on September 25, 1948 in St. Alphonsus, his family's parish church on Chicago's North Side. Nick, who was born on February 4, 1920 in Sterling, Colorado, was a graduate of the well-known Lane Technical High School in Chicago. Catholic families tended to be large at the time and his was especially so. His parents, Nicholas Sr. and Elizabeth Holzman née Nahm, had nine children—six boys and three girls.

Our subsequent reunion with Esther and Nick in Chicago in mid-March 1950 did not, unfortunately, bring much happiness for any of us. At the time, Esther and Nick were still living at home with his parents at 626 W. Buckingham Place and saving up to buy a home in the adjoining suburb of Oak Park. Not long after their purchase of a small stucco house on South Oak Park Avenue and after we had moved in, Mutti and Esther were engaged in almost daily verbal combat with Esther taking the offensive and Mutti doing her best to fend her off.

It appears that Esther was extremely unhappy with the prospect of having to support her three younger siblings by the half blood while Mutti was making an insufficient contribution to the family finances and, on top of that, was talking about temporarily returning to Germany to take care of some unsettled business there. My two younger siblings and I were unfortunately caught up in the cross-fire. What we did not know before of Esther's character and persona, we now found out the hard way even though even Mutti seemed surprised by a complete transformation in her daughter's personality. According to Mother, back in Stuttgart Esther was mild-mannered and kind and after just over three years in America had turned mean and ruthless. After Mutti returned to Germany in June 1951, Esther had wasted no time sending the three of us back to Stuttgart to join her.

After Mutti's return to the States in mid-November 1951 and my own in early April of the following year, Mutti reached out to Esther and we all got together again. Nick continued to be employed as a truck driver for Continental Distributing Company which was one of Chicago's largest distributors of Scotch and Bourbon whiskies and other alcoholic beverages. His territory was the Gold Coast and northern suburbs where he serviced the country clubs and better restaurants in the area.

During one of my summers off from college, I too worked for this company and was assigned as a helper on Nick's delivery truck. I could tell that my brother-in-law was not well liked by his co-workers because he was exceptionally hardworking and, in their view, too close to management. The company tried to make him a scheduling supervisor but he steadfastly refused saying he preferred to work with his customers in the field. That was probably the smart thing to do because with the Teamsters Union he had job security which would not have been the case in management.

Until the early summer of 1955, Esther too was employed working for a small firm known as Henry & Son. That company had set up shop on one of the floors of an old factory building on Chicago's West Side to manufacture specialty clothing items such as party aprons. Esther got me a job there during one of my high school summer vacations. Like Nick, Esther was not popular with her co-workers but highly thought of by Mr. Henry, Sr. and his son. She was their top producer and once Esther sat down at her high-speed sewing machine, she was completely focused working diligently all day and only occasionally taking a short break to eat her bag lunch or go to the bathroom. She was friendly but never socialized with any of her co-workers.

Just about this time Esther decided that she too wanted to drive like most other suburbanites. This would make her less dependent on Nick and on that not always reliable Chicago public transportation system for getting around. Esther took driving lessons and when it was time for her to take the examination in Chicago, she took me along. As I sat in the back seat of the car, the examining officer sitting next to her in the front seat had her go through the required maneuvers. After some jerky starts and stops followed by a wild ride about the area which had me hold onto my seat, the officer told Esther that he would pass her so she could get her license but entreated her never to drive if she could possibly avoid it. She prudently took the officer's advice and never took the wheel of a car again but held on to her driver's license having it reissued whenever it was up for renewal. This document was very useful at the time because it was the only means of providing official identification where such was required.

Chasing The American Dream

Like most immigrants, Esther was eager to share in the American Dream which to most people meant material prosperity and financial independence. More specifically, living the dream meant a college education, a well-paying corporate job, an attractive home in a leafy suburb with good schools for the children's education, and a car or two in the garage. It was something that had largely been absent in the lives of their Old World ancestors but, in the land of opportunity, was eminently achievable through ingenuity and hard work.

Esther was somewhat handicapped in not having enjoyed much formal education but she soon realized that one way to achieve the American Dream was through investment in real estate. Past experience had shown that prices in land and buildings always went up over the years and consequently the acquisition of real property was universally touted as the best possible investment especially for people who did not care to deal with the risks and vagaries of the stock market. It provided a strong hedge against inflation and the timely buying and selling of houses could yield extraordinary profits. Furthermore, owning real estate provided tax advantages since the mortgage interest was income tax deductible. Not surprisingly, every American family's dream after the war was to own their own home.

Nick and Esther had made a good start in this direction with the purchase of the single family home at 515 South Oak Park Avenue in April 1950. By the time Mutti was back from Germany a year and a half later, however, my sister and brother-in-law had already sold their house and were renting a small apartment four blocks down the street at 925 South Oak Park Avenue. This move, although it seemed counterintuitive, made sense, since with Mutti and the rest of us back in Germany, the two no longer needed all that room nor the big mortgage that came with it and there was a much better option available to them.

This option was to buy rental property which not only gave them a place to live but also provided a source of income to help pay off the mortgage. In line with this idea, Nick and Esther purchased a 2-story stucco building located on the northeast side of the village, at 143 North Taylor Avenue. While the couple lived on the second floor, they rented out the downstairs plus a studio apartment located under the roof. This was the beginning of Esther's profitable venture into rental property.

After having made a good start with a small piece of property, Esther was ready for a more significant move. Sometime in 1962, Esther and Nick sold their place on North Taylor Avenue and purchased a 3-story apartment building located just south of the Lake Street "L" in Oak Park at 122-124 South East Avenue. Esther never explained where the funds for this substantial purchase came from. They had, of course, built up some equity in their Taylor Avenue property but that would surely not be enough. One source was a huge restitution program set up by the West German government (BRD) after the war to compensate death camp survivors, *Mischlinge* like Esther, and others adversely impacted by the Nazi regime. According to Elke, who heard it from Ute, Esther became a beneficiaty of this program although the amount she received is not known and neither Esther nor Mutti ever revealed any such payment or payments to me. Additional funds were presumably provided by Uncle Charles. From a greeting card I received from him and our aunt in December 1962, they had enjoyed a visit from Esther and Ute during the past summer. That could have been the time when the loan was arranged. Esther once mentioned such a loan to me and her intention to pay Uncle Charles back as soon as possible.

Their newly acquired property was a handsome brick structure of a lemon color with an ornate stone and brick front and fancy oak and glass entrance door. Dark brown awnings over the front windows shielded from the midday sun. The building had one small basement unit and two large apartments each on three floors separated by a central stairwell. Attached to the back of the building was the usual wooden staircase leading to the apartments' back entrances. Behind the property stood a frame garage for tenant parking which faced the back alley. Esther, Nick, and Steffi moved into one of the two apartments on the top floor, the one on the left as one faced the building.

The apartment was ideally suited for a small family or a retired couple but had an unusual layout. The large living room, which faced the street, took in the entire width of the apartment. Branching off the short hallway leading from this room, was a small bedroom, which was occupied by Steffi, followed by the bathroom. At the end of this hallway was a rectangular dining room which again took up the width of the apartment. The other side of this room led to the kitchen on the right and to the master bedroom on the left, i.e., bedroom and kitchen shared a common wall. A large French door separated the dining and the master bedrooms while a door at the further end of the kitchen gave access to the back stairwell.

Esther expertly managed the rental property herself selecting new tenants, signing leases, and keeping her investment in top shape by tending to all necessary repairs and improvements. To have the right sort of tenants, she was very selective in whom she took in. References from prior landlords were required and well-to-do elderly residents preferred to less affluent younger ones. Tenants were not allowed to own pets. The substantial rental income on the six units she rented out allowed for the early repayment of Uncle Charles' loan, a progressive reduction in the outstanding mortgage, and the accumulation of substantial equity in the property to the point where Nick and Esther almost owned it outright.

The Pop Singer

For people with talent, there had always been another road to riches besides real estate and the volatile stock market and that was by becoming a popular entertainer. The 1950s was an especially profitable decade for male and female vocalists who could belt out the popular hit tunes of the day. Radio and the new medium of television popularized singers and their songs and the sale of long-playing records (LPs) made many of them rich and famous. Among the numerous pop singers of the day were Rosemary Clooney, Perry Como, Eddie Fisher, Patti Page, Elvis Presley, Dinah Shore, Frank Sinatra, and Kay Starr.

It was not long before Esther too began to warble and see herself as a popular singer and recording artist with the money and glamour that came with it. First, however, she had to take voice lessons. Actually, Esther had been exercising her voice even before she came to America because I remember that during my audition for the school choir, I told my music teacher at the Schickhardt Oberschule in Stuttgart, Herr Bähr, that I had an older sister who also much enjoyed singing. Choral singing especially of volkslieder had always been a feature of German musical culture and Chicago had several choral societies known as *Liederkränze* [garlands of songs] to uphold this tradition. These were led by music directors well known in the German-American community who, to supplement their incomes from regular employment, usually gave private singing lessons as well.

Determined to become a real professional, Esther procured the services of one of these people to make her dream come true. For several years Esther diligently took voice lessons and practiced her art at home. One Saturday, Esther took me along with her to this man's studio on North Lincoln Avenue. As she practiced her scales and tried a couple of popular songs, it became clear to me that my sister would never be able to match the great pop singers of the day because when she sang her voice sounded strained and wobbly and she had difficulty holding a tune. It was embarrassing to listen to her but I did not dare mention my concerns.

I was already away in college when I heard from Mutti what happened next. Even though Esther's voice teacher had warned her that she was not yet ready for a public performance, she nevertheless arranged for a recital at one of the German restaurants around Lincoln Square. The affair turned out to be a complete disaster. After her performance, there was some muted, polite applause but most of the audience just sat there in stunned silence. Esther, mortified and disgusted, ran out of the place and immediately fired her voice coach who followed close behind her. Poor Esther was never heard to sing again neither at home nor in public.

Even before her ill-fated singing debut, Esther had made arrangements to have some of her songs recorded. The task of hand-delivering the phonograph records to various Chicago radio stations was entrusted to me. For cutting the records, she had enlisted the services of William (Bill) L. Klein, the founder in 1927 of the *Germania Broadcast*, the most popular and longest running German language program in the Midwest. It came on daily for an hour in the evening and two hours on Sunday mornings and featured German *Schlager* [hit tunes], volkslieder, and operetta music. The show's sponsors were local German-American business establishments including retailers, restaurants, and travel agencies. Bill Klein, who was Jewish, and Esther hit it off well together. Mr. Klein owned a recording studio where he produced the *Germania Broadcast* in addition to radio and television commercials.

One day in the fall of 1953, when I was a junior in high school, Esther informed me of Mr. Klein's wish to see me. He invited the two of us to Fritzel's which was a fancy German-American restaurant in downtown Chicago. Much to my sister's embarrassment, I immediately committed a faux pas. During our conversation, Mr. Klein told me he had heard that my mother and I did most of our shopping at Marshall Field's. "Marshall Field's," I protested without thinking, "Mutti and I can barely afford Sears, Roebuck." (Marshall Field's was the most exclusive and pricey department store in town). On our way home, Esther chided me for mouthing off again. Nevertheless, Mr. Klein evidently liked what he saw and heard because he asked Esther to find out what my favorite German songs were. A short time later, she delivered his gift of a half dozen LPs.

Starting A Family

Nick and Esther were looking forward to having a family. They had been married seven years when, at the end of August 1955, a new chapter in their lives began with the birth of Stephanie Maria. Everything surrounding the birth was kept very hush-hush. The reason became apparent somewhat later. Steffi, as her parents called her, had the misfortune of having come into the world physically handicapped in that her limbs, while perfectly formed, did not grow normally. As far as Mutti could find out, the fetus was defective and was about to be prematurely discharged from the womb when Esther's gynecologist, Dr. Chester Gajewski, made every effort, by injections and other means, to retain it.[1] As might be expected, Steffi's parents were extremely distraught with Nick, a very pious man, appearing to adjust to the situation better than his wife.

Steffi's condition energized Esther and she set out determined to find a cure for her daughter no matter where it took her or what it cost. Whenever she heard or read of some research on dwarfism being done anywhere in the country or abroad, she contacted the place and made an appointment for herself and Steffi to get the latest information and hopefully some help. One time she even traveled to Germany where some quack proposed a cure using a special formula based on bee's honey.

When President Richard Nixon proposed cutbacks in medical research, Esther was indignant and went public. A *Chicago Today* article from the December 1, 1969 issue shows Steffi, then age 14, perusing some of the thousands of petitions she received in support of their fight. Esther took these to Washington to present them to members of Congress and urge them to vote against the cutbacks but was disappointed as most of the senators who were expected at the hearing did not show up. Despite Esther's heroic efforts on Steffi's behalf, all was in vain and she had to resign herself to the fact that their daughter would never grow into a normal-sized adult and would instead become a member of a select group known as little people.

Something that was common knowledge within the family but completely unknown to me for many years was the fact that Bill Klein was more than Esther's friend and business partner but also her paramour. One time Mother got very angry with Esther because of some recent affront and, in her straightforward but slightly comical way said to me, "*Die Esther soll uns mal erzählen wo die Steffi herkommt.*" [Let Esther tell us sometime where Steffi comes from]. When I pressed her to explain what she meant, she blurted out the whole story of Esther's missteps. According to Mutti, not long after Esther and Bill Klein met, the two had an affair and he got her pregnant with Steffi. At the time, Esther had complained to Mother about her humdrum and boring existence with Nick in Oak Park. She told Mutti that she planned to leave Nick and move to Chicago's Gold Coast where the rich and famous lived and all the action was.

Mutti had reminded her daughter of her marriage vows and implored her not to leave Nick who had been a faithful husband and good provider to her. While she was able to persuade Esther not to move out, our mother was apparently not successful in preventing Esther from getting romantically involved with the more glamorous Mr. Klein. Much of this was later confirmed to me by Ute who heard about the affair when she worked for Bill Klein during one of her high school summer vacations. Most remarkable was that Nick, who apparently knew that the newest family member was not his child, just adored Steffi and treated her as if she were his own flesh and blood. This according to Elke who lived in our sister's household from the time Steffi was just three years old. In fact, everyone marveled at the exceptionally strong bond that existed between the two. No child could have hoped for a more caring and loving father than Nick.

A Time For Travel

The summer of 1962 saw Esther, Nick, and Steffi in Germany and Switzerland. In Stuttgart they stopped off to see Josef and Anny Thonemann, the two people of Mutti's acquaintance whom we addressed as *Onkel Josef* and *Tante Anny*, before going on to Geneva to visit with Aunt Emmi and Uncle Charles. In a letter she wrote me in late August of that year, after their return, Esther said, "Aunt Emmy kept calling me and I finally saw her, she is the same. She says she loves Steffi a lot etc.. One day this the other that you know. I told her hello from you. She asked how you were doing." Uncle Charles, who was an investment banker, had given Esther "the lowdown as far as stocks go," she wrote, and she was passing the information on to me. Evidently, our uncle looked at the percentage changes in net incomes of major multinational corporations over a 5-year period to guide his portfolio selections. Xerox Corporation with a +50% change was at the top of his list with AT&T at only +6% at the bottom. Esther went on to complain about the incredibly high prices in Europe for lodging, food, and clothing. People could afford to eat meat only once or twice a week despite making good salaries, she wrote.

Four years later Esther was in the planning stages of another European tour but this one more wide-ranging that would take in Germany, Austria, Italy and Switzerland. A high point would be a few days in Geneva to visit with Aunt Emmi but, more importantly, with Uncle Charles. As fate would have it, our uncle unexpectedly passed away a few months earlier than the scheduled visit—on February 11, 1966—which also happened to be Esther's 39th birthday. She heard about it a few days later but not from Aunt Emmi but a friend in Geneva, she wrote.

Uncle Charles had developed a severe infection in the only kidney he had left and an emergency operation could not save him, according to Esther. "I think I am loosing (sic) my mind, he was the only friend I had left," Esther wrote. According to an April letter from her, Uncle Charles had been looking forward to their arrival because our aunt "locked uncle into the house without food" and "Uncle wanted Nick to get him out this time, but it is to (sic) late now." A lawyer she knew in Geneva told her that our aunt was "not quite right in her mind." In a second letter written the same month, Esther had this to say about our aunt:

> *Well take it from me, [our] aunt has not got what she likes everyone to believe. She is living on money she got from the sale of her home in Grasse + holds a few shares of stock. She never paid any taxes on her sale or other income—so I believe the government will start asking a few questions soon—since uncle paid for the upkeep on the house in Geneva which is old + outdated. Uncle told me that when she dies the state will take most, if at all some is left for 30 some jears (sic) back taxes. She always talked big and mother believes her—I know better. Most of uncle's money went into his stamp collection, his only enjoyment. Well, I hope she leaves enough so mother gets the fare out of it. Uncle's sister writes me once in a while—she seems like a nice person; but scared of aunt; well I am not— uncle is dead now [and] as far as I am concerned she is finished. I told her we would stay at the Richemond if she wants to see us fine otherwise I could not care less.*

The trip was taken as scheduled and in July 1966 the threesome flew to Frankfurt am Main to visit the graves of our grandparents in Schwanheim, then on to Stuttgart to see our friends, the Thonemanns, and from there to Munich where they picked up a rental car for visits to Salzburg, Linz, St Moritz, lakes Como and Maggiore, Chamonix, and Geneva. From there they flew to Paris for a couple of days of sightseeing.

I never did find out whether Esther met up with Aunt Emmi but I doubt it because, needless to say, our aunt had little liking for her niece. Esther did, however, get to meet Uncle Charles' sister, Mme. Evelyn de Pogranyi-Hirzel, in Berne whom she described as "a very nice woman just like uncle, tall and lively." As far as it is known, it was the first and only time the two met although Esther would later claim that this lady was a major influence in her life.

To her credit, Esther's real estate expertise was of much benefit to Mother and me when she arranged for the purchase of Mutti's Place on Augusta Street and North Harlem Avenue in Oak Park in July 1965. I was employed in Virginia at the time and gave Esther a power of attorney to handle all transactions from selecting the property to the closing, which took place on August 16. In line with the real estate motto "location, location, location," Esther found the townhouse unit in the best part of the village (the furthest removed from Chicago's undesirable West Side) and near public transportation—we could not have done much better.

She also did a terrific job negotiating with the owner so that the property cost me less than $20,000 when similar properties on the market were selling for several thousand dollars more. Still, it was an enormous sum for me at the time and I had to take on a mortgage for most of the purchase price. When it was discovered that there was a second mortgage of a few hundred dollars on the property, Esther had the closing attorney trace down the paper's owner and advanced me the money to pay it off.

Esther also helped Mutti with furnishing the place. The bedrooms and dining room were brought over from our flat on Home Avenue but for the living room Esther helped Mutti purchase an elegant sofa, two easy chairs, a 4-piece set of coffee and end tables with inlaid stone tops, plus diverse other items. For behind the sofa, Nick was able to procure a beautiful 3'x 4' still life in oil featuring an assortment of roses and fruits and signed by one B. R. Davis. It had once hung in a fashionable North Shore restaurant that had closed. I was able to show the family my appreciation when they came to visit me in Virginia in August of that year when I took them around Colonial Williamsburg, Jamestown, and other places of interest.

A Friend Of The Family

The good times did not last very long as towards the end of the 1960s, Esther became ever more despondent and eventually suffered a mental breakdown. Various factors were cited as contributing to her mental illness including change of life (she was in her early 40s), the irreversible situation with Steffi who was then in her early teens, and the stress from managing her rental property with her difficult and demanding tenants. Mutti came to the rescue by providing as much assistance to her daughter and her family as she could. At the time, Nick was working at his daytime job with Continental Distributing Company, Steffi was in school, Mutti was on the night shift at her job with Jewel Foods while I was in New York City completing my studies for a business degree.

On a typical day, Mutti had hardly come home from work on the bus early in the morning when she got a desperate phone call from her daughter saying she needed help and to please come over immediately. Mother hurriedly changed clothes, fed her two cats and rushed off to spend the day at Esther's place. Going by bus required a transfer and too much time so that she hurriedly traveled the roughly two miles on foot from her new home. Mother usually found her daughter in bed weeping and after tending to her personal needs, she prepared the meals, cleaned house and afterwards tried to get some sleep on the living room sofa before taking off for work again. It was doubly tough for Mutti whose Jewel Foods job was stressful enough because her son-in-law, who could be a complete jerk at times, continuously complained about her cooking, her housekeeping, and everything else he could find fault with, according to Mutti.

Esther was in and out of the hospital where all kinds of tests were done on her. In the meantime, all her regular physician, a Dr. Earle (now deceased), could do for her was to prescribe antidepressants, sedatives, and sleeping pills. When he recommend she sell the apartment building to rid herself of the stress, Esther got angry. She claimed the doctor was just envious because he and his family lived in a nondescript little stucco house, which happened to be right across the street from her place, and was as poor as a church mouse despite his good income as a physician. Esther's situation in the spring of 1970 was evident from a note she scribbled in block capital letters on a piece of paper found in Mutti's files:

> *Nick:*   *Thursday April 1970*
>
> <u>*Please*</u> *take care of my* <u>*mother*</u> *+* <u>*Steffi*</u> *– Please.*
> <u>*I love you all.*</u> *Esther*
> *Dissolve the trust on the building.*
> *Esther*
> *My love to Peter too.*

Esther's illness had put a severe strain in her relationships with Mutti and me. By early 1971, however, she had gotten over the worst of what she had described as a "nightmare." She had been told that her delicate mental and emotional state required her to be free of any stressful or unpleasant situations. I was away from home at the time and evidentially Mother kept pestering her daughter with too many phone calls and petty problems which began to get on her nerves.

Esther was inadvertently drawn into a dispute Mutti had with a neighbor regarding the renewal of the paved walkway between the two townhouse buildings which Mutti thought unnecessary. This neighbor, Charles Lindberg (now deceased), had shown up at Esther's door on South East Avenue demanding immediate payment of our one-twelfth share of the cost and I had asked Esther to put out the $157 until I could pay her back on my return to the States. This prompted Esther's letter of early June 1971 to me in Frankfurt am Main just 10 days prior to Mother's departure to visit me there:

> *Will pay the money to Mr. Lindberg within the week. I must tell you that this is the last I can do for you—after all you and mother must understand that if the picture was reversed and Nick's family needed help I might not look to (sic) kindly upon such an arrangement. Mother is going on my nerves. I can not be her wailing-board for the unrealistic things she does + advises. My doctor does not want me to get involved in anything—my illness (change of life) might go on for years. Both you and mother must*

understand this, and stand on your own 2 feet. We are expected
to take care of the cats which (while on our vacation) will cost us
another $60. It seems quite amazing to me what has been asked of
us throughout the years and aspecially (sic) at this stage of my life
when tension + illness are a constant threat.

Clearly, Esther felt used and imposed on and I could not blame her. She had done much for Mother and me over the years and we had not always shown the appreciation we should have. But as our mother once wrote me, Esther always talks about what she did for us but never mentions what we, especially Mutti, have done for her and as recently as a year earlier. Incidentally, Esther never made the payment she promised and the very irate Mr. Lindberg had to await our return from Europe in mid-August to get his money.

Real help for Esther came by way of an Oak Park psychiatrist by the name of Dr. Frank H. Murrin. She was presumably referred to him because he was a well-known practitioner in the field of electroconvulsive therapy, also known as electroshock or shock therapy, and it was believed that this technique was the most likely to succeed in bringing Esther out of her depression. Dr. Murrin did the procedure on Esther at Riveredge Hospital, a mental health facility in neighboring Forest Park. The shock treatments produced the expected benefits so that Esther eventually became functional again although not completely cured and continuing therapy was called for.

Naturally, Esther felt most grateful to Dr. Murrin and eventually had an opportunity to show her appreciation. It seems that the doctor was going through a mental health crisis of his own. He had married a woman who had been a patient of his and had subsequently committed suicide. Following his wife's death, Dr. Murrin had become extremely distraught and eventually found himself on West Madison Street in Chicago, commonly known as Skid Row, frequenting the cheap saloons there and drinking heavily. (Oak Park was "dry" meaning that no alcoholic beverages could be sold or served within the village).

Esther, on hearing about the sad state of affairs surrounding her former benefactor, sent Nick to Skid Row to find the doctor and invite him to live with them. When I first met Dr. Murrin at Esther's place on South East Avenue, probably in early 1975, he had moved in with Nick, Esther, and

Steffi and become part of the family. A cot on wheels had been set up in the apartment's dining room for him to sleep on. It stood right outside the master bedroom door. Dr. Murrin, a tall, handsome man of Irish-Catholic descent with a very congenial and friendly manner, asked me to simply call him Frank and I was happy to oblige.

Frank came from a prominent Oak Park family and had a most impressive background and career.[2]

As Mutti eventually found out, there was more to the relationship between Esther and Frank than mere friendship. Mother had always been worried by what people might think and say about Esther and the two men living with her. In order to preempt any rumors and squash others already circulating, Mutti went out of her way to assure everyone that there was no hanky-panky going on between the two. She always insisted that it was a Platonic friendship devoid of anything else. One day Mutti and I were grocery shopping on South Harlem Avenue in neighboring Forest Park when she spotted one of Esther's tenants who had the apartment directly below Esther's. Mother excused herself to talk to the woman in private to set her straight. When Mutti returned from her brief encounter with this lady, she seemed devastated and near tears. Surmising that the woman had set Mother straight rather than the other way around, I did not press Mother to tell me what she had learned.

Many years later, on Christmas Eve 1996, Patti, our neighbor, came over to bring us some home-baked cookies. We started talking about Esther when Patti took me aside and let me in on a secret she had been keeping from me for a very long time. Patti's mother Helen was the personal secretary to the manager of the Marshall Field's branch store in Oak Park. One of the employees there, Eleanor by name, happened to be one of Esther's tenants. Eleanor told Patti's mother that after Nick came bolting down the back stairs in the morning to drive off to work, a number of the women in the building would gather in the apartment below Esther's. There they supposedly listened to the shrieks and groans coming from upstairs as Esther and her psychiatrist friend had their early morning romp. These sessions were apparently part of a program of therapy devised by Dr. Murrin to rid Esther of her affliction.

Esther's arrangement with Frank worked out rather well to most everyone's satisfaction. The doctor's continuing therapeutic efforts kept

Esther on an even keel. He became her loyal companion and counselor and since he had a car and she did not drive, he soon came along on all of Esther's trips outside the house. His title added to Esther's prestige and feeling of self-worth and she proudly introduced him as her friend Dr. Murrin or, at times, as her uncle or Nick's cousin. Nick, who was of the same age as Frank, too seemed comfortable with the arrangement and treated Frank with much deference and respect. According to Ute, Nick had consulted his parish priest about the fix he found himself in but had been told that for a Catholic divorce was out of the question and to just make the best of the situation. Only Steffi, who dearly loved her father, remained openly hostile to Frank.

Mutti was especially delighted with the arrangement since Esther had assured her that she and Frank were just good friends but even after she found out the truth, she continued to maintain a favorable view of their relationship because of the doctor's beneficial impact on her daughter's life. The family all went to the same church, St. Edmund Catholic Church on South Oak Park Avenue, which was closest to their home. To guard against wagging tongues in this very conservative and respectable community that was Oak Park, Frank attended Saturday evening mass by himself while Nick, Esther, and Steffi worshipped on Sunday mornings.

Frank also managed to endear himself to me. One Sunday, when Nick and Esther usually came by Mutti's Place after church, my sister confided in me that Frank had expressed his astonishment at my (supposedly) remarkable intelligence. Never having been blessed with an overabundance of self-esteem, and coming from Esther who was not known for handing out compliments especially to me, this revelation did wonders for my ego. Henceforth, I considered Frank my good friend.

For Frank the bargain was obviously very beneficial. He had a good home and all his personal needs were taken care of. Most importantly, Esther kept Frank dry by not allowing any alcohol in the house. That meant that Nick, who enjoyed an occasional beer, had to do without except when they stopped by Mutti's Place. Mother always stocked up to keep her son-in-law happy.

Moving Further West

By the late 1970s and after nearly two decades in their apartment building, Esther decided it was time to move on. Steffi was no longer at home and Esther, Nick, and Frank were tired of apartment living and looking forward to be in more spacious and comfortable quarters. Perhaps even more importantly, Esther was in near panic mode about developments in the village that put her investment at risk. Their building on South East Avenue was just a few blocks west of the Austin neighborhood of Chicago and the population in that area had rapidly undergone major changes in recent years as more and more African-Americans from Chicago's South Side had migrated north to escape the ghettos and high crime rates found there.

In fact, the eastern part of Oak Park was already turning black and for property owners that was an alarming development. Invariable in those days, when blacks moved into a house, people in surrounding homes would put their places on the market. To ensure a quick sale, they often had to drop the price. This had a domino effect so that a neighborhood could turn from entirely white to entirely black in a matter of months. Those who held onto their property the longest were bound to lose the most as property values continued to plummet. Panic selling was the order of the day.

Owners of rental property were especially vulnerable because with the new civil rights and anti-discrimination laws in place, they could no longer freely choose their tenants and turning away African-Americans opened them up to lawsuits. Esther's tenants were all white and she knew that once she had rented out one apartment to a black person, most of her other tenants would move out as soon as their leases had expired. With the new tenants, the premium rents of former days would no longer be possible.

From a human and moral standpoint this was obviously not the way things should have been but they nevertheless represented the economic facts of life at the time. To get out of their dilemma, rental property owners came up with a novel solution which Esther too adopted. She got out of the rental business by converting all seven apartments into individually owned condominiums. The conversion process was costly on account of certain required building improvements, such as the installation of individual utility meters, plus permit and attorney fees and taxes.

Still, Esther turned a handsome profit because, on one hand, property values in still stable neighborhoods such as hers had been steadily rising over the years and, on the other, the sum total of the sell prices of the individual units exceeded the value of the building as a whole. A number of her tenants bought the units they had been renting or another one in the building while others moved out at the end of their leases.

Esther proved very tough-minded with her tenants. Next door to her lived an elderly brother and sister named Lodeski who had been residing in the building for much of their adult lives. The brother had been Frank's chemistry teacher at Oak Park and River Forest High School around the mid-1930s and both Frank and Esther had befriended them. If these people thought that their friendship with their landlady would call for special consideration, they were sadly mistaken. When Esther decided to sell and these two tenants were, for some reason, not ready to buy their unit on short notice and asked instead for an extension of the lease, Esther would not accommodate them. The two had to move their possessions, including a sizable library, to another apartment building in the village where the sister, who had a heart ailment, died shortly after.

Sometime in 1981, Esther, Nick, and Frank left Oak Park to move further west and settled in adjoining River Forest. Unlike Oak Park, that sister village did not yet have "changing neighborhoods." Their new domicile was a single family home just south of what was then Concordia Teachers College and is now Concordia University. The house they purchased, located at 924 Bonnie Brae, was a handsome 2-story brick building, an upscale version of a Chicago-style bungalow, with plenty of space for a comfortable lifestyle. For Esther to live on Bonnie Brae was especially comforting because her gynecologist, Dr. Chester Gajewski (now deceased), lived just a couple of blocks south with his wife and family. Esther was partial to doctors and, according to Mutti, had a secret crush on him. (Dr. Gajewski was also Mutti's physician at the time).

This move brought a big improvement in the lives of all three and especially for Frank who could now exchange his rollaway bed, and later Steffi's bedroom after she left home, for the large master bedroom suite on the second floor facing the street. While their new home was just three blocks away from Mutti's Place and within easy walking distance, Esther preferred to keep Mother, whom she considered neurotic, at arm's length. This was to ensure she had the peace and tranquility she was told she needed for her own mental wellbeing. We therefore rarely got to see any of them except for Sunday mornings when Esther and Nick continued to stop by the house after church.

In the fall of 1983, I was between jobs and living at home trying to get a pricing consultancy started. Frank and I had become good friends as we had much in common. Unlike Esther and Nick, we had both enjoyed a good education and loved to exchange opinions on many diverse topics. It turned out that we were both aspiring authors. Frank wanted to write a couple of popular books in the field of mental development and human behavior while I planned to do so in my own specialty which was the pricing of products and services. According to Frank, he was busy working on two manuscripts. The books were to be entitled *Who am I?* and *Journey Through the Human Mind*. I loved the titles because I thought they were wonderfully catchy and sure to attract many readers. Fancying myself as having some writing skills, I volunteered to help him do the writing and get the books published.

Meanwhile, I had told him of my own efforts to solve the old problem of how products and services should be priced to maximize company profits. Why would a company's sales revenue often go up while profits went down and vice versa? What must be the optimum sell price for a product or service to achieve maximum revenue or maximum profit? What decision rules applied to determine whether prices should be raised or lowered and what formulas could be used to calculate optimum sell prices? I had invested considerable time studying the pricing literature and formulating my own theory to solve these riddles and hoped to someday publish a book entitled *The Pricing Manual* for the use of pricing and marketing managers. Frank was as enthused about my project as I was about his.

A Growing Estrangement

For some reason, Esther got increasingly jealous of my close relationship with Frank and did her best to keep us apart. Maybe she thought we would be talking about her own mental state which one could tell was very precarious. Her movements seemed automated and almost zombie-like possibly on account of heavy medication for depression. One Sunday morning in early October of that year (1983) when she and Nick came by after church, I told Esther that Frank and I had agreed to meet the following morning, which happened to be Columbus Day, to talk about a few things of mutual interest. "That will not be possible," Esther pronounced, "because I have to see my hairdresser in Oak Brook at 10 in the morning." I told her that there were 24 hours in a day and Frank could presumably spare just an hour of his time.

Esther, sitting on the sofa and leafing through a magazine, remained silent. Then Mutti spoke up and asked her, "Why don't you want Peter to see the doctor?" Esther did not reply. Then Nick said that he thought that Frank was certainly able to make up his own mind whom he wants to talk with. To this I added, "Sometimes I wonder if Frank is allowed to do so." That was enough for Esther. Visibly angry, she slammed down her magazine on the coffee table, got up and told Nick they were leaving. Shouting, "I have heard that garbage long enough," she stormed out the back door with Nick following close behind.

Very exasperating to me was Esther's insistence that everything occur around her schedule without any regard of whether it fit in with anybody else's. There was no negotiating about the time and place of a get-together. It was always the time and place of her choosing. She and Nick could have gone to an earlier mass on Sundays, just as I went to the early worship service at our church, but it had to be the one at 11 o'clock. Consequently, the two never got to Mutti's Place until well past noon. Sometimes, they stopped somewhere else after church which made them show up even later. Often during the pleasant days of spring and fall, when the Rhem Park outdoor pool was closed, I wanted to take Mutti for lunch in Lake Geneva or Fontana followed by some window shopping or a boat ride on the lake. By the time we got up there around 2:30 p.m. at the earliest, most of Sunday was shot.

While I would not have hesitated to suggest to Esther a more convenient time for her weekly visit, it would have upset Mutti and hence I chose never to speak up. Ever concerned of further injury to Esther's already damaged and delicate psyche, Mutti insisted that I keep quiet and let Esther maintain her chosen routine. In fact, I rarely joined in the conversation because one had to be extremely careful of what one said. Any perceived slight brought out the customary response from her. She would abruptly get up shouting "Nick, let's go" and stomp out without saying good-bye even to our mother. This would inevitably bring Mutti to tears and ruin her day which is something I did not savor. After I accepted another position in January 1984, this one on Long Island, I fortunately no longer had to put up with Esther and her oppressive and egotistical behavior for some time.

As to Steffi, despite her physical handicap she did quite well for herself career-wise. After we watched her graduate from Oak Park and River Forest High School in a beautiful outdoor ceremony in June 1974, she went off to college attending Arizona State University in Tempe followed by Brigham Young University in Salt Lake City. Thereafter, she worked in the Southwest for a number of firms including a major credit card company. When I learned from Esther that the ups and downs of corporate employment were taking a toll on my niece, I suggested to my sister that Steffi would be better off working for the federal government since a civil service position offered relatively more job security than the private sector. I had been a civil service employee two decades earlier and knew what I was talking about. Consequently, in mid-1986, Nick took Steffi to Washington, DC for a series of interviews. The happy outcome was that Steffi was offered and as of August 1 of that year accepted a civil service position with the U.S. State Department. She subsequently moved into an apartment in Alexandria, VA where her parents and Frank visited her several times every year.

The North Shore Beckons

The threesome was not destined to stay in their River Forest home very long. By at least early 1986 Esther was making plans to move far north into Chicago's exclusive North Shore suburb of Lake Forest near the Wisconsin border. In fact, in the summer of that year I heard from Mutti that they had already sold their house and moved into an apartment in the northern suburb of Des Plaines in preparation of their relocation to Lake Forest. According to Mutti, Esther had purchased a lot in that town and planned to build a big mansion there. As ever with Esther, everything was very hush-hush. She did reveal to Mutti, however, that building materials were already being delivered to the site on a daily basis. As it turned out, none of this was true and they had never purchased a lot there let alone built a house on it but, instead, Esther was conducting a search for a home for sale which met her requirements.

Two reasons impelled Esther to move far north. One was her concern for property values and her persistent fear of what the influx of minorities, especially African-Americans, would do to the price of real estate. She was certain that what was happening in Oak Park, which was rapidly becoming integrated, would soon also befall River Forest. It was time to move on. Her second reason, also economic in nature, had to do with a mail order business she had started in 1984. The new venture involved selling knockoff perfumes and facial creams from her home by mail.

By using the phrase "our version of" Esther could advertise and sell the popular name-brand fragrances and creams of the day at a heavily discounted price without running afoul of the trademark laws. Operating out of exclusive Lake Forest would add luster to the venture because, as Esther said, the perfume business was all about image. After my permanent return home to Oak Park at Thanksgiving 1986 and the threesome's move into their new Lake Forest home on 970 Northcliffe Way on that holiday, Mutti and I often visited them and they, in turn, occasionally stopped by Mutti's Place.

Due to her precarious mental state, Esther was an unusually moody person with many ups and downs. Catering to her many whims and fancies put a severe strain on any kind of relationship with her. Mutti and I were much looking forward to celebrating Mother's 80th birthday in March 1989 in Lake Forest. We had picked up a *Schwarzwälder Kirschtorte* [Black Forest cherry torte] and other pastries at the Café Lutz when, at the last moment, Esther called claiming she was not feeling well and asking us not to come. The following day when Mutti called to see how she was doing, Esther was perfectly fine again. As Mutti had often said about her unpredictable daughter, *"Bei der Esther weiß man nie wo man dran ist"* [With Esther you never know where you stand].

At other times, Esther could be very charming and gracious. Getting invited at Thanksgiving, Christmas, or Easter was quite a treat because it meant a delicious turkey dinner with all the trimmings. Esther would make a 15- pound turkey that was so tender and juicy that even Mutti could not resist it. Turkey had been unknown to us in Germany, where goose or ham was the traditional holiday fare, and Mutti could never get used to turkey claiming it was too dry and tasteless. Along with the good food and drink, there would be pleasant conversation on diverse topics of interest to Esther, especially gossip about our Swiss aunt.

Esther and Frank continued their close relationship as his education and experience in the field of psychiatry were of obvious benefit to Esther who more than ever relied on him for advice, emotional support and, of course, transportation. Unexpectedly, in mid-January 1990 Frank suffered a heart attack which was described as mild but which nevertheless laid him up for many weeks during which he needed complete rest. During this time Nick was required to do the chauffeuring for Esther. Frank's coronary could have been prevented, I felt, had he followed a more healthy diet but he was fond of juicy, well-marbled steaks which were soft enough for him to gum since, like Mutti, he had problems with his ill-fitting dentures. Esther fed him steaks at home and Frank invariably ordered a steak, cooked rare, whenever they ate out.

I once asked Esther whether she thought it good for the doctor to continuously eating such fatty and cholesterol-heavy foods and she replied, "That's what he wants and that's what he gets." Frank apparently thought the baby aspirin he was taking daily was sufficient to keep his arteries unclogged. As a medical doctor he should have known better or perhaps he just did not care.

When Esther, Nick, and Frank returned to Virginia in the fall of 1990 to spend Thanksgiving with Steffi, they also traveled to Charlottesville to inspect properties on the market. I knew the town well after having gone to school there in the late 1960s and recommended the place to them as a retirement home. They were immediately drawn to the town especially after learning that attached to the University of Virginia was an excellent hospital. This would be especially important for Frank now that he had suffered a coronary and needed to be close to good medical facilities. Frank, I heard, even had his Illinois medical license transferred for practice in the state of Virginia after they moved there.

Esther and Frank returned to Charlottesville for two or three more years checking out various homes for sale. While these properties were very pricey, even more so than those in exclusive Lake Forest, Esther believed that profits from her mail order operation plus the prospect of an eventual windfall from our aunt in Geneva would bring it all within reach. She eventually gave up on that venture figuring, probably correctly, that it was impractical to buy something in Charlottesville while Steffi was living in rent in Alexandria close to her place of employment. Consequently, nothing came of Esther's plans for her, Nick, and Frank to leave Illinois.

In The Fragrance Business

One time in my younger days when I was still highly idealistic and lamented the shortcomings of life in our adopted country, Esther let me know what it was all about. "America may have its faults," she told me, "but it's a good place to make money." After real estate, she turned her attention to two more ventures. The stock market is a risky business especially for novices looking for quick profits but that is where Esther turned next. When Mother and I visited her in Lake Forest she often spent considerable time on the phone behind closed doors talking with her stock broker and others who could furnish her with investment tips. She also subscribed to various business publications such as *Barron's*, the business weekly, and *Fortune* magazine to get the inside scoop on what and when to buy and sell. Undoubtedly she was inspired by our Uncle Charles and may have even obtained some advise from him. The ever secretive Esther never discussed these dealings with me. Her stock market activities were, however, of relatively short duration.

All of a sudden Esther stopped mentioning stocks and bonds, no longer talked to her broker on the phone when we were there, and cancelled all her subscriptions. Presumably, like others out for quick profits, being more of a speculator than an investor she got burned. Our uncle may have even advised her to stop putting her money at risk since she was inclined to be too impetuous to follow a long-term investment strategy such as he would have done.

The focus of Esther's most energetic and longest lasting business venture was into the booming fragrance and cosmetics industry. As it turned out, Esther was a born entrepreneur and gifted with a rich imagination. Once the family had relocated to Lake Forest in late 1986, all of Esther's energy was channeled into her budding perfume business.

She launched a mail order business called Holzman & Stephanie Perfumes, Inc. and used a small brochure and price list entitled *The Romantic World of Perfumes* to sell her versions of the popular fragrances of the day including such trademarked brands as Chanel No. 5, Charlie, Coco, Giorgio, Joy, L'Air du Temps, Lauren, Miss Dior, and Madame Rochas. According to one such brochure, the originals sold for $90 to $190 a bottle while her versions could be had for only $20 to $25.

The use of the same quality oils as the originals was promised and there was a money-back guarantee with unused portions returnable within 15 days of purchase. Obviously, these were huge savings that would appeal to women who wanted to wear these scents but either could not afford the originals or were unwilling to pay the stiff prices charged. For a business address, the brochure listed a Lake Forest post office box number and a phone number which was also the home phone number.

Selling knockoff fragrances was a highly competitive business with innumerable small vendors doing essentially the same thing. Profit margins were extremely low or non-existent and consequently most of these operations were run at a loss. After about three years into her new venture, Esther confided in me that she was still several thousand dollars in the hole. It just so happened that I knew something about marketing and pricing and, although my expertise was mostly in industrial rather than in consumer products, I gave Esther some advise that I felt should be valid in the fragrance business as well.

Whenever possible try to avoid competing on price, I told Esther, because it ruined any chance of making money for any of the competitors. To avoid price competition, companies try to differentiate their products and services from those of their competitors. In fact, I told Esther, she was in the wrong segment of the perfume business. I suggested to her to drop her knockoff perfumes and lotions and develop her own line of designer products that would appeal to a more select and affluent clientele. Such specialty products, if properly promoted, would command the higher prices needed to make her venture profitable provided she was able to build enough sales volume.

I also suggested to her to aggressively promote her product line by getting as much free publicity as she could by attending trade shows, issuing press releases, and obtaining interviews with newspaper columnists and fashion magazine editors. Esther liked the idea and later acknowledged that my advice was the great turning point in her business.

Consequently, Esther wasted no time phasing out her knockoff perfumes and creating and marketing her own line of fragrances. She had a wonderful gift for giving her products unique and catchy names such as *Misuki* (1987), *Je T'aime* (1987), *La Parisienne* (1989), *Holzman's Fascination* (1990), and *Très Chic* (2000). Because, according to Esther, "one should not have to spend a fortune on perfume," prices for these fragrances ranged from only $22 to $40 for a 2.17 ounce bottle.

Esther described her most famous creation, *Misuki*, as "a fragrance so exclusive and beautiful that it was chosen as the catalyst for the award wining film *Scent of a Woman* with international star Al Pacino." According to my sister, she got the name *Misuki* from a make of Japanese motorcycles. Esther sought trademark status for the brand and in January 1996 *Misuki* became a registered trademark on the Principal Register.

Esther also soon realized that the perfume business was highly secretive so that it was difficult for her to get much information from people already in it. This undoubtedly was the reason that she would not divulge many details of her own operation even to Mutti and me. Only Steffi, Frank, and Nick were privy to Esther's activities and plans at the time.

One of the benefits enjoyed by an immigrant to the United States is that one can completely remake oneself and even take on a new identity. One could shed one's skin like a snake and start anew. During the naturalization process to become an American citizen one is even asked whether one wants to drop one's name and assume a new one or at least anglicize it. Hardly anyone knows or really cares about what one was or did in the Old Country and nobody would bother to check up on one's story however fantastic.

Esther took good advantage of this situation in the interviews she gave to promote her business. They revealed much about Esther's character and veracity or, more correctly, lack of it. On Mother's Day 1988, the *Chicago Tribune* published a piece on Esther in its TempoWoman section which read in part:

- **Esther R. Holzman**

Age 50, president, Holzman & Stephanie Perfumes Inc., Lake Forest.

Holzman has a specific concept of how professional women should look: "The main thrust for my company and myself is to project an image of unerring refinement."

Holzman started her business four years ago with her daughter, Stephanie. It's a mail order business that sells perfumes and face creams.

Born and educated in Germany, Holzman, who came to the U.S. in the late 1950s, has a degree in organic chemistry. "I understand oils," she says, "and that's what perfumes are all about."

She also understands the importance of presenting a good image, but she doesn't like that word.

"The word 'image' is plastic," Holzman observes. "I feel what I project is a lifestyle, one of refined elegance—and it takes time to do that."

It's important, she says, "to look well-groomed, and I stress good make-up. I also believe that wearing perfume enhances one's feeling of total elegance."

An "inborn" knowledge of how to act and react with other people is another essential, Holzman says.

"Act natural. Realize your own potential and act on it in a realistic, self-fulfilling way."

You don't have to be wealthy, to project, what Holzman calls "quiet elegance." Daily exercise is important, she says. "I walk two miles every day in 30 minutes. It keeps my weight down, my muscles in good shape and gives me a good outlook on life."

About this time, Esther finally realized her dream of adding a number of local boutiques as another channel through which she could offer her products. She launched her fragrances and facial creams at a popular Lake Forest boutique with much fanfare. There were pastries from the Café Lutz in Chicago, champagne, and flowers provided by a florist active on the North Shore social scene. During this occasion in November 1991, a staff writer from the *Lake Forester* was there and gushed:

From the Villa La Rato Penado nestled in the hills above Grasse, France, the perfume capital of the world, where Esther Holtzman spent her summers, came the inspiration for a line of inexpensive but truly French perfumes. Holtzman spent the summers with her aunt, the Baroness Emmy von Hirzel, but it was the inspiration of another aunt, Countess Evelyn de Prograny, that made Holtzman go into the business with her daughter, Stephanie who lives in Virginia.

The article concluded with nine of Esther's dos and don'ts for wearing perfumes. "DON'T test fragrances by sniffing from the bottle" and "DON'T chose (sic) a fragrance because you like it on another woman" but "DO apply perfume to your pulse points" and "DO use fragrance throughout the day" was some of the advice given. Presumably, Esther picked up these tidbits from the trade journals and fashion magazines she read. According to the article, she was hoping to soon have her products sold in a major department store but which one was still a secret.

Incidentally, this department store venture proved unsuccessful. Beauty and fragrance products in those venues were firmly in the hands of the major cosmetic and fragrance houses which usually leased counter space and brought in their own specially trained sales personnel. The stores themselves were not interested in carrying low-volume, little-known merchandise with marginal profit potentials, Esther learned.

A British Web site devoted to beauty aids chose Esther's fragrances as a featured product with these laudatory words:

> Even as exotic and exclusive perfumes go, they do not come much more exotic or exclusive than the **Holzman & Stephanie Fragrance Collection** from **Holzman & Stephanie Perfumes**. What is perhaps most surprising is that they offer elegance and exclusivity at an affordable price, a combination rare in any product, but particularly in the heady world of perfumes. Esther Holzman (pictured opposite), President of the prestigious house of **Holzman & Stephanie**, has a background as exotic as any of her company's exclusive products. She spent her youthful summers in Grasse, France, the perfume capital of the world, at the enchantingly beautiful home of her aunt, the Baroness Emmy de Hirzel. Another of her aunts, the Countess Evelyn

de Prograny, inspired her to study organic chemistry and to enter the perfume business. Together with her widely-traveled daughter, Stephanie, educated in America with a Masters Degree in Science, she established her own perfume house some 15 years ago. Two of her most famous creations, 'Misuki' and 'Je T'aime' are dedicated to her titled and inspirational aunts...The family's country home is in the exclusive village of Lake Forest, Virginia, providing the perfume house with its alternative name, *Lake Forest Perfumes*.

The undated advertisement also states that the company insists on "Natural Essences," because "[a]s a chemist I know that at no time will you get this kind of response from synthetic compounds. They simply do not hold their scent, but change their composition and are hard and irritating." Incidentally, the writer inadvertently placed Lake Forest in Virginia.[3] Also, the name of Uncle Charles' sister is misspelled.

It is, of course, not unusual for businesspeople to boast of their backgrounds and lavishly praise their product and services. Customers generally do not mind puffing, the practice of making exaggerated claims, as long as they suffer no injury from it. Esther's claims, while undoubtedly not harmful to anyone, nevertheless much exceeded the acceptable limits because many were obviously totally false and misleading. Thus, Esther had no degree in organic chemistry and, in fact, had no formal education beyond elementary school. She did take a short course in chemistry from a Dr. Binder in Stuttgart but that did not make her a chemist. She did work with oils, as she claimed, but not the type of oils used in fragrances but rather with engine oils. Esther came to the United States in 1946 and not in the late 1950s as she told her interviewers. The later date made it plausible that she arrived with a university education and extensive experience as a chemist.

As much as she would have liked to enhance her image and that of her business, none of our relations belonged to the nobility. The only way our aunt could have become the Baroness Emmy von Hirzel (or Baroness Emmy de Hirzel), is if our Uncle Charles had been a baron and our aunt was married to him. Neither was the case. Likewise, Uncle Charles' sister, Evelyn de Pogranyi-Hirzel, while married to a member of the lower nobility, was not a countess. Furthermore, it was absurd to suggest that

Uncle Charles' sister inspired Esther to study organic chemistry and go into the fragrance business.

In a more benign form of puffing, Esther made her prospects and customers believe she ran a large and prosperous company with a busy staff including phone operators and other employees. Anytime one called the company and home phone number one would get a recorded message, in Esther's voice, saying: "This is Holzman and Stephanie Perfumes. Our operators are busy handling other calls. Please leave a message and we'll return your call. Thank you for calling Holzman and Stephanie Perfumes." She had, of course, no phone operators or any other employees with only Steffi, Nick, and Frank helping out at various times.

For handling production, storage, and shipment of her merchandise, Esther employed a so-called fulfillment house. These operations typically provided the same services for a number of other vendors and presumably even competitors. When Esther told a newspaper reporter in November 1990 that she had "65,000 clients throughout the world," she was fantasizing. She may have had a marketing firm do a mailing for her to that many people but there is obviously a big difference between prospects and paying customers. Had she accumulated the number of customers she mentioned, it would have been logistically impossible for her to service them since she had no outside office help. In my estimation, if she had 100 repeat customers she was doing very well. That number, however, would have been insufficient to cover her considerable costs and turn a profit.

In or about the year 1999, the year after our mother had passed away, Esther purchased a second house, a 3-story townhouse located on 5423 Barrister Place in Alexandria, Virginia This would provide Steffi, who had been living in rent, with a more spacious and comfortable home and allow the family perfume business to be conducted from there. In that year Esther also started her own impressive website, www.holzmansteffi-perfumes.com, to promote her business. It was up for 10 years, between November 2, 1999 and November 2, 2009, and carried information on the company and its five fragrance offerings, an order form, and the home address and phone number in Alexandra.

A welcome page showed the façade of an elegant building with the company's name above the front door and, on entering, a room suggestive of an exclusive boutique. One could also click on some of Esther's writings including *The Swiss Conspiracy Book* and *Musings*. In an *About Us* section on this website Esther again repeated the story about her studies of organic chemistry at the exclusive private school of one Professor Dr. Binder, as well as her childhood spent at the Grasse home of her aunt, the Baroness Emmy de Hirzel but "[i]t was the inspiration and driving force of the Countess Evelyn de Prograny (sic), another of Mrs. Holzman's aunts, that made her decide to go into the fragrance business," she wrote. "*Misuki* is dedicated to the Countess and *Je T'aime* to the Baroness Emmy." "Stephanie," according to the Web site, "resides at the family's country house in Virginia where she promotes the perfume line."

Each fragrance was artfully described with *Misuki* as being "so exclusive and beautiful that it was chosen as the catalyst for the award winning film: *Scent of a Woman* with international star Al Pacino." Each 2.17 oz. bottle of these five perfume creations was now priced at $95 plus shipping with a 5-vial sampler costing $10. The order form gave their new home in Alexandria as the business address for Holzman & Stephanie Perfumes, Inc. and a phone number there.

As previously mentioned, an important item on Esther's website was *The Swiss Conspiracy Book*, which was the title of a book she intended to write telling all about how the City of Geneva, with the help of the Geneva court system, fraudulently came into possession of her aunt's estate. "Esther Holzman writes a story of unforgettable greed, deception, betrayal, and blackmail about great wealth, of a beautiful love affair between her Uncle—the scion of one of Berne's great Patrician families, son of a former Swiss ambassador to the U.S. born in America holding dual citizenship and her Aunt. A love that spanned 30 years of marriage." The article promised that "[o]nce you start reading this fascinating tale of deception and callous arrogance you will not be able to put it down." There is no evidence that *The Swiss Conspiracy Book* was ever published..

A few months before Esther closed down her website in November 2009 she had taken leave of her loyal customers with a seemingly contradictory statement: "To our customers and friends! I have retired to write books that I had for years on our site and hope to get into the market come Christmas with *Je T'Aime Peter*—please look for us here. I like to take this opportunity to thank all of our many customers through the 35 years, your friendship was much appreciated! Esther and Stephanie Holzman." Her new perfume *Je T'Aime Peter*, probably named for her dog named Peter, also never appears to have come to market.

While her perfume business most likely never made her any money and remained a drain on her limited resources throughout its existence, it must have provided Esther with at least one important benefit. This was the psychic satisfaction she received from owning and running a company as its president and the status, prestige, and feeling of self-worth she so desperately craved.

More Sad News

After our mother's passing in late May 1998, Esther had the misfortune of losing two more members from her inner circle in short order. Despite my suspicion that Dr. Murrin was terminally ill and his demise imminent, the news of his death just a little over a week after our mother's was still a shocker. Naturally, I would much have liked to attend my erstwhile friend's funeral but because the notice did not appear in the *Chicago Tribune's* obituary column until Tuesday, June 9, and the funeral had already taken place that very morning, I was unable to do so. The short notice read in part: "Frank H. Murrin, M.D., of Lake Forest, June 6, 1998, father of Michael Francis Murrin; brother of Vernile Morgan; and friend of the Holzman family." Visitation was scheduled for Tuesday morning at 10 a.m. at the Wenban Funeral Home followed by a funeral mass at the Church of St. Mary, and interment in St. Mary Cemetery in Lake Forest. Contributions could be made to the American Cancer Society.

Frank's death at age 78 left me with mixed feelings. On one hand, I felt sad that none of his writing projects in the fields of psychiatry and human behavior came to fruition because his total involvement with Esther left him with no time for anything else. On the other hand, he took part in the scheme to remove Mother from her long-time home and bring her to Lake Forest when, as a psychiatrist, he must have known that it would be a traumatizing experience for her. He had also been a signatory of the "Designation of Guardian" document certifying that she was of sound mind and memory when he knew that was not true. In addition, he had done nothing by word or deed to help settle the differences between Esther and me but, on the contrary, supported my sister in all her destructive schemes.

With Frank, Esther had lost a close and trusted friend and companion. The job of Esther's attendant and chauffeur now fell back on Nick who, not being a psychiatrist, could obviously not provide the same kind of emotional support as Frank had done. The result could only mean a further deterioration in Esther's mental and emotional state.

Since Dr. Murrin's passing in early June 1998, I had made it a habit to peruse the *Chicago Tribune's* obituary columns every morning in case these had more surprises in store for me. They did and I was stunned to read the following notice in this paper's December 2, 1999 issue: "Nicholas J. Holzman, 79, of Lake Forest, died suddenly at his home, Nov. 30, 1999, beloved husband of Esther; devoted father of Stephanie Maria Holzman, of Washington, D.C.; dear brother of ...." Listed among his siblings were four brothers, two living and two deceased, and three living sisters. Visitation was scheduled for the following day at the Wenban Funeral Home with the funeral mass to take place in the Church of St. Mary, Lake Forest, on December 4. Interment was to be private. One of Nick's living brothers, Joseph, had been omitted and a corrected version of the death notice was published the following day.

Nick's passing was totally unexpected because, unlike Frank, he had always been in robust health. He was known to have a mild form of asthma but never exhibited shortness of breath nor had I ever observed him use an inhaler in the many years I knew him. I immediately called Ute and we began to speculate whether Esther had perhaps done Nick in for some reason such as wanting to collect on his life insurance. She had, after all, threatened to have me killed on several occasions and had bragged she would get off scot-free because she would plead insanity. Shame on Ute and me for harboring such dark thoughts about our sister. According to his death certificate, Nick died in the emergency room of Lake Forst Hospital of an acute infarct (stroke) due to atherosclerosis and aging. His body, like Mutti's, was cremated at Mt. Olivet Cemetery in Zion, Illinois.

Not having been invited to Nick's funeral, I wanted to pay my respects and attended anyway. The funeral mass in St. Mary's Catholic Church in Lake Forest was quite impressive. The Holzman clan and friends numbering some 40 people sat near the altar on the right side of the aisle as one entered the sanctuary while Esther and Steffi by themselves sat on the other. I arrived shortly after the service had already begun and sat down behind Esther but in a pew all the way to the rear near the entrance. As I perused the faces of the mourners from the side, I did not recognize any of them. I had met some of Nick's siblings as a young boy when we first came over from Germany and briefly lived with their parents in Chicago. But that was nearly half a century ago and I had only seen Nick's brother Joe a couple of times since then.

After the priest's eulogy, in which he mentioned Nick's sudden and unexpected death, Esther got up to read a passage from St. Matthew followed by Steffi who recited a short verse she had composed for her father. From the balcony was heard a small chamber orchestra playing sacred music while a tenor sang Schubert's *Ave Maria*.

After the service, the casket was rolled out followed by Esther and Steffi who positioned themselves near the church entrance. I left the sanctuary right behind them. Steffi, who looked devastated after the sudden loss of her beloved father, and I exchanged a few words in which I expressed my deep sorrow in her loss. Esther and I had nothing to say to each other and I only caught a glimpse of her. She wore a mink jacket over a black dress and stood erect and solemn like a soldier with eyes fixed in a blank stare. Her face was like a lifeless, plastic mask that showed no emotion. It would be the last time I would see either her or Steffi. Not having been an invited guest and feeling like an intruder, I did not stay around to talk with anybody and immediately left for home.

The negative opinion of Nick I had originally harbored has changed considerably and become more charitable over the years. My two sisters and I had always looked on him as the ultimate wimp who let himself be completely taken over by his domineering wife much to the detriment of everybody else in the family. He did whatever he was told to do without ever having had the courage to object to any of her schemes. Without his active participation, Esther's plan to clandestinely carry Mutti off to Lake Forest and keep her isolated there could not have been accomplished. And what married man would allow another man to come into his house and live there as the de facto partner of his wife? Elke, especially, harbored a strong dislike for her brother-in-law. When I informed her of his passing, she wrote back (translated from the German):

In my opinion, Nick was a deceitful person who enjoyed doing
what Esther wanted. I compare him with Iago in Shakespeare's
drama Othello because he loved fights and often instigated them
among the Zells especially between Esther and Mutti or Esther and
me or Mutti and me. He always appeared to be very nice but was
very treacherous and deceitful when I lived with him and Mutti.

I have since come to realize that Nick had few options open to him and he undoubtedly suffered considerable humiliation at his wife's hands. According to Ute, Esther denied her husband the customary marital privileges and once told him that the only reason she was keeping him around was for his paycheck. Nick had many fine qualities and was basically a good and decent man who tried to make the best of the strange situation he found himself in. He was good-natured and loving especially in his relationship with Steffi. He showed the same loving care for Mutti as he sat for hours watching over her at home and at the Westmoreland nursing home. I could tell that his concern for her health and wellbeing was genuine and that he had developed a real affection for Mother. He was also very empathetic towards me in my battle with Esther during Mutti's last illness. Nick was essentially a family man who would have been perfectly happy to live in a small house behind a white picket fence and surrounded by a loving wife and children. He would have been, as indeed he was, a faithful husband and a doting father. He and Esther were, unfortunately, a complete mismatch as to their individual backgrounds, personalities, and aspirations. That was the tragedy of Nick's life.

The death of Jerome (Jerry) Wetmore, Esther's full and my half-brother, earlier that same year, on January 24, 1999 at age 70, did not affect Esther very much as the two were not close. I saw Jerry only twice. The first time was in the Bronx when I was 15 and he was 23 and the second time many years later when Mutti and I came to visit his grandmother in Gary, Indiana, where she had moved to be close to her family, and Jerry was again living with her. I remember his showing me a photo album with pictures of him surrounded by his young buddies in boarding school in England. These were evidently very happy days for him. I later wished I had made the effort to get to know him better.

We never got in touch with each other and Mutti too had no contact with Jerry and never talked about him. Bodo had, after all, been taken from her after she and Fritz got divorced in April 1934 when he was just five years old. A few years later, he was sent off to England and from there to America to join his father. There was little opportunity for mother and son to bond. Esther did not hear about our brother's passing until a month later when she left a message on my answering machine. Jerry had died in Jersey City, NJ, the same place as his father 20 years earlier. According to Esther's message, she was "on her way up there to take care of things."

What little else I know about Jerry comes from a letter Volker wrote me in September 2002 according to which he briefly met our brother when he and his grandmother came to visit Mutti at our townhouse flat on Home Avenue in Oak Park in the late 1950s. According to Volker, towards the end of World War II Jerry had been a member of a regimental band with the U.S. Army and supposedly played the saxophone. (He would have been just 17 when he enlisted). The band members apparently kept in touch and during the Korean War five years later, Jerry was the only one of the group not to reenlist. When all of his former buddies died in combat one after the other, Jerry's mind supposedly snapped. After that experience, according to Volker, Jerry was never fully functional again and spent much time in veterans hospitals.

Closing The Estate

When our mother passed away at the end of May 1998 it did not, unfortunately, resolve all the outstanding issues and problems because the case was still in court pending Esther's final report to the court as guardian of our mother's estate. It had been my hope that with Mutti's passing, I could be rid of Esther and get her out of my mind. This was not to be, however, as she managed to intrude into my life for some time to come. At the beginning of October of that year, she had the audacity to call me. "Aren't you interested in Geneva anymore?" she wanted to know. I did not take the bait and immediately hung up. She was evidently unaware that I knew that the Swiss supreme court had ruled in favor of the City of Geneva back in March already. For me that ended the matter. A few days later Nick called back saying, "Why don't you talk with your sister once?" I replied that I had no interest to have anything more to do with her.

On the same day I received a fax from her with this message: "I am working with the city of Geneva's lawyer. I don't know what will come of it. (A deal). Any letters from Aunt E would be helpful." Why would the City of Geneva be interested in a "deal" with Esther (on behalf of our mother) after the city had already been awarded practically Aunt Emmi's entire estate? And how would our aunt's letters further the cause at this late stage? It made absolutely no sense to me and I did not respond.

At the end of that month, a package arrived from Esther. In it were about 40 letters mostly ones I had written to Mutti over the years and she had retained plus some rental documents from my Palm Harbor property. Presumably Esther had rifled these from the house when she was visiting Mother taking whatever she thought useful to her. Inside the package was a tiny scrap of paper on which she wrote in block letters, "P. Mother asked me before she died to contact you—and so I did. E. Mother's ashes are here. If I hurt you I am sorry." Coming from Esther, I knew she felt no true remorse. I could simply not accept her trite and phony apology and did not respond.

Knowing that Esther and her lawyers were full of surprises, I thought it a good idea to now and then stop by the clerk's office in Chicago's Richard J. Daley Center to ask for the case file and check on any court filings I had not been made aware of. There, for the first time, I saw a document filed by Esther's lawyers entitled "Petition for Payment of Expenses" and attached to it as Exhibit A the "Budget of Monthly Expenses." According to this exhibit, which had been approved by the court, Esther was charging our mother $500 for housing, $160 for food, $144 for hair and personal care, $80 for laundry and dry cleaning, $70 for clothing, shoes and personal items, and $60 for transportation or a total of a little over $1,000 a month. That exceeded Mutti's monthly income from American and German social security benefits by $200 and was twice the amount she was charging Dr. Murrin for monthly expenses.

During the 10 years we lived in our Oak Park townhouse together, Mutti and I had shared weekly expenses and it would never have occurred to me to collect more than half of Mother's income for housing or to charge her for the other items. In fact, there were always a couple of hundred dollars left over every month from Mother's income which I duly used to put into her savings account or to purchase utility and corporate stock with good dividend yields over the years for her portfolio. To me, Exhibit A was just another piece of evidence that Esther's primary motivation for carrying off our mother to Lake Forest was money.

When, after my permanent return to Oak Park in 1986, I learned that Mutti's had used her entire dividend income for birthday and holiday gifts to Esther and her family, it made me furious especially when I found out that our mother had been struggling to pay her bills during my three year absence. When Esther's birthday came up and I asked Mother if she wanted to make out a check to her, Mutti replied, "Esther might not like it." It turned out that her daughter wanted all gifts to her and her family in cash. The probable reason was that she did not want me to know about them. In fact, Mutti never added her substantial dividend income from her stock portfolio to her checking account but cashed all checks to have the money available for her generous gifts. Practically all of Mutti's dividend income went to her supposedly affluent daughter and her family. Needless to say, when I subsequently reduced these individual payments from $100 to $50, in line with Mutti's means, and had her make out personal checks rather than pay cash, it did not endear me to my sister.[4]

A final hurdle to be overcome before the case file could be closed was the approval by the court of a document entitled "First and Final Account" which was an accounting by Esther, the plenary guardian, of how the funds in our mother's estate were spent. It should have been a straightforward and simple matter since all the facts and figures were readily available but, instead, it turned into another acrimonious battle. The new fight took up much of the latter part of 1999 and all of 2000.

Anxious to rid myself of further contacts with Esther as soon as possible, I had contacted Attorney Mike to inquire about the status of the closing documents since it had been over a year since Mother's passing. As a concession to his client, I agreed to be satisfied with a document entitled "Final Report in Lieu of First and Final Account" which would not be a detailed accounting but be less time-consuming and easier for her and her lawyers to prepare. It also spared Esther's lawyers from disclosing their fees which ultimately came out of Mutti's estate and which I surmised were substantial. It is well known that in such acrimonious family litigations the only winners are usually the lawyers.

When this "Final Report" dated September 24, 1999 arrived from Esther's lawyers, I was appalled. The assets I had turned over to Esther in late July 1997, and which Mike had signed for, were inexplicably listed as having come into my possession! According to this document, only $15,500 went to Esther from the estate, all from American bank accounts, plus $10,850 in American and German social security income. All the remaining assets, including Mutti's entire stock portfolio, and the money in her German savings account supposedly went to me by operation of law on our mother's death.

The "Receipt of Distribution" that accompanied the "Final Report" and which I was asked to sign had me acknowledge receipt of all of the corporate stock plus Mutti's Stuttgart bank account. Naturally, I refused to do so and warned Mike not to file the "Final Report" with the court because it was false and potentially fraudulent. Mike came back saying that the documents had unfortunately been prepared by an incompetent paralegal in their office. When I called this paralegal, he told me that he was unaware of the receipt signed by Mike and had relied solely on the information furnished by their client.

When Esther continued to deny having received the passbook from the Landesgirokasse in Stuttgart, which I had mailed to Mike for forwarding to Lake Forest, I wrote to that bank requesting information on the status of the account. The bank, which in the meantime had been renamed Landesbank Baden-Württemberg (State Bank of Baden-Württemberg), wrote back in November 1999 that the account had been closed in June 1998 and the funds in the amount of 19,719 DM ($10,727) transferred to an account in Lake Forest, Illinois.

Another court battle seemed imminent when Esther continued to deny having received most of the funds that were turned over to her while I refused to sign off on court filings that were patently false and fraudulent. This made me decide to secure the services of a lawyer with experience in probate law and in March 2000 hired Attorney John Wolff, an acquaintance of mine with offices in downtown Chicago, to help resolve the dispute.

It was not until December of 2000 that Esther and I could agree, through our respective attorneys, on the contents of the "Receipt of Distribution" and the "Final Report in Lieu of First and Final Account."

Her attorneys apologized saying they had much difficulty getting Esther to cooperate with them. Subsequently, the two documents went through a number of additional revisions. In the final version of the "Final Report" and to which I subscribed, Esther admitted to having received assets totaling $51,000 from our mother's estate including $8,000 in income from American and German social security.

As to her disbursements, this paragraph applied: "From the date of her appointment, July 25, 1997 to the date of the death of the Ward, May 29, 1998, the Guardian disbursed from the Estate a total of $51,000 for room, board, caregivers, medical supplies, physician expenses, clothing and personal items, and administrative expenses of guardianship, including $20,059 paid to the Westmoreland Nursing Home." Since all the Ward's assets had been disbursed for her care, the guardian asked the court that the "First and Final Account" be waived, the Estate be closed, the Surety Bond be cancelled, and she be discharged as guardian of the Person and Estate of Anne Marie Zell.

Even though I never believed that Esther used up nearly all of our mother's life savings for her care in the just 10 months she served as our mother's guardian, I did not object to her claims. For me the important thing was that the "Final Report" would truthfully state the assets Esther received from the estate of our late mother and not some fictitious and much lesser amount.

The final act took place on January 5, 2001 in Judge Richard J. Dowdle's courtroom for a last hearing to have the judge approve the "Final Report" and sign the "Order of Discharge." Janna Dutton was there to represent Esther, who did not show up, while I joined John Wolff to put this case to rest. The judge asked Janna whether all the names listed as siblings had been notified and when she replied that they could not be located, he understandably shook his head.

While Janna did not know their location, I knew the whereabouts of two of them but had good reason not to speak up. Ute and Elke feared and despised Esther and were afraid that if she knew where they lived, she would give them nothing but trouble. Based on past injuries they had suffered at their sister's hands, they were determined to have nothing more to do with her. To insure their privacy, their last names and addresses could not be made part of the public record. My omission was not harmful to their interests because I kept Ute fully informed of the court proceedings and gave her copies of the court filings so that she, as well as Elke, were always fully appraised. Jerry had died two years earlier while nobody had as yet been able to locate Volker.

After comparing the "Final Report" with the "Inventory" of assets filed by Esther's lawyers in September 1997, and correctly noting that Mutti's savings account holding $2,700 had been omitted from the "Inventory," the judge signed the "Order of Discharge" with this notation: "Ward died Estate exhausted Distribution of joint tenancy by operation of law." We thanked the judge who seemed as pleased as we all were to see the end of this lengthy and rancorous affair.

During this court appearance, I got news about something I had long suspected but did not know for certain. Before our case was called, Janna asked John and me to join her outside the courtroom for a quick conference. Janna suggested that there should now be no further claims since our mother's estate had been exhausted and Stephanie Holzman too should be agreeable since no value had been placed on the furniture and household goods. When I asked Janna how this concerned Steffi, she announced that Mother had prepared a new will in which my niece was named a beneficiary. Checking with the clerk's office after the hearing, I found that on April 6, 2000 a second will had indeed been filed for Mutti besides the one I had filed on November 17, 1998. (The will prepared by Attorney Anthony Basile and dated February 28, 1978).

By this new (pour-over) will our mother left all of her tangible personal property in equal shares to "Esther Rose Holzman, Stephanie Maria Holzman and H. Peter Zell" while she gave all the remainder of her estate, real or personal and wherever located, to Esther as trustee under a separate living (inter vivos) trust agreement. Esther was named the executor of the will and her bank, The Northern Trust Company, successor executor.

This last will was dated March 11, 1993, the same date as "The Designation of Guardian" and signed by the same three witnesses, namely, Addis E. Hull, the senior attorney with Esther's Lake Forest law firm, and the two psychiatrists, John W. Hanni, M.D. and Frank H. Murrin, M.D., who all certified that they believed "the testator to be of sound mind and memory at the time of signing." Clearly, these documents had been prepared shortly after Michael Susman, the Oak Park attorney, had declined to prepare testamentary documents due to Mutti's mental incapacity as certified by her physician, Dr. A. Z. Khan.

For me personally, the financial outcome was a wash. The joint tenancy stock to which I had held on to was a few thousand dollars more than the 5-figure legal expenses I had incurred to secure visitation rights and safeguard Mother's assets from piecemeal seizure by an unscrupulous sibling.

It was undoubtedly not the first or last time someone made sacrifices taking care of a loved one for many years only to find himself or herself left out of that person's will with another individual in his or her place. But if the good deed was done, as here, without expectation of financial gain, there should be no cause for complaint and for me there was no cause. In fact, I never held the matter against either our mother or my sister. Mutti may well have felt that Esther had made the greater sacrifices over the years and was more deserving. Furthermore, she had always been impressed by Esther's assertion that Aunt Emmi had promised to leave her entire estate to her. It is therefore plausible that the papers our mother signed represented her true wishes.

On the other hand, Esther exerted substantial influence over her. When she brought Mother to her Lake Forest lawyers, Mutti could hardly have been expected to refuse her signature. She was 84 years old at the time and no longer able to look after her finances while her understanding about the extent or whereabouts of her financial holdings was minimal. In addition, she would not have understood the legalese of the documents she was signing. Who knows what Esther told her was in them? Clearly, a case could have been made that Mother's most recent last will was invalid because of undue influence and mental incapacity but I had no desire to contest it and was just happy it was all over.

After being left with not much more from Mother's estate than some near-worthless furniture from the 1950s and 1960s, I was fortunate I did not also lose my Oak Park home because Esther had wanted that too or at the least half of it. "Just a reminder that half or perhaps more of your house is mine because I paid Mother part of her rent with the understanding that the house was hers," she had faxed me as early as October 1996, and "If you can not pay me the monies—I suggest you take out a mortgage on the house."

Regarding the rent claim, I suppose Mutti's monthly payment of $200 at the time to help out with real estate taxes and insurance could be considered rent although neither Mother or I did so when we agreed on this arrangement when she first moved in. I do recall that for a few months while I was overseas and Mother was between jobs, Esther had helped out by mailing Mutti a $70 check payable from her Holzman & Stephanie Perfumes, Inc. account. Perhaps that was the rent support Esther had in mind. At any rate, Esther struck out here too.

It was Esther's lawyer, Tony Basile, of all people, who had saved me from losing my home. Shortly after its purchase in August 1965, I went to see him to have my will drawn up with a provision that would make Mutti co-owner of the property so that it would immediately pass to her in case of my death. Mr. Basile strongly advised against it and recommended instead that I bequeath Mother the townhouse in my will. This is exactly what I did in a will he prepared for me.

When Esther now claimed that she would take the matter up with her lawyers, I had nothing to worry about because I knew that all dealings in real estate needed to be in writing to be legally enforceable. I had told Mutti that I was buying the home for her and that I wanted her to think of it as her property. Fortunately, I had never put anything down on paper prior to seeing the attorney.

The irony of all this was that when on March 10, 1998 the Swiss supreme court confirmed the lower court rulings leaving Aunt Emmi's estate to the City of Geneva, it was within a day of the 5th anniversary of Esther's taking our mother to her Lake Forest lawyers to make out a new will leaving all of Mutti's assets to her. Consequently, instead of getting everything Mother was expected to inherit from her sister, Esther ended up with nothing. It was a marvelous example of poetic justice.

A Downward Spiral

After the litigation was finally over at the beginning of 2001, I tried to put Esther out of my mind and have nothing more to do with her. Indeed, it was utter bliss not to hear from her for a couple of years when on Saturday, February 1, 2003, I received an unexpected message from her. That day, incidentally, was an awful one in the nation's history. When I turned on the television set in the morning to watch the CNN news, the screen showed a clear blue sky with the camera locked on three tiny white objects descending rapidly towards earth. There was no audio but the caption said it all: "Space Shuttle Columbia Breaks Up Over Texas." On board were seven astronauts, including an Israeli air force colonel and a woman medical doctor, who all perished in the fiery crash. It was a portent of things to come most notably Operation Iraqi Freedom, the invasion of Iraq, six weeks later on orders of a president who just happened to be the former governor of Texas. One great disaster directly pointed to an even greater one. Esther's typed note read:

> HI PETER: 1-22-2003
> I AM CLEANING OUT MY HOUSE FOR A MOVE TO VIRGINIA.
> THERE ARE SEVERAL GERMAN TAPES LEFT FROM MOTHER—
> IF YOU WANT THEM PLEASE LET ME KNOW. IS UTE ILL?

The envelope was marked PLEASE FORWARD and her note reached me in Arizona on that date where I had moved a month earlier after selling Mutti's Place in Oak Park. I would have loved to have these VCR tapes back but thought it prudent not to again get involved with Esther and therefore did not respond. As to the inquiry about Ute, she was not ill but just wanted nothing more to do with our sister. Esther subsequently sold her Lake Forest property and moved into her townhouse on Barrister Place in Alexandria. Poor Steffi, forced to live in the same house with a domineering and mentally disturbed mother, was not too happy with the new arrangement. There was friction between the two from day one and eventually they even stopped talking to each other.

According to Ute, as reported to me by Elke, after moving to Virginia, Esther located Ute on the Internet and entreated her to come to her assistance. She desperately needed help. For reasons Elke and I found perplexing, Ute finally warmed up to Esther despite all the past injuries she had suffered at her hands. Ute's change of heart may well have been motivated by sisterly compassion. There may also have been something else—Ute assumed that our sister was wealthy and financially independent as indeed Esther made everyone believe. According to Elke, as an added incentive Esther made Ute a gift of some expensive jewelry. For whatever reason, the two sisters renewed the friendship that had ended on Ute's wedding day in July 1963 when Esther and Mutti chose not to attend. Now the two regularly exchanged phone calls and e-mail messages.

Since Elke had told Ute not to talk to her about Esther, whom she loathed, nothing more was heard about Esther for some time. Then, in a birthday message in August 2005, Elke let me know that Ute had visited our sister in Alexandria and found her in very bad shape. Two doctors told Ute that Esther required placement in a mental hospital. According to Ute, Esther was planning to return to Illinois and entreated her to remain with her but, being married and with her own household to take care of, Ute could not accept. Esther then contacted Danielle with an offer to work for her as a caregiver but, not surprisingly, her niece's response was negative. In February 2007, when Esther turned 80, I sent her a birthday card with a friendly and upbeat message congratulating her on reaching this important milestone in her life. I did not expect a response and did not receive one.

Esther was known for doing brash things and prided herself in acting resolutely and always "taking the bull by the horns." Often when she proposed doing something that seemed off the wall to me she would follow up with, "You know me—I'll do it." It therefore did not come as much of a surprise to us when we learned that in April of 2009 Esther had sold her place in Alexandria, Virginia and had returned to Lake Forest, Illinois. According to a realtor listing for her Virginia property, the sales price was a little over $400,000. Back in Lake Forest in May of that year Esther purchased a large one-story brick home on 380 Deerpath Square. Because Steffi and her mother had been feuding when Esther sold her Virginia property, she callously sent her daughter packing giving her no choice but to move into rented quarters again. This resulted in a final rupture in the relationship between mother and daughter who would henceforth never be in contact again.

By August of that same year Esther was in Lake Forest Hospital seriously ill. Ute told Elke that she was at Esther's house and found it in such a mess that it took her several days to make it livable again. By September, Esther had recovered and again pleaded with Ute to stay and take care of her because "family is very important and much better than strangers." She could not understand, according to Ute, why everybody had turned against her insisting over and over that she had never hurt anybody in the world. Ute again declined to stay but did hire a caregiver for her sister. Esther then resorted to plying Ute with a continuing stream of phone calls and e-mails every day asking for help. Resorting to some of her old tricks, she let Ute know that she wanted to die and was ready to commit suicide if Ute did not come back. What might have frightened Mutti into compliance was not successful with Ute who remained away.

One can only speculate why Esther decided to return to Illinois because she never divulged her plans or financial affairs to Ute nor to anybody else. Most likely it was because she felt it was her home where she had spent most of her life beginning with her arrival from upstate New York in the late 1940s. She would also be closer to Ute in Michigan who was now the only family member who still wanted to have anything to do with her. What seemed to defy logic was her decision to again make exclusive Lake Forest her home because she no longer needed a prestige address for her perfume business which she had just recently given up unless, of course, she intended to resurrect it.

It made little sense for Esther to purchase a sprawling ranch style home sitting on a lot of over half an acre for $½ million when she was now living by herself and already in her early 80s. According to Ute, our sister took out a reverse mortgage on her new home. This may have been a big mistake because unlike traditional forward mortgages, reverse mortgages are very complex and expensive transactions that are difficult for an average homeowner to understand. It is not uncommon for a mortgagee to lose his or her home to foreclosure because the lender can ask for full repayment of the loan for any number of reasons including non-payment of property taxes or insurance premiums or failure to keep the property in good repair.

During the next few months Ute became increasingly annoyed and disenchanted with her sister for several reasons. Specifically, Esther refused to follow her doctors' orders to treat her various ailments, kept dismissing the caregivers Ute had hired, and continued "lying through her teeth," according to Elke. Most importantly, by mid-October, Esther's finances were in disarray to the point where she was headed for bankruptcy. Evidently, she had accumulated much debt but was spending money as if it was going out of style. Dr. Murrin supposedly left her $200,000 which she had quickly spent. Her caregivers were costing her a bundle every year.

In need of cash, she tried selling her possessions but could find no buyer for some of her most valuable ones including her oil paintings.

Not particularly helpful in Esther's new relationship with Ute may have been some things Esther said to her which would have made Ute cringe. For one, Esther kept defending Mutti by insisting that she had been a good mother. Ute obviously had the opposite opinion. Furthermore, Esther kept reminding Ute that she could have done much better by marrying somebody other than Tom as she had recommended. According to Elke, Esther's doctors told Ute that our sister could no longer live by herself and one psychiatrist bluntly called Esther crazy saying she belonged in a psycho ward.

The year 2010 turned out to be an especially bad and memorable one for Esther. "Stephanie hates her mother and cannot forgive her for what she did to her father..." Elke e-mailed me in January. In the meantime, Esther made increasingly more demands on Ute pestering her with a daily barrage of e-mails and phone calls causing Ute to become increasingly more frustrated with her sister's demands on her time. She was especially disgusted with Esther's fantasizing of great wealth including the claim of having a $½ million equity in her home. Ute knew better. According to Elke, Ute finally came to accept the fact that Esther only manipulates people to her own advantage. She wished she had never restarted their relationship. In fact, according to Elke, Ute became so fed up with the situation that she cut Esther loose by refusing to continue to manage her affairs under the power of attorney she had given her.

This is when Esther apparently thought of me again. At the end of March of that year, I received a surprise phone call from her. The exchange was very short and caustic. "This is Esther," the caller said and after my query "who?" she replied, "This is Esther, your sister." "Why are you calling me," I wanted to know. "Ute gave me your number—is there a problem?" she responded. "Yes there is," was my answer, "because I never want to talk to you again." "I didn't know that" she replied to which I said, "Well, now you do." "Okay," she said, and hung up. Since she had something in her possession I desperately wanted, I called her back on Easter Sunday (April 4) and asked her if she had anything to tell me. Yes, she said, she wanted to let me know that I could have Mother's ashes if I wanted them. Of course, I did, I told her, and asked her about the particulars. She could not talk because she had someone with her, she said, but maybe we could discuss it some other time. I figured Esther would be up to her old tricks and try to do some tough bargaining with me. To my great surprise, less than a week later the urn with Mutti's ashes arrived at my Arizona home.

A Ward Of The State

With Esther no longer able to function on her own, Ute having given up on her, and Steffi wanting nothing more to do with her mother, Esther was adjudged a disabled person and in late April 2010 had become a ward of the state of Illinois. Esther was desperate, we heard, to remain in her home and fought tooth and nail to prevent from being moved out. She was not successful and on Monday, May 31, according to Elke, the authorities came and removed our sister "kicking and screaming" from her home and brought her to an assisted living facility in a neighboring town. Her lender had foreclosed on the reverse mortgage she had obtained on her new home on Deerpath Square. Everything our sister owned was now auctioned off.

A week after her placement, she left a message on my answering machine to please call her back because she had something important to discuss with me "pertaining the law." I did not return her call because Elke had warned me that our sister was looking for someone willing to take Ute's place and accept her power of attorney. That was one assignment I could do without. Then, very early on Saturday morning, July 3, Esther left this message on my answering machine:

> *Peter, this is Esther. I need some help as far as a guardianship is concerned. Since you are a lawyer, I wonder if you could help me out. I don't have a telephone number yet. My telephone is not connected but the telephone number of Sunrise Assisted Living is 847-856-8100. The reason we are here is because I'm having some work done on the house. I had an accident with a little fire and I crawled down on the floor to get to the telephone line and somebody saw me and reported that I was crawling around the room like I wasn't all with it, you know, and that's not the case. Anyway, I don't have anybody that could help me. So, if you can be of help, Peter, call me at 847-856-8100. They will give me a message when*

I get to my telephone. I don't know how long I'm going to be here.
Somebody came out and got a guardianship and I wasn't aware of
that. I fell on the stove. While I was out in the hospital, somebody
threw the papers away and I wasn't aware that somebody wants to
be my guardian. Heavens, I don't need a guardian. I don't have
anybody to help me. Ute is busy and Elke I don't hear from and
that's about it. Thank you very much and have a good day.
Bye-bye.

The phone number Esther gave me was for Sunrise Assisted Living on 500 N. Hunt Club Road in Gurnee, Illinois. It was quite sad for me to hear that our sister had become a ward of the state and had now also lost her battle to remain in her home. Nevertheless, I remained unmoved and did not return the call. How could I succeed in helping Esther when Ute, a very competent and caring person, had so miserably failed? For me, it was not a matter of tit-for-tat. My Christian faith told me to forgive not once but a thousand times and to offer help when called upon especially by a sibling. I felt no more animosity toward my sister. The intervening years had completely extinguished any lingering anger or hatred I had for her. But my survival instincts also told me that I should not again be drawn into Esther's orbit and open myself up to further manipulations and abuse. I felt that in her condition she was best off as a ward of the state not only for her own good but to prevent her from doing any more harm to others. Our dear mother, who always looked out for Esther's best interests, would undoubtedly have agreed with me to leave well enough alone.

The court appointed a Joseph Vogler of Waukegan, Illinois, as Esther's guardian. He was the Public Administrator and Guardian for Lake County, Illinois, after his appointment by the governor, I learned. The guardian, in turn, contacted Ute urging her to contribute to her sister's upkeep because there were insufficient funds available to keep her at Sunrise Assisted Living. Ute, who by now had washed her hands of the whole affair, refused to provide any financial support whatsoever. When asked about my whereabouts, according to Elke, Ute declined to give them any information about me. On Thanksgiving (November 25), Elke had all family members including her two daughters and grandchildren at her house in Valparaiso for the traditional turkey dinner and had also invited Ute and her family.

Before proceeding to Valparaiso, Ute , Tom, and Danielle stopped by Esther's assisted living home for a brief visit. They found Esther ensconced in a small room which she was sharing with another lady. Weeping and wailing, Esther entreated them to take her with them. Her big fear was that the public guardian would place her in a state-run nursing home. Not only are these usually not among the more desirable places to live out one's life but it would mean she would have to give up Peter, her dog and longtime companion, because these facilities normally do not allow pets. She is frantic, Ute reported to Elke, because she has been told that her removal is imminent.

By January 2011, Esther's worst fears had come true—she was removed from her assisted living home in Gurnee and taken to a state-funded nursing facility. Her new home was Brentwood North Healthcare and Rehabilitation Center on 3705 Deerfield Road in Riverwoods, Illinois. Brentwood North was a relatively large nursing home which was both Medicare and Medicaid approved. Fortunately for Esther, her new home had an overall rating of better than average for similar institutions. She clearly appeared to be in good hands. Despite this, according to Ute who occasionally still called her, Esther continued to wail and weep and insist that Ute do more for her. Whenever Ute told her sister that she should be thankful for being in such good hands and that she could, unfortunately, do nothing more for her, Esther would angrily hang up.

Esther's long and tortured life came an end at 5:35 o'clock in the evening of Wednesday, February 27, 2013 at Advocate Condell Medical Center in Libertyville, Illinois. She had reached her 86th birthday just two weeks earlier. According to Ute, our sister was in Hospice care and suffering from congestive heart failure. Her death certificate listed Aspiration pneumonia as the immediate cause with additional issues being hypertension and dementia. According to this document, Esther's body was cremated at Lakewood Crematorium in Green Oaks, Illinois, on the following day. Surprisingly, for a person obsessed with last wills and testaments in which she might be a beneficiary, according to the Lake County records office she left no last will of her own. I did not hear of Esther's passing until mid-March when Elke informed me of this important family event in an e-mail reading:

> *I just received the news that Esther has died. I am ashamed to say that I feel no sense of loss with her passing. Esther certainly did nothing to make the world a better place. She spread discord among family members and treated them cruelly for most of her time on earth.*
>
> *P.S.: Peter, I'm not sure whether I should send you a sympathy card to give you solace. After all, you had contact with her for many years which was not the case with me. But she treated you too so cruelly especially after Mutti died. I can therefore not imagine that you are in deep sorrow. Yet I know that you are able to forgive your fellow man much easier than I.*

No family member was present when Esther passed away, not even Steffi. Naturally, my feelings about our late sister were more complex and conflicted than those of Elke. Even though Esther was the most cruel, mean-spirited, and vindictive individual I had ever encountered in my life, I still felt a big loss and sorrow on hearing the news. It was probably because she had such an immense impact on my and our mother's lives that it was hard to contemplate that she was suddenly gone. I had to remind Elke that Esther had her good side too because if it had not been for our sister, she would most likely never have made it to America to enjoy the opportunities that were given her. According to our faith, to be forgiven our sins we ourselves must first be able to forgive, I wrote.

Reflections On A Tragic Life

It is never possible to know precisely what motivates people to do the things they do or fail to do because one cannot read their minds. One can only speculate and this was especially true of Esther. As she herself said in one of her early fragrance mail-order catalogs, "A woman who wears our perfumes speaks of self-worth, confidence, and mystery." Esther was and remained a mystery to all who knew her. She never opened up about herself and preferred to keep her ideas, thoughts, and plans mostly to herself. Thus, she never divulged the details of her real estate dealings or mail order operation, the precise nature of her illness, or many other things that people normally share with other family members. Presumably only her innermost circle including Frank, Nick, and Steffi were privy to some of these.

Esther was the most secretive person I have ever known. Thus, Mother and I were not aware that Esther had converted her apartment building on South East Avenue into condominiums until we happened to see a "For Sale" sign outside the place and even then she would not divulge any details. We never saw any physical evidence of her mail order operation which she presumably ran out of the basements of her River Forest and Lake Forest homes. Most everything I came to know about Esther's business, including the names of her fragrances, came from her promotional brochure, her website, and other sources.

As to her mental and emotional problems, Mutti reported that she was alternatively euphoric and depressed. From one day to the next, she could be joyful and energetic and then seclude herself and weep uncontrollably. While she evidently went through the usual physiological and psychological changes associated with menopause at the time, her condition seemed much more severe than normal. Dr. Frank Murrin's intervention, unfortunately, did not cure Esther of her affliction but only moderated it to allow her to function in a passable manner. Dr. Khan had told me that her symptoms were suggestive of a bipolar disorder, i.e., she was most likely manic-depressive. Knowing that a person has a severe affliction such as a mental illness normally causes others to become more caring and sympathetic towards him or her. Unfortunately, in Esther's case that was not possible because not only did she consistently deny there was anything wrong with her but her meanness and ruthlessness caused people to soon lose empathy and instinctively turn away.

One of Esther's worst character traits had been her inability to stick to the truth. She just could never desist from saying things that were patently untruthful if that was needed to gain an advantage. It was probably a survival strategy she picked up during the Nazi era where, being a *Mischling*, she often had to deny her identity and background and make herself into something she was not. On one of Esther's and Frank's visits to our home, he brought along a book. When I wanted to see what he was reading, he scrambled to hide it from me. Still, I got a glimpse of its title which was *Hallucinations*.

It seemed fairly obvious that our friend was reading up on one of Esther's smorgasbord of mental problems. She was hallucinating which meant that she probably had difficulty keeping truth and fiction apart. That might explain why her lying was almost pathological in nature. Most people who came in contact with her noticed and commented on it. But no matter what its origins, her habit of spreading falsehoods and lies resulted in much damage to anyone who crossed her.

Esther's relations with her siblings, including myself, were ill-favored from the beginning. According to Mother, when Esther was still quite young she once asked her why she, Mutti, had her other children when she already had her. I did not ask Mutti what her response was. Esther always had difficulty accepting the rest of us. One reason may well have been that, unlike her, we were not only born out of wedlock but presumably all had Nazi or at least Aryan fathers. That was certainly not our fault but a direct consequence of our mother's strenuous effort to save her daughter's skin. Esther survived because of us! She was cruel towards Elke whom she financially exploited and Ute whom she injured emotionally. She became extremely hostile towards me because of my close relationship with Mutti and her fear it would put her expected inheritance from Geneva at risk.

The big tragedy of Esther's live was her fixation on our Aunt Emmi who served as her role model and whom she tried to emulate. Regrettably for her, she did not measure up to our aunt in terms of looks, personality, or intelligence. In her younger days, Aunt Emmi was in a class by herself in regard to all three of these traits and the times were very different then. Esther could not hope to have the same kind of lifestyle however she tried. Both started life with virtually nothing to their names and aspired to become wealthy. While our aunt succeeded remarkably well, Esther did not.

Realizing perhaps that she would not become rich through her own efforts, Esther became ever more obsessed with Aunt Emmi's fortune. Both women had few scruples in achieving their goals. Aunt Emmi and Max had taken off from Berlin for Switzerland with their landlady's possessions in tow while Esther removed our mother from her happy home in Oak Park to her place in Lake Forest. It gave her additional income and ensured she had the one person in her house and under her control who was likely to inherit our aunt's estate.

Other behavior similarities between our aunt and Esther existed. Both women were highly secretive and distrustful of others especially other family members. And like our aunt, Esther felt comfortable being at the center of a ménage à trois. Aunt Emmi had Max and Charles while Esther had Nick and Frank. But while Esther was married to one and having an affair with the other, our aunt was single and free to do as she pleased. The men in both of their lives predeceased them and both women were destined to live out their last days forsaken and alone.

At the same time, I had much cause to resent Esther's egocentric ways and especially what I saw as excessive greed. For most of my career while I worked and lived elsewhere, Mutti had lived in our Oak Park townhouse virtually rent-free while, at the same time, Esther was profiting from her real estate holdings. Needless to say, I was much upset when, after I returned home in 1986 and started to manage our mother's finances, I realized that while I was subsidizing Mutti, Esther had accepted hundreds of dollars in cash gifts from our mother while, unbeknownst to me, she was struggling to make ends meet.[4]

Despite having lived in America since the age of 19, Esther essentially remained an ethnic European of the older generation in her evaluation of people and her relationships. The only people that mattered to her were titled, such as members of the nobility, academics with doctor degrees, or otherwise very successful and affluent ones. Most everybody else was a no-count and in her dealings with such people she was patronizing and condescending. Nick's family was working-class and Esther wanted nothing to do with them. Mother and I never saw any of them on our visits to Esther and I never heard of Esther visiting them. She undoubtedly disdained me for not measuring up to her high expectations. "You never amounted to anything," she once said to me, "look where you are."

One thing Esther learned from our aunt and used to devastating effect was to isolate people once they were under her control. During Uncle Charles' last illness, our aunt kept both Esther and his sister, Evelyn de Pogranyi, from seeing him. It prevented them from exerting any unwanted influence. Similarly, Esther cruelly kept Frank away from his son. I saw Michael Murrin only once and that was just after his father had moved in with Esther and her family. My sister and Mike, who was a teenager then, were walking on Oak Park Avenue when I ran into them and Esther introduced him to me.

A short while later I heard that Mike and Esther had an altercation when Mike showed up at her apartment building to see his father and Esther refused to let him in. In fact, she forbade Mike to ever come to the building again. I never once saw father and son together in Oak Park, River Forest, or Lake Forest. Unknown to me is whether Esther ever allowed Frank to visit his son. That was the heavy price Frank had to pay as part of his bargain with her. Esther later unsuccessfully attempted the same scheme on me, of course, trying to keep me and our mother apart.

The one person who consistently stood by Esther throughout her life was our mother who slavishly indulged her every whim and fancy. Esther was, after all, her first-born and the issue of a happy marriage. They had shared many years of joy and sorrow, and also of anxiety and fear, especially from Esther's birth up to the end of the war. In her relationship with her daughter, Mutti seemed strongly motivated by feelings of guilt for the rough time and humiliation Esther experienced as a child and teenager being a *Mischling* in Nazi Germany. A strong bond between the two was inevitable.

For Mutti, Esther was numero uno and everybody, including myself, always knew and accepted that. Later, when Esther went through her mental crises, Mutti was in constant fear of Esther hurting herself and possibly taking her own life. Esther knew of the hold she had on our mother and used it to get her way. I got the impression that Esther had learned to use her handicap as a tool to use, manipulate, and even tyrannize those around her and especially Mutti.

Mother knew of Esther's shortcomings but always defended her finding all sorts of excuses for her often brutish and bizarre conduct. She claimed Esther was a good and loving girl in Germany and only turned mean and ugly after she came to America. It was the highly competitive and cutthroat American lifestyle that led Esther to become as cold and ruthless as she was, Mutti maintained. She also blamed Nick for what Esther was doing to us. He always hated us, Mutti claimed, and kept egging Esther on against us out of jealousy. Had she lived long enough and seen Esther's pathetic end, Mutti would have portrayed Esther's life as a Greek tragedy—a basically good person brought down by fate and no fault of her own.

One time Mutti said something to me that went in one ear and out the other because I had become tired of her apologies for Esther: "*Sie kann nichts dafür, es liegt ihr im Blut.*" [She can't help it, it's in her blood]. Years later, when her words came back to me and I reflected on them, I realized what Mutti was trying to say, namely, it was not Esther but her genes that were responsible for her conduct. The Nazis, in trying to incite the people against the Jews, had always painted them as cold-blooded, greedy, and unscrupulous exploiters of others. It was in their genes, these virulent racists had maintained. I am certain Mutti never believed any of these slurs herself but they now came in handy in defending Esther against these very charges.

Despite Mother's devotion and loyalty toward her daughter, she could also lash out against her especially when she felt slighted. In many of Mother's letters to me, written while I was employed out of state or in Europe, she often commented about her daughter's cold and strange behavior. In one of these, written in February 1982, Mother wrote that for Esther's 55th birthday, she had picked up some German rye bread and cold cuts from Meyer's Deli on North Lincoln Avenue and wanted to bring them over but Esther had no time for her. She was having workers in to remodel her kitchen, she told Mutti on the phone. She also informed her that an attractive pewter plate I had mailed Steffi from Munich was going to the Salvation Army because they had no use for it.

It was typical of Esther's insensitive and tactless ways. "*Keine Liebe, kein Gefühl, nur alles Business!!!*" [No love, no feelings, just only business!!!], was Mutti's sad lament. On the same theme, Mother wrote me in August 1984 (in translation): "When I think of all I had to go through during the 57 years of her life and, additionally, did everything for her I found possible, but everything, it's incredible how she treats her mother. She only wanted us here [in America] to work and save for her and nobody except her to get somewhere! Sad!!!"

One of the many questions I should have asked Mutti while her memory was still intact was why Esther was not sent to Geneva to live with Aunt Emmi during the Nazi regime where she would have been safe from both the Allied bombings and the Nazi pogrom against the Jews. It would seem to have been the perfect solution to Mutti's dilemma and she would not have had to endure the humiliation she suffered under the Nazis and bring children into the world she did not care to have. Did Mutti not want to let go of Esther? Did Esther not want to live with her aunt and uncle in Geneva? Did our aunt not want her niece around except perhaps only for short periods of time? Did the Swiss government make it difficult or even impossible for Jews and *Mischlinge* from moving to Switzerland at the time? One can only speculate.

It may, however, be safely assumed that Esther occasionally got to visit our aunt and uncle in Geneva and Grasse during the war. Esther was 12 years old when war broke out in September 1939 and a teenager during most of it. This would explain why Mutti always maintained that Esther worked hard and long hours in the Hirzel-Zell household and, in turn, was promised that she would become sole heir to her sister's estate.

Esther's American Dream turned into an American nightmare for which she had only herself to blame. Her past eventually caught up with her, and at the end she had to pay a very steep price. In her relentless pursuit of money, prestige, and social status she was absolutely ruthless and without scruples. The old adage, "What goes around comes around," is as true as ever. One cannot help but reflect on how swiftly and dramatically Esther's fortunes had changed. She seemed so powerful and intimidating when she strutted about, the ever loyal Dr. Murrin at her side, bragging about her wealth, her lawyers, and the things she had done and was yet to do. Then, in the time span of less than two years, her life became completely unraveled as in quick succession she lost everything close and dear to her—her devoted mother, her loyal friend and confidant, and her faithful and long-suffering husband while, at the same time, her lifelong ambition of becoming a wealthy heiress was dashed.

In her glory days, Esther had gone out of her way to make enemies of family and friends and then, when she needed them most, found out that she had neither. She was hardly the first person this has happened to and will not be the last. One thing Esther belatedly learned is that money, prestige, and social status are a poor substitute for family, friends, and relationships which are, in the long run, the only really important things in life other than one's faith in the Almighty.

UTE'S STORY

A Tough Beginning

Mutti's last three children were born in Stuttgart after she and Esther had relocated there in late 1938 after her father's death in Heidelberg. Born near the end of November 1939, Ute was the second of the new arrivals after our mother's divorce from Fritz Würzburger. At the time, the world was once again in turmoil with the Second World War having started less than three months earlier. Ute was baptized into the Christian faith and given the name Ute Walfrieda Zell. On her birth certificate under *Eltern* [parents] only "Anna Maria Zell, *evangelisch*, resident of Stuttgart" appears with no mention of her father. Ute apparently got Mutti to reveal his name which was Franz Lodzin. The Prussian-born Lodzin served with the Wehrmacht as a private and fell in southwestern France in April 1944, just prior to the Normandy invasion.[5] His lowly army rank and age (37) at the time of his death would suggest that he was not a career soldier but drafted into the Wehrmacht and presumably a member of *die Partei* or at least what was important at the time—a member of the so-called Aryan race.

Ute's childhood was an exceptionally unhappy one. Few rays of sunshine seem to have pierced her world of gloom and doom. Ute once told me that she felt abandoned and rejected when she was living in Schruns in the Tyrolean mountains where Mutti and I had visited her in the fall of 1944. Presumably she, along with Volker, was out in the country as part of the *Kinderlandverschickung (KLV)* program organized by the state to get children out of harm's way during the Allied bombing raids on German cities and towns. In fact, Ute remembered being caught up in at least one such air raid during the war. Perhaps she was too young to understand why she was not living in Stuttgart with our mother, Esther and me and ever after attributed it to neglect and callousness on our mother's part.

After her foster mother, Frau Pfeifer, turned her and Volker over to Mutti and me on Lake Constance in September 1946, Ute later recalled, she got her first real taste of "the hell we were going to be subjected to" when we were all on the train to Stuttgart. Mother supposedly slapped Volker across the face because he used a bad word. At the time Ute was nearly seven and Volker four years old. Strangely, I do not remember the incident and, in fact, I do not even recall having been along to pick up my two siblings at the German-Austrian border.

Ute never was an outgoing and friendly child but quiet and reclusive. For reasons unknown, according to Ute, our mother never liked her and showed her no affection. Perhaps Mutti heard of an incident I vaguely remember from my days as a young boy in Forst. One day Ute came for a visit. Since she was three years younger than I and therefore quite small, she must have come in the company of someone else. This must have been just before she was sent to Austria. All that I recall was that Ute was at a neighbor's house when the woman gave her a bagful of apples to take home. Instead of doing so, Ute stopped by our outhouse in the courtyard, ate part of each apple, and threw the rest down the privy. It scandalized all who heard the story and Mutti may have picked up on this childhood indiscretion and saw in it a major character flaw.

Ute's Stuttgart years, according to my sister, were miserable ones. She claimed that Mutti was both verbally and physically abusive. Ute was saddled with choice names and got herself slapped around for even minor infractions. Mutti's favorite expression for Ute was *Duckmäuserin* [sneak, underhanded person] and that is how Mutti mostly felt about her. Had Ute spoken up now and then to defend herself, it might have helped her cause but she was unusually timid and, instead of expressing her true feelings, just sulked.

One bright moment for Ute came in the summer of 1948 when Aunt Emmi invited her to spend some time with her and Uncle Charles in Geneva and their second home in the south of France. Incidentally, I had been accorded the same privilege the year before although my visit was confined to Geneva and I never saw Grasse and the French Riviera. When Mutti and I saw Ute off at the Stuttgart Hauptbahnhof, I had brought along my new box camera to record the event. The photographs show Ute wearing a pretty new dress and a fancy bow in her hair but, as usual, looking sad and forlorn. Most likely she again felt abandoned because she was just eight years old and, as far as I know, traveling alone at least until she got to the border where someone would have escorted and placed her on a train to Geneva. In Geneva, she evidently enjoyed and endeared herself to Uncle Charles who became quite fond of her.

Ute was 10 years old when we all arrived in the States in March 1950 and, like the rest of us, lived with Esther and Nick in their first house on South Oak Park Avenue. She subsequently experienced all the turmoil we went through when Esther locked Mutti and her brood out of the house and sent us all back to Stuttgart in July 1951 when Mutti had returned there after essentially abandoning us. When our mother returned to the States in November of that year, Ute and I were left in the care of Robert and Liesel Sokolov in our apartment on Adlerstrasse while Volker was placed in a children's home. While Mutti sent for me in April of the following year, it took until November 1954 before she brought over Ute and Volker. In the meantime, she had to get the money together for the travel expenses, to have a secure job to support us all, and to find us a place to live. Ute was just short of her 15th birthday on her return and was enrolled as a freshman at Oak Park and River Forest High School where I was a senior.

Although I never witnessed Mutti being verbally or physically abusive toward Ute while we lived on Home Avenue, I did get an inkling that there were problems in their relationship. One morning I remember being in my home room at Oak Park High when the dean of freshmen girls sent me a message to immediately report to her office. I did so and when she told me she wanted to talk to me about Ute and our mother, I felt imposed on. It galled me to have to report to a girls dean and, never being the timid type, gave the lady a piece of my mind telling her that the proper procedure would have been for her to contact the dean of senior boys. With that, I simply walked out of her office. Obviously, I should have listened to her and then talked to our mother about the matter. Because I did not, I never learned the particulars about Ute's complaint.

Until my transfer in the fall of 1958 to the main campus of the University of Illinois, all four of us lived together on Home Avenue in what appeared to me in complete harmony. Ute did well in school and at home played the flute. The two of us got along very well. She had learned to type and on occasion typed a paper for me while I attended the school's undergraduate campus in Chicago. I can unequivocally say that during our time together in Oak Park I never witnessed any form of abusive behavior on our mother's part toward either Ute or Volker nor show any kind of hostility. On the contrary, many photographs from the period attest to some very good times we all had together including attending the annual German-American festivities in Chicago's Riverview Park and visiting some of the many Chicago museums and other big-city amenities. It is a mystery to me how all this alleged abuse Ute later complained about could have happened right under my nose without my being aware of it. Neither Ute nor Volker ever said one word to me about it.

Things Are Looking Up

Ute graduated from Oak Park High in June 1958 with a scholarship to study at a church-affiliated Midwestern college, Valparaiso University, where she took up accounting. The 7-page letter she wrote me from school in early February 1961 while I was serving with the U.S. Army in New Mexico was exuberant and full of joie de vivre. Beginning with "Dear *Bruderherz* " [brother of my heart], she informed me that she had again made the Dean's List and just defeated three other girls for the presidency of the Associated Women Students (AWS), an organization to which every woman student belonged on matriculating. She was looking forward to attending the AWS national convention in April which, alas, was being held at the University of Wisconsin and not in Arizona as in the prior year where she could have come to visit me. In the romance department, things seemed a little complicated:

> *Now since we are on the subject of girls and guys let me tell you about my problems with them. You know that I've been going with this Steve for some time. Well, I don't want to go with him any longer. I still like him but somehow he just doesn't have what I want and need in a boy. For one thing, I think he is much too young for me (he's a few months younger than I am), and for some reason we just don't understand each other. We don't argue or anything but we can never discuss anything; everything seems to be small talk*

and, you know, after a while that gets pretty boring. Besides that, he doesn't exactly know where he is going—not much ambition in other words (according to my standards anyway). Couldn't you just see me somewhere in North Carolina in a small dead town as a housewife. You know, I want to do things and see places. I am a very restless person and would be bored to death doing nothing but housework all day for the next few years anyway. Besides that, I never kidded myself as being in love with him although I did and do like him better than anyone else I have dated.

My sister went on to write:

Now with that said I'll tell you what caused me to realize all this. (Are you yawning yet??). Here I met this boy from River Forest with whom I graduated from Oak Park High. He went to Yale where he goofed off too much and transferred here. He wants to finish at Yale though. Anyway, I've talked to him quite a bit because he is in my French class, and he calls me rather frequently, and we talk for about ½ to ¾ of an hour each time. Undoubtedly you have guessed that I think he is pretty sharp because he is so well versed in everything. Now the problem in this case is this. Why doesn't he ask me out? He always makes sure that we go home together, either by train or his parents come to pick us up and he calls with the most trivial questions. Wouldn't this indicate that he is interested? Does he need a push? If so, he is not getting it from me. Oh well, I guess only time will tell in this case too.

Whatever problems Ute may have had with our mother before, by the time of Mutti's 52nd birthday in March of 1961, these seemed to have disappeared without lingering effects. On that day, Ute gave our mother a cardboard-framed photo portrait of herself. At age 21, Ute was a pretty young woman with a radiant smile. On the inside cover, she had written a warm dedication in German wishing Mutti many more happy years in good health.

The Wedding Disaster

The marriage of a family member is normally a big event and for Ute that time had come. Her fiancé was Tom, who like her and his twin Ted, were graduates of Valparaiso University. After leaving college, my sister was employed by the prestigious Chicago law firm of Baker, McKenzie & Hightower at their offices at One North LaSalle Street in downtown Chicago. From there she wrote me in Virginia, where I had found employment after getting out of the service, in mid-May of 1963:

> *I don't want to say too much, but to put it quite briefly, I'm sure you've gotten wind about Esther's and Mother's feelings about my wedding and their professed opinions on how my marriage will turn out. Now there is no doubt in my mind that it will work out very well and that our love and understanding will see us through many happy and sorrowful hours. The next point is how you feel about it. I realize you know nothing about Tom or his background other than what you've learned from Mother and Esther. But I think you realize that I'm old enough to pick my own partner. Therefore, should you accept the idea of giving me away July 6 (and I hope you do) I would like to be sure that you can do so without reservation......This cat and mouse game we've been playing here in Oak Park is not my cup of tea. Although I've been accused of being two-faced, it certainly is not my nature because I think I'm much too sensitive for that, and I think that's why I worry so much about little things. You studied psychology, what do you say? So now to roll everything in a little neat bundle, Peter, I would very much like you to give me away to Tom if you have no qualms about it and really feel you would like to do this for me.*

She and Tom were taking Mother, Elke, and his parents to dinner in the evening for Mother's Day, she wrote. In a postscript she added, "Well, well, in the meantime I just couldn't take all the belittling that had been going on through a special envoy (you guessed who!) and I went and had a king-size fight with Esther. Of course, no one is coming to the wedding as of now. Are you? Please do!"

Actually, I had not "gotten wind" about the family feud regarding the impending wedding as our mother never wrote me anything about it.

Without consulting Mutti or Esther, I immediately accepted the invitation. Tom wrote me a thank-you note saying that, while there were some caustic verbal exchanges between the four of them, he was still hopeful Esther and Mother would come. Ute and Tom were married on July 6, 1963 in suburban Clarendon Hills and I had come up by train from Newport News, Virginia to attend. Incredibly, Esther had decided to visit her grandmother, Mathilde, in Gary, Indiana on that very day and had talked the always compliant Mutti into coming along. Nick drove and they also brought along Steffi and Elke. Completely unbeknownst to me at the time was that Elke had been scheduled to be Ute's chief bridesmaid.

As it turned out, I found myself the only one of Ute's family to be at her wedding. It was a beautiful if subdued ceremony at my new brother-in-law's Lutheran parish church followed by a reception and catered wedding meal. Tom's parents, Theodore (Bud) and Esther, whom I met for the first time, were noticeably cool towards me and kept their distance. In fact, other than to say hello we never talked to each other. They sat next to the bride and groom while I was assigned to the end of the table next to their pastor. Afterwards, I busied myself taking photographs of the newlyweds which, according to Ute, turned out to be the best pictures of the wedding.

There were probably a number of reasons for the bad blood between Mutti and Esther on one side and Tom and his family on the other but likely centered on Esther's opinion that Ute had picked a man whom she regarded unsuitable to be her husband. According to one account, while Ute was with McKenzie, a German lawyer in the office, a *Doktor* so-and-so, had shown an interest in her. (By German custom, an academic title, such as Juris Doctor, becomes part of the name and the person is addressed as *Herr Doktor*). Esther, who was always impressed with titles, thought the lawyer would make a good match for Ute. To her great dismay, however, Ute did not respond to the lawyer's overtures and nothing came of the matter.

Tom's parents too did not seem to have impressed Esther and Mother even though Bud was a successful stock broker. When I asked Mutti what she thought of Tom's parents, she referred to them as "a couple of Polacks." This comment was very uncharacteristic of Mutti who never made ethnic remarks and must have heard it from Esther.

Another big contributing factor to Mother's and Esther's animosity was that Ute's fiancé smoked. Many years after they were married, Mutti was still fuming when she told me that Tom had insisted that Ute take up the habit too. Nobody in our family had ever smoked and Ute was no exception. Both Mutti and Esther had come to this country with a strong aversion to that addiction because during the Third Reich it was condemned as being foreign, decadent, and a threat to the health of the *Volk*. In America, with its large tobacco industry, the reverse was true. Smoking and drinking stood for worldliness and sophistication as exemplified by Hollywood stars whose standard pose was to hold a cigarette in one hand and a cocktail glass in the other. Tom evidently felt that Ute was too much Old World and pressed her to take up the habit which she did becoming an avid smoker for much of her life. There were other, more trivial, issues between the two sides.

The scandalous absence of Esther, Elke, and our mother at Ute's wedding left deep wounds in Ute's psyche that never healed and the repercussions were lasting. After the wedding, according to Mutti, Ute and Tom gave her an ultimatum to choose between them and Esther because they saw no way they could ever get Esther to accept Tom as a friend. If Mutti decided for Esther, she would never see Ute and Tom again, she was warned. Not surprisingly, Mutti, always loyal and devoted to her eldest child, chose Esther over them. This ended all contact between the two sides of the family.

As a consequence, Ute and Tom chose to break off relations with me too because of my close bond with our mother. They may also have been disappointed to see me come to the wedding by myself. Presumably Tom's letter was intended for me to use my influence to change Mutti's and Esther's minds but I had no intimate knowledge of the nature of the feud between the two sides at the time. In fact, if I had I would have preferred not to get involved in a catfight among our mother and my two sisters about something that would have been of little consequence to me. If Ute and Tom were happy together, I felt, who cares? After their wedding, Mutti and I never heard from Ute and Tom and his parents again and simply put them out of our minds.

A Reunion

Nearly 35 years had passed when, about a week before Christmas 1997, I received a phone call from a woman who said her name was Ute and that she was trying to locate her lost brother. She found my name on the Internet in a listing of Illinois lawyers, she said. After some careful probing, I realized that it was indeed my sister. "Are you an attorney?" she wanted to know. I told her that I was indeed but not in practice. Overjoyed at having again found each other, we talked for nearly an hour. Ute told me that she and Tom had two grown children. She was also in contact with Elke, she said, who too was married and had two grown daughters of her own. Only Volker was still missing.

Ute never mentioned our mother and so I brought up the subject telling her that Mutti was suffering from terminal colon cancer and Alzheimer's. I asked her how she felt about Mutti. Her words "anger, rage, and hatred" quite shocked me. I then asked her if that was her feeling even though our mother was not expected to live much longer. "Yes," she replied, and she felt the same way about Esther. But, according to Ute, she always had a warm spot in her heart for me because I had always defended her. (That was news to me).

According to Ute, she was 58 years old now but no longer working because of an auto accident nine years earlier when she was rear-ended on her way to work and suffered a spinal cord injury. Tom, she said, was 57 and employed by an insurance company. His job investigating big-ticket insurance fraud required him to be on the road much of the time, she said. She gave me her address and phone number in Brighton, Michigan and we agreed to stay in touch. My reply to Ute in my letter just before Christmas summed up my feelings at the time:

> *Words do not suffice to describe my happiness at hearing from you again. I can hardly believe it's been 35 years since we last saw each other. Thank God you and your loved ones are well and that Elke too is all right. That leaves only our dear brother Volker unaccounted for and I have often wondered what happened to the poor guy. ... I just got back from Lake Forest where I visited our dear little mother now 88 years old. I get to see her every other Sunday as well as on Tuesdays and Fridays. As I had mentioned*

to you, she has Alzheimer's. At the beginning of May she was also diagnosed with colon cancer and given just six months more to live. I pray for her every day and it's a miracle that she is still with us and apparently doing well even without treatment. The poor soul is so happy when she sees me but leaving is always a heartbreak because she pleads with me to take her back home with me. However, since July 23, Esther is Mother's legal guardian and I agreed in court to be content with visitation rights. I figured that Esther and her two men could probably also take better care of Mother's physical needs. ... Ute, it was sad for me to hear how you feel about our dear mother. It is not right to blame her for what Esther has done to us. I hope you will find it in your heart to see our mother before she dies. I am sure we could arrange a reunion without Esther's involvement.

In mid-January 1998, Tom stopped by for a first visit at Mutti's Place. He said his dad was living in a retirement home in neighboring Lombard and he was visiting him on the first anniversary of his mother's death. Ute, he said, still harbors deep feelings of hurt and anger towards our mother for not coming to her wedding. I told him that it was unfair for her to blame it all on our mother when it was really Esther's fault. Mutti just could never stand up to her strong-willed daughter. Ute's near fatal auto accident she suffered on her way to work in 1989, Tom said, injured the base of her spine and she is in constant pain. She takes no pain medication for fear of becoming addicted to it, he said, and relies entirely on acupuncture treatments which appear to help. According to Tom, Ute earned a master's degree in accounting and, before the accident, had risen within her company to become vice president and comptroller. He said Ute and Elke were very close and in constant contact with each other.

Elke, he said, was teaching high school German and English and was already completely gray. He would not give me her last name or where she lived. Before he left, I showed him around Mutti's Place and gave him Ute's high school graduation photograph which Mutti had framed and kept on top of our television console.

There followed some more lengthy phone calls before Ute and I finally got to meet. Each time Ute held forth about her miserable childhood and her mistreatment by our mother. According to Ute, when she talks with

Elke they always refer to our mother not as Mother or Mutti but as "Mrs. Zell." I asked Ute to be more charitable towards our mother who had a tough life and was less a victimizer than a victim. She suffered much both during the Nazi era and even afterwards when she came to America as an immigrant with no language or job skills requiring her to work hard and for long hours at subsistence wages, I explained. "How do you know this? Did she talk to you? When did she tell you all this?" she asked. From Ute's questions, it was apparent that, other than Esther, I was the only one privy to Mutti's past and that she had never confided much in either Ute or Elke.

I was much hoping to convince Ute that, at heart, Mutti was a very warm-hearted and compassionate person, which she truly was, and induce her to visit and make peace with our mother before she passed away. Mutti had entered Westmoreland Nursing Center at the end of February and it could therefore be easily arranged for Ute not to inadvertently run into Esther whom she despised.

My effort was unsuccessful and Mutti died on May 29 without seeing Ute or Elke again. I thought it extraordinarily hard-hearted for either of my two sisters to fail to make an effort to see our mother in her last days in this world. Had they come, Mutti would surely have remembered and joyously received them with hugs and kisses. She had turned into a love sponge and even her caregivers were given this treatment. But it was not to be. When I called Ute on Sunday, which was the day after I heard of Mutti's passing, she took the news very calmly expressing her sympathy because, she said, she knew how much our mother meant to me.

Our reunion took place on the following Sunday, June 7, when I drove up to see Ute and her family in Brighton. Ute had originally invited me to visit them on Easter Sunday (April 12) but I had postponed the trip because I wanted to be with our mother on this day which I knew would be her last Easter in this world. The family greeted me warmly. Their home was a handsome 2-story structure in a leafy Brighton neighborhood. I was somewhat shocked to see Ute look so old and drawn that I barely recognized her. The auto injury had taken its toll and she was in obvious pain. Most of the time she preferred to stand which was more comfortable than being seated. According to my sister, after obtaining her accounting degree at Valparaiso University, she obtained an MBA from Michigan State University and was lastly employed as Vice President of Finance with Kaleidoscope Industries of Howell, Michigan, makers of window treatments.

Also present during my visit were their two adult children. Son Tommy, a dark haired, handsome young man, had just turned 30 a few days earlier. He had been a high school tennis star, I learned, and subsequently been recruited by Kalamazoo College to play tennis for them. Tommy had studied political science and public administration, served in the Peace Corps, and was about to leave for an Eastern European country on behalf of a U.S. government agency to set up an Internet system. Danielle, his sister, was two years his senior and had been adopted by Ute and Tom. She had studied retail management and was employed by a major national retailer. Judging from the colorful, swirling paintings she had done, she was also an accomplished artist.

A Difficult Relationship

My gifts were well-received except for the framed 8" x 10" photo portrait of Mutti, showing her at age 84, which Ute eyed with utter disdain. Ute again let me know what she thought of our mother which was not much. She told me of her and Elke's continuing bitterness and rage. Elke blamed me, Ute told me, for not standing up for her so that she could come to Ute's wedding. I replied that, while I knew of the family feud from Ute's letter, I was completely in the dark about the wedding arrangements and, specifically, that Elke was expected to be a bridesmaid. I was hopeful the two sides would settle their differences beforehand. This, unfortunately, did not happen and when I came up from Virginia the day before, the plans for the trip to Gary, Indiana, had already been made and I was completely unaware of them. Had Elke spoken up when I arrived home, I would naturally have insisted that she come along if for no other reason than I would not have been by myself entering what I feared would be hostile territory.

Last but not least, Ute let me know that our mother's births were timed three years apart so that she could get money and a certificate of appreciation from the Nazi state. I had never heard nor seen such a certificate and hence this too was news to me and clearly meant to demean our mother. All my efforts to set the record straight and defend Mutti fell on deaf ears. I stayed at my sister's house overnight and left for home early next morning wondering whether I had made a mistake in coming.

In late August, Ute and Tom came for a first visit to see Mutti's Place together and I gave them a short tour. They had just been in neighboring Lombard for a family gathering with Tom's father. Tom again mentioned that on account of her auto accident and damaged spine, Ute was in constant pain and had recently lost her thyroid gland. Then, on the day after Thanksgiving (November 26), Ute came for a second visit bringing along Danielle and, to my great surprise, Elke. Tom was in Moldova over Thanksgiving to be with son Tommy where the U.S. government had sent him on an assignment. Ute and Danielle had picked up Elke at her home in Valparaiso on their way down to Oak Park. Elke and I had no contact since Ute's wedding and it was quite a surprise to see her again.

Elke was now 53 years old and surprisingly youngish looking despite a head of gray hair. She wasted no time to let me know of the physical and emotional abuse she suffered at the hands of first Esther and then our mother. When I countered that I had never suffered abuse at Mutti's hands, my two sisters claimed that I was our mother's favorite. They cited as an example that after I left for college, Mother had treated the front room in our Home Avenue flat like a shrine and forbade any of them to enter it. As with Ute, I offered my sincere apologies to Elke for Mutti's conduct explaining that our mother was going through some very stressful times and regretfully and unfortunately vented her frustrations on them.

According to Elke, much had happened in her life since she abruptly left home. She had gotten married and she and John had two daughters, Ute and Monica. Daughter Ute was married and had three small children while Monica was still single. According to Elke, she has been teaching high school German and English ever since graduating from the same college as Ute, namely, Valparaiso University.

Realizing that neither Ute nor Elke knew much about our family background, I gave them a short lesson with the help of some photographs of our ancestors and other relatives. Naturally there were many questions especially from Elke who seemed entirely clueless about anything relating to our family. According to Elke, her two daughters had often asked her about their maternal grandparents and other ancestors and she had to tell them that she simply did not know much about them because our mother had never volunteered any information and she had learned not to ask too many questions because of the negative responses she always received.

After introducing my visitors to some neighbors, we drove through the village and past Oak Park High which Elke hardly recognized again because the original school building and field house had been transformed into a college-style campus. A pleasant lunch at a Chinese restaurant, to which I had invited them, concluded their visit. Being described as the favorite of a mother who treated both of her daughters so shabbily, suggested to me that my two sisters most likely harbored strong resentments towards me too. Nevertheless, we parted with hugs and kisses and an assurance from Elke that she would soon let me know her married name and address. This she eventually did in a conciliatory letter to me.

During the last year of the old century and the first two of the new, Ute and I had much of an opportunity to bridge the great divide between us stemming primarily from our very different relationships with our mother. Holidays were occasions for get-togethers either at Ute's house in Brighton or at the home of Tom's twin brother Ted and his wife Karen in Grand Rapids. The two families came together at least three times during the year, viz, Thanksgiving, Christmas, and Easter.

When I visited Ute on Thanksgiving 1999, which happened to fall on her 60th birthday, she and Tom had just moved into their new, smaller home on a golf course in Brighton where he could indulge his love for that game. Our conversation centered on the trips we had recently taken. Ute and Danielle had been on their annual sojourn to Europe a month before while I had just returned from my first visit to Arizona where I was planning to retire. There was also an exchange of tidbits about various family members, but I dared not bring up Mutti because of Ute's strong negative feelings about her.

On Thanksgiving 2001, I drove to Brighton again where I got to meet the entire clan for the first time including Ted and Karen, their son Todd, his wife Wendy with their two small daughters, Anna and Julia, and their two younger children, Andrew (Andy) and Kim. Together with Tom, Ute, Danielle, Tommy, and Bud, there were 14 of us in the largest gathering of family members I had ever attended. Ute, with Tom's assistance, had prepared a Thanksgiving dinner including a huge roast turkey with all the trimmings. The meal was as well done and delicious in every respect as Esther's famous turkey dinners had been. Needless to say, I did not dare tell Ute because mentioning Esther or our mother, for that matter, would surely have ruined her appetite.

The following Christmas, the family gathering was at Ted and Karen's home in Grand Rapids. Bud, or Opa as they affectionately called him, had a room there, as he did at Tom and Ute's, so that whenever he drove up from Lombard, which he still did regularly despite being in his upper 80s, he had a place to stay. Late in the afternoon of Christmas Eve, all of us except Ute attended services at the local Lutheran church and, after a delicious meal, exchanged presents under the beautifully decorated Christmas tree. The giving of presents on Christmas Eve rather than the morning of Christmas Day was according to the old German custom, of course, and came as a pleasant surprise considering that the families were as American as could be.

Ute and Tom had come up from yet another family gathering in Valparaiso, Indiana. They had spent time with Elke, her husband John, and their two daughters, Ute and Monica. Ute, my niece, her husband Brian, and their three small children, Sadie and twins Cole and Mason, had flown in from New England for the holiday. In the meantime, Ute and I had come to bond as much as we could considering that Ute had not softened her stand on our mother and was, in fact, getting even more resentful towards that person she always referred to as "Mrs. Zell."

When I came up for the next family affair, which was at Easter 2002 (March 31) in Brighton, I was determined to convince Ute to let go of her hatred for our mother and therefore make it easier for us to enjoy a more normal relationship. I had brought along some photo albums and letters as a backup for my efforts. The day before Easter Sunday, Ted and his family joined us for a delicious meal featuring baked ham and many side dishes. They left again towards evening, along with Opa, preferring to be home for Easter and attend worship services in Grand Rapids. On Easter Sunday, Tom and Tommy picked me up at my motel, and after attending Easter services at their parish church, St. George Lutheran, we returned to their house where Ute awaited us with Danielle joining us later. The day also happened to be Tom's and Ted's 61st birthday.

After a small lunch of Easter dinner leftovers, I had a chance to discuss our mother and her adventures during the Nazi era pointing out that one had to do many things to survive during this dictatorship which one would not normally have done, I told Ute. Fearing for Esther's life, Mother did what she believed would most likely ensure our sister's safety which was to find refuge in the favored and protected status of motherhood. Ute appeared bored by my explanation. Her response, "So! What does that have to do with me?" amazed me because it seemed terribly self-centered. My efforts to apologize for our mother's ill treatment of her during her childhood fell on deaf ears. Tom even had the audacity to say to me about his mother-in law, "She looked on them [her children] as a business." When I brought up the subject of our lost brother, Ute told me she had located Volker at a halfway house in Oregon and would probably get in touch with him after making sure he did not become a liability.

A Severe Judgment

A rupture in the carefully nurtured relationship between Ute and me appeared imminent and ironically was brought about by way of Volker. Sometime toward the end of April 2002, I suddenly realized that April 19 had been Volker's 60th birthday and decided to send him a birthday card if I could locate him. Ute had told me during my Easter visit the month before that she had traced Volker to Oregon via the Internet and found his name, address, and phone number there. When she called the place, she was startled to find that it was a halfway house. It just so happened that back in 1996, I had purchased a book on family genealogy entitled *The World Book of Zells* published by Halbert's Family Heritage. It contained a world-wide listing of all people with the surname Zell giving addresses by country and, for the United States, by state. No phone numbers were listed. After reading something about the history of the family name and its coat of arms, I had shelved it. It had not occurred to me at the time to search for Volker since I did not know where he lived.

To my great surprise, when I now looked under Oregon, I found a Mr. Erwin V. Zell listed living in Salem. Not knowing whether it was our lost brother, I sent off my greeting card. Volker finally wrote back a month later, on May 30, expressing his joy on us finding each other again. He was "flabbergasted," he wrote, that I found him in a genealogy book under a temporary address after he had been unsuccessfully searching for me for over three decades. "Thanks for the birthday card. Yes, I turned 60 on 19 April 02, one day before Hitler's birthday. I sometimes wonder what reward Mother would have gotten if she could have stuffed me back in for another day," he wrote. "Tell Ute & Elke to please get in touch with me & send them a copy of this letter, please," he continued. In a postscript he added, "No! Don't send money! I got enough!" I immediately forwarded copies of our brother's letter to Ute and Elke.

Ute and Volker had been close ever since they had returned from Austria together after the war. When Ute told me about having found Volker living in a halfway house, she surmised he had been in trouble and would ask her for money. She must now have felt embarrassed that it was I and not she who had the first contact with Volker again. I might have let Ute know that I had found Volker too and would be writing him a birthday card but did not because I was not yet sure that the name and address I had found were really his. Ute now felt she had to backtrack and explain to Volker why she did not get in touch with him when she obviously knew his address and phone number. In her first letter to Volker on June 11, 2002, of which our brother sent me a copy, Ute wrote:

> At this point in time what is most annoying to me is that Peter had your address and decided not to share it with me ?? When I pressed him about it, he said he got your address from "the book of Zell family genealogy." So there is something I'm missing, and I don't understand how he was able to contact you and wish you a happy 60th birthday. There is not a year that has gone by that I haven't thought about you on your birthday, wishing I could share those days with you....Mrs. Zell found us with some pretty sick telephone calls. How did she get our address and telephone number? Rightly or wrongly, we believed that it was from you. My hatred of her and my bitterness toward her cost me my relationship with you; and I am truly sorry for that!.... I noticed that you haven't lost your sense of humor amidst your trials and tribulations. Your comment about your birth one day before Hitler's was interesting because I always suspected that Mrs. Zell was paid to have us. If true, that would explain a lot!

Ute went on to tell Volker something about her family. Tom and she lived in Illinois, Utah, and California, she wrote, before settling in the Midwest in 1978. Their children Danielle, nearly 36, and Tom, just turned 34, are single and "in no hurry to tie the knot." Danielle, she wrote, is a retail manager in charge of human resources and Tommy is a senior program manager for a non-profit organization. Tom went back to work for an insurance company after retiring from another a few years earlier. Ute then described her auto accident in 1989 that ended a successful 14-year career in finance. In an addendum to this letter dated two days later, Ute wrote, "By the way, I figured out how Peter got your address. It is on a pay-for-information website. In addition to Erwin V. Zell, an Erwin Victor Zell is also listed at the same address." It was a nice try by Ute but ludicrous because at that time I owned no personal computer, had never used one, and had never searched the Internet. Ute was, of course, well aware of all that and had even urged me to get a PC so we could correspond by e-mail.

As ridiculous and trivial as it may now seem, another bone of contention between Ute and me was our different idea as to who represented the "family." In her June letter to Volker Ute wrote: "We began a relationship, which at first was and still is difficult because of his [Peter's] attachment to his mother and his unwillingness to listen to my story. Nevertheless, Tom, I, the children, and the rest of the family have embraced him as a member of the family." "I'm thankful you found him [Peter] & restored him to the 'family.' There is nothing worse than having family & having lost it—I'm the expert, folks," Volker wrote back a week later. That did not sit well with me. I had, after all, been the one who had stayed behind and for 10 years taken care of our aging mother while the rest had been away looking out for themselves. Responding to Ute's remark about my having had Volker's address and not sharing it with her and Volker's comment about my having been restored to the family, I wrote Volker in mid-August:

> I must say that sister Ute has long been a mystery to me. I do not think that she always plays with a a full deck......Speaking of family, I did not think much of your remark to Ute "I am thankful that you found him and restored him to the family." In what respect is Ute and her family now "the family" and how was I "restored" to it? Was I an orphan wandering the streets looking for a home or the prodigal son perhaps? To me "the family" was our mother and

her children or whoever is now left. I know you meant to slobber up to sister Ute a little but to me your remark sounded awfully patronizing.

My comments undoubtedly got back to Ute adding further to the conflict between us.

After my return from my Easter 2002 visit, I felt very down and decided not to attend any more of these gatherings with Ute's family. Mutti had been gone nearly four years but I was still grieving and would have liked to have someone to talk with to ease my pain and find closure. Instead of commiseration, all I could expect from my visits was more animosity and resentment. Besides, these many trips of nearly 300 miles each way were becoming a burden and it seemed to me that I was no longer leading my own life but had become part of somebody else's agenda.

In mid-July, we had our 14th annual townhouse party, which was held on the lawns between the two buildings, and Ute and Tom stopped by bringing along their Opa whom they had visited at his retirement home in Lombard. I showed them Mutti's Place after it was remodeled in preparation of its sale and my forthcoming move to Arizona. While Tom and his father enjoyed the party, Ute and I took a long walk through the Frank Lloyd Wright Historic District and other parts of the village. Our conversation predictably centered on our childhood and our very different experiences during those days. Ute was as bitter as ever. This visit turned out to be the last time we would see each other. She called me on my birthday in August and during our conversation lamented the fact that while she was working for Bill Klein, Esther's friend, and Tony Basile, Esther's attorney, she had to turn over every penny to our mother. "I paid for your education, " she said. Since I had never received a red cent of financial support from Mutti, Esther, or any other family member and had financed all of my education through my own efforts, this spurious claim really angered me.

A letter from Ute near the end of 2002 widened the rift between us when she wrote something that no child should ever say about a parent regardless of whether it was true or not, and what she wrote was patently false:

With heavy heart I feel compelled to express some thoughts to you. I don't know the outcome of this process, but I hope it will be a positive one in the long run. First of all, I want to tell you how much you influenced my healing process after so many years of confusion and lack of understanding of what happened to me in my childhood. I will always be grateful to you for that! Second, as this healing process has progressed, other concerns have emerged. I will get right to the point. I sense, perceive or whatever you want to call it, that you blame your siblings for your mother's hardship in life. I wonder whether or not you disdain your younger siblings in the same manner Esther disdains you from what you have told me. It's wonderful that you were "the love child" and, thus, had a special relationship with your mother. The fact that Elke, Volker, and I had Nazi fathers does not mean, in my opinion, that we are tainted and, therefore, cannot contribute to the good of mankind. What it does mean is that your mother "produced" us for the monetary rewards and economic benefits she received. Does that mean that we deserved less than a loving and nurturing environment?

In her letter, Ute claimed that toward Elke and her our mother "behaved like a monster." Elke, she wrote, gave her permission to speak on her behalf. When I read the letter I was livid. To me, the allegation that Mutti had been motivated by money was slanderous with not a shred of evidence to support it and contrary to all known facts. I was so angry that I made a copy of the letter and mailed it to Esther with whom I had no contact in a long time. Esther responded with a short note to Ute defending our mother which I forwarded. Ute's remarks concerning the "Nazi fathers" was in response to a letter I wrote to Volker in mid-June in which I explained to him the circumstances of our births, as far as I knew them. I told him of my suspicion that we all had fathers "who were card-carrying members of the Nazi Party."

In my last letter to Volker, in October 2002, I explained to him that I was simply stating the facts to further explain Mutti's past. "When I wrote that Ute, Elke, and you most likely had Nazi fathers, I was not making a value judgment of your lives or slight you or imply I was in any way superior to you," I wrote him. Naturally, I had to agree with Ute on the two points she made. For one, just because one's father happened to be a member of the Nazi Party or some other disreputable group or organization does not in itself make one a good or bad person. Nobody is given the opportunity to choose his or her parents. Ute was also correct, of course, in saying that every child deserves a loving and nurturing environment regardless of the circumstances of its birth. These were truisms one could not argue with.

A Final Break

When Mutti passed away at the end of May 1998, she left nothing to her estranged three youngest children which I always thought harsh and unjust. Consequently, during one of Ute's first visits to our house after Mutti's passing I asked her if there was anything she wanted of our mother's possessions. I almost immediately regretted opening my mouth when she pointed to the foot-operated sewing machine that had been Opa's last gift to Mutti before he passed away and said, "This is what I want." The piece had obvious sentimental value for Ute because she had become a talented dressmaker in her early years and had honed her sewing skills on this machine. I told Ute that she could have the piece but that I wanted to hold on to it until I left for Arizona a few years hence. When the time came for my relocation, I had second thoughts, however, and decided to take the sewing machine with me. I did not think it proper for me to hand over Mutti's most priced possession to a daughter who absolutely despised and hated her. Reneging on my promise must have much angered Ute although I did not anticipate just how much at the time.

Near the end of January 2003, I let Ute know that I had found my dream home in one of the Del Webb retirement communities northwest of Phoenix and that I would give her the street address as soon as the sale had closed. It was raining cats and dogs when I moved into my new house on Thursday, February 13. Near the end of the month, I received a computer-generated greeting card from Ute with a photo taken in my new community and the date February 14 imprinted on it. Ute's message was that they had spent a long weekend in my village to visit friends. "Unfortunately, with only a p. o. box as your address, we were unable to find you. The first day we were there, Thursday, it poured. All our friends could talk about was how unusual it was to have so much rain in one day. The rest of the weekend was beautiful," she wrote. It was difficult for me to believe that they could not locate me especially since I already had phone service from the 10th of the month (the closing date), my name and address were registered with the homeowners association, and any realtor in the area would have known about the transaction and provided my name and address.

Had they come to see my place before I could even invite them for a visit? Their supposed friends were never revealed to me. To me it was vintage Ute. She also let me know that she had mailed me a package containing our mother's photograph because I had once expressed regret giving it to her. "Life is too short to have regrets," she wrote. The packaging was flimsy and Mother's portrait arrived with the glass shattered and the frame broken. This episode ended all contact between us. I did send greetings to the two on their golden wedding anniversary and the birth of their first grandchild but received no reply. This could have been predicted because, as Elke once reminded me, our sister was never the forgiving type.

Life's Ups And Downs

Like that of most people, Ute's life had many significant ups and downs. A highpoint was her marriage in July 1963 to Tom despite the boycott by her mother and older sister. Ute correctly and courageously stuck to her plan based on her conviction that their love would endure. She was correct because it did. They remained faithful to each other and in July 2013 the two could celebrate their golden wedding anniversary in which Elke too was present after having been cruelly denied participating in the original ceremony. The adoption in 1966 of Danielle and the birth in June 1968 of Tommy added to their happiness. Both children have been a constant source of joy. Tom and Ute even became wealthy not so much through their own efforts as to the generosity of an ancestor. In mid-August 2009, just one week before his 96th birthday, Bud passed away. Bud had been living in a nursing home close to Ted when he fell breaking his arm. With the constant and severe pain resulting from the accident plus his diverse other ailments, he had no desire to continue and looked forward to dying.

Bud had done well as a stock broker and on his passing was able to leave a very substantial amount of money to each of his twin sons. The inheritance allowed Tom and Ute to enjoy a more comfortable lifestyle that included several trips for Ute and Danielle to Europe and taking up residence in Florida during the winter months. In fact, the day after New Year's, the family leaves for Destin in the Florida Panhandle where, for a couple of months, it rents a vacation apartment large enough to accommodate family members and friends before returning to Michigan.

Ute had long been looking forward to having grandchildren but neither Danielle nor Tommy seemed ready "to tie the knot" when in June 2011 Tommy and his longtime lady friend Peggy did just that. Tommy had converted to Catholicism and the couple was married in a Roman Catholic church near Philadelphia where they made their home. According to Elke, who attended the ceremony, the wedding party numbered some 50 people. Early in December of the following year Evan Thomas was born. It was a day of great joy for all but especially Ute who was then 73 years old and did not expect to ever become a grandmother. Then, in April 2015, little Evan got a sister his parents named Ava. Tommy and Peggy are both employed in well-paying jobs and with Peggy being allowed to work out of their home two days a week, the couple hired a nanny to look after the two children during the remaining weekdays.

For Ute, the past few years have brought health issues to the forefront. Besides having to cope with the after-effects of her auto accident, Ute developed problems with the lower portion of her esophagus which did not allow her system to accept food. It led to a dramatic weight loss and when Elke visited our sister and her family in April of 2014, Ute looked very thin and emaciated.

Our mother had Alzheimer's disease, of course, and her children feared that they eventually too would get it. That angst, unfortunately, became reality with Ute. Elke had noticed that something was not quite right from her occasional visits in Michigan and daily e-mail contacts with our sister and feared that "she might be loosing it." In June 2016, Ute fell down a flight of stairs to the basement when she opened the wrong door in her home. Fortunately, she suffered no major injuries. In March 2017, Ute was found to be suffering from a severe depression but refused to take prescribed medication because she was leery of side effects. Then, after a battery of tests, in mid-August of 2018, Ute was officially diagnosed with Alzheimer's.

Since then, there have been a few other developments. Just when Ute was beginning to gain some weight again and her Alzheimer's appeared to have stabilized, our sister suffered another severe blow to her health. In early December 2019, the family was invited to dinner by a friend and neighbor and when, after their meal, Ute stepped into the kitchen, the couple's dog savagely attacked her. Ute was rushed to the hospital where an emergency room nurse saved her from bleeding to death because the bite had punctured a major blood vessel. The incredibly deep wounds took 20 stitches to close. Incidentally, the animal, an Alaskan husky, which apparently had been kept isolated and not introduced to other people before, was picked up and put down in accordance with state regulations.

Despite this unfortunate incident, the family kept to its yearly routine and the day after New Year's 2020, Ute, Tom, and Danielle left by car for their 2-month vacation in Florida where Elke visited them. Ute's dog wounds had mostly healed, according to Elke, but she was no longer able to use her PC for the customary daily e-mail exchanges. Interestingly, during these Ute insisted on writing in German while Elke was to reply in English. According to Elke, our sister did not want to lose proficiency in her mother tongue.

In the meantime, Tom is enjoying retirement and indulging in his favorite pastime in both Michigan and Florida which is playing golf. Both he and his twin Ted were heavy smokers and had the misfortune of getting cancer. In mid-April 2015 Tom was found to have a cancerous tumor behind one eye and given less than a year to live but thanks to experimental treatments he is receiving at a Philadelphia hospital, his cancer has been in remission. His twin Ted was less fortunate. He developed cancer of the mouth and throat that quickly spread throughout his body. When Ted passed away in May 2017 after a long illness, Tom was devastated but not enough to give up smoking.

Daughter Danielle has been much of a blessing to her parents especially during the past few years. She never married choosing the life of an unfettered bachelorette. She is exceptionally well educated having earned an undergraduate and two graduate degrees in education and the arts and all paid for by her doting parents. Danielle has variously been employed as an educator in the Michigan school system and by several local and national retailers. At one time she was personnel manager for the national retail chain Target where she left because the position proved much too stressful.

After obtaining a Master's in Art Education, she found a new calling as an English teacher in China. In her last position there she taught at a university in Guangzhou (Canton) where she made friends with other American expatriates and was very happy. She and her parents kept in touch by Skype and in October 2013 Ute even traveled to China by herself for a visit. Afterwards, mother and daughter moved on to Paris to spend some time there sightseeing and shopping. Danielle remained in China for seven years before returning home in October 2016 just in time to be with her parents when they began to need her assistance with daily living. For a time, she also taught English and citizenship to adult immigrants from Middle Eastern countries.

Danielle had lived with her parents keeping house, cooking the family's meals, and tending to their special needs and in gratitude, in July 2018, they purchased her a house similar to theirs and located close by so that she too would have a place to call her own. According to Elke who saw it, Danielle is absolutely delighted with her new home and has furnished and decorated it beautifully like a pro. Both Elke and I had been wondering how our niece would make out once retired since she has paid very little into the Social Security system and, in fact, nothing during the years she taught in China. Her existence would obviously have to depend on the generosity of her parents. That problem appears to be solved. Ute and Tom promised her that, in consideration of her being such a loving and caring daughter throughout the years, they have sufficiently provided for her support in their will.

Ute's Alzheimer's has had a devastating effect on the entire family but especially on Elke. The two sisters had met for the first time in Oak Park some months after Elke's arrival from Stuttgart in September 1958. At the time of that event, both Ute and I were away at college. Ute and Elke have been the best of friends and soul mates for over six decades now. Naturally, Elke is watching developments with much anxiety. In lieu of e-mail exchanges as in the past, the two sister nowadays stay in touch using their smartphones.

Nothing more, unfortunately, can be done for our sister because no cure for Alzheimer's is yet in sight despite decades of world-wide, intensive medical research and the expenditure of enormous funds to combat this dreadful disease. Nevertheless, Ute, who turned 80 in November 2019, has the good fortune of being surrounded by a loving and caring family which will do anything in its power to help her cope with this very difficult time in her life.

VOLKER'S STORY

***

A Troubled Teen

Most people are justly proud of famous relatives or distinguished ancestors and they will gladly share the details of their lives with friends and strangers alike whenever the opportunity presents itself. The story is quite different with misbegotten and disreputable family members whose existence nobody is willing to admit. They become skeletons in the family closet and are never talked about within the family let alone mentioned to strangers. That is why it is with some trepidation that I open the closet door to expose a family member who brought disgrace to the family but who by now has departed this world to meet his Maker. I speak of my Brother Erwin Volker, called Volker by his family, for whom too much freedom in the land of freedom became his undoing. He was the only person in the long history of our family who spent time in prison. How he got there is a complex story which is only partly known and almost entirely based on his letters to his siblings and his revelations to Ute and Elke who visited him not long before he passed away.

According to his birth certificate issued by the registrar of Stuttgart-Bad Canstatt, Erwin Volker Zell was born at 2 in the morning of April 19, 1942 to Anna Maria Zell, a stenographer, *evangelisch*, of Stuttgart-Untertürkheim. The certificate states that the mother was divorced by order of the 7th Civil Chamber of the Landgericht (state court) in Frankfurt am Main, effective March 7, 1934. At the time of his birth, our mother was employed as a typist with Daimler-Benz A.G., makers of Mercedes-Benz automobiles, in the Stuttgart suburb of Untertürkheim.

On his birth certificate, in common with those of his three siblings, there is no mention of his father and his paternity is uncertain. According to Ute, Volker's father was one Hans Ziegler which is also the name listed on his death certificate. Presumably Ute heard the name from Esther or

Mutti herself. No other information about him could be found because the name Hans Ziegler is fairly common in Germany. With nothing but a name to go by, an online search proved unsuccessful in identifying him but presumably he passed the Aryan racial test.

Another and less credible story on the identity of his father comes from Volker himself. According to a letter Volker wrote me in June 2002, our mother had informed him back in 1960 that his father was one Karl-Heinz Butterweck, a wealthy industrialist from the Ruhrgebiet (an industrial region in western Germany). Volker had needed the information, he wrote, because when, during his army service as driver for a General Walker in Germany, he was required to have top secret clearance and for that he had to furnish the names of both parents. Incidentally, Volker referred to General Walker as "the guy that bailed us out in Korea by re-engaging the enemy half-way up the peninsula & thereby cutting off their supplies to the South."[6]

Volker was a an 8-year-old when we all came to America in March 1950. He had then been sent back to Germany along with Ute and me the following year. Volker returned to the States in the company of Ute in November 1954 as a 12-year-old. During the three years between then and the time of our mother's return to the U.S. in November 1951, he lived in an Evangelical (Lutheran) children's home near Stuttgart.

After Volker returned to Oak Park, he again attended Emerson elementary school and upon graduation in June 1956, entered Oak Park and River Forest High School in the fall of that year but did not graduate. In fact, he was expelled after supposedly throwing a set of keys at his homeroom teacher's head in a fit of anger. Volker was an emotionally troubled and rebellious teenager and when he got out of control at around age 16, Mutti called the authorities and he was sent to juvenile detention. I was away in college at the time and unaware of the turmoil at home as our mother never informed me.

At age 17, Volker wanted to join the U. S. Air Force and had already passed flight training to become a pilot but, because he was underage, he needed our mother's approval. This she refused to give and Volker never forgave her for that claiming it ruined his life. Our mother later told me that he wanted to become a fighter pilot and she feared for his safety because she felt that he was too young and immature to fly a plane let alone a fighter. Instead of the Air Force, Volker enlisted in the U.S. Army. After basic training at Fort Leonard Wood, Missouri, and additional schooling at Fort Sill, Oklahoma, the Army sent him to Germany. Ute and I wrote him during his army training but he never responded .

For what happened to him in the service, I must rely on a letter Volker wrote on Christmas Eve 1960 and addressed to *"Liebste Mutti"* [Dearest mom]. Written in German on stationary of the Sheridan Service Club in Augsburg (Bavaria), it reads in part and in translation:

> *Please be not angry with me for not writing for so long. Please hold on to your chair so you won't fall off. On December 27, 1960, I will be transferred to Fort Dix, N.J. and in January discharged from the army. I could bang my head against the wall for having done what I did. I had a girl in my jeep and let her ride into town with me where I let her off. Somebody saw me and for that I am being sent home. They did not want to discharge me here or else I would have remained in Germany. People are much friendlier here and I also wanted to look out for my darling. Her name is Jutta Werther. When I am back, I will immediately look for work.. ...If you let Peter know, write him it's "Article 209, general discharge," and he will understand. It's really not as bad as many people think. Many, many thanks for the package. It arrived yesterday. Mutti, now that I have been away from you for some time, I finally realize that you always only meant the best for me but I also learned from your mistakes and will be ready when I have children of my own. I still bite my nails and am a smoker. Jutta is a very, very sweet girl. She came from the East Zone in July 1960 and we met at the Augsburg swimming pool at the beginning of September.*

Volker went on to say that he was sending several packages home including two wooden boxes of which one contained a gift for Mutti and the larger was for them both. Volker's discharge was a big disappointment and embarrassment to me because I had just gone on active duty as a 2nd lieutenant with the U.S. Army Reserve.

After his return, Volker lived with Mutti in our apartment on Home Avenue in Oak Park where Ute again met up with him. In her long February 1961 letter she wrote me from college, Ute included a paragraph about Volker (she called him Erwin) that said much about our brother:

When I was home between semesters I saw Erwin once. He still looks the same. From what he says, he must have lost all respect for girls and for himself for that matter. You should have heard him. I was so embarrassed; I could have crawled in a hole and stayed there. I just never have been able and will probably never be able to understand him fully. His ideas seem warped, and he is too old to change. In a way I feel sorry for him because most likely he will never experience the happiness and satisfaction that comes from accomplishment and success. Oh well, who knows, he may show up both of us. Only time will tell.

Volker was still just 18 years old at the time. I much wished it had been otherwise, but Volker fell far short of showing up any of us. There seemed to be a self-destructive element in his psyche that prevented him from reaching his full potential. While he was bright (on an Air Force IQ test he took at age 17 he supposedly scored 148) and could be very charming, he did have emotional problems and a short fuse. Every time things were going well, he managed to ruin it all by doing something especially impertinent and foolish. What Volker lacked most was self-control and what would later become self-evident, a moral compass.

On The Skids Again

For a short time after returning to the States, Volker was doing very well before he was on the skids again. He needed a job and so I wrote Bruno Vogel, the German-born plant superintendent at Delta-Star Electric, a Chicago manufacturing company that had employed me during two summers while attending college, recommending Volker for an apprenticeship. Volker's letter of August 1961 to me was consequently fairly upbeat. At work, he wrote, he had been trained on hydraulic presses, lathes, screw and drilling machines, and had worked in assembly. According to Volker, he got along well with Bruno and had even been given a small raise. "At least that's one place where I haven't ruined my name," he wrote. He had saved up $400 and was planning to return to school in the fall. He still had his girlfriend in Germany, he wrote, and even let Mutti read her letters to him. Mother liked what she heard and read about Jutta and agreed with Volker that she was the girl for him.

He did have one problem, Volker admitted. "As you have probably heard, I've joined those millions of people who hope to catch lung cancer one of these days. The only problem with it is, it's so confounded hard to quit the habit (smoking)," he wrote. Parenthetically, I had been more fortunate in dealing with this scourge. When the large American tobacco companies gave away free packs of cigarettes during Army basic training to get young recruits hooked on nicotine, which they knew was addictive and extremely unhealthy, I refused to take the bait and gave mine away. It was truly a shame that so many of my brothers in arms could not resist the temptation to smoke and had to suffer the often horrible consequences later in life as my brother eventually did.

Less than two years later, everything Volker had accomplished, together with his hopes and dreams, had vanished. By then, he had been fired at Delta-Star Electric for unknown reasons. Mutti had kicked him out of the house and he was living in a Chicago apartment on West Diversey Avenue. Most irritating to Mother was Volker's chain smoking that left the apartment constantly enveloped in cigarette smoke thick enough, as the saying goes, to cut with a knife. Besides the foul air, Mutti was fearful he would smoke in bed and start a fire. There were constant arguments between the two until Mother finally had enough and told him to move out. Volker had his 21st birthday on April 19, 1963 and I had sent him greetings from Virginia where I was employed at the time.

Volker wrote back at the end of the month blaming everybody but himself for his failures. "Nobody in the family ever had brains enough to sit down with me and try to explain things to me. Right now I'm learning things that other kids have known for years," he asserted. "Sure I feel sorry for myself," he continued, "All I wanted was to be an average kid. I couldn't even be that. Mother always had her eye out for you. Right now you pay $30 a month for a room that I had to pay $30 a <u>week</u> for and I don't earn half as much as you do. It seems every time I had a chance to get ahead, mother killed it...." Volker then listed a number of automobile bills that were due. Evidently he had an accident and needed to come up with the insurance premium before he was allowed to drive again. He conclude his letter on this sad note:

I've lost every ounce of ambition I have ever had. I just live day in day out. I don't care about anything or anybody and am hoping for my end to come soon. Guys like me end up in jail and that's another thing mother said that's all I deserve. I've got nothing more to say and please don't write. I'll just send it back.

I took Volker at his word and did not answer him. I figured that to write back and send him money would solve no long-term problems and just lead to a lifelong dependency. That I could do without. Rightly or wrongly, I came to the conclusion that my brother was a loser and nothing and nobody could save him from his fate and himself. Ute and Elke too had broken off contact with him to prevent Esther and Mutti from knowing their whereabouts. (They suspected that Volker would pass on any information he had on them). From now on, Volker was on his own and nothing more was heard from him for nearly four decades.

The Move West

Ute and I finally reconnected with Volker in 2002 after I had gotten in touch with him on the occasion of his 60th birthday in April of that year. It was a year of heavy correspondence between the three of us after decades of separation. How Volker came to leave the Chicago area and settle in the Pacific Northwest was revealed in a 14-page letter he wrote Ute on June 23, of which he had mailed me a copy, and one to me in early September of the year. After moving into his own apartment in Chicago, he wrote, he had little contact with our mother. Then, in the fall of 1965 he went to see Mutti to introduce his fiancé. At the time Mutti had just moved into our new townhouse home near North Harlem Avenue and Augusta Street and it took some effort on his part to locate her. According to Volker, he felt deeply hurt because our mother would not even talk to him or the young lady he had brought along and made him feel that she no longer cared about what he was doing. It was the last time mother and son would see each other.

According to Volker, he came to Salem, Oregon in November 1967 during the days of the so-called flower children, a hippie movement that grew out of the turmoil of the Viet Nam War. There he moved into a

"Christian commune (farm)." "I should mention that Salem, Oregon was/ is a major hub for the mentally ill & MR/DDs (Mentally Retarded / Developmentally Disabled)," Volker wrote Ute. "I was a patient twice at the 'State Hospital' for suicidal depression which resulted from childhood abuses & eventually went from psychological to physiological. 20 mg of 'Paxil' has kept me stable since 1998." According to Volker, he came to live in a Christian mission house in 1989 and has been there on and off.

Volker called himself an "emotional cripple" most of his life which undermined any success he might have enjoyed. "I never had a mentor to show me how to grow up & take responsibility for what I do. (I wish Peter could / would have done that as my big brother). So I always saw myself as a victim of the 'misdeeds' of others & blamed them thereby maintaining my immature feelings. In brief, I never grew up," he wrote Ute. His hot button, he wrote her, was rejection: "Let me tell you what the magic bullet was that split you, Elke & me up. 'Rejection.' I can't handle that from anyone, even to this day, whether intentionally, or not. Currently I am much more stable about it, but it still feels terrible when I sense it." He then went on to describe all the times he felt rejected by his sister.

Crime And Punishment

Volker's letter of May 30, 2002 in response to my greetings on his 60th birthday the previous month, was a real shocker. He was living in a mission house, he wrote, "a place for low lives, down & outs, and homeless like me. How's that for a success story? You still want to hear from me?" Volker went on to write:

> *If you think being homeless is bad, it gets worse. I am now officially an ex-con. In a nutshell, after 3 years & 10 months in prison for "Burg I" I am doing 3 years post prison supervision starting 24 Oct. 01. But don't fret. This isn't over yet. I've spent my time studying law & am filing a "Petition for Post Prison Relief," whereby I can & will challenge my entire prosecution. In brief, I got screwed / tricked out of my rights by a self-serving, court-appointed attorney. They don't like to work too hard at $35/hr, paid from the county coffer, when they ordinarily charge $150/hr.*

> *I'll fill you in on this later. There's more. After 35, or so, years of*
> *smoking, I've got a grand case of C.O.P.D.—Chronic Obstructive*
> *Pulmonary Disease, i.e., asthma, chronic bronchitis & emphysema*
> *in advanced stages. I quit smoking in '97, but only have 20% of my*
> *lungs still functioning. I often need an oxygen tank to get around.*
> *Other than that I'm doing fine. So much for the bad news. There*
> *isn't any other.*

Things obviously could not be much worse for Volker. It had been nearly 45 years since we last saw each other and, in the meantime, he had become a convicted felon, had an incurable disease and was living in a homeless shelter. In my reply of mid-June, I brought him up to date on the many changes that had occurred with the rest of us including the death of our mother four years earlier. I enclosed a check for $100 for him to enjoy a good meal with a friend or two and expressed these thoughts:

> *Your revelations about yourself have shocked me to the core. I could*
> *hardly believe what I was reading! While I realized from early on*
> *that you were on some kind of mission to destroy yourself and that*
> *little could be done for you without complete immersion in your*
> *many problems, I never dreamed it would come to this. I don't*
> *believe that anything like this ever happened in the Zell family*
> *before. But as the French say "C'est la vie.".... Volker, I am deeply*
> *saddened by all the awful things that have happened to you. You*
> *are always in my thoughts and prayers and I wish you the very best.*

During 2002, Volker and I exchanged 7 letters two of which have already been mentioned. Volker's letters were in the stream of consciousness mode, i.e., they were long and rambling to the point where they severely tested my patience and I had to ask him at least once to stop his long winded whining or, in the alternative, to unload his diverse thoughts, emotions, and opinions on his two sisters and leave me out of the loop. His monologues obviously served as a form of therapy as he recounted all the physical abuse and neglect he supposedly suffered as a child at our mother's hands and all the other bad things people had done to him over the years. Towards me personally, he was alternatively accusatory and apologetic, contemptuous and admiring, hateful and loving. I wished he had been more forthcoming about the facts and details of his life since we had parted ways.

From what I could gather from his letters, after having had a rough start in life things never got much better afterwards. In his 5-page letter he wrote me in June of that year, he vividly described the abuse he supposedly had suffered at our mother's hands:

> "*She had a heart of gold & was good to anyone who treated her with kindness & respect. You were not one of them*," you wrote. *That hurts. But then you never knew nor did Ute: When we lived at 8 Adlerstrasse in Heslach we had a coal locker in the basement. One day when Mother had one of her severely violent, angry fits (you don't know about those, but I sure do) which only occurred whenever you and Ute were gone, as in school, she decided that beating me with a large, wooden cooking spoon or belt didn't provide enough satisfaction for her & took me to the coal bin where she kept a heavy rubber hose, which was long enough to double over, & decided to whip me with that. Those whippings I got with that hose I cannot ever forget because they were so severe & terrible that she had once thought she had killed me (that's what I've concluded) or caused permanent damage. I had been beaten unconscious & woke up with her crying & attending to my bloody wounds. That was the last time she beat me (with hose) after dozens of times. I remember that I never knew why I was being beaten & what had set off such fury and hatred for me. Looking back I can easily see how I became the target for whatever terrible things were happening to her, e.g., if I weren't around etc., etc. ...*

Now, Volker was known for hyperbole and hence all he wrote and said cannot be taken at face value but must be heavily discounted to get to the truth, Thus, in his long letter to Ute he reminded her of the time when he met her and Tom on a sidewalk in Chicago and Tom had "snapped my head clean off, right at the shoulders" and that "I still carry the scar of that terrible episode." He had evidently made a disparaging remark that infuriated our brother-in-law. Yet, despite Volker's penchant for wild exaggerations, one must assume that there was at least some truth to his story. The alleged beatings must have happened when Volker was between five and eight years old. It was a side of Mutti I never knew. To be sure, she had slapped Ute now and then but I never saw our mother in the type of angry, violent outbursts as described by Volker. On the contrary, to me she always appeared perfectly calm, rational, and even-tempered.

It is especially the severity and frequency of the alleged beatings that I came to question. It would seem that had Volker been beaten as brutally and as often as he described, welts and bruises would have covered much of his body which would have been visible to Ute and me and also to his teachers at the Lerchenrainschule. The latter would have been required by law to report such abuse to the authorities and, no doubt, they would have done so. There were no such physical signs on Volker and he never said anything to either Ute or me about these supposed beatings. He always appeared happy and contented.

Elsewhere in his June letter to me, Volker paid tribute to the beneficial influence Mutti had on his life. Mother taught all her children good manners and how to behave in different social settings. On a streetcar, for example, we were required to give up our seat to any adult without one while greeting an adult required a deep bow or a curtsy in the case of girls. In Volker's words: "I always knew Mother came from high grade stock. No second class person could have pulled off what she did. She taught us all high class behavior & manners which was a constant source of compliments to us from strangers. We lived in a new apartment building on the hill in Heslach, etc., etc., & we never went hungry."

In the same letter, Volker expressed some hope for the immediate future. He was getting monthly Social Security disability payments of $777, he wrote. That was obviously not much but enough to get by considering that as of January 2003 he was eligible for federally assisted housing. Once in his apartment, he was looking forward to using his 1998 Toshiba personal computer and an Encarta disk on which he even found the village of Korntal-Pfenningen, the location of the children's home he stayed in. He wrote of having to get about with an oxygen tank on a cart until he had a lung reduction operation to cut out all the dead lung tissue. "I started smoking in the army & paying for it now," he wrote. After the operation, he hoped to be able to lightly jog again and be rid of all the medications that kept him breathing.

Volker went on to write, "Peter, I am anxious to hear [about] all the places you went & worked for all these years, since 1958. Ok? Also, you failed to state <u>your</u> birth source. Were you born Jewish, or Aryan, like the rest of us? And who is Jerry? I thought he was born <u>before</u> Esther & left for America with his father." In a postscript Volker added, "Peter: Check with Ute to make sure she got this letter. Mailed [the] same day. That airhead forgot to include her last name <u>anywhere</u>; we have mailmen that refuse to deliver mail without a name in Salem & I won't argue with them—they shoot people nowadays."

In addition to my correspondence with him, Volker and Ute exchanged a number of letters. Of these, I became privy to only the 14-page letter he wrote our sister in June, two days after he wrote me. (In the meantime, I had asked him to stop copying each other because our disclosures could only cause problems between us). In it he addressed the "oversight" directly. "Hey! You got a last name," Volker wrote. "Yeah, ding-a-ling, you left that little detail out of your letter & off the envelope. You realize me not knowing that, or Elke's last name, kept me from getting even to first base looking for you." Incidentally, it is doubtful that not giving out their married names was an oversight by Ute and Elke. His two siblings were obviously still playing it safe.

This feeling of rejection Volker wrote about may well have triggered the incident that led to his downfall. He apparently felt rejected not only by his mother and siblings but his wife as well. According to Elke, who later heard it from Volker, while he owned Westronix, an electronics repair shop in Salem, his business partner became enamored of his wife and when he caught the two in a compromising situation together, he almost went berserk. After getting a gun, he threatening to kill his rival in a standoff with the police that lasted several hours. They finally succeeded in talking Volker out of shooting the fellow and he peaceably surrendered.

That offense got Volker sent to prison even before the burglary he mentioned in his letter. Thus, when Volker wrote that he was now officially an ex-con, he was being less than candid because he had been convicted of lawless activity even before the latest felony.[7] Incidentally, Volker always signed his letters using his first name, Erwin, when he had always been known to us as Volker. As he explained to Ute, he changed his middle name from Volker to Victor because the people he associated with had called him either Vulgar or Fucker.

Empathy And Introspection

Of considerable interest to me in his letter to Ute was Volker's vigorous defense of our mother against our sister who had apparently been raking Mutti over the coals as she was wont to do. Perhaps he did it to get on the good side of me since I would be receiving a copy of his letter to Ute but his argument was still impressive for the wonderful insight he was able to gain of Mother's dire situation during the Nazi regime.

> *This business with "Mother" (not Mrs. Zell) will get settled & I will settle it because I know more about Mother at this time than any of you. If that pushes your nose out of joint, Ute, so be it. I love you, Ute, but don't bad-mouth Mother anymore in the future. I have more right to blame, hate, etc., Mother than anyone in the family because I suffered the most abuse—things she would be imprisoned for nowadays for many years as child-abuse but I won't. Please understand, Ute, & bear with me. What Mother suffered during her life was more terrible than any of us are willing to admit but it meant survival or die. Which would you choose? I will eventually explain to you what happened to "Mother" before & after WW II. ... Mother told me that in order to survive she had to "put out," i.e., bear children for the Nazi regime. That's why we lived in a newly built apartment & never went hungry. I'm quite certain that Peter is also an "Aryan" child but he failed to mention that & explain why Mother chose to favor him all these years. Of course, I may be wrong since Peter was born in 1936 & may well have been fathered by the Jew. That would explain a lot. I'm waiting for Peter to tell me which, rather than resort to alternative.*

In his letter to Ute, Volker kept returning to the same subject, namely, our mother and her past trials and tribulations. Clearly, he was as much bothered as I was by our sister's complete lack of understanding for Mutti's situation as evidenced by her persistent attempts to portray our mother as an absolutely evil and immoral person who turned her womb into a baby factory for personal gain and profit. The Old Testament admonition to honor one's father and mother obviously meant little to our sister. Volker continued:

I am flabbergasted that you know nothing of family history. I simply assumed you knew all this as I did. Yes, we are all from different Aryan fathers & yes she got rewarded for it—she and Esther were spared the concentration camps & were allowed to live. Now you, as a woman with a family, how would you like Tom & Tommy to take off for parts unknown never to be seen again & you & Danielle remain behind only to learn that your marriage to Tom turned into a life-threatening issue unless you comply with the state to voluntarily "prostitute" yourself to total strangers, then raise the little bastards. Really, Ute. I want you to immerse yourself in this scenario & feel the fear & terror of that kind of life, for years. Yes, Mother had a gentle, loving side to her when things went well. She did exceptionally well whenever Peter was home & even occasionally made a point to "demonstrate" to him what an evil person I was & what "hell" I was putting her through. What does that tell you? How about you, Peter? Unfortunately, Peter was rarely around, by Mother's design, when the crap hit the fan & whatever Mother told him he believed & still does. Let's face it, I became an animal, but it never occurred to him (Peter) how I got that way. Does he really believe I was self-made?

Volker continued with some more speculation about my origins and concluded with some very good advice for his two older siblings:

The bottom line regarding Mother is that she suffered a life so terrible & frightening, it was beyond her ability to cope. I'm more inclined to believe that Peter is Jewish or that Mother actually loved his Aryan father. I prefer the Jewish connection, which seems much more logical. After Esther left, Mother became attached to Peter & catered him with her devotion, & targeted me with all her hatred for what happened to her, nearly killing me in the process. The damage to me followed her throughout the years which she, Esther & (Peter ?) blamed me for. That same damage to me, psychologically, destroyed my family connections/relationships & much of my life. It took me most of my life to learn (mostly through Christ—not psychology) what had happened to me. I'm not angry or bitter toward Mother because I feel she suffered more than I & would have never done to me what she did under normal circumstances. Furthermore, I gladly forgive her for all that she *did to me that was bad. I'm grateful to Peter that he was able to provide her with a com- fortable life these past 30 years or so. She deserved it. Ute! Mother started out a good person, like you, but simply couldn't handle it. Mother & I had some long talks when we lived alone together on Home Avenue. She could be <u>very</u> loving, then turn into a devil without notice. I understand that <u>now</u>, but not then. Neither Peter or you are wrong about Mother. She was <u>both</u>, a loving, kind person and an evil tyrant. Peter needs to stop his denial & the rest of us need to stop condemning her. Mother did not choose her life, it was forced on her by politics. Who knows what any of us would do given the same circumstances.*

None of us could know at the time, but when he wrote that marvelous letter of self-examination and forgiveness for our mother to Ute in June 2002, Volker had just a little over two more years to live.

Despite his talks with Mutti, Volker's letters demonstrated many information gaps and misconceptions. His speculation with Ute whether I was Jew or Gentile ("Aryan") was a case in point. These I tried to answer in a long letter I wrote him in mid-August. "I must commend you for standing up for Mother in your letter to Ute," I wrote. "Your insight and analysis of Mother's desperate situation in Nazi Germany is truly remarkable and very much to the point." I also explained to him that I was never Mutti's favorite child, as he seemed to believe, but a distant second to Esther. Mutti and Esther shared a very special bond for very obvious reasons. Having never been the jealous type, I had always fully accepted this.

Even when Mutti focused her attention on me after Esther left for America, I wrote him, I did not get a free ride. She put me on assignments from an early age which she herself should have taken care of. Even when we came to America and Esther was around, Mutti kept relying on me. "If there was a problem to be fixed, she sent me," I wrote Volker. I reminded him that it was I, and not Mutti, who bailed him and Ute out when they had gotten themselves in trouble at Wieboldt's department store on Lake Street and Harlem Avenue.

Volker responded in his September letter saying, "It is easily explained psychologically. You can't expect a child to understand cause & consequences of something you never bothered to teach them. I'd love to punch the lights out of every parent that disagrees with that." My question to Volker would have been, Was Mutti negligent by not explicitly telling her children that to steal is wrong? She did not have to tell me yet I knew. Of course, it is not uncommon for young children to occasionally take things especially if they are deprived of such childhood essentials as toys.

What Volker wrote next in his September letter left me puzzled:

> *Although I do not remember <u>that</u> time, I do remember another time I went to Wieboldt's and packed up all the stuff I could carry. I <u>clearly</u> recall going up to the checkout counters, found all of them full with long lines & decided it would be quicker to squeeze backwards through one of the two turnstiles. As I walked up the stairs (toy dept. was in basement) a few patrons hollered that I had to come back & go through the checkers' line. I didn't know what they were talking about & kept on going. I had absolutely no idea I was doing anything wrong. Why was I such an idiot at 12/13 yrs. old? As soon as I got home & Mother saw the stuff she & I went back to return it. Now why do you suppose I did that & didn't know it was wrong? Or don't you believe it?*

I did not believe Volker because I found the notion that a 12- or 13-year old boy did not know that it was wrong to walk out of a department store with merchandise he had not paid for completely absurd. And it was ludicrous to imply that it was all our mother's fault for never telling him that to steal was wrong. To me this episode meant that Volker was destined for a life of crime from an early age because he did not and would never know right from wrong.

When I did not respond to his latest missive, Volker wrote again a month later alternately feeling sorry for himself and accusing me of rejecting him and my siblings. "When things went wrong it was easy to blame others, get angry & feel contempt & even unbridled hatred, all the while telling myself how justified I was for having those feelings. My fiercest episodes included cursing God up one side & down the other. Here I was doing my level best to do what's right, but end up getting pooped on anyway," he wrote. He continued:

> *Until 1965, the last time Mother had the opportunity to <u>reject</u> me, she never would give me your address, or let me know <u>anything</u>*

about you. Until you filled me in via your recent letter about our
separate birth origins I always considered you my brother, wanted
to stay in touch with you, & couldn't understand why you seemed
to have no desire to stay in touch with me. I concluded you simply
didn't care about me, which hurt me terribly. Is that what you
wanted to do?

After so many years of separation, Volker obviously had a lot to get off his chest and had I been less busy at the time I might have been more patient in taking in what he had to say. As it was, I had my townhouse on the market and many things to do in anticipation of my planned move to Arizona. I just could not be bothered with reading more of Volker's voluminous letters of self-pity and victimization and answering these in a meaningful way. At the same time, Ute and I continued to be at loggerheads over the issue of our mother with Elke sharing our sister's hard-nosed attitude. Besides attacking our late mother, Ute had also been very critical of me. "Ute, don't be concerned about Peter's seemingly strange behavior," Volker had written her, and, "He seems to have been a very private person all his life & careful about whom to trust. Hopefully he will loosen up with me & share his life with me & let me share it with you & Elke."

It was my impression, rightly or wrongly, that all three shared a common bond as the perennial, blameless victims of a terrible mother. The best thing for me, I felt, was to cut them loose. Volker closed his latest letter with, "You once said you would keep me in your prayers. Please do so. Hopefully we can build on that. I am a devout Christian." With that as a cue, I ended my follow-up letter of October to Volker with, "I hope the three of you can sort things out together without my further intervention. I am afraid the chasm between us is too large to be bridged in our lifetimes. Try to find comfort, healing, and closure through faith in Christ!" Volker took the hint and did not write me for over a year.

During the following year, 2003, we did not correspond except that at Christmas of that year, I again sent Volker my traditional greeting and this time he immediately replied with a computer-generated greeting card. "I can't believe you never adopted computers," Volker wrote. "You have no idea how incredibly easy they make writing of any kind. That's the main reason I haven't written you—I found my computer at the mission, where I had stayed, & getting acquainted with it finally—learning how to use it—so I can write & edit any letters to you & hopefully meet your demands regarding the quality of my letters—I simply don't want to hear you <u>whining</u> about it again." But instead of then using his PC, he wrote in his own hand and in block letters as in all his recent missives. He closed with this comment:

> *Your bragging about how <u>you</u> were your mother's "love child" amazes me about how naive & stupid a son you were. To understand your mother and her motives you have to be "street-wise" as I am. Do you <u>truly</u> believe she <u>loved</u> you? It was a <u>common</u> practice to favor the <u>first</u>-born (which you were of her <u>new</u> family) by mothers in order to insure "<u>their own</u>" wellbeing. <u>You</u> were <u>special</u> to her to insure that you would take care of her when old. She succeeded. I gladly challenge you to share all that <u>private</u> & special information she shared <u>only</u> with you, with <u>private</u> information she shared with me. The bottom line is that <u>you</u> were as much of a bastard as the rest of us but <u>you</u> were <u>dedicated</u> to the task of taking care of her in her old age. She made sure <u>you owed</u> her that much & you did, didn't you? You got suckered. I still love you. Bye.*

Needless to say, I had never bragged to anybody about being Mutti's "love child." His claim was as absurd as it was false and came directly from Ute. More importantly, Volker's tough life had made him an absolute cynic. He could not know or understand what these last 10 years or so of our mother's life meant to me. I did not feel burdened but privileged to be able to take care of someone in her dotage who had taken such good care of me throughout much of my life. For me these were years of fulfillment and satisfaction as I had never known before. For the first time in my life, I had looked out for somebody other than myself. Volker was so very wrong as he was about so many other things.

The Final Year

Ute and Elke kept in touch with Volker while Elke, in turn, kept me abreast of what was happening with him. To my surprise, my two sisters decided to visit him in Salem and in her birthday greeting to me in late July 2003, Elke let me know of her and Ute's somber reunion with Volker. He had moved into a cozy little apartment and they spent three days with him reminiscing about the past, taking him out to eat, and doing some essential chores like washing his clothes and cleaning the place. Actually it was Elke who did most of the work because Ute was suffering from her chronic back pains. Naturally, I was not too happy that my sisters had kept their visit a secret but nevertheless found it a very kind and loving thing to do.

Ute and Elke stayed in a nearby hotel and rented a car to get about. One day the three drove around Salem and Portland as Volker described the major places of interest in these towns and his life there during his many years since arriving in Oregon. During their conversations, Volker told his sisters of the horrible prison conditions he had to endure including having been assaulted and sodomized by three fellow inmates. Volker came out a broken man and henceforth needed a portable oxygen tank to breathe and get about, I was told.

With the planned lung reduction surgery coming up, Ute and Elke advised him not to have the operation because they feared the doctors were only going to experiment on him. Nevertheless, Volker was evidently willing to take the chance. Elke wrote me at the end of July 2004 that our brother had been operated on at the VA hospital in Portland two weeks earlier. While the operation was described as successful, he had contracted bacterial pneumonia. He was no longer able to speak, she wrote, and Ute was calling the doctors daily for an update on Volker's condition.

The following month saw a dramatic turn of events when, on the afternoon of August 28, I received a surprise telephone call from Elke telling me that she and Ute were at the VA hospital in Portland after Volker had contacted Ute asking her to come as quickly as possible. His life had become unbearable, he told her, and he was ready to put an end to it. Ute and Elke had immediately flown there without, however, first informing me about the matter. Perhaps it was just as well as I was spared being a witness to what must have been a gut-wrenching experience.

According to Elke, Volker communicated with doctors and nurses by writing on an erasable white tablet with a black marker. When she and Ute entered his room, Volker wrote on his tablet, "Where is my brother?" and after our sisters had given some plausible explanation, he wrote, "Tell him I always loved him." Naturally, I was much touched to hear of our brother's warm sentiments just before his death. Volker must have remembered the day we last saw each other many years earlier when he was still in his mid-teens and I had embraced and told him, "You are my brother and I will always love you."

Elke had just stepped out of his hospital room because she could not bear to see his end when she called me. Ute stayed behind holding Volker's hand. Shortly thereafter Elke called me back saying that the doctor had just stepped outside to tell her it was all over.[8]

Volker's death certificate, issued by the State of Oregon, lists his name as Erwin Victor Zell with "divorced" as marital status. According to this document, he passed away at the Portland VA Medical Center on August 28, 2004 at 4:45 p.m. aged 62 with a physician in attendance. The cause of death is listed as Chronic Obstructive Pulmonary Disease and Pneumonia and the manner of death as "natural." Volker's body was cremated and my two sisters divided his ashes between themselves. Elke buried her share under a tree in the backyard of her Valparaiso home.

After retiring from the Valparaiso school system, Elke had moved to New England and whenever she returns to her old hometown on a visit, she stops by that tree to say a prayer for our late brother. According to Elke, in a touching display of kindness and empathy, the new owners of her erstwhile home placed a stone marker at the site of Volker's ashes bearing his name and birth and death dates.

In memory of our brother Elke also mailed me a very attractive plastic bookmark prepared by Autumn Funerals, Cremation & Burial of Portland with one side showing an eagle in flight with the poem *On Eagle's Wings* and the other Volker's obituary from *The Oregonian* of September 12, 2004 according to which Volker moved to Portland in 1971 and to Salem in 1976 where he owned Westronix. His brother and three sisters are listed as survivors.

According to Elke, during their visit they briefly met Volker's ex-wife and daughter Stephanie but were shocked by their uncaring attitude towards him and decided not to have anything more to do with them.[9]

Volker evidently died in abject poverty and left what little he had to the mission he had stayed at. The three of us agreed to share the expenses for our brother's cremation. Ute took care of the financial matters and closed the estate. When she went through Volker's papers, she found the money order I had mailed Volker two years earlier. Inexplicably, he had not cashed it and I asked Ute to donate it, together with another substantial gift, to the mission.

"Volker's life during the past ten years was terribly hard," Elke wrote me in mid-November, "Nobody really knew how bad things were for him. Well, the dear Lord has ended his misery and called him home." According to Elke, Volker did at least one good deed for his fellow man when he left this world—he donated his eyes to an eye bank.

In Retrospect

Everyone failed Volker including our mother and four of his siblings. Mutti's physical abuse of him as a young child, supposing that really was the case, was inexcusable in itself but also because it must have led to his later developmental problems. As to her later rejection of him, she could only do so much. Mother did her best to show our brother the difference between right and wrong being herself a wonderful example of propriety and decency. During his formative years, she tried to keep him out of trouble and lead a decent life. While he was in the military, she was very supportive sending him gift packages and fostering his relationship with his new-found girlfriend. Then, after his Army discharge and return to the States she took him back in and provided him with a comfortable home.

Regrettably, our mother finally had to tell Volker to move on because she could no longer cope with his dissolute lifestyle, his nicotine addiction, and his many emotional problems. Had he heeded her warnings about the dangers of heavy smoking and made a serious effort to quit, he would not have died under the terrible circumstances he did. But young people rarely pay much attention to the well-meant advice of their elders and can learn only from their own personal experiences. They always know better and Volker was the quintessential know-it-all.

Volker led a tortured life that unfortunately ended in tragedy. A major factor in his going astray must have been the absence of the steady hand of a father and role model. Lacking such an anchor, he went adrift in very dangerous waters. As the older brother, I must share at least some of the blame. Despite Mutti's good intentions to keep this problem-prone brother away from me, I should have attempted to stay in touch with him. Instead of reaching out to him, I wrote him off as a failure and put him out of my mind.

It would have required considerable time, effort, and money to keep Volker on the straight and narrow and out of trouble, and I was simply not prepared to make the sacrifice. His treatment by his three sisters was not much different as they too had abandoned him. Despite all this, I find much comfort in the thought that it was through my efforts, however belated they were, that our brother was brought back into the fold so that in his final two years of life he was not alone among strangers but had family that cared for and looked out for him.

ELKE'S STORY

All Alone In The World

Elke's is a Cinderella story worthy of *Aschenputtel* [ash putterer], the well-known folktale by the Brothers Grimm. She was the only one of Mutti's six children to be born after the war. When she came into the world in September 1945 in Stuttgart's Marienhospital, the Second World War had ended just five months earlier with the defeat of the Third Reich by the combined military forces of the Anglo-American and Soviet empires. The world was about to enter a period of over 40 years that came to be known as the Cold War after the two victorious powers had a falling out over their different political and economic philosophies and how the post-war world should be governed.

The ideological, economic, and military divide known as the Iron Curtain ran right through the center of Germany splitting the country into East Germany (German Democratic Republic) and West Germany (Federal Republic of Germany). The eastern side of the country was essentially a Communist dictatorship dominated by the Soviet Union while the western part became a liberal democracy under the tutelage of the three victorious western powers, chiefly the United States. Like the rest of us, Elke was fortunate to find herself on the western side of the divided country with its greater personal freedoms and home to the post-war *Wirtschaftswunder* [economic miracle].

Elke's christening took place six days after her birth but not in the heavily damaged Evangelische Matthäuskirche, our evangelical (Lutheran) parish church in the Heslach neighborhood of Stuttgart, but at the Marienhospital where she was born. Officiating at the ceremony was not our long-time pastor, Gottfried Lang, but an assistant clergyman. Presumably, at this time right after the war *Pfarrer* Lang could not conduct this service personally because he was sitting in an American jail for storing

Wehrmacht weapons in the basement of his church during the closing days of the Third Reich and for vehemently denouncing the Anglo-American occupiers for their wanton wartime destruction of Stuttgart's houses of worship including his own.

During her early years, Elke was a ward of the state since our mother never bothered to bring her into the family. According to Elke, until she was about 11 years old, she thought she was a full orphan because nobody could or would provide any information about her background. She had the great misfortune of being an unwanted child. Mutti did not even bother to give Elke a middle name as she did with the rest of her children and as was common practice at the time. And when Mutti gathered her brood about her to have a studio portrait taken around Christmas 1948 to send to Esther in Chicago, Elke was conspicuously absent. In fact, aside from a group photo from her grade school graduation, no photos from Elke's childhood have ever surfaced while her siblings were photographed numerous times.

Elke's birth certificate, like that of her siblings with the exception of the two Würzburger offspring, makes no mention of her father. While Elke was living with Esther and Nick for some time after having been brought to America in her early teens, Nick's brother Joe let Elke know that she was illegitimate and that Esther was only her half-sister. When Elke once asked Ute if she knew who her [Elke's] father was, she learned that it was one Paul Fischer, a furniture manufacturer in Stuttgart.[10] According to Esther, the tall, square end table of solid oak with an inlaid ceramic tile top, which Mutti had brought over as a gift for Esther and still stood in their apartment, had been made by Herr Fischer. Esther never liked the bulky piece, which she had called junk, and later gave it to Ute who, in turn, enlisted Danielle and the two brought it to Elke who now cherishes it as a memento of a father she never knew.

Both Ute and I got to know Paul Fischer on a visit to him but only Ute picked up his name or the details concerning our visit. That was remarkable because Ute was about 9 years old, which was three years younger than I. Ute remembers our meeting Herr Fischer in a "bar" in the Stuttgart suburb of Zuffenhausen where Mutti supposedly pressed him for money to buy clothing for little Elke. Ironically, Elke was in a faraway orphanage at the time and, according to Elke, neither our mother nor Herr

Fischer ever came to visit her there. Ute, however, was wrong in saying that we met in a bar because it was in an ordinary *Gaststätte* [tavern, restaurant]. Another time I remember seeing Herr Fischer, although I did not know his name nor the purpose of our visit, was when Mutti, Ute, and I visited him at his furniture factory and I busied myself watching furniture being made while Ute and our mother sat at a table with him.

Most likely Paul Fischer was the Nazi who, according to Mutti's April 1984 letter to me, had defended her before the Gestapo near the end of the war. It must have galled our mother that, in order to keep Esther from harm, she had to put up with this man at a time when everyone knew that the war and the Nazi regime were about to come to a cataclysmic end. Besides that, she could not have been too thrilled to carry a child during these final perilous days of the war with its incessant day- and nighttime Allied bombings of Stuttgart and the rest of the country when one had to be agile and unencumbered to survive. Mutti was, after all, already 36 years old when Elke was born. This could have been one reason Mutti was never able to bond with Elke who was a living reminder of some very bad times.

Life In Orphanages

Before coming to America, Elke spent her childhood in three *Waisenhäuser* [orphanages] in different parts of the country and each associated with the Evangelical (Lutheran) Church. Not long after her birth, Elke was placed in a home in Korntal, a small town a few miles northwest of Stuttgart. Institutionalized and never having been shown much affection or personal attention, Elke became a rebellious little girl who often misbehaved and fought with the other children. At about age five, after an incident involving a caregiver, she was transferred to a *Heim für schwererziehbare Kinder* [home for difficult to raise children], the Hoffmannhaus in Wilhelmsdorf.

Wilhelmsdorf was a small village near Ravensburg, a town about 100 miles southeast of Stuttgart near the Bodensee (Lake Constance) which had been founded by Pietists in the early 19th century. The Hoffmannhaus, a huge building that housed the children, boys on one side and girls on the other, was surrounded by several farm buildings housing livestock, feed, and farm implements as the Hoffmannhaus was largely self-supporting.

It was managed by a caregiver couple, a *Hausvater* [house father] and *Hausmutter* [house mother], who lived in a comfortable apartment on the upper floor of the main building.

The daily care of the children was entrusted to *Erzieherinnen* [governesses] who followed a strict regimen of prayer, school, and work. Elke's situation was aggravated by the fact that she regularly wet the bed and, as children are wont to do, was taunted and harassed as a *Bettnässerin* [bed wetter]. Elke recalls becoming so angry with some of her tormentors that she beat them up, both girls and boys alike.

Elke has few fond memories of the Hoffmannhaus. Life was harsh and regimented and the living conditions deplorable. The building itself was ancient and decrepit with no indoor plumbing or modern toilet or bathing facilities. The privy on the first floor, consisting of a number of wooden seats, was home to swarms of aggressive flies that stung the users. According to Elke, she was always covered with itching scabs making life miserable. The children were expected to earn part of their keep by working—the girls milked the cows, the boys helped clean out the stalls of the farm animals while in the fall both boys and girls were dispatched into the surrounding fields to bring in the harvest of potatoes, sugar beets, and other produce.

The children's daily diet, except for Sundays when the fare was somewhat better, was a thick gruel in the morning and mostly boiled potatoes and cabbage for lunch and dinner. The children were not offered any of the milk produced by the estate's dairy cows because that was sent to a processing plant in the village and sold for income. The deficient diet was the likely cause of a goiter Elke developed which was surgically removed when she was in her mid-teens.

As might be expected of a place that was essentially a reform school, discipline was liberally and swiftly administered. The most common offense, mouthing off at a staff member, was met with an instant slap across the face while more serious infractions were dealt with by the *Hausvater*. Funerals are generally associated with the elderly and certainly not with children's homes, but Elke remembers attending several child funerals as many children died from diverse ailments but mostly dysentery.

Elke's overriding emotion was a feeling of shame and humiliation brought about by her and the other children's complete segregation from the other villagers. They were not allowed to leave the home except when accompanied by one of the *Erzieherinnen* or handlers, as Elke prefers to describe them, for their lack of human feelings. Rather than being allowed to attend the village Volksschule, all their classes were held at the Hoffmannhaus so that no interaction with the other Wilhelmsdorf children was possible.

When they went to church on Sunday morning they were led there in a group and required to sit in the last row of pews. Elke, never timid, often spoke up when she felt some condition was especially onerous or hypocritical. One time she pointed out the incongruence between Christian teachings and their treatment in church when she promptly received a slap in the face that gave her a bloody nose. She, in turn, wiped off the blood and flung it at her *Erzieherin* splattering her dress.

Elke had a chance to visit the Hoffmannhaus again sometime back in the summer of 1996 when her daughter Ute wanted to retrace the venues of her mother's childhood. When the two came to Wilhelmsdorf and Elke saw the Hoffmannhaus in the distance, she became physically ill and nauseous and they immediately left the area. They also visited Stuttgart together where they saw Elke's birthplace, the Marienhospital, and stopped by the Wilhelmspflege in the Stuttgart-Plieningen, the last of the three homes Elke lived in.

While Elke is reluctant to admit it, despite the oppressive atmosphere, her stay in Wilhelmsdorf appears to have produced several salutary results. Her penmanship is immaculate which attests to a good foundation having been laid in school there. Like our mother, she was taught *Handarbeit* including knitting, crocheting, and sewing which has remained a favorite and practical pastime. Because all the children were required to help out with household and other chores, Elke early learned the value of work and has since never shied away from labor of any kind. Finally, being in a Christian institution, the children were instructed in the faith and told of the dire consequences of a sinful life. Elke took her lessons to heart and has remained a faithful and practicing Christian ever since.

Daily communal prayer was part of the regimen and the children said eight prayers every day—a morning and evening prayer and a prayer before and after every meal. Since both boys and girls took their meals together in the large Hoffmannhaus dining room, all the children prayed together six times a day. The prayers they were taught were in rhymed verse with the evening prayer consisting of four stanzas which Elke can still recite to this day. Clearly, the Hoffmannhaus caregivers appear to have accomplished their task of instilling good and lasting values in their charges although the means they used were not the most humane and certainly not very Christian. Obviously, their objectives could have been achieved in a more loving and nurturing atmosphere.

According to Elke, one day her caregivers told her that two relatives of hers had come for a visit. Her visitors, Elke learned, were her Aunt Emmi and Uncle Charles, a very wealthy couple from Geneva, Switzerland. She had, of course, known nothing of the existence of these people or any other relatives. Needless to say, the news electrified not only Elke but also the staff and the other children. The prospect of trading her humdrum existence in an institution in the German countryside for life in an affluent household in a Swiss city seemed almost too good to be true. And it was.

According to Elke, her hopes were quickly dashed when her aunt and uncle discovered that she still wet her bed after Aunt Emmi had invited Elke to share a guest bed with her. The two had spent the night in the spacious apartment of the caretaker couple and left early next morning without even saying goodbye to her. Naturally, the matter was a terrible disappointment and embarrassment for Elke, especially when some of the staff and the other children chided her for being so undesirable that her own family wanted nothing to do with her. Yet, if the visit was more out of simple curiosity and Aunt Emmy was indeed contemplating to adopt Elke, it is unlikely that Mutti would have simply turned Elke over to her sister because of the long-standing animosity between the two.

In retrospect, the incident was unfortunate for the entire family. Had Aunt Emmi been willing and allowed to adopt her, Elke would undoubtedly have made a loving and caring daughter who would have brought joy to her life and comfort and assistance in her old age. Elke would have, for the first time, been able to lead a normal life. Furthermore, our aunt would presumably have left most, if not all, of her estate to her niece and adopted daughter and thereby kept the wealth in the family. Instead, the Swiss courts were left to deliver our aunt's estate, by artful and devious means, to the City of Geneva.

Elke would have remained in Wilhelmsdorf had it not been for the intervention of a very kind and pious elderly couple we called *Onkel Josef* and *Tante Anny* who lived in a *Wohnung* in the Gablenberg district of Stuttgart. As a boy, I saw them only a few times but I did leave Uncle Josef my few possessions, including my accumulated second-hand copies of *Das Neue Universum*, when we first left for America in March 1950. Before her return to the States in 1951, Mutti gave the couple her parent's dining room set and also asked them to temporarily hold on to the grandfather clock Opa had received as a retirement gift from I.G. Farben. (Mother later had this clock shipped to America where it arrived but, unfortunately, severely damaged).

Incidentally, in one of his letters Volker highly praised Uncle Josef and Aunt Anny for often visiting him during the time he was in a children's home in Korntal before his return to the States. At the time, Ute and I were living in our apartment on Adlerstraße in the care of the French-German couple.

The Thonemanns insisted that Elke be brought back to the Stuttgart area where they could visit each other. Consequently, in 1956 Elke was sent to the Wilhelmspflege in Stuttgart-Plieningen, another orphanage, where she stayed for two more years. The Wilhelmspflege had been founded in 1817 as a foundling home by Queen Katharina of Württemberg (a former grand duchess of Russia) and in 1841 named for King Wilhelm I of Württemberg.

Living conditions at the Wilhelmspflege were considerably better than in Wilhelmsdorf. The facilities were newer and the atmosphere more congenial. Every other Sunday Elke was allowed to visit and spend her day with this elderly couple. That was as close as Elke came to being with her family although, interestingly, they were not even related to us. Elke learned that the Thonemanns were longtime friends of our grandparents and that Opa Peter had asked them to please look out for his Annemarie. According to Elke, during her visits Aunt Anny, who was born in 1888, loved to reminisce about the good old *Kaiserzeit* [imperial age] when life was good and orderly. Our Opa Peter had, of course, expressed similar sentiments and this was probably one reason the two families were so close.

On one of her visits, Elke was introduced to our Aunt Irma and Cousin Marga who had come for a visit. The year was probably 1957 when Elke would have been 12 years old. According to Elke, she was somewhat confused about who the two were and what they had to do with her since she had always been told that she was an orphan.

It was at the Thonemann home where the ground was laid for Elke's later emigration and to be, for the first time, with her family. Nobody had bothered to tell her that she had a mother and siblings living somewhere. In fact, when Elke made inquiries about her past, Aunt Anny always rebuffed her saying *"Ich weiß es nicht"* [I don't know]. It was Uncle Josef who finally broke the ice telling Elke that her mother had left the country and now lived in America.

According to Elke, Uncle Josef encouraged her to write our mother to let her know how helpful she was to her aunt and uncle by doing various chores like carrying up the coal from the cellar, cleaning house, doing the laundry, and polishing the couple's shoes and to ask our mother to send for her. This she did and Uncle Josef then mailed the letters but without giving Elke her mother's address. Sadly, Elke never received a reply from Mutti but, quite unexpectedly, it was Esther who arranged for her coming to America. Incidentally, Elke kept in touch with Uncle Josef until he passed away in 1967, just a year after his beloved Anny did.

More Misery

When Elke met her mother and sister for the first time, in early September 1958, she was just days short of 13 and about the same age I had been on my first arrival in the States in the company of Mutti, Ute and Volker nearly a decade earlier. While our crossing was still by steamship, by the late 1950s commercial air travel was well established and this is how Elke made her way to America. At the time, such a trip was still an adventure with a flight taking over twice as long as today. Elke fondly recalls that before she left on her journey into the unknown, the staff and children from the Wilhelmspflege assembled at the Stuttgart airport in Echterdingen to bid her an emotional farewell singing, *Nun Ade, du mein lieb Heimatland* [Now, adieu my dear homeland], a popular Volkslied. Elke and many of the children and caregivers were in tears. Elke's Pan Am flight took her to Chicago via Dublin, Oslo, and Detroit.

Elke arrived at Chicago's O'Hare International Airport after a strenuous 16-hour flight and Nick, Mutti, and Esther were there to greet her. She immediately committed a somewhat comical faux pas. Having seen no photographs of Mutti or Esther, she had no idea as to who was who and so she zeroed in on one of the two, curtsied and offered the customary south German greeting, "*Grüß Gott, Mutti.*" [God be with you, Mutti]. The person she so addressed happened to be not our mother but Esther. After Mutti had identified herself, she informed Elke that she would not be living with her but her sister.

Without much further ado, Nick and Esther drove Elke home which was their 2-flat on North Taylor Avenue in Oak Park. There Elke, being tired from her long and strenuous journey immediately turned in and, much to the surprise and annoyance of her sister, wet the bed. Incidentally, on Elke's arrival both Ute and I were away at college and Volker too was away from home so that we did not get to meet our sister until sometime later.

Elke shudders when she speaks of her time in the Holzman household, consisting of Esther, Nick, and Stephanie, in which she lived for over two and one-half years. Shortly after her arrival, she was enrolled in William Bye Elementary School. Since she spoke no English, she was put in 5th and 6th grades for six weeks each and finished out the school year in 7th grade. Elke graduated from William Bye in June 1960, the same year I graduated from college.

Esther, who was never known for her warm personality let alone for any display of affection, was singularly cool towards Elke. In fact, according to Elke, Esther seemed as if she had ice flowing through her veins and treated her more like an outcast than a sister. Perhaps Elke's habit of wetting her bed, which continued for another year or so, had something to do with that. At the time, Steffi was just three and in need of special care and undoubtedly our fastidious older sister did not relish having a second member of the household with a major handicap.

Fortunately for Elke, her misery at home was assuaged at William Bye where she met a compassionate and supportive teacher, a Miss Randall by name, who became her mentor and a beneficial and lasting influence in her life so that Elke was inspired to become a teacher herself.

Why Esther had brought Elke over in the first place has been controversial. According to Elke, her sister did not do so out of the goodness of her heart but because she needed someone to take care of little Steffi. As much as I sympathize with Elke in the shabby treatment she received, I cannot agree with her assertion, which originated with Ute, because it makes no sense from a practical or economic standpoint and Esther always saw the financial implications of all her moves.

The help Esther could have received from Elke in caring for Steffi would have been marginal at best since, during the daytime, Elke would be attending school and in the evenings be busy with homework. Esther could have hired part-time help, if she needed it, that would have cost far less than the outlays required for bringing Elke to America and the full-time support of a teenager for several years to come. This is not to say that Esther did not intent to use her sister in some way during her high school years to get her money back which, in fact, turned out to be the case.

It must also be assumed that both Mutti and Esther felt some moral obligation to bring Elke to the States and, with Mother not able to afford the expense and Nick in a well-paying job, it fell to Esther to come through for Elke. Esther often complained to our mother about the ingratitude shown by her siblings after all she had done for them.

Elke entered Oak Park and River Forest High School in September 1960. Remarkably, considering that she came to William Bye only two years earlier with no English language skills, she began high school without special classes or tutoring taking all the regular courses as her classmates. Her years while attending Oak Park High were not very happy ones. While she did well academically, some of her fellow students were openly hostile taunting her with chants like, "Hatsi, tatsi, Elke is a Nazi."

At home, Esther continued to be cold and antagonistic toward her. Her sister tried to keep Elke isolated by not allowing her to participate in any school activities such as ball games or private parties. One Friday in May 1961, a girl classmate asked Elke to stop by her house for a visit when Elke informed her that she was not allowed to associate with other kids outside of school. The following day, Esther, Elke, and Steffi had walked to a nearby grocery store where this girl's mother confronted Esther berating her for not allowing Elke to come to their house and telling her that if she did not like to associate with Americans she should go back to where she came from.

After they came home and Elke had lugged a week's worth of groceries upstairs, Esther suddenly flung open a window of their apartment and, without saying another word, threw out the little cardboard suitcase Elke had arrived with from Germany followed by her few other belongings. "Get out," Esther shouted. When Elke asked where she should go, Esther replied, "I don't give a damn." After walking to Mutti's flat on Home Avenue, Elke found our mother waiting for her only to give her a sound thrashing.

Life with Mother was no picnic either. In fact, Elke has described the time she lived with Mutti and Esther as "five years in hell." She found conditions worse than in Wilhelmsdorf because here her tormentors were not outsiders but her own mother and sister. Like Ute and Volker before her, Elke suffered her share of verbal and physical abuse at our mother's hands. According to Elke, Mutti often called her stupid telling her she would never amount to anything beyond being a *Putzfrau* [charwoman]. Calling a child stupid is obviously a very poor example of good parenting. It was especially mean of Mutti to claim that Elke was running and "whoring" around when her daughter was, in fact, a singularly pure and upright young lady who never gave the slightest grounds for such allegations.

Besides being verbally abusive, according to Elke, Mutti could also get physical and try to strike her on occasion. Fortunately for Elke, she was not the submissive type as she had already demonstrated in Wilhelmsdorf. She was already bigger than our mother and athletic and whenever Mutti was throwing one of her tantrums and ready to strike her, said Elke, she simply held on to Mother's hands until she had calmed down.

Worse than all the verbal and physical abuse, Elke sensed that she was being exploited by both Mutti and Esther who were treating her more like an indentured servant than a daughter and sister. When Elke started living with her, Mother was employed at Brach Candies but on Saturdays she continued to do housework for the Peterson family for whom she had previously been working during a stretch of unemployment. Mutti now brought Elke along and that job remained part of Elke's weekend routine for the rest of her stay with Mutti. In addition, throughout her high school years, early in the morning Elke helped out in the school infirmary and then during the lunch break in the teacher cafeteria which earned her a free lunch.

After Esther and Nick had purchased their apartment building on South East Avenue in 1963, Mutti sent Elke there on Sundays where Esther had her clean and vacuum the front entrance and staircase, wash down the back stairs, and do other menial chores. According to Elke, every weekend she was playing *Putzfrau* for Mutti and Esther and never received a red penny in compensation from either one. Elke could have used some money to buy herself desperately needed underclothing and hygienic items but, according to my sister, Mutti denied her every request.

Elke had many other unpleasant experiences living with Mutti. Besides working for Esther on Sundays, she was often sent to other homes for housecleaning chores. According to Elke, Mother sometimes even called her high school with the story that her daughter was sick and then sent her somewhere, such as Mutti's physician, Dr. Fritz Herz, to clean house. Our mother did not even give her bus fare so that she always had to walk to the homes she cleaned. Mutti accused her daughter of being on the phone too much and terminated telephone service even, according to Elke, she rarely used the phone because she had nobody to talk with.

Elke remembers meeting me for the first time sometime after she started living with Mother when I came home for Christmas. According to Elke, my Christmas present to her was a camera I had purchased at a local Oak Park store. She was delighted because she had rarely received a gift from anybody and never one from Mutti or Esther. Her joy was short-lived, however, because as soon as I had left again our mother had her return the camera to the store to get the money back which Mutti then pocketed.

It is difficult for me to reconcile what I heard from Elke about physical and verbal abuse and grievous financial exploitation with the more benign mother I knew. Undoubtedly, when Ute and later Elke lived with her at home, Mother ran a tight ship but it still came as a shock to hear what Elke had to endure at our sister's and then our mother's hands. My only explanation is that Mutti followed Esther's instructions as she was completely beholden to her daughter. Had Esther asked Mutti to jump off a bridge, I believe Mutti would have done so because she was entirely under her daughter's spell.

Esther most likely looked on the whole matter concerning Elke as a fair business transaction. She had spent good money to bring Elke to America and now felt that having her sister do the necessary chores at her apartment building without remuneration was just compensation for her outlays. Esther had, after all, asked me too to reimburse her for her expenses in bringing me to the States and I had done so from the money I earned from my job as a paperboy.

In talking and corresponding with Elke, I could not help but notice that my sister was very familiar with all the places Mutti and I had visited on North Lincoln Avenue earlier. Since Elke had left town right after high school, I surmised that the only way she could have come to know the area was through our mother while they were living together. However, I was evidentially wrong. While Elke confirmed that indeed she and Mutti had visited Chicago's German neighborhood together, it was only once or twice during her entire stay with her.

Elke does not recall seeing any of our beloved *Heimatfilme* at the Deutsches Kino or being taken to the Café Kleinert for coffee and cake afterwards. According to Elke, she did not really get to know the area until years later when she taught high school in Valparaiso and took her German classes there. What she does remember is being with Mother when they saw *Exodus*, an epic film on the founding of the State of Israel, in Chicago and attending some German-American festivities in Chicago's Riverview Park when Ute too came along.

Flying The Coop

According to Elke, the turning point in her life came when Ute and Tom got married in July 1963 and Mutti and Esther would not allow her to attend the wedding and, in fact, stayed away themselves. It was then that she decided that she must part company with the two and leave as soon as she reached legal age. That is exactly what she did. On the very day she turned 18 in September of that year, Elke "flew the coop." It was obviously a very courageous move because she had just started her senior year at Oak Park High and had never been on her own. Ute and Tom counseled her against leaving home and to wait until she had graduated but once Elke had made her decision, her sister and brother-in-law were very supportive.

Our mother was caught completely off guard. Mutti had started working for Jewel Foods earlier that year and was on the night shift. When she came home early the next morning, she found Elke's short note telling her she was now of age and had decided to leave.

When Elke first moved in with Mutti, I was in the service where Mother wrote me that she was having problems with my sister including her continuously mouthing off. Consequently, when Mutti wrote me in Virginia, where I had found employment after my tour of duty had ended, that Elke had unexpectedly left home, I wrote back that it was probably the best thing that could have happened to both of them. As to Mutti's claim in her letter that she had even baked Elke a birthday cake, I knew that was pure baloney because she had never baked one for me nor Esther let alone for anyone else. Even Mutti was not above telling a little white lie now and then for dramatic effect.

After leaving home, Elke moved to an Oak Park rooming house and supported herself with an evening job at Illinois Bell and, on Saturdays, cleaning house for the Petersons. For the first time in a long time she had her Sundays to herself.

Two important milestones in Elke's life happened in quick succession. In February 1964, she became an American citizen with Ms. Randall serving as her sponsor and the following June she received her diploma from Oak Park and River Forest High School. In the meantime she had obtained a scholarship from Valparaiso University in Indiana, commonly known as Valpo, a private school closely associated with the Lutheran Church-Missouri Synod. In this she followed in Ute's footsteps who had previously received a scholarship from the same school.

Sometime in mid-1963, before she left home, Elke had also met our brother Volker for the first time when he stopped by on Home Avenue to show Mutti his new car. The two had much in common in that they were only three years apart in age and had both suffered abuse at the hand of our mother. Not surprisingly, the two hit it off well together. According to Elke, Volker really understood her and the two enjoyed a warm relationship. She, Ute, and Volker often met and had a good time together until Ute and Elke came to suspect that their brother was keeping Mutti informed about their whereabouts and activities and broke off their relationship with him.

Years Of Fulfillment

After six years in Oak Park, in the summer of 1964 Elke relocated to Valparaiso, Indiana, where she made her home for nearly half a century. During her freshman year at college, the past once more briefly intruded into her life when, according to Elke, Mutti wrote her threatening letters which made her fearful of losing her scholarship.

In 1965, in order to throw Mutti off the track and prevent her from sending her more hostile missives, Elke formally changed her name to Elke Zell Peterson. The Petersons, Ray and Elsa, were the elderly couple Mutti, and later Elke, had cleaned house for. Elsa's father, Otto Wolf, worked for the *Chicago Tribune* and, Mutti was told, introduced color printing at Chicago's premier newspaper. The Petersons, who lived on 1117 South Wesley Avenue in Oak Park, were very good to Elke, as they had been to Mutti before, and allowed her to use their name. Elke was, however, not adopted nor assumed Eve as her first name as Mother had mistakenly believed.

This arrangement with the Petersons solved Elke's problem as she heard nothing more from Mutti or anybody else in the family with the exception, of course, of Ute. The two sisters and their respective families stayed in touch and frequently visited each other since they lived only a little over three hours apart by car. At Valparaiso University, Elke realized her dream of becoming a teacher earning a B.A. degree in English and German followed by her Indiana teacher's certificate. Subsequently, she taught at a local high school for three years during which time she continued her education at the university earning a master's in English and Education.

Less than a year after arriving in Valparaiso, Elke met John who was three years her senior and teaching history and athletics at Wheeler High School. They fell in love and in early August 1966, while she was still an undergraduate, they were married. By then, John had left his teaching job to become director of employment at a Bethlehem Steel plant. The marriage took place in her Ev. Lutheran Church but not before John, at her insistence, had himself baptized. Elke herself had been confirmed in an Oak Park Ev. Lutheran Church but not until age 18 after she had already left home. The late date came about because Esther had insisted that Elke attend Catholic services with them on Sunday mornings and Elke finally decided to return to her religious roots.

The couple's daughter, Yvonne Ute (Ute), was born in March 1968 just prior to Elke's receiving her degree while her sister, Monica, followed in December 1973. Both children too were baptized into the Christian faith. After a six year sabbatical to tend to her two young children, Elke returned to the classroom in 1979 teaching English and German at Valparaiso High School.

The following years were especially happy and productive ones for Elke. During a typical school year she taught five honors classes—two in American literature and three in German, and during the summer, a couple of special needs courses. Ute once jokingly said of our sister that she may have been the only high school English teacher in the country with a German accent. At least once a year, she took her German Club and language students to North Lincoln Avenue in Chicago for a taste of German culture and customs. In addition, two times during her tenure she escorted about 40 students to German-speaking Europe, i.e., Germany, Austria, and Lichtenstein, for a couple of weeks of sightseeing and immersion in the cultural landscape there.

Besides being a popular educator, Elke was also an excellent administrator and became chair of her high school's world languages department. In addition, she served as coach of the school's girls volleyball team for 20 years. During her teaching career at Valparaiso High, she was honored a number of times by her school and the state of Indiana and in 1990 received the coveted Outstanding Teacher Award from the University of Chicago. Elke retired in June 2011 after a teaching career spanning some 35 years.

Getting Together Again

Getting together with me again was especially difficult for Elke because of my closeness to our mother who had caused her so much grief and pain. For the sake of her own sanity, she had made a complete break with the past and did not want to be reminded of it again, she told me. She actually felt betrayed by Ute when she heard that our sister had made contact with me. In fact, it was Ute who convinced her to change her mind and reach out to me. Nearly a year passed from Ute's first phone call to me a week before Christmas 1997 and Elke's surprise visit in Oak Park in the company of Ute and Danielle at the end of November 1998. Two weeks after her visit, I received her first letter thanking me for our lunch and conversation. Elke circumscribed our new relationship thus:

> *I apologize for my late acknowledgment, but it took me some time to reflect about the past, which I had attempted to bury for the past thirty-five years. Today I am really glad that you opened the door to the past—not for my sake, but for the sake of my children, who are fascinated by our tumultuous family history. As Ute may have already told you, I am very close to her. We have been best of friends from the day I moved out of 108 Home Avenue. She remains my role model, my confidant, the wind beneath my wings. I love her as dearly as you may have loved our mother. The only request that we have is that you never give Esther any information about us, especially since we have no desire to see her again. Her avarice has totally consumed her, and she could only have a destructive effect on those who have the misfortune to come in contact with her.*

On the subject of Esther we were, of course, in total agreement. All of us, including our mother, suffered greatly under Esther's demonic rule. Much of the correspondence between the two of us was, not surprisingly, focused on our older sister. In mid-April 1999, Elke wrote:

> *Before I close, I wanted to ask you exactly what happened to Esther during the Hitler years. I remember asking Esther's grandmother Wetmore about the war years and promptly received a slap in the face by Mother for having asked such a question. At that time, I was totally unaware of the Holocaust, since nobody in Germany deemed it necessary to inform students about the atrocities committed against mankind. But Esther never was in a concentration camp, from what I know, so how was her life that much more difficult from anyone else living in Germany at that time? If you have any insight into why that woman is so wicked and callous, I certainly would welcome any light you can shed on her background.*

In my reply a week later, I gave Elke a brief rundown of Esther's life during the Third Reich and my assessment of her: "I think Esther was just born evil—her one and only god has always been money." I concluded by inviting Elke to examine the other side of the coin, a side she did not get to see on account of her good fortune of having been born after the war and not prior to or during it:

> *Regarding the Holocaust, it is true that we were never informed about the crimes committed against humanity. But how many American students have been educated about the firebombings of Dresden, Hamburg, Cologne, and other European and Japanese cities by the Americans and British during that same period? Mother, Esther and I barely escaped with our lives when a British bomb hit our air raid shelter under the Marienplatz in Stuttgart. That was our Holocaust. Most people are anxious to remember other people's crimes; they conveniently forget their own.*

Elke was especially taken aback by Esther's capacity for dishonesty when she wrote me in June 1999:

> *Our sister Ute showed me the perfume brochure Esther had made for "Holzman and Stephanie Perfumes." I was aghast at the lies printed in that brochure. Precisely when and at which university did Esther study organic chemistry? How could she be so brazen as to take eleven years off her age? What kind of role model can she be for Stephanie? What did not surprise me is her dragging Mother and her own daughter Stephanie into that circle of deception. That woman has lived a life of evil, and some day she will pay a very high price for all the destruction she has caused in her lifetime. There are times when I cannot believe that we had the same mother.*

To help Elke get over her pain and cement our new relationship, I suggested to her that we meet now and then and break bread together. One of the unexpected problems Elke encountered was her husband John's difficulty in adjusting to the new situation. In March of 1999, Elke had written:

> *You are right, Peter, that we should get together on a more frequent, informal basis. I must admit, however, that my husband is a bit leery about meeting you, especially since he had never met you during the 32 years he and I have been married. I have told him a lot about you since our first meeting last year, and I think he feels threatened by my desire to build a strong and lasting relationship with my real family from the past. He is very much aware of my love for our sister Ute, but the idea of a brother is difficult for him to grasp. Add to that his and Kurt's reliance on me (to care for them), and it makes it difficult for me to get away. Nevertheless, I will make a more concentrated effort to visit with you.*

John and I met only once and that was on Independence Day in 1999 when I drove up to visit him and Elke. Their home, which was located within walking distance of Valpo High, was an attractive 2-story white frame building surrounded by a cluster of ancient trees. Besides my sister and John, also present were Kurt, John's brother, and their Labrador retriever Max. John was surprisingly civil and after some pleasantries we had a delicious meal including porterhouse steaks done on their outdoor grill. Afterwards, Elke and I had an opportunity to talk privately.

Elke filled me in on more of her life story and gave me another hefty dose of past injuries she had suffered at Esther's and Mutti's hands. Perhaps she felt the need to justify her abrupt departure from home. As usual, the best I could do was to again hear Elke out, let her know that I understood her pain, and try to explain our mother's difficult situation at that brief period of time which would account for her mean behavior. On the other hand, my explanation could never serve as an excuse for her abusive conduct, I told Elke.

In my note thanking her and John for their hospitality, I wrote: "Thank you, dear Elke, for not holding my love for our dear mother against me in light of the awful childhood and teenage years you had to endure. You have a loving and generous heart!...You have been richly blessed by having a loving husband, children, and a grandchild, and a fulfilling and rewarding occupation as a dedicated educator. I am truly proud to have you for a sister and rejoice with you in your happiness!"

Elke came to see me in Oak Park twice that year (1999), minus John, and both times we took along my neighbor and friend Patti to help us sort out some of our issues and problems. On her visit on a Sunday in May, near the first anniversary of Mutti's passing, I decided to bring Elke to Lake Forest to see the places where our mother had spent her last days including Lake Forest Hospital and the Westmoreland nursing home.

At Westmoreland, I asked Claudette, the nurse who was in Mutti's room when she died, whether Esther had pulled the plug on our mother since I had become suspicious after viewing Mother's body in the hospital morgue. The nurse's answer was evasive. Mutti's leg had again turned blue, she said, and removal of the IV tubes which only kept her hydrated and did not supply nutrients would have made no difference since she was dying.

Meanwhile Elke had a private talk with another caregiver who gave Elke a rundown of all that went on between Esther and me at the home. She referred to Mutti as "a doll" on account of her sweet and loving disposition. Afterwards Elke suggested that it may have been selfish of me to insist that Mutti be kept alive when she was comatose, suffering, and close to death. That thought had not occurred to me but she may have been right. Are we not all basically selfish?

During Elke's next visit, on the last day of October, also a Sunday, we drove up to Lake Geneva where I showed Elke the places Mutti and I had spent much time, including Popeye's on the Lake, where we had a traditional German meal. Elke and Patti got along very well since they both could commiserate in their relationships with their respective mothers. Patti's mom was an alcoholic who, when she came home from work at Marshall Field's in the evenings and on weekends, drank herself into a stupor. When she died in 1986, Patti got so distraught that she threw all the family photos and other mementos in the trash can and had the Salvation Army pick up the precious furniture and artifacts her mother had accumulated over many years.

Despite my best efforts to help Elke to let go of the past, I continued to be only partly successful. Deep down she remained inconsolable and her anger now and then flared up as when I made a critical comment about her in regard to our mother and she replied in mid-April 2000 with this message:

> *In response to your final comment about my inability to share your grief in Mother's passing away, I can only say that I was never loved or nurtured by her the way you and Esther were, and I had to sever all ties with her for the sake of my own survival and sanity.*

Yes, it is a very sad commentary on our dysfunctional family, but nevertheless a cruel reality created by the very woman you so dearly love. I, too, am very sorry that I never had a mother who loved me or whom I could love. It is an empty feeling that has accompanied me all my life, a feeling far worse than the loss of a loved one.

Elke could also be very generous in her expression of sympathy. Many years later, in March 2007, in an e-mail exchange on the day Mutti would have been 98 years old, Elke wrote (in translation):

Yes, I know today is Mutti's birthday. When I still lived with her, we never celebrated her nor my birthday. I always found that very sad. I know you much miss Mutti. You gave her many beautiful years, Peter, and you were probably the only one of six children who loved his mother unconditionally. All her other children expected something from her but not you and I am really glad that she had at least you in this world because you always gave her such joy. You were then and are to this day a very loving person.

Needless to say, I was deeply touched to read that from someone who had been so terribly hurt not only by our mother for her neglect and abuse but by me as well for my aloof and indifferent attitude towards her in years past.

Divorce

Few lives are without the occasional disappointment, and Elke suffered a large one which, while very distressing at the time, left her stronger and altogether better off. In her somber message of July 2004 in which she wrote me of Volker's post-operative condition, she also informed me that she and husband John had permanently parted company. Alerted by an article appearing in the local paper showing him in the company of another woman made her realize that her husband of 37 years had been unfaithful. That was not all. Elke knew that John liked to gamble. He had at least three times persuaded her to come along on trips to Las Vegas. While he gambled, Elke had stayed in their room and read a novel. Nevertheless, she did not realize the extent of his addiction until one day IRS agents came calling after he had not declared $8,000 in gambling winnings on their income tax return.

Although the Valparaiso years were mostly happy and fulfilling ones for Elke, life was no bed of roses either. She was loaded down with work because John was content to let his wife tend to all things requiring manual labor. Not only was she expected to hold down a full time job which meant teaching classes, grading papers, and tending to all the administrative duties involved, but also raise their two daughters, do the normal household chores, and tend to the maintenance and repair of the house. In addition, she took care of John's father, who lived with them for 5 years, and Kurt, who was afflicted with Down syndrome, for 13.

Not that Elke minded the work or complained about it because she enjoyed being busy and feeling needed but, still, she could not help but realize that she was being used. John called the shots pertaining to almost all important decisions and Elke was left to follow his directives. In that respect things were not too different from what they had been back in Oak Park when Esther was in charge and the rest, including Mutti, had just followed her whims and fancies.

Elke was oblivious to most of her husband's extracurricular activities and even when he started to attend many out-of-town tourism conferences and seminars (John had made another career move and become a county tourist director) she was not concerned since she fully trusted him. It turned out that many of his so-called meetings took place at the blackjack tables of Las Vegas and other gambling venues. There were other financial issues as well.

Despite her husband's despicable conduct, Elke was ready to forgive him if he promised to mend his ways. She was also fearful of suddenly being by herself because in the past he had taken care of everything important. John, however, wanted to relocate to Florida while she thought it prudent to continue teaching until she reached retirement age. This made a divorce necessary. With Indiana's no-fault divorce law, Elke was entitled to only one-half of the remaining equity in their house and she had to assume a mortgage that at one time had been nearly paid off.

After a period of initial angst, Elke felt truly liberated and now much enjoys her new-found freedom. She has no intention to ever get married again, she told me. As to her ex-husband, he did move to Florida as he had promised. When he moved out, he took his handicapped brother Kurt with him relieving Elke of a considerable burden. In Florida, John met a woman who shared his love for gambling and married her. Elke was sufficiently bitter to consider dropping her married name, as our mother had done on her divorce, but her two daughters persuaded her to keep it for their sake. Evidently, while John may have been an unfaithful husband, he was also a caring father and Ute and Monica see him at least once a year.

Travels Here And Abroad

After I had relocated to Arizona in early January 2003 and Elke still taught school in Valparaiso, she visited me twice for long weekends of three or four days. Her first visit in mid-February 2008 was the first time we had seen each other since we met in Oak Park on my return from a trip to Germany and Rome in September 2006. On her visit, we toured my neighborhood by car and on foot, worshipped in my church on Sunday morning, and exercised and swam in our two fitness centers. She met my neighbors some of whom we took to dinner. Elke also got to see much of Arizona as we took day trips to Wickenburg, a former mining town with a famous Western museum, to Prescott, once Arizona's territorial capital before it became a state, to Jerome, another old mining town, to Sedona, an artist colony and spiritual center in Arizona's Red Rock country, and to Tucson, home of the University of Virginia and the Arizona State Museum with its marvelous collection of Indian artifacts.

During her second visit, at the end of June 2009, we also took in the Grand Canyon, Arizona's number one tourist attraction, on an overnight trip. On both occasions Elke and I got to know each other better and began to bond as we realized that we shared the same views on most topics we talked about. We did have to make some adjustments in our habits. While we both liked to turn in early, for Elke that meant about nine in the evening and for me two in the morning. Somehow we managed to accommodate each other.

Elke had been helping out in daughter Ute's household during spring and summer breaks flying in from Valparaiso to wherever the family found itself during her son-in-law's early career moves. For many years

Brian was employed as a corporate executive in Atlanta, Georgia, where their three children were born. To show their appreciation, Ute and Brian now decided to treat her to a special gift on the occasion of her upcoming 65th birthday.

In early July 2010, Brian, Ute, Elke and the three children, Sadie, Cole, and Mason, took off for a three week tour of Germany. In Munich, they rented a minibus and traveled the country visiting such tourist sites as the university town of Heidelberg, King Ludwig II of Bavaria's fantasy castles, medieval Rothenburg, and the island of Lindau where they took a bike ride along Lake Constance. When told they would stop by in Stuttgart, I was anxious for Elke to visit Adlerstrasse 8, where the family lived before our emigration, and drew her a detailed map how to get there. Unfortunately, they never saw the house (which is partly hidden from view by trees from the street below) but they did locate the Marienhospital next door. Their tour ended with three days of sightseeing in Paris. Altogether, according to my sister, it was the most wonderful birthday present she had ever received.

On the tour, they also stopped off at the Wilhelmspflege in Stuttgart-Plieningen, the third and last of the three orphanages Elke lived in. There Elke and her family received a very cordial welcome and were given a tour of the facilities. The home had, in the meantime, been reorganized and given a new mission, namely, to serve children and teens with special needs. The facilities had been completely remodeled and all were astonished when Elke could recall precisely how everything looked in her days there. She also learned that a number of former charges had successfully sued the Evangelische Kirche (Evangelical Lutheran Church) for the illegal use of child labor which resulted in a financial settlement.

In Retirement

A new phase in Elke's life began with her retirement in June 2011 and subsequent move to a picturesque little town in New England to be closer to Ute and her family. After selling her Valparaiso home and living first with her daughter and family and then in rent for a while, Elke was able to move into her new home in May 2012. It had been four years since she had visited me in Arizona and Elke thought it was high time I came to visit her and her family and see her new house. This I did for 10 days in early June 2013. We had a wonderful time together enjoying many little adventures. Elke is a typical Hausfrau in the best sense of the word—she is an excellent cook, housekeeper, gardener, and handyman. Finances are tight and she is also frugal avoiding unnecessary outlays and even collects rainwater in a barrel which she uses to water the trees and plants in her expansive backyard.

Elke's white frame ranch-style home is one of eight in a condo association and located on a quiet street off the main road. The association members are all good neighbors and friends with several coming by to greet me. Her 2-bedroom home, which includes a large dining room next to a spacious kitchen, a comfortable living room with fireplace, is bright and airy with big picture windows all around. The inside is a veritable doll-house filled with family photos, paintings (some by her grandchildren), and knickknacks making it wonderfully gemütlich. Another nice feature of her home is a fully finished basement. Next to one side of her home is a fenced-in garden while the expansive lot in the rear is bounded by a small stream.

Best of all, Elke and Ute and her family live only six miles apart and on the day after my arrival, we were invited for dinner at their house—a 3-story timber wood building on a 4½ acre lot complete with tennis and basketball courts and flower and vegetable gardens. There, for the first time, I met Brian and 12-year-old twins Cole and Mason. Ute and Sadie, age 15, were off on a high school basketball tournament and I did not get to see them until their return a few days later.

As to Ute and Brian, they were married in 1996 in the Valparaiso Ev. Lutheran Church Elke and her family had attended. The two had met at Dartmouth College where both took bachelor of arts degrees. Ute played basketball for the school while Brian was an Ivy League track & field star with several records to his name. Brian and his two brothers were born into a well-to-do family in Wayne, New Jersey. Before their retirement, his father was an attorney with a law practice in New York City while his mother taught high school mathematics. His parents own homes in South Carolina and Maine where their grandchildren spent much time during school vacations.

Brian and his family had left Atlanta for New England after he was offered a position with a public utility company where he is now a top executive. At the time of my visit, Ute was a part-time teacher and head coach of the high school girls basketball team. Sadie played basketball on her mother's team while the twins were into Little League baseball, basketball, and soccer. We went to several games watching all three kids play.

If my niece did not welcome me with open arms, there was presumably a good reason. "Where has this guy been these past four decades," she most likely said to herself, "before showing up at our doorstep." There was also some angst, I heard, that I would try to lure her mother away to live with me in Arizona just when she needed extra help around the house and with driving the kids to school and various sports events while she was coaching and teaching. Of course, I had no such sinister intentions although I did tell Elke that she was always welcome to share my home in the sun.

Rather than remain home, Elke and I decided to drive north and visit parts of nearby Canada including the French-speaking province of Quebec for its old-world ambience and charm. It turned out to be great idea because we had a most enjoyable time together. Our first stop was Montreal where Elke was impressed by the grand architecture in the town center and especially Notre Dame Cathedral which I had previously seen when Mutti and I visited the city in July 1974. We next drove on to Quebec where we stayed two nights in its Old Town to sample all this charming place had to offer including its fine restaurants. We took a bus tour of the city and went on walking tours of the Citadel and the Quebec provincial Parliament.

Before returning home, my sister and I stopped off at Canada's capital Ottawa. There we rode up the Peace Tower in the Parliament building. Both in Quebec's Citadel and here we were astonished to find much memorabilia from the World War I battle of Arras, France. That engagement had been won by Canadian troops and here tribute was paid to their sacrifice and valor. Arras rang a bell with me because it was in Arras where Mutti's older brother Karl had met his tragic fate at the young age of 18 and just out of school. It made us reflect on how strangely interconnected people, places, and events can be despite them being worlds apart.

An Active Family

Since these early contacts much has happened in Elke's life and the lives of her loved ones. Her family can now only be described as awesome. Daughter Ute has become a local celebrity by leading her high school girls basketball team to five consecutive state championships while in 2017 being named girls basketball coach of the year. Her girls rarely lose a game and the entire family, including Elke, is usually there to cheer them on even if it sometimes means traveling out of state. While playing on her mom's team, Sadie was named girls high school basketball player of the year for her state by a national organization. The twins, Cole and Mason, too are natural athletes and played basketball on their high school teams with Cole being especially talented.

Daughter Monica, who studied accounting at the University of Florida, is employed in outside sales by a major pharmaceutical company while husband Craig, who is Australian-born, markets imported wines. The couple owns an attractive home in Fort Lauderdale.

Elke's family is very close-knit and gets together whenever there is a good opportunity. Most every Sunday, Elke has Ute and her family over for dinner of popular American and German dishes. Brian much enjoys his mother-in-law's German cooking including *Jägerschnitzel* [schnitzel with mushrooms] or Bavarian *Weißwurst* [white sausage] with sauerkraut and mashed potatoes, the latter two according to her special recipes. Other family favorite include Hungarian goulash, Georgia peach chicken, and grilled Australian lamb chops.

As is the case with most American families, Thanksgiving is the time for the yearly family reunion. On this occasion, Monica and husband Craig fly up from Florida for the traditional turkey dinner at Brian's and Ute's house. Both Brian and Craig are excellent cooks and do the gobbler while the rest of the family tends to the side dishes and desserts.

Another occasion for a get-together is the yearly mother-daughter retreat in September, Elke's birth month, when she is a guest of her two daughters for three or four days with all expenses paid. It is a custom Ute and Monica started right after their mother's divorce. In the past they have visited such popular vacation spots as Montreal, Quebec, Las Vegas, New

Orleans, Newport, and New York City. On top of that, whenever Monica gets lonely to see her mom, Elke flies in for a visit of a week or so.

Elke is a dynamo and always on the go. Much of her activity is centered around her church, a small congregation of the Lutheran Church - Missouri Synod, where she sits on the church council. As chair of its Encouragement Committee, she stays in touch with members by phone and individually written get-well, sympathy, and condolence cards.

Every day of the week, she visits a German-born lady and church member named Maria, a widow. Maria was very active in church affairs until some years ago when she suffered a severe stroke leaving her unable to speak. Elke spends about an hour with Maria during which they pray together and Elke reads her a German short story and verses from Scripture. Her visit concludes with their singing of a popular Volkslied.

In the past, Elke has also taught English and citizenship classes for immigrants and special classes for home schooled children in her congregation. In addition, she does much entertaining. Every other month she has her pastor and his family over for dinner. Individual church members and members of an area German Club are frequent dinner guests as well.

Not surprisingly for one steeped in literature as she is, when her day's chores are done, Elke likes to read a piece of fiction, preferably on some historical theme, or a good biography. She subscribes to *The New Yorker* magazine and on weekends receives the *Sunday New York Times*. In addition, to keep up with her German heritage, Elke gets the weekly *New Yorker Staats - Zeitung & German Times* and the bi-monthly *German Life* magazine.

About three times every year, Elke is on the road to meet up with family and friends scattered over four states. Each tour usually includes visits to Ute, Tom, and Danielle in Brighton, Tommy and Peggy and their two children in Philadelphia, Peggy's parents in Greensburg, Pennsylvania, her best friend Donna in Johnstown, Pennsylvania, and friends and former colleagues in Valparaiso and Chicago. Donna is practically part of the family since she and Elke raised their children together in Valparaiso. She, in turn, visits Elke and her family about twice a year.

Besides all these travels, Elke managed to find time for two-week visits to my Arizona home in the spring of 2016 and again two years later.

The first time we again toured the state including the Grand Canyon but the second we decided to stay close to home and just enjoy each other's company.

It was the summer of 2019 and six years since my first New England trip when Elke and I decided it was time for a return visit especially since the twins had recently graduated from high school and were about to leave for college while I had another birthday coming up. This time, a week in early August, I was warmly received by the entire family. Elke and I decided to stay close to home and, as always, had a wonderful time together beginning with a birthday party in my honor to which she had invited some members from her church.

Our daily routine usually began with a brisk one-hour walk, sometimes accompanied by Ruby, her family's chocolate Labrador retriever, followed by a delicious breakfast of blueberry pancakes, crepes, or some other delicacy. As part of Elke's daily routine, I also got to meet her good friend Maria, a very bright and charming lady who astounded me with her expert knowledge of Scripture and German literature. On Sunday morning we attended worship services at Elke's church in a neighboring town. On a Tuesday evening, she had her pastor and his family over for a tasty meal and spirited conversation on religious topics. Elke also took me to Stowe for a visit to the Trapp Family Lodge and other places of interest in the Greater Boston area.

At the time of my visit, Ute was looking forward to September and leading her high school girls basketball team to a possible 6th consecutive state championship. She also planned to teach an honors class in American government. The twins were now 19 years of age and 6'-3" tall, the same height as their father, and still growing. I got to see them only one day at dinner at a local restaurant because the following day they were off to Montreal to celebrate their graduation with their classmates, and immediately thereafter the entire family left for a bike and hike tour of Yosemite National Park in California's Sierra Nevada Mountains.

Meanwhile, Sadie was in Colorado taking tourists on hikes on trails along the Rocky Mountains. She was attending Tufts University where she was majoring in applied mathematics and physics with an expected June 2020 graduation date. She had been recruited to play basketball for her school which had her parents and Elke scrambling to watch all of her games one way or another.

Both Cole and Mason earned high SAT scores which helped with entry into prestigious colleges in Ohio and Pennsylvania, respectively. Shortly after my visit, the two, who have always been close despite their very different personalities, left for college and for the first time lived apart. Neither has yet decided on a college major but while Mason is leaning toward economics, Cole, following in the footsteps of his mom and older sister, began playing basketball for his school.

Since then something quite unexpected happened that has affected the lives of millions around the world including Elke's family, namely, the deadly Covid-19 or coronavirus pandemic. It arrived in the United States earlier in 2020 and attacks the respiratory system of its victims. Scientists have determined that the disease is best contained by social distancing, frequent hand washing, the wearing of facial masks, and temperature checks in confined spaces. The need for social distancing, in turn, has meant the closing of schools and colleges with students required to do their studies online from home.

Despite these handicaps, Sadie completed her studies and in mid-May 2020 received her bachelor's degree in mathematics and physics. Sadly, there was no on-campus graduation ceremony at her school this year but her mom mailed out a studio photograph to relatives and friends showing Sadie in the traditional cap and gown. The entire family is, of course, immensely proud of her and celebrated her achievement on her return home in mid-June. Cole and Mason had come home at the beginning of March already and successfully finished their college freshman years online. In the meantime, the twins finished their summer jobs and have begun their sophomore year studying off-campus while Sadie has found her first permanent position teaching advanced mathematics at a prestigious New England school. Elke is happy to have most of her family close by again and over for Sunday dinner just like in the good old days.

Finding Peace Through Faith

Despite her tough childhood and teenage years, Elke is one of the most cheerful and outgoing people I know. The two of us have, in the meantime, bonded and become the best of friends. We are in continuous contact with one another. Since we both also see the comical side of life, when we are together or on the phone, lots of laughter is part of our conversation. We are on the same page on most issues although in the political arena Elke is considerably more on the liberal side. Fortunately, my sister no longer harbors that strong feeling of loathing she once felt for our mother as I have been able to convince her that in her own way Mutti was a very decent and caring person who did much good while in the world.

According to Elke, she does not hold anything our mother did during the war years against her because she lived through some very difficult times and did whatever she had to do to survive. Had she only shown her a little of the love she so desperately craved. She will never understand how Mother, she told me, could be such a loving and supportive parent to two of her children and totally reject the other four. Therein lies a great riddle about one can only speculate.

Mutti obviously disregarded a cardinal rule of good parenting which is to never show favoritism in the treatment of one's children and, most importantly, never to be abusive physically or emotionally. Someone needed to sit down with her to explain the damage her conduct was doing to the lives of her three youngest children but nobody did. If somebody had, everything would have turned out much differently.

The foregoing is, of course, only a small part of Elke's story. The first 18 years of her life were, needless to say, very traumatic and after her retirement, and encouraged by her two daughters, she decided to a write a memoir of those times. In mid-August 2020, she informed me that she had just become a published author and that I would soon be receiving a signed copy of her book but feared that her revelations about Mutti would shock and upset me. My sister, Elke Zell Bowman, entitled her book *Enduring Shame*. When I read Elke's autograph copy of her book, I was, quite frankly, stunned and dismayed. It is perhaps not surprising that, on account of our very different relationships with her, our opinions of and feelings for our mother would also differ sharply. Nevertheless, we both agreed that the matter will in no way affect our relationship and the friendship and affection we have developed over the years for one another.

Elke has always taken her Christian faith very seriously. It has given her the strength to endure in the face of great hardships. During my 2019 visit she told me that from childhood on she always felt and believed that Jesus loved her when no one else did.

Her joy would be complete were it not for the fact that her family, in line with modern trends, is not religious and unchurched. Having her family with her during worship service is a dream that comes true only once in a while, such as on Christmas Eve, when Ute and the children usually come along as a special favor.

The fact that none of her three grandchildren is baptized is cause for deep concern but Elke hopes and prays that they all will eventually find their way to the faith.

In a note to me about her teenage experiences, she once summed up her Christian faith in these words: "I believe that God looked out for me. After I ran away from home life became wonderful. That's why I thank God every day for all the 'miracles' he has wrought me and still does." What a precious example of a life triumphant over adversity through faith!

NOTES

1. In the mid-1950s many babies around the world were being born deformed with some of them missing limbs or limbs that did not grow normally. The cause was traced to a drug named Thalidomide which had first been produced by a West German pharmaceutical company and marketed over the counter to pregnant women to deal with the side effects of pregnancy such as anxiety, sleeplessness, and morning sickness. Thalidomide was later found to attack the fetus if taken during pregnancy resulting in miscarriages and deformities. By the time the drug was finally taken off the market late in 1961, about 12,000 deaths and cases of severe birth defects were counted world-wide. It is not known whether Esther actually took this drug or a similar medication because she never talked about the matter. It is possible that the cause of Steffi's dwarfism had nothing to do with Thalidomide but was due to a genetic defect. Interestingly, Thalidomide is still marketed and approved by the World Health Organization (WHO) for the treatment of certain cancers.

2. Frank's parents, Dr. Frank H. and Esther B. Murrin, made their home at 1112 Fair Oaks Avenue in Oak Park where they raised their two children, Frank and Vernile. The father was a respected Oak Park physician. Esther's friend, born on April 14, 1920, was a 1945 graduate of the Northwestern University Medical School and certified by the American Board of Psychiatry and Neurology. Following his graduation, he served two tours of duty with the U.S. Navy. Dr. Murrin made scholarly contributions in his field and in 1948, at age 28, became co-author of *Progress in Neurology and Psychiatry*, Volume 5. After the Navy, there followed a career of about 25 years as a teacher, administrator, and practitioner in neuropsychiatry and neurology in the Chicago area. He taught at the Loyola University Stritch School

of Medicine in Maywood and was Director of Psychiatry at Cook County Hospital, one of the biggest such facilities in the nation.

Frank's sister, Vernile, too did very well for herself. Vernile Murrin became a well-known radio actress who starred in a number of mystery plays including the series *Curtain Time* on WGN, Chicago's premier radio station. Vernile had been offered but declined a Hollywood contract preferring to stay in the Chicago area where she met and married the retired chairman of United States Gypsum, Graham J. Morgan. Thereafter, Vernile Morgan became active as a philanthropist and board member of several civic organizations.

Vernile's stepdaughter, Heather Morgan, then Director of the Chicago Council of Fine Arts, married Michael A. Bilandic, a corporate attorney, whom the Chicago city council had chosen as acting major after Mayor Richard J. Daley had dropped dead of a heart attack in his doctor's office in mid-December 1976. Shortly after, a blizzard struck Chicago effectively shutting down the city for days, Mr. Bilandic was blamed for the fiasco and lost the Democratic primary. He was succeeded by Jane M. Byrne, an anti-machine candidate, who became the first female major in Chicago history. Mr. Bilandic then served on the Illinois Supreme Court for 10 years, the last three as chief justice, before his death in January 2002.

3. The four referenced articles promoting Esther's beauty care business appeared in these publications:

* Carol Kleiman, "A portrait that works: How do you project a confident image?" *Chicago Tribune*, Section 6 (TempoWoman), May 8, 1988, 7.
* Laurie Levy, "Mother/daughter duo makes scents," Shoptalk North Shore/November 1990.
* Sheila Richard, "Champagne, flowers greet new Lake Forest Perfume," *Lake Forester*, 28 Nov. 1991, 5.
* http://i4beauty.co.uk/personal/beautyparlour/featuredprod/holzmanstephani.html. (The undated advertisement was located on this website on April 19, 2007).

4. Admittedly, Esther was not entirely at fault for the difficulties between the two of us. Thus, I had long harbored strong feelings

of resentment towards her especially for what I saw as her callous treatment of our mother over the years. Instead, I should have reached out to her especially since she obviously had mental and emotional problems. I definitely should have praised her now and then for her accomplishments, some of which were truly impressive, and I should have shown some love and more care which I neglected to do. Susan, my attorney, told me that she had heard from Attorney Mike that Esther considered me a jellyfish who usually backed down in any confrontation with her. She must therefore have felt perfectly safe taking away our mother only to experience anger, shock, and surprise when I fought back. She had been misled by my past willingness to always let her have her way because I did not want to upset our mother.

5. According to the records of the Volksbund Deutsche Kriegsgräberfürsorge e. V., the German War Graves Commission, Ute's father, Franz Lodzin, was born on October 14, 1906, in Altbraa, Pomerania (now part of Poland) and was a Wehrmacht private. He fell on April 22, 1944 in Égletons, France, and is buried in the German military cemetery in Berneuil which holds the graves of over 8,300 Wehrmacht soldiers. Ute, accompanied by Danielle, visited her father's gravesite in early October 2013 after both had returned from the People's Republic of China, where Danielle was teaching at the time, to spend some time in Paris and the French countryside.

6. When the original version of *Just Passing Through* was published in 2011 the identity of General Walker, for whom Volker claimed to have been driving while serving with the U.S. Army in Germany, was still a mystery. It could not have been General Walton Walker, commander of the 8th Army in Korea, because that officer had died in a vehicle accident there in 1950. The puzzle was coincidently solved when, on November 22, 2013, the Public Broadcasting System (PBS) aired a program commemorating the 50th anniversary of President John F. Kennedy's assassination which I happened to be watching. According to this report, the president's assassin, Lee Harvey Oswald, had on April 10, 1963 also tried to assassinate an Army general by the name of Edwin A. Walker.

An online search revealed that in 1960, while Volker was serving with the U.S. Army in Augsburg, Germany, General Edwin A. Walker was commander of the 24th infantry division stationed in Augsburg.

This must have been the General Walker Volker had been driving for. The records further indicate that General Walker was relieved of his command on April 17, 1961 because of impermissible right wing political activities. Edwin A. Walker was born on November 10, 1909 and had served both in World War II and the Korean war. He left the service in 1962 and died on October 31, 1993. Since an Army private would not have been entitled to a jeep, it must be assumed that the jeep Volker took on a joyride into town was General Walker's. When I wondered about the nature of Volker's Army discharge, Ute contacted the Department of Veterans Affairs and received a laudatory Presidential Memorial Certificate for Erwin V. Zell which she forwarded to me.

7. An Internet name search revealed that Erwin Victor Zell was first arrested in December 1969 in Oregon for recklessly endangering another. He was 27 at the time and had arrived in that state just two years earlier. During subsequent years he was arrested and charged with various misdemeanors and felonies including burglary, assault, harassment, menacing, and unlawful use of a weapon. He was either acquitted, put on probation and at least once sent to prison. One case from this time was argued before an Oregon appellate court (*State v. Zell*, 749 P.2d 1196) and decided on February 10, 1988. In his trial his lawyers appealed "his conviction for harassment contending that the trial court erred in denying his motion to withdraw his previously entered plea of no contest." The appeal was dismissed. The decision is cited in several subsequent cases involving other defendants.

8. Physician-assisted suicide (PAS) a.k.a. Dying With Dignity (DWD) statutes for the terminally ill who choose to end their lives prematurely exist in a number of foreign countries and ten American jurisdictions including Oregon. Everywhere else the practice is still illegal and criminally prosecuted. One can endlessly discuss its morality and there is something to be said for either side. On one side, all religions strongly condemn suicide because it is, after all, a murder. Murder even if it is not of another person can never be condoned or excused according to this view. On the other hand, there are occasions where the practice seems fully justified on humanitarian grounds if it is meant to put an end to needless suffering. One such scenario occurs

when, as in Volker's case, a person cannot get enough air in his or her lungs to breathe and is essentially being slowly and cruelly asphyxiated. It must be one of the most terrible dying experiences that no human being should be required to endure. Our Maker, a God of love and compassion, has undoubtedly forgiven Volker and will not deny him his place in Heaven on account of it.

9. Volker's marriage in Oregon appears to have been his second after an earlier one in Chicago. In early November 2013 a JoAnn Carrington contacted me through one of the social media sites to which I was then subscribing telling me that when she googled to obtain information on her former husband, pages from my *Just Passing Through: A German-America Family Saga* (original edition) came up. According to JoAnn, "I was the fiancé that met his mother in the book" and added "I hope I am not bothering you" and "I would love to hear from you." She was married to Volker, she wrote, when she was just 16. Their marriage ended in divorce after two years and they had a daughter. In my reply I informed JoAnn that Volker had remarried and had died in Oregon in August 2004. Naturally, I was happy to hear from her and suggested we stay in touch via e-mail but heard nothing more from her. When I told Elke, she contacted Ute who confirmed that JoAnn had been Volker's first wife and that their daughter was given up for adoption.

10. As might be expected, Elke always wanted to know more about her father, Paul Fischer, and during the time she lived with our mother on Home Avenue in Oak Park, she came across some of Mutti's belongings in a storage area of the apartment which she hoped might provide some clues. Among her discoveries was a so-called *Hitlerbuch* which was chockfull of photographs of the Führer surrounded by adoring crowds including mothers and children. I vaguely remember seeing this book, which was of an oversized format, and casually leafing through it once. Elke's search, alas, revealed nothing about her father. Presumably, Mutti was given the book in appreciation for her three Aryan children born during the Third Reich and, incredibly, brought it over in one of the crates of our belongings she had shipped to the States. The book apparently did not survive her move to our townhouse home on North Harlem Avenue in Oak Park because it was never seen again. According to Ute, who got the information from Esther, Elke's father died in 1955 from lung cancer.

AN AUTOBIOGRAPHICAL SKETCH

Getting An Education

My narrative begins in Oak Park, Illinois with my entry into Oak Park and River Forest High School (Oak Park High) in the spring of 1952 after my return from Germany. I was again fortunate being able to attend a very good school that provided me with a solid foundation for my future education. Oak Park High was rated one of the best in the country and had produced a number of luminaries in diverse fields including the Nobel laureate Ernest Hemingway (1899-1961) who famously described his hometown as a village of "broad lawns and narrow minds." Ray Kroc, the founder of the McDonald's restaurant empire, too attended Oak Park High but did not graduate and, like Hemmingway, served with the American Red Cross in Europe during the First World War as an ambulance driver.

The high school, like the village itself, was a somewhat snobbish place and a bastion of the ruling elite, viz., White Anglo-Saxon Protestants (WASPs). There was not one black student in my graduating class although nobody, including myself, took note at the time. Being an immigrant and a paperboy who had to walk his paper route early in the morning before coming to school, I was near the bottom of the totem pole in social rank and popularity which, however, did not bother me in the least.

Required reading in English class was the standard high school fare at the time that included a couple of Shakespeare plays (*Hamlet* and *The Merchant of Venice*), *David Copperfield*, the *Forsythe Saga*, *Giants in the*

Earth, and *The Red Badge of Courage*. Charles Dickens became my favorite author and I read several of his novels. Shakespeare too left an indelible impression on me and, with my paperboy money, I immediately bought a volume of his complete works. As I read through several of his plays, I discovered a multitude of rhymed verses the most meaningful ones of which I wrote down and committed to memory much as I had done with some German poetry at the Oberschule in Stuttgart. The subjects I enjoyed most were English, history, Latin, mathematics, physics, and gym.

Back in Germany, math was my Achilles' heel and algebra remained a complete mystery. That all changed when as a freshman at Oak Park High our algebra textbook was *Algebra for Problem Solving*. One of its three authors, Elsie Parker Johnson, was chairman of our mathematics department. For the first time I became aware of the beauty and power of mathematics. From then on, I took every math class being taught including advanced algebra, solid geometry, and trigonometry. My graduation from Oak Park High on June 16, 1955 was pretty much a nonevent as nobody in my family attended. Mutti was at work and the rest, including Esther, were apparently busy or not interested.

It was my good fortune to be selected, based on the results of a competitive examination and years of service, as one of 27 newspaper delivery boys to win a scholarship from The Newspaper Distributors Association of Chicago. As part of the prize, we were guests of the U.S. Navy which flew us to their Pensacola Naval Air Training Station in Florida for a four-day stay at the end of June of that year. The well-known World War II naval hero Rear Admiral Daniel V. Gallery served as our guide. There was a tremendous amount of publicity surrounding the trip and we were interviewed and photographed by the major Chicago dailies. On our return, the *Chicago Tribune* asked us to write an article on our experiences and mine was published on September 8, 1955.

The scholarship award of $500, together with my savings, allowed me to go to college. I chose the University of Illinois which then had its Chicago undergraduate division at Navy Pier, a former military installation that jutted out into Lake Michigan. Following my maternal grandfather's footsteps and with my love of math and physics, I decided to study engineering matriculating in September 1955.

A major milestone in my life came on January 3, 1956, when I was sworn in as an American citizen at the federal courthouse in Chicago with my boss at the Village Newspaper Agency, Tom Doherty, serving as my sponsor.

At the "U of I," I joined the Reserve Officers' Training Corps (ROTC). If I was going to serve in the Army, I decided, it might as well be as an officer. The program director, Major Frank McClenahan, an artillery officer who had fought against the Wehrmacht during World War II, was surprisingly friendly toward me and became my mentor. I quickly rose up the ranks becoming one of three cadet company commanders. At a mass formation on January 9, 1958, I was presented with the Chicago Tribune Silver Medal for military merit.

In February of that year, I transferred to the main campus in Champaign-Urbana to complete my course work. Many of my fellow students, some of whom were studying on the GI Bill, found the engineering curriculum very tough and dropped out of school, switched to other programs, or hung on by the skin of their teeth. I was in the latter category. To keep my grade point average up (a minimum of 3.0 out of 5.0 was required to stay in school), I took a number of what to me were "soft courses," such as psychology, in which I could expect to get at least a "B" without too much effort. I was also fortunate in having an exceptional memory that allowed me to easily retain pages of engineering textbook formulas and class notes for use during examinations.

My two friends at school, John and Richard, and I graduated on June 18, 1960 with bachelor of science degrees in Electrical Engineering while I, in addition, received my commission as a second lieutenant in the U.S. Army Reserve and assigned to the Signal Corps. Mutti, Esther, and Nick came down from Oak Park to join me for the graduation ceremonies.

During the summer of 1959, I was sent for ROTC basic training at a Signal Corps camp in Fort Gordon (near Augusta, Georgia) where all nearly came to a bad end for me. While World War II had ended over a decade ago, there was still much lingering antipathy against Germans especially among some members of the U.S. military. Numerous nasty incidents by officers, especially captains, and noncoms let me know that I did not belong.

In one field exercise the technique used to string communications wires between trees had been demonstrated to us—a harness with a spike was attached to each shoe and one climbed a tree by sinking the two spikes, one after the other, into the trunk while holding on to it with arms extended. Each member of my platoon practiced the technique in turn by climbing just half-way up and down again under the watchful eye of an instructor. I was the last in line and the captain told me to climb the tree all the way to the top. When I got there and looked down, the officer and everybody else had left the scene. Keeping my arms extended but not too far lest I lose my grip (we were not given safety belts), I jammed each spike in succession into the tree trunk hoping the one spike would support my weight as I slowly descended. Within a few feet of the ground I fell without, however, suffering any injuries.

A jeep finally came by to pick me up with the driver apologizing for having forgotten about me. The outcome would have been disastrous for me had I fallen from a greater height. Satan had sent me up that tree, I came to realize, but the good Lord had once again intervened on my behalf.

In Government Service

My next eight years or so were spent, broadly speaking, in government service. My 6-year U.S. Army commitment included two years on active duty in the U.S. Army Signal Corps and I was called up on September 10, 1960. After a brief stint at the Signal Officer School at Fort Monmouth, NJ, I was sent to the White Sands Missile Range in New Mexico where I first served as a headquarters staff officer and then as Upper Range Area Signal Officer. My base of operation was Stallion Site in the northern part of the range near the village of Socorro, a small community of mostly Spanish speaking people.

My landlord in Socorro was an old-timer named Clarence Barrett who, as a parting gift, gave me a copy of his booklet entitled *Pot O' Gold*, a charming account of his boyhood with his father (his mother had died when he was just three) prospecting and trading in furs and hides along the old Rio Grande River. Socorro happened to be not far from Alamogordo and I had the opportunity to visit historic Trinity Site where on July 16, 1945 the U.S. Army detonated the first atomic bomb.

In September 1962, I was released from active duty with the permanent rank of First Lieutenant in the U.S. Army Reserve and returned to Oak Park. My service obligation ended in June 1966 with an honorable discharge.

On my return to Oak Park, I searched for and found my first job. The National Aeronautics and Space Administration (NASA) was planning for a lunar landing and needed engineers. After answering a job ad in the *Chicago Tribune*, I was offered a position as an Aero-Space Technologist with the Langley Research Center in Hampton, Virginia. I accepted and became a career conditional employee on November 1, 1962.

At Langley, I was assigned to the Electrical Experimental Equipment Section and eventually specialized in the design and development of high-voltage capacitor discharge facilities. These were used to accelerate small particles to simulate micrometeorites whose impact on various types of spacecraft exteriors was being tested with the object of finding the most impact resistant. I much enjoyed my work because it utilized my mathematical skills and allowed me to make a genuine contribution not only to the art of high voltage capacitor discharge technology but to the overall lunar mission as well.

NASA believed in continuing education and encouraged employees to obtain advanced degrees by taking courses at Langley during regular working hours. I enrolled in a program leading to a master's degree offered by the University of Virginia taking some courses at Langley and spending the first semester of the 1965/1966 school year at the main campus in Charlottesville. Incidentally, the University of Virginia had been founded in 1817 by Thomas Jefferson, the author of the *Declaration of Independence* and later the third president of the United States.

My work was also my hobby and I devoted almost all of my time to it so that I had little in the way of a social life. Sometimes on weekends, I would drive from Newport News, where I lived, to nearby Colonial Williamsburg to enjoy its ambiance and indulge my other hobby, namely, photography. Most of the time after work and even past midnight found me engaged in some work related activity such as reading technical literature, making calculations, or writing on my master's thesis.

To satisfy the engineering school's thesis requirement, I was able to arrange for several months of experimental research at Langley to test out a mathematical model I had developed. While my thesis entitled *An Investigation Into the Factors Affecting Projectile Velocity in an Exploding Foil Hypervelocity Gun* was highly mathematical with a minimum of verbiage, one of the three examining professors said to me: "Mr. Zell, this is an engineering thesis—did you really have to use all that flamboyant language?" Well, at least I kept them from falling asleep reading through it, I thought.

My work effort culminated on August 12, 1967 with the degree of Master of Electrical Engineering. (Shortly after I received my M.E.E. degree, the title for a degree requiring a thesis was changed to Master of Science in Electrical Engineering). During my time at Langley, I also published two technical articles—one in *EDN* (Electrical Design News) magazine (June 1968) and one in *Design News* (November 1968).

My career progress at the NASA was exceptionally good. A year after my appointment as a GS-7, at a salary of $6,500, I was promoted to civil service grade GS-9. Two years later, on November 1, 1965, I became a career tenured employee which was followed a year later by a promotion to grade GS-11. My step increases within the grade levels came unusually fast thanks to my boss, Bernard (Ben) Ellis, who was most helpful in advancing my career. Ben, who happened to be Jewish, was a career civil service employee who knew all the intricacies of operating within the federal system and I benefited much from his expertise.

Ben urged me to study management engineering which would take me out of design and development and on track for a management position with the NASA. The School of Government and Business Administration of George Washington University of Washington, D.C. just happened to offer an off-campus program at Langley. I applied and in April 1968 was accepted as a candidate for the degree of Master of Science in Administration. Things were looking up for me and I was quite satisfied with my life and work when I abruptly decided that, after six years at the NASA and living in Virginia, I needed a change and it was time for me to move on. It was a decision I came to regret after some years in the corporate world.

Two things prompted my move to leave the NASA. First, I wanted to study business in preparation for a hopefully more glamorous and exciting career in private industry. The second thing, and something that really worried me, was the rumor of a RIF (reduction in force) within the NASA which was to take place shortly after the planned Apollo 11 mission to land a man on the moon. I felt that this event, which was less than a year away, was sure to affect me since most of my colleagues had many years of seniority over me. Being terminated would leave me very vulnerable because my work experience in high-voltage capacitor discharge technology was not readily transferable to private industry.

It was quite a surprise and shock to everyone when I announced my resignation from the NASA effective September 20, 1968 to go to business school. I am sure Ben and his superiors felt let down after their investment of time and effort in me. My colleagues thought I was foolish to make a career change when I was already 32 years old and would be competing for jobs with much younger men. Mutti, who was 59 at the time and working for Jewel Foods, was aghast when I told her and pleaded with me to reconsider. Perhaps she knew the value of a good job better than most anybody. My subsequent career in marketing and selling technical and industrial products was not as glamorous as I had expected and was spent mostly in middle management.

In Corporate America

With letters of recommendation from Ben Ellis and Professor E. C. Stevenson, my University of Virginia thesis advisor, I applied to three business schools and chose the Graduate School of Business at Columbia University in New York City. The school had a sterling reputation and was on a trimester system so that, if I took no break, I would have my degree in less than a year and a half.

My career change and decision to study business management came at the height of the Vietnam War. Antiwar demonstrations had erupted in all major American cities and the country was in turmoil. Students were protesting the draft and many college campuses were focal points of unrest. Worrisome was the fact that in May of 1968 student protesters had taken over several buildings at Columbia because of the university's involvement in research connected with the war and the protests were ongoing. Leaving my new car, a 1967 Mercury Cougar, with Nick and Esther in Oak Park, who kept it in the garage behind their apartment building, I took the train to New York. There, I rented a room in one of the university properties on the corner of Broadway and West 113th Street.

After matriculating in September 1968, I chose marketing and international business as concentrations because marketing was flaunted as the panacea for all the ills afflicting business firms at the time. While I may have chosen the right school, I am sure that I chose the wrong curriculum and much regretted not to have taken up international finance instead. I did rather well with two appearances on the Dean's Honor List and was awarded the Master of Business Administration (MBA) degree on February 25, 1970.

With an MBA from Columbia, the world was my oyster—at least for a while. I had some very good job interviews at the school and my education and experience were in demand. Unfortunately, nobody was ready to send me to Europe where I wanted to work. The only option for me now was to travel there on my own. Aunt Emmi had invited me to stay with her in Geneva and conduct my job search from there and in early April 1970, I sailed for Europe after having sent my car ahead on a freighter.

After some job interviews in Germany, I accepted the offer of Digital Equipment GmbH, the German subsidiary of Digital Equipment Corporation (DEC) of Maynard, MA, as a sales engineer for their line of small digital computers. About the same time, I was also invited by a large German electrical company, Siemens A.G., to come in for an interview at their Munich headquarters but, perhaps foolishly, declined because I had just accepted the DEC offer.

I started work for DEC on June 1, 1970 in their Cologne office and was then sent for three months of training to their Maynard headquarters then ensconced in an abandoned textile plant. After my return to Germany, I was assigned to their sales office in Frankfurt am Main, then located in the suburb of Neu-Isenburg, and given the job of prospecting for customers among the universities and research centers in the Frankfurt metropolitan area. These early computers for scientific and industrial use were difficult to program (using machine language), word length was just 12 bits, and computer memory was very limited. The little expensive machines, called PDP-8s, were consequently a very tough sell.

In Maynard I had met Kenneth Olsen, DEC's cofounder and CEO, and in mid-March 1971 wrote him proposing a new line of compact digital computers that would replace cumbersome machine language with everyday English and could be used by both businesses and the general public for many activities requiring data analysis and computation. The device would have a typewriter keyboard for entering data in English, an auxiliary memory, a digital processor, and an attached vertical monitor for displaying the results. Mr. Olsen's response was disappointingly negative as he questioned the feasibility of such a device. Some years later, in 1977, he was famously quoted as saying, "There is no reason why anyone would want a computer in their home."

After a while it was apparent that I was in the wrong job and at the end of July 1971 resigned. Mutti came to visit me and, using my apartment in Frankfurt-Sachsenhausen as a base, we toured Germany for several weeks in my Mercury Cougar visiting relatives and friends and taking in the usual tourist sites.

I did not return to work until Mutti's 63rd birthday on March 6, 1972 when I joined the Delta-Star Division of the H. K. Porter Company, Inc. of Pittsburgh, a conglomerate. Delta-Star Electric Company had been founded in 1908 in Chicago to serve the electric power industry and taken over by H. K. Porter in 1950. The company was not new to me as I had worked there on the factory floor during the summers of 1956 and 1957 while attending the University of Illinois at Navy Pier. Chicago's West Side, where the factory was located, was then known as America's workshop for all the many manufacturing companies, both large and small, located there. During these years of industrial expansion, Delta-Star was humming with activity as there was great demand for the company's pioneering products which were considered the Rolls Royce of the industry.

Delta Star's product line included indoor and outdoor air-break disconnect switches that were used by electric power companies in their power distribution substations to isolate transformers, circuit breakers, and other apparatus from the power grid for service and maintenance. Some of the disconnect switches were huge, motor-operated devices rated at up to 500,000 volts. All the country's major electric utility companies such as American Electric Power, Commonwealth Edison, Duke Power, and Consolidated Edison were longtime customers.

The West Fulton Street factory was fully equipped to produce the entire product line and had a model shop, a foundry, a tool- and die-making shop, a welding shop, and a galvanizing shop in addition to the customary machinery including drilling and boring machines, automatic lathes, milling machines, and specialized machinery of every sort. One of the buildings held a high-voltage engineering laboratory where the latest switch designs could be tested. It had been an exciting place to work at.

Things at Delta-Star had much changed during the intervening 15 years and mostly for the worse. Intense price competition had made operations unprofitable and this unit of H. K. Porter was losing money. I was hired in when many managers were being terminated and the work force reduced. Delta-Star was obviously not the place for someone looking for job security. Nevertheless, I was willing to give it a try since I had grown very fond of the company and its great products and hoped I could help turn it around.

During my 4½ years at Delta-Star, I served in various management positions including marketing services, product sales, and assistant marketing manager. I soon realized that the major problems were not local but much higher up in management. There were at least two. For one, Delta-Star was committed to develop an oil-filled interrupter switch which was to replace an oil circuit breaker and its associated disconnect switch. The project reportedly consumed millions of dollars to design, develop, and test. Independent market research had shown that the product was not feasible because it did not have the required current interrupting capacity of a circuit breaker and was too costly for use as just a disconnect switch. Not one unit was ever sold. The second major problem at Delta-Star was that top management insisted on a "cost plus" pricing model. It caused the company to price itself out of the market and in 1980, after escalating losses, the plant was shut down.

With the Delta-Star plant doomed to close sooner or later, I was fortunate to attract the attention of C. R. (Bud) Hintz, the vice president of the electrical division, who, at the beginning of November 1976, transferred me to the profitable Peerless Motors Division of H. K. Porter Company, Inc.. This company was located in Warren, Ohio, a blue-color town and base for several large manufacturing plants. Porter/Peerless, located in an old brick building on West Market Street, had complete in-plant manufacturing facilities for many types of electric motors. In 1965 it became the first company to offer a line of direct current permanent magnet servomotors specifically designed for the machine tool industry. Using permanent magnets to create the required magnetic field made these motors less bulky, more efficient, and less expensive than standard direct current motors.

Porter/Peerless had a number of European distributors and large original equipment manufacturer (OEM) accounts but no offices there and Bud came up with the idea of having me establish a presence to further penetrate the European market. West Germany was of special interest because of its large and well-known machine tool industry. After training on motors in Warren, I was sent to Europe arriving in Amsterdam at the end of March 1977.

My assignment was to provide technical support to our customers and go prospecting for new accounts among the manufacturers of machine tools, i.e., milling machines, numeric controlled lathes, and the like. I called on just about every machine tool OEM in West Germany promoting the Porter/Peerless line of permanent magnet motors and collecting information on each company on product usage and competitor activity. Working out of Frankfurt am Main, I set up a repair facility for Peerless motors there to serve all of the company's European customers. Sometimes Bud had me on assignments for other electrical division products as well.

My new job carried an impressive title, namely, Divisional Sales & Technical Manager - Europe but it was far from ideal. Because it had been created for me in short order, there were organizational problems and it never became quite clear which of the four executives and managers who thought were in charge of me was my real boss. Besides Mr. Hintz, there was the H. K. Porter Director of Marketing with offices in midtown Manhattan, the Warren works plant manager, and the motors product manager. The main issue was whether I should be selling directly to machine tool OEMs, which would short-circuit some of our large distributors who were themselves selling to these accounts, or confine my activities to finding new accounts.

Another big problem for me was the absence of any administrative support. The studio apartment I had rented in Sachsenhausen (in the same high rise I had lived when I was with DEC) also served as my office. For transportation, I used a rental car which I surrendered on weekends to save on costs. I was with this H. K. Porter unit for 2½ years when in May 1979 I decided to leave my old employer for another firm.

After seven years with H. K. Porter, I joined the Gettys Manufacturing Company, a profitable young company with modern manufacturing and administrative facilities located in Racine, WI. The company had been founded by Roger Hill, who had formerly been an engineer with the Oster Company, his wife Emily, and some associates to design and manufacture electronic tracers for the machine tool industry. The Gettys Pacesetter tracer had a stylus that followed (traced) the contours of a model while parallel work stations shaped metal pieces into clones of the model. The company had sales and service subsidiaries in Germany, France, Italy, and the United Kingdom and a manufacturing plant in Ireland.

After some initial work in a number of departments and making a review of company pricing practices, I was made Manager of International Marketing reporting to the Vice President–International. My duties included managing Gettys' foreign sales, providing technical and administrative support to the subsidiaries, and developing and monitoring the foreign sales forecast. During a 9-month period ending in late June 1982, I gained additional foreign sales experience working out of Gettys GmbH in Munich.

The change in employers proved a good career move even though my good fortune did not last as long as I would have liked. The job was interesting and challenging, my salary took a quantum jump and, like most employees, I was enrolled in Gettys' profit sharing program. The working environment was very congenial and the company's location, just across the Illinois border, ideal in that I could return home to Oak Park on most weekends.

Then something quite unforeseen happened. For the first nine months of 1980, Gettys' sales and net income had risen by 15% and 65%, respectively, compared to the previous year but by late 1980, sales began to drop dramatically. When Roger called on one of Gettys' major stateside machine tool accounts, Cincinnati Milacron, he was told that their orders backlog had recently been shrinking to an alarming degree. The same was heard from other customers. Another economic recession was on the horizon.

The Hills and the other stakeholders in the company now decided that this was an opportune time to sell out. It just so happened that a major electronics company, Gould Inc. of Rolling Meadows, IL, had a strong interest in acquiring Gettys because the Gettys line of servomotors and drives would fit in perfectly with management's goal of becoming a world leader in factory automation. Gould, which had its beginnings in 1950 in the battery business, had recently bought up other companies to achieve this goal. A deal was struck and in mid-January 1981, Gettys became the Gettys Motion Control Division of Gould Inc. in exchange for Gould common stock valued at $20.9 million. The not unexpected sharp decline in sales and income materialized and continued into 1982 prompting Gould's management to drastically trim the Gettys payroll. Many employees were let go and towards the end of 1982, I too was placed on permanent layoff. Incidentally, Gould's venture into factory automation proved a failure and the continuing heavy financial losses led to its liquidation in 1993.

The economic downturn meant that management jobs were in short supply especially in industrial marketing and sales. I therefore appreciated Gould's offer to pay for professional outplacement counseling services with a Milwaukee consulting firm. While conducting my job search, I decided to start my own management consultancy by conducting in-house *Pricing For Profit* seminars. The Delta-Star disaster, which resulted in large numbers of employees losing their jobs, sparked my strong interest in the profitable pricing of products and services and to develop my own pricing theory. Not much came of this venture because towards the end of 1983 one of my resumes found its way to a well-known German executive search firm. One of their clients was looking for a German-speaking vice president of marketing and sales for their American subsidiary on Long Island. Would I be interested?

An Employer With A Connection

The company I came to work for was Alexander Wiegand GmbH, also known as WIKA, a leading manufacturer of pressure instrumentation founded in January 1946 by Dip.-Ing. Alexander Wiegand. Its location was Klingenberg am Main, a small town southeast of Frankfurt. At the time, I had never heard of the company but the town's name rang a bell because Mutti had once mentioned it to me as the place her father and his superior sometimes went to visit an I.G.-Farben warehouse there. Before I left home, I had been told that I would be in Klingenberg for either a day or two, if they did not think that I was their man, or for three weeks of orientation and product training if they did.

After a series of meetings in Klingenberg with WIKA's owner, Ursula Wiegand, her second in command, Hans-Georg Ehlich, and a few of the other top managers, I was hired in January 1984. During my first stay in town, which lasted nearly 7 weeks, I had the privilege of being given the spacious apartment in a guesthouse next to the Erlenbach mansion where Frau Wiegand resided plus a company automobile for my personal use.

My employment contract with one year's duration and renewable thereafter made me Vice President, Marketing & Sales of WIKA Instrument Corporation, the company's American subsidiary. The position reported administratively to the executive vice president of the American company and operationally to the foreign sales manager of the parent company. WIKA was a highly successful firm with over 20 sales offices and manufacturing subsidiaries world-wide and a product program encompassing the entire spectrum of pressure instrumentation including dry and liquid-filled gauges, contact gauges, process gauges, precision test gauges, chemical seals (for measuring corrosive materials), and electronic pressure transducers and instruments. The Klingenberg factory encompassed several modern buildings each housing the latest in specialized machinery plus a research laboratory. The entire workforce was highly trained in their respective job functions. The American subsidiary was located in Hauppauge on Long Island, NY, in a modern building that housed the corporate offices and some limited assembly and product customizing facilities.

WIKA's most impressive and valued asset was undoubtedly Frau Wiegand who, belying her diminutive size and self-effacing demeanor, was an extraordinarily aggressive and tough-minded businesswoman. At any meeting she presided over or was present, it was a good idea to be well prepared. Ursula Wiegand was the widow of Dr. (juris) Alexander Wiegand, the founder's son, who in 1967 had been shot dead by the company's accountant. The story goes that Dr. Wiegand had been visiting his employee at a hospital when the latter pulled a gun from under the covers and shouting "you made me sick" killed him. Frau Wiegand immediately faced a challenge from the fledgling company's bank creditors who wanted to seize the company's assets. After a prolonged legal battle Ursula Wiegand prevailed becoming its sole owner.

My reception at the American corporate headquarters in Hauppauge in mid-March 1984 was chilly even though Herr Ehlich was there to introduce me to the staff. The American subsidiary was headed by Paul Eberle, a Swiss-American from Zurich, who held the title of executive vice president and was therefore my boss administratively. He had, unfortunately, not been consulted when I was hired and it had been rumored that he was on his way out and that I had been chosen to be his replacement. He had run afoul of the owner for being too intransigent and not aggressive enough to fully exploit the American market potential. Most importantly, the American subsidiary was losing money.

Paul had every reason to be unhappy because if it had not been for him, the company might not have an American presence. He evidently saw the potential for the company's line of oil-filled pressure gauges and pioneered their use in the American petrochemical industry which bought the German product in large quantities. The profits generated by his sales efforts had substantially contributed to the growth of the parent company which was still in its infancy and in need of cash. Needless to say, it was a difficult situation for me to be in. Despite my difficulties, I found the work, which covered every aspect of industrial marketing and sales and drew on my education and past work experience, very challenging and rewarding.

"It's a small world," is an often heard expression and this was proven out in my association with my new employer. While on vacation with Mutti in Oak Park in early October 1985, I showed her the new WIKA company brochure that had been produced for the American market earlier that year. Regarding WIKA's history, it stated:

> The founder of the company Dipl.-Ing. Alexander Wiegand was born in 1888 in Fulda. After graduation in Darmstadt and München [Munich] he joined the welding gas division of IG-Farben in Frankfurt-Griesheim. For 25 years he held the position of Chief Engineer and in 1946 he founded the WIKA company. Dipl.-Ing. Alexander Wiegand died in 1951.

When Mutti saw the founder's photograph in the brochure, she immediately recognized him as her father's superior at I.G.-Farben in Griesheim. He was the one who used to come by their house and sometimes he and Opa would travel to the company warehouse in Klingenberg together. Indeed, the above description fit in perfectly time-wise with my grandfather's tenure with I.G.-Farben. Thus, by a curious coincidence, I now found myself employed by the widow of the son of Opa's erstwhile superior.

When, after the war, the Allies took over I.G.-Farben and broke it up because it was a monopoly with Nazi affiliations, Herr Wiegand was presumably dismissed. He then took the logical step of setting himself up in Klingenberg. Welding technology required the use of certain gases and gauges for gas pressure measurements and that is the product he chose for his business. Incidentally, the name WIKA was derived from the names of the two founders—Alexander Wiegand and Philipp Kachel. Herr Kachel later broke away to run his own company specializing in the manufacture of temperature measurement instruments until 1986 when WIKA took over the Kachel company adding thermometers to the company's product line.

The inherent organizational problems and resulting personality conflicts could, alas, not be resolved. Although I had no aspirations to take his job and tried to put him at ease, I was unable to overcome Paul's angst-driven hostility. In the meantime, I had become very concerned about Mother back in Oak Park and realized that sooner or later I would have to return home and take care of her. When I told my bosses not to include me in their future plans, my contract was not renewed.

I left WIKA at the end of October 1986 with my salary payable for another three months. Incidentally, soon after my departure Frau

Wiegand made good on her promise and put Paul out to pasture. In fact, she hired a new general manager, disposed of the Hauppauge property, and moved the American subsidiary into new office and manufacturing facilities near Atlanta, Georgia. This move away from Long Island made good sense since it brought the company closer to its major market in the petrochemical industry. Ursula Wiegand passed away at age 59 in 1996, the 50th anniversary of the company's founding, and left the firm to her son also named Alexander.

From Business To Law

After my return to Oak Park, I was in a quandary on what to do next. Another position in international marketing and sales, which would have taken me away from home for extended periods of time, was out of the question because Mutti, who was then 77 years old, had difficulty coping and needed my presence. Management positions in general were difficult to come by in the mid to late 1980s, especially in the overrun area of marketing and sales. Most companies were downsizing and aggressively dropping middle managers from their payrolls to reduce costs and improve profitability. The digital computer had replaced many middle management functions and positions. After a long and futile search for a management job in the Chicago area (all job offers came from out-of-state), another career change seemed in order. I had always been interested in legal matters and now decided to study law. With a business and a law degree, I should be able to find a position in a corporate law department.

Considering my advanced age, only modest financial resources, and other considerations, I ruled out applying to one of the more prestigious Chicago law schools and chose The John Marshall Law School (now part of the University of Illinois in Chicago) in downtown Chicago instead. John Marshall, named for the most famous chief justice to sit on the U.S. Supreme Court, had been established in the late 19th century to allow less privileged members of American society to enter the legal profession. Especially important for me was that at John Marshall courses could be taken throughout the year which made it possible to complete the course work in considerably less time than the three years normally required for a Juris Doctor (JD) degree.

To test the waters, I matriculated in early January 1988 in the evening program with a reduced work load but nevertheless completed my course work in record time obtaining my JD on August 31, 1990. In his opening remarks to the incoming class, a professor informed us that their aim was not to teach about justice or fairness but the law. That was news to me because I had previously thought that these were what the law was all about. My major interests were in corporate, intellectual property, and antitrust law and I did rather well considering that I was twice the age of my fellow students most of whom were already in the legal profession working as paralegals for Chicago law firms. After taking the usual series of preparatory courses, I sat for the next scheduled Illinois state bar examination, which was held over a two-day period at the end of February 1991 at Northwestern University's Chicago campus, and passed on my first try.

When I took my oath of office at Chicago's McCormick Place on May 9, 1991, I was just short of 55 years old and probably the oldest one of the 674 new attorneys admitted to the practice of law in Illinois. The swearing in ceremony was presided over by Illinois Supreme Court Justice Michael Bilandic, a distant relative of Dr. Frank Murrin. Mutti, Esther, and Frank were in attendance and after the ceremonies I took us all to lunch at the Como Inn. This ceremony was followed on June 28, 1991 by a similar but smaller one (no family or friends were allowed) at the federal district court for the Northern District of Illinois in the Everett McKinley Dirksen Courthouse in downtown Chicago.

As it turned out, I could have saved myself the considerable expense and effort of becoming a lawyer because it never led to a full-time legal position. Attorneys, like middle managers, were not much in demand at the time, not even ones with an MBA degree, and especially not ones at my age with no prior legal experience. For a new and inexperienced lawyer to go solo would be extremely difficult, I was told, and not recommended.

The only activity in the legal area I did engage in was as a certified arbitrator for the Circuit Court of Cook County in downtown Chicago. For about 7 years before leaving the Chicago area, I served part-time on a 3-person panel of arbitrators. Arbitration was a mandatory program that had been set up by the state to unclog the overloaded judicial system and provide for speedy adjudication of civil cases filed with the circuit court in which liability for monetary damages was the only issue. Most of these cases involved automobile and slip-and-fall accidents. Each panel heard on the average of four cases a day and panel members were paid on a per case basis. All the rules and procedures of a regular court hearing were followed and litigants, usually represented by their attorneys, had the right to reject the arbitrators' rulings and have their cases heard before a judge.

Coasting Into Retirement

With another seven or so years left before I could retire with reduced benefits under Social Security, I decided to lower my sights and pick a job in a line of work I could do and that was as close to home as possible. I consequently found my calling in retail sales in and around Chicago. Since it was as bad to be overqualified as it was to be under-qualified for a job, I found it prudent not to mention my many degrees on my job applications which made me look like a professional student.

My first retail job was with a company named Polk Brothers at their new flagship store in neighboring Melrose Park. (Their first store, a huge, warehouse-like building had burned down in June 1987). This company was a furniture and appliance discounter and a Chicagoland icon with a huge following of loyal and satisfied customers. Sales people were on straight commission, i.e., they received no salary but earned a commission on each of their sales from which they drew a certain amount, known as the draw, to give them a consistent weekly income. Customer traffic was very good so that the established sales quotas were easily met. With the Polk Bros. commission rates one of the highest in the retail business, I soon had a respectable income again.

Unfortunately, in mid-June 1992, only four months after I had joined the company, the owners decided to leave the retail business and put the proceeds from the sale of the company into a charitable trust, the Polk Bros. Foundation. The news was unexpected and came as a shock to employees and customers alike. Soon thereafter, all the stores were closed, the employees let go, and the remaining inventory auctioned off.

My next stop was Marshall Field's, Chicago's premier department store and another Chicago retail icon, where I started at the beginning of September 1992 as a sales associate. Their downtown flagship store on State Street, where I had applied and found employment, was famous for its opulent interior and upscale merchandise that yearly attracted tens of thousands of shoppers including tourists from abroad The company had been founded over a century earlier to cater to the carriage trade and offered only quality, brand-name merchandise. People used to proudly carry about the store's dark green shopping bags, which bore an image of its famous clock attached to a corner of the downtown building, for the social status it conferred.

I was assigned to a specialty boutique known as the Charvet / Field's Afar Shop. The Charvet part of the shop featured custom-made shirts, ties, and cummerbunds from Charvet Place Vendôme of Paris. As the name Fields Afar suggested, it featured exotic and expensive gift items from around the world. Also offered were jewelry, silver, and other precious items from estate sales. The work was very enjoyable and I received a number of citations for excellent customer service. The subsequent sale of Marshall Field's to an out-of-town department store chain with a different retail philosophy and clientele brought an end to an era and was greeted with sadness throughout the city and suburbs. Even though the new owners kept the name, the house's character and image changed much for the worse.

Field's Afar and then the Charvet shop were closed and I was assigned to the men's accessory department which soon took on the character of a discount operation with low-cost merchandise at bargain-basement prices. This was not the kind of selling I could get used to and after three years, I left the company. Incidentally, Marshall Field's was eventually taken over by Macy's of New York.

An upscale retailer, Plunkett Home Furnishings of Hoffman Estates, was my last employer. When the company's owner, Hugh Plunkett, a big man of Irish decent, hired me as a sales associate shortly after New Year's of 1997 I was already 60 years old and knew little about furniture. My place of employment was his furniture store on North Avenue in River Forest, one of several he owned, and which was ideally located within walking distance of Mutti's Place. Hugh's young son Dan was the store manager and my immediate superior.

Plunkett's had a loyal and discriminating clientele among homeowners and apartment dwellers in Chicago and the near western suburbs. The company offered name brand case goods and upholstery in the medium to upper price ranges, upholstery customizing services, oriental rugs, and accessories including mirrors and original works of art. The monthly sales quota of $25,000 was not easy to reach but, thanks to some supportive colleagues and loyal customers, I managed to stay with the company for over 5 years.

The furniture retail business was highly competitive with many Chicago area furniture stores failing over the years especially those catering to the more price-sensitive segment of the market. Fortunately, Hugh was an expert merchandiser and promoter who knew how to buy and sell and keep his customers coming back. Now and then Hugh himself would stop by to give us a pep talk. He also liked to kid his employees and once said of me, "Look at Peter, he came to America to be a brain surgeon and wound up selling furniture."

Perhaps ending one's business career as a furniture salesman is not something commendable but I was philosophical. At least I was gainfully employed when so many qualified people were systemically excluded from the job market because of their age. Over the years, I had made some financial investments in corporate bonds and stocks with good yields and, together with my Social Security income, could now comfortably retire. My retirement at age 65 on Sunday, March 10, 2002 was made memorable by a wonderful dinner-party my colleagues gave me at a local restaurant.

Incidentally, Plunkett's prospered for another few years when it became a victim of both the Great Recession (2007-2009) and the Internet. The latter had drastically changed the way people bought furniture and other products. Prospective furniture buyers could now come into stores to find something they liked and then go online to purchase the same or a similar item directly from the manufacturer at deeply discounted prices. Plunkett's was forced to close its doors in late 2009.

After my retirement, there was no good reason for me to remain in the Chicago area and, like other retirees, I decided to move to a part of the country with a warmer and more agreeable climate. A neighbor had suggested one of the Del Webb retirement communities in Arizona's Valley of the Sun to me and there I moved, after several visits, a few days after New Year's of 2003. After a short search, I found my dream home and by a happy coincidence at the very same price I had sold Mutti's Place a short time earlier. That real estate is a good investment was proven again because the value of my initial Oak Park townhouse investment had increased by a factor of eight.

I have lived there since enjoying the many amenities of the place and devoting my time to keeping physically fit, reading and writing, and travel.[1] Like most people, if given a chance to lead my life over again and knowing what I know now, I would have done many things differently. Most likely, I would have remained with the NASA in Virginia, gotten married, and started a family. Divine Providence had other plans for me. A low libido has allowed me to lead a chaste and moral life and fully devote myself to my assigned task. If I were asked to sum up my life I would do so in the words a great poet used near the end of his life.[2]

> Tasted have I like a hummingbird on the wing
> Life's sweet nectar and now with the great Goethe sing:
> Ye happy eyes, what ye have seen
> Let come what may, how fair it's been.

Special Gifts

Nature loves diversity and it is therefore not surprising that everyone in this world is a special creation with interests, talents, strengths and weaknesses, and life experiences unique to that individual. As Paul wrote: *Having then gifts differing according to the grace that is given to us, whether prophecy, let us prophesy according to the proportion of faith; Or ministry, let us wait on our ministering: or he that teaches, on teaching; ......* (Romans 12:6-8). Many of us have been endowed with special and extraordinary gifts and I am no exception.

Having been blessed with the gift of life and the gift of faith, I was also given the gift of poetry. In my youth, I had perused the poetry in Shakespeare's plays and later came across Goethe's tragedy *Faust II* (in an English translation). What had attracted me to rhymed verse was not only its beauty but the fact that it contained so much irrefutable truth. In fact, it can be said that poetry is truth! When my interests changed to mathematics and the sciences and later to economics and business management, reading poetry was no longer part of my life. Consequently, I never became familiar with the works of the great poets of the past. When I now run across an occasional piece in a newspaper by one of the major living poets, I am invariable appalled at what has become of that great literary genre. Rhymed verse has, sadly, gone out of style and been replaced by so-called free verse which to me is just unintelligible, frivolous literary rubbish lacking in substance and dressed up and promoted as poetry.

My poetic gift came to me late in life, at Christmastime 1985, when I was already going on 50. Unexpectedly, I became the recipient of a rhymed quatrain which was followed in quick succession by others. My poetic venture resulted in a large number of rhymed couplets and quatrains. These were very diverse in nature—historical, inspirational, patriotic, personal, philosophical, prophetic, and religious. So many, especially the earliest ones, had a very apocalyptical bend to them so that I named the series *Poems for the End of the Age.*

Another set of poems was the product of war. Mid-March 2003 witnessed the unprovoked attack on Iraq, the cradle of western civilization, by coalition forces led by the United States. Like most people around the world, it angered me because it was not a war of necessity but one of choice. As bombs and missiles rained down on ancient Baghdad, my heart went out to the inhabitants and especially the hapless woman and children who would be cowering in the basements of their homes as Operation Shock and Awe engulfed them.[3] As a child, I too had once been a victim of the same type of aerial terror and needed to speak out. Powerful rhymed verse seemed the best means to do so.

Since I had never written any poetry by design, I was again happily surprised when I became the recipient of a major poem that occupied me, on and off, from mid-February to mid-November 2004. The new poem turned out to be exactly 100 quatrains in length and in the form of a stage play in which four characters—an American, a German, an Israeli, and a Poet (the moderator)—discuss their views on past and present events. Its title *Discourse on the Mosel* derived from the fact that its venue was Trier, located on the Mosel (Moselle) River, and Germany's oldest town.

Incidentally, Trier was founded by the Romans in 15 BC as *Augusta Treverorum* and once known as *Roma secunda* for its importance to the ancients. The Roman Emperor Constantine I (later to be known as "the Great") and his mother Helena resided here where in 310 AD he had the Basilica of Constantine a.k.a. the Aula Palatina erected, one of the largest extant buildings from antiquity. I subtitled the poem *The Century Poem* for its 100 verses following the example of the 16th century French seer Nostradamus who had divided his prophesies into ten "centuries" of 100 quatrains each.

The gift of prophesy is very rare and one that can be a mixed blessing. While it would be presumptuous of me to claim prophetic gifts, I have nevertheless been able to gain insights into certain important biblical prophesies and specifically ones appearing in the final book of sacred Scripture variously known as *The Revelation to John, The Revelation of St. John the Divine*, or the *Apocalypse*. These new interpretations, supposing they are valid, have left me conflicted and deeply troubled because they are truly frightening. It goes without saying but I love this world and this country and, as a childhood survivor of a horrible war that left tens of millions of people dead and caused immense destruction to cities, towns, and cultural landmarks throughout the world, I have no desire for a repeat performance.

Nor do I relish being the bearer of bad tidings and be despised for it as all predictors of bad times are. And why would anyone with my lowly origin, having been born to an unwed mother in an ancient inn in an obscure village, come to be favored with such an important mandate? As always, I looked to Scripture and found a possible answer in a letter St. Paul wrote to the Corinthians: *But God hath chosen the foolish things of the world to confound the wise; and God hath chosen the weak things of the world to confound the things which are mighty; And base things of the world, and things which are despised, hath God chosen, yea, and things which are not, to bring to nought things that are: That no flesh should glory in his presence.* (I Corinthians 1:27-29). God works in mysterious ways and has rarely chosen powerful people born in great houses but the lowly and inconsequential ones for such tasks.

In my humble opinion, *Revelation* has been misinterpreted from almost the beginning of Christianity. As I read through the standard interpretations offered by the church fathers and biblical scholars of this very complex and mysterious work, it became apparent to me that they could not possibly be correct. Clearly, John of Patmos was not prophesying about ancient Rome or its rival Parthia or modern Rome and the apostate Catholic Church, as American evangelicals would lead one to believe, but rather this very time we live in. It was a future time which happens to be our time John was addressing. The future is here! The *Four Horsemen of the Apocalypse*, the *City of Babylon,* the number *666,* and other mysteries are not about the past but the present.[4] In view of my premonition of a catastrophic happening in the very near future, I end my work with a personal view of the present East-West conflict and a plea for peace. The reader should be forewarned that my views are controversial and do not conform to the prevalent Western ones of the day. They will be offensive to many but revelatory to others.

In Search Of World Peace

Mankind is on a fateful journey on the road to Armageddon that will end in all likelihood, barring divine intervention, in less than a decade from now in a nuclear holocaust of biblical proportions. That is my frightening and sad conclusion after carefully reading and reinterpreting *Revelation* and other prophesies in light of the escalating East-West conflict. Eventually the confrontation between the two dominant military powers of the day, namely, the United States of America and the Russian Federation, will plunge the world into the abyss that will bring unimaginable horrors to our beloved planet. It was nearly six decades ago, on September 25, 1961, when President John F. Kennedy went before the United Nations General Assembly and delivered this powerful warning:

> *Mankind must put an end to war or war will put an end to mankind.....Today, every inhabitant of this planet must contemplate the day when this planet may no longer be habitable. Every man, woman and child lives under a nuclear sword of Damocles, hanging by the slenderest of threads, capable of being cut at any moment by accident or miscalculation or madness. The weapons of war must be abolished before they abolish us.*

The speech was given during the height of the Cold War, a political and military standoff between the United States of America and the Union of Soviet Socialist Republics (USSR) that had the potential of escalating into a real war. It almost did a year later during the Cuban Missile Crisis (October 1962) when the Soviet Union began installing missiles in Cuba to deter the United States from invading the island which under Fidel Castro had turned Communist. When the Russians succumbed to an American blockade of Cuba and demands to remove their missiles, it was hailed as a great American diplomatic victory. Later it was learned that, in return, the United States had secretly agreed to pull its ballistic missiles, which were directed at the Soviet Union, out of Turkey. In the meantime, with the development of more advanced weapons systems, the emergence of cyber warfare, and ever more conflicts erupting in different parts of the world, life on this planet has become even more precarious.

My interpretation of parts of the *Apocalypse* has convinced me that not only is our planet destined for an apocalyptic event in the very near future but that leading this march to ruin is none other than the United States of America. This will come as a shock to most Americans who have always considered their country exceptional among the nations of the world because of its supposed goodness, decency, and righteousness in dealing with others. In fact, many American Christians identify America with that *city that is set on a hill* from Jesus' Sermon on the Mount. (Matthew 5:1-7:29). Part of exceptionalism is the belief that because of its laudable qualities, the United States is in a special relationship with the Almighty and uniquely blessed and protected. The United States is indeed unique and exceptional but not for its goodness and righteousness but for its unrivaled power as a global military empire and vast ambitions to, what has been euphemistically called, "lead" the world.

Military empires have never been known for their benevolence or righteousness. In fact, the history of all military empires is written in blood. All military empires eventually fall and end up on the trash heap of history not for their goodness but for their evil. The globe is littered with the pathetic remnants of once proud and mighty empires. Of all military empires it may be said, *Pride goeth before destruction, and an haughty spirit before a fall*. (Proverbs 16:18).

Why is the existence of a military empire worthy of God's blessing nearly impossible? The reason is that the crimes and sins of military empires are legion. Military empires are engines of war—they are born of war, they are sustained by war, and they perish in war. Military empires may differ in their degree of evil but they do not differ in kind. In their glory days military empires are, without exception, arrogant, brutal, corrupt, deceiving, dishonest, immoral, hypocritical, oppressive, self-righteous, and unrepentant. They achieve their goals of hegemony and domination by any means necessary including coercion, extortion, intimidation, threats, and no-holds-barred wartime violence and covert acts of violence against adversaries during times of peace. When two or more military empires war against each other it is not a struggle between good and evil but between evils and the best mankind can hope for is for the lesser evil to prevail. If it does, the outcome does not put an end to the malice inherent in military empires but allows it to continue in the surviving one or ones.

A Clash Of Superpowers

Over the past quarter of a millennium the United States has grown from 13 North American colonies within the British Empire to become the most powerful military empire the world has ever known. Its founders modeled it on the *Imperium Romanum*, the most powerful military empire of antiquity. This American Empire ("the Empire") is the first and only global military empire in world history. The Empire's leaders have divided the entire planet into several so-called Unified Combatant Commands, each headed by a four-star general or admiral, to preside over the world. Few countries are left where the Empire does not have a direct or indirect military presence. The Empire's army, air, naval, and special forces bases dot the globe. It has surrounded itself with a coterie of allies to do its bidding and to use as staging areas for further imperialistic expansions under the false banner of freedom and democracy. Many of these allies are former enemy states which have been incorporated into the Empire not by their choice but as a result of defeat and subjugation. The Empire's claim of freedom is false because once a country is allied with the Empire it is no longer free but must subordinate its own best interests to that of the

Empire. The "free world" which the Empire's leaders claim to be leading simply does not exist and has never existed.

The Empire's power is nearly absolute. It openly or clandestinely wages war, militarily, politically, and economically, to affect regime change anytime and in any country it considers a challenge to its economic, military, or political power. It reserves to itself the exclusive right to wage war whether UN-sanctioned or not if its interests are threatened and seeks to deny it to all others where their interests are at stake. The Empire spends more on its military than the rest of the world combined. Its arsenal of weapons of mass destruction is by far the largest of any country and sufficient to destroy the world many times over. It is the world's largest arms exporter and profiteer from the sale of weapons. It shuns and unilaterally reneges on international treaties and agreements unless these give it a clear advantage over its treaty partners. The Empire's economy is the world's largest and its economic, financial, and political clout such that it can dictate to most of the world's nation-states whom they may trade with and in what commodities and whom they are forbidden to do so or face severe economic and political sanctions. It flaunts established international law and seeks to make its own laws the law of the planet. Never before in world history has one country been able to amass such power and exert such unbridled control over the affairs of mankind.

The present times are uniquely dangerous because the Empire's world supremacy is being increasingly challenged by several powerful players on the world stage, both old and new, not least of which is the Russian Federation, the successor state to the now defunct Soviet Union. As ever since the end of the Second World War, the world is economically, militarily, and politically divided into two hostile camps. History teaches that whenever a military empire finds itself challenged in its perceived role as the world's leading power, military confrontations and ultimately war with its rival or rivals are the inevitable outcomes.

The dissolution of the USSR, effective with the final days of 1991, brought a unique opportunity for the end of this perennial East-West conflict. Sadly, it was not taken largely because the Empire's leadership at the time was more interested in exploiting and solidifying the Empire's world hegemony than in deescalating the conflict with its chief rival. "By the grace of God, America won the Cold War....A world once divided into two armed camps now recognizes one sole and pre-eminent power, the United States of America.....the leader of the West has become the leader of the world" President George H. W. Bush had triumphantly proclaimed in his 1992 State of the Union Address. It was the beginning of a new world order and a *Pax Americana*, a later version of the *Pax Romana*, meaning a peace enforced by and for the benefit of the Empire.

The end of the Soviet Union also brought an end to the Warsaw Pact, a military alliance the Soviets had forged as a counterweight to NATO, an organization founded in April 1949 in Washington. The Russian Federation subsequently withdrew its forces from the Warsaw Pact countries including the former East Germany and Poland. Did the United States and its NATO allies follow suit and withdraw from their member countries including the reunited Germany? Quite the contrary. Despite assurances given by President George H. W. Bush that it would not happen, NATO rapidly expanded eastward and now numbers 29 member states stretching from North America across the whole of Europe into Eurasia (Turkey).

To the chagrin of the Russians, in 1997 three former Warsaw Pact countries, namely, Poland, the Czech Republic, and Hungary were also invited to join. This expansion was not difficult to accomplish because NATO membership held the prospect of European Union membership and generous military and economic assistance. The Russians have justly viewed this eastward expansion of the Empire as an act of military aggression. Should it come as a surprise that they are alarmed to see a power hostile to their interests, the Empire, now ensconced just outside their borders?

The more recent Ukraine and Crimea crises have reinvigorated this lingering East-West feud. Briefly, in 1922 the Ukrainian Soviet Socialist Republic became a founding member of the USSR. When the Soviet Union was dissolved in 1991, Ukraine chose independence which resulted in a split in allegiance among the populace with Ukrainians in the eastern part, the one closest to the newly created Russian Federation, being mostly pro-Russian while those in the western part desiring closer ties with the European Union. The outcome was political turmoil, widespread government corruption, the rise and fall of several governments, and increasing violence between the two factions. In April 2014 fighting erupted between the Ukrainian government and Ukrainian separatist forces. The latter were backed by Russia and in August the Russians intervened military in Eastern Ukraine. Not surprisingly, a hue and cry went up in the West about Russian military aggression. The Empire's leadership wasted no time punishing the Russians by using NATO to funnel weapons and military aid to Western Ukraine and imposing diverse economic sanctions that caused considerable damage to the Russian economy.

The situation was exacerbated by the situation in Crimea, a peninsula on the southern edge of Ukraine that juts into the Black sea. The territory had been part of Russia since the late 18th century when Czarina Catherine the Great incorporated it into the Russian Empire. In February 1954, the Soviets under Nikita Khrushchev, in a gesture of goodwill, made the peninsula part of the Ukraine. With Ukraine in turmoil, in early 2014 the Supreme Council of Crimea voted to declare its independence from Ukraine and join the Russian Federation pending approval by the people in a referendum. This referendum, on March 6, 2014, produced a record turnout with over 90% of voters in favor of accession. The following day the Crimea parliament declared its independence from Ukraine and on March 18 Crimea signed a petition of accession to the Russian Federation which was immediately granted. The high approval rating would have suggested a rigged election but no protests were heard to that effect from the Crimean people as hoped for in the West. The reason was that nearly two-thirds of Crimeans are ethnic Russians who view the Russian Federation as their homeland.

The United States and its European client states immediately denounced the Crimean referendum as being invalid, the reunification termed an "annexation," and Russia's President Vladimir Putin reviled and turned into the Empire's favorite outcast. This is not to say, of course, that President Putin's conduct has been anything approching exemplary and his reputation as a militant nationalist and international troublemaker not well deserved. Why should the outcome of this referendum be questioned and the desire of the Crimean people to rejoin their Russian countrymen be unacceptable to the West? The simple answer is that the Empire's leaders want to support Ukraine in its claim to Crimea in order to wean the country away from Russia and turn it into a loyal ally.

Ukraine obviously has major differences with its powerful neighbor but does that mean that it is at war with Russia and allied with the Empire as some of the Empire's leaders are wont to claim? Most likely not. The fact is that Ukrainians and its newly elected leadership are anxious to resolve their problems with the Russians in order to restore domestic tranquility. They are, in fact, committed to neither the Empire nor the Russian Federation. The Ukrainians are not averse to accepting military and economic aid from the West when offered. Like other countries caught up in the maelstrom between East and West, including India and Turkey which are also often cited as being the Empire's loyal friends and allies, Ukraine seeks good relations with both sides while avoiding to become beholden to either.

The second superpower to challenge the Empire in its global leadership role is the People's Republic of China (PRC). China is not as yet a major military power but it is a commercial one and the world's second largest economy. The PRC is a member of the UN Security Council, the world's most populous country (its population is over four times that of the U.S.), and a strong ally of Russia. The United States and China are presently engaged in a limited trade conflict but, despite interim agreements on some issues, a full-scale trade war is looming.

The conflict began when President Donald Trump charged the Chinese leadership with engaging in unfair trade practices that resulted in a huge trade imbalance between the two countries. To "level the playing field" he imposed ever escalating import duties on Chinese goods and placed certain Chinese companies on a black list of firms that American firms are forbidden to do business with ostensibly for national security reasons. The Chinese have reacted with surprising nonchalance probably because the damage to their economy is minimal. Despite President Trump's claim that the U.S. is collecting billions in import fees, it is not the Chinese who are paying them but the importers and ultimately the American consumer. The Chinese are not without some leverage in this dispute. Thus, they can modulate their purchases of American agricultural products or their holding in U.S. treasury bonds which help finance U.S. government debt.

The quarrel between these two superpowers was inevitable because President Trump's America First (AF) policy and Chinese President Xi Jinping's Belt and Road Initiative (BRI) are irreconcilable. The BRI calls for vast Chinese investments for infrastructure construction and economic development throughout Asia and East Africa. China needs raw materials and a market for its goods and hence this arrangement with developing countries is mutually beneficial. For many of these countries BRI is an attractive alternative to American aid because the latter is invariable tied to some form of military alliance and cooperation. Many countries are unwilling to accept such arrangements with the Empire because of a concomitant loss of national sovereignty as it would mean the establishment of American military outposts and even the stationing of troops there. China's Belt and Road Initiative is thus an obvious challenge to the Empire and is the source of much of the American hostility directed at the PRC.

Adding to the trade conflict is the fact that the Chinese will be unwilling to open up their country to foreign businesses as much and as quickly as the United States would like. The Chinese leadership is understandably very protective of its huge market and refuses to surrender it to foreigners, and especially Americans, because their countrymen have walked this road before.[5]

Two other hotspots that have the potential of escalating into a major military confrontation are the Islamic Republic of Iran and the Democratic People's Republic of Korea. Iran has long been in the crosshairs of the American Right and America's Christian fundamentalists which see the country as a threat to the State of Israel. In May 2018, President Trump withdrew the United States from the Joint Comprehensive Plan of Action a.k.a. the Iran Nuclear Deal signed in July 2015 which limits Iran's nuclear capabilities in return for the removal of economic sanctions. He did so, in his words, because it was "a bad deal." The European Union was part of this "bad deal" as were the Russian Federation, the People's Republic of China, Japan, the European Union, and the rest of the world because it was felt to be the best agreement possible under the circumstances. Iran itself has a long history of grievances against the Empire which underlies the feud.[6]

The Trump administration subsequently renewed its economic sanctions against Iran preventing. it from selling oil, its major source of income, on the open market with devastating consequences to its economy. The aim is to force the country's leadership into negotiating a new agreement more in line with the Empire's interests. This is not likely to happen anytime soon as Iran's supreme leader has shown no willingness to renegotiate it. A second objective, namely, to destabilize and bring down the regime is likewise unlikely to be met because people are usually willing to endure great hardship and stay with their leadership rather than give in to a hostile power.

In his 2002 State of the Union Address, President George W. Bush singled out North Korea as part of an "axis of evil," which also included Iraq and Iran, because of its nuclear missile program. As in the case of Iran, the Empire imposed severe economic sanctions against the country. A strong response was inevitable. Since 2012, under the leadership of Kim Jon-un, a grandson of the country's founder, North Korea has been aggressively challenging the Empire by launching missiles of ever longer ranges with the latest being able to reach America's West Coast. The country is, of course, the venue of the Korean War (1950-1953) which ended in a stalemate at the very point it began., namely, at the 38th parallel separating South and North Korea.

During that war, the United States waged an intense bombing campaign on North Korea's cities and towns that nearly spilled over into China. North Korea would have long ago succumbed to the Empire's economic sanctions were it not for the economic and moral support it is receiving from its powerful neighbor. The Chinese have obviously no interest in North Korea's collapse which would result in the Empire, via South Korea, being ensconced on their southern border.

The Myth Of Infallibility

Most Americans have been led to believe that their country is special among the nations in its goodness and righteousness in dealing with others. In a Thanksgiving proclamation in 1982, President Ronald Reagan spoke of America as "an anointed land" that was set apart by a "divine plan" so people from every corners of the world could make America "a land of morality, fairness, and freedom." Less than a year later he gave a speech to the National Association of Evangelicals in which he called the Soviet Union an "evil empire" and "the focus of evil in the modern world." He termed the struggle between the two superpowers as one "between right and wrong and good and evil."

President Reagan's views were held by a majority of his countrymen. Americans had always believed that as a nation they were morally superior to every other nation and people and therefore in a special relationship with God. But this is a deceptive fable. The reality is that the United States is not just another nation-state peaceably coexisting with other nation-states but a global military empire with vast ambitions and that no such empire can in the least be qualified to claim moral superiority over others. As one prominent American historian has written, "They [Americans] must cast away centuries-old notions of themselves as God's chosen people. In today's world, such pretensions cannot fail [but] to alienate others."[7]

Could it even be that, instead of being favored by the Almighty, the almighty Empire is on a collision course with God with the inevitable outcome? Could it be that He intents to make an example of the Empire to teach it and the world a lesson on who created and rules the world? What makes many of the Empire's leaders think they own the world? When a people, no longer content to play the roles of men start playing God, divine retribution cannot be far off!

No nation-state, empire, or people has clean hands and least of all the Empire or the American people. Americans must stop self-righteously preaching to their adversaries and start listening to them. They must recognize the fact that the American is not a model society to be admired and aspired to by all others but is seriously flawed as are all societies the world over. They must try to understand other peoples' points of view and put themselves in their places. It goes almost without saying but belligerence, confrontation, and hubris as practiced by the Empire's political and military leaders are not survival strategies for our age while good will, humility, and repentance for past crimes and sins are.

If it is true that the Empire is on the forefront of the march to an impending catastrophe, it must be because of two dark forces at work which are uniquely American. These seek to thwart the best efforts of decent people around the globe to achieve peace.

The first major dark force is made up of the worshippers of the Empire who have made it their Golden Calf. These are the millions of expansionists, imperialists, and ultranationalists who feel compelled to spread "American values" throughout the world by economic and political clout, or, if necessary, by military force. Their crusade under the false banner of freedom and democracy is uncompromising towards other forms of government, economic systems, or lifestyles.

Many of these modern-day crusaders like to equate democracy with Christianity when, in fact, there is absolutely no support for this notion in Scripture. Christ's Sermon on the Mount makes no mention of political or individual freedom. In neither the Old nor the New Testament of the Bible is the word democracy to be found even though Athenian democracy has been around since the 6th century BC. Interestingly, when the disciples wanted to find a successor to Judas Iscariot they did not choose Matthias by taking a vote but by casting lots! (Acts 1:23-26). If democracy and personal freedom had been part of God's plan for mankind, why do they not show up in Scripture? The obvious answer is that they are not. Yet the Empire's superpatriots continue to count on Providence for protection believing in American exceptionalism. To them the world is an evil place with only the United States and some of its most trusted allies on the path to righteousness. For them the Empire can do no wrong in spite of all the historical evidence from the beginning of the republic to the contrary. Americans may be exceptional in many praiseworthy respects but "they are not exceptional," another American historian concluded, "in any sense of moral innocence or purity."[8]

While American values may mean individual freedom, representative government, and the free enterprise system, the Empire's fiercest champions ignore the fact that other peoples have their own value systems and priorities that are different from their own but just as valid. Many people, such as the Chinese and Russians, are comfortable with more authoritarian rule because they are distrustful of democratic forms of government with their inherent instability and polarization of society into hostile camps. The best example is the very model of republican government, namely, the United States. Often ignored by America's Right is that many people throughout the world are less concerned with individual freedoms than with the welfare of their society as a whole. They do not mind more authoritarian rule and certain restrictions on their individual freedoms if they believe it is for the good of their country. No better proof of the validity of this claim is that in a referendum held at the end of June 2020, nearly 80% of Russian voters approved changes to their country's Constitution that would allow their autocratic and long-serving president to remain in office for two more 6-year terms. Russians are simply fearful of political turmoil that may follow President Putin's reign.

For millions of Americans one of their most cherished rights is to own and carry handguns (open or concealed) up to and including military assault weapons. Most of the planet's people have no such rights and, furthermore, have no desire to have them. They need only point to America's gun culture and the havoc it has brought to American society with mass shootings in schools, houses of worship, shopping centers, and other venues, and homicides rates that are the highest in the world. America's values are not the world's values!

Much of the world justly rejects many other aspects of the "American way." One is American style capitalism. European countries have long discarded America's Darwinist approach in favor of a social market economy which tends to be more humane and just. They have enjoyed the right to universal health care since the late 19th century while in America this basic right is still being hotly debated. Millions of Americans have no or inadequate health insurance and must suffer the consequences. In the United States severe economic downturns inadvertently results in mass unemployment and long lines at food banks. Europeans use short-time work (*Kurzarbeit* in German) that keeps all workers in their jobs working part-time at close to full wages while their governments compensate employers to do so until the crisis has passed. In Europe and Asia, free public education extends through college while millions of American students are dependent on loans so that a good portion of their early careers are spent paying them off.

Another fact these flag-wavers blissfully ignore is that the U.S. has the world's highest incarceration rate, a law enforcement apparatus that exceeds in size the standing armies of most countries, a long history of human rights violations and racial tensions, and one of the highest poverty rates of any developed country, especially among children. The American criminal justice system, which is based on the English common law, is at variance with Europe's civil law because its major aim is retribution while the latter's is rehabilitation. Consequently, despite all the extradition treaties in effect, most countries do not turn over their citizens for trial in the United States and not even citizens of other countries if the American indictments appear politically motivated.

Another dark force peculiar to the Empire consists of the millions of Christian fundamentalists who actively seek war in the Middle East, especially against Iran, to speed the Second Coming. They hope thereby to secure for themselves a place among the select few to be taken up into Heaven in the so-called "rapture." American evangelicals are clearly misguided because Christianity is not a warrior religion but, on the contrary, one that extols peace. In His Sermon on the Mount, Christ called the peacemakers blessed *for they shall be called the children of God.* (Matthew 5:9). He also admonished his flock to *not tempt the Lord thy God.* (Matthew 4:7). By seeking conflict in the Middle East and elsewhere, these people are trying to do just that, namely, tempt and provoke.

Peculiar to American evangelicals is their lockstep support of the State of Israel and their devotion to the Old Testament to the point where the New Testament becomes a mere appendage to the former. The Roman Catholic and mainline Protestant churches rightly hold the opposite view by putting Christ at the center of their Christian faith and recognizing the New as the fulfillment of the Old Testament and God's final word to mankind. (See, for example, John 14:6 and Matthew 5:17).

American evangelicals have, unfortunately, become such a prominent and influential force in American society that much of the Empire's foreign policy is driven by their warped and dangerous views. Former President Jimmy Carter, himself a Baptist and American evangelical, weighed in on this very issue when he wrote, "One of the most bizarre admixtures of religion and government is the strong influence of some Christian fundamentalists on U.S. policy in the Middle East."[9] Well-known is the fact that several recent American presidents as well as members of Congress, cabinet members, and presidential appointees would not have come into or stayed in office without the strong backing of American evangelicals.

The Empire's mass media too must share much of the blame for the existing tensions with other nation-states and societies, especially adversaries, by relentlessly beating the war drums. Freedom of the press is one of the pillars of a democratic form of government and that is why freedom of speech and the press is enshrined in the First Amendment to the U.S. Constitution. The papers and other media do a marvelous job exposing and publicizing overreach by governments, corruption and malfeasance in government and industry, violation of citizens' individual rights, injustice and judicial misconduct, endemic police brutality, and other important concerns. On the domestic front they are indispensable.

Yet it never fails to amaze how some American newspaper editors, broadcasters, and journalists can extol the gay lifestyle, support same-sex marriage, endorse abortion on demand, and celebrate other liberal causes but when it comes to relationships with adversaries always come out on the extreme right. They spew out a litany of disinformation, half-truth, and innuendo against rival governments, leaders, and institutions to besmirch, discredit, and demonize all and everything that does not subjugate itself to the Empire and its value system.

They rarely have anything positive to say or write about any of the Empire's many adversaries. When was the last time Americans have heard or read anything favorable about China? This despite that country's impressive economic and social advances that took it from an impoverished, backward country to an economic superpower in just over four decades. China bashing has become the favorite pastime of both politicians and media moguls which, unfortunately, has not advanced the cause for peace. America's mass media keep accusing their adversaries, including China, of human rights abuses despite the Empire's own long history of such abuses that continue to the present day.

They lambaste the media of their adversaries for spreading state propaganda when they themselves act as mere sounding boards for the Empire's own propaganda. America's mass media do little to clarify the issues by presenting both sides in an unbiased and factual manner. The news presented is artfully managed and selected to sway public opinion which in no way differs from the state controlled media of their adversaries.

Instead of giving the American public the straight facts so it can decide for itself, the mass media brain-wash it with masses of heavily distorted opinions and wild speculations. Rarely do they bring new insights to an issue. Exaggerated patriotism, even if false, obviously sells newspapers and raises viewership but it solves no problems. The mass media should be building bridges between people, nations, and cultures, but instead they erect walls to keep people apart.

Lest one forget, it was two newspaper publishers who, using sensationalism to build readership, instigated the Spanish-American War of 1898 which, like the Mexican-American War of a half century earlier, was a war of aggression and conquest. One of these early media moguls, Joseph Pulitzer, is today honored by having a prize for journalistic excellence named after him!

Quo Vadis?

The new millennium began with an ominous event. On September 11, 2001 (9/11) Islamic militants, using four fully loaded commercial airliners, brought down the twin towers of New York's World Trade Center, heavily damaged the Pentagon in Washington, DC, and came close to destroying the White House. This spectacular deed shocked the Empire together with much of the rest of the world. Perhaps it was meant as an omen for this new age. The attack did not come out of nowhere but was triggered by another one of the Empire's military adventures—this one into the Muslim world. In August 1990, President George H. W. Bush, in anticipation of Operation Desert Storm against Iraq, had obtained approval from the Saudi regime to station American military personnel in Saudi Arabia, the venue of two of the holiest sites to Islam, namely, Makkah (Mecca) and Medina.

The result was the rise of Islamic extremism and the Empire's war on terrorism which has been called "the endless war." In February 1998, Osama bin Laden, a Saudi who had founded al-Qaeda ten years earlier, and other Muslim extremists declared "Jihad [holy war] against Jews and Crusaders" of which 9/11 was the ultimate outcome. During President Barack Obama's administration targeted assassinations were considered the most effective way to deal with Islamic terrorism and in May 2011 U.S. special operations forces killed bin Laden. But far from ending the war, it spawned other extremist groups and it appears that the Empire will be occupied with this scourge for years to come.

The risk of a global military confrontation between the three major powers of the day has substantially increased with the divisive America First policy of President Trump. This pseudopopulist president has managed to completely unravel what was once an ordered world. After withdrawing the United States from the Iran Nuclear Deal in May 2018, in early August 2019 the president also withdrew the United States from the 1987 Intermediate-Range Nuclear Forces (INF) Treaty after accusing the Russians of non-compliance and citing China's non-participation. The

INF Treaty between the Soviet Union and the United States required both parties to eliminate and foreswear all nuclear and conventional ground-based ballistic and cruise missiles with ranges between 500 km and 5,500 km (310 - 3,450 miles). That agreement, originally signed by Mikhail Gorbachev, the Soviet secretary-general, and President Ronald Reagan and later ratified by both countries, was a much-hailed milestone on the road to universal peace. Now, the arms race is on once more with possibly catastrophic consequences.

Under the Trump administration, the Empire's relations with its European allies have become strained to the breaking point. In November 2019, the president took the United States out of the 2015 Paris Agreement (*L'Accord de Paris*) on climate change and again because it was supposedly "a bad deal for America." This UN-sponsored agreement, with nearly 200 signatory countries, has the goal of limiting the average temperature increase to well below 2°C over pre-industrial levels because of the proven, disastrous consequences of global warming. Both the Iran Nuclear Deal and the Paris climate accord have the strong support of French President Immanuel Macron and German Chancellor Angela Merkel. Both leaders are committed to the European Union, strong supporters of existing international agreements and organizations, and in favor of a constructive, non-confrontational approach in relations with both Russia and China.

Then in late December 2019, President Trump signed legislation with the disingenuous and provocative title Protecting European Energy Security Act of 2019 which seeks to preempt EU energy procurement and distribution laws for environment friendly energy and, specifically, to scuttle a gas pipeline project called Nord Stream 2 to run between Russia and Germany under the Baltic Sea. The administration is opposed to it ostensibly because it would make Germany too dependent on Russian gas. The real reasons are twofold, namely, the pipeline would deprive Ukraine (the Empire's supposed friend and ally) of gas transit fees and compete with a U.S. scheme to sell its more expensive liquid gas to the Continent. Should it not be left to the Germans to decide where they want to buy their gas and themselves evaluate the risks involved in working with the Russians to fill part of their energy needs? Why should the Empire's leadership feel entitled to coerce its so-called partner and ally into a decision that may not be in Germany's best interests?

The president celebrated the beginning of the pivotal decade of the 2020s by, on January 3, 2020 ordering the assassination of Iran's top general, Qasem Soleimani, in a targeted drone strike near the Baghdad (Iraq) airport. The general was revered by Iranians who for days after filled the streets of Tehran shouting "Death to America."

Then early in March of the year, Secretary of State Mike Pompeo denounced the International Criminal Court (ICC) as "an unaccountable political institution masquerading as a legal body" and "a renegade, unlawful, so-called court." The ICC had dared to rule against the United States on a human rights issue in Afghanistan. This court, which sits in The Hague, Netherlands, was established in 2012 under the Rome Statute to try cases involving war crimes, genocide, crimes against humanity, and aggression. Most of the world's countries recognize the ICC's jurisdiction with few exceptions including the United States and the Russian Federation. The U.S. had always supported the court before especially when its decisions were in line with American interests and had even instigated prosecutions of foreign individuals and regimes.

In May, President Trump announced his intention to withdraw the United States from the Open Skies Arms Control Treaty (OST), signed in 1992, that allows member nations to conduct unarmed surveillance flights over each other's territory with 72 hour notice. He again claimed Russia had been violating the treaty but, more importantly, China is not a treaty member and, in fact refuses to participate in any treaty between Russia and the United States. It is not likely that his move will change the minds of China's leaders and join in a new treaty. More recently, in the middle of the coronavirus pandemic, the president announced the withdrawal from the World Health Organization (WHO) because that organization is supposedly beholden to China. There are not many international treaties left before the Empire has completely isolated itself from the rest of the world.

In the search for peace, NATO, the Empire's military arm in Europe, deserves special scrutiny. When the alliance was founded its purpose was to "keep the Soviet Union out, the Americans in, and the Germans down," according to General Hastings Ismay, Winston Churchill's chief military advisor and NATO's first secretary general. Until the collapse of the USSR at the end of 1991, it met all three objectives but what has been its purpose since? Recent opinion polls have shown that two-thirds of Europeans no longer consider Russia a threat. Indeed, few people think it very likely that President Putin is interested in launching a military assault on Western Europe with or without the NATO alliance. Just about everyone agrees that it would be impossible for the Russians to impose their rule over any part of central or western Europe they chose to invade.

This poses a dilemma for the Empire's leadership, namely, How do we continue to keep NATO relevant to the Europeans and thereby maintain control over them? The answer is simple—it is to continue to represent the Russians as aggressors and a direct military threat by using Ukraine and Crimea as examples. That is why many in the higher echelons of the U.S. government want to keep the Ukraine and Crimea issues alive and tensions with the Russians high. The only country to consistently endorse this war-mongering propaganda is Poland.

NATO has always been a great boon to the Empire because of all its members it is its only real beneficiary. The alliance allows the Empire to establish and maintain military bases in Europe over which it exerts complete control and which are essential to its global reach. These bases serve as staging areas for military operations in the Middle East and Africa and allow its leadership to strike at its enemies and conduct warfare wherever and whenever it pleases. Thus, U.S. drone operations in the Middle East, which include surveillance flights and targeted assassinations, are conducted from Germany and the big American airbase near Ramstein, Germany, is a major hub for Middle East operations of the Empire's military.

The supposed protection the Empire offers its NATO allies is not free but partially paid for by the people so protected with direct and indirect payments and subsidies for the maintenance of these bases. Furthermore, NATO member states make most of their military purchases in the United States to be assured of the latest technology and for the purpose of standardization. To operate these weapon systems, especially fighter aircraft, NATO members spend more large sums to send military personnel to the U.S. for training. This is a major reason President Trump has been clamoring for more European defense spending. It would mean more American jobs and for the Empire's defense contractors higher sales and profits. Just recently, to placate him, the NATO leadership agreed to reduce the Empire's payments to 16% of NATO's budget while cajoling

Germany, which derives no overt benefits from NATO, to increase its payments to the same amount.

Few Europeans fully realize what danger the NATO alliance has put them in and how great the imbalance is of benefits received. The alliance is entirely under American control. It is headed by an American general who reports directly to the U.S. president while its secretary general is typically a European but essentially serves at the pleasure of the president. Despite his impressive title, this official has little influence on policy or its implementation with his primary function being to keep Europe aligned with the Empire's plans and objectives. He does not and never has been a true representative of European interests.

With both top officials of NATO beholden to the same authority, the Continent is essentially committed to a military alliance over which it has little control. By Article 5 of NATO's charter, an attack on one member country is an attack on all which means that any military conflict between the U.S. and another power could drag Europe into an unwanted war. In such a war all major decisions would be made in Washington and these would be foremost aimed to protect the Empire's homeland with only minor consideration given to the security and welfare of its European dependencies.

The Road To Peace

Now more than ever, it is imperative that all means be employed to diffuse the present East-West tensions before they escalate into a Third World War. The key to peace rests with the Empire and its leadership. As the most powerful nation on the planet and the first and only one to have used atomic weapons to subdue an enemy, the United States has a special obligation to avoid war and work for peace. The Anglo-American Manhattan Project, which produced this weapon of mass destruction, was arguably the most devilish and diabolical project ever undertaken by a national government outside the Holocaust. While the evil of the Holocaust was around for just a decade or so, the evil spawned by the Manhattan Project has been with mankind for three quarters of a century and is yet to reach its final fruition.

Both sides are presently engaged in updating their nuclear arsenals and developing hypersonic missiles carrying nuclear warheads against which there can be little, if any, defense. It has also become clear that their targets will not be military installations but their opponent's major cities. It would be a replay of the immense slaughter and destruction of the Second World War but on an immeasurably larger scale and this time go beyond Europe and Asia to include North America as well. Not to be ignored is the fact that sitting at the pinnacle of world power and endowed with huge and vulnerable population centers, in any nuclear exchange the Empire would have the most to lose.

While Americans as individuals may be among the world's most benevolent, generous, kind, patriotic, and religious people, they are also among the most misguided because humility, introspection, and penitence have never been part of the American national experience. Their admirable personal qualities have never been translated into their conduct as a nation making them arguably the most arrogant, hypocritical, proud, and self-righteous people on earth. Hypocrisy, the practice of accusing adversaries of flagrant wrongdoing such as human rights violations or military aggression while engaging in the same vile acts themselves, appears to be an especially well developed American trait on the national level.

Morality and decency have been replaced by the "national interest." If it is in the national interest everything has become good and righteous. To bring about peace on this planet, it is essential that Americans step down from their moral ivory tower on which they have ensconced themselves without just cause. They must finally acknowledge their own shortcomings as a nation and society and begin to deal with other peoples, including adversaries, in a way that is conciliatory and in good faith. Above all, they must begin to respect other people, be they friends or adversaries, and their ways just as they want others to respect them and their ways.

How then, specifically, might de-escalation of tensions to avoid a disastrous war be accomplished? The key is for America's leadership to engage in Realpolitik which is politics of the achievable rather politics based on doctrine, principles, and ideals especially where these are not universally accepted. In the case of the Russian Federation, the Empire and its European client states, must finally accept the fact that its leadership will never give up the Crimean peninsula because it is rightfully part of the Russian Federation. Crimea's largest city and port, Sevastopol, is home to its Black Sea fleet and has been since the days of the Czars. It is unrealistic to assume that any kind of economic sanctions and other pressures will drive the Russians out of Crimea. It is as unrealistic as to expect the Empire to give up its naval base in Naples, Italy, the homeport of its Mediterranean fleet, or any other military base around the world it considers vital to its national security.

So why sanctions and other hostile acts including NATO military exercises on Russia's borders such as Poland and the Baltic states? Why keep imposing economic and other sanctions on a country when these will have no effect whatsoever on that country's conduct and only serve to increase hostilities?

It is high time to change course by putting an end to trade sanctions against the Russian Federation by a gradual reduction and finally an elimination of these altogether. In return, Russia's leadership could be expected to actively cooperate in resolving issues in several hotspots around the world including Afghanistan, Iran, Libya, and Syria, and in the fight against Islamic terrorism. Most of these issues, including Russian interference in American presidential elections, exist as a direct result of sanctions and other hostile acts by the Empire. Most importantly, the Russian leadership can be expected to halt their support of Ukrainian separatists.

There is an excellent chance that an agreement could be negotiated which would amount to a win-win situation for both superpowers. For the Russians it would remove an immense burden on their economy and allow them to again function in a normal manner while the Americans would be relieved of an enormous military and financial burden in conducting military and clandestine operations and propping up unpopular regimes friendly to the Empire around the globe. Both countries could reduce their enormous military budgets and use their resources on much needed infrastructure projects and other worthwhile causes. Most importantly, such cooperation would reduce hostilities between the two superpowers and the risk of war.

The major obstacle to such an agreement with Russia will undoubtedly be the Empire's decision makers especially in the United States Congress. That branch of government has always been a crowded roosting place for war hawks opposed to any peaceful resolution of this or any other conflict with adversaries and especially the Russian Federation. Many senators and representatives on both sides of the aisle are paranoid in their conviction that Russia represents an existentialist threat to the Empire but, incredibly, instead of attempting to deescalate the conflict they do everything in their power to magnify it by bellicose acts and rhetoric. One can only surmise that many of these individuals believe that either a war with Russia, which is likely to include China, will not happen but, if it should, it would be winnable. History is likely to prove them wrong on both counts.

Another world war is a strong possibility and in its outcome there will be found no victors but only losers. Even if the Empire were able to completely obliterate its adversary, perhaps by a preemptive nuclear missile attack, it is very likely that "the seat of Empire" (in George Washington's words), its major cities, and much of the remainder of the country would be laid waste and made uninhabitable for decades, even centuries, to come because, given its huge territory, Russia will retain sufficient military resources to strike back no matter what the Empire undertakes.

Could the Empire's leaders then claim to have won a victory? It would be a pyrrhic victory at best! That is why all of these haughty, pompous, war-mongering fools in high government positions should be identified and removed from office for the good of the country and the world.

As distasteful as Communist dictatorships and Islamic theocracies may be, the Empire must accept the fact that these exist and are not likely to disappear anytime soon. In the case of the People's Republic of China, it is unrealistic to presume that U.S. import duties and other punitive measures will deter the Chinese leadership from making major changes in its economic goals or behavior. It may agree to accommodate the United Stats in the short term but it will never give up its long-term goal of becoming an economic and technological superpower on a par with the Empire. In short, China will not be denied its rightful place among the great powers of the world.

The Empire must finally accept the new realities and end its hostile attitude towards the PRC. In its trade negotiations it must lower its sights to achieve what is achievable. China's leadership has no known plans to turn their country into a military power to rival the Empire any time soon. So why provoke it by belligerent rhetoric and acts to do just that because it feels militarily threatened?

A major issue with the PRC is advanced technology and especially in the area of artificial intelligence. It would obviously not be in the interest of the West if China won the technology race such as, for example, in the deployment of 5G (5th generation) wireless technology. To counter Chinese efforts may mean more expenditures on research and development by the federal government, better coordination of research efforts between private industry and government, not allowing the purchase of American companies or technologies or allowing American companies to set up shop in China in critical areas, and restricting Chinese students in the U.S. to areas of study that will not expose them to advanced research in areas important to national security. Some of these measures have already been implemented and undoubtedly there are many other ways the United States can protect itself without unduly increasing tensions with China.

At the same time China's right to prevent its economic and financial exploitation by the West must be recognized. Just a handful of hugely powerful and profitable American-owned multinationals including Amazon, Facebook, Google (Alphabet), and Microsoft, dominate cyberspace in not only the American but also the European and Japanese markets. At one time the American public was protected from monopolistic business practices by the Sherman Anti-Trust Act (1890). Unfortunately, this and similar laws are no longer being enforced mainly because most of the monopolizers are American firms. Nowadays the Justice Department and Federal Trade Commission spring into action only to enforce the antitrust laws in the case of foreign, especially Chinese, companies.

Few rules and regulations yet exist to curb the sometimes shady operations of these behemoths which include using diverse schemes in the EU to avoid paying taxes where they make their profits, dodging EU privacy and anti-competition laws, and generally making a mockery of EU laws and regulations because they are big and powerful enough to do so. Since almost all of these cyberspace giants are American-owned and therefore completely beholden to the U.S. government and its laws and regulations, and, furthermore, by their nature, collectors and custodians of vast amounts of personal and business data, it is not reasonable to assume that they will ever be given free reign in China.

In the case of North Korea, the Empire's leadership and the mass media keep assailing North Korea and its supreme leader, Kim Jong-un, for its pursuit of weapons of mass destruction and ballistic missiles program notwithstanding the obvious fact that the Empire itself is not only the biggest custodian of such weapons but keeps expanding its arsenal. It is another case of immense hypocrisy on the Empire's part. The reason the North Korean leader seeks such weapons is to deter the Empire's leaders from mounting a preemptive military strike against his regime, as occurred in Iraq. They will not likely do so if they can expect a potent military response

A number of high level meetings between President Trump and Kim Jong-un have not resulted in much conflict resolution because the North Koreans have made dropping their weapons program contingent on the lifting of trade sanctions while the Americans want the North Koreans to cease weapons production without giving anything in return. Things just do not work that way. The key to better relations is again the lifting of trade sanctions.

Much of the Empire's attention is focused on Iran which it suspects of wanting to acquire a nuclear arsenal. No one anywhere wants this to happen. A miscalculation by its leadership or an accident could set off a global chain reaction of attacks and counterattacks with dire and unpredictable consequences. The only question is how such a scenario could be avoided. The Empire's method is, as ever, blunt force through punitive measures like economic, financial, and political sanctions accompanied by "fire and fury" threats by the president.

A far more productive approach would be for the West to share some of its nuclear technology with the Iranians that would allow them to achieve their dream of joining the rest of the world, including Israel, in the peaceful uses of such technology including the production of electricity and other benign purposes. This has been, in fact, their stated goal and not weapons development. Would it not be possible to prevent such development by UN-sponsored on-site inspections and other means as had been successfully done in Iraq? Why must the Empire's leaders keep confronting and challenging Iran and other countries in pursuing their legitimate goals instead of cooperating with them to make the world a safer and more peaceful place?

In the meantime, the American electorate has given the country new leadership in President Joe Biden and Vice President Kamala Harris. The outcome of this hotly contested race for the White House and vacancies in the U.S Congress did not give the winners an overwhelming and decisive mandate underscoring the polarization of American society on most issues of the day. This suggests that divisive and troublesome times lie ahead. President Biden has promised to undo much of the damage done by his predecessor's combative and capricious reign. The big question now is, Will he succeed in pulling the country together to follow his leftist agenda in the face of strong opposition from an entrenched and powerful Right? Most importantly, Will the Biden era bring about the hoped for rapprochement among the major powers or will tensions remain high and possibly even escalate? The prospects for world peace continue to be very uncertain.

A Concluding Note

If these international conflicts were not enough, the unexpected appearance on the world stage of the deadly coronavirus or Covid-19 has added to mankind's woes. Within three months after its first emergence in Wuhan, China, in mid-December 2019, it had appeared in over 100 countries causing the World Health Organization (WHO) to declare it a pandemic.

The virus quickly spread with Italy and Spain becoming new epicenters followed by the United States where the disease has been especially devastating. In fact, the U.S. has become the world leader for cases of both infections and deaths. With less than 5% of the world population, the country accounts for one-quarter of global coronavirus infections. By mid-November 2020, the American Covid-19 death toll stood at one-quarter million which number is expected to reach the staggering one-half million mark by early 2021. Like the so-called Spanish flu of a century ago which killed on the order of 50 million people world-wide, Covid-19 too will eventually come to an end. In fact, health care providers and the general public are already being treated with powerful new vaccines that came on the market in less than a year after the pandemic began.

All crises, such as the present one, cause people to reflect on mankind's precarious existence on this planet. Things can happen unexpectedly and life for most of the world's population change drastically and almost instantaneously never to be the same again. The coronavirus pandemic is a humbling experience for all people and a time for reflection. For people of faith it is a special time for spiritual renewal and the need to strengthen the bonds with their faith and the Almighty.

Some Christians ask if this pandemic might be part of the prophesied tribulation preceding the Second Coming. Is this the time of which it is written, *And except those days should be shortened, there should no flesh be saved: but for the elect's sake those days shall be shortened*? [Matthew 24:22]. It is quite possible because in those days *nation shall rise against nation, and kingdom against kingdom: and there shall be famines, and pestilences, and earthquakes, in diverse places.* [Matthew 24:7]. This points to a devastating war of apocalyptic proportions and like nothing seen in the world before. The present pandemic, therefore, must not blind people to the danger of such a war. It will be a war in which the Lord judges the nations and peoples of the world. All crime and sin committed on earth is avenged on earth and His wrath will not be found wanting.

Predictions about the future have been made since the beginning of recorded history. Things were no different in the days of Jesus. The Second Coming was discussed among His disciples even while the Lord was still among them so that He had to admonish them to watch and remain vigilant because *of that day and that hour knoweth no man, no, not the angels which are in heaven, neither the Son, but the Father.* [Mark 13:32]. Accordingly, it would be utterly presumptive and ill-advised to attempt to fix a time for the Second Coming. Nothing written above should therefore be construed as trying to foretell that event. As noted before, all predictions about future events, including those described herein, are necessarily speculative. Yet, considering that the year 2028 marks the 2000th anniversary of Christ's crucifixion, resurrection, and ascension into Heaven and also lies at the beginning of the third day (II Peter 3:8), it is conceivable, although not at all certain, that this particular date, give or take a year, will not pass without a major happening to commemorate that momentous event in human history.[10]

This new decade may well be a defining moment in the history of mankind. All that has been achieved and created by human hands during the past two or three thousand years may perish in as little as an hour along with millions upon millions of human beings. This is because the prospects for a peaceful resolution of existing conflicts do not look promising especially as long as the United States of America and the

Russian Federation continue to follow their vainglorious and mutually destructive paths.

Belligerent nationalism and militarism, usually in the guise of some honorable and virtuous cause, are once again on the rise in the world. Ambitious men in high places with world dominion on their minds and malice in their hearts are misleading the people and drawing the world ever closer to a nuclear holocaust. One can only hope and pray that the forces of good will prevail and a merciful and righteous God intervene to save mankind from this ultimate catastrophe. President Kennedy concluded his speech to the United Nations on a hopeful note which will also serve as a fitting conclusion to this book:

> *Ladies and gentlemen of this Assembly, the decision is ours. Never have the nations of the world had so much to lose, or so much to gain. Together we shall save our planet, or together we shall perish in its flames. Save it we can—and save it we must—and then shall we earn the eternal thanks of mankind and, as peacemakers, the eternal blessing of God.*

NOTES

1. Since my retirement I had made it a habit of celebrating my birthday somewhere overseas and when my 80th came around in 2016, I decided to make it a special one by joining a Christian tour group to the Holy Land. It was an exhilarating experience during which I came to love the Israelis and their country. On that special day, I found myself walking the streets of Jesus' de facto home town, Capernaum, standing on the Mount of Beatitudes, and taking a boat ride on the Sea of Galilee. The tour also took us to Jerusalem and the Yad Vashem, Israel's official memorial to victims of the Holocaust. After touring the museum, I donated a copy of my *Just Passing Through: A German-American Family Saga* (original edition) as a contribution for ongoing research on the subject. Very memorable was a Saturday, the Jewish Sabbath, that found us on the fortress of Masada where our cable car broke down requiring us to walk down the 2-mile long Snake Path. It was a huge challenge for someone my age.

   Being of German birth, I was apprehensive as to my possible reception in Israel but I had nothing to fear as I was received as a dear friend. Shopkeepers who saw my name on my credit card immediately began talking to me in German. To my surprise, in my hotel room I could watch TV programs directly from Germany. Clearly, despite of what had happened in the not too distant past, the Israeli and German people have become good friends and partners. The Federal Republic has spent billions in restitution to victims of Nazism and much of the new state's infrastructure was donated by Germany after its reunification in October 1990. The Federal Republic continuous with its generous economic support to this day.

2. Rudolf Magnus, *Goethe as a Scientist*, trans. Heinz Norden (New York: Henry Schuman, 1949), 241.

3. Shock and Awe was the codename given to the initial stage of the Iraq War which began on March 20, 2003 when President George W. Bush ordered the invasion of Iraq "to disarm Iraq of weapons of mass destruction, to end Saddam Hussein's support of terrorism, and to free the Iraq people." The operation, which bore a striking similarity to the Blitzkrieg of Nazi Germany, was conducted by a coalition of troops from the United States, Britain, Australia, and Poland and came to a victorious conclusion one month later with the fall of Baghdad and the ouster of the country's dictator. To feign popular support among the populace, American news reports showed a colossal statue of Saddam Hussein in Firdos Square being pulled down supposedly by Iraqis when, in fact, Iraqis were visibly unenthused by the Americans' arrival and the statue was toppled not by them but by an American armored vehicle.

In early May 2003, President George W. Bush, supposedly piloting a fighter aircraft, landed on the aircraft carrier USS *Abraham Lincoln* in the Persian Gulf and under a banner reading "Mission Accomplished" proclaimed that "major combat operations in Iraq have ended." It was wishful thinking as the war continued for another decade as a result of an insurgency against the invaders and sectarian violence between Sunni and Shiite Muslims that cost the lives of tens of thousands of Iraqis.

The allegations against the Iraq leader later proved to be entirely false and deliberately contrived to justify a war which President George W. Bush, with the strong support of British Prime Minister Tony Blair, had long been planning. The pending war was widely unpopular in Europe with millions of people taking to the streets in mass protests against it. It was euphemistically labeled Operation Iraq Freedom, despite having nothing to do with freedom for the Iraqi people. George W. Bush's election to his first term was highly controversial due to voting irregularities in Florida where his brother, "Jeb" Bush, served as governor at the time. In fact, he lost the popular vote.

There is a strong likelihood that Mr. Bush started the Iraq War to help his reelection which had been denied his father, George H. W. Bush. For the junior Bush it would be a win-win situation. If the war was of short duration and victorious, he would be a national hero and easily win reelection. If the war dragged on, as it did, he could call himself a "wartime president" and be assured of a second term because Americans characteristically do not change leadership during wartime. The strategy worked and George W. Bush easily won reelection in 2004.

4. Readers interested in more details regarding my interpretation of parts of the *Apocalypse* and/or my poetical writings can find these in three previously published works, namely, *A Poetical Offering With Commentaries* (2006), *Visions of the Apocalypse* (2015), and *Poems for the End of the Age* (2016). All were published by Xlibris LLC and are available in print (hardcover or paperback) or in digital format. These writings were published under an assumed name, John Peter Allemand, to keep them apart from my other books including one on business management, namely, *Pricing For Profit: The Manager's Guide to Market Oriented Pricing*, also published by Xlibris (2014).

5. After the opium wars during the mid-19th century, the Chinese economy was dominated by the British. The First Opium War (1839-1842) came about when the British East India Company began smuggling opium from India into China causing millions of Chinese to become addicted. The Americans joined this illicit trade by importing opium from Turkey. When the Qing emperor tried to intervene, the British Navy and army were brought in resulting in a devastating defeat for the Chinese who were forced to sign the infamous treaty of Nanking which ceded Hong Kong to the British Empire. Essentially, the leaders of the British Empire had successfully consummated an armed robbery. The Second Opium war was no less disastrous leading to further foreign incursions. These wars had a devastating effect on the Chinese economy and caused the disappearance of any semblance of Chinese national sovereignty. The Chinese people remember this epoch in their history as one of shame and humiliation. In July 1997 Hong Kong was finally returned to Chinese rule as a semi-autonomous region.

Since then, major developments have taken place. The year 2019 saw mass protests, under the banner of freedom and democracy, against authoritarian Chinese rule. Parenthetically, the protesters appear to have forgotten that Hong Kong was never truly free. As a crown colony of the British Empire, its government was headed by a royal governor and the country economically and financially exploited like all British colonies from Australia to South Africa. To finally bring Hong Kong under its control, at the end of June 2020 China's National People's Congress passed a national security law which will punish acts of subversion and other hostile acts against the state. Predictably, the Trump administration responded with more sanctions and other hostile acts thereby adding to the escalating tensions between the two superpowers.

The Western politicians and mass media, especially in the U.S., have long lambasted the PRC for its human rights violations in Hong Kong and its supposed ill-treatment of its Muslims minority. Then, near the end of May 2020 something shocking happened right here in the United States. While his fellow officers looked on, a white police officer in Minneapolis kneeled on the neck of a black American, George Floyd, while he was lying handcuffed on the ground. He did so for nearly 9 minutes until his prisoner was dead. "I can't breathe," Mr. Floyd was repeatedly heard saying in the filmed incident. It was another example of endemic police violence against America's black minority. When it appeared that the officer would again go scot-free, street demonstrations erupted around the country and around the world.

With this unfortunate incident the world was again reminded of American hypocrisy and the stark difference between its self-proclaimed ideal of justice for all under the law and reality. The lesson to be learned is that Americans. must clean up their own act before they can sit in moral judgment of other peoples. America cannot keep masquerading as the world's moral leader while at the same time allowing conditions at home that are reminiscent of a police state. Hopefully, all this will lead to real change in the American legal system which presently holds the country's police virtually immune from prosecution for even the most egregious of crimes. Will America's politicians and media moguls now feel sufficiently chastened to temper their virulent verbal and written assaults against adversaries, especially China, or will they be emboldened to keep them up in an effort to use the failings of the Chinese and others as a smokescreen to hide their own? Time will tell.

6. Iranian grievances against the Anglo-Americans go back to at least the reign of the Shah of Iran (Mohammad Reza Pahlavi). In the

1940s, British interests owned and ran the Iranian oil industry. In 1951 the democratically elected Iranian prime minister, Mohammad Mosaddegh, nationalized the industry after obtaining parliamentary approval. Under President Dwight D. Eisenhower, a joint Anglo-American operation involving America's CIA and the M16, it's British counterpart, forced Prime Minister Mosaddegh from office. The Shah and Anglo-American oil interests then jointly ran Iran's oil industry for a quarter of a century in a deal that was mutually beneficial—the Anglo-Americans received cheap oil while the Shah spent the proceeds from the oil sales on American fighter jets and other armaments leaving the people impoverished.

After increasing unrest, the Islamic Revolution of 1978 forced out the Shah and returned the Ayatollah Ruhollah Khomeini from exile in Paris. A theocratic constitution was drafted and approved in a referendum which replaced the previous absolute monarchy with an Islamic republic in which the Ayatollah became the supreme leader. Ayatollah Khomeini understandably had no love for the United States and called the country the "Great Satan." The Iran Hostage Crisis followed during which Iranian students held 52 Americans hostage in the American embassy in Tehran for 15 months.

7. George C. Herring, *From Colony to Superpower*, 963.
8. Walter Nugent, *Habits of Empire: A History of American Expansion*, 317.
9. Jimmy Carter, *Our Endangered Values*, 113, 114.
10. The Christian era did not begin with the year 0, i.e., Christ was not born in 0 AD (anno Domini) as is commonly assumed. His birth year actually falls in the pre-Christian era due to a dating error by a Roman monk named Dionysius Exiguus who in 526 AD had been assigned the task of creating a Christian calendar with the feast days of the Church. Exiguus fixed Christ's birth in the Roman year 754 which was five years off. Consequently, if it is assumed that Christ was about 30 years of age when he began His ministry (Luke 3:23) and that it lasted three years, the year of Jesus the Christ's death and resurrection must have been 28 AD give or take a year.

Interestingly, Christianity's Messiah was born during a great epoch in human history, namely, the reign of Caesar Augustus (63 BC - 14 AD) who was the grandnephew of Julius Caesar (on his mother's side) and became the first emperor of the powerful *Imperium Romanum*. The Roman Empire facilitated the spread of Christianity especially after Emperor Constantine the Great issued the Edict of Milan (313 AD) which ended the persecution of Christians. Constantine's mother, the Roman Empress Helena, also known as Saint Helena, was a devout Christian who had a profound influence on her son. She visited Jerusalem at his behest and around 326 AD had the Church of the Holy Sepulcher built. Just prior to his death in May 337 AD, Constantine had himself baptized into the faith and thus became the first Christian Roman emperor.

APPENDIX

A. Family Crest & Motto

GOTT MEYN TROST

B. Family Relationship Diagram

Johann Peter Zell[1]
(1814 - 1895, E)
m. 1872 (Krefeld)

Louise Kirchhoff
(1839 - 1896, E)

August Sareika[2]
(1839 - 1886, E)
m. 1874 (Strassburg)

Maria Catharina Wormer[3]
(1848 - 1925, K)

▲ Peter Zell
"Opa" (1872 - 1938, E)
m. 1898 (Frankfurt a. M.)

▲ Augusta Rosa Sareika
"Oma" (1875 - 1932, E,)

▲ Carl Peter Zell
"Uncle Karl" (1899 - 1918, E)

▲ Ludwig Friedrich Clemens Zell
"Uncle Lulu" (1901- 1943, E)
m. 1931 (Bitterfeld)

▲ Irma Lina Schellberg
"Aunt Irma" (1911 - 2002, E)

▲ Max Aeschbach
"Uncle Max" (1895 - 1976, E)
m. 1933 (Luzern)

▲ Louise Emma Zell
"Aunt Emmi" (1903 - 1993, E)

▲ Friedrich Würzburger[5]
"Fritz" (1901 - 1979, J)
m. 1928 (Frankfurt a. M.)

▲ Anna Maria Zell
"Mutti" (1909 - 1998, E)

Marga Annerosel Zell
"Cousin Marga" (1931 - 1999, E)

▲ Peter Karl Rolf Zell
"Cousin Peter" (1937 - 2017, E)

▲ Helmut Ludwig Zell
"Cousin Helmut" (1939 -, E)

▲ Esther Rosa Würzburger[4]
Esther (1927 - 2013, J)

▲ Friedrich Würzburger
Bodo (1928 - 1999, J)

⬥ Hans Peter Ludwig Zell
Peter (1936 -, E)

⬥ Ute Walfrieda Zell
Ute (1939 -,E)

⬥ Eruin Volker Zell
Volker (1942 - 2004, E)

Notes

K = "Katholisch" (Roman Catholic); "Evangelisch" (Evangelical Lutheran); "Jüdisch" (Jewish); E

1 Johann Peter Zell was previously married to Anna Maria Backhaus, E

2 On August Sareika's baptismal certificate his surname and that of his parents is spelled Schareika

3 After the death of August Sareika, Maria Catharina Sareika née Wormer married Clemens Schaub, K

4 Esther converted to Catholicism prior to her marriage to Nickolas ("Nick") Holzman

5 After their arrival in America, the Würzburgers changed their name to Wetmore

C. Port of New York Arrivals of Würzburger & Zell Families

Name	Birth Place	Age	Ethnicity/ Nationality	Port of Departure	Arrival Date	Ship
Friedrich Wuerzburger	Hoechst	36	Hebrew	Hamburg	1 Apr 1938	Washington
Friederick Wuerzburger	Frankfurt	11	Hebrew	Liverpool	17 Apr 1940	Scythia
Israel Julius Wuerzburger	Thuringia	67	Hebrew	Lisbon	2 Sep 1941	Mouzinho
Sara Mathilda Solinger Wuerzburger	Bavaria	63	Hebrew	Lisbon	2 Sep 1941	Mouzinho
Esther Wurzburger	------	19	German	Bremen	13 Dec 1946	Ernie Pyle
Herbert Wuerzburger	Germany	35	Hebrew	Liverpool	21 Jun 1940	Britannic
Erwin David Wurzburger	Frankfurt	35	German	Liverpool	13 May 1946	Drotningholm
Anne Zell	------	40	German	Le Havre	11 Mar 1950	America
Peter Zell	------	13	German	Le Havre	11 Mar 1950	America
Ute Zell	------	10	German	Le Havre	11 Mar 1950	America
Volker Zell	------	7	German	Le Havre	11 Mar 1950	America
Anne Marie Zell	------	41	German	Hamburg	15 Nov 1951	Homeland
Peter Zell	------	15	German	Bremerhaven	7 Apr 1952	Neptunia
Ute Zell	------	15	German	Bremerhaven	6 Nov 1954	Gripsholm
Volker Zell	------	12	German	Bremerhaven	6 Nov 1954	Gripsholm

Notes

1) Information taken from "New York Passenger Lists, 1820 -1957," at http://www.ancestrylibrary.com

2) In the ship manifests of alien inbound passengers the name Würzburger (with the umlaut) is spelled either Wuerzburger or Wurzburger

3) Like all Jews during the Nazi era, Julius and Mathilda Würzbuger were required to add Israel and Sara, respectively, to their given names

4) Erwin, the youngest of the Würzburger brothers, lived in England during the war

5) Elke Zell (not listed above) arrived from Stuttgart by air in early September 1958 at age 13

D. Bibliography

Bailey, George. *Germans: The Biography of an Obsession*. New York: The Free Press, 1991.

Beschloss, Michael. *The Conquerors: Roosevelt, Truman and the Destruction of Hitler's Germany, 1941-1945*. New York: Simon & Schuster, 2002.

Carter, Jimmy. *Our Endangered Values: America's Moral Crisis*. New York: Simon & Schuster, 2005.

Friedrich, Jörg. *The Fire: The Bombing of Germany, 1940 -1945*. Trans. Allison Brown. New York: Columbia University Press, 2006.

Hansen, Randall. *Fire and Fury: The Allied Bombing of Germany, 1942-1945*. New York: Penguin Group, 2008.

Hastings, Max. *Armageddon: The Battle For Germany, 1944-1945*. New York: Alfred A. Knopf, 2004.

Herring, George C. *From Colony To Superpower: U.S. Foreign Relations Since 1776*. New York: Oxford University Press, 2008.

Irving, David. *Apocalypse 1945: The Destruction of Dresden*. London: Focal Point Publications, 2007.

Lindner, Stephan H. *Inside IG Farben: Hoechst During the Third Reich*. Trans. Helen Schoop. New York: Cambridge University Press, 2008.

Lowe, Keith. *Inferno: The Fiery Destruction of Hamburg, 1943*. New York: Scribner, 2007.

Nugent, Walter. *Habits of Empire: A History of American Expansion*. New York: Alfred A. Knopf, 2008.

Roosevelt, Eleanor. *The Autobiography of Eleanor Roosevelt*. New York: Da Capo Press, 1992.

Samuel, Wolfgang W. E. *The War of Our Childhood: Memories of World War II*. Jackson: University Press of Mississippi, 2002.

Stargardt, Nicholas. *The German War: A Nation Under Arms, 1939-1945*. New York: Basic Books, 2015.

Toland, John. *Adolf Hitler*. Garden City, NY: Doubleday & Co., 1976.

In German

Arbeitskreis Heimatmuseum. *Suenheim Sweinheim Schwanheim*. Frankfurt-Schwanheim: Josef Henrich Verlag, 1971.

Beck, Waltraut, Josef Fenzl, and Helga Krohn. *Die Vergessenen Nachbarn: Juden in Höchst*. Frankfurt a. M.: Jüdisches Museum der Stadt Frankfurt am Main, 1990. [The Forgotten Neighbors: Jews in Höchst].

Burda, Heinz. *Stuttgart im Luftkrieg 1939-1945* (Veröffentlichungen des Archivs der Stadt Stuttgart, Band 35). 2nd ed. Stuttgart: Klett-Cotta Verlag, 1985. [Stuttgart During the Air War 1939-1945].

Dussel, Konrad. *Graben: Vom Bauerndorf zur modernen Industriegemeinde*. Heidelberg: Verlag Regionalkultur, 2006. [Graben: From Peasant Village to Modern Industrial Community].

Müller, Norbert. *Sagen, Geschichten Und Gereimtes aus dem alten Schwanheim und seiner Gemarkung*. Frankfurt am Main: Heimat und Geschichtsverein Schwanheim e.V., 1997. [Folklore, Stories, and Rhymes of Old Schwanheim and its Environs].

Schukraft, Harald. *Wie Stuttgart wurde, was es ist: Ein kleiner Rundgang durch die Stadtgeschichte*. Tübingen: Silberburg Verlag, 1999. [How Stuttgart developed, what it is: A small journey through city history].

Vater, Aenne et al. *1100 Jahre Schwanheim: Ein Festbuch zum Jubiläumsjahr 1980*. Frankfurt am Main - Schwanheim: Verein 1100 Jahre Schwanheim, 1980. [1100 Years Schwanheim: A Celebratory Publication For The Jubilee Year 1980].

Wagner, Wilhelm J. *Neuer Bildatlas Zur Deutschen Geschichte*. Munich: Chronik Verlag, 2002. [New Illustrated History of Germany].

E. Acknowledgements

I am much indebted to a number of sources in France, Germany, Switzerland, and the United States for genealogical information on my ancestors including birth, marriage, and death certificates. Many of the German *Urkunden* [genealogical documents] relied on herein are from the collection of my late Cousin Peter Zell who came to be the official keeper of the *Ahnenbuch* [book of ancestors] when he inherited a large cache of family document from his mother, my Aunt Irma, after she passed away. These papers had been collected by his father, Ludwig, to show proof of his so-called Aryan ancestry which was a prerequisite to becoming a member of the NSDAP (Nazi Party) during the Third Reich. In a major undertaking, Cousin Peter photocopied most of these documents and mailed them to me over a period of years beginning in October 2002. For that I am most grateful.

Since my cousin's father had to account only for forebears that were in direct line to him, many family members were not included in his document list. In fact, their existence was not known to either my cousin or me until I conducted my own genealogical researches in preparation for the first edition of *Just Passing Through: A German - American Family Saga* published in March 2011. Prior to this research we did not know, for example, that our Great-grandfather Johann Peter Zell's marriage to Louise Kirchhoff was his second—he had previously been married to a Anna Maria Backhaus with whom he had several children. Nor did we know that our Great-grandmother Maria Katharina née Wormer had married a Clemens Schaub some years after the death of August Sareika. Peter's knowledge about our ancestors necessarily proved limited because he was only five years old when he last saw his father who served with the Wehrmacht while his mother talked little about her husband's side of the family.

Birth, marriage, and death certificates do not suffice, of course, to tell the story of a person's life and I was fortunate to be able to draw on my mother's knowledge of family history and particularly about her parents, grandparents, and their backgrounds. This information allowed me to flesh out the data from my cousin's papers, the documents on our family left by Mother, and genealogical information subsequently acquired by me from various sources. My big regret is that I rarely asked Mutti any questions and just listened to whatever she volunteered to tell me leaving me to later speculate about many things I could have known for certain if I had simply asked. To my cousin's daughter Trixi, I owe thanks for transcribing a number of *Urkunden* from the old German script, known by the name of its inventor as *Suetterlin*, into readable German and providing assistance in obtaining and analyzing diverse items of other genealogical data.

For additional *Urkunden* pertaining to the Zell family of Krefeld including our Grandfather Peter Zell's siblings, I employed the services of a professional genealogist, Andrea Thausing of Essen, who searched through the archival church records and constructed a partial family tree. I had previously contacted the Evangelische Kirche in Krefeld for these documents and they had passed my request on to her. For information on the final resting places of relatives who served with the Wehrmacht in World War II, I am much indebted to the researchers of the Volksbund Deutsche Kriegsgräberfürsorge (German War Graves Commission) of Kassel, Germany.

Documents and information were obtained from a number of parish offices, city registrars, and archival services in France, Germany and Switzerland. Some individuals in these need special mention and thanks for assistance that went beyond the ordinary. Laurence Perry of the Strasbourg city archives obtained the birth certificate of my maternal grandmother, Augusta Rosa Zell née Sareika, and informed me about the exact location of her birthplace. Frau Angelika Herkert of the Karlsruhe municipal archives traced down the records concerning the suicide of my Great-grandfather August Sareika, first revealed to me by Mutti, while Frau Irene Ehler of the Karlsruhe office for municipal services and protection located the marriage certificate of my great-grandmother, Maria Katharina Sareika née Wormer, with Clemens Schaub.

Other contributors were Dr. Marion Stascheit of the Hochschule Mittweida who graciously provided me with a copy of an original prospectus from the year 1893, and copies of my Grandfather Peter Zell's courses and grades at the school as well as the correspondence between the school administrators and my Great-grandfather Johann Peter Zell. I also owe thanks to Jean-Claude Lavanchy, Kurator Philatelie, of the

Museum für Kommunikation of Berne who mailed me a biography of Charles August Hirzel including a rare photograph of him. I am also indebted to Dr. Roland Müller of the Stuttgart municipal archives who found the information related to my childhood experience during the 1944 bombing of Stuttgart and answered a number of my questions. Last but not least, Christine Wern of the Jüdisches Museum Frankfurt provided me with a copy of *Die Vergessenen Nachbarn: Juden in Höchst* [The Forgotten Neighbors: Jews in Höchst] which provided me with valuable information on Mutti's in-laws, the Würzburger family, and their Jewish friends.

France, Germany & Switzerland

Archives de la Ville et de la Communauté Urbaine, 67076 Strasbourg Cedex, France

August-Gräser-Schule (formerly Schwanheimer Volksschule), 60529 Frankfurt am Main, Germany

Das Telefonbuch, www.dastelefonbuch.de

Deutsche Dienststelle (WASt), 13403 Berlin, Germany

Deutsches Rotes Kreuz, Generalsekretariat Suchdienst, 81549 München, Germany

Erzdiözese Freiburg, Erzbischöfliches Archiv, 79095 Freiburg, Germany

Evangelische Martinusgemeinde, 60529 Frankfurt-Schwanheim, Germany

Evangelisches Pfarramt Graben-Neudorf, 76676 Graben-Neudorf, Germany

Frankfurter Neue Presse (Höchster Kreisblatt), 60327 Frankfurt am Main, Germany

Graben-Neudorf, Gemeindeverwaltung, 76676 Graben-Neudorf, Germany

Heimat-und Geschichtsverein Schwanheim e.V., 60529 Frankfurt-Schwanheim, Germany

Hochschul- und Landesbibliothek RheinMain, 65185 Wiesbaden, Germany

Hochschule Mittweida, University of Applied Sciences, Hochschularchiv, 09648 Mittweida, Germany

Katholisches Pfarramt St. Michael Neuweier, 76534 Baden-Baden, Germany

Klett-Cotta Verlag, 70178 Stuttgart, Germany

Kontor für Ahnenforschung, Andrea Thausing, 45134 Essen, Germany

Museum für Kommunikation, CH-3005 Bern, Switzerland

Pompes Funèbres Générales Genève SA, CH-1227 Carouge, Switzerland

Sanofi-Aventis Deutschland GmbH, Hoechst GmbH, 65926 Frankfurt am Main, Germany

Schillerschule, Schulleitung, 60596 Frankfurt am Main, Germany

Stadt Baden-Baden, Stadtarchiv, 76530 Baden-Baden, Germany

Stadt Baden-Baden, Standesamt, 76534 Baden-Baden, Germany

Stadt Bruchsal, Notariat, 76646 Bruchsal, Germany

Stadt Burg, Regionales Zivilstandsamt Menziken, CH-5736 Burg (AG), Switzerland

Stadt Eschborn, Stadtarchiv / Museum, 65734 Eschborn, Germany

Stadt Frankfurt am Main, Institut für Stadtgeschichte, 60311 Frankfurt am Main, Germany

Stadt Frankfurt am Main, Presse- und Informationsamt, 60311 Frankfurt am Main, Germany

Stadt Frankfurt am Main, Standesamt, 60275 Frankfurt am Main, Germany

Stadt Frankfurt am Main, Standesamt (Höchst) Mitte, 60311 Frankfurt am Main, Germany

Stadt Karlsruhe, Bürgerservice und Sicherheit, 76133 Karlsruhe, Germany

Stadt Karlsruhe, Stadtarchiv, 76124 Karlsruhe, Germany

Stadt Krefeld, Standesamt, 47798 Krefeld, Germany

Stadt Stuttgart, Kulturamt, Stadtarchiv, 70178 Stuttgart, Germany

Stadt Zürich, Bevölkerungsamt, Ausweise und Auskünfte, CH-8004 Zürich, Switzerland

Volksbund Deutsche Kriegsgräberfürsorge, 34112 Kassel, Germany

Zentrales Verzeichnis Antiquarischer Bücher, https://www.zvab.com

United States

America's Obituaries & Death Notices, https://www.newsbank.com

Ancestry Library Edition, https://www.ancestry.com

Association for Postal Commerce (PostCom), https://www.postcom.org

Chicago Historical Society, 60614 Chicago, IL

Google Search, https://www.google.com

FamilySearch, https://www.familysearch.org (The Church of Jesus Christ of Latter-day Saints)

Illinois Department of Public Health, Division of Vital Records, Springfield, IL 62702

MyHeritage DNA, http://www.myheritage.com

National Archives and Records Administration, Archives II Reference Section, 20740 College Park, MD

New York Passenger Lists, 1820-1957, http://search.ancestrylibrary.com

Oregon Health Authority, Oregon Vital Records, Portland, OR 97293

Simon Wiesenthal Center, Los Angeles, CA 90035

United States Social Security Death Index (SSDI), https://www.familysearch.org

Wikipedia, the free encyclopedia, https://en.wikipedia.org

A Note on Ancestry Research in Germany

For Americans of German descent who wish to trace their forebears, the following information should be helpful. The key year for such researches is 1870. In that year Germany was united under the leadership of Prussia (Second Reich) and Kaiser Wilhelm I's prime minister, Chancellor Otto von Bismarck, instituted a number of nation-wide reforms. Among these were the establishment in each town of a *Standesamt* [registrar's office] which was charged with keeping birth, marriage, and death records for the populace. Prior to then, these records were kept exclusively in the offices of the parish churches. Therefore, if information is desired for an ancestor who lived before 1870, the *Pfarramt* [church office] in the village or town he or she was born in should be contacted. This will require the researcher to know whether the person was *katholisch* [Roman Catholic] or *evangelisch* [Evangelical Lutheran] especially if the village was large enough to have churches of both confessions. The church offices are generally understaffed and do not have the resources to search their records but can usually provide the name of a local genealogist who will do this search for a fee. For records after 1870, these may be found in either one of two places. The *Standesamt* will keep records for the past few decades after which they are sent to the *Stadtarchiv* [city archives]. A good place to start is the *Standesamt* in the village or town the ancestor was born in. Its address and/or website can be located on the Internet or the envelope simply addressed to "Standesamt" in the appropriate village or town. If not much more is known than the ancestor's name, the LDS Family History Library in Salt Lake City, Utah may have the person on file. Their vast collection of church records is accessible through their website given above.

F. People & Places

1.

2.

3.

4.

5.

6.

7.

8.

9.

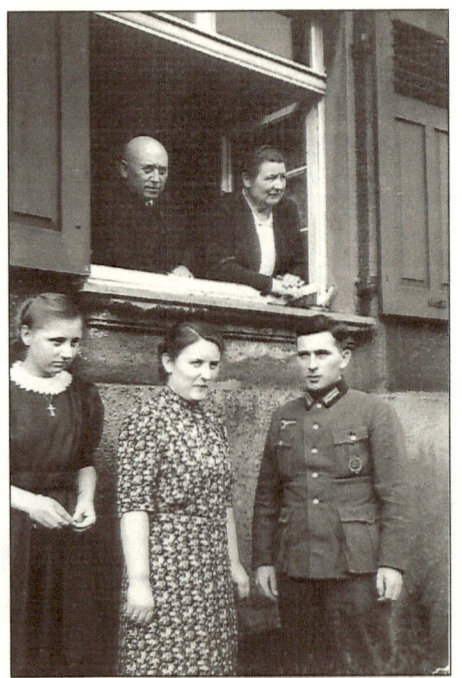

10.

11.

12.

13.

14.

15.

16.

17.

18.

19.

20.

21.

22.

23.

24.

25.

26.

27.

28.

29.

30.

31.

32.

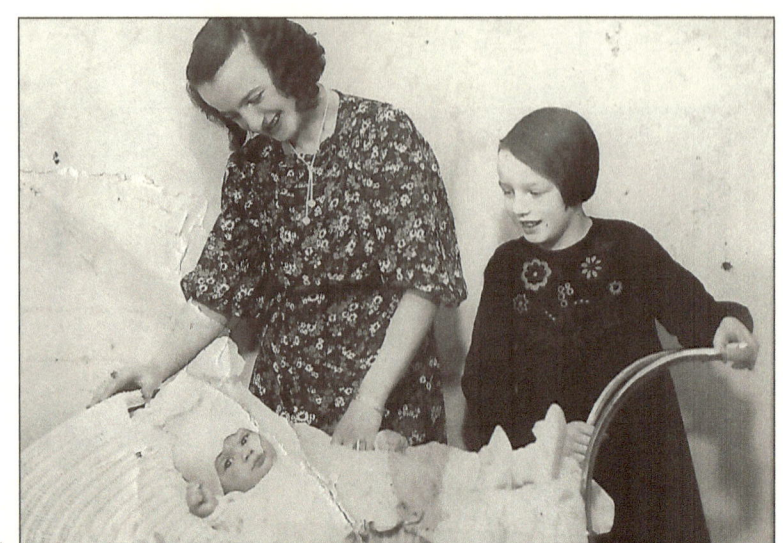

33.

34.

35.

36.

37.

38.

39.

40.

41.

42.

43.

44.

45.

46.

47.

48.

49.

50.

51.

52.

53.

54.

55.

56.

57.

58

59.

60.

61.

62.

63.

64.

65.

G. Photo Notes

These photographs, chosen from a large trove of family and other prints Cousin Peter turned over to the author as well as from the author's own files of prints and photo slides, are meant to complement the text by showing the principal characters at various stages of their lives. For some ancestors mentioned in the book no photographs have, unfortunately, survived.

1. Auguste Rosa and Anna Maria Zell with one of the family's Irish Setters
    Undated studio photo, but probably from 1924, taken in Höchst am Main showing Oma and Mutti as a young girl. On the reverse of this postcard (which is not addressed) appears an affectionate message from his parents to Ludwig Zell (Uncle Lulu) congratulating him on his 23rd birthday. (At the time he was serving in the French Foreign Legion).

2. The unknown ancestors
    Undated studio photo taken in Karlsruhe and possibly showing the parents of Clemens Schaub, the husband of Maria Katharina Schaub née Wormer, after the death of August Sareika.

3. Johann Peter Zell
    Undated photo portrait of the author's great-grandfather taken in Crefeld (Krefeld).

4. Louise Zell née Kirchhoff
    Undated photo portrait of the author's great-grandmother taken in Crefeld (Krefeld).

5. Peter Zell as a young man
    Undated photo portrait of the author's grandfather (Opa) taken in Bruchsal.

6. Peter Zell with sports medals
    Undated photo portrait of Opa taken in 1898 (at age 26) in Frankfurt-Sachsenhausen.

7. Peter Zell in mid-life
    Undated photo portrait of Opa.

8. Auguste Rosa and Louise Emma Zell with Maria Katharina Schaub née Wormer
    Undated studio photo from about 1905 taken in Karlsruhe showing Oma, Aunt Emmi, and the author's great-grandmother.

9. Ludwig Friedrich Zell
   Undated photo portrait of the author's Uncle Lulu.

10. Uncle Lulu in Wehrmacht uniform with wife and daughter
    Uncle Lulu at Easter 1940 with Aunt Irma and Cousin Marga. In the window appear Opa's full brother, Carl Wilhelm, an architect, and his wife, Bertha Emilie née Klein.

11. Louise Emma Zell in Berlin
    Undated studio portrait of Aunt Emmi probably from the mid- to late 1920s.

12. Louise Emma Zell in Geneva
    Undated studio portrait of Aunt Emmi probably taken in the late 1940s.

13. Charles August Hirzel
    Undated studio portrait of Uncle Charles, a banker and Aunt Emmi's life partner.

14. Emmi Zell with the author
    Aunt Emmi on an outing with her nephew to Mont Salève, France, near Geneva. (April 1982).

15. Annemarie Zell as a young girl
    Undated studio photo of the author's mother (Mutti) from about 1921 taken in Höchst am Main.

16. Mutti in Berlin
    Photo taken in Berlin in June 1931 at age 22 when she was visiting her sister Emmi.

17. Mutti (right) with unknown lady friend
    Undated studio photo taken in Karlsruhe.

18. Annemarie with Ute and Peter Zell
    Photo taken in August 1958 in Chicago's Riverview Pak during Schwabenpicnic showing Mutti (age 49), Ute (18), and the author (22).

19. Annemarie with Volker and Peter Zell
    Photo taken in July 1958 in Chicago's Riverview Park during German-American Day showing Mutti (age 49), with Volker (16) and the author (21).

20. Annemarie and Elke Zell with Esther Holzman
    Mutti with daughters Elke (left) and Esther in front of Esther's apartment building (not visible). Photo taken by the author. (August 1962).

21. Mutti with the author
    Visiting Mutti after her recent surgery in Oak Park, Illinois. (August 1967).

22. Mutti keeping informed
    Mutti studying the Chicago Tribune in our townhouse apartment in Oak Park, Illinois. (August 1964).

23. Mutti at President John F. Kennedy's grave
    Mutti (in black) in Arlington National Cemetery, Washington, DC. (June 1964).

24. Mutti with Putzi
    Mutti with her favorite pet cat, Putzi, at Mutti's Place in Oak Park. (Late 1960s).

25. Mutti in front of her home in Oak Park
    Mutti in front of Mutti's Place. (August 1973).

26. Mutti with Esther and Nick at Steffi's high school graduation
    Watching Steffi's graduation in the Oak Park and River Forest High School football stadium. (June 1974).

27. Mutti with Julius and Erika Kuchenbeißer in Graben-Neudorf, Germany
    Mutti with Aunt Erika and Uncle Jule during a stay in their home. (July 1971).

28. Mutti with Maria (Marie) and Robert Gartner
    Mutti and the author on a visit to Mama Gartner and Robert in Karlsruhe. (June 1982).

29. Mutti on an outing with classmates
    Mutti (in sunglasses) on a bus tour with her lady friends from the Jahrgang [birth year] 1909 at the Schwanheimer Volksschule. (July 1971).

30. Photo portrait of Mutti
    Mutti (age 84) in a photo taken in Chicago prior to the author's trip to Geneva, Switzerland. (April 1993).

31. Mutti near the end of her life
    Mutti in Deerfield, Illinois, before her passing the following May at age 89. (August 1997).

32. Esther with Nick and Steffi Holzman
    In the rear of Mutti's Place. (September 1972).

33. The author (Peter) as a baby with Mutti and Esther
    Undated photo probably taken in 1937 in Graben, Germany. Mutti would have been 28 and Esther 10 at the time.

34. The author as a schoolboy
    Photo taken in Forst probably in 1943 when the author would have been 7. It appears on the back of a postcard written on June 10, 1948 and addressed to "Fräulein (Miss) Frieda Reichert, Seegasse 16, Kronau near Bruchsal" by Maria Gartner, the author's foster mother (Mama Gartner). In her message to her sister, she announces the date of her forthcoming visit and tells her of a schoolgirl named Doris who has been living with her for 18 days. It is signed "Marie and the children Doris and Wolfgang." Doris was evidently a new foster child. (The author received the postcard from Ms. Reichert on a visit to Kronau).

35. The author in an American passport photo
    Photo portrait taken in July 1951 in Oak Park, Illinois (at age 14) prior to his being sent back to Germany.

36. The author's confirmation photo
    Postcard photo taken in March 1952 near the Matthäuskirche in Stuttgart, Germany.

37. Photo portrait of the author
    The author at work in his company's Munich office. (May 1982).

38. Peter Karl Zell with the author
    At Cousin Peter's home in Bad Soden-Salmünster. (August 2006).

39. Sister Elke with the author
    At Ernest Hemingway's Oak Park birthplace after the author's return from a trip to Germany and Rome. (September 2006).

40. Ute Walfrieda Zell
    Photo portrait (in cardboard folder) of the author's Sister Ute, which she gave our mother on the occasion of Mutti's 52nd birthday with a dedication (translated from the German): "Dear Mutti, on your birthday today, I wish you all the best and many beautiful and healthy years to come, your Ute 1961." Ute was 21 at the time.

41. Erwin Volker Zell
    Undated photo portrait of the author's Brother Volker.

42. Photo portrait of the author's Sister Elke
    Elke in a photo taken while teaching high school in Valparaiso, Indiana. (Early 1990s).

43. Maria (Marie) Gartner

Photo of Mama Gartner taken by the author (with his box camera) in March 1950 as the train from Stuttgart stopped in Bruchsal on the way to Paris during the family's emigration.

44. The Würzburger Sons

Friedrich (Fritz), Herbert, and Erwin Würzburger in 1915 showing Erwin, the youngest, dressed as "kaiserlicher Offizier" [imperial officer]. From "Juden in Höchst: Die Vergessenen Nachbarn" by Waltraut Beck et al. © 1990 Jüdisches Museum der Stadt Frankfurt am Main, 21. By permission of the Jüdisches Museum Frankfurt.

45. Ludwig Zell's family

Studio photo taken in 1948 in Bitterfeld showing Aunt Irma with Helmut (left), Marga, and Peter Zell.

46. Mutti with three of her six children

Studio photo taken at Christmas 1948 in Stuttgart showing Mutti (age 39) with Ute (9), Volker (6), and Peter (12).

47. Esther and her family

Photo taken in Mutti's Place showing (clockwise) Dr. Frank Murrin, a family friend, Steffi, Nick, Esther and Mutti. (Christmas 1975).

48. Ute and her family

From a family gathering in Brighton, Michigan, showing Ute up front holding Libby. In the back row: Ted, the brother of Ute's husband Tom with wife Karen (sitting in front of him), their daughter Kim, and Tom with daughter Danielle and son Tommy. In the middle row: Opa Bud with Ted's children Todd and Andy. In the front row: Todd's wife Wendy and their children Anna and Julia. (Thanksgiving 2001).

49. Elke and her family

From a family gathering in Valparaiso, Indiana, showing Elke in the center with our sister Ute and Ute's husband Tom (holding Daisy). In the back row: Elke's daughter Ute with husband Brian (left) and her daughter Monica with husband Craig. In front are her grandchildren Sadie, Mason, and Cole. (Thanksgiving 2006).

50. Peter Karl and his family

From a visit to Bad Soden-Salmünster, Germany, showing at the top center Cousin Peter standing next to Hella, son Matthias' life partner (partly hidden) and Michael, daughter Trixi's husband. A step down appear his son Matthias and daughter Dörte with her husband Thomas. In the third row: His grandson Felix and granddaughter Neele. Up front are his wife Karen, daughter Trixi, granddaughter Julchen, and grandson Tjard. (August 2011).

51. The original Zell family home in Schwanheim am Main
Postcard photo of the building on Feldbergstraße 8 (now Blankenheimer Straße 8) in about 1925. The family lived here in rent until 1930 when it moved to Vogesenstraße 40. Out front, and barely visible, are Annemarie with the family's two Irish Setters.

52. The Zell family home after its renovation in Frankfurt-Schwanheim, Germany
The house on Blankenheimer Straße 8 (formerly Feldbergstraße 8) where the family lived in rent. (September 2011).

53. The Würzburger Eck in Höchst am Main
Photo from 1910 shows the men's clothing store operated by the Würzburger family from the 1890s until the early 1930s when the Nazis came to power. The corner on the right, at the intersection of Bolongarostraße and Königsteiner Straße, was known as the Würzburger Eck. From "Juden in Höchst: Die Vergessenen Nachbarn" by Waltraut Beck et al. © 1990 Jüdisches Museum der Stadt Frankfurt am Main, 19. By permission of the Jüdisches Museum Frankfurt.

54. The former Würzburger Eck in Frankfurt-Höchst, Germany
This building housed the Würzburger men's clothing store until the early 1930s when The Würzburger family lost the property in a forced sale during the Nazi era. The building was heavily damaged during the World War II bombings and rebuilt. The top floor appears to be a post-war addition. (September 2006).

55. The author's birthplace in Graben-Neudorf, Germany
The house on Rheinstraße 2-4 where the author was born on the second floor of the building's left side. The right side was a Gaststätte [inn] called Zur Sonne. (June 1982).

56. The Evangelische Kirche in Graben-Neudorf
The Evangelical (Lutheran) church in the center of Graben where the author was baptized. (August 2011).

57. The author's childhood home in Forst after its renovation
    The house of the Leibold family on Burgweg 13 where the Gartner family lived in rent. The person at the entrance is Andreas, Wolfgang Gartner's son, who accompanied the author to Forst from Karlsruhe. (September 2006).

58. The Pfarrkirche St. Barbara in Forst
    St. Barbara's Catholic church which the author attended as a young boy. (August 2011).

59. The Schloßplatz in Stuttgart
    Central Stuttgart with the jubilee column and the Neues Schloß (New Palace) and Altes Schloß (Old Castle), both rebuilt after the World War II bombing of the city. (September 2011).

60. Stuttgart's Schillerplatz in the late 1950s
    Stuttgart's historic center, showing Thorvaldsen's Schiller monument and the rebuilt Stiftskirche (Founder's Church) dating from the early 13th century. By permission of Dieter Geißler, professional photographer.

61. The author's boyhood home in Stuttgart
    The building on Adlerstraße 8 showing the Zell family's apartment on the second floor facing the camera. (August 2017).

62. The Evangelische Matthäuskirche in Stuttgart
    The rebuilt Evangelical (Lutheran) church of St Matthew in which the author was confirmed. (August 2017).

63. Aunt Emmi's home in Geneva, Switzerland
    The villa on the Plateau de Champel which was the home of Uncle Charles and Aunt Emmi. (May 1993).

64. Esther's home in River Forest, Illinois
    The home on Bonnie Brae where the family moved after selling their Oak Park apartment building. (August 1981).

65. Auguste Zell's (Oma's) birthplace in Strasbourg, France
    The author's grandmother was born in this house near the Münster (cathedral) in the town then known as Strassburg, Germany. (August 2011).